MW00811597

REVELATION 8-22
AN EXEGETICAL COMMENTARY

Robert L. Thomas

MOODY PRESS

CHICAGO

All Scripture quotations, unless otherwise noted, are the author's
translation.

Library of Congress Cataloging in Publication Data

Thomas, Robert L., 1928–
    Revelation 8-22 : an exegetical commentary / Robert L. Thomas.
    p.   cm.
    Includes bibliographical references and index.
    ISBN 0-8024-9267-3
    1. Bible. N.T. Revelation VIII-XXII—Commentaries.   I. Title.
II. Title: Revelation eight-twenty-two.
BS2825.3.T462   1995
228'.07—dc20   95-4176
                                                            CIP

1 3 5 7 9 10 8 6 4 2

Printed in the United States of America

Dedicated to
my children,
Barbara
Bob
Jon
Mark
Mike,
five overcomers whose faith in Christ has been a great encouragement

Written especially for the informed layman, student, and scholar, all exegesis and exposition is based on the original languages of the Bible books. Translations used are those of the author. Textual criticism and word study are included where appropriate.

This in-depth commentary also includes extended excursuses on important topics of theological and historical interest.

The text is interpreted according to a historical and grammatical hermeneutic and propounds a conservative, evangelical theology. But the reader will not get a narrow view of problem passages. This commentary interacts with a range of major views, both evangelical and nonevangelical.

REVELATION 8-22

Through the centuries since its writing, the book of Revelation has captured the fascination of the Christian church. Earliest Christians were unanimous in understanding its prophecies as descriptions of events surrounding the premillennial second advent of Jesus Christ, but alongside their exclusively futuristic and premillennial view other hermeneutical approaches to the book began to emerge in the third century. These clouded, and added complexity to, the task of explaining the book's meaning. For most of the Christian era, consequently, many readers have viewed this last of the NT writings as though it were hopelessly embedded in an aura of deep mystery. An avalanche of interpretive literature has evidenced remarkable interest in the book's contents, but along with the interest has come widespread bewilderment.

In post-Reformation times detailed commentaries on the Greek text of Revelation from a futurist and premillennial perspective have been scarce and perhaps even nonexistent. As a follow-up to *Revelation 1-7* (Moody, 1993), this second of two volumes continues the filling of that void with its exegetical analysis of the last fifteen chapters of the Apocalypse. It reaffirms the basic framework of eschatology espoused by ancient Christianity, but with added help from centuries of maturing thought and doctrinal progress in the Body of Christ.

About the author

Robert L. Thomas (B.M.E., Georgia Institute of Technology; Th.M., Th.D., Dallas Theological Seminary) is professor of New Testament language and literature at The Master's Seminary, Sun Valley, California. He has written *Understanding Spiritual Gifts* and "1, 2 Thessalonians" in the *Expositor's Bible Commentary* and has edited *A Harmony of the Gospels (NASB)* and *The NIV Harmony of the Gospels*. He is also general editor of the *New American Standard Exhaustive Concordance*.

Table of Contents

Introduction

Whereas the various areas of biblical criticism receive at least brief treatment in this volume, the principal emphasis of the commentary is exegesis. Exegesis means the application of generally accepted hermeneutical principles to the original (Hebrew, Aramaic, and Greek) biblical text with a view to unfolding (lit. "leading out," Gk. *exēgeomai*) its correct, contextual meaning. The method followed is commonly referred to as grammatico-historical exegesis.

This is a commentary on the Greek and Hebrew texts of the Bible, not on an English translation. Consequently Greek and Hebrew words and phrases appear in their original scripts, but with English transliterations and translations provided at their first occurrence. After that, transliterations alone normally suffice. However, only the original scripts are employed in the Additional Notes and footnote discussions, since scholars and specialists would be the ones most interested in that more technical material (e.g., word studies, grammatical or syntactical points, etymologies, textual variants in the original languages, specialized bibliographies, etc.). Unless otherwise indicated, all Scripture translations are those of the author.

This commentary stresses the development of the argument of Revelation and its central theme. An attempt has been made to show how each section of a book fits together with the preceding and following sections. The reader must not become so preoccupied with the trees (analysis) that he fails to see the forest (synthesis).

Most of the abbreviations and transliterations follow the guidelines of the *Journal of Biblical Literature (JBL)*. The only abbreviations listed are those not found in *JBL*.

Asterisks in either the Translation or the Exegesis and Exposition section refer the reader to discussions of text-critical problems in the Additional Notes section, though these are not the only kinds of discussions one will encounter in the Additional Notes sections (see above).

May this commentary be used by God to advance the cause of a more exegetically-based, and so more accurate, biblical interpretation and biblical theology. An increased understanding of Revelation will bring many Christians to a higher plane of Christian living and cause them to join with John as he prayed, "Amen, come, Lord Jesus" (Rev. 22:20).

Preface to Revelation 8-22

This is a brief supplement to the "Preface" in the companion volume, *Revelation 1-7, An Exegetical Commentary*. In one sense this volume is the second of a two-volume set. However, these companion volumes are not being published as volumes 1 and 2 because each book has its own distinguishing title. References to *Revelation 1-7* in the footnotes of this volume will follow the usual form of documentation. Numerous parenthetical citations to the companion volume occur in the text. The first of these in each chapter will contain the author's last name, the short title, and page numbers. Subsequent citations will appear, for example, as "(Thomas, pp. 1-3)."

A number of works not cited in the "Selected Bibliography" of *Revelation 1-7* appear in the documentation of this volume. Many of these, but not all, are works that have become available since the earlier publication. The documentation in the footnotes will suffice for those desiring to pursue further research in these sources.

I want to express gratitude to Moody Press for its decision to proceed with the publication of the two volumes of this commentary. The historic significance of this commentary is simply this: the body of Christ has never had access to a thoroughgoing treatment of the last book of the Bible from the perspective of dispensational, pretribulational, premillennial eschatology. This is the approach that Moody Bible Institute has traditionally honored. I thank the staff for its commitment in seeing this project through to its completion.

Further, I want to express appreciation to the board and the administration of The Master's College and Seminary for granting me a sabbatical to complete the manuscript on *Revelation 8-22*. Without their encouragement and wholehearted support, this project would have been much longer in reaching fruition. In addition, I am greatly indebted to Michael Canham for his immense help in compiling the indexes of ancient literature, modern authors, and Scripture for both *Revelation 1-7* and *Revelation 8-22*. Likewise, Ted Bigelow, Rick Carmickle, and Tim Dane deserve much credit for their indispensable contributions in helping with the index of subjects. My special thanks to these four men.

May God use this work to strengthen His people for the tasks remaining before the coming of our Lord Jesus Christ.

Abbreviations .

In addition to those standard abbreviations found in the *Journal of Biblical Literature*, Instructions for Contributors, please note the following:

EBC	*The Expositor's Bible Commentary*
EDT	*Evangelical Dictionary of Theology*
GTJ	*Grace Theological Journal*
NA	Nestle-Aland, *Novum Testamentum Graece*, 26th ed.
GEL	*Greek-English Lexicon*, ed. J. Louw and E. Nida
NIDNTT	*New International Dictionary of New Testament Theology*, ed. Colin Brown
TrinJ	*Trinity Journal*

14

The Seventh Seal
and the First Six Trumpets

The intercalation on "The Servants of God" having ended, the numerical sequence of the seals picks up from the end of chapter 6 as the Lamb opens the seventh and last seal.

9. THE SEVENTH SEAL: THE SEVEN TRUMPETS AWAITED (8:1)

Translation

1And when he opened the seventh seal, there came a silence in heaven for about a half hour.

Exegesis and Exposition

8:1 The repetition of ἤνοιξεν (*ēnoixen*, "opened") in the first clause, Καὶ ὅταν ἤνοιξεν τὴν σφραγῖδα τὴν ἑβδόμην (*Kai hotan ēnoixen tēn sphragida tēn hebdomēn*, "And when he opened the seventh seal"), signals a continuation of the seal-series from 6:12 (cf. also 6:1, 3, 5, 7, 9).[1]

As this action occurs, the scene has shifted back to the throne room of chapters 4-5 with the Lamb as the approved representative for opening the seals.

The breaking of the final seal brings an unexpected result: "there came a silence in heaven for about a half hour" (ἐγένετο σιγὴ ἐν τῷ

---

1. James Moffatt, "The Revelation of St. John the Divine," in *The Expositor's Greek Testament*, ed. W. Robertson Nicoll (Grand Rapids: Eerdmans, n.d.), 5:401.

οὐρανῷ ὡς ἡμίωριον [*egeneto sigē en tō ouranō hōs hēmiōrion*]). This silence differs markedly from results of the six previous openings and has proven to be a puzzle for interpreters, causing them to advance at least five proposals: (1) It is the silence at the beginning of the sabbatical rest or the Millennium.² (2) It is not literal silence because of the continuing heavenly songs, but is a brief cessation in judgment.³ (3) It is a temporary suspension of the revelations granted to John.⁴ (4) It is a pause in the heavenly praises to allow the prayers of the saints to be heard before the throne.⁵ (5) It is a dramatic pause to symbolize the awe and dread with which the heavenly hosts await the events about to happen.⁶

Viewpoint 1 fails to recognize that the silence is in heaven, not on earth as would be true of the Millennium. Besides, silence is not a characteristic of heavenly rest, so it is exegetically irrelevant to connect this silence to millennial rest (Swete). The most conspicuous failure of the first view is, however, its assignment of an outcome that is diametrically opposed to the results of the other six seals.⁷ They are displays of the wrath of God against earth's rebels, but this view wants to make the seventh a picture of blessing. This is not what the seals portray.

This same consideration rules out view 2 as a solution. The first six seals denoted judgment. To have the seventh picture a cessation of judgment is inconsistent and unacceptable. The third proposed solution has merit in recognizing that the absence of an elder or angel speaking, of a chorus of praise or cry of adoration, and of thunder from the throne points to a temporary cessation of revelation.⁸ Yet it is more accurate not to call it a cessation of revelation, because the period of silence is part of the revelatory process. The fourth view has

---

2. Henry Alford, *The Greek Testament* (London: Longmans, Green, 1903), 4:630.
3. Walter Scott, *Exposition of the Revelation of Jesus Christ* (Swengel, Pa.: Bible Truth Depot, n.d.), pp. 168-69.
4. Henry Barclay Swete, *The Apocalypse of St. John* (London: Macmillan, 1906), p. 107.
5. R. H. Charles, *The Revelation of St. John*, ICC (New York: Scribner, 1920), 1:223.
6. Isbon T. Beckwith, *The Apocalypse of John* (New York: Macmillan, 1919), p. 550; J. A. Seiss, *The Apocalypse*, 3 vols. (New York: Charles C. Cook, 1909), 2:17; John F. Walvoord, *The Revelation of Jesus Christ* (Chicago: Moody, 1966), p. 150; Robert H. Mounce, *The Book of Revelation*, NICNT (Grand Rapids: Eerdmans, 1977), p. 179; Homer Hailey, *Revelation, an Introduction and Commentary* (Grand Rapids: Baker, 1979), p. 214.
7. George E. Ladd, *A Commentary on the Revelation of John* (Grand Rapids: Eerdmans, 1972), p. 122.
8. Archibald Thomas Robertson, *Word Pictures in the New Testament* (Nashville: Broadman, 1933), 6:356.

contextual advantage in the observation that a half hour was about the length of time necessary for the priest to perform the offering of incense required by the law (cf. Lev. 16:13-14; Luke 1:10, 21) and suggested by 8:3-4.[9] It also parallels the Talmudic tractate *Hagigah* (12*b*) where God silences the angels by day so that He may hear the prayers of Israel.[10] The chief disadvantage of this explanation is sequential; the prayers of the saints in this context come after the period of silence, not during it.

The fifth theory that views the silence as preparatory for what is about to happen is most consistent with the immediate context of chapter 8. It is a hushed expectancy that makes the judgments about to begin more impressive (Beckwith, Seiss, Scott, Mounce, Hailey, Walvoord). This kind of silence corresponds to OT occurrences of the same in conjunction with reverence for God and awesome expectation of His judgment (cf. Hab. 2:20; 3:3; Zeph. 1:7-8, 15, 17-18; Zech. 2:13).[11] So the silence prepares for what is to come in 8:2 ff.

The limit of the silence to about a half-hour[12] duration is an interesting accommodation of heavenly actions to a human limitation. One must think of heaven under the immediate rule of the eternal God as not subject to time limitations, but for the sake of the prophet a specifically short restriction applies to the period of silence. For the seer this was an impressive intermission in the rapidly moving drama into which his vision had drawn him (Swete, Mounce, Walvoord).

If the silence is only preparatory, what then is the essence of the seventh seal? The answer to this question is a crucial factor in determining the structure of the whole apocalyptic portion, 4:1–22:5. The far-reaching impact of this issue should be in mind in the resolving of this issue.[13] Two major possibilities have prevailed in the analysis of Revelation's structure. One recommends that the trumpet series in 8:6 ff. covers essentially the same ground as the seals have covered by

---

9. Lee, "Revelation," 4:595; David Chilton, *The Days of Vengeance* (Fort Worth, Tex.: Dominion, 1987), pp. 229-30.
10. G. R. Beasley-Murray, *The Book of Revelation*, NCB (Grand Rapids: Eerdmans, 1978), p. 150.
11. Moffatt, "Revelation," 5:401; J. Massyngberde Ford, *Revelation*, vol. 38 of AB (Garden City, N.Y.: Doubleday, 1975), p. 134; Philip Edgcumbe Hughes, *The Book of Revelation, A Commentary* (Grand Rapids: Eerdmans, 1990), p. 101.
12. The noun ἡμίωριον is a rare word and occurs only here in the NT. It is a combination of ἥμι, "half," and ὥρα, "hour" (Robertson, *Word Pictures*, 6:356).
13. The "Introduction to the Commentary" in the earlier volume has anticipated the crucial importance of this issue. Robert L. Thomas, *Revelation 1-7, An Exegetical Commentary* (Chicago: Moody, 1992), p. 43 n. 161.

describing events that are chronologically parallel but not necessarily identical with what the seals speak about.[14] "Recapitulation" is the term usually applied to this type of explanation. The other structural plan, called the "telescopic" or "dovetailing" view, sees the seventh seal as composed of the seven trumpets with the consequence that the trumpets are chronologically subsequent to the first six seals in their fulfillment.[15]

Brief notice should be given to a third view which proposes that the structure follows neither strict chronological arrangement nor a systematic retracing of the same period. It holds that the development is merely literary and is not intended to portray a corresponding historical development.[16] It is proper to credit the writer for his literary art (Mounce), but it is hermeneutically unacceptable to conclude that such expertise excludes rational comprehensibility (contra Mounce).[17] No factor dictates that a description cannot be graphic if it follows a logical scheme. A perfectly logical apocalypse is *not* a contradiction in terms (contra Mounce).[18]

Concerning the first of the two major structural possibilities—recapitulation—probably the strongest argument is the similarity between the sixth seal judgment (6:12-17) and events said to follow the Tribulation in Matt. 24:29. Accordingly, the similarity places the sixth seal on the threshold of the end, leaving no other option than for the trumpets to return and cover the same ground again.[19] Other phenomena presented in support of recapitulation include the occurrence of the storm theophany in connection with each seventh member (8:5; 11:19; cf. 16:18) and the presence of an indication of the arrival of the end at each seventh member (Alford).

A response to pro-recapitulation evidence notes that the similarity between Rev. 6:12-17 and Matt. 24:29 is only a similarity. Earlier dis-

---

14. Lee, "Revelation," 4:595; William Hendriksen, *More Than Conquerors* (Grand Rapids: Baker, 1944), pp. 139-40.
15. E. W. Bullinger, *The Apocalypse* or *"The Day of the Lord"* (London: Eyre and Spottiswodde, n.e.), pp. 301-2, 306; W. G. Scroggie, *The Book of Revelation* (Edinburgh: Book Stall, 1920), p. 167; C. A. Blanchard, *Light on the Last Days* (Chicago: Bible Institute Colportage, 1913), p. 58.
16. Martin Kiddle, *The Revelation of St. John*, HNTC (New York: Harper, 1940), pp. xxix-xxxiii; J. W. Bowman, "The Revelation to John: Its Dramatic Structure and Message," *Int* 9 (1955): 436-53; G. V. Caird, *A Commentary on the Revelation of St. John the Divine*, HNTC (New York: Harper & Row, 1966), p. 106; Mounce, *Revelation*, p. 178.
17. Thomas, *Revelation 1-7*, pp. 32-36.
18. See Excursus 3 at the end of this volume.
19. R. C. H. Lenski, *The Interpretation of St. John's Revelation* (Columbus, Ohio: Lutheran Book Concern, 1935), p. 271; Alan F. Johnson, "Revelation," in *EBC*, ed. Frank E. Gaebelein (Grand Rapids: Zondervan, 1981), 12:490.

cussion has noted the difficulty in making the two fulfillments identical (Thomas, *Revelation 1-7*, pp. 451-52). The use of the storm theophany is also questionable as proof. These incidents signal only that the end will come in conjunction with that seventh member. The seventh members could begin at different times—i.e., the seventh trumpet later than the seventh seal—and be of extended durations and still end at the same time. This would allow all the trumpets to be subsequent to the first six seals. The same observation applies in reference to other seventh-member indications that the end has arrived. The seventh members could be sequential in their beginnings, but still terminate together.

Contextual considerations are heavily on the side of a telescopic-type structure. The vision of the angels with the trumpets (8:2) comes immediately after the opening of the seventh seal. Since the text assigns no other content to the seventh trumpet, the full impression is that the seals and trumpets are successive.[20] These angels are intimately interwoven with the seventh seal and are an integral part of its action through their introduction in 8:2 and their reintroduction in 8:6.[21] Coupled with this specific observation is a more general one that notes the significant increase in intensity in the trumpet series over that of the seals (Scott, Johnson). The judgments become more severe as the period advances toward the personal return of Christ. This must mean chronological progression. Support for the telescopic analysis of the structure involves other factors that relate to the broader context. At the end of this volume Excursus 3—"The Structure of the Apocalypse: Recapitulation or Progression?"—provides a fuller discussion of all the issues than is possible at this point.

The correctness of the telescopic understanding, therefore, leads to the conclusion that the silence of v. 1 purposes to prepare for the awful consequences of the seven trumpet judgments that will commence shortly. Earlier chronological placement of the first six seals in the first half of the prophetic week of Daniel (Thomas, pp. 452-53) dictates that the first trumpet happen early in the last half of that week.

Additional Notes

8:1 A difference between the temporal clause introducing the other six seals and that of the seventh seal is the use of ὅταν in 8:1 instead of

---

20. Merrill C. Tenney, *Interpreting Revelation* (Grand Rapids: Eerdmans, 1957), p. 71.
21. Friedrich Düsterdieck, *Critical and Exegetical Handbook to the Revelation of John*, in Meyer's Commentary, trans. and ed. Henry E. Jacobs (New York: Funk & Wagnalls, 1887), pp. 261-63; Ladd, *Revelation*, pp. 121-23; M. Robert Mulholland, *Revelation, Holy Living in an Unholy World* (Grand Rapids: Zondervan, 1990), p. 185.

the ὅτε in the other six places. Rather than assuming that the change brings the tone of uncertainty into this seventh usage (Alford, Swete, Simcox), one should allow that the Koinê Greek writers sometimes used ὅταν with the aorist indicative to depict a definite occurrence.[22] Yet the probable shade of meaning is probably somewhere between definiteness (ὅτε ἤνοιξεν, aorist indicative) and indefiniteness (ὅταν ἀνοίξῃ, aorist subjunctive) (Swete).

B. THE SOUNDING OF THE SEVEN TRUMPETS (8:2–11:19)

1. THE SETTING OF THE TRUMPETS: THE PRAYERS OF THE SAINTS (8:2-6)

Translation

2And I saw the seven angels who stand before God, and seven trumpets were given to them. 3And another angel having a golden censer came and stood at the altar, and much incense was given to him that he might dispense it on behalf of the prayers of all the saints on the golden altar which is before the throne. 4And the smoke of the incense ascended before God with the prayers of the saints from the hand of the angel. 5And the angel took the incense, and filled it from the fire of the altar and cast [it] to the earth; and [peals of] thunder and voices and [flashes of] lightning and an earthquake occurred. 6And the seven angels who had the seven trumpets prepared themselves that they might sound.

Exegesis and Exposition

8:2 A new occurrence of καὶ εἶδον (*kai eidon*, "and I saw") marks a new phase of John's seventh-seal vision. This scene follows the half hour of silence and includes preparatory actions for the trumpet series (8:2-6) and the sounding of the first four trumpets (8:7-12), the next *kai eidon* not coming until 8:13.[23]

John saw "the seven angels who stand before God" (τοὺς ἑπτὰ ἀγγέλους οἳ ἐνώπιον τοῦ θεοῦ ἑστήκασιν [*tous hepta angelous hoi enōpion tou theou hestēkasin*]). Because of the article with *angelous* ("angels") and because of an alleged correspondence with seven archangels in Jewish tradition, some have identified these angels as a special group consisting of Uriel, Raphael, Raguel, Michael, Saraqâêl, Gabriel, and

---

22. Archibald Thomas Robertson, *A Grammar of the Greek New Testament in the Light of Historical Research* (Nashville: Broadman, 1934), pp. 958, 973; idem, *Word Pictures*, 6:356; R. C. H. Lenski, *The Interpretation of St. John's Revelation* (Columbus, Ohio: Lutheran Book Concern, 1935), p. 266.
23. J. B. Smith, *A Revelation of Jesus Christ* (Scottdale, Pa.: Herald, 1961), p. 137.

Remiel.[24] The perfect participle *hestēkasin* ("stand") indicates that they were in position before God and had been there some time as a special class of angels would be. Another strength of this identification is a similar description of Gabriel's position in Luke 1:19. Though the Bible never calls him an "archangel," it does represent him, one of the traditional group, as stationed in that location.[25]

Two reasons militate against the proposed identification, however. These seven are missing from the heavenly company described in Revelation 4-5 (Beckwith), and the agreement of the present context with Jewish angelology is not complete (Alford). It is an angel distinct from this group who offers the prayers of the saints in 8:2-5. If this were such a special group, certainly one of them would have performed this task. The position of these angels before God does not automatically equate them with the traditional archangels. It simply puts them in a position similar to that of Gabriel (Walvoord).

The preferable course is to explain the article as pointing out a specific group, not necessarily the one known in Jewish tradition.[26] What makes them special is their commission to sound the trumpets. Their position before God marks their readiness for service, in this case the service of symbolically initiating the trumpet afflictions. This is the natural sense of the words, and no reason has arisen to point to another understanding (Scott, Walvoord).

John saw the seven angels receive seven trumpets: καὶ ἐδόθησαν αὐτοῖς ἑπτὰ σάλπιγγες (*kai edothēsan autois hepta salpinges*, "and seven trumpets were given to them"). Trumpets played a major part in the national life of Israel, finding use in ceremonial processions (e.g., Josh. 6:1; 1 Chron. 15:24), in assembling people for war, journeys, and special feasts (e.g., Num. 10:9-10), in warning of the coming day of the Lord (e.g., Joel 2:1), and in announcing the new year (e.g., Num. 29:1) (Seiss, Walvoord, Mounce). As a signal for war, the trumpet found a natural association with judgment (Moffatt). Here they are precursors of divine judgment in the Day of the Lord (cf. Zeph. 1:14-16) (Scott, Smith).

8:3 Before the trumpets sound, however, an interlude sets the tone for them: Καὶ ἄλλος ἄγγελος ἦλθεν καὶ ἐστάθη ἐπὶ τοῦ θυσιαστηρίου

---

24. Alford, *Greek Testament*, 4:632; Beckwith, *Apocalypse*, p. 550; Robertson, *Word Pictures*, 6:356; Morris, *Revelation*, p. 119; Mounce, *Revelation*, p. 180. Extrabiblical references to these angels, also known as "Angels of the Presence," include the *Book of Jubilees* 1:27, 29; 2:1-2, 18; 15:27; 31:14; *Tobit* 12:15; *1 Enoch* 20:2-8.
25. Mounce, *Revelation*, p. 180; Hughes, *Revelation*, p. 103.
26. Alford, *Greek Testament*, 4:632; Leon Morris, *The Revelation of St. John*, TNTC (Grand Rapids: Eerdmans, 1969), p. 119; Mounce, *Revelation*, p. 180.

ἔχων λιβανωτὸν χρυσοῦν (*Kai allos angelos ēlthen kai estathē epi tou thysiastēriou echōn libanōton chrysoun*, "And another angel having a golden censer came and stood at[27] the altar"). As John watched, another angel with a golden censer came into the picture and stood before the altar. Attempts to identify this angel as Christ have rested mainly on the theological consideration that only Christ as high priest can help the prayers of the saints.[28] A basic canon of interpretation, however, states that one must never depart from the plain meaning of words because of an alleged doctrinal principle (Alford). To insist that the angel is Christ results from reading concepts from the epistle to the Hebrews into this context. Besides, careful observation of what the angel does reveals that the angel performs no mediatorial service in making the prayers completely acceptable; he only enforces the prayers (Beckwith, Lenski, Morris).

A more satisfactory identification is that the angel is another created being like "another angel" in 7:2 (Alford, Lenski). This is an angel of the same kind (*allos*, "another of the same kind"[29]) as those in 8:2. He does not engage in angelic invocation. He simply takes the provided incense and facilitates the prayers of the saints. Had this been Christ, He would have needed no incense.[30] A suggestion is that the angel may be one of the twenty-four elders who hold the incense in Rev. 5:8 (Charles). This view is possible, but it cannot be proved.

The identity of the altars, two in v. 3 and one in v. 5, has been a subject of debate. Hints at 6:9 and 7:15 compare the heavenly scene of John's visions to a temple, though heaven is not expressly called a temple until 11:19 (Moffatt). Whether the heavenly temple has one or two altars has been the major question (Thomas, pp. 517-19: Excursus 2). Proponents of the two-altar theory usually find both of the altars here, the altar of burnt offering in vv. 3*a*, 5 and the altar of incense in v. 3*b* (cited by Beckwith, Ladd). This approach has the angel going first to the altar of burnt offering to secure some coals (v. 3*a*) and taking

---

27. "stood at." Ἐστάθη ("stood") is an ingressive aorist of ἵστημι: the angel came and "took his place." A number of uses of ἐπί in the LXX favor the meaning of "at" or "by" rather than "upon" in such a situation as this (cf. Gen. 24:13, 43; Amos 9:1) (Swete, *Apocalypse*, p. 108; Charles, *Revelation*, 1:226). A use in Acts 5:23 also argues for this meaning (Beckwith, *Apocalypse*, p. 552).

28. Scott, *Revelation*, p. 180; Seiss, *Apocalypse*, 2:26-27; H. A. Ironside, *Lectures on the Book of Revelation* (New York: Loizeaux, n.d.), p. 146; Robert Govett, *Govett on Revelation* (1981 reprint; Miami Springs, Fla.: Conley & Schoettle, 1961), 1:310.

29. Richard Chenevix Trench, *Synonyms of the New Testament* (Grand Rapids: Eerdmans, 1953), pp. 357-61.

30. William R. Newell, *The Book of Revelation* (Chicago: Moody, 1935), p. 121; Walvoord, *Revelation*, p. 152.

them to the altar of incense (v. 3*b*) where he places the coals taken from the altar of burnt offering. He then returns to the altar of burnt offering (v. 5) to take fire to cast into the earth. This reconstruction is vivid, but it fails in not connecting the altar of v. 5 with the incense of v. 4 in accord with the contextual flow. Moreover, the two-altar theory itself is open to question. The assumption that in Revelation every part of the earthly temple has its prototype in the heavenly temple is ill-founded (Alford, Charles).

The single-altar theory better satisfies the present context and the context of the whole book (Charles). Attention in this passage is upon the incense. This, along with later references to the altar of incense (cf. 9:13; 14:18; 16:7), effectively excludes the possibility of this being the altar of burnt offering (Beckwith). Only the altar of incense was made of gold (v. 3*b*) (Lenski). Identifying this with the altar of incense also best satisfies the two OT analogies with John's current experience, where Isaiah's coal came from the altar that was within the ναός (*naos*, "temple") (Isa. 6:6) and Ezekiel's coals of fire were from between the cherubim who were in closest proximity to God (Ezek. 10:2). The altar of incense must have been the source of both of these (Charles). The reason why the stipulation "before the throne" comes with the second instead of the first mention of the altar in v. 3 is to emphasize nearness to God in proximity to the prayers of the saints, not to distinguish the altar in v. 3*b* from the one in v. 3*a* (contra Smith).

The "golden censer" (*libanōton chrysoun*), sometimes referred to as a "firepan," was an implement used in the Solomonic temple (cf. 1 Kings 7:50; 2 Kings 25:15; 2 Chron. 4:22; Jer. 52:18-19). Derived from λίβανος (*libanos*, "frankincense") (Matt. 2:11; Rev. 18:13), λιβανωτός (*libanōtos*) in the OT referred to "incense" or "frankincense" (e.g., 1 Chron. 9:29, LXX). It is found only in Rev. 8:3, 5 in the NT, and it means "censer."[31] The adjective *chrysoun* ("golden") decides for "censer" instead of "incense."

The next step in the drama was for the angel to receive from God much incense to offer on the altar for the prayers of the saints: καὶ ἐδόθη[32] αὐτῷ θυμιάματα πολλὰ ἵνα δώσει ταῖς προσευχαῖς τῶν ἁγίων πάντων ἐπὶ τὸ θυσιαστήριον τὸ χρυσοῦν τὸ ἐνώπιον τοῦ θρόνου (*kai edothē autō thymiamata polla hina dōsei tais proseuchais tōn hagiōn pantōn epi to thysiastērion to chrysoun to enōpion tou thronou*, "and much incense was given to him that he might dispense it on behalf of the prayers of all the saints on the golden altar which is before the

---

31. Swete, *Apocalypse*, p. 108; Beckwith, *Apocalypse*, p. 553; W. Michaelis, "λίβανος, λιβανωτός," *TDNT*, 4:264.
32. As customary, the verb ἐδόθη (*edothē*) is singular because of the neuter plural subject θυμιάματα (*thymiamata*).

throne"). Though the source of the gift of incense is unstated, custom-ary usage of *edothē* ("was given") throughout Revelation indicates that it was God (cf. 6:2, 4, 8, 11; 7:2; 9:1, 3, 5; 11:1, 2; 13:5, 7, 14, 15; 16:8; 19:8; 20:4) (Alford).

Incense had a prominent place in OT worship (e.g., Ex. 30:34-38) and serves as a reminder that intercessory prayer is like sweet perfume before the Lord (Walvoord). In the temple ritual, the priest poured the saucer of incense over the burning coals on the altar of incense. At the same time, the Israelites bowed in prayer as the fragrant cloud of smoke ascended heavenward. A similar connection between incense and the prayers of the saints occurs in Rev. 5:8, except there the in-cense and the prayers are one and the same.

In 8:3 "much incense" is either the same as or distinct from the prayers of the saints. Of course, the analogy of 5:8 argues for identify-ing the two (Seiss), and grammatically *tais proseuchais* ("the prayers") can mean "consisting of the prayers of the saints."[33]

But this metaphor differs from 5:8, with the prayers corresponding to the live coals on which the grains of incense fall. The meeting of the incense and the hot coals produces the fragrant smoke cloud, a symbol of divine acceptance (Swete). It is better to observe the contextual distinction between the incense and the prayers.[34] The angel adds "much [more] incense"[35] to the prayers to increase greatly the volume of aromatic smoke (Lenski). The prayers and the incense ascend to-gether (8:4), but this does not require a merging of the two.

The preferable understanding of *tais proseuchais* ("on behalf of the prayers") is as a dative of advantage. The offering of incense is to help the prayers, i.e., to make them more acceptable to God. This does not assign a mediatorial role to the angel, but it simply says that the pray-ers rise directly to God, being enforced by the accompanying incense (Beckwith). In the context of the Apocalypse the prayers are unques-tionably the cries of the saints during the future Great Tribulation for judgment against their persecutors as the present paragraph will shortly reveal (8:4-5; cf. 6:9-10; 9:13; 14:18).[36] This being the case, it is

---

33. "Consisting of" is possibly equal to the Hebrew ל ot definition (F. F. Bruce, "The Book of Revelation," *A New Testament Commentary*, ed. H. C. D. Howley [London: Pickering & Inglis, 1969], p. 646), or it can be construed as a dative of reference, "in token of the prayers" (Caird, *Revelation*, pp. 103, 107).

34. Alford, *Greek Testament*, 4:633; William Lee, "The Revelation of St. John," in *The Holy Bible*, ed. F. C. Cook (London: John Murray, 1881), 4:598; Mounce, *Revelation*, p. 182.

35. Note the plural noun θυμιάματα (*thymiamata*).

36. Clarence Larkin, *The Book of Revelation* (Philadelphia: Clarence Larkin, 1919), p. 69.

improper to see them as the prayers of all the saints of all time.[37] Martyrs in heaven will perhaps cry the loudest, but the number of these future saints will not be limited to them (Alford). The destination of their prayers is the golden altar before God's throne, the place of power and the source of the trumpet judgments about to be initiated.[38]

8:4 Leaving the angel's hand, the smoke followed an upward route to arrive in the presence of God: καὶ ἀνέβη ὁ καπνὸς τῶν θυμιαμάτων ταῖς προσευχαῖς τῶν ἁγίων ἐκ χειρὸς τοῦ ἀγγέλου ἐνώπιον τοῦ θεοῦ (*kai anebē ho kapnos tōn thymiamatōn tais proseuchais tōn hagiōn ek cheiros tou angelou enōpion tou theou*, "and the smoke of the incense ascended before God with the prayers of the saints from the hand of the angel"). The smoke is that resulting from the burning of incense (*ho kapnos tōn thymiamatōn*, "the smoke of the incense"). Because of the ripeness of the season in the divine purpose, it denotes acceptability. Prayers unanswered until now become welcome and receive an immediate reply (Alford).

An inflectional form identical to one in v. 3, *tais proseuchais*, performs a different function in v. 4, where it is an associative instrumental.[39] The smoke produced by the burning incense rises "in the company of the prayers." The association of the two guarantees divine acceptance of the prayers for God to act in vengeance.

8:5 The next step in the interlude before the trumpet series brings earth's inhabitants into the picture: καὶ εἴληφεν ὁ ἄγγελος τὸν λιβανωτόν, καὶ ἐγέμισεν αὐτὸν ἐκ τοῦ πυρὸς τοῦ θυσιαστηρίου καὶ ἔβαλεν εἰς τὴν γῆν (*kai eilēphen ho angelos ton libanōton, kai egemisen auton ek tou puros tou thysiastēriou kai ebalen eis tēn gēn*, "And the angel took the incense, and filled it from the fire of the altar and cast [it] to the earth"). The angel does so by taking[40] and filling his golden censer with coals from the fire on the altar and hurling them earthward. This connotes judgment about to be imposed in answer to the prayers connected with

---

37. William Henry Simcox, *The Revelation of St. John the Divine* (Cambridge: Cambridge U., 1893), p. 104; Caird, *Revelation*, p. 107; Ladd, *Revelation*, p. 125.

38. Excursus 2 (Thomas, *Revelation 1-7*, pp. 517-22) develops the close association of this scene with 6:9-11, which also involves the altar and the prayers. See also John Paul Heil, "The Fifth Seal as a Key to the Book of Revelation," *Bib* 74 (1993): 232-33; Grant R. Osborne, "Theodicy in the Apocalypse," *TrinJ* 14NS, no. 1 (Spring 1993): 75-76.

39. Robertson, *Grammar*, p. 529; Mounce, *Revelation*, p. 182.

40. See 5:7 for a discussion of the perfect tense of εἴληφεν. The dramatic perfect function preferred there is the best here also (cf. Robertson, *Grammar*, p. 899; Lenski, *Revelation*, p. 271). Perhaps the angel had laid aside the censer after its use in 8:3-4, and now takes it up again, though εἴληφεν may simply be pleonastic (Swete, *Apocalypse*, p. 109; Beckwith, *Apocalypse*, p. 554; Morris, *Revelation*, p. 121).

that same altar in 8:3-4 (Alford, Swete, Charles, Beckwith). The connection between the divine wrath about to fall upon the earth and the prayers of God's people is conspicuous (Lenski, Morris). The censer normally used for offering incense has become a symbol of judgment in response to prayer (Swete, Walvoord), an action similar to the one in Ezek. 10:2-7 where the hands rather than a censer carry the hot coals (Moffatt).

Fire is a frequent symbol for divine torment of the wicked (Seiss).[41] The hurling of the fire into the earth recalls the saints' question of 6:10, "How long?" and signals that an answer to those prayers is on the way in the form of judgmental visitations against the earth.[42] The interaction between the sovereignty of God and the prayers of His people is part of the ultimate mystery of existence (Beasley-Murray). The saints pray for justice and their prayers play a part, but it is God's business to determine the time and nature of actions against their persecutors.[43]

The second announcement of the storm theophany (cf. 4:5) follows: καὶ ἐγένοντο βρονταὶ καὶ φωναὶ καὶ ἀστραπαὶ καὶ σεισμός (*kai egenonto brontai kai phōnai kai astrapai kai seismos*, "and [peals of] thunder and voices and [flashes of] lightning and an earthquake occurred"). The thunder, voices, and earthquake are in marked contrast with the silence of 8:1 (Lenski). They along with the lightning are physical disturbances that accompany the manifestation of God's wrath against an impenitent world (cf. Ex. 19:16-19; Rev. 11:19; 16:18) (Moffatt). They see in the string of catastrophes in the coming trumpet series the accomplishment of what God set out to do in "the hour of trial that is about to come upon the whole inhabited earth, to try those who dwell upon the earth" (3:10; cf. 4:5). By the time the seven trumpets have run their course, also marking the completion of the seventh seal, God's purging of this creation will be complete. This is the implied import of the storm theophany.

The earthquake is an added feature not found in the earlier theophany of 4:5. In the mind of the prophet John, this enhanced even more the magnitude of the importance of what he was witnessing. Whether literal or not, in his state of being "in the spirit" the earthquake was undoubtedly an experience of reality for him.

8:6 To close the interlude, the seven trumpet angels reappear and prepare to sound: Καὶ οἱ ἑπτὰ ἄγγελοι οἱ ἔχοντες τὰς ἑπτὰ σάλπιγγας

---

41. This fire possibly bears a direct connection with the fire that is part of the first three trumpets (Mounce, *Revelation*, p. 186).
42. Alford, *Greek Testament* 4:634; Kiddle, *Revelation*, p. 146; Johnson, "Revelation," 12:489.
43. J. P. M. Sweet, *Revelation* (Philadelphia: Westminster, Pelican, 1979), p. 160.

ἡτοίμασαν αὐτοὺς ἵνα σαλπίσωσιν (*Kai hoi hepta angeloi hoi echontes tas hepta salpingas hētoimasan autous hina salpisōsin,* "And the seven angels who had the seven trumpets prepared themselves[44] that they might sound"). Their preparatory activity, probably in a deliberate arranging of themselves in the proper order and raising their trumpets in readiness to sound, heightens the sense of expectancy even more.[45] The signal for them to prepare was the presentation of incense on the altar (8:3) and the casting of fire to the earth (8:5) (Lee).

Following the pattern of the seal series, the first four trumpets are different in kind from the last three. These four set in motion the forces of nature to achieve their destructive effects on natural objects. Of the fifteen items affected by the plagues of the first four trumpets, one-third receives injury or destruction in twelve instances (8:7, 10, 11 being the exceptions) (Charles). God uses the world of nature to punish mankind.

On the other hand, in the last three trumpets, sustaining human life in the face of demonic onslaughts is the major concern, particularly among earth's godless inhabitants (Moffatt). Like the bowls to follow (16:1 ff.) the trumpet series has reminiscences of the OT plagues against Egypt—the first trumpet paralleling the seventh Egyptian plague (Ex. 9:24), the second trumpet resembling the first plague (Ex. 7:19-20), the fourth trumpet recalling the ninth plague (Ex. 10:21), and the fifth trumpet paralleling the eighth plague (Ex. 10:12). Both series are judgments against the enemies of God's people and comprise steps toward deliverance of the saints (Lee, Beasley-Murray).

Additional Notes

8:2 Ἑστάναι ἐνώπιον translates עמד לפני (cf. 1 Kings 17:1; 18:15; 2 Kings 3:14; 5:16; Jer. 15:19). It means to "attend upon," "be the servant of" (Charles). How long the angels had been in that position is uncertain. They may have arrived just before or just after the hour of silence, or they may have been like Gabriel or other special angels who stand before God continually (Seiss).

8:3 Other proposed functions of the dative ταῖς προσευχαῖς have been dative of indirect object after δώσει (Alford) and dative of reference because of the sense carried over from 5:8.[46] The indirect object possibility would have required προστίθημι in place of δίδωμι which

---

44. As occasionally happens, the intensive pronoun αὐτούς functions here as a reflexive.
45. Albert Barnes, *The Book of Revelation* (New York: Harper, 1851), p. 223; Seiss, *Apocalpyse*, 2:41; Scott, *Revelation*, p. 183; Mounce, *Revelation*, p. 183.
46. Caird, *Revelation*, pp. 103, 107.

normally does not mean "add." The dative of reference will not satisfy, because it is a vague and rather awkward way of equating the prayers with the incense, which is the goal of the suggestion.

8:4 Besides the associative instrumental function of ταῖς προσευχαῖς, suggested uses have included (1) the dative of advantage (Beckwith, Charles, Seiss, Lenski), (2) the dative of indirect object (Alford), (3) the dative of reference (Swete), and (4) the dative of possession (Lee). In regard to (1), the notion of benefit present in 8:3 pales into the idea of accompaniment in 8:4 (Mounce). Views (2) and (3) rest on inadequate meanings for the same form in 8:3. The possibility of (4) finds its basis in the functioning of the dative, like the Hebrew ﬥ, to show possession (cf. Gen. 9:5; Deut. 1:3; 2 Sam. 3:2, LXX) (Lee). This is interesting, but lacks credibility because of the rarity of the dative of possession in the NT. The key consideration that favors the associative instrumental in v. 4 is the difference between the verbs in vv. 3 and 4: in v. 3, δώσει lends itself to the idea of advantage, and in v. 4, ἀνέβη to that of association.

8:6 To view the first four trumpets as the end of the Jewish nation before the outbreak of war with the Romans in the late sixties A.D.[47] is purely imaginative and without any valid exegetical evidence. It is also the height of unwarranted allegorism to limit the scope of the trumpets to Judea and Jerusalem.[48] This does flagrant injustice to the worldwide scope of the prophecy.

2. THE FIRST TRUMPET: BURNING OF A THIRD OF VEGETATION (8:7)

In contradistinction to the last three trumpets, the first four afflict natural objects, i.e., earth, trees, grass, sea, rivers, and the like. The fifth and sixth have men as their special objects,[49] and unlike the first four which are connected and interdependent, are separate and independent. In contrast to these two, the first four have only an indirect effect on mankind. Besides these differences, the voice of the eagle in 8:13 separates the trumpets into two groups (Alford, Swete, Beckwith, Sweet).

God's people are not the objects of the trumpet judgments, but a world violently hostile toward God is (Mounce, Morris). The visitations purpose to lead unbelievers to repentance (cf. 9:20-21). This purpose is realized in only exceptional cases, however (Moffatt, Caird). They mark an increase in severity compared to the seals, with afflic-

---

47. Chilton, *Days of Vengeance*, p. 236.
48. Ibid., p. 237.
49. The seventh trumpet is the same as the fifth and sixth, but will be developed in connection with the seven bowls of wrath.

tions that are of a more supernatural nature, but the wrath of God will become even more evident in the series of bowls yet to come (Beckwith). The third part affected in the first through the fourth and the sixth trumpets is an indication that, bad as they are, these plagues are not the ultimate ones (Kiddle).

The judgments now beginning were those held back in 7:3 until the servants of God were sealed.[50]

Translation

7And the first sounded; and hail and fire mixed with blood came, and were cast into the earth; and the third part of the earth was burned up, and the third part of the trees were burned up, and all green grass was burned up.

Exegesis and Exposition

The words Καὶ ὁ πρῶτος ἐσάλπισεν (*Kai ho prōtos esalpisen*, "And the first sounded") launch the reader into the trumpet series.[51] The immediate consequence of the first sounding is the arrival of χάλαζα καὶ πῦρ μεμιγμένα[52] ἐν αἵματι (*chalaza kai pyr memigmena en haimati*, "hail and fire mixed with blood"). This combination resembles the results of local volcanic activity in Asia Minor that John may have witnessed. However his constant use of OT material argues for a background of Ex. 9:24 in this description (cf. Ps. 105:32) (Mounce). Hail and stones fell in a shower of blood as hail and/or volcanic fireballs commonly fall in a shower of rain. The allusion to the seventh Egyptian plague (Ex. 9:23-27)—which spared the Israelites—is clear, except here blood is an added feature (Alford). The combining of fire and blood recalls an eschatological feature connected with the Day of the Lord in Joel 2:30 (Charles).

God is probably the unnamed agent who casts this unfathomable deluge into the earth: καὶ ἐβλήθη εἰς τὴν γῆν (*kai eblēthē eis tēn gēn*, "and were cast into the earth"). History of both the first century A.D. and the twentieth century has recorded upheavals of nature resembling this plague (Swete, Moffatt), but none nearly so awful. Just how dreadful it will be depends somewhat on whether the phenomena connected with the plague are literal or only symbolic.

Resolution of this issue depends largely on one's basic philosophy

---

50. Thomas, *Revelation 1-7*, pp. 456-66; Alford, *Greek Testament*, 4:637.
51. The verb form ἐσάλπισεν occurs to initiate each of the seven trumpets (cf. 8:8, 10, 12; 9:1, 13; 11:15).
52. This perfect passive participle is neuter in agreement with the neuter πῦρ and plural because of the compound subject χάλαζα καὶ πῦρ (Robertson, *Word Pictures*, 6:358).

for interpreting Revelation as a whole. A symbolic interpretation assumes the absence of strict realism in a vision of this sort because of the introduction of illogical results, such as the darkening of a part of the luminaries diminishing the duration rather than the intensity of light, a single burning star falling on a third part of all rivers and fountains, and fire burning amid a rain of hail and blood (Beckwith).[53] The prophet describes a marvelous scene without attention to realistic details. Advocates of the symbolic approach generally chalk up these inconsistencies to the nature of apocalyptic literature in its orientation toward symbolism.[54]

Yet Revelation is according to its own self-claim primarily a prophecy rather than a typical apocalyptic writing,[55] and works of prophecy require no such hermeneutical predisposition toward symbolism. The OT prophets understood that the miracles of Egypt were to be repeated in the future (e.g., Isa. 10:22-25; 11:12-16; 30:30; Jer. 16:14-15; 23:7-8; Ezek. 38:22; Mic. 7:15) (Govett). At several points the prophet Amos uses God's miraculous work of deliverance from Egypt as a reference point for the way He will deal with His people in the future (cf. Amos 2:10; 4:10; 8:8-9; 9:5-7). The same principles of interpretation apply in prophecies as in historical narrative. To contend otherwise is to stand in judgment over the text rather than listening to its message.[56]

Furthermore, the proposal that apocalyptic literature cannot be logically cohesive because of its essentially poetic or artistic bent cannot stand. This assumption stems mostly from reading into the Apocalypse characteristics that apply to nonbiblical apocalypses. One cannot make such an across-the-board comparison, however, because Revelation is divinely inspired and the other apocalypses are not. It is fundamentally prophetic, not apocalyptic, and hence falls into an entirely different category of hermeneutics. No one has made a thorough case against the possibility of a prophecy's being scientifically and logically consistent *and* artistically effective in its imagery as well. Nor will such a case be made, because rationality and artistry are not mutually exclusive.

In addition, symbolic interpretation leads to a hopeless quagmire

---

53. Other indications that this is the language of ecstatic experience and scenes cannot fit into a consistent pattern include the prohibition not to hurt the green grass (9:4) after all the grass has already been burned up (8:7) and the falling of a great star from heaven (8:10) after all the stars have already fallen (6:12) (Ford, *Revelation*, p. 132; Mounce, *Revelation*, p. 184).
54. Morris, *Revelation*, p. 123; Beasley-Murray, *Revelation*, p. 157; Vern Sheridan Poythress, "Genre and Hermeneutics in Rev 20:1-6," *JETS* 36/1 (March 1993): 48-52.
55. Thomas, *Revelation 1-7*, "Introduction to the Commentary," pp. 23-29.
56. Ibid., pp. 29-38.

of contradictions. For instance, the earth, grass, and trees are symbols for nations and men in the first trumpet (8:7), but in trumpets 3, 5, and 6 these objects of nature appear side-by-side with men (8:11; 9:4, 15). This type of explanation leads to endless conjecture and turns Revelation into an incomprehensible riddle (Seiss). As Alford observes, "all analogy requires that in the same series of visions, when one judgement is to destroy earth, trees, and grass, and another not to injure earth, trees, or grass, . . . the earth, trees, and grass bear the same meaning in the two cases."[57] Symbolic presuppositions cannot constitute a reasonable pattern for interpreting any literature. Only the text under scrutiny can justify figurative understanding by indications of its own, none of which is present at this point.

In view of the resemblances of the trumpet visitations to five and possibly six of those against Egypt in Moses' day, the plain literal sense of the plagues is far superior to the fanciful associations attached to them by those who spiritualize the text.[58]

The casting of the hail and fire mixed with blood has a threefold result: καὶ τὸ τρίτον τῆς γῆς κατεκάη,[59] καὶ τὸ τρίτον τῶν δένδρων κατεκάη, καὶ πᾶς χόρτος χλωρὸς κατεκάη (*kai to triton tēs gēs katekaē, kai to triton tōn dendrōn katekaē, kai pas chortos chlōros katekaē*, "and the third part of the earth was burned up, and the third part of the trees were burned up, and all green grass was burned up"). The destructive power of this plague lies in the fire that burns significant portions of earth's vegetation (Alford). It was the hail in the comparable Egyptian plague that wrought the destruction of vegetation (Ex. 9:25) (Lee). The first object is the cultivated soil on earth's surface apart from the sea (cf. 8:8-9) and the inland bodies of water (8:10-11), a third of which was burned up (Alford, Beckwith, Mounce). The second object is a third of the trees, a particular part of cultivated area already named (Mounce). Fruit trees in particular were important to life in Palestine and in Asia Minor (cf. Matt. 7:17; Jude 12). Flames destroyed these too.

The third element of vegetation to be burned is πᾶς χόρτος χλωρός (*pas chortos chlōros*, "all the green grass"). This poses a dilemma, because grass still exists when the fifth trumpet arrives (9:4). It is hermeneutically wrong to see this as an inconsistency retained to achieve artistic effect (contra Morris, Hailey). Also, the text does not

---

57. Alford, *Greek Testament*, 4:635.
58. Ibid.; Swete, *Apocalypse*, p. 110; Bullinger, *Apocalypse*, pp. 299-300; Robertson, *Word Pictures*, 6:358; Walvoord, *Revelation*, p. 153.
59. Κατεκάη is an aorist passive indicative from κατακαίω, a κατα- prefix intensifying the simple verb καίω, with the meaning "I burn up." The threefold repetition of the verb in v. 7 is for dramatic effect (Robertson, *Word Pictures*, 6:358).

allow a limitation of "all the green grass" to that within a third part of the earth (Alford). Two considerations help to resolve the quandary. First, a time lapse between the first and fifth trumpets allows time for grass to be regrown after the burning, but before the assault of the fifth seal. Second, in most parts of the earth grass is not green the year round, but is seasonal. Burning of all the grass that is green during a particular season would leave the remainder untouched until its season of dormancy is over (Simcox). Whether the affected portion was one-third or some other percentage, the text does not say. The description simply says "all" that is green at the time of the plague. Either of these two explanations allows for taking "all" in its literal sense without contradicting 9:4.

3. THE SECOND TRUMPET: DESTRUCTION OF A THIRD OF SEA LIFE (8:8-9)

Translation

8And the second angel sounded; and [something] like a great mountain burning with fire was cast into the sea; and the third part of the sea became blood, 9and the third part of the creatures which were in the sea, which had life, died, and the third part of the ships were destroyed.

Exegesis and Exposition

8:8 What John heard and saw next was, Καὶ ὁ δεύτερος ἄγγελος ἐσάλπισεν· καὶ ὡς ὄρος μέγα πυρὶ καιόμενον ἐβλήθη εἰς τὴν θάλασσαν (*Kai ho deuteros angelos esalpisen; kai hōs oros mega puri kaiomenon eblēthē eis tēn thalassan*, "And the second angel sounded; and [something] like a great mountain burning with fire was cast into the sea"). Opinions regarding the meaning of ὡς ὄρος μέγα πυρὶ καιόμενον (*hōs oros mega puri kaiomenon*, "[something] like a great mountain burning with fire") are in three camps. One opinion sees the mountain as representative of spiritual Babylon or some other great kingdom.[60] Besides the occasional figure of a mountain to represent a kingdom in the OT (e.g., Ps. 48:1; Jer. 51:25), this explanation lacks for support. The variety of suggested identifications—i.e., Babylon (e.g., Swete), Zion (e.g., Hailey), a heathen nation (ibid.), Rome (e.g., Lee)—reflects the subjectivity of this viewpoint. Most crippling, however, is the use of ὡς (*hōs*, "like") to indicate it was not an actual mountain, but a burning mass so large as to look like one.[61] It confuses figures of speech to have the mountain in a metaphorical sense, and then to use it as a simile to identify the object (Walvoord).

---

60. Lee, "Revelation," 4:601; Ironside, *Revelation*, p. 150.
61. Alford, *Greek Testament*, 4:636; Robertson, *Word Pictures*, 6:359.

A second opinion has connected the fall of the mountain-like object with local volcanic activity in the area (Moffatt, Mounce). But this also falters in that it was not something from the mass, but the mass itself that fell into the sea (Alford, Simcox, Swete). The third explanation takes the mountain-like mass to be a meteoric chunk, ablaze with fire (Alford, Walvoord). This allows for the comparative *hōs* and falls into the category of the falling stars from heaven under the sixth seal (6:13). This maintains a basically literal approach to the text that incorporates provisions for figurative language when the text itself so indicates (Walvoord).

"The sea" into which the burning mass is thrown is the sea as a whole, not just the Mediterranean Sea (Alford). The result was, "The third part of the sea became blood" (καὶ ἐγένετο τὸ τρίτον τῆς θαλάσσης αἶμα (*egeneto to triton tēs thalassēs haima*). Was this actual blood or only a blood-like color? The sea around Thera, an island near Patmos where volcanic eruptions were frequent, was often a bright orange color (Moffatt, Kiddle). This may be what the description means, but it is doubtful, because the text says the sea becomes blood, not *like* blood. On the basis of his vision, John believed that a large part of the sea would, quite literally, turn into blood as it had under the first deliverance in Egypt (Kiddle; cf. Ex. 7:20; Ps. 78:43-44). On a natural plane it is impossible for an object like a burning mountain to turn one-third of the sea into blood, cause one-third of marine life to perish, and destroy one-third of the shipping vessels. On a supernatural one it is not, however. The advances of modern science are staggering to the human mind, but the impact of this trumpet is even beyond that. Man is in no position to question the extent and manner of what God devises and implements.[62]

8:9 The account continues by telling the impact on sea-life and shipping: καὶ ἀπέθανεν τὸ τρίτον τῶν κτισμάτων τῶν ἐν τῇ θαλάσσῃ, τὰ ἔχοντα ψυχάς, καὶ τὸ τρίτον τῶν πλοίων διεφθάρησαν[63] (*kai apethanen to triton tōn ktismatōn tōn en tē thalassē, ta echonta psychas, kai to triton tōn ploiōn diephtharēsan*, "and the third part of the creatures which were in the sea, which had life, died, and the third part of the ships were destroyed"). As under the first Egyptian plague (Ex. 7:21; cf. Zeph. 1:3), the fish in the blood-filled environment perished (Moffatt).

---

62. J. O. Yoder, in Smith, *Revelation*, p. 139.
63. The διά prefix of διαφθείρω adds a perfective force to the simple verb φθείρω. The verb occurs again in 11:18 where its objects are personal. Proximity to the plural πλοίων probably explains the plural number of διεφθάρησαν (Beckwith, *Apocalypse*, p. 557; Robertson, *Word Pictures*, 6:359).

Κτίσμα (*Ktisma*, "creature") refers to something created (cf. 1 Tim. 4:4; James 1:18), which in this situation must be fish.

The seagoing vessels are hard hit too. To take τῶν πλοίων (*tōn ploiōn*, "the ships") to stand for little states which become engulfed along with the Roman Empire (Lee) is untenable. These are literal ships on the high seas at the time the calamity strikes. They meet with destruction, διεφθάρησαν (*diephtharēsan*, "were destroyed") attributing "a quasipersonal life to the ships in view of their human masters and crews" (Swete).

Additional Notes

8:8 The second trumpet blast brings a phenomenon similar to something described in *1 Enoch* 18:13, "seven stars like a great burning mountain." The dating of *1 Enoch* is uncertain, but among those placing the section with this quote before Revelation, some feel that this trumpet is possibly an allusion to the Enoch passage mentioned (e.g., Swete). But John simply wrote what he saw, though his visions were part of his total experiences—physical, psychic, and spiritual. In the last analysis, his judgment did not determine what he was to write. The phenomena he saw portray eschatological judgment and exceed any natural explanation (Mounce).

8:9 The nominative participle τὰ ἔχοντα is in apposition with the genitive τῶν κτισμάτων. This appositional nominative, a grammatical rarity, is rather common in the Apocalypse (cf. 2:13, 20; 3:12; 9:14; 14:12).[64]

4. THE THIRD TRUMPET: POISONING OF A THIRD OF THE FRESH WATER (8:10-11)

Translation

[10]And the third angel sounded; and a great star burning as a torch fell from heaven, and fell upon the third part of the rivers and upon the fountains of waters. [11]And the name of the star is called "Wormwood." And the third part of the waters became wormwood, and many among men died from the waters, because they were made bitter.

Exegesis and Exposition

8:10 The sound of the third trumpet brings another object falling from heaven: Καὶ ὁ τρίτος ἄγγελος ἐσάλπισεν· καὶ ἔπεσεν ἐκ τοῦ

---

64. Alford, *Greek Testament*, 4:572, 637; Charles, *Revelation*, 1:234; Beckwith, *Apocalypse*, p. 557; Robertson, *Word Pictures*, 6:359.

οὐρανοῦ ἀστὴρ μέγας καιόμενος ὡς λαμπάς, καὶ ἔπεσεν ἐπὶ τὸ τρίτον τῶν ποταμῶν καὶ ἐπὶ τὰς πηγὰς τῶν ὑδάτων (*Kai ho tritos angelos esalpisen; kai epesen ek tou ouranou astēr megas kaiomenos hōs lampas, kai epesen epi to triton tōn potamōn kai epi tas pēgas tōn hudatōn*, "And the third angel sounded; and a great star burning as a torch fell from heaven, and fell upon the third part of the rivers and upon the fountains of waters"). This time the falling object is ἀστὴρ μέγας καιόμενος ὡς λαμπάς (*astēr megas kaiomenos hōs lampas*, "a great star burning as a torch"). The symbolically inclined interpreters have seen the star as representing a false religious leader,[65] a deluding influence given the people as an act of judgment (Lenski), and an angel (Johnson). The first two suggestions are hard-pressed to survive, because heresy is hardly a judgment inflicted on men as a penalty for sin (contra Lee). All three symbolic interpretations fail in the absence of any textual indication that the star is a symbol for something else. Most naturally understood, this is a literal star or meteor (Walvoord). Ancient usage of λαμπάς (*lampas*, "torch") to denote a meteor shooting through the air confirms this conclusion.[66] An apparent contradiction in light of earlier words about the stars falling from the sky (6:13) (Moffatt) is resolved by identifying these stars with the earlier stars as falling meteors (Thomas, pp. 453-54). Stars remain in the sky until the time of the third and fourth trumpets.

The star lands on and pollutes a third of the rivers (8:10)—the "third" (τὸ τρίτον [*to triton*]) stipulating the partial nature of the trumpet judgments once again—and falls on all the springs of water, but pollutes only a third of them (8:11) (Alford; Simcox; Beckwith). This again recalls the first Egyptian plague with its contamination of the drinking-water supply (Ex. 7:21).[67] This was a familiar token of divine punishment (cf. Jer. 9:15) (Beckwith). Pagan worship of spirits associated with rivers and springs was widespread in John's time, so this could be an expression of God's displeasure with such (Mounce). It is more probably His punishment of all people for their diverse kinds of ungodliness (Kiddle).

8:11 The star has a name: καὶ τὸ ὄνομα τοῦ ἀστέρος λέγεται ὁ Ἄψινθος. καὶ ἐγένετο τὸ τρίτον τῶν ὑδάτων εἰς ἄψινθον (*kai to onoma tou asteros legetai ho Apsinthos. kai egeneto to triton tōn hudatōn eis apsinthon*, "And the name of the star is called 'Wormwood.' And the third part of the waters became wormwood"). Ἄψινθος (*Apsinthos*, "Wormwood"), a word found nowhere else in the Greek Bible (Ladd), is a plant with a bitter taste appearing in several varieties in Palestine.

---

65. Ironside, *Revelation*, p. 151.
66. LSJ, p. 261.
67. Robertson, *Word Pictures*, 6:359.

At Marah a tree made the bitter water sweet (Ex. 15:23-25; cf. 2 Kings 2:19-21), but here the reverse occurs (Walvoord). This is probably a reminiscence of the bitter water forced on the rebellious Israelites of old (Kiddle). Wormwood in the OT was a symbol for divine punishment (Jer. 9:15; 23:15; Lam. 3:15, 19), an appropriate background for this trumpet (Beckwith). Wormwood itself was not a poison, though poisonous effects were sometimes connected with it (e.g., Jer. 3:15). Its bitterness at times could sometimes lead to death, however (Beckwith).

The remainder of v. 11 indicates that some deaths do result: καὶ πολλοὶ τῶν ἀνθρώπων ἀπέθανον ἐκ τῶν ὑδάτων, ὅτι ἐπικράνθησαν (*kai polloi tōn anthrōpōn apethanon ek tōn hydatōn, hoti epikranthēsan*, "and many among men died from the waters, because they were made bitter"). One perspective is that πολλοὶ (*polloi*, "many") is simply a stylistic variation referring to the one-third that is customary in this series (Kiddle, Mounce). This, however, would amount to a duplication of the destructive effect of the sixth trumpet (9:18). The unlikelihood of *polloi* referring to one-third is shown also in this writer's freedom to repeat specific figures with no concern for stylistic variation (e.g., three occurrences of τὸ τρίτον [*to triton*] in 8:7 and five in 8:12). The plain statement is that many, not all, who drank the water died. If a third of mankind drank it, they all suffered, but the suffering did not always result in death (Beckwith). The death here is only incidental. The first four trumpets are to punish, not necessarily to kill (ibid.).

Additional Notes

8:11 The construction ἐγένετο . . . εἰς is common in the LXX and in the NT when citing the OT (cf. 16:19; John 16:20; Acts 5:36).[68] Wormwood mixed with water does not kill, but this construction could indicate that the water became wormwood (Swete; contra Charles and Mounce). The text does not say the water became *like* wormwood. Yet the ἐπικράνθησαν in 8:11 mandates that the water was not transformed into wormwood, but only embittered by it. Probably the εἰς would have been omitted from the construction as in 8:8 if the waters had become literal wormwood (Charles, Mounce).

5. THE FOURTH TRUMPET: DARKENING OF A THIRD OF THE HEAVENLY BODIES (8:12-13)

Translation

12And the fourth angel sounded; and the third part of the sun and the third part of the moon and the third part of the stars were

---

68. Moffatt, "Revelation," 5:405; Robertson, *Word Pictures*, 6:359.

stricken, so that the third part of them was darkened and the day did not brighten for a third part of it, and the night likewise. [13]**And I looked, and I heard an eagle flying in midheaven saying with a loud voice, "Woe woe woe to those who dwell on the earth because of the rest of the trumpet-sounds of the three angels who are about to sound."**

Exegesis and Exposition

The sun, moon, and stars receive the immediate brunt of the fourth trumpet: Καὶ ὁ τέταρτος ἄγγελος ἐσάλπισεν· καὶ ἐπλήγη τὸ τρίτον τοῦ ἡλίου καὶ τὸ τρίτον τῆς σελήνης καὶ τὸ τρίτον τῶν ἀστέρων, ἵνα σκοτισθῇ τὸ τρίτον τῆς σελήνης καὶ τὸ τρίτον τῶν ἀστέρων, ἵνα σκοτισθῇ τὸ τρίτον αὐτῶν καὶ ἡ ἡμέρα μὴ φάνῃ τὸ τρίτον αὐτῆς, καὶ ἡ νὺξ ὁμοίως (*Kai ho tetartos angelos esalpisen; kai eplēgē to triton tou hēliou kai to triton tēs selēnēs kai to triton tōn asterōn, hina skotisthẹ̄ to triton autōn kai hē hēmera mē phanȩ̄ to triton autēs, kai hē nux homoiōs*), "And the fourth angel sounded; and the third part of the sun and the third part of the moon and the third part of the stars were stricken, so that the third part of them was darkened and the day did not brighten for a third part of it, and the night likewise"). Ἐπλήγη (*Eplēgē*, "Were stricken") is a verb form of the noun πληγή (*plēgē*), which means "plague." The verb occurs in Ex. 9:31-32 [LXX] to describe the devastating effects of the hail on the crops (cf. Ps. 102:4) (Mounce). This trumpet has no mention of the instrument used to strike the heavenly bodies, the idea perhaps being that the instrument should not receive as much attention as the plague itself (Alford).

Darkening (cf. σκοτισθῇ [*skotisthẹ̄*, "was darkened"]) is a symbol for judgment throughout the OT. The particular parallel with this trumpet is the ninth Egyptian plague (Ex. 10:21-22). Amos called the Day of the Lord a day of darkness (Amos 5:18; cf. Isa. 13:10; Joel 2:2; Mark 13:24). The fourth trumpet fulfills this anticipation (Mounce). A questioning of the literality of the plague arises once again. The non-literal explanation sees this as a removal of the light of the truth (Lee, Scott, Kiddle), but this reads into v. 12 something that is not there, resulting in a wide variety of meanings such as a reference to the spiritual darkness of Mohammedanism (Lee) or the fall of long-established governments in the western empire (Scott). The literal understanding of an actual reduction of light to serve as a suitable warning for more severe judgments to come (cf. 8:13) is more satisfactory (Walvoord).

How the fractional darkening of the heavenly bodies can produce a reduced duration[69] of daylight, moonlight, and starlight is a puzzle

---

69. In τὸ τρίτον αὐτῆς, τὸ τρίτον is an adverbial accusative to express the duration of the "not shining" of the day.

(Swete). Yet man's ability to grasp the "how" of the cause and effect is no basis for attributing inconsistency to the author. The way this works out belongs to the altogether supernatural region of the visions (Alford). The Creator of all things can certainly devise a means by which a partial eclipse can result in a shortening of duration from the light-bodies.

The verse mentions no direct effect of this judgment on mankind, but clearly the impact will be great. Almost every area of life—agriculture, navigation, human health, productivity, and the like—are bound to feel the consequences of this plague. The dread of plagues yet to come as signaled by the darkness is over and above all these.

8:13 John signals a new scene in his vision with his usual καὶ εἶδον (*kai eidon*): Καὶ εἶδον, καὶ ἤκουσα ἑνὸς[70] ἀετοῦ πετομένου ἐν μεσ-ουρανήματι λέγοντος φωνῇ μεγάλη (*Kai eidon, kai ēkousa henos aetou petomenou en mesouranēmati legontos phonē megalē*, "And I looked, and I heard an eagle flying in midheaven saying with a loud voice"). The beginning of this scene is a transition from the first four trumpets (8:7-11) to the last two trumpets (9:1-21) (Alford, Mounce).

"Eagle" (ἀετοῦ [*aetou*]) has much stronger MS support than "an-gel" (ἀγγέλου [*aggelou*]), the rendering of the KJV in this verse (Lee). The ability of the eagle to speak (λέγοντος [*legontos*]) is insufficient ground on which to conclude it is symbolic (contra Johnson). Animate creation other than mankind receive that ability occasionally in Scrip-ture (cf. Gen. 3:1-5; Num. 22:28-30). The picture is that of a strong bird rushing to its prey, in this case referring to the rapid approach of God's remaining vengeance (cf. Deut. 28:49; Hos. 8:1; Hab. 1:8; cf. also *2 Baruch* 77.17-22; 87.1).[71] The depredatory nature of eagles is in view in this choice of birds (Mounce). "Vulture" is the rendering of this word sometimes (cf. Luke 17:37), a meaning that would not be com-pletely inappropriate here.[72] At one extreme, the eagle speaks of the salvation of God for Israel, reminding that the plagues are but the birth pangs of God's new age (cf. Deut. 32:9-11; Ex. 19:4; Mark 13:8), but at the other, it is a bird of prey, associated with blood, death, and rotting flesh (cf. Job 39:27-30).[73]

Μεσουρανήματι (*Mesouranēmati*) fixes the eagle's position in "mid-heaven," the position of the sun at noon. This is a place where all can

---

70. This form of εἷς which usually means "one" represents the English indefi-nite article "an" in this instance as it does elsewhere in the book (cf. 9:13; 18:21; 19:17) (Beckwith, *Apocalypse*, p. 559; Robertson, *Word Pictures*, 6:360; Lenski, *Revelation*, p. 283). It is not a reference to "one solitary" eagle (Morris, *Revelation*, p. 125).
71. Alford, *Greek Testament*, 4:639; Robertson, *Word Pictures*, 6:360.
72. Mulholland, *Revelation*, pp. 192-93.
73. Caird, *Revelation*, p. 117; Chilton, *Days of Vengeance*, p. 241.

see him (Alford, Swete). His "loud voice" (φωνῇ μεγάλῃ [*phonē mega-lē*]) assures that all will hear him. Broad coverage is important, for the disasters he announces will touch earth-dwellers in every part of the world (Kiddle).

The eagle's announcement is brief, but vital: Οὐαὶ οὐαὶ οὐαὶ τοὺς κατοικοῦντας ἐπὶ τῆς γῆς ἐκ τῶν λοιπῶν φωνῶν τῆς σάλπιγγος τῶν τριῶν ἀγγέλων τῶν μελλόντων σαλπίζειν (*Ouai ouai ouai tous katoikountas epi tēs gēs ek*[74] *tōn loipōn phōnōn tēs salpiggos tōn triōn angelōn tōn mellontōn salpizein,* "Woe woe woe to those who dwell on the earth because of the rest of the trumpet-sounds of the three angels who are about to sound"). The past trumpets have been woeful in themselves, but this announcement forebodes that the remaining three will be especially grievous, so much so as to have the name "woe" reserved for each of them (Swete, Beckwith). One reason for using this word that usually refers to great calamity is that these will have people, not objects of nature, as their direct objects (Alford, Mounce). Double "woes" are for emphasis in Ezek. 16:23; Rev. 18:10, 16, 19, but the triple woe refers to the three remaining trumpet blasts (cf. 9:1, 12; 11:14).

The objects of the coming vengeance, τοὺς κατοικοῦντας ἐπὶ τῆς γῆς (*tous katoikountas epi tēs gēs,* "those who dwell on the earth"), are the same as the ones on whom martyrs in 6:10 invoke vengeance, so this is a further step in the answer to their prayers (Alford). They comprise only the wicked according to regular usage in Revelation (cf. 3:10; 9:4, 20). From this point on their future is especially bleak.

Additional Notes

8:12 Beckwith views ἵνα σκοτισθῇ . . . μὴ φάνῃ as a result clause because the analogy with the first three trumpets requires it. As important as analogy may be, however, the normal function of ἵνα is to express purpose: the purpose of the smiting is to produce these effects. If accented on the ultima, φάνῃ would be aorist passive, but this accentuation on the penult makes it an aorist active.[75]

8:13 Τῆς σάλπιγγος is singular here because it defines or characterizes the plural φωνῶν. The plural is unnecessary since the noun draws the reader's attention, not to the plurality of the trumpets, but to the "trumpetlike" sound proceeding from each of the angels (Swete, Beckwith).

---

74. The preposition ἐκ denotes the source whence the woes spring (cf. usage in 8:11) (Alford, *Greek Testament*, 4:639). "As a result of" is a possible rendering for it here (Robertson, *Word Pictures*, 6:360).
75. Robertson, *Word Pictures*, 6:360.

6. THE FIFTH TRUMPET: DEMONIC LOCUST PLAGUE (9:1-12)

Translation

1And the fifth angel sounded and I saw a star, fallen from heaven into the earth, and the key of the pit of the abyss was given to him. 2And he opened the pit of the abyss, and smoke came up from the pit as smoke of a great furnace, and the sun and the air were darkened because of the smoke of the pit. 3And locusts came out of the smoke into the earth, and authority was given to them as scorpions of the earth have authority. 4And it was said to them that they should not hurt the grass of the earth or any green [thing] or any tree, except [they should hurt] men, such ones as do not have the seal of God upon their foreheads. 5And it was given to them that they should not kill them, but that they should be tormented for five months; and their torment [was] as the torment of a scorpion when it stings a man. 6And in those days men will seek death and will in no way find it, and they will desire to die, and death will flee from them.

Exegesis and Exposition

Already introduced by the eagle's proclamation in 8:13, the fifth trumpet sets the tone for the last three trumpets through its specificity and independence of the two to follow. This feature marks the last three seals too. The seventh trumpet also resembles the seventh seal in the way it solemnly concludes the whole and contains the next series within in its scope. As with the seals also, two episodes intervene between the sixth and seventh members. In so doing, the episodes set the stage for the seventh trumpet.

9:1 The lengthy description of the fifth trumpet falls into two parts: the impact of the locusts (vv. 1-6) and the characteristics of the locusts (vv. 7-12).

The impact of the locusts (9:1-6). With the sounding of the fifth trumpet, the seer beholds yet another fallen star: καὶ εἶδον ἀστέρα ἐκ τοῦ οὐρανοῦ πεπτωκότα εἰς τὴν γῆν, καὶ ἐδόθη αὐτῷ ἡ κλεὶς τοῦ φρέατος τῆς ἀβύσσου (*kai eidon astera ek tou ouranou peptōkota eis tēn gēn, kai edothē autǭ hē kleis tou phreatos tēs abyssou,* "and I saw a star, fallen from heaven into the earth, and the key of the pit of the abyss was given to him"). This star differs from those under the sixth seal (6:13) and third trumpet (8:10), however. The star's receipt and use of "the key of the pit of the abyss" (vv. 1-2) shows that it stands for an intelligent being (Lenski, Johnson). Suggested identifications of this intelligent being have abounded.

The idealist approach to Revelation usually tries to dodge the issue of identification by saying the star could be any one of a number of persons throughout history (Lee, Beasley-Murray). Yet as much information is available here as has been for other trumpets where attempts to specify have been made. The suggestion that he is the Antichrist (Scott) has very slim evidence. Considerable input has gone into efforts to prove the star is a man like Mohammed. The possibility of stars being personified as men as in the OT (e.g., Judg. 5:20; Job 38:7) and Jewish apocalyptic (e.g., *1 Enoch* 88:1; 90:24) is part of the argument.[76] The tie to Mohammed lies in the leader's reputation for gathering armies and leading them against corrupt Christianity as Mohammed did, although the elect are left unharmed.[77]

Besides ignoring the possibility that the masculine pronoun αὐτῷ (*autō*, "to him") could refer to an angel just as well as to a man, this view goes too far in assuming that every true Christian remained untouched by Mohammed's conquests (Alford). It also goes beyond revealed truth to assume that Mohammed or any other man had a heavenly origin. This could characterize only an angel. To a large degree, the participle πεπτωκότα[78] (*peptōkota*, "fallen") in v. 1 is determinative in this issue. If it is simply another way of noting an angel who had descended from heaven on a divine mission (Charles, Lenski), the star is one of God's angelic agents (cf. Judg. 5:20; Job 38:7). If on the other hand the participle has the theological connotation of casting from heaven because of divine disapproval (Alford, Lee, Kiddle, Walvoord, Sweet), this must be either Satan (Alford, Swete) or an unidentified evil angel (Simcox), the former being the more probable (cf. Luke 10:18; Rev. 12:7-9). The edge of probability in deciding between an unfallen angel and Satan favors the unfallen angel as the star's identification, because to make the participle *peptōkota* refer to Satan's one-time fall from heaven is to attach too much theological significance to a passing detail in the unfolding of one of the trumpet judgments (Morris). Besides this, "fallen" to describe a star rather than an angel divests the word of the notion of divine judgment (Charles). So this star must be an unfallen angel dispatched on a divine mission to advance the next stage of God's punishment against the rebellious earth-dwellers.

No angel retains permanent possession of the key of the abyss, so God had to give it to him (ἐδόθη αὐτῷ [*edothē autō*]) for use on this

---

76. Moffatt, "Revelation," 5:406; J. Massyngberde Ford, *Revelation*, vol. 38 of AB (Garden City, N.Y.: Doubleday, 1975), p. 143.
77. Barnes, *Revelation*, p. 211; E. B. Elliott, *Horae Apocalypticae* or *A Commentary on the Apocalypse, Critical and Historical*, 4th ed. (London: Seeleys, 1851), 1:414-22.
78. The perfect tense of πεπτωκότα indicates that the star was already on earth, not in the midst of his fall, when John saw him.

special occasion (cf. 20:1 also) (Alford, Charles). The term ἄβυσσος (*abyssos*, "abyss") rendered the Hebrew תְּהוֹם (*tĕhôm*) in the LXX when the latter referred to "deep waters" (cf. Gen. 1:2; 7:11; Ps. 105[106]:9; 106[107]:26) or to the depths of the earth (cf. Ps. 70:21[71:21, English]) (Swete). Etymologically, the alpha privative combines with βυθός (*bythos*, "depth") to mean "without depth," but in usage the word means "bottomless."[79] Seven of the nine NT uses of the word are in Revelation (cf. Luke 8:31; Rom. 10:7). Here it is the picture of a subterranean cavern connected to earth's surface by a "shaft" or "well" (τοῦ φρέατος [*tou phreatos*]) whose opening has a secured lid of some type (Moffatt). Its inhabitants include the demonic prince of 9:11 and the beast from the abyss mentioned in 11:7; 17:8 (Sweet).

Making the abyss emblematic of the accumulated power of evil in the world (Caird) is too imaginative to be plausible. With this kind of fanciful interpretation, one could make the passage say almost anything he wanted. Another position is to make the abyss synonymous with hell since, of the two other-world places, heaven and hell, it could not be heaven (Lenski). This reasoning is too simplistic, however, because Jesus in Luke 16:19-31 showed distinctions between different parts of the underworld. The ultimate destiny of the Devil and his angels, the lake of fire, differs from this abyss and is more deserving of the title "hell" (Matt. 25:41; Rev. 19:20; 20:10) (Lee, Charles). Better judgment dictates that the abyss is the preliminary place of incarceration for fallen angels from which some of them are about to be released under this trumpet. Luke 8:31, as well as the other six uses in the Apocalypse (9:2, 11; 11:7; 17:8; 20:1, 3), supports this opinion.[80]

9:2 The angel proceeds with his mission of releasing the occupants of the abyss: καὶ ἤνοιξεν τὸ φρέαρ τῆς ἀβύσσου, καὶ ἀνέβη καπνὸς ἐκ τοῦ φρέατος ὡς καπνὸς καμίνου μεγάλης, καὶ ἐσκοτώθη ὁ ἥλιος καὶ ὁ ἀὴρ ἐκ τοῦ καπνοῦ τοῦ φρέατος (*kai ēnoixen to phrear tēs abyssou, kai anebē kapnos ek tou phreatos hōs kapnos kaminou megalēs, kai eskotōthē ho hēlios kai ho aēr ek tou kapnou tou phreatos*, "and he opened the pit of the abyss, and smoke came up from the pit as smoke of a great furnace, and the sun and the air were darkened because of the smoke of the pit"). The divine agent used the key given to him to unlock (ἤνοιξεν [*ēnoixen*, "he opened"]) the shaft leading to the underground chamber. When he did so, smoke rose from the shaft as from an erupting volcano, but this was no volcano (Swete). This was literal smoke that John saw, not a figurative representation of extreme deceptions and error propagated by Satan (contra Hailey). The literal understanding of the trumpets up to this point verifies this. In Revelation smoke may per-

---

79. Robertson, *Word Pictures*, 6:361.
80. Ibid.; Walvoord, *Revelation*, p. 159.

tain to holy things (8:4; 15:8), but most of the time it is in connection with judgment, doom, and torment (9:17, 18; 18:9, 18; 19:3) (Smith). This unfavorable tone applies here too. The smoke is a vivid reminder of divine judgment at Sodom (Gen. 19:28) and Sinai (Ex. 19:18).[81] The volume of smoke compares to that produced by a large smelting furnace, usually used for purifying metals (ὡς καπνὸς καμίνου μεγάλης [*hōs kapnos kaminou megalēs*]) (cf. 1:15).

The volume is so great that it darkens the light of the sun and the air through which that light must pass (Alford). Under the previous trumpet the striking of the luminaries had obscured their light too, but this is a hindering of the sun's effect (ἐσκοτώθη [*eskotōthē*]), not an enfeebling of its ability to illuminate (Swete, Charles).

9:3 From the cloud of smoke emerged a swarm of locusts: καὶ ἐκ τοῦ καπνοῦ ἐξῆλθον ἀκρίδες εἰς τὴν γῆν, καὶ ἐδόθη αὐταῖς* ἐξουσία ὡς ἔχουσιν ἐξουσίαν οἱ σκορπίοι τῆς γῆς (*kai ek tou kapnou exēlthon akrides eis tēn gēn, kai edothē autais exousia hōs echousin exousian hoi skorpioi tēs gēs*, "and locusts came out of the smoke into the earth, and authority was given to them as scorpions of the earth have authority"). This trumpet parallels the eighth of the Egyptian plagues (Ex. 10:12-20), but these locusts are not ordinary locusts. They have a leader (cf. 9:11) unlike locusts of the earth (cf. Prov. 30:27), and unlike regular locusts, their power to hurt is in their scorpion-like tails (ἐξουσία ὡς ἔχουσιν ἐξουσίαν οἱ σκορπίοι τῆς γῆς (*exousia hōs echousin exousian hoi skorpioi tēs gēs*, cf. 9:5).[82]

The irresistible destructive power of locusts is proverbial in the OT (e.g., Deut. 28:38; 2 Chron. 7:13; Joel 2:25) as is their seemingly limitless number (e.g., Ps. 105:34; Nah. 3:15) (Lenski). The central OT passage about locusts is Joel 1-2 which describes a locust-visitation that serves as a harbinger or component of the Day of the Lord. The fifth-trumpet locusts similarly serve as a part of end-time events (Beckwith, Mounce). Locusts were also part of the diet of John the Baptist (Matt. 3:4; Mark 1:6).

But these locusts are different, and it remains to establish their identity. One perspective is that they signify human armies, either Arabic[83] or Oriental.[84] The parallel with Joel 2:1 ff., which shows the analogies between a locust swarm and a human army, is probably the chief factor favoring this opinion. The characteristics differentiating

---

81. Hughes, *Revelation*, pp. 108-9.
82. Alford, *Greek Testament*, 4:640; Swete, *Apocalypse*, 115; Moffatt, "Revelation," 5:406; Charles, *Revelation*, 1:242; E. W. Bullinger. *The Apocalypse* or *"The Day of the Lord"* (London: Eyre and Spottiswoode, n.d.), p. 279.
83. Elliott, *Horae Apocalypticae*, 1:264-68.
84. Barnes, *Revelation*, pp. 212-13.

these locusts from ordinary ones are a serious obstacle to this view, however.

The view that takes the locusts to represent God's superhuman judgment against the consciences of men (Scott) is too vague to do justice to the details of the passage. The passage contains no hint of this kind of symbolism.[85] To fall back on taking these as ordinary locusts according to the Exodus pattern (Morris) because of the ways they differ from "normal" locusts is another alternative. As noted above, however, their leadership pattern and means of inflicting harm contrast with ordinary locusts. Ordinary locusts do not breed in the center of the earth, the origin of this swarm.[86] These locusts do not eat grass (cf. 9:4) like natural ones (Caird, Johnson). So it is out of the question to see these as locusts of the type in the eighth Egyptian plague.

Heavy evidence favors the identification of these locusts as demons or fallen angels who assume a locust-like form. They have an angel as their leader (9:11). They come from the abyss where evil spirits are imprisoned (Beckwith, Lenski). Their attack against men rather than consuming of green vegetation points to their demonic nature (Beasley-Murray). They have a form such as no human being has ever seen (Bullinger, Seiss, Walvoord). The ability of demons to assume an assortment of material forms is further illustrated in 16:13 where three demons appear as frogs (Smith).

What emerges to afflict rebellious mankind, then, is a horde of supernatural creatures bent on spreading as much misery as possible. Divine permission (ἐδόθη [*edothē*]) allows them the stinging power of scorpions in their tails (cf. vv. 5, 10) (Swete) to inflict their agony. The scorpion belongs to the largest and most malignant of all insect tribes. Its general appearance is like a lobster, but much more hideous. Its sting located near the end of its tail is not always fatal, but can be. It ranks with the snake in its hostility toward human beings (cf. Luke 10:19; 11:12).[87]

9:4 The locusts have strict limitations assigned: καὶ ἐρρέθη αὐτοῖς ἵνα μὴ ἀδικήσουσιν τὸν χόρτον τῆς γῆς οὐδὲ πᾶν χλωρὸν οὐδὲ πᾶν δένδρον, εἰ μὴ τοὺς ἀνθρώπους οἵτινες οὐκ ἔχουσι τὴν σφραγῖδα τοῦ θεοῦ ἐπὶ τῶν μετώπων (*kai errethē autais hina mē adikēsousin ton chorton tēs gēs oude pan chlōron oude pan dendron, ei mē tous anthrōpous hoitines ouk*

---

85. Jack MacArthur, *Expositional Commentary on Revelation* (Eugene, Oreg.: Certain Sound, 1973), pp. 207-8.

86. Henry M. Morris, *The Revelation Record* (Wheaton, Ill.: Tyndale, 1983), p. 158.

87. Swete, *Apocalypse*, p. 116; Charles, *Revelation*, 1:242; Robertson, *Word Pictures*, 6:362; *Collier's Encyclopedia*, 20:512-13.

echousi tēn sphragida tou theou epi tōn metōpōn, "And it was said to them that they should not hurt the grass of the earth or any green [thing] or any tree, except [they should hurt] men, such ones as do not have the seal of God upon their foreheads"). The one issuing these limitations is unnamed, but the unexpressed agent of the passive action ἐρρέθη (*errethē*, "it was said") is probably the same as the unexpressed agent of the three uses of ἐδόθη (*edothē*, "it was given") in 9:1, 3, 5—God Himself. God exercises His sovereignty to control this plague. The demons can go only as far as He permits. Their release was in order to do their own wills up to a certain point (cf. Ezek. 9:4-6) (Bullinger, Lenski, Mounce).

The restraint did not allow the demonic locusts to touch what locusts usually destroy, the vegetation (cf. Ex. 10:5, 12, 15). Damage to plant life came earlier (cf. 8:7). The grass damaged under the first trumpet has regrown by now, but the locusts are to leave it alone. Men, not foodstuffs, are the objects.[88] Εἰ μὴ τοὺς ἀνθρώπους (*Ei mē tous anthrōpous*, "Except [they should hurt] men") states the exception to the "do not hurt" limitation. Ironically it is a group of people in rebellion against God who are victims of demons who themselves are in rebellion against God (Beasley-Murray). This is a classic example of the confusion and irrationality of the forces of evil which logically should have formed an alliance with one another.

The demons may not afflict all humans, however, only "such ones as do not have the seal of God upon their foreheads" (οἵτινες[89] οὐκ ἔχουσι τὴν σφραγῖδα τοῦ θεοῦ ἐπὶ τῶν μετώπων [*hoitines ouk echousi tēn sphragida tou theou epi tōn metōpōn*]). Those whose foreheads lack the seal of God will receive the torment. Those with the seal, the one granted earlier to the 144,000 in 7:4-8, are secure against this physical pain. As Israel in Egypt escaped the plagues that punished their neighbors (cf. Ex. 8:22 ff; 9:4 ff.; 10:23), the servants of God will be exempt from the attack of the locusts (Swete, Smith, Sweet).

9:5 The demonic horde receives a further limitation: καὶ ἐδόθη αὐτοῖς ἵνα μὴ ἀποκτείνωσιν αὐτούς, ἀλλ᾽ ἵνα βασανισθήσονται[90] μῆνας πέντε· καὶ ὁ βασανισμὸς αὐτῶν ὡς βασανισμὸς σκορπίου, ὅταν παίσῃ ἄνθρωπον (*kai edothē autois hina mē apokteinōsin autous, all᾽ hina basanisthēsontai mēnas pente; kai ho basanismos autōn hōs basanismos*

---

88. Swete, *Apocalypse*, p. 116; Bullinger, *Apocalypse*, p. 319; Robertson, *Word Pictures*, 6:362.
89. Οἵτινες apparently retains its qualitative force here (cf. 1:7; 2:24; 20:4) (Robertson, *Word Pictures*, 6:362).
90. The future passive indicative with ἵνα is relatively rare in the NT, but occurs several other times in Revelation, e.g., 3:9; 6:4; 8:3; 13:12 (Charles, *Revelation*, 1:243).

skorpiou, hotan paisę anthrōpon, "and it was given to them that they should not kill them, but that they should be tormented for five months; and their torment [was] as the torment of a scorpion when it stings a man"). They have permission to torment, but not to kill. Under the third trumpet, death was possible (8:11), but not here.

In the NT, βασανίζω (*basanizō*, "I torment") entails acute pain, either physical (Matt. 8:6; Rev. 12:2), mental (Matt. 8:29; 2 Pet. 2:8), or metaphorical (Matt. 14:24; Mark 6:48). In Revelation where persecution is so much in view, the thought of torment as punishment is uppermost (cf. 9:5; 11:10; 14:10, 11; 18:7, 10, 15; 20:10). Revelation 12:2 is the only exception.[91]

The duration of the torment is five months.[92] This corresponds to the normal season of pillaging by ordinary locusts, beginning in May and extending through September. The continuous-historical school of interpreting Revelation, by understanding the period nonliterally, has suggested at least seven "fulfillments" of the five months during the Christian era (Lee). Major motifs involved in the consummation of the age do appear throughout Christian history, but the locust imagery of this prophecy relates to the ultimate conflict between God and Satan at the close of the age (Mounce).

Beyond this, precise understandings of the five months have varied. Most views search for a hidden or figurative meaning. Definiteness of time is one meaning assigned to the five-month period (Swete).[93] Some suggest that the period signifies a long period of time (cf. Beasley-Murray). Some see an allusion to a limited or brief period of time (Lee, Scott, Kiddle, Sweet). (Comparing this time-frame to the "ten days" in 2:10 is unjustifiable, however, because there it is a genitive expressing the kind of time and here it is an accusative of duration of time.) Lastly, some understand the five months figuratively with no chronological connotation (Lenski, Mulholland), in spite of the absence of any indication in the text that nonliterality is intended.

An acceptance of the text's plain meaning is satisfactory. The habit of ordinary locusts furnishes the starting point for the description of this demonic swarm.[94] There is no good reason for changing the normal meaning of the time element. The objections that normal locusts do not remain stationary (Beasley-Murray) and do not wreak their havoc continuously for the stated period (Beckwith, Lenski, Hailey) are not valid. The torment of this plague could be intermittent and

---

91. Swete, *Apocalypse*, p. 116; Robertson, *Word Pictures*, 6:362.
92. Μῆνας πέντε is an accusative of the extent of time.
93. Düsterdieck, *Revelation*, p. 277.
94. Ibid., p. 278; Alford, *Greek Testament*, 4:641; Charles, *Revelation*, 1:243; Walvoord, *Revelation*, p. 161.

move from place to place too. But it continues doing so for five months. Such torture may be offensive to some modern minds (Sweet), but this is a divinely appointed method of punishing sin.

9:6 The painfulness of the scorpion sting brings men to desperation: καὶ ἐν ταῖς ἡμέραις ἐκείναις ζητήσουσιν οἱ[95] ἄνθρωποι τὸν θάνατον καὶ οὐ μὴ[96] εὑρήσουσιν αὐτόν, καὶ ἐπιθυμήσουσιν ἀποθανεῖν καὶ φεύγει ὁ θάνατος ἀπ᾽ αὐτῶν (*kai en tais hēmerais ekeinais zētēsousin hoi anthrōpoi ton thanaton kai ou mē heurēsousin auton, kai epithymēsousin apothanein kai pheugei ho thanatos ap᾽ autōn*, "and in those days men will seek death and will in no way find it, and they will desire to die, and death will flee from them"). The words καὶ ἐν ταῖς ἡμέραις ἐκείναις ζητήσουσιν . . . (*kai en tais hēmerais ekeinais zētēsousin . . .*) ("and in those days men will seek . . .") mark a change in style from a witness of visions to a prophet predicting the future. Since 4:1, John has been an apocalyptic reporter, but he now switches to being a direct organ of the Spirit (Alford). This confirms the distinctly prophetic, as opposed to an apocalyptic, nature of the Apocalypse, and along with it the literal mode as the correct way of interpreting such material (Thomas, pp. 23-40).

Ἐν ταῖς ἡμέραις ἐκείναις (*En tais hēmerais ekeinais*, "in those days") covers the five-month period of v. 5. Hopefully the scorpion sting would bring repentance, but instead it evokes a quest for death (Swete, Bullinger, Charles). Physical pain, not depression, is their reason for seeking death (Mounce). Even though the death-quest is prompted by a vehement desire, as the strong word ἐπιθυμήσουσιν (*epithymēsousin*, "they will desire") indicates, death will escape them.[97] This motive for wanting to die is quite different from Paul's desire to die so as to be with Christ (Phil. 1:23). This is a fleeing from the misery on this side, but for Christians death is gain because of what is on the other side of death (Alford, Swete). The motivation for dying in 1 Kings 19:4, Job 3:21, and Jer. 8:3 resembles that of these fifth-trumpet victims, though the circumstances differed in each case.

The meaning and form of φεύγει (*pheugei*, "will flee") emphasizes the elusiveness of death. As a futuristic use of the present tense, it not only predicts the flight of death, but it also affirms the certainty of that flight.[98] Death will not be just hard to find. It will aggressively run away from those pursuing it.

---

95. The article is generic, pointing out the category that includes all people (Robertson, *Word Pictures*, 6:363).
96. The strong double negative οὐ μὴ expresses emphatic negation. By no means will men find the death they desire (Alford, *Greek Testament*, 4:641).
97. Alford, *Greek Testament*, 4:641; Robertson, *Word Pictures*, 6:363.
98. Alford, *Greek Testament*, 4:363; Charles, *Revelation*, 1:244; Robertson, *Word Pictures*, 6:363; Robertson, *Grammar*, p. 870.

Additional Notes

9:3 Sinaiticus and a few other MSS have the masculine αὐτοῖς instead of the feminine αὐταῖς. This views the locusts as personal agents rather than as locusts. External evidence for the feminine is stronger, however.

The characteristics of the locusts (9:7-12). With the effects of the locust plague in mind, the author now turns to describe the locusts themselves.[99]

Translation

⁷And the likenesses of the locusts [were] similar to horses prepared for battle, and upon their heads [something] like crowns as of gold, and their faces [were] as faces of men. ⁸And they had hair as the hair of women, and their teeth [were] as [those] of lions, ⁹and they had breastplates as breastplates of iron, and the sound of their wings [was] as the sound of chariots of many horses running into battle. ¹⁰And they have tails like scorpions and stings, and their authority in their tails is to hurt men for five months. ¹¹They have a king over them, the angel of the abyss, whose name in Hebrew is Abaddon and in Greek he has the name Apollyon.

¹²The first woe has passed away; behold, two woes still come after these things.

Exegesis and Exposition

9:7 In his description of the locusts, John uses the words ὡς (*hōs,* "as") and ὅμοιος (*homoios,* "like") nine times to convey a picture of the demonic locusts (Moffatt, Charles). He begins his description with an etymological relative of the latter adjective ὁμοιώματα (*homoiōmata*): Καὶ τὰ ὁμοιώματα τῶν ἀκρίδων ὅμοιοι ἵπποις ἡτοιμασμένοις εἰς πόλεμον, καὶ ἐπὶ τὰς κεφαλὰς αὐτῶν ὡς στέφανοι ὅμοιοι χρυσῷ*, καὶ τὰ πρόσωπα αὐτῶν ὡς πρόσωπα ἀνθρώπων (*Kai ta homoiōmata tōn akridōn homoioi hippois hētoimasmenois eis polemon, kai epi tas kephalas autōn hōs stephanoi homoioi chrysǭ, kai ta prosōpa autōn hōs prosōpa anthrōpōn,* "And the likenesses of the locusts [were] similar to horses prepared for battle, and upon their heads [something] like crowns as of gold, and their faces [were] as faces of men"). He begins with the head and moves progressively toward the tail of the creatures (Smith). Opinions differ widely about the meaning of each comparison.

Broadly speaking, the description has occasioned three views. It is an idealized depiction of a natural swarm of locusts (Moffatt), an

---

99. Düsterdieck, *Revelation,* pp. 278-79.

idealized picture of an army of men (probably Mohammedan warriors),[100] or a representation of the demonic locusts who will torture men for five months (Swete, Charles, Lenski). The comparative terminology might justify a reference to natural locusts (Moffatt, Charles), but some parts of the description could not apply to them (e.g., tails like scorpions). Some might construe these comparisons to refer to frightening military strength,[101] but the creatures are like locusts, not men, and no events of history can match the details of this visitation (Walvoord). Viewing this as a representation of demonic locusts is preferable, because it partially explains the unusual features of the afflictors. Basically, they are like locusts, but their supernaturalness adds a degree of dreadfulness to their appearance for the sake of enhancing their terrifying effect.[102] As for the objection that demons cannot assume a physical shape (Walvoord, Ladd), Jesus' experience in the gospels nullifies this (e.g., Matt. 8:30-32; Mark 5:11-13; Luke 8:32-33).

A resemblance between natural locusts and horses, particularly those with armor, is the reminder brought by ὅμοιοι ἵπποις ἡτοιμασμένοις εἰς πόλεμον (*homoia hippois hētoimasmenois eis polemon*, "similar to horses prepared for battle").[103] This similarity occasioned a similar comparison in Joel 1-2 (Swete, Charles). It is without foundation to think that John at this point had in mind the mythical monsters called centaurs whose upper bodies were like human beings and lower parts like horses (contra Ford).

The creatures also had something like crowns on their heads: καὶ ἐπὶ τὰς κεφαλὰς αὐτῶν ὡς σπέφανοι ὅμοιοι χρυσῷ (*kai epi tas kephalas autōn hōs stephanoi homoioi chrysō*, "and upon their heads [something] like crowns as of gold"). Suggested associations of these have included the yellow-tipped antlers of a natural locust (Lenski), the golden turbans of the Muslim hordes (Moffatt), the bronze helmets of the Roman legionnaires (Ford), and a feature distinctive to these demonic locusts (Lenski). Earlier discussion favors the last of these in pointing to the success to be enjoyed by the locusts throughout the five months (Swete, Lenski, Kiddle). The victory implication derives from the symbolic import of στέφανος (*stephanos*, "crown" or "wreath") (cf. 14:14).

The end of v. 7, καὶ τὰ πρόσωπα αὐτῶν ὡς πρόσωπα ἀνθρώπων (*kai ta prosōpa autōn hōs prosōpa anthrōpōn*, "and their faces [were] as faces of men"), suggests that the creatures have the intelligence and capaci-

100. Elliott, *Horae Apocalypticae*, 1:414-22.
101. Hughes, *Revelation*, p. 110.
102. Düsterdieck, *Revelation*, p. 279; Alford, *Greek Testament*, 4:642.
103. Robertson, *Word Pictures*, 6:363.

ties of human beings, not just that of insects (Lenski, Swete). Because of this comparison, some have concluded they are literal men, but the whole imagery opposes the picture of men afflicting men (Lenski). In fact, men and locusts are distinct from each other in 9:3-4. The creatures are not a product of nature, but are creatures of superhuman evil.

9:8 Verse 8 adds two more attributes of the locusts' appearance: καὶ εἶχον τρίχας ὡς τρίχας γυναικῶν, καὶ οἱ ὀδόντες αὐτῶν ὡς λεόντων ἦσαν (*kai eichon trichas hōs trichas gynaikōn, kai hoi odontes autōn hōs leontōn ēsan*, "and they had hair as the hair of women, and their teeth [were] as [those] of lions"). The reason why the hair of the creatures cannot refer to the antennas of natural locusts (contra Beckwith) is that two relatively short organs of sensation protruding from the head can hardly be called hair (Mounce). The reason the reference cannot be to hair on the legs or bodies of natural locusts (contra Mounce) is that the text says it must be like the hair of women which is on their heads. This must be another feature that differentiates the creatures from natural insects and adds to the gruesomeness of the demonic army (Alford, Lenski).

Ordinary locusts have teeth (cf. Joel 1:6), but not the powerful teeth of these creatures. These lionlike teeth denote voracity (Bullinger, Beckwith). Yet in spite of their fierceness, these demons do not tear their victims apart (Mounce).

9:9 Two additional characteristics resemble aspects of forces on the battlefield: καὶ εἶχον θώρακας ὡς θώρακας σιδηροῦς, καὶ ἡ φωνὴ τῶν πτερύγων αὐτῶν ὡς φωνὴ ἁρμάτων ἵππων πολλῶν τρεχόντων εἰς πόλεμον (*kai eichon thōrakas hōs thōrakas sidērous, kai hē phōnē tōn pterygōn autōn hōs phōnē harmatōn hippōn pollōn trechontōn eis polemon*, "and they had breastplates as breastplates of iron, and the sound of their wings [was] as the sound of chariots of many horses running into battle"). One was their iron breastplates. The noun θώραξ (*thōrax*) referred originally to the human chest—i.e., the area from the neck down to the navel. From this it developed the meaning of a breastplate of armor covering the chest and the back.[104] It has this meaning here and in its other NT usages (cf. 9:17; Eph. 6:14; 1 Thess. 5:8). The material of which it was made, iron, adds the connotation of invincibility to the description of the demonic locusts. The scaley backs, thoraxes, and flanks of literal locusts may be in view in this element of the likeness (Alford), but this too may be another element distinctive to the creatures of this plague to denote their invulnerability (Lenski). Earlier considerations in this discussion make the latter more probable.

---

104. Ibid., 6:364.

The other battlefield resemblance lies in the sound made by the wings of the agents of misery. The loud rushing sound of the swarm creates a formidable psychological problem for mankind and implies the hopelessness of resisting them. Joel compares the noise of locusts' wings to the clatter and clangor of chariot wheels and the hoofbeat of horses moving swiftly into battle (Joel 2:4-5; cf. 2 Kings 7:6; Jer. 47:3). The same is the picture here.

9:10 As awesome to the eye and ear as these other elements of the special locusts are, they are only peripheral in comparison with the damage caused by their tails: καὶ ἔχουσιν¹⁰⁵ οὐρὰς ὁμοίας σκορπίοις καὶ κέντρα, καὶ ἐν ταῖς οὐραῖς αὐτῶν ἡ ἐξουσία αὐτῶν ἀδικῆσαι τοὺς ἀνθρώπους μῆνας πέντε (*kai echousin ouras homoias skorpiois kai kentra, kai en tais ourais autōn hē exousia autōn adikēsai tous anthrōpous mēnas pente*, "And they have tails, like [the tails of] scorpions, and stings, and their power in their tails is to hurt men for five months"). This is a further detailing of v. 5. The power to inflict torture lies in these scorpionlike tails with stings (Swete, Bullinger, Beckwith). The word for "stings" (κέντρα [*kentra*]) derives from κεντρέω (*kentreō*), a verb meaning "I prick" or "I sting."¹⁰⁶ The noun designated the goad used for oxen (cf. Prov. 26:3, LXX) and the spur, quill, or sting of an insect.¹⁰⁷ Its only other NT uses are in Acts 26:14, Paul's kicking against "the goads," and 1 Cor. 15:55, "the sting" of death (Swete, Charles).

What was referred to as torment in v. 5—βασανισθήσονται . . . βασανισμὸς (*basanisthēsontai . . . basanismos*, "they may be tormented . . . torment")—in v. 10 becomes a power to "hurt" (ἀδικῆσαι [*adikēsai*]) for five months' duration.

9:11 A further characteristic of this locust swarm is their leader, another indication that these are no ordinary earthbound locusts (cf. Prov. 30:27): ἔχουσιν ἐπ᾽ αὐτῶν βασιλέα τὸν ἄγγελον τῆς ἀβύσσου· ὄνομα αὐτῷ¹⁰⁸ Ἑβραϊστὶ¹⁰⁹ Ἀβαδδὼν καὶ ἐν τῇ Ἑλληνικῇ ὄνομα ἔχει Ἀπολλύων¹¹⁰ (*echousin ep᾽ autōn basilea ton angelon tēs abyssou; ono-*

---

105. As a follow-up to the two imperfects of ἔχω in vv. 8-9, this present tense must be a historical present to heighten the vividness of the tails' description (Mounce, *Revelation*, p. 197).
106. G. A. Abbott-Smith, *A Manual Greek Lexicon of the New Testament* (Edinburgh: T. & T. Clark, 1950), p. 244.
107. M. R. Vincent, *Word Studies in the New Testament*, 2d ed. (McLean, Va.: MacDonald, reprint of 1888 ed.), 1:615.
108. See Rev. 6:8 for this same dative of possession with ὄνομα (cf. also John 1:6; 3:1; 18:10).
109. The adverb Ἑβραϊστί appears only in John's writings in the NT (cf. John 5:2; 19:13, 17, 20; 20:16; Rev. 16:16) (Swete, *Apocalypse*, p. 119; Charles, *Revelation*, 1:245).
110. The nominative case of Ἀπολλύων is retained though the proper name is in apposition with accusative ὄνομα (Robertson, *Word Pictures*, 6:365).

ma autō Hebraisti Abaddōn kai en tē Hellēnikē onoma echei Apollyōn, "they have over them the angel of the abyss as king, whose name in Hebrew is Abaddon and in Greek he has the name Apollyon"). The resemblance of the advancing locusts to an army suggests the need of a commander to coordinate the battle plan (Beckwith). The identifying of this commander-king as an angel is further evidence these are not regular locusts.

Some prefer not to attempt a definitive identification of this king, relegating him to the sphere of symbolic delusion or imagination (Swete, Charles, Lenski, Mounce). Yet according to 9:6, the fulfillment of this vision will be much more than a delusion. The verse gives the leader a name (two, in fact), calls him an angel, and assigns him a role as king of the demonic locusts. He cannot be disgarded as a delusion, not having actual existence.

Another idea has been that he is Satan,[111] but the fact that Satan is "the prince of demons" (Matt. 12:24) does not necessarily make him king over the demons confined in the abyss. His domain is the heavenly places, not the lower parts (cf. Eph. 6:12).[112] Nowhere does Satan have a connection with the abyss until being cast into it later (cf. 20:1-3).[113] Satan will become prominent later in the book (cf. Rev. 12 ff.), but it is unlikely that this obscure reference introduces him this early (Beckwith, Mounce). When he does enter the sequence, his introduction is dramatic (cf. 12:3, 9) (Alford).

On the other hand, a significant case exists for identifying this king as an otherwise unknown angel who is in charge of the abyss. Satan has leaders and sub-leaders under his command (cf. Eph. 6:12), so this could easily be one of those (Swete). The angel's title assures that the demon locusts obey his orders (Swete). Demons were assigned specific responsibilities like this in the Jewish thought of the day.[114] The highly developed angelology of Judaism had a special angel assigned to many spheres. Consequently, this is simply an angel whose name and responsibility in the hierarchy of evil the text discloses.

John gives the angel's name in two languages (Ἑβραϊστὶ . . . ἐν τῇ Ἑλληνικῇ [*Hebraisti . . . en tē Hellēnikē*, "in Hebrew . . . in Greek"]) because the end-time plague will afflict both groups (Seiss). Then too, John had to transfer his Hebrew thought-mold in order to communicate with his predominantly Gentile readership in Asia Minor (cf. Rev. 16:16). In the NT, the habit of supplying information bilingually char-

---

111. Theodore H. Epp, *Practical Studies in Revelation* (Lincoln, Neb.: Back to the Bible, 1969), 2:117; Smith, *Revelation*, p. 145; Walvoord, *Revelation*, p. 163.
112. H. Morris, *Revelation*, p. 164.
113. Newell, *Revelation*, p. 132.
114. Beckwith, *Apocalypse*, pp. 70, 445, 563.

acterizes only the gospel of John and Revelation in the NT (cf. John 1:38, 42; 4:25; 6:1; 9:7; 11:16; 19:13, 17, 20; 20:16; Rev. 1:7; 3:14; 12:9) (Lee, Johnson).

The name Ἀπολλύων (*Apollyōn*) comes from ἀπόλλυμι (*apollymi*) which means "I destroy." So the Greek term has the same meaning as the Hebrew Ἀβαδδὼν (*Abaddōn*), "Destroyer." This is expressive of the effect to be wrought by the demonic locusts whom the angel leads (Charles, Beckwith). The suggestion that John is sarcastically associating the angel with the god Apollo (Moffatt, Kiddle, Beasley-Murray, Mounce, Johnson), tempting as it is, is hardly correct. John calls him an angel, not a god, and Apollo was never associated with the abyss. To propose that the king is a figure of speech for death (Kiddle) takes the OT usage of the Hebrew name into account, but it fails to acknowledge that the angel is a real being and not merely a personification. Reasons for not identifying him as Satan appear in the discussion above. The name is simply an appropriate designation given to the fallen angel who rules the locusts from the abyss.

9:12 With the description of the fifth trumpet complete, the announcement of the completion of the first woe and the anticipation of the remaining two are in order: Ἡ οὐαὶ ἡ μία ἀπῆλθεν· ἰδοὺ ἔρχεται ἔτι δύο οὐαὶ μετὰ ταῦτα* (*Hē ouai hē mia apēlthen; idou erchetai eti dyo ouai meta tauta*, "The first woe has passed away; behold, two woes still come after these things"). This is probably a parenthetic word by John, but it could be a continuation of the eagle's announcement from 8:13 (Moffatt, Johnson). Mankind will welcome the passing of the first woe, but they have no room to heave a sigh of relief. Two more are yet to come (Beckwith). When John writes ἀπῆλθεν (*apēlthen*, "has passed"), he means, of course, in the future time of fulfillment. The woe had not passed away at the time Revelation was written (Beckwith, Lenski, Ladd).

The present tense ἔρχεται (*erchetai*, "comes") following ἰδοὺ (*idou*, "behold") makes this announcement quite dramatic. The second woe commences with the conclusion of this announcement and continues until 11:14, with an intervening intercalation in 10:1–11:13. Μετὰ ταῦτα (*Meta tauta*, "After these things") shows that the woes are not contemporaneous, but consecutive (Lee, Smith). Two woes are still to come after the first.

Additional Notes

9:7 Ἵπποις is an associative instrumental in function, as occurs frequently following ὅμοιος in this book (cf. 1:15; 2:18; 4:6; 9:10, 19; 11:1; 13:2, 11).[115]

---

115. Robertson, *Word Pictures*, 6:363.

Instead of ὅμοιοι χρυσῷ, some MSS have the rare plural form χρυσοῖ, and a few others read χρυσοῖ ὅμοιοι χρυσῷ. Χρυσοῖ has the support of more MSS and is the harder reading because of the rarity of the plural, but its witnesses are of a much later date. Χρυσοῖ ὅμοιοι χρυσῷ is an obvious conflation of the other two readings, and besides, has only weak MS evidence.[116] Besides having the support of stronger witnesses, ὅμοιοι χρυσῷ is more in accord with the style of Revelation.[117] Though not the more difficult reading because of this stylistic agreement, it still receives the nod as the correct reading.

9:10 Οὐρὰς ὁμοίας σκορπίοις is a condensed idiom whose expanded meaning would be "tails like [the tails of] scorpions." A similar idiom appears in 13:11 (cf. Matt. 5:20; 1 John 2:2).[118]

9:11 βασιλέα being anarthrous, is the predicate accusative in apposition with the accusative of direct object, τὸν ἄγγελον.

Ἀβαδδὼν is a transliteration of the Hebrew word אֲבַדּוֹן (cf. Job 26:6; 28:22; 31:12; Ps. 88:11; Prov. 15:11; 27:20). The LXX renders it by ἀπώλεια which means "destruction." In the OT it refers to destruction, parallel to Sheol (Job 26:6; Prov. 15:11; 27:20), death (Job 28:22), and the grave (Ps. 38:11). The Greek rendering "Apollyon" comes from the name's association with ἀπώλεια in the LXX.

9:12 Οὐαί used substantively is usually neuter, but the feminine article occurs here, perhaps because John was thinking of θλίψις or ταλαιπωρία, both of which are feminine (Beckwith).

Μία (Mia) is an ordinal number meaning "one," but here its use is as a cardinal in place of πρώτη, "first" (cf. 6:1; Mark 16:2).[119]

Though the subject of ἔρχεται is the plural δύο οὐαί, the verb is singular because it comes before its subject in the sentence. This is commonly called a "Pindaric" construction: "a third person singular verb occurs in the clause prior to its subject which may be plural and is placed in the singular regardless of the number of the subject."[120]

The καὶ that begins v. 13 either disappears or is moved to a position before μετὰ ταῦτα in a number of respected MSS including p47. To move the καὶ or do without it is also the harder reading, because it differs from John's usual pattern for introducing the trumpet angels.

---

116. Bruce M. Metzger, *A Textual Commentary on the Greek New Testament* (New York: United Bible Societies, 1971), p. 743.
117. Ibid., p. 743.
118. Robertson, *Word Pictures*, 6:365.
119. Ibid., 6:366.
120. James Home Moulton, *A Grammar of New Testament Greek. Prolegomena*, 3d ed. (Edinburgh: T. & T. Clark, 1908), p. 58; cf. Düsterdieck, *Revelation*, p. 282; Alford, *Greek Testament*, 4:644.

This variation has the effect of reading μετὰ ταῦτα with the beginning of v. 13 rather than with the end of v. 12.[121]

Substantial witnesses, including Alexandrinus, also stand in support of leaving the καὶ where it is at the beginning of v. 13, thereby keeping μετὰ ταῦτα as the conclusion of v. 12. This too can be construed as the harder reading, because usually in this book the phrase begins a sentence or clause. With an evenly divided external testimony, the decision comes down to deciding between two "harder" readings. Because the removal or relocation of καὶ is so hard that it is probably impossible, the reading that leaves it at the beginning of v. 13 is the preference.[122]

7. THE SIXTH TRUMPET: DEATH TO A THIRD OF EARTH'S INHABITANTS (9:13-21)

Translation

[13]And the sixth angel sounded, and I heard a voice from the horns of the golden altar which is before God, [14]saying to the sixth angel who had the trumpet, "Loose the four angels who are bound at the great river Euphrates." [15]And four angels, who were prepared for the hour and day and month and year, were loosed that they might kill a third of men. [16]And the number of the armies of cavalry [was] twenty thousands of ten thousands; I heard the number of them. [17]And thus I saw the horses in the vision and those sitting upon them, having breastplates of fire and hyacinth and brimstone; and the heads of the horses [were] as heads of lions, and from their mouths issued forth fire and smoke and brimstone. [18]From these three plagues were killed the third [part] of men, from the fire and the smoke and the brimstone which issued from their mouths. [19]For the authority of the horses is in their mouth and in their tails; for their tails are like serpents, having heads and with them they do harm.

Exegesis and Exposition

The deadly attack (9:13-19). With the sixth trumpet, the severity of the judgments increases even more than with the fifth. A voice from the golden altar responds to the sounding of the sixth angel: Καὶ ὁ ἕκτος ἄγγελος ἐσάλπισεν· καὶ ἤκουσα φωνὴν μίαν ἐκ τῶν [τεσσάρων]* κεράτων τοῦ θυσιαστηρίου τοῦ χρυσοῦ τοῦ ἐνώπιον τοῦ θεοῦ (*Kai ho hektos angelos esalpisen; kai ēkousa phōnēn mian ek tōn [tessarōn]*

---

121. Metzger, *Textual Commentary*, p. 743.
122. Ibid.

keratōn tou thysiastēriou tou chrysou tou enōpion tou theou, "And the sixth angel sounded, and I heard a voice from the horns of the golden altar which is before God"). In this case, for the first time, the trumpet angel in addition to blowing his trumpet assumes an active role in initiating the visitation.

What John heard (ἤκουσα [*ēkousa*]) in this vision replaces—but has the same force as—what he saw (εἶδον [*eidon*]) in most of the others. He heard a voice from the horns of the golden altar. Whose voice it is that speaks to the angel is the puzzle. Assigning the voice to the Messiah[123] is rather far-fetched in this context. It could be the voice of the altar itself if 8:3, 5 mean that the altar spoke as a result of the prayers of the saints (Alford). However Revelation never explicitly says an inanimate object speaks. John heard a voice from somewhere near the altar.[124] Others say that this could be the unified voice of the prayers of the saints that so consistently are associated with the altar (cf. 6:9-11; 8:3-4) (Alford, Swete, Lee). Yet the facts that the saints nowhere else issue a command to an angelic agent and that the noun φωνὴν (*phōnēn*, "voice") is singular in number render this view improbable. Taking God as the One speaking has merit in that the altar is in the vicinity of the throne.[125] God certainly has the authority to set the second woe into action. Furthermore, a voice from the throne in 19:5 is probably God's (Beasley-Murray). Even if this is true in 19:5, though—and it is doubtful—a voice emanating from the altar in 16:7 is clearly not God's, because He is the One addressed (Beckwith). To identify this as the voice of the angel of the altar in 8:3 captures the strong points of earlier views, but eliminates their weaknesses. The stated connection of this angel with the golden altar and with the altar-requests of the saints for this judgment, is ample reason to understand him to be the one giving direction to the sixth angel (Swete, Smith, Mounce). The triple use of the article τοῦ . . . τοῦ . . . τοῦ (*tou . . . tou . . . tou*) with the identical phrase in 8:3 (τὸ . . . τὸ . . . τὸ [*to . . . to . . . to*]), supplies corroboration for this conclusion. This is "*the* altar, *the* golden one, *the* one before God" in both places.

The horns of the altar were four in number, one at each corner. The voice coming "from" (ἐκ [*ek*]) them probably implies an origin "from the midst of" them (i.e., an implied (μέσου [*mesou*]) (Alford, Beckwith). The horns simply belonged to the surroundings, though one suggestion is that they recall God's sovereignty and judicial judg-

---

123. James Glasgow, *The Apocalypse* (Edinburgh: T. & T. Clark, 1872), p. 262.
124. Moses Stuart, *A Commentary on the Apocalypse* (Edinburgh: Maclachlan, Stewart, 1847), p. 577; Barnes, *Revelation*, p. 225.
125. Stuart, *Apocalypse*, p. 577; Barnes, *Revelation*, p. 225.

ment (Walvoord). It is better to see the voice as coming from the surface of the altar lying between the four corners (Alford, Beckwith).

9:14 The instructions to the sixth angel are explicit: λέγοντα τῷ ἕκτῳ ἀγγέλῳ, ὁ ἔχων τὴν σάλπιγγα, Λῦσον τοὺς τέσσαρας ἀγγέλους τοὺς δεδεμένους ἐπὶ τῷ ποταμῷ τῷ μεγάλῳ Εὐφράτῃ (*legonta tō hektō angelō, ho echōn tēn salpinga, Lyson tous tessaras angelous tous dedemenous epi tō potamō tō megalō Euphratē*, "saying to the sixth angel who had the trumpet, 'Loose the four angels who are bound at the great river Euphrates'"). To avoid misunderstanding as to which sixth angel, the parenthetical words ὁ ἔχων τὴν σάλπιγγα (*ho echōn tēn salpinga*, "who had the trumpet") clarify that it is one of the seven introduced in 8:2, 6 (Swete).

His instruction is to "loose the four angels who are bound at the great river Euphrates" (Λῦσον[126] τοὺς τέσσαρας ἀγγέλους τοὺς δεδεμένους ἐπὶ τῷ ποταμῷ τῷ μεγάλῳ Εὐφράτῃ [*Lyson tous tessaras angelous tous dedemenous epi tō potamō tō megalō Euphratē*]). The article τούς (*tous*) indicates that these four angels are familiar figures, but the reason for their familiarity is unknown. They appear nowhere else in the biblical record until this point where they apparently serve as leaders of the invading host (Beckwith). Some have seen them as good angels because of a supposed resemblance to the angels of 7:1, but those are at the four corners of the earth, not bound at the river Euphrates (Swete, Charles). Good angels are never bound (cf. 2 Pet. 2:4; Jude 6; Rev. 20:1 ff.) (Seiss, Walvoord). To take these angels as symbols of heathenism[127] is also unjustified, because nowhere else in the Apocalypse are angels symbolic. It is true that ἀγγέλος (*angelos*) without qualification occurs nowhere else in Revelation to refer to an evil angel (Lee), but in this one instance the context makes evident that this is an evil angel. They are fallen angels who are kept bound (δεδεμένους [*dedemenous*]) until the divinely appointed time for them to perform as agents of God's wrath.[128]

"The great river" (τῷ ποταμῷ τῷ μεγάλῳ [*tō potamō tō megalō*]) is a standing epithet for the Euphrates in the OT (cf. Gen. 15:18; Deut. 1:7; Josh. 1:4) as it is later in this book (Rev. 16:12) (Beckwith). It forms one of the borders of the land promised to Abraham (Gen. 15:18) and is the river that the enemies of God will cross prior to the last conflict before the Millennium (Rev. 16:12). Its headwaters are in the moun-

---

126. Λῦσον is an ingressive aorist carrying the force of "let loose" (Robertson, *Word Pictures*, 6:366).
127. John Peter Lange, *The Revelation of John*, Lange's Commentary, ed. E. R. Craven (Grand Rapids: Zondervan, 1968), p. 211.
128. Alford, *Greek Testament* 4:645; Swete, *Apocalypse*, p. 121; Robertson, *Word Pictures*, 6:366.

tains of Armenia, and it joins the Tigris in lower Babylon, the two rivers combining for a length of 1,800 miles. It separated Israel from her two chief enemies, Assyria and Babylon. The name refers not to just the river itself, but to the whole region drained by the river.[129] This was also the frontier between Rome and her enemy to the east, the Parthian Empire (Moffatt). The area beyond the Euphrates to the east is traditionally the source from which enemy attacks came against Israel (Beckwith). Some have ventured to understand this "Euphrates" in a symbolic way (e.g., Lee, Hailey), but its OT background requires that it be literal. Mingling literal designations of places with mystic language is quite uncommon in Scripture (Alford).

9:15 The sixth angel complies with his instructions and releases the four angels: καὶ ἐλύθησαν οἱ τέσσαρες ἄγγελοι οἱ ἡτοιμασμένοι εἰς τὴν ὥραν καὶ ἡμέραν καὶ μῆνα καὶ ἐνιαυτόν, ἵνα ἀποκτείνωσιν τὸ τρίτον τῶν ἀνθρώπων (*kai elythēsan hoi tessares angeloi hoi hētoimasmenoi eis tēn hōran kai hēmeran kai mēna kai eniauton, hina apokteinōsin to triton tōn anthrōpōn*, "and four angels, who were prepared for the hour and day and month and year, were loosed that they might kill a third of men"). The four angels were in a state of readiness (ἡτοιμασμένοι [*hētoismasmenoi*, "prepared"]) awaiting the appointed time to swing into action. Though they had fallen from divine favor, they still had experienced divine preparation for their nefarious task. Other instances of divine preparation, in either a positive or negative sense, occur in Matt. 25:34, 41; Mark 10:40; Luke 2:31; 1 Cor. 2:9; Rev. 12:6; 16:12 (Swete).

"The hour and day and month and year" (τὴν ὥραν καὶ ἡμέραν καὶ μῆνα καὶ ἐνιαυτόν [*tēn hōran kai hēmeran kai mēna kai eniauton*]) has been the basis for various chronological calculations as though the article τήν (*tēn*, "the") were not present or as though it appeared with each noun (Lee). One article governing all four nouns shows that duration is not in view, but that the occasion of each one of the time designations is one and the same: the appointed hour occurs on the appointed day in the appointed month and in the appointed year. The four angels await the signal that this hour has arrived.[130] Once again, this sounds the note of divine providence that recurs so often in this book (e.g., δεῖ [*dei*] in 1:1, μέλλει [*mellei*] in 1:19) (Moffatt). God's actions are not accidental, but planned and precise in time, to the point of a fixed hour of a fixed day of a fixed month of a fixed year

---

129. Beckwith, *Apocalypse*, p. 266; Glasgow, *Apocalypse*, p. 262; Moffatt, "Revelation," 5:408; Vincent, *Word Pictures*, 1:616; Mounce, *Revelation*, p. 201.
130. Vincent, *Word Pictures*, 1:616; Alford, *Greek Testament*, 4:645; Swete, *Apocalypse*, p. 122; Charles, *Revelation*, 1:252; Bullinger, *Apocalypse*, p. 329; Robertson, *Word Pictures*, 6:367.

(Johnson). All the forces of history are under His sovereign control (Mounce).

The purpose of the angelic preparation is "that they might kill a third of men" (ἵνα ἀποκτείνωσιν τὸ τρίτον τῶν ἀνθρώπων [*hina apokteinōsin to triton tōn anthrōpōn*]). Ἵνα (*Hina*, "That") expresses the goal of the mission as it does in v. 5, but there the goal was torture, not death (Alford, Charles). This must be physical death, not spiritual or metaphorical death. Physical death has already plagued the world under the fourth seal (6:7-8) and the third trumpet (8:10-11) (Beckwith), but not to the same extent as this. The fifth trumpet has brought torture in the physical sense (9:5), so the present trumpet naturally supersedes it, bringing death in a physical sense (Swete). A later reference to the survivors in v. 20 (οἱ λοιποί [*hoi loipoi*, "the rest"]) confirms that the afflicted are no longer on the scene after the plague.

"A third of men" (τὸ τρίτον τῶν ἀνθρώπων [*to triton tōn anthrōpōn*]) is a third of "those who dwell on the earth" (τοὺς κατοικοῦντας ἐπὶ τῆς γῆς [*tous katoikountas epi tēs gēs*]), i.e., the earth-dwellers who are the designated objects of the three woes (8:13) (Alford, Charles). The designated proportion does not include any of God's servants who were explicitly excluded under the fifth trumpet (cf. 9:4). The account of the sixth trumpet is not that explicit about the exclusion, but the word about the unrepentant two-thirds who escape in 9:20 implies that the plague had nothing to do with those whose repentance had already placed them in God's service (Sweet).

The fractional "one-third" represents an increase in intensity over any plague so far. One-quarter of earth's population earlier met the same fate under the fourth seal, so this trumpet signals the nearing of the climax of the period of wrath. Perhaps the one-third mortality will not be numerically much larger than the one-quarter already slain, but proportionately it will be a significantly larger percentage than any death-toll before it.

9:16 Abruptly the armies used to kill the large portion of humanity appear on the scene: καὶ ὁ ἀριθμὸς τῶν στρατευμάτων τοῦ ἱππικοῦ δισμυριάδες μυριάδων· ἤκουσα τὸν ἀριθμὸν αὐτῶν (*kai ho arithmos tōn strateumatōn tou hippikou dismyriades myriadōn; ēkousa ton arithmon autōn*, "and the number of the armies of cavalry [was] twenty thousands of ten thousands; I heard the number of them"). The four angels, once they are set free, turn into a huge force of cavalry. No explanation tells the source of the armies. It is only by implication that their origination has something to do with the four angels. Perhaps each of four armies (plural, τῶν στρατευμάτων [*tōn strateumatōn*]) has one of the angels as a leader,[131] but this is not verifiable.

---

131. Glasgow, *Apocalypse*, p. 132.

The identity of the armies' constituents has raised questions. Are they men or demons? The presence of the four angels in the area of the Euphrates River is a point in favor of these being men (cf. 16:12) (Walvoord). God's use of human armies of heathen nations to fulfill His purposes in the OT accords with this understanding (cf. Isa. 10:6-7, 25-26; 44:27–45:7; Hab. 1:6-11; Jer. 51:11, 28) (Hailey). If the two witnesses can breathe fire from their mouths in 11:5, the fire and brimstone spewing from the horses' mouths in 9:17 could pertain to mortals too (Seiss). The fact that the horses rather than the riders are the destructive agents and that they and their riders wear brightly colored breastplates matching the destructive forces proceeding from their mouths suggests that the combination of horse and rider is of superhuman origin.

The determining aspect in favor of these being demons is the description of the horses that differs so greatly from any ordinary horse that these horses must be of another order. Couple with this the association with the four demonic angels of 9:14 (Seiss), the fire, smoke, and brimstone proceeding from their mouths (Charles, Beasley-Murray), and the nature of the visiting hordes under the fifth trumpet (Seiss), and a case strongly favorable to seeing these as angels emerges.

The armies resemble a force composed of mounted troops (τοῦ ἱππικοῦ [*tou hippikou*, "of cavalry"]). A comparable term τὸ πεζικός (*to pezikos*) would have denoted infantry.[132] The horses rather than the horsemen are the active members of this group (Beckwith). They are quite numerous, δισμυριάδες μυριάδων (*dismyriades myriadōn*, "twenty thousands of ten thousands") giving their number as two hundred million. The feeling on one side is that the number is too large to be precise. Until modern times, rarely if ever has an army that large been assembled.[133] But these armies are demonic, not human, so the largeness of the number is no obstacle (Bullinger). Some have used ἐν τῇ ὁράσει (*en tē horasei*, "in the vision") as a ground for interpreting the number figuratively, but this would require allegorizing throughout the book. This phrase is no different from John's frequent εἶδον (*eidon*, "I saw").[134] Probably an exact number of two hundred million is intended; otherwise, some specification such as in 5:11 ("ten thousands of ten thousands and thousands of thousands") or 7:9 ("which no one could count") would have been used (cf. Ps. 68:17; Dan. 7:10; Heb. 12:22; Jude 14) (Morris, Ford). John is careful to point out how he knew the number. "I heard the number of them" (ἤκουσα τὸν ἀριθμὸν

---

132. Robertson, *Word Pictures*, 6:367.
133. Swete, *Apocalypse*, p. 122; BAGD, p. 199.
134. Düsterdieck, *Revelation*, p. 288; Smith, *Revelation*, p. 148.

αὐτῶν [*ēkousa ton arithmon autōn*]) indicates the figure came to him as part of the vision.[135]

9:17 After hearing the number of the horsemen, John saw what they looked like: καὶ οὕτως εἶδον τοὺς ἵππους ἐν τῇ ὁράσει καὶ τοὺς καθημένους ἐπ᾽ αὐτῶν, ἔχοντας θώραχας πυρίνους καὶ ὑακινθίνους καὶ θειώδεις· καὶ αἱ κεφαλαὶ τῶν ἵππων ὡς κεφαλαὶ λεόντων, καὶ ἐκ τῶν στομάτων αὐτῶν ἐκπορεύεται[136] πῦρ καὶ καπνὸς καὶ θεῖον (*kai houtōs eidon tous hippous en tē horasei kai tous kathēmenous ep' autōn, echontas thōrakas pyrinous kai hyakinthinous kai theiōdeis; kai hai kephalai tōn hippōn hōs kephalai leontōn, kai ek tōn stomatōn autōn ekporeuetai pyr kai kapnos kai theion*, "and thus I saw the horses in the vision and those sitting upon them, having breastplates of fire and hyacinth and brimstone; and the heads of the horses [were] as heads of lions, and from their mouths issued forth fire and smoke and brimstone"). He proceeds to describe the manner (οὕτως [*houtōs*, "thus"]) in which they appeared.

The mention of horses in the Bible is usually in connection with warfare.[137] The horses John saw in his vision are no exception. Grammatically ἔχοντας (*echontas*, "having") could modify the horses and the riders or the riders alone, assigning the breastplates to both or to the riders only. The first impression is to assign it to the riders only because τοὺς καθημένους (*tous kathēmenous*, "those who sat") is nearest to ἔχοντας (*echontas*) (Swete). On the other hand, with this as the first feature in the description the stronger probability is that it applies to the horses as well, because they are the main subject of the rest of the description.[138] For horses to wear such apparel was not unheard of in ancient times (Moffatt). This is the only detail given about the horsemen's appearance. They have defensive armor only, a characteristic agreeing with their subordinate role (Beckwith).

Θώραχας πυρίνους καὶ ὑακινθίνους καὶ θειώδεις (*Thōrakas pyrinous kai hyakinthinous kai theiōdeis*, "Breastplates of fire and hyacinth and brimstone") may refer to the actual materials which compose the breastplates, but it is difficult, perhaps impossible, to conceive of material objects made of these. Besides, in the LXX ὑακίνθινος (*hyakinthinos*) is a dye the color of blue smoke (cf. Ex. 25:4; 27:16) (Swete, Moffatt). Even though the same word in Rev. 21:20 is a precious stone,

---

135. Lange, *Revelation*, p. 211.
136. The verb ἐκπορεύεται is singular in agreement with the nearest member of the compound subject, because it appears before the compound subject (Robertson, *Word Pictures*, 6:368).
137. Vincent, *Word Pictures*, 1:617.
138. Düsterdieck, *Revelation*, p. 289; Beasley-Murray, *Revelation*, p. 165.

the color connotation fits better here as matching the καπνὸς (*kapnos,* "smoke") that proceeds from the horses' mouths. So the other two materials must represent colors too. Though no ὡς (*hōs*) appears, its presence is strongly implied.[139] The breastplates were the color of "fire and hyacinth and brimstone."

Πυρίνους (*Purinous,* "Of fire") represents a fiery red color (Alford). As noted above, ὑακίνθινος (*hyakinthinos*) referred to a dark-shaded color including that of sulphurous smoke.[140] Θειώδεις (*Theiōdeis,* "Brimstone") described something made of sulphur and also something with a sulphurous hue or light yellow. Brimstone was traditional as an accompaniment of God's wrath.[141] The association of the three colors recalls the fate of the cities of the plain in Gen. 19:24, 28 (Swete). It also denotes the relationship of these horses with the lake of fire introduced later in the book (cf. 14:10-11; 19:20; 20:10; 21:8) (Beckwith). They are of the nature of those who will eventually arrive at such a fate.

The likeness of the horses' heads to those of lions (ὡς κεφαλαὶ λεόντων [*hōs kephalai leontōn*]) suggests that the army combines the swiftness of horses with the majestic bearing of lions (Swete). Lions elsewhere in Revelation betoken terror (their roar in 10:3), ferocity (their teeth in 9:8), and destructiveness (their mouth in 13:2) (Scott). Here their eminence seems to be in view.

The most destructive facet of the horses was their mouths which emitted "fire and smoke and brimstone" (πῦρ καὶ καπνὸς καὶ θεῖον [*pyr kai kapnos kai theion*]). The word στόμα (*stoma,* "mouth") appears three times in vv. 17-19, as it does in connection with the sixth bowl judgment too (cf. 16:13). It is impossible to determine from the text whether all three elements come from the mouth of each horse or whether each element alone proceeds from the mouths of one-third of the horses (Alford, Lee). Probability is on the side of the former, however.

9:18 It is through these three plagues that a third of mankind perishes: ἀπὸ τῶν τριῶν πληγῶν τούτων ἀπεκτάνθησαν τὸ τρίτον τῶν ἀνθρώπων, ἐκ τοῦ πυρὸς καὶ τοῦ καπνοῦ καὶ τοῦ θείου τοῦ ἐκπορευομένου[142] ἐκ τῶν στομάτων αὐτῶν (*apo tōn triōn plēgōn toutōn*

---

139. Robertson, *Word Pictures,* 6:367.
140. Alford, *Greek Testament,* 4:646; Swete, *Apocalypse,* p. 123; J. H. Moulton and G. Milligan, *The Vocabulary of the Greek Testament* (Grand Rapids: Eerdmans, 1974), p. 647.
141. Stuart, *Apocalypse,* p. 579; Barnes, *Revelation,* p. 228; Moffatt, "Revelation," 5:409-10.
142. The participle ἐκπορευομένου is singular in agreement with last member of the series of three. In sense, it modifies all three, however (Lee, "Revelation," 4:616).

apektanthēsan to triton tōn anthrōpōn, ek tou pyros kai tou kapnou kai tou theiou tou ekporeuomenou ek tōn stomatōn autōn, "from these three plagues were killed the third [part] of men, from the fire and the smoke and the brimstone which issues from their mouths"). Πληγή (*Plēgē*, "Plague") is the term applied to the threefold destructive capacity of the horses. It is the same word used in the LXX to name the plagues of Egypt (e.g., Ex. 11:1). It will appear frequently from here on in the Apocalypse also (cf. 9:20; 11:6; 13:3, 12, 14; 15:1, 6, 8; 16:9, 21; 18:4, 8; 21:9; 22:18).[143]

For further emphasis the preposition ἐκ (*ek*, "from") repeats the threefold way people will die by echoing the ἀπό (*apo*, "by") from earlier in the verse. Ἀπό (*Apo*) is used with a passive verb to express agency in 12:6 also (Charles), but agency depicted indirectly as the direction or the source from which the result comes (Alford, Swete).

The repeated article with each of the destructive mediums (τοῦ . . . τοῦ . . . τοῦ (*tou . . . tou . . . tou*, "the . . . the . . . the") indicates that each element is a separate agency of destruction (Swete). The three together will be responsible for the largest death-toll in human history up to that point.

9:19 The prophecy continues by explaining the power of the horses: ἡ γὰρ ἐξουσία τῶν ἵππων ἐν τῷ στόματι αὐτῶν ἐστιν καὶ ἐν ταῖς οὐραῖς αὐτῶν· αἱ γὰρ οὐραὶ αὐτῶν ὅμοιαι ὄφεσιν, ἔχουσαι κεφαλὰς, καὶ ἐν αὐταῖς ἀδικοῦσιν (*hē gar exousia tōn hippōn en tō stomati autōn estin kai en tais ourais autōn; hai gar ourai autōn homoiai ophesin, echousai kephalas, kai en autais adikousin*, "for the authority of the horses is in their mouth and in their tails; for their tails are like serpents, having heads and with them they do harm"). Verse 19 has two uses of γὰρ (*gar*, "for"), the first appearance of the conjunction since Rev. 3:2. The first of them furnishes an explanation that the general power of the horses lies in their mouths and tails. Prior discussion has already elaborated on this power in vv. 17-18. This is the first mention of the power of their tails, however (Beckwith).

Because the contribution of the tails to the plague is new, the second *gar* explains what the power of the tails is. They resemble snakes, including the heads, which are capable of inflicting painful injury to their victims. This detail would have been especially meaningful to the church at Pergamum where the temples in honor of the gods Zeus and Asklepios emphasized the role of snakes in their worship (Thomas, p. 179; Beckwith, Mounce). The description of fire-breathing demonic horses with tails like snakes is grotesque, causing some to interpret them as figurative references to the serpents on the

---

143. Swete, *Apocalypse*, p. 124; Abbott-Smith, *Lexicon*, p. 364; Robertson, *Word Pictures*, 6:368.

pagan altars or to the custom of the Parthians of binding their horses' tails to look like serpents (Charles, Kiddle). Great variety has marked the assortment of mystical meanings attached to the tails (Lee). The ὅμοιαι (*homoiai*, "like") gives a basis for some figurative understanding of the tails, but most suggestions ignore the power attributed to the tails. The tails were not actual serpents, but they did *function* like serpents. The power of the tails enables the horses to hurt (ἀδικοῦσιν [*adikousin*, "they do harm"]) people physically. They torture with the pain of a snake-bite as the locusts of the previous trumpet did with a scorpion sting. The sting is the extent of the pain from the locusts, but the demonic horses not only inflict comparable or worse pain; they also kill (cf. v. 15) (Beckwith).

Additional Notes

9:13 An accusative object φωνὴν follows ἤκουσα here, but in 8:13 the object is genitive. Sometimes this distinction denotes a difference between the sound only (Acts 9:7, genitive) and understanding the sense of what is heard (Acts 22:9, accusative). Here this differentiation between the two cases does not apply, however, for the sense was clear in both cases.[144]

Whether to understand μίαν as a simple indefinite article or as reflecting singleness is a question. It is the simple article in 8:13 and 18:21 (Charles), but the adjective may deserve more attention as calling attention to the singleness of the voice though it came from four horns (Swete). In favor of the former possibility is John's inclination to show the influence of Hebrew usage in his style (e.g., Dan. 8:3, אֶחָד) (Charles). The context has no strong indication of any intention to emphasize singularity, so the probability of μίαν function as an indefinite article is stronger.

The two strongest MSS, p[47] and A, omit τεσσάρων from the text, yet the witnesses for including it are almost as impressive. The omission could have been accidental because of the word's similarity to κεράτων, but it could also have been added to match the four angels bound at the Euphrates (9:14) or as an antithesis to the *one* voice John heard. Most decisive, however, is the consideration that the omission is the harder reading, because it was a well-known fact from the OT that the altar had four horns. So it would have been easier to add it than to leave it out. The omission is correct.[145]

9:14 The nominative participle ἔχων is in apposition with the dative ἀγγέλῳ, a phenomenon that occurs also at 2:20; 3:12; 14:12.[146]

---

144. Robertson, *Word Pictures*, 6:366.
145. Metzger, *Textual Commentary*, p. 744.
146. Robertson, *Word Pictures*, 6:366.

9:15 Compare ἐλύθησαν to δεδεμένους in v. 14. Λύω is the regular correlative of δέω (cf. Matt. 16:19; 18:18; Mark 11:4-5; Luke 13:16; 1 Cor. 7:27) (Swete).

The preposition εἰς following ἑτοιμάζω commonly means "with a view to" or "for" (cf. v. 7; 2 Tim. 2:21) (Alford).

9:16 The accusative case of the thing τὸν ἀριθμὸν about which one hears follows the classical rule for a direct object after ἀκούω.[147]

9:17 Some are of the opinion that οὕτως along with ἐν τῇ ὁράσει points backward to v. 16,[148] but the adverb can look forward. This context requires it to refer to what follows as it does frequently (e.g., Matt. 1:18; 2:5; John 21:1; Heb. 4:4).[149] John would not repeat v. 17 by telling that he saw what he heard, as the backward reference would require. This would be redundant.

The phrase ἐν τῇ ὁράσει occurs nowhere else in the book, though it is frequent in Daniel (cf. Dan. 7:2; 8:2, 15; 9:21) (Beckwith). It could possibly mean "in appearance, not in reality" (Lee), but this is quite remote. "In the vision" is preferable, though the phrase is pleonastic coming after εἶδον.

9:18 The verb ἀπεκτάνθησαν is plural even though the subject τὸ τρίτον is singular. The reason is that τὸ τρίτον is neuter singular to capture a collective concept.[150]

The response of the survivors (9:20-21). The loss of a third of the earth's population and the suffering of many more hopefully would cause the survivors to be more responsive to God, but it does not.

Translation

20And the rest of men, who were not killed by these plagues, did not even repent of the works of their hands, that they should not worship the demons and the idols of gold and of silver and of brass and of stone and of wood, which can neither see nor hear nor walk, 21and they did not repent of their murders or of their sorceries or of their fornication or of their thefts.

Exegesis and Exposition

9:20 In spite of the plain evidences of God's wrath all around them, the remaining earth-dwellers continue adamant in their obduracy toward God: Καὶ οἱ λοιποὶ τῶν ἀνθρώπων, οἳ οὐκ ἀπεκτάνθησαν ἐν[151] ταῖς

---

147. BDF, par. 173.
148. Vincent, *Word Pictures*, 1:616; Lenski, *Revelation*, p. 304.
149. Lee, "Revelation," 4:615; Barnes, *Revelation*, p. 228.
150. Robertson, *Word Pictures*, 6:368.
151. The preposition ἐν is clearly used instrumentally here (Swete, *Apocalypse*, p. 124; Beckwith, *Apocalypse*, p. 569).

πληγαῖς ταύταις, οὐδὲ* μετενόησαν ἐκ τῶν ἔργων τῶν χειρῶν αὐτῶν, ἵνα μὴ προσκυνήσουσιν τὰ δαιμόνια καὶ τὰ εἴδωλα τὰ χρυσᾶ καὶ τὰ ἀργυρᾶ καὶ τὰ χαλκᾶ καὶ τὰ λίθινα καὶ τὰ ξύλινα, ἃ οὔτε βλέπειν δύνανται οὔτε ἀκούειν οὔτε περιπατεῖν (*Kai hoi loipoi tōn anthrōpōn, hoi ouk apektanthēsan en tais plēgais tautais, oude metenoēsan ek tōn ergōn tōn cheirōn autōn, hina mē proskynēsousin ta daimonia kai ta eidōla ta chrysa kai ta argura kai ta chalka kai ta lithina kai ta xylina, ha oute blepein dynantai oute akouein oute peripatein*, "And the rest of men, who were not killed by these plagues, did not even repent of the works of their hands, that they should not worship the demons and the idols of gold and of silver and of brass and of stone and of wood, which can neither see nor hear nor walk").

The text is quite explicit in identifying "the rest" (οἱ λοιποὶ [*hoi loipoi*]) as those "who were not killed by these plagues" (οἱ οὐκ ἀπεκτάνθησαν ἐν ταῖς πληγαῖς ταύταις [*hoi ouk apektanthēsan en tais plēgais tautais*]). These are the survivors of the visitation of the demonic cavalry. It is an outside possibility that "these plagues" refers to all the judgments of chapters 8-9 (Johnson), but contextual support favors limiting them to the three instruments of death—fire, smoke, and brimstone—under the sixth trumpet (cf. 9:18) (Beckwith).

The survivors shunned repentance. The adverb οὐδὲ (*oude*, "not even") intensifies negating of μετενόησαν (*metenoēsan*, "repent") and the force of the tragic statement about the ones who remained alive. They absolutely failed to change their conduct, their creed, or their attitudes toward God, which would have appeared to be the least they could do in light of what the world had just experienced.[152] This is the first mention of repentance since 4:1, though the seven messages in chapters 2-3 had a number of references to it (cf. 2:5 (twice), 16, 21, 22; 3:3, 9). The only remaining occurrences are 9:21; 16:9, 11 (Ford). In all cases in the apocalyptic portion of the book, the word about repentance is negative as here. God's loving care for His people is repeatedly evident, but opportunities to repent, though they are there, are rare (Beckwith).

Μετανοέω ἐκ (*Metanoeō ek*, "I repent of") in Revelation denotes a change of mind in rejection of something that is anti-God (cf. 2:21, 22; 9:21; 16:11). What they failed to turn away from here was τῶν ἔργων τῶν χειρῶν αὐτῶν (*tōn ergōn tōn cheirōn autōn*, "the works of their hands"). Throughout Scripture the works of man's hands stands for idolatry (Deut. 4:28; 27:15; 31:29; 2 Kings 19:18; 22:17; 2 Chron. 32:19; 34:25; Ps. 115:4; 135:15; Isa. 2:8; 17:8; 37:19; Jer. 1:16; 10:3, 9; 25:6, 7, 14; 32:30; 44:8; Hos. 14:3; Mic. 5:13; Hag. 2:14; Acts 7:41) (Alford,

---

152. Robertson, *Word Pictures*, 6:368.

Bullinger, Scott). Worshiping idols has been a longstanding problem for earthlings and will continue to be into the future as this prophecy anticipates. Even something so great as the deaths of a significant portion of the world's people will still be insufficient to deter men from this practice, though presumably God's servants will have warned them against it repeatedly.

Like Paul (Rom. 1:18-32), John was utterly intolerant of any kind of pagan worship. Such was the fountainhead of moral corruption and the primary cause of the outpouring of God's wrath against mankind (Beasley-Murray). To worship idols is to rob God of the glory due Him alone (cf. Rom. 1:23) and to consort with evil spirits who excel in the corrupting of man (cf. 1 Cor. 10:19-20) (Johnson). The negative purpose of not repenting (ἵνα μὴ προσκυνήσουσιν . . . [*hina mē proskynēsousin . . .*, "that they should not worship . . ."]) elaborates on the forms of idol worship. Repentance would have led to the abandoning of the worship of unclean spirits and of the idols that represent them, but failure to repent does just the opposite. It perpetuates the continued worship of idols representing demons, whether made of gold, silver, brass, stone, or wood (Alford, Swete).

Τὰ δαιμόνια (*Ta daimonia*, "the demons") clearly refers to unclean or evil spirits, as the gospels call them. On the surface, the demons carry the appearance of idols, but throughout the Bible worship proffered to idols is ultimately the worship of demons (cf. Deut. 32:17; Ps. 106:37; 1 Cor. 10:21) (Alford, Swete). The continuation of demon worship enhances the irony of the situation: the very demons who were agents in inflicting such wide-scale death under the sixth trumpet continue to be the objects of worship for the remaining two-thirds of mankind (Kiddle).

Τὰ εἴδωλα τὰ χρυσᾶ καὶ τὰ ἀργυρᾶ καὶ τὰ χαλκᾶ καὶ τὰ λίθινα καὶ τὰ ξύλινα (*Ta eidōla ta chrysa kai ta argyra kai ta chalka kai ta lithina kai ta xylina*, "the idols of gold and of silver and of brass and of stone and of wood") tells the outward form that demons assume in order to receive worship. Εἴδωλον (*Eidōlon*, "Idol") refers to any image that represents a heathen god. John could hardly forget the innumerable pagan shrines around him, where false priests and prophets led their followers in bowing down before the representations that claimed to be gods. Nor could he ignore the rapid increase in temples devoted to emperor-cult worship (Kiddle). Sins of idolatry mostly characterized his Gentile readers, but the moral sins in v. 21 marred the lives of both Jews and Gentiles (Lee).

He reminds his readers of the helplessness of these idols, a fact which they undoubtedly knew already: ἃ οὔτε βλέπειν δύνανται οὔτε ἀκούειν οὔτε περιπατεῖν (*ha oute blepein dynantai oute akouein oute peripatein*, "which can neither see nor hear nor walk"). This is an oft-repeated formula from the OT (cf. Deut. 4:28; Ps. 115:5-7; 135:15 ff.; Isa. 44:12-20; Dan. 5:23) (Charles, Mounce). It highlights the senselessness of idol worship.

9:21 Not only are the earth-dwellers unrepentant of their sins against the first table of the Mosaic law through their worship of other gods, but they also have a general disregard for the cardinal principles of the moral code (Kiddle): καὶ οὐ μετενόησαν ἐκ τῶν φόνων αὐτῶν οὔτε ἐκ τῶν φαρμάκων* αὐτῶν οὔτε ἐκ τῆς πορνείας αὐτῶν οὔτε ἐκ τῶν κλεμμάτων αὐτῶν (*kai ou metenoēsan ek tōn phonōn autōn oute ek tōn pharmakōn autōn oute ek tēs porneias autōn oute ek tōn klemmatōn autōn,* "and they did not repent of their murders or of their sorceries or of their fornication or of their thefts"). Men are no less unwilling to repent of their social sins than of their idolatries (Swete, Beckwith, Charles, Lenski). Three of the Ten Commandments—the sixth, seventh, and eighth—explicitly prohibit three of the four vices listed— murder, fornication, and theft (Ex. 20:13-15). The NT condemns the same three (Luke 18:20; Rom. 13:9) (Mounce).

The fourth of the sins, φαρμάκων (*pharmakōn,* "sorceries") is a broader word than the variant φαρμακειῶν (*pharmakeiōn,* "sorceries") in that it can refer to poisons, amulets, charms, drugs, magic spells, or any object that is supposed to possess holiness, elicit lust, or be otherwise enchanting.[153] It can refer to witchcraft too. Usually drugs were involved in such practices. If the use of the drugs is to cause an abortion or infanticide, this is tantamount to the sin of idolatry (v. 20) on the one hand and to murder and fornication on the other (v. 21) (Lee). If the drugs create magic spells as practiced in Asia to incite illicit lust, this is equivalent to fornication (v. 21) (Moffatt). Sorceries were common in Asia (cf. Acts 19:18-19) (Sweet). The Bible sternly denounces this form of sin (cf. Ex. 22:18; Lev. 20:27; Deut. 18:10-12; cf. also 1 Sam. 28:7; Acts 8:9; 13:8; 19:13-15).[154]

"Murderers," "fornicators," "sorcerers," and "idolaters" are in the lists of those excluded from the New Jerusalem in 21:8 and 22:15, doubtless because of their failure to repent of their law-breaking.

Additional Notes

9:20 Instead of οὐδὲ some sources have οὔτε and still others have οὐ. It is possible to eliminate οὐ from consideration because its external support is very weak and it is the easiest of the readings. External support for the other two variants is about equal. Both are also harder readings by virtue of their normal function as adverbs but used as

153. Glasgow, *Apocalypse,* p. 273; Moffatt, "Revelation," 5:410; Vincent, *Word Pictures,* 1:617-18.
154. Scott, *Revelation,* p. 215; Chilton, *Days of Vengeance,* p. 258.

conjunctions here.[155] Beyond this, however, οὔτε is easier to explain in that scribes would try to match the correlative οὔτε . . . οὔτε at the end of v. 20 rather than trying to insert a reading that differs here.[156] In this light οὐδὲ is preferable.

9:21 Some respected MSS, including Alexandrinus, read φαρμακειῶν instead of φαρμάκων. The former also appears in 18:23 as well as in Gal. 5:20. The latter occurs nowhere else in the NT. The former has the added advantage of matching more easily the other categories listed in v. 21 as belonging to the second table of the law. Nevertheless, φαρμάκων enjoys stronger external support and is the harder reading because of being a *hapax legomenon*.[157] So it is the chosen reading.

Πορνείας is the only sin in the list that occurs in the singular, perhaps because of the nature of the sin. It is one never-ceasing impurity with those whose hearts are so tainted. The term represents sexual sin in general, not a specific act of fornication (Morris).

---

155. Metzger, *Textual Commentary*, p. 744.
156. Ibid.
157. Ibid.

15

Preface to the Seventh Trumpet

With the completion of the sixth trumpet, also called the second woe, the seventh trumpet does not come immediately, but awaits the setting of the stage for its sounding. Two preliminary elements must prepare the way for this last in the trumpet series: the announcement of the end of delay (10:1-11) and the measurement of the temple and its worshipers (11:1-14).

8. THE ANNOUNCEMENT OF THE END OF DELAY (10:1-11)

Translation

¹And I saw another strong angel descending from heaven, clothed in a cloud, and the rainbow was over his head, and his face was as the sun, and his feet were as pillars of fire, ²and he had in his hand a little scroll opened. And he placed his right foot on the sea and his left on the land, ³and he cried with a great voice as a lion roars. And when he cried, the seven [peals of] thunder uttered their own voices. ⁴And when the seven thunders spoke, I was about to write; and I heard a voice from heaven saying, "Seal the things which the seven thunders spoke, and do not write them." ⁵And the angel whom I saw standing on the sea and on the land lifted his right hand to heaven ⁶and swore by the one who lives forever and ever, who created the heaven and the things which are in it and the earth and the things which are in it and the sea and the things which are in it, that there will no longer be delay, ⁷but in the days

of the sound of the seventh angel, when he will sound, then the mystery of God will be completed, as he preached the good news to His own slaves the prophets. [8]And the voice which I heard from heaven again spoke with me and said, "Go, take the scroll which is opened in the hand of the angel who stands on the sea and on the land." [9]And I went away to the angel, requesting him to give me the little scroll. And he says to me, "Take and eat it, and it will make your stomach bitter, but in your mouth it will be sweet as honey." [10]And I took the little scroll from the hand of the angel and ate it, and it was in my mouth as sweet as honey; and when I ate it, my stomach was made bitter. [11]And it was said to me, "It is necessary for you to prophesy again concerning many peoples and nations and tongues and kings."

Exegesis and Exposition

Some prefer to include 10:1–11:13 as part of the sixth trumpet judgment because of the declaration of 11:14 that at that point the second woe has passed.[1] This conclusion is uncalled for, however, in light of the clear indication of 9:20-21 that the sixth trumpet has ended there. After that comes an interlude that is a transition from the second to the third woe, making it as though 11:14 joins immediately with 9:21.[2] Just as a two-vision interlude precedes the seventh seal (cf. 7:1-17), so here the visions of the angel with the little scroll (10:1-11) and of the two witnesses (11:1-13) intervene before the seventh trumpet, which is also the third woe.[3]

This section is parenthetical to the sequential movement of the trumpet judgments. It contains no reference to the judgment of the earth-dwellers, but consoles believers by reiterating God's role as the sovereign over earthly affairs, who will not only judge the wicked, but also will exalt the suffering faithful in due time. The interlude prepares for the final trumpet-blast by reviewing developments leading up to that moment, particularly those related to the city of Jerusalem. The climactic angelic announcement of the imminence of the end

---

1. Friedrich Düsterdieck, *Critical and Exegetical Handbook to the Revelation of John*, in Meyer's Commentary, trans. and ed. by Henry E. Jacobs (New York: Funk & Wagnalls, 1887), pp. 295-96; E. W. Bullinger, *The Apocalypse* or *"The Day of the Lord"* (London: Eyre and Spottiswodde, n.d.), p. 335; J. B. Smith, *A Revelation of Jesus Christ* (Scottdale, Pa.: Herald, 1961), p. 149.
2. Homer Hailey, *Revelation, an Introduction and Commentary* (Grand Rapids: Baker, 1979), p. 241.
3. Archibald Thomas Robertson, *Word Pictures in the New Testament*, 6 vols. (Nashville: Broadman, 1933), 6:370.

(10:6-7) anticipates a time after the sixth trumpet, but immediately before the seventh sounds.[4]

Chapter 10 is in two parts: a climactic announcement (10:1-7) and the recommissioning of John (10:8-11).

A climactic announcement (10:1-7).

10:1 Καὶ εἶδον (*Kai eidon*) in 10:1 introduces another scene in the larger vision of the trumpets: Καὶ εἶδον ἄλλον ἄγγελον ἰσχυρὸν καταβαίνοντα ἐκ τοῦ οὐρανοῦ, περιβεβλημένον νεφέλην, καὶ ἡ ἶρις ἐπὶ τὴν κεφαλὴν αὐτοῦ, καὶ τὸ πρόσωπον αὐτοῦ ὡς ὁ ἥλιος, καὶ οἱ πόδες αὐτοῦ ὡς στῦλοι πυρός (*Kai eidon allon angelon ischyron katabainonta ek tou ouranou, peribeblēmenon nephelēn, kai hē iris epi tēn kephalēn autou, kai to prosōpon autou hōs ho hēlios, kai hoi podes autou hōs styloi pyros*, "And I saw another strong angel descending from heaven, clothed in a cloud, and the rainbow was over his head, and his face was as the sun, and his feet were as pillars of fire"). This scene marks a significant change in John's literary method. Here his personality re-emerges as it did briefly between the sixth and seventh seals (7:13-14),[5] but now for the first and last time in this drama, he leaves the observer's corner and occupies the very center of the stage (e.g., 10:9-11).[6] This new role also involves a change in location from heaven to earth, as the angel descends from heaven (10:1) and stands upon the earth where John hears a voice from heaven (10:4, 8) and goes to him (10:8) (Beckwith). The new style is one element among others that heightens the anticipation and accentuates the solemnity of the apocalyptic events to follow.[7]

Attempts to identify "another strong angel" (ἄλλον ἄγγελον ἰσχυρόν [*allon angelon ischyron*]) have included equating him to a well-known angel, either Gabriel or Michael.[8] The prominence of these two

---

4. G. R. Beasley-Murray, *The Book of Revelation*, NCB (Grand Rapids: Eerdmans, 1978), pp. 168-69.
5. James Moffatt, "The Revelation of St. John the Divine," in *The Expositor's Greek Testament*, ed. W. Robertson Nicoll (Grand Rapids: Eerdmans, n.d.), 5:411.
6. Isbon T. Beckwith, *The Apocalypse of John* (New York: Macmillan, 1919), p. 573; Moffatt, "Revelation," 5:411; Walter Scott, *Exposition of the Revelation of Jesus Christ* (Swengel, Pa.: Bible Truth Depot, n.d.), p. 218; John F. Walvoord, *The Revelation of Jesus Christ* (Chicago: Moody, 1966), p. 169.
7. Henry Alford, *The Greek Testament* (London: Longmans, Green, 1903), 4:648-49.
8. R. H. Charles, *The Revelation of St. John*, ICC (New York: Scribner's Sons, 1920), 1:258-59; Smith, *Revelation*, pp. 153-54; J. P. M. Sweet, *Revelation* (Philadelphia: Westminster, Pelican, 1979), p. 177; Robert H. Mounce, *The Book of Revelation*, NICNT (Grand Rapids: Eerdmans, 1977), p. 207; Alan F. Johnson, "Revelation," in *EBC*, ed. Frank E. Gaebelein (Grand Rapids: Zondervan, 1981), 12:496.

in the book of Daniel on which Revelation so strongly relies enhances this possibility (cf. Dan. 8:16; 9:21; 10:13, 21; 12:1) (Charles, Sweet, Mounce, Johnson). In view of the many angels besides these two who have a part in Scripture, it is purely guesswork to limit the possibilities to these, however. The strength (ἰσχυρόν [*ischyron*]) of the angel is no assurance that the reader will know his name. After all, he is ἄλλον (*allon*, "another"), i.e., one in addition to someone elsewhere. He is not unique.

Another proposal identifies him with the strong angel mentioned in 5:2 because both speak with a loud voice (cf. 5:2; 10:3) (Alford, Moffatt). This, of course, disregards the differentiation between the two by the adjective *allon* ("another"). "Strong" angels are probably numerous, because yet another appears in 18:21.

A number of favorable elements support saying this angel is Christ. Both descend in a cloud (cf. 1:7). The description here is similar to that of Christ in 1:12-16, particularly the face and feet. The rainbow suggests a theophany (cf. 4:3; Ezek. 1:28) (Scott). The comparison of the angel's voice to a lion's roar (10:3) looks back to the voice of God in the OT (e.g., Hos. 11:10; Amos 1:2; 3:4, 8) (Moffatt). It was God who held the seven-sealed scroll until Christ took it in chapter 5. The angel held the little scroll until he gave it to John (Scott).

Yet, unless this is an exception, Christ is never called an angel in Revelation, particularly "another of the same kind" (*allon*) and not unique.[9] When referring to the unique Son of God, the text is never ambiguous (Alford). What absolutely forbids this angel being Christ is the oath sworn by the angel in 10:5-6, one that could never come from the lips of the second person of the Trinity (Beckwith, Mounce).

The best identification is to see this angel as similar to but distinct from the angel in 5:2. That is the only strong angel mentioned earlier, so the *allon* must compare the two (Alford, Smith). This is as close as it is possible to come, given the available data, to saying who this obviously significant angel is. The angel's strength is attributable to his appearance and the actions he performs.[10]

John sees the angel in the process of his descent from heaven καταβαίνοντα ἐκ τοῦ οὐρανοῦ (*katabainonta ek tou ouranou*, "descending from heaven") as he does the angel in 20:1 also (Swete).[11]This confirms that John has moved from heaven, where he has been since

---

9. Henry Barclay Swete, *The Apocalypse of St. John* (London: Macmillan, 1906), p. 123; Charles, *Revelation*, 1:259; Bullinger, *Apocalypse*, p. 336.
10. R. C. H. Lenski, *The Interpretation of St. John's Revelation* (Columbus, Ohio: Lutheran Book Concern, 1935), p. 311.
11. For the combination of καταβαίνω and ἐκ elsewhere, see 3:12; 13:13; 16:21; 18:1; 20:1, 9. In all but 20:9 where it is aorist, καταβαίνω is present tense.

8:2, to the earth.[12] Being "clothed in a cloud" enhanced the glory of the angel's appearance.[13] Clouds are often the vehicles on which heavenly beings ascend or descend, usually in an eschatological setting (Ps. 104:3; Dan. 7:13; Isa. 19:1; Acts 1:9; Rev. 1:7), but here they are the angel's clothing (Mounce). The cloud does more than reinforce the angel's dignity, however. It shows his mission to be related to judgment. Of the twenty other occurrences of νεφέλη (*nephelē*, "cloud") in the NT, nine come in connection with scenes of judgment (cf. Matt. 24:30; 26:24; Mark 13:26; 14:62; Luke 21:27; Rev. 1:7; 14:14, 15, 16). This context falls into that category because of the angel's function in relation to the trumpet judgments past and future (Walvoord).

Ἶρις (*Iris*) is the same word for "rainbow" as the one in 4:3 that encircles the throne in heaven. It brings its association with divine majesty there into this context to add to the impressive stature of this angel. In 4:3, the rainbow, likened to an emerald, was a number of shades of green (Thomas, *Revelation 1-7*, pp. 343-44), but here a rainbow with its variegated colors and glories, caused by the sunshine of the angel's face, was a kind of glorious headdress (Swete, Scott, Ladd). But the rainbow denotes more than just heavenly glory (contra Beckwith) or the prismatic effect of the cloud upon the sunlight (contra Swete, Mounce). It betokens mercy in the midst of judgment as it did in Noah's day,[14] the same significance as it had in the initial vision of the throne room (Alford).

Comparing the angel's face to ὁ ἥλιος (*ho hēlios*, "the sun") recalls the depiction of Christ in 1:16 and invests the angel with glory and great majesty (cf. Luke 9:26) (Alford, Swete, Scott). The angel of 18:1 manifests divine glory too (Alford). Πόδες (*Podes*, "Feet") includes the angel's legs also, as the description στῦλοι πυρός (*styloi puros*, "pillars of fire") indicates. The word πούς (*pous*, "foot") had such a connotation in secular Greek[15] and earlier biblical Greek (cf. Ex. 24:17; Lev. 1:13; 8:21; 9:14, LXX) (Charles). The likening of the legs and feet to "pillars of fire" (ὡς στῦλοι πυρός [*hōs styloi pyros*]) brings a recollection of the columns of fire that mercifully led the Israelites under

---

12. Beckwith, *Apocalypse*, pp. 579-80; Moffatt, "Revelation," 5:411; William R. Newell, *The Book of Revelation* (Chicago: Moody, 1935), p. 140; Leon Morris, *The Revelation of St. John*, TNTC (Grand Rapids: Eerdmans, 1969), p. 136.
13. George E. Ladd, *A Commentary on the Revelation of John* (Grand Rapids: Eerdmans, 1972), p. 141.
14. Robert Govett, *The Apocalypse Expounded by Scripture* (London: Charles J. Thynne, 1920), 1:448-49; Alford, *Greek Testament*, 4:650; Scott, *Revelation*, p. 220; H. A. Ironside, *Lectures on the Book of Revelation* (New York: Loizeaux, n.d.), p. 175; Robert L. Thomas, *Revelation 1-7, An Exegetical Commentary* (Chicago: Moody, 1992), p. 343.
15. Beckwith, *Apocalypse*, p. 580; LSJ, p. 1456.

Moses in the wilderness darkness (cf. Ex. 13:21-22; 14:19, 24).[16] This association adds reinforcement to the theme of judgment, suggested by the fire, tempered by mercy already seen in the rainbow (Alford).

10:2 One more detail about the angel opens v. 2: καὶ ἔχων ἐν τῇ χειρὶ αὐτοῦ βιβλαρίδιον ἠνεῳγμένον (*kai echōn en tē cheiri autou biblaridion ēneōgmenon*, "and he had in his hand a little scroll opened"). Here the angel holds the little scroll *in* (ἐν [*en*]) his hand in contrast to 5:1 where the scroll lay *upon* (ἐπί [*epi*]) the hand. In the former case it was perhaps too large to be grasped *in* the hand. It is probably in the left hand of the angel to allow him a little later to raise his right hand (presumably empty) to utter the oath (10:5).[17]

The "little scroll" is a diminutive of βιβλάριον (*biblarion*) which is itself a diminutive of βιβλίον, βίβλος (*biblion, biblos*, "scroll"). The word apparently distinguishes this scroll from the one in 5:1 ff. (Alford). It is a rare word and in the NT occurs only in Rev. 10:2, 9, 10. Its rarity probably accounts for the wide variety of different readings in this verse and in 10:8-10 (Mounce).

Controversy reigns over the contents of the little scroll as it did regarding the scroll of chapter 5. Some want to link it to the earlier scroll as the title deed to the earth.[18] The earlier scroll is now "opened" (10:2), as this one is, with the breaking of the last seal in 8:1 (Smith). A "mighty angel" was associated with the earlier seal as the one is here too (Sweet). This explanation will not do, though, because of the rejection of that identification of the first scroll (Thomas, pp. 376-77). Besides that, the prophecy makes no direct allusion to the contents of this scroll as it did to the contents of the chapter 5 scroll (Beckwith).

A further suggestion that this little scroll contains Revelation 12-22 as the first one contains chapters 1-11 is unsatisfactory because of the relative size of the two. The *little* scroll would not contain more than the scroll that is written on front and back (Ladd). Another proposal limits the contents of the little scroll to the vision of 11:1-13 because it is "little," and thus differs from the scroll of chapter 5 (Charles, Bullinger). It notes that the necessity of John's prophesying again in 10:11 finds its fulfillment in the immediate sequel of the opening part of chapter 11 (Charles). The bitter-sweet contents of the little scroll (10:9-10) is a fitting parable of the church's suffering and triumph as portrayed in 11:1-13 (Beasley-Murray). But this definition of the little

---

16. Swete, *Apocalypse*, p. 126; Martin Kiddle, *The Revelation of St. John*, HNTC (New York: Harper, 1940), p. 169; Mounce, *Revelation*, p. 207.

17. Alford, *Greek Testament*, 4:750; M. R. Vincent, *Word Studies in the New Testament* (McLean, Va.: MacDonald, n.d.), 1:618.

18. Alford, *Greek Testament*, 4:650; Swete, *Apocalypse*, p. 126; J. A. Seiss, *The Apocalypse* (New York: Charles C. Cook, 1909), 2:227-29; Ironside, *Revelation*, p. 170; Smith, *Revelation*, p. 54; Mounce, *Revelation*, p. 214.

scroll would mean that the earlier scroll ends at 9:21 with the sixth trumpet, whereas the scene in chapters 4-5 implies that the contents of that scroll carry through to the consummation of the kingdom. This is intolerable also because it separates the seventh trumpet from the other six (Beckwith).

It is somewhat more satisfying to allow that the little scroll contains a portion of what the former scroll contained since it is "little" and the other one is not (Alford). It must carry through to the end if it includes "the mystery of God" (10:7). It must also pertain to John's recommissioning in 10:11.[19] Yet it is misleading to relate the two scrolls, one of which was sealed and the other opened (Lenski). No hint of the continuing trumpet visions occurs in the little scroll, but that series is a primary backbone of the larger scroll (Beckwith). In the parallel case of Ezekiel the prophet, he ate the scroll which turned out to be God's command (Ezek. 3:2, 11) (Lee). It was an object lesson that amounted to a recommissioning of the prophet (cf. Rev. 10:9-11 with Jer. 1:10). So is it here (Beckwith, Beasley-Murray). The bitterness of the coming trumpet in which the judgments of God will reach their climax comes through in the bitterness John experiences in eating the scroll. It is fitting just before the climax to renew John's prophetic call (Ladd). This explanation of the scroll, of course, does not exclude the "little scroll" from the contents of the first scroll, but it does emphasize the prophet's call as the content rather than the details of the succeeding visitations.

The "opened scroll" (βιβλαρίδιον ἠνεῳγμένον [*biblaridion enegg-menon*]) is an allusion to Ezek. 2:9-10. This signifies the revealed counsels of God. The contents of the scroll in 5:1 were sealed closed, only to be revealed by the action of the Lamb (Scott, Morris). The undisclosed meaning of the seven thunder-voices (10:3) also contrasts with open disclosure of this "opened scroll."

The strong angel next assumes a symbolic position: καὶ ἔθηκεν τὸν πόδα αὐτοῦ τὸν δεξιὸν ἐπὶ τῆς θαλάσσης, τὸν δὲ εὐώνυμον ἐπὶ τῆς γῆς (*kai etheken ton poda autou ton dexion epi tes thalasses, ton de euonymon epi tes ges*, "and he placed his right foot on the sea and his left on the land"). By planting his feet on sea and land, the angel displays his purpose to take possession of both (cf. Deut. 11:24). This asserts the divine right and determination to execute judgment against a world that exhibits its rebellion through idolatry and immorality (cf. 9:20-21) (Bullinger, Mounce). The angel's gigantic size and encompassing stance intimates that his message pertains to the whole world (Swete, Charles, Ladd), not just to the Mediterranean Sea and the land

---

19. Düsterdieck, *Revelation*, pp. 307-8; Alford, *Greek Testament*, 4:654.

of the Asiatic mainland, the area of which John was a resident (Beckwith). The symbolic import of the angel's position is emphatic by virtue of its repetition twice more in this chapter (10:5, 8).[20]

Various understandings of the angel's position have arisen. One says its purpose is to portray his immense size (Mounce). The size is interesting and important, but it is not the main emphasis of his stance. Another view sees the sea as representing the instability of mankind, yet its ability to sustain the angel's weight (Swete). This approach furnishes no comparable explanation of the land, however. Still another way to view his posture is to emphasize the wide spread of his feet as illustrating "many peoples and nations and tongues and kings" (10:11) to whom John was to prophesy (Lenski, Hailey). But this view rests on an aspect of posture not expressed in the text. A better interpretation takes the sea and land as offering a comprehensive picture of the whole earth, to whom John will address his message (Beckwith, Moffatt). This is the connotation of comparable expressions in the OT (cf. Ex. 20:4, 11; Ps. 69:34; cf. also Rev. 7:2) (Swete, Mounce).

10:3 In addition to planting his feet in a symbolic pose, the strong angel cried out, his cry being accompanied by seven peals of thunder: καὶ ἔκραξεν φωνῇ μεγάλῃ ὥσπερ λέων μυκᾶται. καὶ ὅτε ἔκραξεν, ἐλάλησαν αἱ ἑπτὰ βρονταὶ τὰς ἑαυτῶν φωνάς (*kai ekraxen phōnē megalē hōsper leōn mykatai. kai hote ekraxen, elalēsan hai hepta brontai tas heautōn phōnas*, "and he cried with a great voice as a lion roars. And when he cried, the seven [peals of] thunder uttered their own voices"). The content of his cry is unrecorded, unless his cry is synonymous with his oath in v. 6. The context of the cry, however, suggests that it is a cry of power and vengeance (Seiss). Φωνῇ μεγάλῃ (*Phonē megalē*, "With a great voice") notes the loud volume of the cry. Loud cries appear in the OT (cf. Isa. 40:9; Ps. 24:4; Dan 3:4) and are especially characteristic of Revelation (cf. 1:10; 5:2, 12; 6:10; 7:2, 10; 8:13; 14:7, 9, 15; 18:2) (Swete, Charles). The loudness brings special emphasis to an individual or to what he says.

Comparing the announcement to a lion's roar further accentuates the loudness of the utterance (Swete). The same comparison describes God's voice in Hos. 11:10 and Amos 3:8 (cf. Jer. 25:30; Joel 3:16; Amos 1:2). Μυκάομαι (*Mykaomai*, "I bellow, roar") is an onomatopoeic word for the bellowing of an ox (cf. Job 6:5, LXX) or the lowing of cattle. It can also portray the roar of a lion.[21] The analogy does not mean that the angel's cry was inarticulate; the intelligibility of the accompanying

---

20. The usual order in Revelation is "land," then "sea," but all three times in this chapter "sea" precedes "land" (cf. 5:13; 7:1, 2, 3; 12:12; 14:7).
21. LSJ, p. 1151.

utterance of the seven thunders argues against this. The content of his utterance probably comes in v. 6 (Swete, Beckwith). Other verbs that would have depicted a lion's roar more specifically are ὠρύεσθαι (*ōryesthai*) (cf. 1 Pet. 5:8) and ἐρεύγεσθαι (*ereugesthai*) (cf. Hos. 11:10, LXX), but *mykaomai* probably indicates the depth as well as the volume of the angel's voice in compelling greater attention and inspiring deeper awe (Swete).

The article in αἱ ἑπτὰ βρονταί (*hai hepta brontai*, "the seven [peals of] thunder" or "the seven thunders") assumes that the thunders are well-known to John's immediate readers, but that identity is not clear to present-day readers. A relationship to the thunderous voice of the Father to Christ in John 12:28-29 or to the sevenfold voice of the thunderstorm in Ps. 29:3-9 is possible.[22] The former association is more probable, since God's voice is comparable to a lion's roar in Hos. 11:10 and Joel 3:16 and thunder resembles God's voice in judgment (cf. 1 Sam. 7:10; Job 26:14; Ps. 18:13) (Scott). The thunder is different from the angel's voice, so it could not be the effect—thunder—being by metonymony put for the cause—God's voice (Charles; contra Moffatt, Bullinger). It must have been understandable, not just a noise, because John started to write down the substance of it in 10:4 (Charles). Though the text does not reveal what the thunders said, it is a safe conclusion that they are an audible symbol that God will bring added terror before the end (cf. 8:5; 11:19; 16:18) (Scott, Kiddle, Mounce).

10:4 John's effort to record what the thunders said is forbidden: καὶ ὅτε* ἐλάλησαν αἱ ἑπτὰ βρονταί, ἐμελλον γράφειν· καὶ ἤκουσα φωνὴν ἐκ τοῦ οὐρανοῦ λέγουσαν, Σφράγισον ἃ ἐλάλησαν αἱ ἑπτὰ βρονταί, καὶ μὴ αὐτὰ γράψῃς (*kai hote elalēsan hai hepta brontai, emellon graphein; kai ēkousa phōnēn ek tou ouranou legousan, Sphragison ha elalēsan hai hepta brontai, kai mē auta grapsēs*, "and when the seven thunders spoke, I was about to write; and I heard a voice from heaven saying, 'Seal the things which the seven thunders spoke, and do not write them'"). In obedience to his command in 1:19, John was about to write down what the thunders said (Alford). This apparently means that John used intervals between activity during his visions to do his writing (Lee), or at least to take notes on what he had seen and heard (Swete).

"A voice from heaven" (φωνὴν ἐκ τοῦ οὐρανοῦ [*phōnēn ek tou ouranou*]) stopped him, however. Out of reverence, John usually leaves the personal source of the heavenly voice unidentified (Moffatt). This

---

22. Swete, *Apocalypse*, p. 127; Charles, *Revelation*, 1:261; Robertson, *Word Pictures*, 6:371.

may be either the voice of God or of Christ (cf. 14:13; 18:4) who gave the original commission for him to write (1:11, 19) (Beckwith, Mounce). Σφράγισον (Sphragison, "Seal") is a technical apocalyptic term (cf. 22:10), practically equivalent to μὴ . . . γράψῃς (mē . . . grapsēs, "do not write") (Charles). It alludes to Dan. 12:4, 9 where the command to Daniel was to keep his visions secret until the end (cf. Dan. 8:26; Rev. 5:1). The difference here is the application of the term to unwritten utterances. In effect, it says, "Leave the utterances unwritten," a meaning that is clarified by the following μὴ αὐτὰ γράψῃς (mē auta grapsēs, "do not write them") (Swete, Beckwith). These utterances are the only part of the book that is sealed.[23]

The prohibition to write gives an indirect indication of John's prophetic authority, authority that he claims at the beginning and the end of the book. The reference here is to the inspiration of restraint that must accompany the inspiration of impulse. The inspiration of restraint indicates that the written contents of the Apocalypse were only part of John's total visionary revelation (cf. John 21:25). Paul's unrecorded ecstasies in 2 Cor. 12:1-4 point to the same principle in Paul's prophetic experience. This restraint does something for the prophet subjectively in preparing him for his remaining prophecies (Alford, Moffatt). The suggestion that the cancellation of the seven-thunders revelation amounts to a shortening of the Great Tribulation for the elect's sake (cf. Mark 13:20)[24] cannot be substantiated. The bowl series yet to come argues against this (Beasley-Murray).

10:5 The angel in the symbolic stance now adds to the symbolism of his posture by lifting his right hand to heaven: Καὶ ὁ ἄγγελος ὃν εἶδον ἑστῶτα ἐπὶ τῆς θαλάσσης καὶ ἐπὶ τῆς γῆς ἦρεν τὴν χεῖρα αὐτοῦ τὴν δεξιὰν εἰς τὸν οὐρανὸν (Kai ho angelos hon eidon hestōta epi tēs thalassēs kai epi tēs gēs ēren tēn cheira autou tēn dexian eis ton ouranon, "And the angel whom I saw standing on the sea and on the land lifted his right hand to heaven"). Resuming his picture of v. 2, John describes the angel as lifting his right hand, the customary gesture of one taking a solemn oath. This is a free allusion to Dan. 12:7, the only other passage in Scripture with the combination "he lifted his hand and swore."[25] In the Daniel passage it is God's eternity that is appealed to, but here added to that is His work of creating all things.[26] Also unlike

---

23. Newell, *Revelation*, p. 142.
24. G. V. Caird, *A Commentary on the Revelation of St. John the Divine*, HNTC (New York: Harper & Row, 1966), pp. 126-27; Sweet, *Revelation*, p. 178; Mounce, *Revelation*, p. 211.
25. Charles, *Revelation*, 1:262-63. Genesis 14:22 and Deut. 32:40 have somewhat similar instances of oath taking.
26. Robertson, *Word Pictures*, 6:372.

Dan. 12:7, this angel lifted only his right hand, the little scroll lying open in his left. The direction of the hand is heavenward because that is God's dwelling-place (Alford).

10:6 After lifting his hand, the strong angel committed himself to an oath in the most solemn fashion: καὶ ὤμοσεν ἐν τῷ ζῶντι εἰς τοὺς αἰῶνας τῶν αἰώνων, ὃς ἔκτισεν τὸν οὐρανὸν καὶ τὰ ἐν αὐτῷ καὶ τὴν γῆν καὶ τὰ ἐν αὐτῇ καὶ τὴν θάλασσαν καὶ τὰ ἐν αὐτῇ* (*kai ōmosen en tō zōnti eis tous aiōnas tōn aiōnōn, hos ektisen ton ouranon kai ta en autō kai tēn gēn kai ta en autē kai tēn thalassan kai ta en autē*, "and swore by the one who lives forever and ever, who created the heaven and the things which are in it and the earth and the things which are in it and the sea and the things which are in it"). Meaning "swear" or "affirm by an oath," ὤμοσεν (*ōmosen*) marks this as a moment of increased solemnity because of the nearness of the time of fulfillment. What is about to take place is of ultimate importance (Alford, Smith, Walvoord).

The expression ζῶντι εἰς τοὺς αἰῶνας τῶν αἰώνων (*zōnti eis tous aiōnas tōn aiōnōn*, "the one who lives forever and ever") is common in Revelation to specify the eternal existence of God (cf. 1:18; 4:9, 10; 15:7).[27] The OT frequently calls Him "the living God"[28] as does the NT.[29] His eternity of being strengthens and, as it were, makes more binding the climactic oath of this angel.

As if this were not enough, the angel adds God's work as Creator of all things to reinforce the import of the oath even more. Ἔκτισεν (*Ektisen*) clearly refers to God's creative activity in Gen. 1:1 ff., as is done frequently in the OT (e.g., Ex. 20:11; Pss. 33:6; 102:25; 146:6; Isa. 37:16; 42:5; 45:18; Jer. 32:17; 51:15) (Swete). In the NT, references to God's creative activity are relatively rare outside Revelation (cf. Acts 14:15; 17:24; Heb. 11:3; Rev. 4:11; 14:7) (Charles). The eternal One, the Creator, most certainly will fulfill His purpose for His creation (Beckwith). He has the prerogative of destroying it and replacing it with a new creation, if He so chooses (Alford, Kiddle). The all-encompassing scope of God's creative acts is evident in the expression τὸν οὐρανὸν καὶ τὰ ἐν αὐτῷ καὶ τὴν γῆν καὶ τὰ ἐν αὐτῇ καὶ τὴν θάλασσαν καὶ τὰ ἐν αὐτῇ (*ton ouranon kai ta en autō kai tēn gēn kai ta en autē kai tēn thalassan kai ta en autē*, "the heaven and the things which are in it and the earth and the things which are in it and the sea and the things which are in it").

---

27. Ibid.
28. Cf. Deut. 5:26; Josh. 3:10; 1 Sam. 17:26, 36; 2 Kings 19:4, 16; Pss. 42:2; 84:2; Isa. 37:4, 17; 57:15; Jer. 10:10; 23:36; Dan. 6:20, 26; Hos. 1:10.
29. Cf. Matt. 16:16; 26:63; Acts 14:15; Rom. 9:26; 2 Cor. 3:3; 6:16; 1 Thess. 1:9; 1 Tim. 3:15; 4:10; Heb. 9:14; 10:31; 12:22.

The electrifying buildup[30] sets the stage for the simple, but extremely profound substance of the oath: ὅτι χρόνος οὐκέτι ἔσται (*hoti chronos ouketi estai*, "that there will no longer be delay"). The meaning of χρόνος (*chronos*) is commonly "time," but there is only a minimal preference for that meaning here (Lenski). For the statement to speak of the cessation of time is meaningless here. It is pointless for an angel, after such an elaborate preparation, to make a declaration about the timeless nature of eternity (Mounce). Besides, a future kingdom of one thousand years remains (11:15-19; 20:1-10) before eternity replaces time (Smith). Apocryphal works speak of the absolute cessation of time (e.g., *2 Enoch* 33:2; 65:6-7) (Charles), but the contrast between time and eternity is a philosophical one that has no support in biblical theology.[31]

The only meaning for *chronos* that makes any sense in this context is the sense of "delay." The adversative conjunction ἀλλ' (*all'*, "but") at the beginning of v. 7 is intelligible only if the noun is assigned this meaning (Smith). A strong consensus supports this meaning,[32] but an effort to refer it to the delay before the reign of Antichrist that begins with the third woe (Charles) is futile. This misses the important chronological point that no time advances without the sounding of another trumpet. The events of 10:1–11:14 are not happenings between the sixth and seventh trumpets, so no chronological progression transpires between this point and 11:15 (Morris, Mounce).

The "delay" is best seen as that before fulfillment of the mystery of God (v. 7). The announcement clearly corresponds to the question of the martyrs in 6:10: "How long?" (Moffatt). The verbal similarity indicates that this as a comparison of ἔτι χρόνον (*eti chronon*, "time [or delay] yet") in 6:11 with χρόνος οὐκέτι (*chronos ouketi*, "delay no longer") in this verse. It tells that the answer to the prayers of the saints found in the trumpet series (cf. 8:3-5) is now about to receive its final fulfillment (Swete, Bullinger). The rest of God's plans are now ready to come to fruition. This is essentially the same question answered by the angel in the strikingly similar passage of Dan. 12:7. This explanation matches the continuation of the announcement in v. 7, which serves to clarify what the angel means (Alford, Beckwith).

10:7 That continuation is a strong contrast to the nonexistent de-

---

30. Leonard L. Thompson, *The Book of Revelation, Apocalypse and Empire* (Oxford: Oxford Univ., 1990), p. 67.
31. Oscar Cullmann, *Christ and Time* (Philadelphia: Westminster, 1962), p. 49.
32. Alford, *Greek Testament*, 4:652; Swete, *Apocalypse*, pp. 126-27; Vincent, *Word Studies*, 1:617; Charles, *Revelation*, 1:263-64; Beckwith, *Apocalypse*, p. 582; Bullinger, *Apocalypse*, p. 339; Robertson, *Word Pictures*, 6:372; Hailey, *Revelation*, p. 244.

lay: ἀλλ᾽ ἐν ταῖς ἡμέραις τῆς φωνῆς τοῦ ἑβδόμου ἀγγέλου, ὅταν μέλλῃ σαλπίζειν, καὶ ἐτελέσθη τὸ μυστήριον τοῦ θεοῦ, ὡς εὐηγγέλισεν τοὺς ἑαυτοῦ δούλους* τοὺς προφήτας (*all' en tais hēmerais tēs phōnēs tou hebdomou angelou, hotan mellē salpizein, kai etelesthē to mystērion tou theou, hōs euēngelisen tous heautou doulous tou prophētas,* "but in the days of the sound of the seventh angel, when he will sound, then the mystery of God will be completed, as he preached the good news to His own slaves the prophets"). This clause as a whole corrects the possible false impression that the announcement of the end of delay means an immediate end (Swete). It does not and the strong adversative ἀλλ᾽ (*all'*, "but") makes that emphatic point (Alford, Lee). In contrast to the nonexistent delay, the culmination of the hidden purpose of God has arrived in conjunction with the last of the trumpet judgments (Ladd).

Earlier trumpets have covered a period of time, for example, the fifth which extended for five months (cf. 9:5). The seventh is no different as the words ἐν ταῖς ἡμέραις τῆς φωνῆς τοῦ ἑβδόμου ἀγγέλου (*en tais hēmerais tēs phōnēs tou hebdomou angelou* "in the days of the sound of the seventh angel") indicate. These words mix the fulfillment of the prophecy with the prophecy itself (Alford). Τῆς φωνῆς (*Tēs phōnēs*, "of the sound") must be sort of a subjective genitive, yielding the sense "in the days which the sounding of the seventh trumpet covers" (Beckwith). Ἡμέραι (*Hēmerai*, "days") often denotes a period of time (e.g., Matt. 24:37, 38) as this context requires it to. The period of the seventh trumpet includes the seven bowls (16:1 ff.), which culminate in the destruction of Babylon and consummation of all things (Ladd).

These "days" receive a further definition in the temporal clause ὅταν μέλλῃ σαλπίζειν (*hotan mellē salpizein*, "when he will sound"). The frequent meaning of μέλλω (*mellō*) as "I am about to" in Revelation could argue for the same meaning here (cf. 3:2, 10; 8:13; 10:4; 12:4, 5; 17:8; and possibly 2:10 [twice]). Yet the sense of this statement requires the verb to function as a periphrasis for the future tense: "he *will* sound" (cf. 3:16).[33] The former meaning would express imminence, but that is out of place here. It is contrary to the subsequent facts of the book (Beckwith). The consummation does not come *before* the blowing of the seventh trumpet, but is *simultaneous* as a part of that sounding. The temporal clause is epexegetic of "in the days of the sound of the seventh angel," which relationship dictates that it cannot come before the seventh trumpet.

That sounding marks the completion or fulfillment of the mystery of God. With the aorist tense ἐτελέσθη (*etelesthē*, "will be completed")

---

33. Charles, *Revelation*, 1:264; BDF, par. 356; Mounce, *Revelation*, p. 212; Johnson, "Revelation," 12:497-98.

the angel looks "back" in prophetic anticipation of the days spoken of, from the perspective of when they will be a thing of the past (Alford). The days, though future, are so distinctly present in his mind that he uses an aorist indicative rather than a future indicative (cf. 15:1; 17:17) (Swete). This is usually called a proleptic aorist (Charles, Mounce). Perhaps "will have been fulfilled" is the closest an English paraphrase can come to it.

"The mystery of God" (τὸ μυστήριον τοῦ θεοῦ [*to mystērion tou theou*]) is what reaches its fulfillment in those days. *Mystērion* in the NT denotes a secret revealed by God (e.g., Eph. 3:1-10). In Rom. 16:25-26 it refers to God's redemptive plan, at first hidden in the mind of God, but now revealed and made public to all who listen to the prophetic word (Ladd). In other uses "mystery" refers to the church, the revelation of Antichrist, the kingdom, and that all shall not die (cf. Matt. 13:10-35; Rom. 11:25; 1 Cor. 15:51; Eph. 1:9; 3:1-10; 6:19; Col. 1:26-27; 2:2; 4:3; 2 Thess. 2:6-8). In the present passage it speaks of the great purpose of God in the evolution of human history (Swete, Beckwith). The view of the primitive world that secret purposes were communicated through symbols accounts for the use of *mystērion* with a slightly different meaning of "symbolic representation" in Rev. 1:20 and 17:7 (Moffatt).

The expression *to mystērion tou theou* ("the mystery of God") appears in 1 Cor. 2:1 and Col. 2:2 also. Its precise connotation in this setting needs definition. One opinion limits it to the secret of coming judgment because the sounding of the seventh trumpet leads to the outpouring of the seven bowls of God's wrath (Bullinger). The tie-in between the mystery of God and the "little scroll" that must have something to do with the remainder of the Apocalypse is a valid observation in support of this view, but this is too narrow. The remainder of the book also includes the establishment of God's kingdom on earth and eventually the new Jerusalem. Referring "the mystery of God" to the casting of Satan from heaven (cf. 12:8-9) (Charles) is also too restricted for the same reason. Also, the thanksgiving after the blowing of the seventh trumpet anticipates something greater than this (cf. 11:17-18).

It is preferable to refer the expression to God's purpose in bringing His kingdom to its fruition. This is a purpose that has been hidden from the world, at least insofar as its detailed outworking is concerned. It will finally attain its full realization with the complete salvation of the saints in the perfected kingdom (Beckwith, Moffatt). The fact that He preached it to "his slaves the prophets" shows that the unfolding of the mystery was at least in part in the OT descriptions of the establishment of the kingdom (Walvoord). This meaning coincides with the thanksgiving after the blowing of the seventh trumpet (cf.

11:15 ff.) (Alford) and with the mention of the kingdom in the heavenly song accompanying the seventh trumpet (cf. 11:15) (Mounce). The mystery of God consists of the heretofore unrevealed details unfolded in the chapters from here to the end, chapters that tell of the institution of God's kingdom on earth and eventually in the new heavens and new earth.

This was *good* news to the prophets (εὐηγγέλισεν [*euēngelisen*, "preached the good news"]) (cf. Gal. 3:8) (Alford). Amos 3:7 tells of God's revelation of His "secret counsel" to the prophets. The prophets came to the Israelites who refused the good news about the kingdom time and again (e.g., Jer. 7:25; 25:4). Ultimately the good news is not about the martyrdom of the saints or the judgment of God's enemies. It covers pronouncements concerning the kingdom of the world becoming the kingdom of our Lord and of His Christ (11:15) (Smith). Granted both God's people and His enemies will encounter hardships on the way, but the news is ultimately good.

The fact that ἑαυτοῦ (*heautou*, "his own") is a reflexive pronoun rather than the more usual αὐτοῦ (*autou*, "his") and that the position of the pronoun is emphatic by appearing before rather than after its noun shows God's special attachment to His prophets (Charles). The question is whether these are OT prophets, NT prophets, or both. The inclusion of both groups under one designation (Swete) is unlikely because of the differences that distinguish OT and NT prophecy from each other. The arguments for identifying them as NT prophets are worthy of mention. A few verses later, in 10:11, the mention of prophecy is certainly NT prophecy. The term "mystery" has a special affinity to NT prophecy too (cf. 1 Cor. 13:2; Eph. 3:4-5). The nearness of the consummation had for years been a source of confidence and joy for NT prophets (Moffatt). In addition, δοῦλος (*doulos*, "slave") is a characteristic title for them (cf. 1:1; 11:18).[34] It would also appear that the majority of references to prophecy in this book speak of the NT gift (Beckwith). Yet the relative silence of NT prophecy in regard to the fulfillment of Israel's hope and kingdom is notable. The occurrences of προφήτης (*prophētēs*, "prophet") in the Gospels, Acts, and the Epistles are predominantly reference to OT prophets (Hailey). It was to OT prophets that the good news regarding events of the last days came. So the case for NT prophets is not so clear-cut after all.

A number of considerations make it hard to exclude a reference to OT prophets. It is difficult to ignore the use of this expression "His slaves the prophets" to refer to OT prophets (cf. Jer. 7:25; 25:4; Amos 3:7) and in the NT the dominant use of the noun "prophet" to refer to

---

34. David Hill, *New Testament Prophecy* (Atlanta: Knox, 1979), p. 79.

OT prophets. Couple with these John's heavy dependence on the OT (especially the books of Ezekiel, Daniel, and Zechariah) in Revelation, and the case for understanding OT prophets is quite persuasive.

The recommissioning of John (10:8-11). Following the angel's dramatic announcement, attention now shifts to the prophet John.

10:8 A second command comes to him via the voice from heaven: Καὶ ἡ φωνὴ ἣν ἤκουσα ἐκ τοῦ οὐρανοῦ, πάλιν λαλοῦσαν μετ᾽ ἐμοῦ καὶ λέγουσαν, Ὕπαγε λάβε τὸ βιβλίον[35] τὸ ἠνεῳγμένον ἐν τῇ χειρὶ τοῦ ἀγγέλου τοῦ ἑστῶτος ἐπὶ τῆς θαλάσσης καὶ ἐπὶ τῆς γῆς (*Kai hē phōnē hēn ēkousa ek tou ouranou, palin lalousan met' emou kai legousan, Hypage labe to biblion to ēneǭgmenon en tǭ cheiri tou angelou tou hestōtos epi tēs thalassēs kai epi tēs gēs*, "And the voice which I heard from heaven again spoke with me and said, 'Go, take the scroll which is opened in the hand of the angel who stands on the sea and on the land'"). John hears the same voice as in v. 4 speaking to him. This is the voice of God or Christ, an authoritative voice. Otherwise, John might have been reluctant to approach the strong angel as commanded (Beckwith, Scott, Mounce, Walvoord).

Though not allowed to write the utterance of the seven thunders, John receives instructions to go and take the unsealed and opened little scroll in the angel's hand. The symbolic stance of the angel reminds him for the third time in this chapter (cf. vv. 2, 5) of the angel's complete authority over the whole earthly situation (Walvoord).

10:9 In compliance, John approaches the angel and requests the little scroll: καὶ ἀπῆλθα πρὸς τὸν ἄγγελον λέγων αὐτῷ δοῦναί μοι τὸ βιβλαρίδιον (*kai apēltha pros ton angelon legōn autǭ dounai moi to biblaridion*, "and I went away to the angel, requesting him to give me the little scroll"). Ἀπῆλθα (*Apēltha*, "I went away") indicates that John left his former place as a spectator to assume a role in the drama of which he had been simply an observer until now. He requested[36] the angel to give him the little scroll.

The angel responds by not only giving him the scroll, but also by instructing him to eat it: καὶ λέγει μοι, Λάβε καὶ κατάφαγε αὐτό, καὶ πικρανεῖ σου τὴν κοιλίαν, ἀλλ᾽ ἐν τῷ στόματί σου ἔσται γλυκὺ ὡς μέλι (*kai legei moi, Labe kai kataphage auto, kai pikranei sou tēn koilian, all' en tǭ stomati sou estai glyky hōs meli*, "and he says to me, 'Take and

---

35. Βιβλίον replaces βιβλαρίδιον in naming the little scroll that the latter word names elsewhere in the chapter (10:2, 9, 10). The two are relatively interchangeable (Mounce, *Revelation*, p. 214).
36. Λέγω is the common word for "say," but in this context it takes on the meaning of "bid" or "request" as it does in 13:14 and Acts 21:21 (Robertson, *Word Pictures*, 6:374).

eat it, and it will make your stomach bitter, but in your mouth it will be sweet as honey'"). He tells John to take and devour it. Κατάφαγε (*Kataphage*, "Eat") is a Hebrew idiom for receiving knowledge, similar to the English use of "digest" for considering and meditating on what has been learned (Bullinger). The κατά (*kata*) prefix on the verb has a perfective force to emphasize the completeness of the eating. John's devouring of the scroll is literal to illustrate his thorough assimilation of the scroll's contents (Kiddle). The same type of enactment occurs in Ezek. 3:1-3 and Jer. 15:16.[37]

In instructing John to eat the little scroll, the angel anticipates its effect on him: bitterness in the stomach and sweetness in the mouth. Πικρός (*Pikros*, "Bitter"), a cognate of πικρανεῖ (*pikranei*, "it will make bitter"), refers to anything that is sharp to the senses of sound, taste, or feeling. In referring to sharpness to the taste, it is the antonym of γλυκύς (*glykys*, "sweet"). In the parallel situations of Ezekiel and Jeremiah, the record says nothing of this kind of bitterness,[38] but it is implicit in the rebelliousness of their listeners and the consequent judgment against them (cf. Jer. 15:17; Ezek. 3:7-9, 14).[39] The angel mentions the bitterness first, probably because it is the unexpected part of the prophetic commission. Before the joys of the consummation lay a bitter prelude of national and political predictions that John had to deliver (Moffatt). His κοιλία (*koilia*, "stomach"), the digestive apparatus, is where John will feel the bitter sensation. In other words, when he appropriates his prophecy inwardly, he will sense the bitterness (Walvoord).

The sweetness, likened to honey, perhaps represents the joys of the consummation that are part of the prophecy, but more probably, since it is limited to the mouth, it speaks of John's present satisfaction in being informed of God's will for the future (cf. Ps. 119:103). These same words, when digested, bring sadness over the news of persecutions, apostasies, and judgments (Alford). The bitterness and sweetness do not pertain to different parts of the little scroll, but to sensations of the prophet at different stages in regarding the totality of it.[40]

10:10 John complies with what the angel has told him to do: καὶ ἔλαβον τὸ βιβλαρίδιον* ἐκ τῆς χειρὸς τοῦ ἀγγέλου καὶ κατέφαγον αὐτό, καὶ ἦν ἐν τῷ στόματί μου ὡς μέλι γλυκύ· καὶ ὅτε ἔφαγον αὐτό, ἐπικράνθη ἡ κοιλία μου (*kai elabon to biblaridion ek tēs cheiros tou angelou kai katephagon auto, kai ēn en tō stomati mou hōs meli glyky; kai hote ephagon auto, epikranthē hē koilia mou*, "and I took the little scroll

---

37. Robertson, *Word Pictures*, 6:374.
38. Ibid.
39. Düsterdieck, *Revelation*, p. 305; Ladd, *Revelation*, p. 147.
40. Düsterdieck, *Revelation*, p. 305.

from the hand of the angel and ate it, and it was in my mouth as sweet as honey; and when I ate it, my stomach was made bitter"). He took the little scroll and ate it. Κατέφαγον (*Katephagon*, "Ate") probably refers to a literal eating of the scroll. Because of the Hebrew idiom, some think this is merely a mental digesting of the contents of the scroll, but the context gives the impression that this is a literal eating, as the natural sequence of mouth to stomach suggests.[41] The results are the same as predicted by the angel, except in reverse order—sweetness in the mouth and bitterness in the stomach. This reversal brings the bitterness into closer proximity to the prophet's explicit recommissioning in v. 11. The remainder of his prophetic career will entail the prediction of grievous woes (Beckwith).

10:11 After the lesson from the little scroll, John receives direct guidelines regarding his future ministry: καὶ λέγουσίν μοι, Δεῖ σε πάλιν προφητεῦσαι ἐπὶ λαοῖς καὶ ἔθνεσιν καὶ γλώσσαις καὶ βασιλεῦσιν πολλοῖς (*kai legousin moi, Dei se palin prophēteusai epi laois kai ethnesin kai glōssais kai basileusin pollois*, "and it was said to me, 'It is necessary for you to prophesy again concerning many peoples and nations and tongues and kings'"). The subject of λέγουσίν (*legousin*, "they say"), the source of the commission, is possibly the heavenly voice of vv. 4 and 8 and the angel of 10:9, but more probably it is the third person plural of indefinite reference as in 12:6; 13:16; 16:15.[42] This device expresses reverentially the divine impulse experienced by the prophet (Moffatt). The present tense of *legousin* represents in a vivid and dramatic way how the words came to John.

The particle δεῖ (*dei*, "it is necessary") embodies the thrust of compulsion. It is a logical necessity that John comply. He is bound to prophesy to meet an existing need, and so receives a command supported by divine decree to prophecy (Alford, Swete, Mounce). It is not just a subjective necessity; it is objective necessity that depends on the will of God.[43] Jeremiah and Ezekiel were under a similar compulsion (cf. Jer. 1:10; Ezek. 4:7) (Swete).

The adverb πάλιν (*palin*, "again") shows that this is not a new commission, but the renewal of an old one (cf. 1:19). It links what has preceded with what is yet to come (cf. 11:15).[44] The prophecies of the remainder of the book are in contrast to those that have preceded in

---

41. Ibid., p. 304; Bullinger, *Apocalypse*, p. 342; Robertson, *Word Pictures*, 6:374.
42. Düsterdieck, *Revelation*, p. 305; Alford, *Greek Testament*, 4:654; Lee, "Revelation," 4:638; Beckwith, *Apocalypse*, p. 584; Robertson, *Word Pictures*, 6:374; J. Massyngberde Ford, *Revelation*, vol. 38 of AB (Garden City, N.Y.: Doubleday, 1975), p. 160.
43. Düsterdieck, *Revelation*, p. 305.
44. Robertson, *Word Pictures*, 6:374.

that they are more burdensome than anything prophesied up to now (Beckwith, Beasley-Murray). This new command to prophesy (προ-φητεῦσαι [*prophēteusai*]) puts John side-by-side with Ezekiel, Daniel, and Zechariah. It points to a change in the apocalyptic announcements introduced by 11:1-14 and beginning at 12:1 (Lee).

The subject of his future prophecies is fourfold, ἐπὶ λαοῖς καὶ ἔθ-νεσιν καὶ γλώσσαις καὶ βασιλεῦσιν πολλοῖς (*epi laois kai ethnesin kai glōssais kai basileusin pollois*, "Concerning many peoples and nations and tongues and kings"). Ἐπί (*Epi*, "Concerning") could mean "before," but this would have required objects in the genitive rather than the dative case (Lee). It could carry the meaning "against" because of the air of hostility that prevails among the opponents of the Lamb.[45] The objects of the preposition would more likely have been in the accusative case for this meaning, however.[46] It is better to assign the meaning "in regard to" or "concerning" when the preposition occurs with the dative case (cf. John 12:16; Rev. 22:16) (Beckwith). This is the meaning in the LXX in rendering the Hebrew idiom "to prophesy in regard to" (Ladd). Some of John's remaining prophecies are quite favorable toward the redeemed, so it would be inaccurate to say he must yet prophecy *against* the groups named.

Mention of three of the four groups comes earlier in 5:9—λαοῖς καὶ ἔθνεσιν καὶ γλώσσαις (*laois kai ethnesin kai glōssais*, "peoples and nations and tongues"). The inclusion of βασιλεῦσιν (*basileusin*, "kings") in this list serves notice that God's word through His prophets takes precedence over the highest rank in human authority (Morris, Mounce). "Kings" are actually included in the other three terms, but their specific mention focuses special attention on rulers as distinguished from their peoples. This perhaps anticipates such places as 16:14; 17:10, 12 (Beckwith, Charles, Mounce). Πολλοῖς (*Pollois*, "Many") applies to all four terms in the list and emphasizes the largeness of the scope of the remaining prophecies. Their applicability would go far beyond John's immediate time and geographical circumstances (Swete).

Additional Notes

10:1 The text retains the accusative case with the perfect passive of περιβάλλω to express that with which individuals are clothed as it does in 7:9, 13.[47]

With ἡ ἶρις, the writer drops the accusative case as the object of εἶδον and replaces it with the nominative in his description of the

---

45. Bullinger, *Apocalypse*, p. 342; M. Robert Mulholland, *Revelation, Holy Living in an Unholy World* (Grand Rapids: Zondervan, 1990), p. 202.
46. Robertson, *Word Pictures*, 6:375.
47. Ibid., 6:370.

scene. The article is generic as it is with "the earth," "the sun," and other such expressions.[48]

10:2 The use of the participle ἔχων in place of the imperfect indicative εἶχεν is rather common in this book (cf. 4:7, 8; 12:2; 19:12; 21:12, 14). It is a Semitic idiom.[49]

The original meaning of εὐώνυμον was "of good name, omen, well-named," but to avoid the ill omen usually attached to the left, it came to be used euphemistically for the left hand.[50]

10:3 Ὥσπερ occurs only here in Revelation, but John uses it twice in his gospel (John 5:21, 26). It has the same sense as ὡς, which occurs a number of times in the book.[51]

The reflexive pronoun ἑαυτῶν shows intensive possession: "their own" voices. The voices were and remained "their own," not shared with anyone else and therefore perpetuated (Alford).

10:4 Among a number of textual variants in this verse, the principal one is a substitution of ὅσα for ὅτε. The weight of external evidence heavily favors ὅτε, however, leading to the conclusion that ὅσα was a scribal modification by way of an interpretive rewriting of the text.[52]

The combination of the imperfect ἔμελλον with the present infinitive γράφειν determines this to be an inchoative use of the present infinitive: "I was on the point of beginning to write."[53] Ἔμελλον is one of two ways to write the imperfect of μέλλω (cf. John 4:47; 12:33; 18:32), the other being ἔμελλον (cf. John 6:6; Rev. 3:2) (Swete).

Γράψῃς is an ingressive aorist: "do not begin to write them."[54] The position of αὐτὰ is emphatic: "*them* do not write" (Swete). The content of the things not written contrasts with the things that John was to write (1:19) (Morris).

10:5 The combination ἵστημι ἐπί followed by the genitive as here and in 10:8 means "I stand on." Followed by the accusative it means "I stand at" (Rev. 3:20; 7:1) or "I stand on" (Rev. 8:3; 11:11; 12:18; 14:1; 15:2) (Charles).

10:6 The use of ἐν after ὀμνύω rather than the more usual accusative (cf. James 5:12) corresponds more to Hebrew usage (cf. Matt. 5:34, 36).[55]

---

48. Beckwith, *Apocalypse*, p. 580; Robertson, *Word Pictures*, 6:370.
49. Charles, *Revelation*, 1:256-57; Robertson, *Word Pictures*, 6:370.
50. LSJ, p. 740; G. A. Abbott-Smith, *A Manual Greek Lexicon of the New Testament* (Edinburgh: T. & T. Clark, 1950), p. 191.
51. Robertson, *Word Pictures*, 6:371.
52. Bruce M. Metzger, *A Textual Commentary on the Greek New Testament* (New York: United Bible Societies, 1971), pp. 744-45.
53. Robertson, *Word Pictures*, 6:371-72.
54. Ibid., 6:372.
55. Ibid.

Some authorities omit καὶ τὴν θάλασσαν καὶ τὰ ἐν αὐτῇ, but it was probably accidental, being attributable to homoeoarcton and homoeoteleuton. External evidence favors inclusion of the words as original. They are necessary to complete the angel's formal discourse.[56]

10:7 The καὶ in v. 7 carries the connotation of "then" as is often the case in the apodosis of this type of sentence (cf. first occurrence in 14:10).[57]

Εὐηγγέλισεν is one of the rare uses of εὐαγγελίζω in the active voice in the NT. Another is in 14:6. The middle voice of the verb has an accusative object in Gal. 1:9 and 1 Pet. 1:12.[58]

A few weaker MSS read the dative rather than the accusative case δούλους following εὐηγγέλισεν. Other sources insert a καὶ after the δούλους, but neither is this well supported. Some copyist(s) added the καὶ because of an unfamiliarity with the OT phrase "His servants the prophets" (cf. Jer. 7:25; 25:4; Amos 3:7; cf. also Rev. 11:18). Also, the strongly supported ἑαυτοῦ is stronger than the weakly supported αὐτοῦ that would have been more normal. Ἑαυτοῦ is also the harder reading.[59]

10:8 Ὕπαγε is an exclamation like ἴδε and is common on the NT (e.g., Matt. 5:24; 8:4; 19:21; John 4:16; 9:7). It is probably a Hebraism (e.g., Gen. 27:13; Hos. 1:2).[60]

The participles λαλοῦσαν . . . λέγουσαν are accusative case, agreeing with ἦν, rather than nominative in agreement with φωνὴ, as some MSS have it. Usual style would have expected two imperfects ἐλάλει καὶ ἔλεγεν rather than two participles, but here the participles function as finite verbs. The same idiom occurs in 4:1.[61]

10:9 Λέγει is a dramatic, vivid present tense.[62] In the Gospels, this use of the tense would be called a historical present.

10:10 The external evidence supporting the two readings βιβλίον and βιβλαρίδιον is more evenly divided here than in vv. 2, 9. A decision between the two is further complicated by the use of βιβλίον in v. 8. The external evidence gives a slight edge to βιβλαρίδιον, however, if the impossible reading βιβλίδιον in p[47] is understood to support βιβλαρίδιον.[63]

---

56. Metzger, *Textual Commentary*, p. 745.
57. Charles, *Revelation*, 1:265; Robertson, *Word Pictures*, 6:373.
58. Robertson, *Word Pictures*, 6:373.
59. Metzger, *Textual Commentary*, p. 745.
60. Charles, *Revelation*, 1:267; Robertson, *Word Pictures*, 6:373.
61. Moffatt, "Revelation," 5:413; Robertson, *Word Pictures*, 6:373.
62. Robertson, *Word Pictures*, 6:374.
63. Metzger, *Textual Commentary*, pp. 745-46.

9. THE MEASUREMENT OF THE TEMPLE AND WORSHIPERS (11:1-14)

Translation

¹And a reed like a rod was given to me, saying, "Rise and measure the temple of God and the altar and those who worship in it. ²And cast out the court which is outside the temple and do not measure it, because it has been given to the Gentiles, and they will trample on the holy city forty-two months. ³And I will give [authority] to My two witnesses, and they will prophesy a thousand two hundred and sixty days clothed in sackcloth. ⁴These are the two olive branches and the two lampstands which are standing before the Lord of the earth. ⁵And if anyone desires to hurt them, fire goes forth from their mouths and devours their enemies; and if anyone desires to hurt them, it is necessary thus for him to be killed. ⁶These have the authority to shut heaven, lest it give forth rain during the days of their prophesy, and they have authority over the waters to turn them into blood and to smite the earth with every plague as often as they desire. ⁷And when they finish their witness, the beast who ascends from the abyss will make war with them and will conquer them and kill them. ⁸And their corpses [will be] in the street of the great city, which is spiritually called Sodom and Egypt, where also their Lord was crucified. ⁹And [those] from peoples and tribes and tongues and nations see their corpses three and a half days, and they do not permit their corpses to be placed into a tomb. ¹⁰And those who dwell upon the earth rejoice over them and make merry, and they send gifts to one another, because these two prophets tormented those who dwell upon the earth. ¹¹And after the three and a half days the breath of life from God entered them, and they stood on their feet, and a great fear fell on those beholding them. ¹²And they heard a great voice from heaven saying to them, 'Come up here'; and they went up into heaven in the cloud, and their enemies beheld them. ¹³And a great earthquake occurred in that hour, and the tenth [part] of the city fell, and seven thousand persons were killed in the earthquake, and the rest became afraid and gave glory to the God of heaven."

¹⁴The second woe has gone away; behold, the third woe comes soon.

Exegesis and Exposition

11:1 A simple καὶ (*kai*, "and") joins a description of the temple and its worshipers (11:1-13) with John's recommissioning (10:8-11): Καὶ ἐδόθη μοι κάλαμος ὅμοιος ῥάβδῳ, λέγων, Ἔγειρε καὶ μέτρησον τὸν ναὸν τοῦ θεοῦ καὶ τὸ θυσιαστήριον καὶ τοὺς προσκυνοῦντας ἐν αὐτῷ (*Kai edothē moi kalamos homoios hrabdǭ, legōn, Egeire kai metrēson ton naon tou theou kai to thysiastērion kai tous proskynountas en autǭ*, "And a reed like a rod was given to me, saying, 'Rise and measure the temple of God and the altar and those who worship in it'"). Seemingly, his first task under his renewed prophetic call is to provide information related to the temple and the city where it stands.

John receives a κάλαμος (*kalamos*, "reed"), a plant with a hollow stalk that was often used for measuring because of its light weight.[64] The same plant was used as a walking staff (cf. Ezek. 29:6; Mark 6:8) and a writer's reed (cf. 3 John 13). Ezekiel apparently used a reed nine feet in length for measuring (cf. Ezek. 42:16-19). The plant grew in the Jordan Valley sometimes to the height of 15 to 20 feet (Swete, Smith). The reed resembled a ῥάβδῳ (*hrabdǭ*, "rod"), an implement used for walking or leaning.[65]

The text does not specify from whom John received the reed, but it was probably from the same one who spoke the words introduced by λέγων (*legōn*, "saying").[66]

Some late MSS try to solve this dilemma by inserting the words καὶ εἱστήκει ὁ ἄγγελος (*kai heistēkei ho angelos*, "and the angel stood") just before the participle *legōn*, but the reading shows no sign of being original (Walvoord). Grammatically, *legōn* could modify *kalamos*, but it is difficult to have a reed speaking.[67] The participle must agree according to sense with the unexpressed agent of ἐδόθη (*edothē*, "was given"), i.e., whoever it was who gave John the reed. God is one possible agent of the giving and speaking in 11:1. His last direct instructions to John were in 10:8, and He is often the unexpressed agent of *edothē* in this book.[68] Yet continuity with the end of chapter 10 would point elsewhere. The strong angel who last dealt with John in 10:9-11 is the most probable agent of the giving and speaking. No one has

---

64. Albert Barnes, *The Book of Revelation* (New York: Harper, 1851), p. 267; Robertson, *Word Pictures*, 6:376; Walvoord, *Revelation*, p. 176; Ford, *Revelation*, p. 168.
65. Barnes, *Revelation*, p. 267; Swete, *Apocalypse*, p. 129; Beckwith, *Apocalypse*, p. 596.
66. Düsterdieck, *Revelation*, p. 311.
67. Attempts to equate κάλαμος to the Word of God by noting its relationship to the source of the word for the "canon" of Scripture or to Christ's rod of iron which is His word (cf. Rev. 2:27; 12:5; 19:15) are unconvincing. In the LXX, a passive verb with an unexpressed agent and followed by a nominative participle of λέγω occurs several times, each time points to a personal agent (cf. Gen. 22:20; 38:24; 48:2) (Robertson, *Word Pictures*, 6:376).
68. J. Ramsey Michaels, "Revelation 1:19 and the Narrative Voices of the Apocalypse," *NTS* 37, no. 4 (October 1991): 610.

entered or left the scene since then (Bullinger). Only the angel was present to give John the reed, so he must also be the one giving him the added instructions in 11:1-2.

The angel's word to John is for him to rise and measure the temple of God, the altar, and the worshipers in the temple. Once again, John receives an invitation to become a participant in the action (cf. 1:12; 5:4; 7:14; 10:9-11; 19:10; 22:8) (Smith, Walvoord). He is to perform a symbolic act as some of the prophets of the past. For example, Isaiah walked naked and barefoot as a sign of Egypt's impending captivity to Assyria (Isa. 20:2-5). Ezekiel dug through the wall and carried his luggage out in the sight of Israel as a sign of the coming exile (Ezek. 12:1-7) (Mounce). Measuring in Zechariah 2 and Ezekiel 40 was a symbol for future judgments and the restoration of Israel. Sometimes it was a picture of future destruction (2 Sam. 8:2; 2 Kings 21:13; Isa. 28:17; Lam. 2:8; Amos 7:7-9) (Johnson).

It is pretty obvious that obtaining physical dimensions was not the purpose of John's assignment, so a goodly number have proposed that the measuring is a symbol for preservation from danger and destruction (e.g., Bullinger, Beckwith, Moffatt, Ladd, Ford, Johnson). Similar purposes of measuring in Ezek. 40:2–43:12 and Zech. 2:1-8 support this possibility (cf. Jer. 31:39; Zech. 1:16) (Moffatt, Ladd, Ford, Johnson). Yet this view raises the pertinent question, from whom are the temple and its worshipers to be protected? The very next verse tells of the trampling of the rest of the city by the Gentiles. If the temple and the worshipers stand for the church and the holy city stands for the church, as some say, this can hardly be an assurance of protection. Because of difficulties encountered in identifying the temple, the altar, the worshipers, and the holy city later in v. 1, the preservation view is hard to support. Besides this, John himself does the measuring. He is hardly capable as a provider of protection.

No physical dimensions are forthcoming from John's activity (cf. 21:16-17), so μέτρησον (*metrēson*, "measure") must purpose to glean information of another type. A consideration of the immediate context fixes the measurement as the immediate sequel to his recommissioning in 10:11 and shows its results to be disclosed in the immediately subsequent verses (11:3-14) (Alford). This approximates the sense of μετρέω (*metreō*, "I measure") as used in Matt. 7:2—the sense of forming an opinion about something. But the acquiring of information or forming an opinion is not all that is involved. Since the non-measurement of 11:2 symbolizes territory that is profane (ἔκβαλε ἔξωθεν [*ekbale exōthen*], "cast out"), the measuring must be a mark of God's favor. In other words, John's future prophecies will distinguish between God's favor toward the sanctuary, the altar, and their worshipers and His disapproval of all that is of Gentile orientation because

80

of their profanation of the holy city for half of the future seventieth week. This distinction shows in the case of the two witnesses who in association with the sanctuary and the altar enjoy God's favor (11:5-6, 11-12) and their Gentile foes who oppose them, kill them, and eventually experience a devastating earthquake because of God's disfavor (11:13). The two witnesses enjoy God's favor, but not His protection and preservation from all enemies. So the measuring is an object lesson of how entities favored by God will fare during the period of Gentile oppression that lies ahead.

Ναόν (*Naon*, "Temple") refers more specifically to the sanctuary here, because v. 2 distinguishes the outer precinct of the temple complex as something separate from it (Johnson). The inner court of the Herodian temple had a division for the priests where the altar stood, one for the Israelites, and one for the women. Between these three and the court of the Gentiles was a low wall erected to keep Gentiles from the inner court (Beasley-Murray). A determination of what this "sanctuary" or "temple" is has received extensive attention. Considerable effort has gone into proving this to be a figurative reference to the church. The NT often calls the church the temple of God (1 Cor. 3:16; 2 Cor. 6:16; Eph. 2:21; 1 Pet. 3:5; cf. 1 Cor. 6:19) (Charles, Swete, Kiddle, Beasley-Murray, Hailey). Ναός (*Naos*, "Sanctuary") in particular lends itself to this figurative meaning (Lenski, Hailey). At the beginning of His ministry, Jesus referred to the temple as His Father's house (cf. Mark 11:17; Matt. 21:13; Luke 19:46; John 2:16), but near the end of it, He called it the house of the Jews (Matt. 23:38; Luke 13:35) (Charles).

This figurative interpretation fails for a number of reasons, however. The temple as the dwelling place of God is not in view here. It is the Jewish temple in Jerusalem which is hardly a suitable picture of the church which is largely Gentile (Ladd). Further, the outer court and the entire city experience trampling by the Gentiles (11:2), signifying that the temple and the court stand for something that best contrasts with the Gentiles, i.e., something Jewish (ibid.). The mention of the sanctuary, the altar, the court of the Gentiles, and the holy city shows unmistakably that the discussion at this point is on Jewish ground (Seiss). But most obvious of all is the logical fallacy that if the sanctuary represents the church of the Messianic community, who are the worshipers that are measured along with the sanctuary and the altar? This is an unbearable combining of figurative and literal elements connected only by καὶ (*kai*, "and"). The nonliteral interpretation is woefully inconsistent and self-contradictory. In addition, this figurative explanation results in a hopeless effort to identify the outer court and the holy city in 11:2.

The only way out of this entanglement of internal contradictions is

81

Revelation 11:1-2   Revelation 8-22

to understand this as a literal temple that will exist in actuality during the future period just before Christ returns. The false messiah will desecrate it and turn it into a place for people to worship him (cf. Dan. 9:27; 12:11; 2 Thess. 2:4; Rev. 13:14-15) (Walvoord). This allows for a distinction between the temple and the worshipers in it (Bullinger). Jesus' anticipation of the future abomination of desolation (Matt. 24:15) and Paul's prophecy regarding a future temple (2 Thess. 2:4) require a literal temple in the future (Bullinger, Smith). A distinct hope of Christians is for the future repentance of Israel (Beckwith). This requires a re-institution of the national life of this people, including its temple.

Τὸ θυσιαστήριον (To thysiastērion, "The altar") must be the one where the people could gather, the brazen altar of sacrifice in the court outside the sanctuary. References of the noun to the golden altar throughout the rest of Revelation is no problem for this identification, because elsewhere in the book, the altar is in heaven, not on earth as this one is. Only priests could enter the sanctuary which was the location of the golden altar of incense (Walvoord). Jesus never entered the sanctuary, but He entered the court as a babe (Luke 2:27), sat in it as a boy while being interrogated by the Jewish leaders (Luke 2:46), as a man healed the blind and the lame there (Matt. 21:14), and taught daily in it toward the end of His ministry (Matt. 26:55; Luke 20:1) (Smith).

The combination of μέτρησον (metrēson, "measure") with τοὺς προσκυνοῦντας (tous proskynountas, "the worshipers") as one of its objects is an instance of "zeugma"—a verb governing more than one object, one of which does not fit the verb meaning (Bullinger). Measurement of a building is quite appropriate, but for "the worshipers," another verb such as λόγισαι (logisai, "count" or "number") would usually be more likely here (Moffatt). Worshipers could gather in the court in front of the brazen altar. These worshipers in John's vision represent a future godly remnant in Israel who will worship God in the rebuilt temple. Among them are probably those who will come to Christ through the ministry of the two witnesses (11:13; cf. Ezek. 14:22; Rom. 11:4-5, 26) (Smith).

11:2 John was not to measure the outer court: καὶ τὴν αὐλὴ τὴν ἔξωθεν τοῦ ναοῦ ἔκβαλε ἔξωθεν καὶ μὴ αὐτὴν μετρήσῃς (kai tēn aulēn tēn exōthen tou naou ekbale exōthen kai mē autēn metrēsēs, "and cast out the court which is outside the temple and do not measure it"). "The court which is outside the temple" (τὴν αὐλὴν τὴν ἔξωθεν τοῦ ναοῦ, tēn aulēn tēn exōthen tou naou]) was an uncovered yard outside the house. Usually there were two courts, an outer one between the door and the street and an inner one surrounded by buildings (cf. Luke 1:22; Mark

82

14:66). The reference here is to the outer court, outside the sanctuary, but still within the ἱερόν (*hieron*, "temple"). Gentiles could enter this part, but not the inner court.[69] The distinction is between Jews, the godly remnant, and Gentiles, the wicked without God (cf. 1 Cor. 5:1; 1 Thess. 4:5) (Bullinger, Morris).

John's directions were to "cast outside" (ἔκβαλε ἔξωθεν [*ekbale exōthen*]) and not to measure (μὴ αὐτὴν μετρήσῃς [*mē autēn metrēsēs*]) this outer court. By divine plan, it has been abandoned to the heathen (Alford, Moffatt). Generally, ἐκβάλλω (*ekballō*, "I cast out") in the NT depicts an act of rejection (cf. Luke 4:29; 13:28; 20:15; John 6:37; 9:34-35; Acts 7:58). It speaks of a removal from favor (cf. Matt. 22:13; 25:30; 3 John 10) (Hailey). To remain unmeasured amounts to the opposite of being measured (Beasley-Murray). It marks an exclusion from God's favor.

The angel proceeds to give the cause for the exclusion: ὅτι ἐδόθη τοῖς ἔθνεσιν, καὶ τὴν πόλιν τὴν ἁγίαν πατήσουσιν μῆνας τεσσαράκοντα δύο (*hoti edothē tois ethnesin, kai tēn polin tēn hagian patēsousin mēnas tesserakonta dyo*, "because it has been given to the Gentiles, and they will trample on the holy city forty-two months"). The causal ὅτι (*hoti*, "because") reveals that the outer court has fallen into Gentile hands, and they will control and defile the holy city for forty-two months. In this important statement, "Gentiles," "holy city," and "forty-two months" deserve special attention

One explanation of ἔθνεσιν (*ethnesin*, "Gentiles") is that it refers to those conquering nations over whom Christ will exercise His millennial reign (Alford). However, the death of Christ's enemies at His return will make it impossible for this particular group of nations to be His subjects in the Millennium (cf. 19:21).

Another perspective refers τοῖς ἔθνεσιν (*tois ethnesin*, "the Gentiles") to all people outside of Christ, including Jews. Because this view identifies the church as the temple in v. 1, the designation "Gentiles" is said to include professing Christians who forsake Christ and join the ranks of the beast (Johnson). This analysis falters, however, in its failure to allow for the ongoing distinction between Jews and the remainder of the world's population. This distinction applies, not only in a comparison of 7:4-8 with 7:9, but even in this very passage where the Jewishness of the temple, the altar, and the holy city is so evident.

The best identification of "Gentiles" gives a narrower, technical sense, contrasting them to the Jewish people. This fits the immediate context and allows the noun the same meaning in 11:18 (cf. 14:8;

---

69. Robertson, *Word Pictures*, 6:377.

19:15; 20:3). On the whole, it will be this group in rebellion against God who will oppress the Jewish remnant and wreak havoc in Jerusalem in the period just before Christ's return.

The main question about "the holy city" is whether it is the literal earthly Jerusalem, the heavenly Jerusalem, or false Christianity invaded by the profane world. It can hardly refer to the heavenly city, the one in Rev. 21:2, 10 (contra Charles), because that city belongs to the new creation and this one to the present creation. Seeing "the holy city" as false Christianity invaded by the profane world (Alford, Mounce, Johnson) rests on a preunderstanding that the whole passage is highly symbolical, taking both the temple in v. 1 and the holy city in a nonliteral way. It supposes both the temple and the holy city to be the church. Not only is this a confusing mixture of figures, but in one case the church allegedly enjoys protection and in the other must submit to being despised and mistreated by the Gentiles. These two interpretations mutually exclude each other and cannot represent an accurate understanding of the words.

The preferable identification of "the holy city" is the literal city of Jerusalem on earth. If the temple is on earth (v. 1), the city must be on earth. After all, the heavenly Jerusalem has no temple (Rev. 21:22). Old Testament and NT usage of "the holy city" supports this conclusion (cf. Neh. 11:1, 18; Isa. 48:2; 52:1; Dan. 9:24; Matt. 4:5; 27:53) (Ford). A little later in this chapter, further evidence that this is the earthly Jerusalem surfaces in the identification of the city with the one where the Lord was crucified (11:8) (Johnson). The objection that the Romans destroyed the earthly city twenty-five years before John wrote Revelation[70] ignores prophecies that tell of a rebuilt Jerusalem during the future Tribulation (Walvoord). So this normal straightforward meaning of "the holy city" is the solution.

The issue of the "forty-two months" revolves around whether it is a literal or symbolic time period, and if literal, whether it is the opening half or final half of the seventieth week of Daniel 9. It also involves how this period relates to other periods of comparable length in Revelation—the twelve hundred sixty days (11:3; 12:6), the times, time, and half a time (12:14), and the other mention of forty-two months (13:5). The symbolic interpretation derives from the presumption that all or most of the numbers in Revelation are symbolic (Johnson), but proponents have no substantial evidence that such is true. The suggestions that three-and-a-half is half of seven and therefore denotes something midway in its course, that forty-two is pejorative

---

70. Johnson, "Revelation," 12:502; Kenneth L. Gentry, *Before Jerusalem Fell: Dating the Book of Revelation* (Tyler, Tex.: Institute for Christian Economics, 1989), pp. 165-67.

because it is the result of multiplying six times seven, and that forty-two is Messianic because it results from multiplying three times fourteen—the total of the consonants in David's name—are some attempts to assign symbolic significance to the forty-two months (Ford). Yet sane biblical interpretation requires that words be taken in their natural meaning unless contextual factors require something other than a literal interpretation (Bullinger).

Both of the literal understandings of the forty-two months recognize the impact of the book of Daniel, particularly chapter 9, on the Apocalypse.[71] The principal argument for making the forty-two months the first half of the seventieth week is theological. The first half will be a time when Jewish worship will continue as indicated by the measuring of the sanctuary and the worshipers, but the worship will come to an abrupt halt when beast worship begins at the midpoint of the week.[72] Yet the period of Jewish control in Jerusalem would preclude the need for special favor toward the worshipers as the measuring of v. 1 implies (Walvoord). It also appears that the measuring of v. 1 and the nonmeasuring of v. 2 are simultaneous. A continuation of Jewish worship while the rest of the city experiences Gentile intrusion is impossible. Further, the two witnesses apparently prophesy during the same period of opposition from the beast as the remainder of the chapter indicates (cf. 11:3).

It is better, therefore, to find the fulfillment of the forty-two months during the last half of the seventieth week. A principal reason for this is that the period of ill-treatment by the Gentiles fits the latter half better because of the breaking of the covenant with the Roman prince in the middle of the week (Dan. 9:27) (Walvoord). It also makes for a better connection with the 1260 days in 11:3 (Bullinger). The alleged problems of having a witness in Jerusalem during this period, a period following the flight of the woman in 12:6, 14 (Smith), is not serious. The absence of the bulk of Israelites does not exclude a concurrent witness to the city by the two witnesses. In fact, a witness facing stern opposition is what 11:3-13 describes. So the period is a literal forty-two months just before Christ returns in power (19:11-21).

---

71. See G. K. Beale, "The Influence of Daniel upon the Structure and Theology of John's Apocalypse," *JETS* 27/4 (December 1984): 413-23; John Andrew McLean, "The Seventieth Week of Daniel 9:27 as a Literary Key for Understanding the Structure of the Apocalypse of John" (Ph.D. diss., Univ. of Michigan, 1990); idem, "The Structure of the Book of Revelation and Its Implication for the Pre-Wrath Rapture (Part One)," *Michigan Theological Journal* 2/2 (Fall 1991): 138-67, and "(Part Two)," *Michigan Theological Journal* 3/1 (Spring 1992): 5-40.
72. Smith, *Revelation*, p. 171; Charles Caldwell Ryrie, *Revelation*, Everyman's Bible Commentary (Chicago: Moody, 1968), p. 72.

Πατήσουσιν (*Patēsousin*, "They will trample on") does not predict utter destruction for the city; the city's continued existence is presupposed in 11:3-13 (Beckwith). Just as it survived throughout the earlier parts of "the times of the Gentiles" (Luke 21:24), it will do so during this, the closing phase of that extended period. An effort to apply this forty-two-month period to the days just before the destruction of Jerusalem in A.D. 70 necessitates a date of writing for Revelation in the A.D. 60s.[73] The necessity of combining a literal hermeneutic with a symbolic one in order to support this thesis[74] is a major weakness, however. Only by arbitrarily picking and choosing what is literal-historical and what is figurative-symbolic can one have the temple as representing spiritually the church and the holy city as the literal city of Jerusalem.[75] It also necessitates an equation of the Roman siege of Jerusalem with the forty-two-month period of trodding underfoot.[76] This misrepresents what such a period of oppression is. Siege is not the same as dominant control. Besides, the period of siege was much longer than forty-two months, extending back to 65 or 66 rather than to an alleged beginning in 67.[77]

An assignment of the period to a future defilement and domination of Jerusalem and the rebuilt temple is more satisfactory (Walvoord). This best aligns with consistent literal hermeneutics and allows for the well-known expectation of Israel's restoration and prominence in God's future program (Matt. 24:15; Rom. 9-11) (Bullinger).

11:3 The connection of John's measuring activity with the account of the two witnesses in vv. 3-13 is not immediately obvious, but the connection of the latter to the former by a simple καὶ (*kai*, "and") requires some kind of close continuity (Kiddle): καὶ δώσω τοῖς δυσὶν μάρτυσίν μου, καὶ προφητεύσουσιν ἡμέρας χιλίας διακοσίας ἑξήκοντα περιβεβλημένοι* σάκκους (*kai dōsō tois dysin martysin mou, kai prophēteusousin hēmeras chilias diakosias hexēkonta peribeblēmenoi sakkous*, "and I will give [authority] to My two witnesses, and they will prophesy a thousand two hundred and sixty days clothed in sackcloth"). In brief, that continuity entails God's continuance of getting His message out in spite of Gentile oppression (Mounce). The thousand two hundred and sixty days of v. 3 connected to the forty-two months of v. 2 provides another indication of the continuity from v. 2 to v. 3.

---

73. Gentry, *Jerusalem Fell*, pp. 165-69; David Chilton, *The Days of Vengeance* (Fort Worth, Tex.: Dominion, 1987), pp. 274-75.
74. Gentry, *Jerusalem Fell*, pp. 174-75.
75. Contra ibid.
76. Gentry, *Jerusalem Fell*, pp. 250-53.
77. Contra ibid.

Because of the first person verb δώσω (*dōsō*, "I will give") and pronoun μου (*mou*, "My"), the impression could be that God (Beckwith) or Christ (Swete) begins speaking at this point. The witnesses clearly belong to God and Christ, not to the angel who speaks in vv. 1-2. But the reference to "their Lord" in 11:8 shows that it cannot be Christ speaking (Alford). It is characteristic of Revelation that at times angels apparently become divine mouthpieces to the point of speaking the very words of God or Christ as though deity were the source (cf. 22:7).[78] As the angel continues his description through 11:13, God's voice enters the narrative here in a very inconspicuous manner.

The OT required two witnesses as competent legal testimony to secure a conviction (Deut. 17:6; 19:15; Num. 35:30; cf. Heb. 10:28). Jesus also made the number two a minimum to confirm a point of discipline (Matt. 18:16) or verify truth (John 8:17) (Hailey). Paul too alluded to the need of a plurality of witnesses to validate a judgment (2 Cor. 13:1; 1 Tim. 5:19).

The two witnesses here, though, are two prophetic voices of the future, as the future tenses of δώσω (*dōsō*, "I will give") and προφητεύσουσιν (*prophēteusousin*, "they will prophesy") indicate. Who are they? Some answer that they signify the church (e.g., Morris, Kiddle, Beasley-Murray, Mounce, Sweet, Hailey, Johnson), pointing out that lampstands (cf. 11:4) are symbols for churches earlier in the book (cf. 1:20) (Kiddle, Morris, Johnson) and that the beast would hardly make war (cf. 11:7) with just two people (Mounce, Johnson, Sweet). They also note that people around the world will witness their deaths (cf. 11:9), hardly a possibility if only two individuals are in view (Johnson, Sweet). Beyond this, the approach falls back on an assumption of symbolism throughout 11:1-13, which has never received definitive support.

Objections to the symbolic identification of the two witnesses are rather easy to come by. Only individual persons can wear sackcloth (cf. 11:3) (Seiss). The description represents the two witnesses as individuals having specific power and distinct identities as two ancient prophets did (cf. 11:5-6).[79] The plural number of προφητεύσουσιν (*prophēteusousin*, "they will prophesy") opposes the notion of a corporate identity (Alford). Individuality could hardly find a clearer expression than in 11:5 where a national interpretation regarding the witnesses' opponents is impossible (Alford, Bullinger). The description of the two witnesses is too detailed for them to be representative of a corporate

---

78. Düsterdieck, *Revelation*, p. 314.
79. Düsterdieck, *Revelation*, p. 315; Alford, *Greek Testament*, 4:659; Robertson, *Word Pictures*, 6:378.

body (Ladd). The corporate view would require that all believers of the future undergo martyrdom, denying the possibility of survivors that will remain to populate the Millennium. The obstacles to the symbolic view are insurmountable.

The ancient church, including such as Tertullian, Irenaeus, and Hippolytus, were consistent in identifying the two witnesses as Enoch and Elijah.[80] The principal reason for selecting these two was that both were translated to heaven without seeing death (Gen. 5:24; 2 Kings 2:11). The necessity for all men to die (cf. Heb. 9:27) supposedly requires the return of these two to earth to experience death. Besides this, an early tradition said that Enoch would rejoin Elijah for such a ministry as these two witnesses have (*1 Enoch* 90:31; *4 Ezra* 6:26) (Moffatt, Beasley-Murray). The evidence for this view is refutable, however. For one thing, it is not warranted to conclude that all must die once. The ones alive at the return of the Lord for His church will never meet physical death (cf. 1 Thess. 4:17). Also, the saints alive at the end of the Great Tribulation will enter the millennial kingdom without ever having to die (Smith). A further difficulty for this view is Enoch's failure to match the criteria assigned to the two witnesses in 11:5-6 (Mounce).

A viewpoint easier to sustain makes the two witnesses Moses and Elijah. The OT miraculous signs of those two match those performed here by the witnesses (cf. 11:5-6). Elijah called down fire from heaven (2 Kings 1:10) and shut off the rain from heaven (1 Kings 17:1; cf. Luke 4:25; James 5:17). Moses turned water into blood and struck the earth with plagues (Ex. 7:14-11:10, esp. 7:14-18; 8:12) (Charles, Smith, Bullinger, Mounce). Also, Mal. 4:5 predicted the return of Elijah "before the coming of the great and terrible day of the LORD" (Walvoord), and Deut. 18:15, 18 predicted the coming of a prophet like Moses (Alford, Swete, Moffatt). The two figures seen with Christ on the Mount of Transfiguration in the preview of the coming kingdom were Moses and Elijah (Matt. 17:3; Mark 9:4; Luke 9:30) (Walvoord, Mounce). The mystery surrounding Moses' death (Deut. 34:5-6; Jude 9) and the translation of Elijah (2 Kings 2:11) offer some corroboration of these as the two witnesses (Charles). Finally, the duration of the drought in 11:6 (cf. 11:3) is the same as that under Elijah's ministry, three and a half years (Caird).

This mode of explaining the two witnesses is not without objections. One is that John the Baptist fulfilled the Malachi prophecy about

---

80. Thomas W. Mackay, "Early Christian Millenarianist Interpretation of the Two Witnesses in John's Apocalypse, 11:3-13," in *By Study and Also by Faith*, ed. John M. Lundquist and Stephen D. Ricks (Salt Lake City: Deseret, 1990), pp. 252-65, 310.

Elijah's return. The rejoinder is John the Baptist was only like Elijah. He did not restore all things as required by the prophecy (Seiss, Smith). Another objection is that Moses did die. For him to return as one of the witnesses would have him dying a second time. The reply for this is that though two deaths for the same person is difficult to explain, it did happen in the case of Lazarus whom Jesus raised from the dead. A final objection is that these could be two future individuals who only resemble Moses and Elijah (cf. Matt. 11:14; 17:10-13) (Ladd). This is a possible alternative, but the balance of the evidence is for an expectation of the actual return of the very same persons.

The ministry of the two, when they come, will undoubtedly include a preaching of repentance, but προφητεύσουσιν (*propheteusousin*, "they will prophesy") of necessity includes the foretelling of the future (cf. 10:11; 1 Pet. 1:10; Jude 14) (Alford). The 1,260 days of their ministry will be simultaneous with the trampling of the holy city (11:2) and the work of the false Christ in the world (11:7; 13:5) (Beasley-Murray, Mounce). The sackcloth clothing of the witnesses is in token of needed repentance and approaching judgment (cf. Isa. 22:12; Jer. 4:8; 6:26; Jon. 3:5, 6, 8; Matt. 11:21) (Alford). It marked their lamentation over the treading down of the holy city and the prevalence of evil all around them (Hailey).

11:4 The mission of the two witnesses resembles that of Zerubbabel and Joshua: Οὗτοί εἰσιν αἱ δύο ἐλαῖαι καὶ αἱ δύο λυχνίαι αἱ ἐνώπιον τοῦ κυρίου τῆς γῆς ἑστῶτες (*Houtoi eisin hai dyo elaiai kai hai dyo lychniai hai enōpion tou kyriou tēs gēs hestōtes*, "These are the two olive branches and the two lampstands which are standing before the Lord of the earth"). The two witnesses represent[81] the OT characters of Zech. 4:2, 3, 11-14 in being raised up for a similar mission as they (Bullinger). Just as Joshua and Zerubbabel sought to restore Israel to her land, so will the two witnesses (Alford).

This passage does not state the role of the Holy Spirit in the ministry of these two, but the allusion to Zechariah 4 certainly carries the implication of the Spirit's vital part (cf. Zech. 4:6). John has drawn on this chapter earlier in fashioning a special title, "the seven spirits," for the Holy Spirit (cf. 1:4) (Thomas, pp. 66-68). In Zechariah's vision, the olive oil from the trees provided fuel for the lampstand as an emblem of the light brought through Joshua and Zerubbabel (Swete, Charles, Walvoord). The oil pictured the working of the Holy Spirit. In Zechariah, there was only one lampstand with seven lights, but John's account has two lampstands to picture the two witnesses more dis-

---

81. Εἰσιν carries the meaning of "represent" here as it does in its two occurrences of 1:20 (Bullinger, *Apocalypse*, pp. 354-55).

tinctly. Αἱ ἐνώπιον τοῦ κυρίου τῆς γῆς ἑστῶτες (*Hai enōpion tou kyriou tēs gēs hestōtes*, "Which are standing before the Lord of the earth"), an allusion to Zech. 4:14, is more explicit about the source of the witnesses' power. Their nearness to the almighty ruler of the earth shows their readiness to serve, their acceptableness, and their authority (Seiss, Smith).

11:5 Their power to accomplish their mission is phenomenal: καὶ εἴ τις αὐτοὺς θέλει* ἀδικῆσαι, πῦρ ἐκπορεύεται ἐκ τοῦ στόματος αὐτῶν καὶ κατεσθίει τοὺς ἐχθροὺς αὐτῶν· καὶ εἴ τις θελήσῃ αὐτοὺς ἀδικῆσαι, οὕτως δεῖ αὐτὸν ἀποκτανθῆναι (*kai ei tis autous thelei adikēsai, pyr ekporeuetai ek tou stomatos autōn kai katesthiei tous echthrous autōn; kai ei tis thelēsei autous adikēsai, houtōs dei auton apoktanthēnai*, "and if anyone desires to hurt them, fire goes forth from their mouths and devours their enemies; and if anyone desires to hurt them, it is necessary thus for him to be killed"). As the angel continues his description of the two witnesses, he observes that any attempt to harm them will meet with fire from their mouths that has a deadly effect on the perpetrator. This is the first of several traditional features drawn from the lives of Moses and Elijah (Moffatt, Kiddle).

The first part of v. 5 uses a construction that assumes the actuality of the wish, εἴ τις . . . θέλει (*ei tis . . . thelei*), which essentially means "if anyone engages in desiring." The verb θέλει (*thelei*, "desires") is present indicative and makes the assumption that some will want to harm the two. The last part of the verse varies the construction by using an aorist subjunctive rather than a present indicative, εἴ τις θελήσῃ (*ei tis thelēsē*), the essence of which is "if anyone may desire."[82] The latter is conceived as less likely to happen.[83] The consequence of each is apparently the same, death by fire.

Πῦρ (*Pyr*, "Fire") alludes to Elijah's treatment of Ahaziah's messengers, though here the fire comes from the witnesses' mouths rather than from heaven (2 Kings 1:10-14). The double announcement in v. 5 gives the impression of referring to literal fire (Alford). God will once again use literal fire to protect His messengers who speak on behalf of Israel.[84] The sense of literal fire is also more consistent with the literal drought and plagues spoken of in v. 6 (Mounce, Sweet). James and John sought this ability with a vindictive spirit during Christ's earthly ministry and were refused (Luke 9:54-55), but these two are inspired

---

82. Swete, *Apocalypse*, pp. 135-36; Robertson, *A Grammar of the Greek New Testament in the Light of Historical Research* (Nashville, Tenn.: Broadman, 1934), p. 1017; BDF, par 372[3].
83. Robertson, *Word Pictures*, 6:378-79.
84. Bullinger, *Apocalypse*, p. 358; Walvoord, *Revelation*, p. 180; Robertson, *Word Pictures*, 6:379.

prophets who are vehicles of future divine judgment (Caird). This furnishes them a means of protection in a time of great jeopardy. The necessity of death to any would-be abuser of the two—δεῖ αὐτὸν ἀποκτανθῆναι (*dei auton apoktanthēnai*, "it is necessary for him to be killed")—means the end of physical life. This immediate judgment of God upon the enemies of the witnesses is what protects them and prolongs their ministries (Alford).

11:6 Additional words about the power of the two witnesses shows how well-equipped they are for their task: οὗτοι ἔχουσιν τὴν ἐξουσίαν κλεῖσαι τὸν οὐρανόν, ἵνα μὴ ὑετὸς βρέχῃ τὰς ἡμέρας τῆς προφητείας αὐτῶν, καὶ ἐξουσίαν ἔχουσιν ἐπὶ τῶν ὑδάτων στρέφειν αὐτὰ εἰς αἷμα καὶ πατάξαι τὴν γῆν ἐν πάσῃ πληγῇ ὁσάκις ἐὰν θελήσωσιν (*houtoi echousin tēn exousian kleisai ton ouranon, hina mē hyetos brechę tas hēmeras tēs prophēteias autōn, kai exousian echousin epi tōn hydatōn strephein auta eis haima kai pataxai tēn gēn en pasę plēgę hosakis ean thelēsōsin*, "These have the authority to shut heaven, lest it give forth rain during the days of their prophesy, and they have authority over the waters to turn them into blood and to smite the earth with every plague as often as they desire"). In this context both occurrences of ἔχουσιν (*echousin*, "they have") are futuristic presents pointing forward to power (ἐξουσίαν [*exousian*, "authority"]) of the prophets over the forces of nature (Beckwith, Walvoord).

Their power to shut heaven and stop rain from falling parallels what Elijah accomplished through prayer (1 Kings 17:1, 7; 18:1; James 5:17) and covered 9the same duration of three and a half years (Luke 4:25; James 5:17; cf. 11:3). Τὰς ἡμέρας τῆς προφητείας αὐτῶν (*Tas hēmeras tēs prophēteias autōn*, "During the days of their prophecy") is an accusative of extent of time and covers the entire period of the execution of their prophetic office.[85] In Elijah's time the measure was a punishment for sin (Moffatt). Presumably it will have the same purpose in the future.

Their power to turn water into blood and to smite the earth with plagues alludes to what Moses did (Ex. 7:17-21; 9:14; 11:10; 1 Sam. 4:8) (Alford, Mounce). These future prophets will have the same resources as Moses did to deliver his people from Egyptian slavery (Morris). The third trumpet (8:8) and the third bowl (16:4) will also evidence this power. Their power will even exceed that of Moses because they will call upon it whenever they wish (ὁσάκις ἐὰν θελήσωσιν [*hosakis ean thelēsōsin*, "as often as they desire"]). Moses had to await a divine command before he could inflict a plague (Swete).

11:7 Divine decree has fixed the duration of ministry for the two

---

85. Swete, *Apocalypse*, p. 133; Robertson, *Word Pictures*, 6:379.

witnesses: καὶ ὅταν τελέσωσιν τὴν μαρτυρίαν αὐτῶν, τὸ θηρίον τὸ ἀναβαῖνον ἐκ τῆς ἀβύσσου ποιήσει μετ᾽ αὐτῶν πόλεμον καὶ νικήσει αὐτοὺς
καὶ ἀποκτενεῖ αὐτούς (*kai hotan telesōsin tēn martyrian autōn, to thērion
to anabainon ek tēs abyssou poiēsei met' autōn polemon kai nikēsei
autous kai apoktenei autous*, "and when they finish their witness, the
beast who ascends from the abyss will make war with them and will
conquer them and kill them"). The verb τελέσωσιν (*telesōsin*, "they
finish") carries the import of a work completed or goal attained
(Moffatt, Walvoord, Morris, Mounce). The wording clearly indicates a
point in time when they will have achieved their specific duty that has
as its explicit definition τὴν μαρτυρίαν αὐτῶν (*tēn martyrian autōn*,
"their witness"). They will have completed their divinely appointed
task (Swete, Bullinger).

For the first time and somewhat by way of anticipation, τὸ θηρίον
(*to thērion*, "the beast") enters the description. *Thērion* is a word for a
beast of prey, one with a ravenous appetite, a carnivore like a lion or
panther.[86] It connotes a cunning of unreasoning violence that acts
according to its own cruel nature. It differs from ζῷον (*zōon*, "living
creature") which usually refers to animals also, but lacks the rapacious
connotations.[87] This first of thirty-six references to the archenemy of
God's people in Revelation (Mounce) is a passing reference that notes
the overlap of his rule with the span of the witnesses' ministry and his
antagonism toward them. Chapters 13 and 17 in particular will tell
more about this figure and furnish opportunities for a more precise
identification of the beast, but a preliminary narrowing of the field of
possibilities is advantageous here.

For one thing, the beast is not Satan himself, for a dragon is the
representation of Satan (12:3, 9). In Daniel θηρία (*thēria*, "beasts") are
earthly empires that oppose the saints (Dan. 7:18, 27), opposition that
is quite evident in the beast's war with the witnesses (Swete). In Revelation 13, the healing of his mortal wound (13:3, 12), the use of a
masculine pronoun referring to the neuter (*thērion*, 13:8), and his being an object of worship (13:8) are elements to indicate that the beast
is a ruler who represents himself as Christ (Swete, Charles, Beckwith).
The two possible identities, empire and ruler, are not mutually exclusive of each other, however, because the Scripture tends to view a ruler
of an empire as inseparable from his empire. In 11:7, however, precise
identification must recognize the dominance of an individual who
receives blame for the conquest and death of the two witnesses.

Τὸ ἀναβαῖνον ἐκ τῆς ἀβύσσου (*To anabainon ek tēs abyssou*, "Who
ascends from the abyss") tells the permanent cast of the beast's charac-

---

86. Werner Foerster, "θηρίον," *TDNT*, 3:134.
87. Rudolf Bultmann, "ζῷον," *TDNT*, 2:873.

ter (cf. 17:8). The abyss is the haunt of demons (cf. Luke 8:31), so his demonic orientation is no surprise (Mounce). This passage gives no time frame for his ascent from the abyss (Lenski, Caird), but later discussion will suggest it coincides with his ascent from the sea in 13:1.

The beast's actions—ποιήσει μετ' αὐτῶν πόλεμον καὶ νικήσει αὐτοὺς (*poiēsei met' autōn polemon kai nikēsei autous*, "will make war with them and will conquer them")—is an echo from Dan. 7:21 (Charles). He likewise will make war with the rest of the woman's seed and overcome them too (12:17; 13:7*a*). This will result in physical death for the two witnesses (ἀποκτενεῖ αὐτούς [*apoktenei autous*, "[will] kill them"]) (Walvoord).

11:8 To enhance the insult, he will leave their bodies unburied: καὶ τὸ πτῶμα αὐτῶν ἐπὶ τῆς πλατείας τῆς πόλεως τῆς μεγάλης, ἥτις καλεῖται πνευματικῶς Σόδομα καὶ Αἴγυπτος, ὅπου καὶ ὁ κύριος αὐτῶν ἐσταυρώθη (*kai to ptōma autōn epi tēs plateias tēs poleōs tēs megalēs, hētis kaleitai pneumatikōs Sodoma kai Aigyptos, hopou kai ho kyrios autōn estaurōthē*, "and their corpses [will be] in the street of the great city, which is spiritually called Sodom and Egypt, where also their Lord was crucified"). The worst indignity perpetrated on a person in that culture was to be left unburied after death (cf. Ps. 79:2-3) (Swete, Beasley-Murray, Mounce).

"The great city" in whose street their bodies will lie has the distinction of being "spiritually called Sodom and Egypt" (καλεῖται πνευματικῶς Σόδομα καὶ Αἴγυπτος [*kaleitai pneumatikōs Sodoma kai Aigyptos*]). Πνευματικῶς (*Pneumatikōs*, "Spiritually") shows this to be the language of allegory or metaphor. Neither Sodom nor Egypt is the city's real name (Alford, Beckwith). The figurative likeness suggests utter moral degradation. Isaiah (Isa. 1:9 ff.) and Ezekiel (Ezek. 16:46) gave the name Sodom to Judah in her worst days.[88] Egypt is a symbol of oppression and slavery (Swete, Mounce). The thing that Sodom and Egypt had in common was their unmitigated enmity toward the true God and His people.[89]

This much information has not salvaged "the great city" from controversy over its location, however. One proposal is a classic illustration of the idealist interpretation of Revelation. It does not limit "the great city" to any one location—i.e., Babylon, Rome, or Jerusalem—but says it represents all cities that have opposed the Lord through the centuries (Kiddle, Morris). It points to the mention of "those who dwell on the earth" in 11:10 as indicative of the necessity for a worldwide understanding of the expression (Mounce, Sweet). Yet by assign-

---

88. Barnes, *Revelation*, p. 279; Mounce, *Revelation*, pp. 226-27.
89. Düsterdieck, *Revelation*, p. 317.

ing "every meaning" to the words, this view essentially assigns "no meaning" to them. Verse 8 does not say it is *spiritually* the great city as this explanation would require. Neither can this identification satisfy the last clause, "where also their Lord was crucified."[90] The idealist approach simply gives insufficient attention to the specifics of the prophecy.[91]

A specific suggested location is the city of Rome. Assuming that "Babylon" throughout Revelation means Rome, this view points to seven other references in Revelation where "the great city" has this meaning (cf. 16:19; 17:18; 18:10, 16, 18, 19, 21) (Caird, Mounce). Aside from the uncertainty of the equation of Rome with "Babylon," "the great city" only refers to Babylon in the latter half of the book. This is too early to find a reference to Babylon (Swete). No ground exists for falling back on an allegorical interpretation here. As noted above, *pneumatikōs* ("spiritually") does not apply to this issue, but to the likening of a literal city to historical examples of opposition to God. The Roman interpretation can work only if the two witnesses are figurative for the church, a possibility that has been ruled out in the discussion of 11:3 above.

If language has any meaning at all, it is hard to identify "the great city" as anywhere else but Jerusalem, because it was there "where also their Lord was crucified" (Swete). Many are the connections of Moses and Elijah with Jerusalem, but there are none with Rome (Charles). Ezekiel has a comparison of Jerusalem with Egypt because of her adoption of the customs and vices of Egypt (Ezek. 23:3, 4, 8, 19) (Bullinger). Jerusalem has been in view since v. 1 of this chapter. Why should recourse be to any other locale?[92] Historically, Jerusalem goes by the title of "the great city" (cf. Jer. 22:8) (Bullinger). The desolation of Jerusalem at the time John was writing his Apocalypse is no argument against this solution, because the prophecy was looking forward to a time when Jerusalem would be rebuilt and inhabited by the Jews in the last days.[93] Reference in the last part of v. 8 is unquestionably to Christ's crucifixion. The prophets will die in the same place—note the καὶ (*kai*, "also")—as their Lord did. But instead of immediate burial, they will suffer the disgrace of having their corpses remain in the street of that city (Beckwith).

11:9 For three and a half days they will be a spectacle for all races and nations: καὶ βλέπουσιν ἐκ τῶν λαῶν καὶ φυλῶν καὶ γλωσσῶν καὶ

---

90. Ibid., p. 321.
91. Ibid., pp. 327-28.
92. Robertson, *Word Pictures*, 6:380.
93. Hanns Lilje, *The Last Book of the Bible* (Philadelphia: Muhlenberg, 1955), p. 161.

ἐθνῶν τὸ πτῶμα αὐτῶν ἡμέρας τρεῖς καὶ ἥμισυ, καὶ τὰ πτώματα αὐτῶν οὐκ ἀφίουσιν τεθῆναι εἰς μνῆμα (*kai blepousin ek tōn laōn kai phylōn kai glōssōn kai ethnōn to ptōma autōn hēmeras treis kai hēmisy, kai ta ptōmata autōn ouk aphiousin tethēnai eis mnēma*, "and [those] from peoples and tribes and tongues and nations see their corpses three and a half days, and they do not permit their corpses to be placed into a tomb"). "Peoples and tribes and tongues and nations" is essentially the same enumeration as has been encountered earlier at 5:9 and 7:9, except here they are not the source from which the redeemed come as in the two earlier references. Here the worldwide groupings are the pool from which come those who in league with the beast are for the moment glad to see the end of the two witnesses. These must be members of different nations present in Jerusalem at this critical time (Charles).

Gloating over the dead bodies continues for "three and a half days" (ἡμέρας τρεῖς καὶ ἥμισυ [*hēmeras treis kai hēmisy*]), the correspondence to the three and a half years of prophetic ministry being only coincidental.[94] The ancients regarded this length of exposure as a great indignity. This meant great shame to the dead ones in the eyes of the onlookers, who were also responsible for the prolongation.[95] With the τὰ πτώματα (*ta ptōmata*, "the corpses") John drops the collective force of πτῶμα (*ptōma*, "the corpse"), probably because of the separate handling necessary for two dead bodies (Swete). This variation is further verification that the two witnesses are not symbols for the church.

11:10 The merriment over the deaths of the two witnesses is widespread: καὶ οἱ κατοικοῦντες ἐπὶ τῆς γῆς χαίρουσιν ἐπ᾽ αὐτοῖς καὶ εὐφραίνονται, καὶ δῶρα πέμψουσιν ἀλλήλοις, ὅτι οὗτοι οἱ δύο προφῆται ἐβασάνισαν τοὺς κατοικοῦντας ἐπὶ τῆς γῆς (*kai hoi katoikountes epi tēs gēs chairousin ep' autois kai euphrainontai, kai dōra pempsousin allēlois, hoti houtoi hoi dyo prophētai ebasanisan tous katoikountas epi tēs gēs*, "and those who dwell upon the earth rejoice over them and make merry, and they send gifts to one another, because these two prophets tormented those who dwell upon the earth"). The earth-dwellers are prominent through two mentions in v. 10. Οἱ κατοικοῦντες ἐπὶ τῆς γῆς (*Hoi katoikountes epi tēs gēs*, "Those who dwell upon the earth") is an apocalyptic formula for the unbelieving world, the same as the groupings listed in v. 9 (Swete, Beckwith; see discussion at 3:10 and 6:10 in Thomas, pp. 289, 446). The suggested limitation of these earth-

---

94. Bullinger, *Apocalypse*, pp. 363-64; Robertson, *Word Pictures*, 6:381.
95. This assumes that ἀφίουσιν has the same subject as βλέπουσιν earlier in the verse, which seems natural. It is possible that this is a plural of indefinite statement as in 10:11 (Bullinger, *Apocalypse*, p. 361; Charles, *Revelation*, 1:288-89).

dwellers to people in the land of Palestine might be feasible if it were not for the worldwide scope of the listings in v. 9 and the use of the technical expression for "those who dwell upon the earth" in the rest of Revelation (Charles). A globe-spanning interest in these two deaths is anticipated, but not every single person will see the corpses in person. Because of the cosmopolitan backgrounds of Jerusalem's inhabitants, representatives from all groups will be there to witness it personally, however.[96]

The verbs χαίρουσιν . . . εὐφραίνονται (chairousin . . . euphrainontai, "rejoice . . . make merry") reflect clearly the emotional state of the wicked at the death of the two witnesses. Their celebration and exchange of gifts are both fiendish and childish. They show their state of utter depravity and unquenchable hatred toward Christians (Swete, Beckwith, Lenski). This is an interesting reversal of the picture when the Jews rejoiced over the death of Haman at the first Feast of Purim (Est. 9:19, 22) (Sweet).

The ὅτι (hoti, "because") reveals the reason for the rejoicing: the termination of torment inflicted on the earth-dwellers by the two. Their special powers (11:5-6) had brought suffering and death for three and a half years, but probably the worst torment was that of troubling men's consciences over their sinfulness (cf. 1 Kings 18:17; 21:20).[97] It is sad that such jubilation will mark the end of an opportunity for the world to hear God's spokesmen. Yet the world has always shown this kind of hostility to God (e.g., Mark 6:20) (Mounce).

11:11 The international celebration is short-lived, however. The resurrection of the two witnesses ends it (Mounce): καὶ μετὰ τὰς τρεῖς ἡμέρας καὶ ἥμισυ πνεῦμα ζωῆς ἐκ τοῦ θεοῦ εἰσῆλθεν ἐν αὐτοῖς, καὶ ἔστησαν ἐπὶ τοὺς πόδας αὐτῶν, καὶ φόβος μέγας ἐπέπεσεν ἐπὶ τοὺς θεωροῦντας αὐτούς (kai meta tas treis hēmeras kai hēmisy pneuma zōēs ek tou theou eisēlthen en autois, kai estēsan epi tous podas autōn, kai phobos megas epepesen epi tous theōrountas autous, "and after the three and a half days the breath of life from God entered them, and they stood on their feet, and a great fear fell on those beholding them"). Πνεῦμα ζωῆς (Pneuma zōēs, "breath of life") is a phrase used of the lower animals in Gen. 6:17; 7:15, 22, but here the clear allusion is to Ezek. 37:5, 10, where God sends the breath of life into dead bones, making them live again and stand on their feet (cf. 2 Kings 13:20-21).[98]

The tense change to εἰσῆλθεν (eisēlthen, "entered") signals a

96. J. Otis Yoder, in Smith, *Revelation*, p. 173.
97. Barnes, *Revelation*, p. 281; Swete, *Apocalypse*, p. 136.
98. Swete, *Apocalypse*, p. 136; Charles, *Revelation*, 1:290; Robertson, *Word Pictures*, 6:382.

change in perspective. The prophetic presents χαίρουσιν (*chairousin*, "rejoice") and εὐφραίνονται (*euphrainontai*, "make merry") and the future πέμψουσιν (*pempsousin*, "will send") in v. 10 have switched to an aorist εἰσῆλθεν (*eisēlthen*, "entered"). In the speaker's mind, what was prophecy there has now become fact.[99] In evidence of their resurrection, the two witnesses stood on their feet just as the dry bones in Ezekiel's vision (Ezek. 37:10) and the dead within Elisha's tomb (2 Kings 13:21). The accusative case in ἐπὶ τοὺς πόδας (*epi tous podas*, "upon the feet") matches the accusative of the comparable construction in the LXX of the Elisha account, but differs from the genitive following ἐπί (*epi*, "upon") in the Ezekiel passage.

The dual resurrection brought "great fear" (φόβος μέγας [*phobos megas*) to the spectators, something on the order of making them panic-stricken or terrified. Murder is the ultimate weapon of mankind, so no means remained for them to silence the two (Mounce). The beholders wondered what worse thing could happen to them now.

11:12 After rising, the witnesses hear a voice from heaven summoning them upward: καὶ ἤκουσαν* φωνῆς μεγάλης ἐκ τοῦ οὐρανοῦ λεγούσης αὐτοῖς, Ἀνάβατε ὧδε· καὶ ἀνέβησαν εἰς τὸν οὐρανὸν ἐν τῇ νεφέλῃ, καὶ ἐθεώρησαν αὐτοὺς οἱ ἐχθροὶ αὐτῶν (*kai ēkousan phōnēs megalēs ek tou ouranou legousēs autois, Anabate hōde; kai anebēsan eis ton ouranon en tē nephelē, kai etheōrēsan autous hoi echthroi autōn*, "and they heard a great voice from heaven saying to them, 'Come up here'; and they went up into heaven in the cloud, and their enemies beheld them"). The voice from heaven is probably that of Christ which summoned John to heaven at 4:1 (Smith).

The summons upward ἀνάβατε ὧδε (*anabate hōde*, "come up here") and its response ἀνέβησαν εἰς τὸν οὐρανὸν (*anebēsan eis ton ouranon*, "they went up into heaven") recalls the earlier ascension of Elijah (2 Kings 2:11) and the mysterious circumstances surrounding Moses' death (Deut. 34:5-6) (Sweet). Their ascension resembles that of Christ because of the cloud through which they pass (ἐν τῇ νεφέλῃ [*en tē nephelē*]). A cloud received Christ when He ascended (Acts 1:9). Clouds will also encompass those in Christ when they ascend into heaven (1 Thess. 4:17).

The ascension of the witnesses will be in the full vision of their enemies (ἐθεώρησαν αὐτοὺς οἱ ἐχθροὶ αὐτῶν [*etheōrēsan autous ho echthroi autōn*, "their enemies beheld them"]). Their ascent will be gradual enough for humans to witness as was Christ's ascension (Acts 1:9). The difference is that it was Christ's friends who saw Him ascend (Swete). The snatching away of those in Christ will apparently not be

---

99. Robertson, *Word Pictures*, 6:382; Morris, *Revelation*, p. 151.

that gradual because it will happen quickly as the twinkling of an eye (1 Cor. 15:51-52) (Walvoord).

11:13 A great earthquake occurs in conjunction with the ascent of the two witnesses: Καὶ ἐν ἐκείνῃ τῇ ὥρᾳ ἐγένετο σεισμὸς μέγας, καὶ τὸ δέκατον τῆς πόλεως ἔπεσεν, καὶ ἀπεκτάνθησαν ἐν τῷ σεισμῷ ὀνόματα ἀνθρώπων χιλιάδες ἑπτά (*Kai en ekeinē tēhōrạ egeneto seismos megas, kai to dekaton tēs poleōs epesen, kai apektanthēsan en tǭ seismǭ onomata anthrōpōn chiliades hepta*, "And a great earthquake occurred in that hour, and the tenth [part] of the city fell, and seven thousand persons were killed in the earthquake"). It was "in that hour" of seeing the witnesses ascend that the inhabitants of Jerusalem experienced a great earthquake. This must be a literal movement of the earth's surface that causes the fall of a tenth of the city (Mounce). The whole city of Jerusalem was, of course, in ruins as John wrote (Charles), so this refers to the Jerusalem of the future, rebuilt and standing.

"Persons" is the rendering of ὀνόματα ἀνθρώπων (*onomata anthrōpōn*), which is literally "names of men." The unusual expression perhaps indicates that the number is carefully and precisely stated. This is similar to the usage of ὀνόματα (*onomata*, "names") in 3:4 and ὀνομάτων (*onomatōn*, "names") in Acts 1:15.[100] The studied moderation of the figure seven thousand as well as the fractional value of one-tenth shows that the disaster will be partial and ordinary (Swete). In John's day the figure suits the population of Jerusalem, which was about 120,000, but in no way could it have referred to Rome (Charles).

A further result of the tragedy was a widespread turning to God by the remainder of Jerusalem's populace: καὶ οἱ λοιποὶ ἔμφοβοι ἐγένοντο καὶ ἔδωκαν δόξαν τῷ θεῷ τοῦ οὐρανοῦ (*kai hoi loipoi emphoboi egenonto kai edōkan doxan tǭ theǭ tou ouranou*, "and the rest became afraid and gave glory to the God of heaven"). Some disagree with this understanding of the phraseology, however. They view the glory to God as given under compulsion and not from repentance (Bullinger, Kiddle). They say the magicians of Egypt did the same when they acknowledged, "This is the finger of God" (Ex. 8:19). The reasoning is that "the whole earth" cannot follow the beast (13:3-4) if 90 percent of Jerusalem's population has repented (Mounce). The inherently evil nature of the city (11:8) and the hardness of the earth-dwellers (11:10) preclude the possibility of genuine worship or repentance (Hailey). Yet elsewhere in Revelation, giving glory to God is tantamount to repentance (cf. Rev. 4:9; 16:9; 19:7).

"Giving glory to God" has a positive spiritual connotation else-

---

100. Alford, *Greek Testament*, 4:663; Bullinger, *Apocalypse*, p. 367; Robertson, *Word Pictures*, 6:383.

where in the OT and in the NT too (cf. Josh. 7:19; 1 Sam. 6:5; Isa. 42:2; Jer. 13:16; Luke 17:18; John 9:24; Acts 12:23; Rom. 4:20; 1 Pet. 2:12) (Charles, Ladd, Beasley-Murray). The response here is clearly the opposite of that in 9:20-21. One objection to finding true repentance is that the giving of glory to God apparently results in no postponement of judgment (Seiss). In fact, it does not even forestall the judgment that comes in the very next verse (Scott). Yet this problem is only apparent, because quite conceivably, this response of the Jerusalemites comes chronologically later than part of the bowl series that comes in chapter 16. All in all, the evidence is a bit stronger to support that this is a genuine repentance in response to the great earthquake. It comes toward the end of the bowl series and is the only bright spot in the midst of a predominant hardening of men's hearts. It comes here as an encouragement just before the last stroke of the seventh trumpet falls. The interlude between the sixth and seventh seals offered encouragement at an earlier stage of this "hour of trial." Since the inhabitants of Jerusalem will be mostly Jewish, this could very well be the future repentance of Israel that will accompany Christ's second advent (cf. Rom. 11:26).

These contrite ones will acknowledge "the God of heaven," an OT title for God that distinguished Him from the many gods of the heathen (cf. Ezra 1:2; Dan. 2:18; Jon. 1:9) (Swete, Beckwith, Walvoord). The title occurs once again in Revelation at 16:19.

11:14 A dramatic announcement as a follow-up to those in 8:13 and 9:12 comes at this point to mark the end of the 10:1–11:13 interlude: Ἡ οὐαὶ ἡ δευτέρα ἀπῆλθεν· ἰδοὺ ἡ οὐαὶ ἡ τρίτη ἔρχεται ταχύ (*Hē ouai hē deutera apēlthen; idou hē ouai hē tritē erchetai tachy*, "The second woe has gone away; behold, the third woe comes soon"). Because of this announcement, some would include the interlude as part of the second woe, thereby extending the second woe beyond the end of the sixth trumpet in 9:21.[101] But the announcement of the passing of the second woe in 11:14a does not necessitate this extension. The writer puts the announcement of the second woe's end here to conjoin it with the announcement of the commencement of the third woe in 11:14b, which identifies with the seventh trumpet sounded in the next verse.[102] The material in 10:1-11 especially is hardly in the category of a woe. To maintain clarity, the interlude material must not mix with material in the numbered sequences of the book. Revelation 9:20-21 clearly marks the end of the sixth trumpet, which is the second woe (Hailey).

---

101. Swete, *Apocalypse*, p. 141; Robertson, *Word Pictures*, 6:384.
102. Beckwith, pp. 607-8; Edith M. Humphrey, "The Sweet and the Sour: Epics of Wrath and Return in the Apocalypse," *SBLASP* (1991): 454.

A phrase usually reserved for the imminence of Christ's return describes the coming of the third woe (cf. Rev. 2:16; 3:11; 22:7, 12, 20).[103] This ταχύ (*tachy*, "soon") contrasts with the μετά ταῦτα (*meta tauta*, "after these things") that anticipated the coming of the second woe (9:12). The imminence stems from the fact that events of the seventh trumpet or third woe are those leading into and including the Second Coming ἔρχεται ταχύ (*erchetai tachy*, "comes soon"). These events are imminent because the progression of seals and trumpets has now reached the point that the return of Christ as Warrior-King (19:11-16), which is an integral part of the seventh trumpet, is now imminent.[104] The contents of the third woe will not come until 16:1 ff., after a briefing on all the different subplots of God's providence (Alford). The first two woe-descriptions followed immediately after their respective trumpet-blasts, but because the seventh trumpet is of a much broader scope, a great deal of intervening explanation is necessary (Beckwith).

With the announcement of 11:14, the stage is now set for the next step in chronological movement, the sounding of the seventh trumpet.

Additional Notes

11:1 Ἐν αὐτῷ refers either to the altar—i.e., "in connection with it" (Lenski)—or to the temple—i.e., "in it." The latter appears more probable, since these are worshipers in the temple. Since only the priests could enter the ναός ("sanctuary"), the sense may be "those who worship in connection with the sanctuary."

11:2 Copyists who understood αὐλήν to be the inner courtyard found τὴν αὐλὴν τὴν ἔξωθεν puzzling and changed ἔξωθεν to ἔσωθεν. Sinaiticus was one of the MSS affected. Ἔξωθεν is the preferred reading because of good external support, notably p[47] and A, and because it is the harder reading.[105]

Μῆνας τεσσαράκοντα δύο is an accusative of the extent of time. The period so designated is the period of Gentile triumph, of the ministry of the two witnesses, and the hiding of the woman in the wilderness.[106]

11:3 The construction καὶ δώσω . . . προφητεύσουσιν is Hebraic. It means, "I will commission or give permission to." The combination appears nowhere else in Revelation, but three other constructions with διδόναι have the same sense: (1) διδόναι with the infinitive means "to

---

103. Robertson, *Word Pictures*, 6:384.
104. See Excursus 5 at the end of this volume for a discussion of the extent of the seventh bowl, which is a part of the seventh trumpet. That seventh bowl includes the events of 19:11-21.
105. Metzger, *Textual Commentary*, p. 746.
106. Robertson, *Word Pictures*, 6:377.

permit" (2:7; 3:21; 6:4; 7:2; 13:7, 15; 16:8); (2) διδόναι with ἵνα and the subjunctive (9:5; 19:8); and (3) ἐδόθη αὐτῷ ἐξουσία ποιῆσαι (13:5; cf. John 1:12; 5:27) (Charles).

Sinaiticus and Alexandrinus, among others, have an accusative plural ending for περιβεβλημένοι rather than a nominative plural one.[107] It is better to go with the nominative reading of C, however, because the accusative is an impossible reading.

11:4 The participle ἑστῶτες is masculine nominative plural in agreement with οὗτοι, the subject of the sentence that begins v. 4. Yet the article governing the participle, αἱ is feminine in agreement with ἐλαῖαι and λυχνίαι, which it follows.[108] The position of the ἐνώπιον phrase between the article and its participle, as sometimes occurs in Revelation, probably accounts for the difference in gender (Charles).

11:5 Significant MS variations for θέλει and θελήσει include those in p⁴⁷ which reads the future indicative θελήσῃ in both places, and Ephraemi which reads θέλει instead of θελήσῃ. The present indicative and the aorist subjunctive are most probably correct, however, because both have the support of Sinaiticus, Alexandrinus, and other Greek MSS and Latin versions.

The singular στόματος is a collective use of the noun, corresponding to the collective use of πτῶμα in 11:8 to speak of two corpses (Charles).

11:6 The combination ὑετὸς βρέχῃ is unusual. The more usual has ὁ θεός as the subject of βρέχει (Matt. 5:45), or βρέχει occurs alone (James 5:17). Joel 2:23, LXX, has ὁ θεός as the understood subject of βρέξει and ὑετὸν as its direct object (Swete, Charles).

11:8 Πτῶμα is a collective noun implying a plurality of corpses. This is evident from the plural πτώματα in 11:9. Since its derivation is from πίπτω, it refers to what is fallen, especially what has been slain in battle.[109] It can thus signify that which has fallen, be it one or many (Alford).

11:9 The ἐκ phrase is partitive, implying a plural pronoun "those from among . . ." (Lenski). This implied plural is the subject of βλέπουσιν. Cf. 2:10.[110]

11:11 The article τὰς looks back to the original mention of the three and a half days in 11:9 (Charles).

Φόβος ἐπέπεσεν ἐπὶ is a Lucan phrase in the NT (cf. Luke 1:12; Acts 19:17), but it also has an OT counterpart (cf. Ex. 15:16; Ps. 54[55]:5) (Charles).

107. Ibid., 6:378.
108. Swete, *Apocalypse*, p. 135; Robertson, *Word Pictures*, 6:378.
109. Robertson, *Word Pictures*, 6:380.
110. Charles, *Revelation*, 1:288; Robertson, *Word Pictures*, 6:381.

Θεωροῦντας and ἐθεώρησαν (11:12) are the only occurrences of θεωρέω in Revelation, but the verb appears more than twenty times in John's other writings. Revelation uses other words in its place: ὁράω (2 times), ὄψεσθαι (3 times), εἶδον (56 times), and βλέπειν (12 times) (Charles).

11:12 A case can be made for the reading ἤκουσα rather than ἤκουσαν because John uses the first person singular of ἀκούω about twenty-five other times throughout the book. In addition, the first person has respectable MS support, including p47. The third person plural of ἀκούω has stronger external support, including Sinaiticus, Alexandrinus, and Ephraemi. It is also the harder reading because of the frequency of the first person in this book. Since it fits well with the ongoing narration of the voice of 11:1, ἤκουσαν is the preferred reading.[111]

---

111. Alford, *Greek Testament*, 4:665; Charles, *Revelation*, 1:290; Robertson, *Word Pictures*, 6:383; Lenski, *Revelation*, p. 348.

16
The Seventh Trumpet and Background of the Seven Bowls Begun

The sounding of the seventh trumpet brings a great heavenly celebration over the anticipated establishment of God's kingdom on earth (11:15-19), but a disclosure of the subject matter of the trumpet awaits an extensive examination of background matters (12:1–14:20) necessary to comprehend that trumpet's contents once they are divulged. This chapter will treat the sounding of the trumpet (11:15-19) and the beginning of the background discussion (12:1-18), with the remainder of the background data (13:1–14:20) reserved for the next chapter of the commentary.

10. THE SEVENTH TRUMPET: THE SEVEN BOWLS AWAITED (11:15-19)

Translation

15And the seventh angel sounded; and there came great voices in heaven, saying,
"The kingdom of the world has become [that] of our Lord and of His Christ,
and He will reign forever and ever."
16And the twenty-four elders who were before God sitting upon their thrones fell on their faces and worshiped God, 17saying,
"We give thanks to you, Lord God Almighty, who is and who was,
because you have taken your great power
and begun to reign;

¹⁸and the nations were enraged,
and your wrath came
and the time for the dead to be judged
and to give the reward to your slaves the prophets
and to the saints, even to those who fear your name,
the small and the great,
and to destroy the destroyers of the earth."
¹⁹And the temple of God which is in heaven, was opened, and the ark of His covenant in His temple appeared; and there came [bolts of] lightning and voices, and [peals of] thunder and an earthquake and great hail.

Exegesis and Exposition

11:15 Word about the second woe's conclusion and third woe's imminent arrival (11:14) bids the seventh trumpet-angel to act, thereby resuming the progressive movement following the intercalation of 10:1–11:14: Καὶ ὁ ἕβδομος ἄγγελος ἐσάλπισεν· καὶ ἐγένοντο φωναὶ μεγάλαι ἐν τῷ οὐρανῷ λέγοντες (*Kai ho hebdomos angelos esalpisen; kai egenonto phōnai megalai en tō ouranō legontes*, "And the seventh angel sounded; and there came great voices in heaven, saying"). He sounds his trumpet, yet, as with the seventh seal (8:2-5), no earthly activity of judgment resumes immediately. Instead a dramatic heavenly announcement (11:15*b*) and hymn of thanksgiving (11:16-18) follow at once. Then comes an extended presentation, beginning in heaven and telling of the inner movements that lie behind this climax of human history (11:19–14:20) yet to be described (15:1 ff.).[1]

The absence of any immediate visitation against the earth-dwellers until chapter 16 is indicative of the nature of chronological progression in the fulfillment of the numbered series. Just as the seventh seal included all seven trumpets, the seventh trumpet includes all seven bowls described in 16:1 ff.[2] This "telescoping" of the bowls for incorporation as part of the seventh trumpet agrees with the earlier revelation that the seventh trumpet is not a momentary happening, but occupies a period of time (cf. 10:7). This among other dissimilarities differentiates it from "the last trumpet" of 1 Cor. 15:51-52 (Bullinger, Walvoord).

Because of what will eventually occur after "the various under-

---

1. Martin Kiddle, *The Revelation of St. John*, HNTC (New York: Harper, 1940), pp. 211-12.
2. E. W. Bullinger, *The Apocalypse* or *"The Day of the Lord,"* (London Eyre and Spottiswoode, n.d.), pp. 368-69; George E. Ladd, *A Commentary on the Revelation of John* (Grand Rapids: Eerdmans, 1972), p. 160; see also Excursus 3 at the end of this volume.

plots"³ of chapters 12-14 work themselves out, an outburst of praise accompanies the sounding of the trumpeter.⁴ The voices uttering the hymn are in heaven, and they are loud—φωναὶ μεγάλαι ἐν τῷ οὐρανῷ (*phōnai megalai en tō ouranō*, "great voices in heaven"). This is quite a contrast to the silence in heaven that followed the opening of the seventh seal (8:1).⁵ Whose voices they are is unrevealed, the same indefiniteness prevailing as in 12:10 and 19:6 where φωνή (*phōnē*, "voice") is singular instead of plural as here.⁶ The voices should not be limited to a single category of angels such as the living beings (4:8) or the living beings and twenty-four elders (5:8-10). Neither should the twenty-four elders who sing the next hymn (11:16-18) be excluded from among these singers (contra Alford). It is a response of the whole host of heaven celebrating the coming ultimate victory marked by the seventh trumpet.

John's visional location changes from earth back to heaven to enable him to hear this song, because knowledge of events celebrated in this song are at this point limited to heaven (Beckwith). This heavenly scene helps the reader of his prophecy to connect events on earth with the invisible powers which control them and to view earth's tragedies in the light of this heavenly perspective.⁷

The focus of the heavenly enthusiasm is the kingdom of God: Ἐγένετο ἡ βασιλεία τοῦ κόσμου τοῦ κυρίου ἡμῶν καὶ τοῦ Χριστοῦ αὐτοῦ, καὶ βασιλεύσει εἰς τοὺς αἰῶνας τῶν αἰώνων (*Egeneto hē basileia tou kosmou tou kyriou hēmōn kai tou Christou autou, kai basileusei eis tous aiōnas tōn aiōnōn*, "The kingdom of the world has become [that] of our Lord and of His Christ, and He will reign forever and ever"). Attempts to identify βασιλεία (*basileia*, "kingdom") as the church of the present era by assigning it an abstract sense⁸ are futile, because an abstract sense for the noun is impossible when τοῦ κόσμου (*tou kosmou*, "the world") follows immediately in assigning a realm over which the rule

---

3. Henry Alford, *The Greek Testament* (London: Longmans, Greek, 1903), 4:664.
4. Isbon T. Beckwith, *The Apocalypse of John* (New York: Macmillan, 1919), p. 274.
5. William Lee, "The Revelation of St. John," in *The Holy Bible*, ed. F. C. Cook (London: John Murray, 1881), 4:643; Archibald Thomas Robertson, *Word Pictures in the New Testament*, 6 vols. (Nashville: Broadman, 1933), 6:384.
6. Leon Morris, *The Revelation of St. John*, TNTC (Grand Rapids: Eerdmans, 1969), pp. 152-53; Robert H. Mounce, *The Book of Revelation*, NICNT (Grand Rapids: Eerdmans, 1977), p. 230.
7. Henry Barclay Swete, *The Apocalypse of St. John* (London: Macmillan, 1906), pp. 145-46.
8. G. R. Beasley-Murray, *The Book of Revelation*, NCB (Grand Rapids: Eerdmans, 1978), p. 188; David Chilton, *The Days of Vengeance* (Fort Worth, Tex.: Dominion, 1987), pp. 287-88.

extends. Nor can the singular number of the noun support an abstract sense (i.e., "royal dominion"). The singular views the world as a unit, a single concrete kingdom. This world-empire, once dominated by a usurping power, has now passed into the hands of its true owner. Later celebrations in the book (12:10; 19:6) also observe this transition (Swete). The noun has a consistent concrete rather than abstract force in the NT (e.g., Matt. 4:8). Jesus will return and assume the throne of His father David in this future crisis, at which time He will replace the satanically energized sovereignty of world rulers that has prevailed for so long.[9] The whole theme of Revelation is the purging of evil from the world so that it can become the domain of the King of kings (cf. 19:16). Only a physical kingdom on earth will satisfy this.

The aorist verb ἐγένετο (*egeneto*, "has become") is proleptic. The replacement of the kingdom of the world in fulfillment does not occur chronologically at this point in the series of visions. Rather, the perspective of the verb tense is a point after the action of the seventh trumpet will have run its course.[10] This event is future from the point of progress reached in the series, but the verb views it as an already accomplished fact (cf. Luke 19:9).[11] The seventh trumpet triggers an anticipation of the final triumph when the future visible kingdom of God on earth will become a reality, when a transference of power from the heathen nations to God, as described in Psalm 2, will come.[12] This change has not yet happened, but the time has come for it to happen (Alford). This use of the aorist tense conveys the absolute certainty of these future transactions by speaking of them as already past (Mounce).

The new rulers of the domain of the earth are τοῦ κυρίου ἡμῶν καὶ τοῦ Χριστοῦ αὐτοῦ (*tou kyriou hēmōn kai tou Christou autou*, "[that] of our Lord and of His Christ"). Κυρίου (*Kyriou*, "Lord") is a title for God the Father as the later αὐτοῦ (*autou*, "His") shows. In the NT κύριος (*kyrios*, "Lord") more often refers to Christ, but in Revelation, it designates the Father more frequently.[13] Χριστοῦ (*Christou*, "Christ") refers to Jesus, of course. He is the Father's Anointed One (cf. Luke 2:26;

---

9. J. B. Smith, *A Revelation of Jesus Christ* (Scottdale, Pa.: Herald, 1961), p. 178.
10. R. H. Charles, *The Revelation of St. John*, ICC (New York: Scribner's Sons, 1920), 1:294; Kiddle, *Revelation*, p. 207.
11. Friedrich Düsterdieck, *Critical and Exegetical Handbook to the Revelation of John*, in Meyer's Commentary, trans. and ed. Henry Jacobs (New York: Funk & Wagnalls, 1887), pp. 328-39; Robertson, *Word Pictures*, 6:384.
12. Swete, *Apocalypse*, p. 142; Ladd, *Revelation*, p. 161; Beasley-Murray, *Revelation*, p. 188; Alan F. Johnson, "Revelation," in *EBC*, ed. Frank E. Gaebelein (Grand Rapids: Zondervan, 1981), 12:509.
13. Morris, *Revelation*, p. 153; Robertson, *Word Pictures*, 6:384.

9:20; Acts 4:26).[14] "The Lord and His Anointed (or Christ)" echoes Ps. 2:2, which early in Christian church history received a Messianic interpretation (Charles, Mounce). Themes from Psalm 2 recur frequently in Revelation (cf. 2:27; 12:5, 10; 14:1; 16:14; 17:18; 19:15, 19).[15] The psalm will have its final fulfillment when the Anointed is victor over all the kings of the earth (cf. Ps. 2:9; Rev. 19:17-21) (Smith).

In consequence of the acquisition of the kingdom of the world, the Father and His Christ will rule eternally (βασιλεύσει εἰς τοὺς αἰῶνας τῶν αἰώνων [*basileusei eis tous aiōnas tōn aiōnōn*, "He will reign forever and ever"]). The unity of the joint sovereignty accounts for the singular βασιλεύσει (*basileusei*, "He will reign") (cf. Eph. 5:5) (Beasley-Murray, Mounce). When the Father rules, so does the Son. Sequentially speaking, the kingdom of the Son will ultimately merge with that of the Father (cf. 1 Cor. 15:24, 27-28) (Swete). The eternal nature of this kingdom (εἰς τοὺς αἰῶνας τῶν αἰώνων [*eis tous aiōnas tōn aiōnōn*, "forever and ever"]) harks back to Dan. 2:44; 7:14, 27 (cf. Luke 1:33) (Beckwith, Charles). The heavenly throng is exuberant over this momentous occasion, and rightly so.

It is evident that this looks forward to divine rule in the new creation (22:3-5) (Beasley-Murray). The eternal duration of the kingdom requires this. But whether or not it has the millennial reign over the present creation (20:1-10) in view needs clarification. Since earlier promises to the redeemed include reigning on earth (5:10), this prediction of an eternal reign must include the millennial or earthly phase of Christ's future reign. The central theme of Revelation is the establishment of God's kingdom on earth (Ladd). In addition, OT anticipations from which John draws many of his concepts include the eventual passing of the rule over earth into God's hands (Dan. 2:35, 44; 4:3; 6:26; 7:14, 26-27; Zech. 14:9).[16] Paul also looked forward to a future kingdom in two phases (1 Cor. 15:24-28). The closing chapters of the Apocalypse refer specifically to these two phases, one a kingdom on the earth (20:1-10) and another a kingdom in God's new creation (21:1–22:5). This heavenly announcement must include both.

11:16 One segment of the heavenly throng follows up the dramatic announcement with a song of worship and thanksgiving: καὶ οἱ εἴκοσι τέσσαρες πρεσβύτεροι [οἱ] ἐνώπιον τοῦ θεοῦ καθήμενοι ἐπὶ τοὺς θρόνους αὐτῶν ἔπεσαν ἐπὶ τὰ πρόσωπα αὐτῶν καὶ προσεκύνησαν τῷ θεῷ (*kai hoi eikosi tessares presbyteroi [hoi] enōpion tou theou kathēmenoi epi tous*

---

14. Beckwith, *Apocalypse*, p. 609; Robertson, *Word Pictures*, 6:385.
15. J. P. M. Sweet, *Revelation* (Philadelphia: Westminster, Pelican, 1979), p. 191.
16. John F. Walvoord, *The Revelation of Jesus Christ* (Chicago: Moody, 1966), p. 184.

thronous autōn epesan epi ta prosōpa autōn kai prosekynēsan tō theō, "and the twenty-four elders who were before God sitting upon their thrones fell on their faces and worshiped God"). It has been some time since the elders entered the ongoing action of the book. The last time was when one of the group functioned as an angelic revealer to explain to John the identity of the innumerable multitude in heaven (7:13-14). This time the whole group falls in worship of God as they have previously (4:10; 5:8, 14), this time the added ἐπὶ τὰ πρόσωπα αὐτῶν (*epi ta prosōpa autōn*, "on their faces") dramatizing their worship more graphically. This like all the other worship scenes in Revelation (chaps. 4-5; 7:9-12; 8:3-4; 14:2-5; 15:2-4; 16:5-7; 19:1-8; 22:1-5) transpires in heaven.[17]

11:17 Their song is one of thanksgiving: λέγοντες, Εὐχαριστοῦμέν σοι, κύριε ὁ θεὸς ὁ παντοκράτωρ, ὁ ὢν καὶ ὁ ἦν, ὅτι εἴληφας τὴν δύναμίν σου τὴν μεγάλην καὶ ἐβασίλευσας (*legontes, Eucharistoumen soi, kyrie ho theos ho pantokratōr, ho ōn kai ho ēn, hoti eilēphas tēn dynamin sou tēn megalēn kai ebasileusas*, "saying, 'We give thanks to you, Lord God Almighty, who is and who was, because you have taken your great power and begun to reign'"). The thanks expresses gratitude for God's answer to the prayers of the saints in the form of the trumpets, the seventh of which has just sounded (Alford). The verb εὐχαριστέω (*eucharisteō*, "I give thanks") appears only here in Revelation, but John uses it three times in his gospel (John 6:11, 23; 11:41) (Lee).

The combination κύριε ὁ θεὸς ὁ παντοκράτωρ (*kyrie ho theos ho pantokratōr*, "Lord God Almighty") as a title for God is frequent in this book (1:8; 4:8; 15:3; 16:7; 19:6; 21:22). Παντοκράτωρ (*Pantokratōr*, "Almighty") occurs twice with ὁ θεὸς (*ho theos*, "God"), but without κύριος (*kyrios*, "Lord") (16:14; 19:15). It contributes the thought that none can resist His power. It appropriately speaks of God's all-embracing sovereignty (Morris), a sovereignty that at the point of the song's perspective becomes a visible reality in asserting its direct rule over the world.

The expression ὁ ὢν καὶ ὁ ἦν (*ho ōn kai ho ēn*, "who is and who was") focuses upon God's uninterrupted existence in the present and past. In the future He will be the same as He reigns "forever and ever." A third part of the title—ὁ ἐρχόμενος (*ho erchomenos*, "who is coming") that appeared earlier (1:4, 8; 4:8)—drops out, because at the moment anticipated in the song, He has already come (cf. 16:5).[18] The

---

17. Marianne Meye Thompson, "Worship in the Book of Revelation," *Ex Auditou* 8 (1992): 48-49.
18. Lee, "Revelation," 4:644; Charles, *Revelation*, 1:295; Beckwith, *Apocalypse*, p. 609; James Moffatt, "The Revelation of St. John the Divine," in *The Expositor's Greek Testament*, ed. W. Robertson Nicoll (Grand Rapids: Eerdmans, n.d.), 5:420.

kingdom Jesus told His disciples to pray for (Matt. 6:10) has arrived in connection with the second coming of the King (Bullinger). The song continues by giving the reason for (ὅτι [*hoti*, "because"]) the thanksgiving. God has seized direct control of the world. Εἴληφας (*Eilēphas*, "you have taken") is perfect tense in contrast with the aorist ἐβασίλευσας (*ebasileusas*, "begun to reign"). The perfect tense pictures the permanence of His control (Morris). A perfect of λαμβάνω (*lambanō*, "I take") in contrast with an aorist occurs at 3:3; 5:7; 8:5 also.[19] "Your great power" (τὴν δύναμίν σου τὴν μεγάλην [*tēn dynamin sou tēn megalēn*]) is the final and overwhelming display of power through which God will overwhelm His enemies (Swete, Mounce). The almighty One until this time allows anti-Christian power to control the world, but after the future climax, His direct control will be in place.[20]

The aorist of ἐβασίλευσας (*ebasileusas*, "[have] begun to reign") is ingressive as well as proleptic.[21] From a future vantage point when the reign will have begun, the singers look back to the reign's starting point. This is none other than the visible establishment of God's reign over hostile powers through the vanquishing of all hostile powers (Ladd, Kiddle, Beasley-Murray). The effort to equate this reign with the church age following A.D. 70 and to say that the events of 11:18 are those leading up to the destruction of Jerusalem in that year rests on an extremely allegorical treatment which finds no justification in the text itself.[22]

11:18 The twenty-four elders also sing about the response of the nations and the implementation of God's wrath and of judgment of the dead: καὶ τὰ ἔθνη ὠργίσθησαν, καὶ ἦλθεν ἡ ὀργή σου καὶ ὁ καιρὸς τῶν νεκρῶν κριθῆναι καὶ δοῦναι τὸν μισθὸν τοῖς δούλοις σου τοῖς προφήταις καὶ τοῖς ἁγίοις καὶ τοῖς φοβουμένοις τὸ ὄνομά σου, τοὺς μικροὺς καὶ τοὺς μεγάλους, καὶ διαφθεῖραι τοὺς διαφθείροντας τὴν γῆν (*kai ta ethnē ōrgisthēsan, kai ēlthen hē orgē sou kai ho kairos tōn nekrōn krithēnai kai dounai ton misthon tois doulois sou tois prophētais kai tois hagiois kai tois phoboumenois to onoma sou, tous mikrous kai tous megalous, kai diaphtheirai tous diaphtheirontas tēn gēn*, "and the nations were enraged, and your wrath came and the time for the dead to be judged [came] and to give the reward to your slaves the prophets and to the saints, even to those who fear your name, the small and the great, and

---

19. Swete, *Apocalypse*, p. 143; Robertson, *Word Pictures*, 6:385.
20. Düsterdieck, *Revelation*, pp. 329-30.
21. Robertson, *Word Pictures*, 6:385; Kiddle, *Revelation*, p. 208; Smith, *Revelation*, p. 178. Other proleptic aorists in the song are ἐγένετο (v. 15), ὠργίσθησαν, and ἦλθεν (v. 18) (Beckwith, *Apocalypse*, p. 609; Ladd, *Revelation*, p. 162).
22. Contra Chilton, *Days of Vengeance*, pp. 290-93.

to destroy the destroyers of the earth"). The institution of the hated kingdom of God provokes a defiant rage from the nations (Lee). The verb ὠργίσθησαν (*ōrgisthēsan*, "were enraged") denotes the hostility of the nations of the world against God. Their wrath is quite distinct from the wrath of God by which these same people were terrified (6:17) (Moffatt). The wrath of men is wicked; the wrath of God is holy (Walvoord).

Eventually they will demonstrate their wrath by assembling in great armies to oppose God (16:14, 16, 19; 20:8-9).[23] This last great assault against divine power looks back again to Psalm 2 (cf. 11:15; Ps. 2:1, 5, 12) (Beckwith). The Jerusalem church in Acts 4:25-28 applied Psalm 2 to the treatment of Christ by Herod Antipas, Pontius Pilate, and others, but here the outlook is wider and the fulfillment more ultimate (Swete). This part of the elders' song is reminiscent of the promise to the overcomers in Thyatira, whose promise is to share in the infliction of punishment on the nations (2:26-27) (Kiddle).

The next line of the song is a proleptic statement of the coming of God's wrath (ἦλθεν ἡ ὀργή σου [*ēlthen hē orgē sou*, "your wrath came"]). God's wrath is more than a match for the wrath of the nations. Ὀργή (*Orgē*, "Wrath") is the consistent word in other NT books to prophesy the coming of this wrath (cf. Matt. 3:7; Luke 3:7; Rom. 2:5, 8; 5:9; 1 Thess. 1:10; 5:9) (Smith). The outpouring of God's wrath spells the end of worldly rebellion against God.

The sense of ἦλθεν (*ēlthen*, "came") carries into the next line of the hymn: "the time for the dead to be judged [came]" (ὁ καιρὸς τῶν νεκρῶν κριθῆναι [*ho kairos tōn nekrōn krithēnai*]). Καιρὸς (*Kairos*, "Time") carries the force of "the right time or season" (cf. Mark 11:13; Luke 21:24). Judgment comes only when the time is ripe (Swete, Morris, Johnson). Two other infinitives besides κριθῆναι (*krithēnai*, "to be judged") in the remainder of v. 18 add to the identification of this *kairos*. They are δοῦναι (*dounai*, "to give") and διαφθεῖραι (*diaphtheirai*, "to destroy").[24] In addition to judgment, it is also the right season to give rewards to the faithful and to destroy those who destroy the earth. The judgment of the dead is the first event of the "fitting time."

The judgment of all men at the Great White Throne (20:11-15) is the event seen by some in this reference (e.g., Lee, Charles, Lenski), but a closer look at the Great White Throne will reflect that it is the judgment of the wicked only. The inclusive nature of the judgment is correct, however, because the remainder of v. 18 speaks of both groups, the righteous and the wicked. The elders in their song make no attempt

---

23. Smith, *Revelation*, p. 179; Charles Caldwell Ryrie, *Revelation*, Everyman's Bible Commentary (Chicago: Moody, 1968), p. 75.
24. Düsterdieck, *Revelation*, p. 330; Johnson, "Revelation," 12:509.

to separate the different phases of judgment as they are separated in the closing chapters of Revelation. They simply sing of that future judgment as though it were one event, much on the order of other Scriptures that do not distinguish future judgments from each other (cf. Mark 4:29; John 5:25, 28-29; Acts 17:31; 24:21) (Swete).

The distribution of rewards will, of course, be a part of the judgment. Μισθὸν (*Misthon*, "Reward") is what is due to each person. The payment of it is for everyone an act of God's grace, but rewards will vary in proportion to the works of the recipient (cf. Rom. 4:4; 1 Cor. 3:8) (Swete, Morris). Revelation 21:9–22:5 in particular describes the reward of the faithful (Mounce). The recipients have an extended designation: τοῖς δούλοις σου τοῖς προφήταις καὶ τοῖς ἁγίοις καὶ τοῖς φοβουμένοις τὸ ὄνομά σου, τοὺς μικροὺς καὶ τοὺς μεγάλους (*tois doulois sou tois prophētais kai tois hagiois kai tois phoboumenois to onoma sou, tous mikrous kai tous megalous*, "your slaves the prophets and to the saints, even to those who fear your name, the small and the great"). A division of this compound expression into three groups—the prophets, Jewish Christians (i.e., "saints"), and Gentile Christians (i.e., "those who fear your name")—has the merit of usage in the book of Acts on its side. In Acts οἱ φοβούμενοι τὸν θεόν (*hoi phoboumenoi ton theon*, "those who fear God") frequently denotes Gentiles who as proselytes attached themselves to Jewish synagogues (e.g., Acts 13:16, 43) (Swete). Yet usage in another NT author and from a different era of Christian history is out of place in a book that makes no such distinction between Jewish and Gentile Christians (Beckwith, Moffatt, Lenski).

The better course is to understand two groups of reward recipients, the prophets and the saints, by understanding the καί (*kai*) following ἁγίοις (*hagiois*, "saints") to have the ascensive meaning "even" (Beckwith, Ladd, Mounce). It is important, however, to distinguish the two from each other.[25] The sense of "the prophets and the rest of the saints" has the disadvantages of not limiting τοῖς δούλοις σου (*tois doulois sou*, "your slaves") to the prophets only and of applying τοῖς φοβουμένοις τὸ ὄνομά σου (*tois phoboumenois to onoma sou*, "those who fear your name") to the prophets as well as the saints. Both of these present very unusual combinations. "Your servants the prophets" is a well-known OT designation for OT prophets (e.g., 2 Kings 9:7; 17:13, 23; 21:10; 24:2; Dan. 9:6, 10) (Bullinger). The designations δοῦλοι (*douloi*, "slaves) and ἅγιοι (*hagioi*, "saints") nowhere else apply to the same group in the same passage. Δοῦλος (*Doulos*, "Slave") in Revelation has a nontechnical use to refer to Christians in general, but it

---

25. Beckwith, *Apocalypse*, pp. 610, 687.

also has a technical use to refer to the prophets only. Revelation 1:1 illustrates both uses of the word. In the present verse, the meaning must be technical to refer to the prophets only, resulting in two categories, "your slaves the prophets" on the one hand and on the other "the saints, even to those who fear your name."

Another problematic issue is the identity of these prophets. The linking of prophets with apostles in 18:20 and the angel's reference to them as "your [John's] brethren" in 22:9 shows the impossibility of excluding NT prophets from the term.[26] Their responsibility as vehicles of divine revelation distinguishes them from the saints in general. On the other side, however, "prophets" in 10:7 certainly included and was probably limited to OT prophets. "Your servants the prophets" has an OT ring to it, as cited above. The following rationale indicates that the two meanings do not mutually exclude each other. In Rev. 1:1, John by referring to himself as a *doulos* takes his place alongside the OT prophets. By the time of this writing, deaths of the other apostles had thrust NT prophecy into the limelight,[27] even to the point of making the NT prophet equal in authority with OT prophets. So the probable solution here is to see a reference to OT prophets primarily, but not to exclude NT prophets from the picture completely. The latter take their place in being grouped with that former prestigious company.

"The small and the great" (τοὺς μικροὺς καὶ τοὺς μεγάλους [*tous mikrous kai tous megalous*]) applies to "the saints" only. John is fond of referring to these two categories of humanity (cf. 13:16; 19:5, 18; 20:12).[28] In this case, it means that the lowliest slave among the converts of Christ will receive the same consideration as a convert of imperial rank (cf. Ps. 115:13) (Swete).

The "fitting time" (καιρὸς [*kairos*]) when the dead are judged and the faithful are rewarded will also be the occasion of destruction of earth's destroyers (διαφθεῖραι τοὺς διαφθείροντας τὴν γῆν [*diaphtheirai tous diaphtheirontas tēn gēn*]). Two ideas of who these destroyers are have them as destroyers of every kind (Swete, Lenski) and more specifically the Roman Empire of John's day picturing the forces of the last days (Mounce). Neither view does justice to the specific details of Revelation. The latitude of the expression far exceeds a reference to Rome, and the details of the visions do not allow a reference to just any destroying force. Another viewpoint limits the reference to those alive on earth who rebel against God in the future period just before Christ's

---

26. D. E. Aune, *Prophecy in Early Christianity and the Ancient Mediterranean World* (Grand Rapids: Eerdmans, 1983), p. 196.
27. Aune, *Prophecy in Early Christianity*, p. 197; Mounce, *Revelation*, p. 232.
28. Robertson, *Word Pictures*, 6:386.

return (Walvoord), but this is too restrictive. Chronological sequence is not that critical in this song of the elders. The expression must be broad enough to include all agencies of evil (Beasley-Murray). It better agrees with the context of Revelation to identify the destroyers as Babylon, the beast, the false prophet, and Satan (Charles, Johnson). "Those who destroy" must include Babylon because of the allusion to Jer. 51:25 and the similar identification of Babylon in 19:2 (Smith). Furthermore, it is the destruction of these entities that precedes the final establishment of the kingdom (19:17-21; 20:10) (Kiddle).

11:19 Immediately after the conclusion of the elders' hymn of thanksgiving, the ark of the covenant in the heavenly sanctuary appears: καὶ ἠνοίγη ὁ ναὸς τοῦ θεοῦ ὁ ἐν τῷ οὐρανῷ, καὶ ὤφθη ἡ κιβωτὸς τῆς διαθήκης αὐτοῦ ἐν τῷ ναῷ αὐτοῦ· καὶ ἐγένοντο ἀστραπαὶ καὶ φωναὶ καὶ βρονταὶ καὶ σεισμὸς καὶ χάλαζα μεγάλη (*kai ēnoigē ho naos tou theou ho en tō ouranō, kai ōphthē hē kibōtos tēs diathēkēs autou en tō naō autou; kai egenonto astrapai kai phōnai kai brontai kai seismos kai chalaza megalē*, "and the temple of God which is in heaven, was opened, and the ark of His covenant in His temple appeared; and there came [bolts of] lightning and voices, and [peals of] thunder and an earthquake and great hail"). Verse 19 is a transition verse having a close connection with what precedes and with what follows. If it connects more closely with what follows, it begins a new section. In favor of this division is the stylistic shift from the more usual εἶδον (*eidon*, "I saw") to ὤφθη (*ōphthē*, "appeared") in v. 19 as well as in 12:1, 3 (Moffatt). Verse 19 also relates closely to what is about to be disclosed (Scott). Yet a greater structural break comes with the appearance of "the great sign" in 12:1. Also, the occurrence of the storm theophany as in v. 19*b* usually marks the end rather than the beginning of a new vision.

It is better to view v. 19 as the response to the hymn of vv. 17-18 (Beckwith, Lenski, Ladd, Morris). The ark of the covenant corresponds to the rewarding of the faithful and the cosmic disturbances to the outpouring of God's wrath in that song (Mounce). This is a solemn view of the temple from which the judgment of the dead proceeds (cf. 14:15, 17; 15:5-8; 16:7) (Alford). It is a fitting inauguration of God's final judgments as it is a conclusion for the series initiated by the seventh trumpet.

The prolepticism that characterizes vv. 15-18 applies to ἠνοίγη (*ēnoigē*, "was opened") also. The opening of the temple is very probably the same as the one in 15:5 where the chronological progression resumes with the introduction of the seven bowls.[29] Symbolically it

---

29. Düsterdieck, *Revelation*, p. 331.

means that after the series has run its course human beings will enjoy unmediated fellowship with God (cf. Rev. 21:3) (Ladd). The ναὸς (*naos*, "temple") is now the celestial heavenly temple, the one presupposed but not specifically mentioned in the scenery of chapters 4-5 (cf. 3:12; 7:15; 15:5 ff.) (Moffatt). The sanctuary on earth (11:1) differs from it. It is the point where the prayers of the saints ascended (8:3-4) and from which God's acts of vengeance proceed (8:5; 15:5-8) (Alford). With this as the source and with the appearance of the ark of the covenant, it is clear that the judgments to come relate to the restoration of God's people Israel and the fulfillment of all His covenant promises to them (cf. Gen. 15; 2 Sam. 7) (Bullinger).

"The ark of His covenant" (ἡ κιβωτὸς τῆς διαθήκης αὐτοῦ [*hē kibōtos tēs diathēkēs autou*]) has a rich biblical history. It symbolizes God's presence and the place of atonement (cf. Lev. 16:2 ff.; Heb. 9:3 ff.; 10:20), but used wrongly, it becomes the source of the Philistines' plagues (cf. 1 Sam. 4:8) and Jericho's fall (Josh. 6:1-20) (Sweet). Its proper place was within the second veil of the tabernacle (Heb. 9:4, 24) and in the inner chamber of Solomon's temple (1 Kings 8:6). This scene is of the heavenly counterpart of that earthly ark. John views heaven under the same ritual categories as those found in the OT, with the understanding that the originals of those sacred things on earth exist in heaven (Moffatt, Morris). At some point during OT times the earthly ark disappeared, perhaps perishing when Nebuchadnezzar burned the temple (2 Kings 25:9; Jer. 3:16)[30] or being removed by Shishak (1 Kings 14:26) or Manasseh (2 Chron. 33:7).[31] A tradition has it that Jeremiah hid the ark in a cave on Mount Sinai until the final restoration of Israel (*2 Macc.* 2:4-8). The disappearance of the ark signified a temporary setback that had to be corrected before the bliss of the final consummation. For a Jewish Christian prophet, therefore, this appearance of the heavenly ark indicated that the Messianic crisis was now at hand, God's covenant people and His dealings on their behalf being central subjects of the visions to follow (Alford, Moffatt, Johnson).

The usual storm theophany closes the heavenly response to the seventh trumpet's sounding. Ἀστραπαὶ καὶ φωναὶ καὶ βρονταὶ καὶ σεισμὸς καὶ χάλαζα μεγάλη (*Astrapai kai phōnai kai brontai kai seismos kai chalaza megalē*, "[Bolts of] lightning and voices, and [peals of] thunder and an earthquake and great hail") manifest the divine presence (cf. Ex. 19:16-19; Rev. 4:5; 16:18) (Swete, Ladd) and wrathful judgment of God (Rev. 8:5; 10:3; 16:18) (Beckwith). These combined

---

30. Robertson, *Word Pictures*, 6:386; Mounce, *Revelation*, p. 233.
31. G. V. A. Caird, *A Commentary on the Revelation of St. John the Divine*, HNTC (New York: Harper & Row, 1966), p. 144.

with the first view into the heavenly ναὸς (*naos*, "temple") and the revelation of the long-lost ark of the covenant make this an unusually decisive moment (Moffatt). These phenomena, particularly the earthquake and hailstorm, will come up for further mention in 16:18, 21 (Kiddle).

Additional Notes

11:15 Λέγοντες is a masculine participle to agree with the natural gender of those speaking. Grammatical agreement would have called for a feminine participle to modify φωναί. Personifications of a voice by natural agreement occur at 4:1 and 9:13-14 also.[32]

Τοῦ κόσμου is an objective genitive: "the kingdom over the world." In 17:18 ἐπί is used in place of the objective genitive.[33]

The two genitives τοῦ κυρίου . . . τοῦ Χριστοῦ require that the sense of ἡ βασιλεία be repeated with them.[34]

The genitive of the personal pronoun ἡμῶν recalls that God is sovereign over the heavenly singers as well as over the creatures of His material creation (cf. Matt. 6:10).

11:18 Ὠργίσθησαν and ἦλθεν, like ἐβασίλευσας (v. 17), are other proleptic aorists with an ingressive force. The anger of the nations spoken of here is that which vents itself beginning in 19:19 (Smith).

The accusative case of τοὺς μικροὺς καὶ τοὺς μεγάλους is an anacoluthon, because it stands in apposition with the dative case of ἁγίοις.[35]

C. THE POURING OUT OF THE SEVEN BOWLS (12:1–18:24)

The seventh trumpet has opened the way for a revelation of the seven bowl-judgments, but for that revelation to be meaningful, a sketch of the hidden forces behind this great climax of human history and of the personages that play a part in that climax is necessary (Alford, Mounce).

1. THE BACKGROUND OF THE BOWLS (12:1–14:20)

The introductory background of the seven bowls spans back to view the initial rebellion of Satan and moves forward to show the continuous impact of that rebellion throughout human history, including in particular how it will emerge in developments leading up to

---

32. Swete, *Apocalypse*, p. 141; Robertson, *Word Pictures*, 6:384.
33. Düsterdieck, *Revelation*, p. 328.
34. Robertson, *Word Pictures*, 6:384.
35. Ibid., 6:386.

and including the triumphant return of Christ to earth. This comprehensive survey features the last three and one-half years just before that return.

a. The Woman, the Male-Child, and the Dragon (12:1-18)

Translation

¹And a great sign appeared in heaven, a woman clothed with the sun, and the moon [was] under her feet, and upon her head [was] a crown of twelve stars, ²and she was with child and cried being in travail, even being tormented to give birth. ³And another sign appeared in heaven, and behold, a great red dragon, having seven heads and ten horns and upon his heads [were] seven diadems, ⁴and his tail dragged the third [part] of the stars of heaven and cast them into the earth. And the dragon stood before the woman who was about to give birth, that when she gave birth to her child, he might devour [Him]. ⁵And she gave birth to a son, a male, who is about to destroy all nations with a rod of iron; and her child was caught away to God and to His throne. ⁶And the woman fled into the wilderness, where she has there a place prepared by God, that there they might nourish her a thousand two hundred and sixty days.

⁷And a war occurred in heaven, Michael and his angels had to make war with the dragon. And the dragon and his angels made war, ⁸and yet he did not prevail, neither was a place for them found any longer in heaven. ⁹And the great dragon, the serpent of old, who is called the Devil and Satan, who deceives the whole earth, was cast down—was cast down into the earth, and his angels were cast down with him. ¹⁰And I heard a great voice in heaven saying,

"Now have come the salvation and the power
> **and the kingdom of our God**
> **and the authority of His Christ,**
because the accuser of our brethren has been cast down,
> **who accuses them before our God day and night.**
¹¹And they themselves overcame him because of the blood of
> **the Lamb**
> **and because of the word of their testimony,**
and they did not love their life unto death.
¹²Because of this, make merry, heavens
> **and those who dwell in them;**
woe to the earth and the sea,
> **because the devil has descended to you**
having great anger,
> **knowing that he has little time."**

13And when the dragon saw that he had been cast into the earth, he pursued the woman who had given birth to the male. 14But two wings of a great eagle were given to the woman, that she might fly into the wilderness into her place, where she is nourished there a time and times and a half a time from the presence of the serpent. 15And the serpent cast from his mouth water as a river behind the woman, that he might make her [to be] swallowed up by the river. 16And the earth helped the woman, and the earth opened its mouth and drank the river which the dragon cast from his mouth. 17And the dragon was enraged at the woman, and went away to make war with the rest of her seed, who keep the commandments of God and have the testimony of Jesus; 18and he stood on the sands of the sea.36

Exegesis and Exposition

The first episode of the survey is in three parts, the first of which tells about a woman clad in the sun who gives birth to the Messiah and about the threat to the Messiah posed by a huge red dragon. Most of it deals with the past (12:1-5), but part has to do with the future (12:6). The method of narration beginning at this point differs from anything previous, because it focuses on the secret maneuvers that lie behind the visible conflict to be portrayed under the seven bowls (Kiddle). That future struggle is merely the outworking of a conflict between God and Satan that has lasted throughout history since Satan's fall. This prepares the way for all that is anti-Christian to enter the world at 13:1.37

The dragon's enmity against the Messiah (12:1-6). The first six verses of chapter 12 furnish the plot for the whole background drama. **12:1** Verse 1 introduces the woman: Καὶ σημεῖον μέγα ὤφθη ἐν τῷ οὐρανῷ, γυνὴ περιβεβλημένη τὸν ἥλιον, καὶ ἡ σελήνη ὑποκάτω τῶν ποδῶν αὐτῆς, καὶ ἐπὶ τῆς κεφαλῆς αὐτῆς στέφανος ἀστέρων δώδεκα (*Kai sēmeion mega ōphthē en tō ouranō, gynē peribeblēmenē ton hēlion, kai hē selēnē hypokatō tōn podōn autēs, kai epi tēs kephalēs autēs stephanos asterōn dōdeka*, "And a great sign appeared in heaven, a woman clothed with the sun, and the moon [was] under her feet, and upon her head [was] a crown of twelve stars"). An effort to find John's source for 12:1-6 in pagan mythology has noted the existence of a story familiar in the ancient world. A usurper doomed to be killed by a yet unborn prince plots to succeed to the throne by killing the royal seed at birth.

---

36. Verse 18 of chap. 12 in the Greek text appears in English translations as the opening part of v. 1 of chap. 13. See textual note on ἐστάθη under "Additional Notes" on 12:18.
37. Düsterdieck, *Revelation*, pp. 334-35; Charles, *Revelation*, 1:299.

In the Greek myth of the birth of Apollo, when the child's mother reached the time for delivery, she was pursued by the dragon Python who sought to kill both her and her unborn child. She found refuge, however, and four days after she gave birth to Apollo, he found Python and killed him. Similar myths existed in Egypt and Babylonia too.[38]

John may well have known of these pagan myths, but it is very doubtful that he would use them as a primary source for this account. His antagonism toward paganism reflected elsewhere in the book would forbid that he acknowledge so large an element of credibility in stories that were of pagan origin.[39] Besides, differences between the account and the myths are striking enough to eliminate the possibility that he merely borrowed the material (Morris, Johnson). The only real similarity between the two is its portrayal of a supernatural conflict between good and evil, which is the substratum of all mythologies (Beckwith, Kiddle).

Another proposal parallels the story of 12:1-6 with activities of the emperor Domitian between A.D. 80 and 90. After the death of his ten-year-old son, Domitian proclaimed the boy a god and his mother, the mother of god. Coinage from the times glorifies the son of Domitian as the lord of heaven and savior of the world.[40] The analogy of this with what 12:1-6 describes unduly limits the scope of the vision, however. If there is a connection, Domitian probably borrowed from Christian tradition rather than vice versa.

The possibility that John borrowed from a similar account in the Dead Sea Scrolls (Johnson) is remote, because John was not that familiar with the Qumran Community. John's allusions to the birth of the Messiah through the Messianic community (Isa. 9:6-7; Mic. 5:2) and to the Messianic community (Isa. 26:17; 66:7) show that the OT was a primary factor in John's thinking (cf. Isa. 54:1-6; Jer. 3:20; Ezek. 16:8-14; Hos. 2:19-20) (Mounce, Johnson). These correspondences are not specific enough to satisfy the details of what John writes here, however.

The OT passage referring to the details of this account is Gen. 37:9-11 where in Joseph's dream the sun and moon represents Jacob

---

38. Beckwith, *Apocalypse*, pp. 614-15; Kiddle, *Revelation*, pp. 215-16; Adela Y. Collins, *The Combat Myth in the Book of Revelation* (Missoula: Scholars Press, 1976), chap. 2; Beasley-Murray, *Revelation*, pp. 192-96; Johnson, "Revelation," 12:512.
39. Beckwith, *Apocalypse*, p. 615; Morris, *Revelation*, p. 156; J. Massyngberde Ford, *Revelation*, vol. 38 of AB (Garden City, N.Y.: Doubleday, 1975), p. 188; Mounce, *Revelation*, p. 235.
40. Merrill C. Tenney, *New Testament Times* (Grand Rapids: Eerdmans, 1955), pp. 334-37.

and Rachel, and the twelve stars the twelve patriarchs (Morris, Walvoord). John sees in the woman an ongoing fulfillment of the Abrahamic covenant (Walvoord). This is the only place in Scripture with anything like the description of the woman. Both Joseph and his father understood the meaning of Joseph's dream properly (Bullinger). This primary passage is the background of the vision, therefore, with the rest of the OT supplying indirect clarification.

Immediately after the storm theophany of 11:19 "a great sign" (σημεῖον μέγα [*sēmeion mega*]) confronted John. Σημεῖον (*Sēmeion*, "Sign") shows that the woman who constitutes the sign is not an actual woman, but symbolically represents some other entity or group.[41] The greatness (μέγα[42] [*mega*, "great"]) of the sign shows that it is something remarkable and very significant and vast in its appearance (Alford, Bullinger). Because of references to the sun, moon, and stars in this vision, some want to understand τῷ οὐρανῷ (*tō ouranō*, "heaven") as the sky in this instance,[43] but this is not in keeping with the usual sense of the noun in Revelation. Heaven is the location where the earlier part of the vision takes place (cf. 11:15, 19) (Charles), and heaven is the location from which the dragon is cast out a little later (cf. 12:7-9).[44] So John sees the great sign in heaven portraying events that will happen on earth (Walvoord).

The sign consists of "a woman clothed with the sun, and the moon [was] under her feet, and upon her head [was] a crown of twelve stars" (γυνὴ περιβεβλημένη τὸν ἥλιον, καὶ ἡ σελήνη ὑποκάτω τῶν ποδῶν αὐτῆς, καὶ ἐπὶ τῆς κεφαλῆς αὐτῆς στέφανος ἀστέρων δώδεκα [*gynē peribeblēmenē ton hēlion, kai hē selēnē hypokatō tōn podōn autēs, kai epi tēs kephalēs autēs stephanos asterōn dōdeka*]). The inclination to identify the woman as the Virgin Mary rests on the use of similar terminology in Matt. 1:18, 23 to describe Mary in her pregnancy and similarities in language to the prophecy of the virgin birth in Isa. 7:10-11, 14.[45] This effort faces the insurmountable obstacles of this being a symbolic woman, not a real one, and of the impossibility of this being a single individual in light of "the rest of her offspring" in 12:17.[46] The dragon's persecution of this latter group must be aimed at more than the children of one mother.

---

41. Düsterdieck, *Revelation*, p. 335.
42. The adjective μέγας occurs five more times in this chapter (vv. 3, 9, 10, 12, 14).
43. Beckwith, *Apocalypse*, pp. 616, 621; Mounce, *Revelation*, p. 236.
44. Düsterdieck, *Revelation*, p. 335; Alford, *Greek Testament*, 4:667; Beckwith, *Apocalypse*, p. 653.
45. Chilton, *Days of Vengeance*, pp. 298-99.
46. Robertson, *Word Pictures*, 6:387; Johnson, "Revelation," 12:513.

To identify the woman as God[47] is to leave unexplained how God could bring forth God and then have to flee from the dragon into the wilderness. Identifying her with the people of God from both OT and NT has the advantage of recognizing that in the course of history it was national Israel which begat the Messiah (Moffatt, Ladd, Johnson, Kiddle), but it exceeds the boundaries of justified interpretation in merging the descendants of Abraham with the church to constitute one people of God. For one thing, the woman cannot be *all* the people of God, because "the rest of her seed" in 12:17 shows that there are some in addition to her.[48] The Christian community could hardly be the mother of Jesus, but the Jewish Messiah could be regarded as a child of the Jewish community (Charles). The Messiah, born under the law, was the product of the OT people of God (cf. Gal. 4:4), but the NT church is His bride (2 Cor. 11:2; Eph. 5:25-27, 31-32). No continuity in identity from one people to the next has ever been proven (contra Johnson). Such a supposed continuity would exclude the national identity of Israel that clearly exists in the pages of the Apocalypse.

The evidence for limiting the symbolic meaning of the woman to national Israel is strong. Earlier discussion has shown the connection of various elements of the symbolism with Gen. 37:9-11 (Walvoord, Ford). The figure of Israel as a travailing woman adds to this (Isa. 26:17-18; 66:7 ff.; Jer. 4:31; 13:21; Mic. 4:10; 5:3) (Swete, Morris; Ford). Reference to the ark of the covenant in 11:19 adds to the evidence for this national identification. Another picture of the 144,000 in 14:1 ff. (cf. 7:1-8) renews the emphasis on the Jewishness of this context. It is begging the question to assert that Revelation makes no sharp distinction between the people of God in the OT and the church in the NT (contra Beckwith, Swete). That distinction has already appeared in 7:1-8 and appears once again in the great sign of the woman in chapter 12.

The woman was "clothed with the sun" (περιβεβλημένη τὸν ἥλιον [*peribeblēmenē ton hēlion*]), an allusion to Gen. 37:9-10 where the sun represented Jacob who stood in the lineage to inherit the blessings of the Abrahamic covenant (Walvoord). In the words "the moon [was] under her feet" (ἡ σελήνη ὑποκάτω τῶν ποδῶν αὐτῆς [*hē selēnē hypokatō tōn podōn autēs*]), the moon refers to Rachel, Jacob's wife and the mother of Joseph, another allusion to Gen. 37:9-10. "Upon her head [was] a crown of twelve stars" (ἐπὶ τῆς κεφαλῆς αὐτῆς στέφανος ἀστέρων δώδεκα [*epi tēs kephalēs autēs stephanon asterōn dōdeka*]) contains a clear reference to the twelve tribes of Israel, not only from Joseph's

---

47. M. Robert Mulholland, *Revelation, Holy Living in an Unholy World* (Grand Rapids: Zondervan, 1990), pp. 216-17.
48. Düsterdieck, *Revelation*, pp. 355-57.

dream (cf. Gen. 37:9-10), but also by comparison with the twelve tribes in Rev. 7:5-8 and 21:12 (Alford, Swete, Kiddle). These details of the woman's appearance clinch her identification as a representation of national Israel.

12:2 Further data regarding the woman relates to her condition: καὶ ἐν γαστρὶ ἔχουσα, καὶ* κράζει ὠδίνουσα καὶ[49] βασανιζομένη τεκεῖν (*kai en gastri echousa, kai krazei ōdinousa kai basanizomenē tekein,* "and she was with child and cried being in travail, even being tormented to give birth"). Ὠδίνουσα (⁻*Odinousa*) is a participle from the verb form of the noun ὠδίν (*ōdin*), which means "birth pangs" (cf. 1 Thess. 5:3).[50] This is the figure of Israel as a travailing woman as occurs so often in the OT (cf. Isa. 13:8; 21:3; 26:17-18; 61:7-8; 66:7 ff.; Jer. 4:31; 13:21; 22:23; Hos. 13:13; Mic. 4:10; 5:2-3).[51] Just as a woman feels the pains of childbirth, so did the nation in preparation for the coming of Christ (Lee, Kiddle). The cause of these pains, at least in part, is the persecution of the nation inspired by Satan in an attempt to stop the birth and destroy this people of God. Israel was in travail at the time of Christ's first coming (Walvoord).

The verb βασανίζω (*basanizō*, "I torment") and its cognates describes acute pain whether physical (Matt. 8:6), mental (Matt. 8:29; 2 Pet. 2:8), or metaphorical (Matt. 14:24; Mark 6:48) (Swete). Here for the only time in the NT, it refers to the pains of childbirth.[52] The infinitive τεκεῖν (*tekein*, "to give birth") tells either the purpose of the endured torment[53] or the manner or cause of it (Beckwith). Defining it as purpose accords best with possible uses of the infinitive. The birth she is awaiting is the faithful community's begetting of the Messiah. The reference is to the birth of Jesus at His first coming, but technically speaking this historical event had already occurred when John wrote. So this is a heavenly enactment of that past historical event just as other parts of this vision are enactments of events yet to occur (Walvoord, Ladd, Mounce).

12:3 The appearance of a second sign in heaven is the next thing to catch John's attention: καὶ ὤφθη ἄλλο σημεῖον ἐν τῷ οὐρανῷ, καὶ ἰδοὺ δράκων μέγας πυρρός, ἔχων κεφαλὰς ἑπτὰ καὶ κέρατα δέκα καὶ ἐπὶ τὰς κεφαλὰς αὐτοῦ ἑπτὰ διαδήματα (*kai ōphthē allo sēmeion en tō ouranō, kai idou drakōn megas pyrros, echōn kephalas hepta kai kerata deka kai*

---

49. This καί is epexegetic, because βασανιζομένη is synonymous with ὠδίνουσα (Beckwith, *Apocalypse*, p. 623).
50. Robertson, *Word Pictures*, 6:388.
51. Roger D. Aus, "The Relevance of Isaiah 667 to Revelation 12 and 2 Thessalonians 1," *ZNW* 67 (1976): 254-56.
52. Ibid.; Mounce, *Revelation*, p. 237.
53. Alford, *Greek Testament*, 4:667; Swete, *Apocalypse*, p. 149; Robertson, *Word Pictures*, 6:388.

epi tas kephalas autou hepta diadēmata, "and another sign appeared in heaven, and behold, a great red dragon, having seven heads and ten horns and upon his heads [were] seven diadems"). This second σημεῖον (*sēmeion*, "sign") followed closely after the first and was an integral part of it (Swete).

Καὶ ἰδοὺ (*Kai idou*, "And behold"), as is frequently the case in this book (e.g., 4:1; 6:2, 5, 8), calls special attention to the description of the new sign.[54] Δράκων (*Drakōn*, "Dragon"), probably derived from δέρκομαι (*derkomai*, "I see clearly"), was the name applied to a variety of great monsters in ancient mythology. Homer wrote about a creature with three heads, coiled like a serpent with a diet of poisonous herbs. The Babylonians feared a seven-headed hydra. Typhon was the Egyptian dragon which persecuted Osiris.[55] In Canaanite tradition, it was Leviathan which was closely associated with Rahab, the female monster of chaos (Mounce). These monsters picture Israel's enemies in the OT. Leviathan is Egypt in Ps. 74:14 and Assyria and Babylon in Isa. 27:1 (cf. Job 41:1-8). Pharaoh is the great monster in the rivers (Ezek. 29:3; cf. Job 7:12; Ezek. 32:2; Jer. 51:34). Sometimes Rahab was the main enemy of God's people (Isa. 51:9; Job 26:12-13; Ps. 89:10). On occasion, it was Behemoth (Job 40:15-24) and on others, the serpent (Amos 9:3) (Beckwith, Charles, Lenski, Mounce). John prefers to speak of Satan as a dragon because of the fierceness of dragons in Hebrew thought (cf. 12:4, 7, 9, 13, 16, 17; 13:2, 4, 11; 16:13; 20:2) (Swete).

Establishing the identity of the dragon as Satan is not difficult because of explicit statements of who he is in 12:9 and 20:2 (Alford, Scott, Walvoord). The only attempt to say that he is any other than Satan makes a connection with the Roman Empire. Because of similarity between descriptions in 12:3 and 13:1 and Dan. 7:7-8, 24, some view the dragon to be a combination of the empire and satanic power (Alford, Walvoord). The clear identification of 12:9 eliminates the possibility of this dual meaning.

The dragon is "great" (μέγας [*megas*]) and "red" (πυρρός [*pyrros*]). In other words, he is large and either "flame-colored" to denote destruction (cf. 9:17) or "blood-red" denoting murder (cf. John 8:44; 1 John 3:12) (Swete, Lee). *Pyrros*, occurring elsewhere in the NT only at 6:4, adds to the expression of the dragon's terrible appearance and fierce and cruel nature. Red is the color of blood and harmonizes with his murderous intentions to kill the offspring of the woman.[56] His

---

54. Robertson, *Word Pictures*, 6:388.
55. Ibid.; Ivan M. Benson, "Revelation 12 and the Dragon of Antiquity," *ResQ* 29, no. 2 (1987): 97-100.
56. Moses Stuart, *A Commentary on the Apocalypse* (Edinburgh: Macmachlan, Stewart, 1847), p. 621; Beckwith, *Apocalypse*, p. 623; John Peter Lange, *The*

great size finds confirmation in his control over a third of the stars of heaven (v. 4).[57]

The dragon's seven heads with diadems and his ten horns are a bit ambiguous, because the description does not give the location of the ten horns. If the seven heads stand for seven successive world empires, the ten horns must be on the seventh head to agree with Daniel's placement of the ten horns at the end of time (Dan. 7:24). A full discussion of what the heads, horns, and diadems represent is premature before an examination of 17:9-10, but a few preliminary observations are in order here. To say that they merely represent the great power of the dragon (Lenski, Morris, Ladd) does not fairly represent the details given about them in chapters 13 and 17. The parallel references in 13:1 and Dan. 7:7-8, 20, 24 indicate a connection with a future world empire, perhaps a revived Roman Empire (Walvoord). Repetition of some of the details of the description in 13:1 shows the first beast to be the agency through whom the dragon lies in wait for the woman's offspring (cf. 12:17) (Alford). The seven crowned heads may be either ten kingdoms of the future which have been reduced to seven by the little horn of Daniel 7 (Walvoord), or they may be a symbol for the entire imperial government of the world from beginning to end throughout world history.[58] The shifting of the diadems from the heads of the dragon (12:3) to the horns of the beast (13:1) represents a change of power from the seven kings or kingdoms to ten kings or kingdoms. It shows that the details of the vision are significant (Smith).

In anticipation of a fuller discussion at 17:9-10, the tentative meaning assigned to the heads, horns, and diadems takes the heads to be seven consecutive world empires with the diadems indicating that they are in the process of running their course as John writes. It understands the ten horns to belong to the last of these empires with the shift in diadems at 13:1 indicating the pre-eminence of ten kingdoms during the last three and one half years just before Christ's return. Διάδημα (*Diadēma*, "Diadem"), derived from διαδέω (*diadeō*, "I bind around"), was a blue band with white marking used by Persian kings to bind on their royal crown.[59] It was a symbol for royal power (cf. 13:1; 19:2) in contrast with στέφανος (*stephanos*, "crown"), which denoted victory in the games, civic worth, military valor, nuptial joy, or festal gladness

---

Revelation of John, Lange's Commentary, ed. E. R. Craven (Grand Rapids: Zondervan, 1968), p. 246; Walter Scott, *Exposition of the Revelation of Jesus Christ* (Swengel, Pa.: Bible Truth Depot, n.d.), p. 248.

57. Düsterdieck, *Revelation*, p. 337.
58. J. A. Seiss, *The Apocalypse* (New York: Charles C. Cook, 1909), 2:303.
59. Robertson, *Word Pictures*, 6:389.

(Lenski). So the position of the diadems signified the location of universal earthly domination (Lee).

12:4 The dragon's control of a third of the stars of heaven illustrates his vast authority: καὶ ἡ οὐρὰ αὐτοῦ σύρει τὸ τρίτον τῶν ἀστέρων τοῦ οὐρανοῦ καὶ ἔβαλεν αὐτοὺς εἰς τὴν γῆν *(kai hē oura autou surei to triton tōn asterōn tou ouranou kai ebalen autous eis tēn gēn,* "and his tail dragged the third [part] of the stars of heaven and cast them into the earth"). Yet it is not just a general word to represent Satan's great power (contra Morris, Johnson). To leave it at that divests the details of the text of deserved significance. It is also insufficient to identify the stars with the persecuted martyrs of John's day[60] or to refer to their casting to the earth as the subjugation of political and spiritual agents in the revived Roman Empire (Walvoord). Persecution of the saints is the backdrop of this book, but this vision goes behind the scenes to look at the more transcendental animosity lying behind that persecution.

The stars must refer to angels who fell with Satan in history past.[61] The similarity of this verse to Dan. 8:10, where "the host of heaven" is an apparent reference to angels, shows this. Already in Revelation a star has pictured an angel (9:1). That factor along with the reference to Satan's angels in 12:8-9 adds credence to this explanation (Smith). This is a war in heaven that resulted in the casting of Satan and his angels to earth before the birth of the woman's child, so it belongs to the past. A second war in 12:7-9 is Satan's final attempt to storm heaven, bringing about the child's overthrow after his birth (Charles). The casting of the stars to earth (ἔβαλεν αὐτοὺς εἰς τὴν γῆν [*ebalen autous eis tēn gēn*]) is his leading of these angels to a battle in which they were worsted, when he too was hurled down from his heavenly abode to earth.[62]

In his deposed status, the dragon can do nothing else but take out his animosity on the earthly scene: καὶ ὁ δράκων ἔστηκεν ἐνώπιον τῆς γυναικὸς τῆς μελλούσης τεκεῖν, ἵνα ὅταν τέκῃ τὸ τέκνον αὐτῆς καταφάγῃ *(kai ho drakōn hestēken enōpion tēs gynaikos tēs mellousēs tekein, hina hotan tekę to teknon autēs kataphagę,* "and the dragon stood before the woman who was about to give birth, that when she gave birth to her child, he might devour [Him]"). Verse 4*b* shows the relationship between the two heavenly signs introduced earlier (Swete). The dragon's

---

60. Ibid.
61. R. C. H. Lenski, *The Interpretation of St. John's Revelation* (Columbus, Ohio: Lutheran Book Concern, 1935), p. 356.
62. Robert Govett, *Govett on Revelation* (1981 reprint; Miami Springs, Fla.: Conley & Schoettle, 1861), 2:21-23; William Henry Simcox, *The Revelation of St. John the Divine* (Cambridge: Cambridge Univ., 1893), p. 126; Charles, *Revelation*, 1:320; Lenski, *Revelation*, p. 356.

struggle is primarily with the woman's child, not with her, so he stands before her waiting for the birth to take place. The standing position is unusual when viewed in connection with a serpent (cf. Gen. 3:14), but this was the usual posture of ancient dragons and serpents which sought to devour children (Moffatt).

The dragon's evil intentions toward the woman's unborn child evidenced themselves throughout OT history. Instances of his hostility surfaced in Cain's murder of Abel (Gen. 4:8), the corrupting of the line of Seth (Gen. 6:1-12), attempted rapes of Sarah (Gen. 12:10-20; 20:1-18) and Rebekah (Gen. 26:1-18), Rebekah's plan to cheat Esau out of his birthright and the consequent enmity of Esau against Jacob (Gen. 27), the murder of the male children in Egypt (Ex. 1:15-22), attempted murders of David (e.g., 1 Sam. 18:10-11), Queen Athaliah's attempt to destroy the royal seed (2 Chron. 22:10), Haman's attempt to slaughter the Jews (Esther 3-9), and consistent attempts of the Israelites to murder their own children for sacrificial purposes (cf. Lev. 18:21; 2 Kings 16:3; 2 Chron. 28:3; Ps. 106:37-38; Ezek. 16:20).[63]

The attack of Herod against the children of Bethlehem (Matt. 2:16) and many other incidents during Jesus' earthly life, including His temptation, typify the ongoing attempt of the dragon to "devour" (κα-ταφάγῃ [*kataphagē*]) the woman's child once he was born. The most direct attempt was, of course, in the crucifixion of Christ (Alford, Johnson).

12:5 The snatching away of the child to heaven after His birth frustrated the dragon's attempt to devour Him, however: καὶ ἔτεκεν υἱόν, ἄρσεν,* ὃς μέλλει ποιμαίνειν πάντα τὰ ἔθνη ἐν ῥάβδῳ σιδηρᾷ· καὶ ἡρπάσθη τὸ τέκνον αὐτῆς πρὸς τὸν θεὸν καὶ πρὸς τὸν θρόνον αὐτοῦ (*kai eteken huion, arsen, hos mellei poimainein panta ta ethnē en hrabdǭ sidērǎ; kai hērpasthē to teknon autēs pros ton theon kai pros ton thronon autou*, "and she gave birth to a son, a male, who is about to destroy all nations with a rod of iron; and her child was caught away to God and to His throne"). Ἔτεκεν (*Eteken*, "She gave birth to") refers to Israel's begetting of her Messiah. It was the work of the nation, not of Mary alone.[64] The suggestion referring this to the crucifixion of Christ rather than to His birth follows the concept of Psalm 2 that the birthday of the king is the day of His accession to the throne (Caird). It also finds verification in the words about labor pains in John 16:19-22 (Ford). Yet the kingly theme is not prominent enough in the present context to warrant seeing this as His assumption of the throne (Beasley-Murray).

Though some earlier interpreters took υἱόν, ἄρσεν (*huion, arsen*, "a

---

63. Robertson, *Word Pictures*, 6:389; Chilton, *Days of Vengeance*, pp. 307-8.
64. Robertson, *Word Pictures*, 6:390.

son, a male") to be Christ *and* the church or even the church alone, it is clearly a reference to Jesus Christ (Swete, Seiss). This finds verification in the relative clause ὃς μέλλει ποιμαίνειν πάντα τὰ ἔθνη ἐν ῥάβδῳ σιδηρᾷ (*hos mellei poimainein panta ta ethnē en hrabdō siderā*, "who is about to destroy all nations with a rod of iron"). The words of the clause are from Ps. 2:9 and are applied to the overcomer in 2:27 as they are to the Warrior-King in 19:15 (Alford). For a discussion of the need to translate ποιμαίνειν (*poimanein*) by "destroy," see the earlier discussion at 2:27 (Thomas, *Revelation 1-7*, p. 233). In His triumphant return, Christ will destroy "all nations" (πάντα τὰ ἔθνη [*panta ta ethnē*]) and then have dominion over new nations that will arise when He institutes His kingdom. An iron scepter (ῥάβδῳ σιδηρᾷ [*hrabdō siderā*, "rod of iron"]) is one that cannot be broken or resisted. This picture drawn from Psalm 2 requires that the birth pictured here be that of Jesus Christ (Alford).

The male child is inaccessible to the dragon because of being caught away to God and to His throne (ἡρπάσθη τὸ τέκνον αὐτῆς πρὸς τὸν θεὸν καὶ πρὸς τὸν θρόνον αὐτοῦ [*hērpasthē to teknon autēs pros ton theon kai pros ton thronon autou*]). This visionary view passes over the events of Christ's life, His crucifixion, and His resurrection to focus immediately on His ascension. The verb ἁρπάζω (*harpazō*, "I snatch away") is used of a wild beast catching its prey (John 10:12), but it also refers to the snatching away of Philip after dealing with the Ethiopian eunuch (Acts 8:39) and of being caught up to heaven, either the church at the coming of Christ (1 Thess. 4:17) or Paul when he was caught up to Paradise (2 Cor. 12:2, 4) (Walvoord). The flight of Jesus' parents into Egypt immediately after His birth (Matt. 2:14-15) does not satisfy the conditions of this snatching away, because its destination is the heavenly throne of God. It best refers to Christ's ascension to His Father's throne after the resurrection (cf. Acts 2:33, 34; 5:31; 7:55, 56; Rom. 8:34; Eph. 1:20; Heb. 8:1; 10:12; 12:2; 1 Pet. 3:22). *Harpazō* need not carry the connotation of escape from immediate danger. It is simply another way of describing the action of ἀνελήμφθη (*anelēmphthē*, "was taken up") of Acts 1:2, 22; 1 Tim. 3:16 (Swete). The main purpose of His ascension was not to escape Satan's hostility, but this was a by-product of it. Once the Messiah was in that heavenly presence, Satan had no further access to Him, so he had to redirect his animosity.

12:6 The woman was the only one left for him to attack, so she fled into the wilderness: καὶ ἡ γυνὴ ἔφυγεν εἰς τὴν ἔρημον, ὅπου ἔχει ἐκεῖ τόπον ἡτοιμασμένον ἀπὸ τοῦ θεοῦ, ἵνα ἐκεῖ τρέφωσιν αὐτὴν ἡμέρας χιλίας διακοσίας ἑξήκοντα (*kai hē gynē ephygen eis tēn erēmon, hopou echei ekei topon hētoimasmenon apo tou theou, hina ekei trephōsin autēn hēmeras chilias diakosias hexēkonta*, "and the woman fled into the wilderness, where she has there a place prepared by God, that

there they might nourish her a thousand two hundred and sixty days").
The flight reported in this verse comes chronologically after the warfare in heaven about to be described in 12:7-12, and the woman's
escape receives a more detailed treatment in 12:13-17 (Alford, Charles,
Bullinger). Discussion below will place the heavenly defeat of the dragon and his angels by Michael and his angels at the midpoint of Daniel's
seventieth week, so the 1,260 days of the woman's protection must
correspond to the last half of that week, while the two witnesses are
serving in Jerusalem (cf. 11:3).

To interpret the woman's flight as a general picture of preservation
through evil and tribulation (Lenski, Johnson) does not account for
the vivid details of the picture. To interpret it as referring to the flight
of the Jews to Pella in A.D. 66 as the Romans came to put down the
Jewish rebellion[65] would be meaningless to John's readers in Asia
Minor. That flight may illustrate the future fulfillment of this prophecy, but in this context that earlier Roman invasion is unrelated (Morris). The future flight of Israel to a place of safety midway through the
seventieth week is the best way to understand the reference of the
prophecy of this vision (Walvoord). Israel will have had relative tranquillity during the first half of the week (cf. Dan. 9:27). Jesus spoke of
Jewish oppression and a flight by the Jews during the period after the
abomination of desolation (cf. Matt. 24:15-28; Mark 13:14-22) (Scott).
In spite of his fiercest efforts, the dragon will be unable to reach the
woman.

The "wilderness" or "desert" (ἔρημον [erēmon]) to which the woman fled is in the fulfillment on earth, of course. The vision does not
specify its location, but the territory that elsewhere is a picture of
desolation (e.g., Rev. 17:3) is for the woman a place of liberation and
safety (Caird). ʼΑπὸ τοῦ θεοῦ (Apo tou theou, "By God") shows the
source of her protection. It apparently means "by the command of
God" in this instance (Moffatt), because the verb τρέφωσιν (trephōsin,
"they might nourish") is an indefinite plural (cf. 10:11; 11:9) indicating
that others will see to immediate administration of her needed
nourishment.[66]

The "thousand two hundred and sixty days" (ἡμέρας χιλίας διακοσίας ἑξήκοντα [hēmeras chilias diakosias hexēkonta]) appears at 11:3
also, with equivalent periods expressed in other terms at 11:2; 12:14;
13:5. It synchronizes with the period of prophesying of the two witnesses (Swete). This period of protective care for the woman will also
be the future period of the false Christ's raging (13:5), so it cannot refer

---

65. Chilton, *Days of Vengeance*, p. 309.
66. Alford, *Greek Testament*, 4:669; Robertson, *Word Pictures*, 6:391.

to the whole age between the ascension and Parousia of Christ (Beasley-Murray).

The expulsion of the dragon from heaven (12:7-12).

12:7 Returning to a point before the flight of the woman, the vision now furnishes an additional reason for the rage of the dragon against the woman: Καὶ ἐγένετο πόλεμος ἐν τῷ οὐρανῷ, ὁ Μιχαὴλ καὶ οἱ ἄγγελοι αὐτοῦ τοῦ πολεμῆσαι μετὰ τοῦ δράκοντος. καὶ ὁ δράκων ἐπολέμησεν καὶ οἱ ἄγγελοι αὐτοῦ (*Kai egeneto polemos en tō ouranō, ho Michaēl kai hoi angeloi autou tou polemēsai meta tou drakontos. kai ho drakōn epolemēsen kai hoi angeloi autou,* "And a war occurred in heaven, Michael and his angels had to make war with the dragon. And the dragon and his angels made war"). The thought of v. 7 returns to the end of v. 5 and the frustrated response of the dragon to the ascension of the male child (Moffatt), though some would see Michael, not the dragon, as the initiator of the battle in heaven.[67] Verse 6 is somewhat parenthetical and anticipatory of vv. 13-17. This section includes an account of the battle in heaven (vv. 7-9) and a heavenly hymn of victory (vv. 10-12) (Johnson).

The time of the warfare designated by πόλεμος . . . πολεμῆσαι . . . ἐπολέμησεν (*polemos . . . polemēsai . . . epolemēsen,* "a war . . . make war . . . made war") has been a subject of debate. To make it a war that occurred in John's day as a cosmic prelude to the consummation (Mounce) ignores the prolepticism that pervades this context. This war cannot fit into John's day because Satan did not pursue Christ when He ascended (Beckwith). Some would refer this back to the primordial battle when Satan initially fell (cf. 12:4), but Satan has already fallen and sought to harm the male child before this battle (Beckwith). Further, making this the initial fall of Satan disagrees with the consequences reflected in 12:10-12.[68]

Another view makes this a heavenly battle at some unknown time in the past, the result of which is an ongoing spiritual warfare since the beginning (Beckwith, Hailey). The supporting evidence for this conclusion is John's concern with the present reality of Satan's rage (Beckwith). The birth of the Messiah in the past (12:5) gives precedent for assigning other events of the vision to the past (Ladd). The problem with this understanding is that it offers no place for details such as the involvement of Michael and his angels and the time span of the 1,260 days.

---

67. E.g., Beckwith, *Apocalypse,* pp. 618, 625; Chilton, *Days of Vengeance,* p. 311.
68. Homer Hailey, *Revelation, an Introduction and Commentary* (Grand Rapids: Baker, 1979), p. 273.

Another recommendation finds the warfare transpiring as Christ was on the cross (Caird). Michael was involved in the heavenly counterpart while Christ won the victory in the realm of earthly reality (ibid.). This answer also looks to several of Christ's statements in anticipation of the cross regarding His victory and the fall of Satan (cf. Luke 10:17-18; John 12:31; 16:11, 33).[69] Yet this view denies Satan access to heaven ever since the slaying of the Lamb. The present context has him excluded from that presence for only three and one half years (12:6, 14). This can hardly be the period between the ascension and the second coming of Christ. In this context of Revelation, this war cannot be a reference to Christ's triumph on the cross. It is rather a "cosmic prelude" to the consummation, explaining why the dragon is so severely hostile toward the people of God during the last segment of the Tribulation (Mounce). His expulsion from heaven (12:9, 12) is his reason for "going all out" to persecute anyone of the woman's seed (12:17) he can get to.

The war is an end-time event, occurring midway through Daniel's seventieth week. During this period, Satan's total energies will oppose anyone allied to God, particularly the people of Israel (Walvoord). This accounts for the unusual severity of persecution during that last three and one half years (Scott, Walvoord). It agrees with the "little time" left for Satan after he leaves heaven (12:12). The involvement of Michael in defense of Israel in the last days (Dan. 12:1) also coincides with this conclusion. This is apparently an effort of the dragon to unseat the woman's Son and reestablish himself in the presence of God (Swete). When it ends in failure, he has to leave heaven.

Ἐν τῷ οὐρανῷ (En tō ouranō, "In heaven") indicates the scene of this battle. It is not a spectacle taking place in the sky, but a conflict in heaven itself (Charles, Mounce). Michael who leads the battle against the dragon is the special patron of the people of Israel (Dan. 10:13, 21; 12:1) (Swete, Charles). He is an angel and can by no stretch of reason be seen as the Son of God.[70] This is not his first conflict with the Devil (Jude 9). In this instance, he is leader of a heavenly army that withstands the dragon and his army. As the archangel (Jude 9), he apparently holds a high rank among unfallen angels as the dragon does among fallen angels (Alford).

12:8 The defeat of the dragon in this war results in his losing his access to heaven: καὶ οὐκ ἴσχυσεν,* οὐδὲ τόπος εὑρέθη αὐτῶν ἔτι ἐν τῷ οὐρανῷ (kai ouk ischysen, oude topos heurethē autōn eti en tō ouranō,

---

69. Alford, *Greek Testament*, 4:669; Philip Edgcumbe Hughes, *The Book of Revelation* (Grand Rapids: Eerdmans, 1990), p. 139.
70. Alford, *Greek Testament*, 4:669; Lee, "Revelation," 4:660; contra Chilton, *Days of Vengeance*, pp. 311-13.

"and yet he did not prevail, neither was a place for them found any longer in heaven"). Καί (*Kai*) has a concessive or adversative sense of "and yet" or "but" in this instance.[71] The verb ἴσχυσεν (*ischysen*, "he did . . . prevail") is the equivalent of יָכֹל (*yākôl*) in Dan. 7:21 where it says the little horn "overpowers" the saints. It has an absolute sense of "be victorious" (Charles). Saying that the dragon was not victorious is another way of announcing his defeat. The aorist of this verb is another example of prolepticism, because Satan as "the accuser of our brethren" has and will have access to heaven until this future battle transpires (Lee, Johnson).

The correlative conjunction οὐδέ (*oude*, "neither") introduces the climax of the narrative sequence, the announcement that instead of succeeding in the attempted coup, the dragon found himself excluded from any further access to the heavenly scene.[72] The negation of τόπος εὑρέθη αὐτῶν (*topos heurethē autōn*, "was a place for them found") means absolute and complete exclusion as evidenced by comparable expressions in Dan. 2:35; Zech. 10:10; and Rev. 20:11 (Swete, Charles, Walvoord). The genitive pronoun αὐτῶν (*autōn*, "for them"), referring to the dragon and his angels, is an objective genitive. In the expression of Rev. 20:11, the corresponding pronoun is dative, αὐτοῖς (*autois*, "for them").[73] The adverb ἔτι (*eti*, "any longer") shows that God continues hearing the accusations of the dragon (12:10; cf. 1 Kings 22:19-22; Job 1:6, 9-11; 2:1; Zech. 3:1) until this point, but subsequently He no longer entertains such claims (Swete).

12:9 The exit of the dragon from heaven is by force: καὶ ἐβλήθη ὁ δράκων ὁ μέγας, ὁ ὄφις ὁ ἀρχαῖος, ὁ καλούμενος Διάβολος καὶ ὁ Σατανᾶς, ὁ πλανῶν τὴν οἰκουμένην ὅλην—ἐβλήθη εἰς τὴν γῆν, καὶ οἱ ἄγγελοι αὐτοῦ μετ' αὐτοῦ ἐβλήθησαν (*kai eblēthē ho drakōn ho megas, ho ophis ho archaios, ho kaloumenos Diabolos kai ho Satanas, ho planōn tēn oikoumenēn holēn—eblēthē eis tēn gēn, kai hoi angeloi autou met' autou eblēthēsan*, "and the great dragon, the serpent of old, who is called the Devil and Satan, who deceives the whole earth, was cast down—was cast down into the earth, and his angels were cast down with him"). The threefold repetition of ἐβλήθη . . . ἐβλήθη . . . ἐβλήθησαν (*eblēthē . . . eblēthē . . . eblēthēsan*, "was cast down . . . was cast down . . . were cast down"), the first two redundantly referring to the dragon, emphasizes the ignominious manner of this mass expulsion from heaven (Scott). Satan as the energizer of Babylon had an initial fall from heaven (Isa. 14:12), and Christ earlier related Satan's fall

---

71. Robertson, *Word Pictures*, 6:392.
72. Alford, *Greek Testament*, 4:670; Lee, "Revelation," 4:661; Stuart, *Apocalypse*, p. 624.
73. Robertson, *Word Pictures*, 6:392.

from heaven to the authority of His followers over evil spirits (Luke 10:18) (Lee). He saw His own crucifixion as laying the foundation for the casting out of Satan (John 12:31). Βάλλω (*Ballō*, "I cast down") finds frequent use in the NT in connection with judgment (e.g., Matt. 3:10; 13:42; John 15:6). In its handling of various kinds and phases of judgment, Revelation uses the term twenty-six times.[74] The removal of the dragon from heaven is one of three steps in his demise from this point on. Besides this, he will enter the abyss for a thousand years (20:1-3) and then the lake of fire as his eternal home (20:10) (Scott).

To avoid any possibility of mistaken identity of the leader of this fallen band, v. 9 identifies him in five ways. First, he is ὁ δράκων ὁ μέγας (*ho drakōn ho megas*, "the great dragon"). Repeating the μέγας (*megas*, "great") from v. 3, the writer reiterates the title emphasizing the remorseless cruelty of this being.[75] Second, he is ὁ ὄφις ὁ ἀρχαῖος (*ho ophis ho archaios*, "the serpent of old") (cf. 20:2). Ἀρχαῖος (*Archaios*, "Of old") reaches back to the beginning of the human race and its fall (Gen. 3:1 ff.; cf. 2 Cor. 11:3). Subtlety for which the serpent is noted is another mark of this being (Scott). In leading humans into sin, the serpent had the first occasion to accuse them before God, but this battle marks his last opportunity to do so (Rev. 12:10).

Third, he is ὁ καλούμενος Διάβολος (*ho kaloumenos Diabolos*, "[the one] who is called the Devil"). Διάβολος (*Diabolos*, "The Devil") comes from διαβάλλω (*diaballō*) which means "I defame, slander, accuse falsely" (Walvoord) or "I separate, act as an adversary."[76] This being is the calumniator of God's servants before the divine presence, seeking to separate them from God (Beckwith, Moffatt). *Diabolos* is the usual rendering of שָׂטָן (*śātān*, "satan") in the LXX (e.g., Job 1:6), suggesting that the two words are almost synonymous (Charles). His task is to arraign men before the bar of divine justice. When not actively doing this, he roams the earth collecting evidence for his next prosecution (Caird).

Fourth, he is ὁ καλούμενος . . . ὁ Σατανᾶς (*ho kaloumenos . . . ho Satanas*, "[the one] who is called . . . Satan"). This is a transliteration of the Hebrew שָׂטָן (*śātān*, "Satan"). The name appears fourteen times in the book of Job and elsewhere in the OT at 1 Chron. 21:1; Zech. 3:1, 2. All these refer to a superhuman adversary, who inspired David's census, accused Job, and accused Joshua the high priest. The Hebrew word also referred to a human adversary such as God raised up against Solomon (1 Kings 11:14, 23, 25; cf. 1 Sam. 29:4). It speaks of the angel

---

74. Friedrich Hauck, "βάλλω" *TDNT*, 1:526-27.
75. Scott, *Revelation*, p. 258; Robertson, *Word Pictures*, 6:392.
76. Werner Foerster, "διάβολος," *TDNT*, 2:73.

of the Lᴏʀᴅ who stood in the way of Balaam in Num. 22:22. The name appears sixteen times in the Gospels, two in Acts, ten in Paul, and seven in Revelation.

Fifth, he is ὁ πλανῶν τὴν οἰκουμένην ὅλην (*ho planōn tēn oikoumenēn holēn*, "[the one] who deceives the whole earth"). He is the master of deception with an uncanny ability to mislead people. It is his chief aim and occupation.[77] He tricked Judas into betraying Jesus (John 13:2) and tried to undercut the faith of Peter (Luke 22:31) (Mounce). His cunning in luring people to ruin (cf. 2 Cor. 2:11; 11:3; 1 Tim. 2:14; 2 John 7; Rev. 2:20; 13:14; 18:23; 19:20; 20:3, 8, 10) combines with his adversarial role in accusing them once they have fallen (Moffatt, Beckwith, Johnson). The objects of his deception are "the whole earth," the term οἰκουμένη (*oikoumenē*) rather than γῆ (*gē*, "the earth") being chosen as more specifically depicting earth's inhabitants and the political structure which characterizes their society.[78]

The dragon's army of angels paid the same penalty as he: οἱ ἄγ-γελοι αὐτοῦ μετ᾿ αὐτοῦ ἐβλήθησαν (*hoi angeloi autou met' autou eblēthēsan*, "his angels were cast down with him"). So the purging of heaven was complete.

12:10 The purging elicits a hymn from a loud voice in heaven, which John heard: καὶ ἤκουσα φωνὴν μεγάλην ἐν τῷ οὐρανῷ λέγουσαν, Ἄρτι ἐγένετο ἡ σωτηρία καὶ ἡ δύναμις καὶ ἡ βασιλεία τοῦ θεοῦ ἡμῶν καὶ ἡ ἐξουσία τοῦ Χριστοῦ αὐτοῦ (*kai ēkousa phōnēn megalēn en tō ouranō legousan, Arti egeneto hē sōtēria kai hē dynamis kai hē basileia tou theou hēmōn kai hē exousia tou Christou autou*, "and I heard a great voice in heaven saying, 'Now have come the salvation and the power and the kingdom of our God and the authority of His Christ'"). The song in 12:10-12 is another of the sudden outbursts of praise found in Revelation (cf. 4:8, 11; 5:9-10, 12, 13; 7:10, 12; 11:15, 17-18; 15:3-4; 19:1-2, 4, 6-8) (Mounce). It falls into three stanzas: the arrival of God's kingdom and Christ's authority (v. 10), the earthly victory of the saints who identify with Christ in His witness and death (v. 11), and the celebration over the expulsion of the dragon and warning to earth because of the Devil's ejection from heaven (v. 12).

The identity of the singers is indefinite. It could be the martyrs of 6:10, because they also utter their cry of vindication "with a loud voice" (φωνῇ μεγάλῃ [*phonē megalē*]). The voice mentions "*our* brethren" (12:10), so it cannot be the voice of angels. Angels would hardly refer to mortals as "brethren" (Charles, Kiddle, Walvoord, Mounce).

The adverb ἄρτι (*arti*, "now") introduces the proleptic song, sung as though the anticipated expulsion of Satan were already past (Bull-

---

77. Robertson, *Word Pictures*, 6:393.
78. Otto Michel, "ἡ οἰκουμένη," *TDNT*, 5:157-59.

inger). The joining of ἐγένετο (*egeneto*, "have come") to the adverb conveys the sense, "just now has come, actually, fully, and completely." It shows how recent the downfall of Satan is from the future vantage point of the singers.[79]

The song in part celebrates the arrival of ἡ σωτηρία καὶ ἡ δύναμις καὶ ἡ βασιλεία τοῦ θεοῦ ἡμῶν (*hē sōtēria kai hē dynamis kai hē basileia tou theou hēmōn*, "the salvation and the power and the kingdom of our God"). Σωτηρία (*Sōtēria*, "salvation") occurs in 7:10 and 19:1 also, carrying the connotation of "victory" in both places as it does here. This is victory over the dragon, one more step in the establishment of God's kingdom on earth (Scott). Δύναμις (*Dynamis*, "Power") is the divine power that accomplished this great victory, the power that produced the male child and took Him to heaven (12:5) and provided for the dragon's defeat (12:8-9) (Lenski, Charles). Ἡ βασιλεία τοῦ θεοῦ ἡμῶν (*Hē basileia tou theou hēmōn*, "The kingdom of our God") is the same one celebrated in the earlier song of 11:15. It includes the future temporal phase (20:1-10) and the eternal phase (21:1–22:5) of the kingdom. All three entities, the salvation or victory, the power, and the kingdom belong to "our God" (τοῦ θεοῦ ἡμῶν [*tou theou hēmōn*]) (Beckwith).

A further arrival celebrated in the song is "the authority of His Christ" (ἡ ἐξουσία τοῦ Χριστοῦ αὐτοῦ [*hē exousia tou Christou autou*]). Ἐξουσία (*Exousia*, "Authority") is authority as compared to the physical "power" of δύναμις (*dynamis*) (Morris). This is the same future triumph as is sung about in 11:15. Christ exercises the authority given to Him by the Father (cf. Ps. 2:8; Matt. 28:18; John 17:2) (Swete). The "Anointed One" (cf. Ps. 2:2; Rev. 11:15) will rule in the future kingdom of God, though some would refer this rule to the period beginning with Christ's life, death, and resurrection (Caird, Mounce). To refer it to the present era would mean that the accusing work of Satan is over, according to the next line of the hymn. This can hardly be. The removal of Satan from heaven is in conjunction with the victory of Michael in heaven, not with the cross of Christ. The victory of the brethren through the blood of the Lamb mentioned in v. 11 covers a period preceding that victory of Michael.[80] Only a referral of the kingdom to the future satisfies the proleptic perspective of the singers of this song (Kiddle). The kingdom of God on earth has not arrived at this point in the book's chronological progression, because Satan has further work to carry out on earth (Beckwith). The song looks forward to the con-

---

79. Lee, "Revelation," 4:662; Lenski, *Revelation*, p. 378; Robertson, *Word Pictures*, 6:393.
80. Contra Chilton, *Days of Vengeance*, pp. 315-17.

summation that has not yet occurred in actuality, though it has in principle (Ladd).

The cause of the coming of the salvation, power, and kingdom is the dismissal of the dragon from heaven: ὅτι ἐβλήθη ὁ κατήγωρ* τῶν ἀδελφῶν ἡμῶν, ὁ κατηγορῶν αὐτοὺς ἐνώπιον τοῦ θεοῦ ἡμῶν ἡμέρας καὶ νυκτός (hoti eblēthē ho katēgōr tōn adelphōn hēmōn, ho katēgorōn autous enōpion tou theou hēmōn hēmeras kai nyktos, "because the accuser of our brethren has been cast down, who accuses them before our God day and night"). This is the only time that the NT calls Satan "the accuser," but his names do not leave his adversarial role in any doubt (cf. v. 9). Tradition assigns to Michael the role of advocate on behalf of men (cf. 1 Enoch 40:9) (Alford, Moffatt), but the NT has Christ as the Christian's advocate (Rom. 8:34; 1 John 2:1; Heb. 7:25; 9:24). "Our brethren" (τῶν ἀδελφῶν ἡμῶν [tōn adelphōn hēmōn]) must be the ones still alive on earth at the future time of Satan's casting to earth (Charles). His heavenly role of accuser will end, but his role as persecutor of the brethren will intensify after he no longer inhabits heaven.

The participial clause ὁ κατηγορῶν αὐτοὺς ἐνώπιον τοῦ θεοῦ ἡμῶν ἡμέρας καὶ νυκτός (ho katēgorōn autous enōpion tou theou hēmōn hēmeras kai nyktos, "who accuses them before our God day and night") emphasizes the incessant exercise of the malignant accusations by the accuser (Charles). This emphasis highlights the main point of the current vision that his mouth will at one point be stopped forever. The scene of his accusations, ἐνώπιον τοῦ θεοῦ ἡμῶν (enōpion tou theou hēmōn, "before our God"), is identical with the scene of his accusation of Job, ἐνώπιον τοῦ κυρίου (enopion tou kyriou, "before the Lord") (Job 1:6, LXX). The genitives of time ἡμέρας καὶ νυκτός (hēmeras kai nyktos, "day and night") tell how uninterruptedly he inveighs against the brethren (Charles). It is just as steady as the praises of the four living beings in heaven (cf. 4:8 where the same expression occurs; cf. also 7:15; 14:11; 20:10).

12:11 Next on the agenda for the singers is the earthly victory of the saints who identify with Christ in His witness and death: καὶ αὐτοὶ ἐνίκησαν αὐτὸν διὰ τὸ αἷμα τοῦ ἀρνίου καὶ διὰ τὸν λόγον τῆς μαρτυρίας αὐτῶν, καὶ οὐκ ἠγάπησαν τὴν ψυχὴν αὐτῶν ἄχρι θανάτου (kai autoi enikēsan auton dia to haima tou arniou kai dia ton logon tēs martyrias autōn, kai ouk ēgapēsan tēn psychēn autōn achri thanatou, "and they themselves overcame him because of the blood of the Lamb and because of the word of their testimony, and they did not love their life unto death"). While he was yet accusing, though, Satan was unsuccessful in his thrusts against the brethren. They overcame him despite his cunning by resisting his trickery and refuting his calumnies. The Lamb's earlier defeat of the enemy was the basis of their victory (cf. Col. 2:15) (Moffatt). "They themselves" (αὐτοί [*autoi*]), in addition to Michael, won a victory over the dragon (Mounce). The sojourn of these martyrs on earth is probably the period just before the inauguration of the kingdom on earth. They will not be subject to heavenly accusation during that period, but they will have endured it prior to that and must face the worst that the dragon has to offer when he is cast down to earth. The proleptic nature of this song necessitates this dating of their martyrdom. These are saints who will have overcome because of the blood of the Lamb and the divine word to which they have borne testimony (Beckwith). The martyrdom is still ahead for them at this stage of the book's chronological progress, but the deaths of the martyrs are treated as fait accompli because of the anticipated completion of the mystery of God under the seventh trumpet (cf. 10:7; 11:15).

The aorist ἐνίκησαν (*enikēsan*, "they overcame") is proleptic in the same sense as in 7:9 ff. where the redeemed multitude in a proleptic vision sees the victory as having already been won. The martyrs' fight is over; they are already victors, though they have not yet fully realized their triumph.[81] The victory over Satan is a spiritual one which is won even in the terrible experience of martyrdom (Ladd).

The διά (*dia*, "because of") phrase assigns a twofold cause for their victory, a primary and objective one which is the blood of the Lamb, and a secondary and subjective one, which is their personal labor and self-sacrifice (Swete, Lee). Because the Lamb's blood was shed, they had an answer to the accuser's charges (Alford), and they found a motivation to devote themselves to His service, which was the secondary cause of their victory. In the expression τὸν λόγον τῆς μαρτυρίας αὐτῶν (*ton logon tēs martyrias autōn*, "the word of their testimony"), both μαρτυρίας (*martyrias*, "testimony") and αὐτῶν (*autōn*, "their") are subjective genitives, yielding the sense "the word of God to which they have borne testimony." As usual, the singers attribute special power to the word of God, a characteristic of the word in John's writings elsewhere (cf. John 8:31-32; 15:3) (Beckwith). These brethren have given a faithful testimony and confession even to the point of death and thereby have contributed to their own victory (Alford). This is another of the places where John connects μαρτυρία (*martyria*, "testimony") with the powerful word of God (cf. 1:2, 9; 6:9; 20:4) (Beckwith). The expression refers to their evangelistic confession of Jesus, not to the testimony of their blood as martyrs, though their confession came in situations of martyrdom.[82]

---

81. Düsterdieck, *Revelation*, pp. 348-49; Swete, *Apocalypse*, p. 156; Lee, "Revelation," 4:662.
82. H. Strathmann, "μαρτύς, μαρτυρέω, κ. τ. λ.," *TDNT*, 4:502.

Another aorist indicative, ἠγάπησαν (ēgapēsan, "they did . . . love") pictures the future heroism of these saints. They will put their lives on the line out of loyalty to Christ (John 12:25; cf. Matt. 10:39; 16:25; Mark 8:35-36; Luke 9:24; 17:33). Paul too had this attitude (Acts 20:24; 21:13; Phil. 1:20 ff.) as did Jesus Himself (Phil. 2:8).[83] They will not love their earthly life (ψυχήν [psychēn]).[84] They will consent even to die, possibly a violent death, rather than relinquish their profession and fidelity to Christ.[85] Being ready to die for their faith is the ultimate in Christian faithfulness (Swete, Lenski).

12:12 The song closes on the notes of celebration over the expulsion of the dragon and of warning to earth because of the Devil's ejection from heaven: διὰ τοῦτο εὐφραίνεσθε, [οἱ] οὐρανοὶ καὶ οἱ ἐν αὐτοῖς σκηνοῦντες· οὐαὶ τὴν γῆν καὶ τὴν θάλασσαν, ὅτι κατέβη ὁ διάβολος πρὸς ὑμᾶς ἔχων θυμὸν μέγαν, εἰδὼς ὅτι ὀλίγον καιρὸν ἔχει (dia touto euphrainesthe, [hoi] ouranoi kai hoi en autois skēnountes; ouai tēn gēn kai tēn thalassan, hoti katebē ho diabolos pros hymas echōn thymon megan, eidōs hoti oligon kairon echei, "because of this, make merry, heavens and those who dwell in them; woe to the earth and the sea, because the Devil has descended to you having great anger, knowing that he has little time"). Διὰ τοῦτο (Dia touto, "Because of this") occurs also at 7:15 and 18:8 in this book and is in John's gospel fifteen times (Charles). The antecedent of τοῦτο (touto, "this") is the substance of v. 10, the casting down of the dragon (Alford, Charles), v. 11 being somewhat parenthetical. The thought of intensified persecution (v. 12b) does not quell the spirit of rejoicing, because it is only preliminary to the realization of the kingdom of God and of Christ (Kiddle).

The call to "make merry" (εὐφραίνεσθε [euphrainesthe]) (cf. 11:10; 18:20) apparently echoes Isa. 49:13 and Ps. 96:11 (Mounce). The heavens and the inhabitants of heaven have special reason for merriment because of the elimination of Satan from their surroundings. "Those who dwell in them [i.e., heaven]" (οἱ ἐν αὐτοῖς σκηνοῦντες [hoi en autois skēnountes]) refers to the angels whose actual abode is heaven just as a comparable expression does in 13:6. It cannot refer to the church on earth, as some contend (Lee, Beckwith). The song goes on to bid those on earth to do anything but rejoice.

The woe (οὐαὶ [ouai]) is not the third woe in the series of three mentioned in 8:13 (contra Bullinger, Sweet), because it is not from God and its objects are not the rebellious earth-dwellers. That third woe must await the content of the seventh trumpet in the form of the seven bowl judgments (16:1 ff.). This pronouncement concerns Satan's

---

83. Swete, *Apocalypse*, p. 156; Robertson, *Word Pictures*, 6:395.
84. BAGD, p. 893.
85. Stuart, *Apocalypse*, p. 626.

hostility to the people of God, not the calamities sent on the non-Christian world as in the three woes (Beckwith, Mounce). This woe makes a bold contrast to the rejoicing of the heaven-dwellers. Bad times face the inhabitants of the whole terrestrial world (i.e. τὴν γῆν καὶ τὴν θάλασσαν [*tēn gēn kai tēn thalassan*, "the earth and the sea"] because of the arrival of a new full-time inhabitant.

The reason for the sympathetic warning is given by the ὅτι (*hoti*, "because") clause. The irreversible descent of ὁ διάβολος (*ho diabolos*, "the Devil") is bad enough news, but the manner of his descent is even worse. Ἔχων (*Echon*, "Having") is a modal participle telling that as he descends, the Devil has great rage. He knows it is his last great campaign, so his mean-spirited irrationality provokes in himself the utmost intensity of anger against mankind (cf. Mark 13:19-20) (Moffatt). Θυμὸς (*Thymos*, "Anger") is a more turbulent word than ὀργή (*orgē*, "wrath"). It is a more emotional response than it is a rational one.[86] A portion of a world already in the throes of God's wrath must now add to that the fury of the archenemy of God.

The causal participle εἰδώς (*eidōs*, "knowing") tells why the Devil's anger is heightened. It is his knowledge of the shortness of time available to him. His remaining time corresponds to the three and one half years of the reign of the beast from the sea (13:5) whom he enthrones immediately after his casting out of heaven (Simcox). It is the same as the period designated in 12:6, 14 (Swete). The return of Christ to assign him to the abyss for a thousand years is what makes the καιρὸν (*kairon*, "time") so ὀλίγον (*oligon*, "little") (Alford, Walvoord). The proleptic surroundings of the hymn show that this period is future. It cannot represent the whole course of human history, but must be the period of Satan's final outburst against the righteous (Mounce).

The dragon's pursuit of the woman (12:13-18). John has now furnished an additional reason for the dragon's pursuit of the woman: his expulsion from heaven and consequent shortness of time to vent his anger against the people that brought the Messiah into the world (12:7-12). So the account of John's vision returns to furnish details regarding the flight and protection of the woman (12:13-17).

12:13 The account resumes by repeating the substance of 12:6: Καὶ ὅτε εἶδεν ὁ δράκων ὅτι ἐβλήθη εἰς τὴν γῆν, ἐδίωξεν τὴν γυναῖκα ἥτις ἔτεκεν τὸν ἄρσενα (*Kai hote eiden ho drakōn hoti eblēthē eis tēn gēn, ediōxen tēn gynaika hētis eteken ton arsena*, "And when the dragon saw that he had been cast into the earth, he pursued the woman who had given birth to the male"). The reason for the woman's flight is in v. 6

---

86. M. R. Vincent, *Word Studies in the New Testament* (reprint; McLean, Va.: MacDonald, 1888), 1:423; Walvoord, *Revelation*, p. 194.

only by implication, but here it is explicit. She is fleeing the pursuit of the dragon (Alford, Lee, Beckwith, Mounce). When the dragon saw he could not reach the woman's Son, he turned to the mother to try to hurt the Son through her (Swete).

The dragon's pursuit and the woman's deliverance has been compared to various past happenings: the forty-two stages of the original desert wanderings of Israel, pursuit of the Israelites by Pharaoh, the attempt to drown the male infants in the Nile, the turning of rivers into dry land (cf. Isa. 42:15; 43:3; 50:2), Israel's being carried to safety on eagle's wings (Deut. 32:11) (Kiddle, Caird, Sweet, Mounce), the nourishment of Israel by God (Deut. 8:3, 16) (Alford), and the flight following the outbreak of persecution in A.D. 64 (Swete). Yet aspects of the escape of Israel from Egypt are too different to fulfill the imagery of a dragon-monster chasing a woman (Beckwith). To match any of the above proposals with the present vision requires an extreme allegorization of the details for which the text furnishes no justification.

It is better to allow this flight to be a literal one in the future that corresponds to the flight from Egypt (cf. Ex. 14:5; Josh. 24:6) (Bullinger). It will be the same flight that Jesus predicted in His Olivet Discourse (cf. Matt. 24:15-28; Mark 13:14-23) (Bullinger, Walvoord). Sometimes διώκω (*diōkō*, "I pursue") indicates a hostile pursuit, and this is one of those times.[87] The hostility is an outgrowth of her giving birth to the male Son, as indicated in the qualitative relative clause, ἥτις ἔτεκεν τὸν ἄρσενα (*hētis eteken ton arsena*, "who had given birth to the male"). This clearly refers back to the event of 12:5.

12:14 An adversative καί (*kai*, "but") (Ladd) introduces the explanation of how the woman escaped the dragon's hostility: καὶ ἐδόθησαν τῇ γυναικὶ αἱ δύο πτέρυγες τοῦ ἀετοῦ τοῦ μεγάλου, ἵνα πέτηται εἰς τὴν ἔρημον εἰς τὸν τόπον αὐτῆς, ὅπου τρέφεται ἐκεῖ καιρὸν καὶ καιροὺς καὶ ἥμισυ καιροῦ ἀπὸ προσώπου τοῦ ὄφεως (*kai edothēsan tē gynaiki hai dyo pteryges tou aetou tou megalou, hina petētai eis tēn erēmon eis ton topon autēs, hopou trephetai ekei kairon kai kairous kai hēmisy kairou apo prosōpou tou opheōs*, "but two wings of a great eagle were given to the woman, that she might fly into the wilderness into her place, where she is nourished there a time and times and a half a time from the presence of the serpent"). The passive form ἐδόθησαν (*edothēsan*, "were given") retains its usual apocalyptic sense of being granted by God for His purposes (Alford). God's miraculous intervention explains how the woman accomplished her escape mentioned in v. 6. The dragon is no match for her God-given powers (Swete).

The expression "two wings of a great eagle" (αἱ δύο πτέρυγες τοῦ

---

87. Swete, *Apocalypse*, p. 157; Robertson, *Word Pictures*, 6:395.

ἀετοῦ τοῦ μεγάλου [*hai dyo pteryges tou aetou tou megalou*]) signifies expansive strength and rapid flight and is an echo of terminology used for Israel's deliverance from Egypt (Ex. 19:4; Deut. 32:11; cf. Isa. 40:31).[88] The use of the terminology indicates that this is a further act of God's protecting of Israel (cf. Ps. 91:1-4).[89] Since the woman is a symbol for national Israel, the two wings of the great eagle must also be a figure to portray an as yet undisclosed supernatural means for her deliverance.

The purpose of the wings was to enable her to fly to the wilderness to her place (ἵνα πέτηται εἰς τὴν ἔρημον εἰς τὸν τόπον αὐτῆς [*hina petētai eis tēn erēmon eis ton topon autēs*]). This is a literal flight from Jerusalem, with the literal flight of Israel from Egypt as a background. Τόπον αὐτῆς (*Topon autēs*, "Her place") could refer to the wilderness (τὴν ἔρημον [*tēn erēmon*]) of Sinai (Seiss), but in His advice to the faithful remnant, Jesus told those in Judea to flee to the mountains (Matt. 24:16) (Walvoord). Petra, the ruins of an ancient city of Edom carved out of rock and protected by high mountain walls and with a narrow access, has been a suggested location of the "place,"[90] but this is pure speculation. The only stipulation possible is that it is a place of refuge for converted Israel during the last half of the seventieth week (Lee).

In this place of refuge the woman will receive nourishment (τρέφεται [*trephetai*]) from God just as Elijah received food at the brook Cherith and as Israel received manna in the wilderness (Alford, Walvoord). This is a critical provision because no one will be able to buy or sell without the mark of the beast during this three and one half years (13:17) (Bullinger). The expression καιρὸν καὶ καιροὺς καὶ ἥμισυ καιροῦ (*kairon kai kairous kai hēmisy kairou*, "a time and times and a half a time") uses καιρὸς (*kairos*, "season") to depict the same period as is designated in months (11:2; 13:5) and days (11:3; 12:6) elsewhere (cf. Dan. 7:25; 12:7). It must be the last half of the week because it is the period of the dragon's "last fling" (cf. 12:12). In fact, all three ways of designating the period are talking of the same span.[91] It must be a period of time of this literal length. This designation is not a symbol for some longer period in earlier history (Alford). This is how long the woman receives shelter from the "presence" (προσώπου [*prosōpou*]) of the serpent (τοῦ ὄφεως [*tou opheōs*]), another name for the dragon (cf. 12:9) (Ford).

---

88. Alford, *Greek Testament*, 4:672; Stuart, *Apocalypse*, p. 627; Lenski, *Revelation*, p. 382.
89. Düsterdieck, *Revelation*, p. 352; Walvoord, *Revelation*, p. 195.
90. Norman B. Harrison, *The End* (Minneapolis: Harrison Service, 1948), p. 132.
91. Ladd, *Revelation*, pp. 153, 174.

12:15 Since the serpent could not pursue the woman, he attempted to impose harm by drowning her:[92] καὶ ἔβαλεν ὁ ὄφις ἐκ τοῦ στόματος αὐτοῦ ὀπίσω τῆς γυναικὸς ὕδωρ ὡς ποταμόν, ἵνα αὐτὴν ποταμοφόρητον ποιήσῃ (*kai ebalen ho ophis ek tou stomatos autou opisō tēs gynaikos hydōr hōs potamon, hina autēn potamophorēton poiēsē̞*, "and the serpent cast from his mouth water as a river behind the woman, that he might make her [to be] swallowed up by the river"). Whether the expression ὕδωρ ὡς ποταμόν (*hydōr hōs potamon*, "water as a river") and the term ποταμοφόρητον (*potamophorēton*, "swallowed up by the river") indicate an attempted destruction by literal water[93] or portray the hot pursuit of the woman by an army (cf. Jer. 46:7-8; 47:2-3)[94] is difficult if not impossible to determine. It could be either, but since the serpent's initial effort to pursue met with frustration, this may very possibly be a different tactic through the use of water to accomplish what he could not do otherwise. Certainly it is not referring to the attempt of the Jewish authorities to eradicate the church (cf. Acts 8:1-3) or the river of lies that will threaten the elect in the future (2 Thess. 2:9-11; Rev. 13:14) (contra Mounce). It relates more to a tangible use of force by an authority figure than to either of these proposals.

12:16 Another supernatural provision protects the woman from this new threat: καὶ ἐβοήθησεν ἡ γῆ τῇ γυναικί, καὶ ἤνοιξεν ἡ γῆ τὸ στόμα αὐτῆς καὶ κατέπιεν τὸν ποταμὸν ὃν ἔβαλεν ὁ δράκων ἐκ τοῦ στόματος αὐτοῦ (*kai eboēthēsen hē gē tē̞ gynaiki, kai ēnoixen hē gē to stoma autēs kai katepien ton potamon hon ebalen ho drakōn ek tou stomatos autou*, "and the earth helped the woman, and the earth opened its mouth and drank the river which the dragon cast from his mouth"). The OT speaks of the earth opening its mouth to swallow the Egyptians (Ex. 15:12) and Korah, Dathan, and Abiram (Num. 16:28-33; 26:10; Deut. 11:6; Ps. 106:17). It also uses a flood as a metaphor for overwhelming evil (Pss. 18:4; 124:2-4; Isa. 43:2). The former appears more likely to be a pattern of the present picture, because the woman is in real physical danger (Moffatt, Mounce). Very possibly, through an earthquake whatever water the dragon may send after the woman drains into underground openings (Seiss). Instances of underground rivers in Asia Minor may illustrate this miraculous delivery (Swete).[95]

---

92. Robertson, *Word Pictures*, 6:396.
93. Düsterdieck, *Revelation*, pp. 353-54; Bullinger, *Apocalypse*, p. 416; Smith, *Revelation*, pp. 190-91.
94. Govett, *Revelation*, 2:62-64.
95. The proposal that the earth's swallowing of the river pictures the curse imposed in Gen. 3:17 (Paul S. Minear, "Far as the Curse Is Found: The Point of Revelation 12:15-16," *NovT* 33, no. 1 [1991]: 74-75) pushes alleged analogies between this chapter and Gen. 3:15-20 too far. The deliverance of

12:17 The divine protection given the woman enraged the dragon even more, but all he could do was redirect his animosity: καὶ ὠργίσθη ὁ δράκων ἐπί τῇ γυναικί, καὶ ἀπῆλθεν ποιῆσαι πόλεμον μετὰ τῶν λοιπῶν τοῦ σπέρματος αὐτῆς, τῶν τηρούντων τὰς ἐντολὰς τοῦ θεοῦ καὶ ἐχόντων τὴν μαρτυρίαν Ἰησοῦ (*kai ōrgisthē ho drakōn epi tę̄ gynaiki, kai apēlthen poiēsai polemon meta tōn loipōn tou spermatos autēs, tōn tērountōn tas entolas tou theou kai echontōn tēn martyrian Iēsou*, "and the dragon was enraged at the woman, and went away to make war with the rest of her seed, who keep the commandments of God and have the testimony of Jesus"). Ὀργίζω (*Orgizō*, "I enrage") also tells the reaction of the nations in 11:18. The dragon had to redirect his anger from the Son to the woman in 12:5 when the Son escaped his clutches. That increased his rage. He lost his place in heaven in 12:8, 9, 12, angering him even more. At this point the woman has escaped to a place of refuge, leaving him only the woman's remaining seed to vent his fury on. The repeated frustration of his efforts explains the furious persecution the dragon proceeds to inflict on the faithful. He goes away "to make war with" (ποιῆσαι πόλεμον [*poiēsai polemon*], cf. 13:7) "the rest of her seed" (τῶν λοιπῶν τοῦ σπέρματος αὐτῆς [*tōn loipōn tou spermatos autēs*]) who apparently did not go with their fellow Israelites to the place of refuge. Besides the Son, the woman, earlier identified as national Israel, has other children who are distinguished from the group of Jewish people whom the dragon cannot touch. These are scattered followers of the Lamb who did not reach the appointed place in the wilderness prepared for the main body of people symbolized by the woman.[96] The mention of this remnant prepares the way for the encounter between the beast, representing the dragon, and the faithful (cf. 13:7; Dan. 7:21).

A specific identification of this group entails a choice between four proposals. First, seeing the remaining ones as Gentile Christians as distinct from the Jewish mother-church in Jerusalem falls short in eliminating Jewish Christians from among them and in restricting the woman to the Jerusalem church.[97] Second, taking them to be selected members of the believing community who suffer persecution after the pattern of Christ (Swete, Caird, Kiddle) is only partially right, because it fails to distinguish between the woman and the rest of her seed (Alford). According to this view, she is nothing more than the sum of her children.[98] Distinguishing between the conquerors of chapters 2-3

Israel from Egypt is much more plausible as the source of John's allusions here.

96. Robertson, *Word Pictures*, 6:395.
97. Düsterdieck, *Revelation*, pp. 356-57.
98. Ibid., p. 356.

and the rest of the church[99] or between the ideal church and the empirical church on earth (Ladd) does not overcome this difficulty. Third, the understanding that the remaining ones are a believing remnant and the woman is Israel as a whole (Walvoord), cannot explain why unbelieving Israel is granted divine protection from the dragon.

Fourth and best of all is the identification of "the rest of her seed" as the 144,000 Israelites who were sealed in chapter 7. These have the distinction of being active witnesses throughout the world during the last three and one half years before Christ returns, an opportunity not granted to the larger believing community of Israel who are protected in seclusion (Seiss, Smith). Granting the continuity of 12:1–14:5, one must see the portrayal of the victorious 144,000 in 14:1-5 as a sequel to the battle of the dragon's two emissaries with "the rest of her seed" in chapter 13. The extended section is a connected sequence from this point on with the mention of the dragon's animosity toward that seed here, his stationing of himself on the sands of the sea in 12:18, the appearance of the earthly agents he will use to inflict his damage in 13:1, 11, and the proleptic scene of the victorious victims of his persecution after the conflict is over in 14:1-5. This sequence says rather plainly that "the rest of her seed" is none other than the 144,000.

Earlier discussion has dwelt on the Jewish lineage of the 144,000 (cf. 7:1-8; Thomas, pp. 475-78). This agrees with the identification of the woman of chapter 12 as national Israel (12:1-2). The special mission of that earlier group as slaves of God (7:3) and witnesses for Christ during the last half of the eschatological week also agrees with the special characteristics of this seed as having "the testimony of Jesus" (τὴν μαρτυρίαν ᾽Ιησοῦ [*tēn martyrian Iēsou*]) and of not hiding away with the rest of national Israel during this period (Scott). Their aggressive witness is doubtless one of the factors that makes them the brunt of harsh treatment by the dragon and his beasts.[100] Their keeping of the commandments of God (*tōn tērountōn tas entolas tou theou*) certainly incurs satanic displeasure too. That is the exact opposite of the value system under which the dragon operates.

The genitives τοῦ θεοῦ (*tou theou*, "of God") and ᾽Ιησοῦ (*Iēsou*, "of Jesus") are both subjective: "the commandments which God gave" and "the testimony which Jesus bore," i.e., the truth that He taught. Other occurrences of the latter expression in this book always have this meaning (cf. 1:2, 9; 6:9; 14:12; 19:10; 20:4) (Beckwith, Mounce, Sweet). These are apparently the same saints who receive commendation for their perseverance in 14:12. "The testimony of Jesus" has "the word of God" as its complement quite often in the Apocalypse (cf. 1:2, 9; 6:9;

---

99. Kiddle, *Revelation*, p. 240; Chilton, *Days of Vengeance*, p. 323.
100. Robertson, *Word Pictures*, 6:397.

20:4). This as "the word which God spoke" closely approximates "the commandments which God gave."

12:18 As he plots his war against "the rest of her seed," the dragon takes his station on the sand of the sea: καὶ ἐστάθη* ἐπὶ τὴν ἄμμον τῆς θαλάσσης (*kai estathē epi tēn ammon tēs thalassēs*, "and he stood on the sands of the sea").[101] Unable to reach the woman, he prepares to call his wicked cohorts into action (Mounce). He stops on his way to war to summon his next instrument, the beast from the sea.[102] His place by the sea apparently derives from Dan. 7:2, 3, 7, 8, 19-27 as the source of the "little horn" whose counterpart is about to be described in 13:1 ff. (Moffatt). A discussion of 13:1 will probe the possibility of equating the sea with the abyss of 11:7 and 17:8. This stationing sets the stage for the next development in the dragon's "last gasp" program.

Additional Notes

12:1 Σημεῖον is a frequent word in John's gospel for naming a miraculous sign with a deeper spiritual significance (e.g., John 2:11, 23) (Swete, Johnson). In Revelation, Satan's emissaries perform deceptive signs as a caricature of those done by Christ (cf. 13:13, 14; 16:14; 19:20). Sometimes σημεῖον is associated with τέρας, which denotes the element of wonder provoked by a miracle (cf. Matt. 24:24; John 4:48; Acts 2:22; 5:12). Σημεῖον in itself does not denote wonderment as τέρας does, but on some occasions the marvel-producing element in a σημεῖον is obvious from the context in which the word is used (cf. Luke 21:11; Rev. 13:13, 14; 15:1; 16:14; 19:20).[103] In the remainder of Revelation including 12:1 are seven signs, three in heaven (12:1, 3; 15:1) and four on earth (13:13, 14; 16:14; 19:20). Only this one is void of a reference to evil or judgment (Morris, Johnson).

12:2 Ἐν γαστρὶ ἔχουσα is a technical idiom for pregnancy as in Matt. 1:18, 23 and 1 Thess. 5:3. The participle ἔχουσα probably functions as a finite verb here (Charles), though possibly the phrase parallels the περιβεβλημένη κ.τ.λ. of v. 1 (Swete). Some MSS omit the καί just before κράζει to ease the grammatical irregularity of having no finite verb with ἐν γαστρὶ ἔχουσα, but external support for inclusion of the conjunction is quite strong (ibid.).

12:4 The present tense of σύρει to speak of an event that happened in the past provides the description with vividness much on the order of a historical present tense.

---

101. Verse 18 of chap. 12 in the Greek text appears in English translations as the opening part of v. 1 of chap. 13. See textual note on ἐστάθη under "Additional Notes" on 12:18.
102. Robertson, *Word Pictures*, 6:397; Johnson, "Revelation," 12:523.
103. Robertson, *Word Pictures*, 6:387.

The rough breathing with which ἔστηκεν is pointed takes it as a perfect tense of ἵστημι. It can be pointed with a smooth breathing, ἔστηκεν, making it an imperfect of στήκω.[104] The rough breathing is preferable, though, resulting in a present force "is standing" and adding to the vivid impact of the portrayal of the dragon's challenge of the woman about to give birth.

12:5 Some MSS, including p[47] and Sinaiticus, read the masculine ἄρσενα rather than the neuter ἄρσεν that finds support in Alexandrinus and Ephraemi among others. The noun is in apposition with the masculine υἱόν, which explains why some scribe(s) would think it should be masculine instead of neuter. The neuter ἄρσεν has an explanation, however, being caused by the neuter τέκνον or παιδίον in John's mind as he wrote. The difference in gender between υἱόν and ἄρσεν is perhaps a solecism, but not a problem, because appositions do not require agreement in gender. The two nouns emphasize the gender of the child (Alford, Swete, Lenski).

12:6 The addition of ἐκεῖ after ὅπου is according to the pattern of Hebrew redundancy which uses an adverb or pronoun after a relative pronoun (cf. 3:8; 8:2, 9; 13:8, 12; 17:9; 20:8).[105] The twofold occurrence of ἐκεῖ in the verse marks the definiteness of the place prepared for the woman, where she can be nourished and cared for (Scott).

The phrase ἀπὸ τοῦ θεοῦ is one of the rare uses of ἀπό after a passive verb to denote agency (Charles).

12:7 The infinitive πολεμῆσαι with τοῦ occurs nowhere else in Revelation. Paul and Luke use the construction for a wide range of senses, and Matthew and Mark to a more limited extent. It often has a final (or consecutive) force, though the consecutive force is often so weak that it has no more than an epexegetical sense.[106] The construction in this verse poses a bit of a problem. One solution to the dilemma is the proposal of the insertion of an implied repetition of ἐγένετο from earlier in the verse. The idea would be that Michael "went forth" to make war, taking the initiative in the struggle.[107] The grammatical irregularities of this view, particularly the nominative ὁ Μιχαὴλ καὶ οἱ ἄγγελοι performing the action of the infinitive, are too numerous to be acceptable. Another explanation takes the infinitive as an appositional genitive, the infinitive in apposition with πόλεμος: "the war,

---

104. Ibid., 6:389.
105. Swete, *Apocalypse*, p. 152; Beckwith, *Apocalypse*, p. 624; Robertson, *Word Pictures*, 6:390.
106. BDF, par. 400[8].
107. Düsterdieck, *Revelation*, p. 343; Swete, *Apocalypse*, p. 153; Bullinger, *Apocalypse*, p. 405; Mounce, *Revelation*, p. 241.

consisting of Michael and his angels making war."[108] But again the nominative rather than the accusative case of ὁ Μιχαὴλ καὶ οἱ ἄγγελοι is inexplicable. Of many suggested solutions, the only one that seems to respect all the data is this: the construction is a pure Hebraism, with the force "Michael and his angels *had to fight* with the dragon" (Charles). It reproduces the Hebrew text where the noun is nominative (subject) and is followed by ל plus the infinitive. The construction expresses tendency, intention, or obligation.[109] Putting this together with the author's tendency to use the nominative in place of other cases such as the genitive or dative,[110] one has credible support for this sense of the construction here.

Μετά with the genitive has a hostile sense after verbs of fighting, etc. It denotes the person against whom the warfare is waged.[111] In combination with πολεμέω, it occurs in Rev. 2:16; 13:4; 17:14, but nowhere else in the NT.[112] Some have considered it a Hebraism, but the papyri have it frequently.[113]

In τοῦ δράκοντος and ὁ δράκων, the articles point back to the first mention of δράκων in 12:3 where the noun is anarthrous. The use of the article to point to a previously mentioned substantive is common.[114]

12:8 The plural ἴσχυσαν rather than the singular ἴσχυσεν has good support in MSS such as p47, Sinaiticus, and Ephraemi, and is the reading preferred by some.[115] Yet scribes would hardly have changed a plural to a singular because of the plural subject ὁ δράκων . . . καὶ οἱ ἄγγελοι in v. 7 that carries over into v. 8. Since the singular is the harder reading and has the support of Alexandrinus and other MSS, it is the preferred reading. Its singular number agrees with the principal subject, δράκων (Beckwith).

12:10 The accusative φωνὴν μεγάλην is the object of ἀκούω here as it is in 5:11; 10:4; 14:2; 18:4 because the substance is the main thing,

---

108. Beckwith, *Apocalypse*, p. 625; Ernest De Witt Burton, *Syntax of the Moods and Tenses in New Testament Greek*, 3d ed. (1978 reprint; Grand Rapids: Kregel, 1900), par. 400; C. F. D. Moule, *An Idiom Book of New Testament Greek* (Cambridge: Cambridge Univ., 1960), p. 129.
109. BDB, p. 518a.
110. BDF, par. 400[8]; Nigel Turner, *Syntax*, vol. 3 of *A Grammar of New Testament Greek* (Edinburgh: T. & T. Clark, 1963), p. 141.
111. BAGD, p. 509.
112. Robertson, *Word Pictures*, 6:392.
113. Robertson, *A Grammar of the Greek New Testament in the Light of Historical Research* (Nashville: Broadman, 1934), p. 610.
114. Robertson, *Grammar*, p. 762.
115. E.g., Robertson, *Word Pictures*, 6:392.

not the speaker, yet the object φωνῆς μεγάλης is genitive after the same verb in 11:12; 14:13.[116]

Some MSS, including p[47], Sinaiticus, and Ephraemi, have the regular form of this noun, κατήγορος, instead of the unusual κατήγωρ (cf. John 8:10; Acts 23:30, 35; 25:16, 18). The latter has the support of Alexandrinus, however, and is the harder reading, so it is preferred (Swete). Κατήγωρ was for a while thought to be a transliteration of the Hebrew קטיגור (Swete), but Deissmann found the form in the papyri uninfluenced by Jewish or Christian sources.[117]

12:11 Verse 11 has a distinctly Johannine flavor through its thought and its use of Johannine vocabulary (e.g., νικᾶν, λόγος, μαρτυρία, ἀγαπᾶν) (Beckwith).

Efforts to assign διά with the accusative the meaning of "through," expressing the means of the victory of the brethren[118] are not convincing. The examples used to prove this force are weak. It is better to distinguish the preposition with the genitive ("through") from its use with the accusative ("because of") (Charles, Alford). John uses ἐν with the instrumental to speak of Christ's blood as the means of release and redemption (cf. 1:5; 5:9).[119]

12:12 The case with οὐαί here is the accusative (τὴν γῆν καὶ τὴν θάλασσαν) as it is in 8:13,[120] but the interjection occurs with the nominative in 18:10, 16, 19. The accusative is more usual. Some places use the dative, however (e.g., Matt. 11:21; 18:7).[121]

12:13 Having used the neuter ἄρσεν in v. 5, the writer now refers to the Son with a more expected form, the masculine ἄρσενα (Lenski).

῞Ητις is a qualitative relative pronoun as well as a relative of indefinite reference. In Luke's writings, it often has the same force as the relative of definite reference, but in most of the rest of the NT it retains its qualitative force, as it does here.[122] It seemingly retains its qualitative force throughout Revelation (cf. 1:12; 2:24; 9:4; 11:8; 19:2; 20:4). Also, the relative pronoun carries a secondary causal sense here.[123]

12:14 The article is probably generic, not a reference to the eagle

---

116. Ibid., 6:393; Lenski, *Revelation*, p. 377.
117. Deissmann, *Light from the Ancient East*, trans. Lionel R. M. Strachan, 4th ed. (1978 reprint; Grand Rapids: Baker, 1922), pp. 93-94; Robertson, *Word Pictures*, 6:393-94.
118. Beckwith, *Apocalypse*, p. 627; Chilton, *Days of Vengeance*, p. 315.
119. Robertson, *Word Pictures*, 6:394.
120. BDF, par. 102[2].
121. Alford, *Greek Testament*, 4:671; Robertson, *Word Pictures*, 6:395.
122. Charles, *Revelation*, 1:287; Robertson, *Grammar*, p. 728; idem, *Word Pictures*, 6:395-96.
123. Düsterdieck, *Revelation*, p. 351; Lenski, *Revelation*, p. 382.

mentioned in legend. It is not John's habit of pointing distinctly to an extrabiblical source. He simply wants to designate the strongest and most rapid of wings.[124]

Another pleonastic use of ὅπου . . . ἐκεῖ follows the one in 12:6. This construction followed Semitic usage, but was not unknown in classical and other nonbiblical Greek writings uninfluenced by Semitic sources.[125]

Since the Greek has no dual number, both here and in the LXX version of Dan. 7:25 and 12:7, "two times" is expressed by a simple unqualified plural καιρούς (Lee).

12:15 Ποταμοφόρητον is a rare word with the connotation "immersed in the flood and borne away by it."[126] The word occurs only here in the NT and is not found in the LXX or in classical writers. It was unattested outside the NT until found in some papyrus texts from Egypt, meaning "washed away by the Nile."[127]

The combination τηρεῖν τὴν ἐντολήν is particularly Johannine, being found only twice in the NT outside John's writings and not appearing at all in the LXX. It occurs nine times in the gospel of John and the Johannine epistles and two times in Revelation (Charles).

12:18 A textual variant reads ἐστάθην rather than ἐστάθη. This takes John as the subject, as the one standing on the sands of the sea, and begins a new sentence. If this reading were correct, it would be the only time in the book when John changes his position without being told to do so (Sweet). The probabilities are on the side of ἐστάθη being correct, however, largely because of its external support, including p[47], Sinaiticus, Alexandrinus, and Ephraemi. The first person reading apparently arose when copyists accommodated ἐστάθη to the first person of the following εἶδον in 13:1.[128]

---

124. Düsterdieck, *Revelation*, pp. 351-52; Alford, *Greek Testament*, 4:672; Stuart, *Apocalypse*, p. 627; Beckwith, *Apocalypse*, p. 629; Robertson, *Word Pictures*, 6:396.
125. Robertson, *Grammar*, p. 722; BDF, par. 297.
126. Stuart, *Apocalypse*, p. 628; cf. Lenski, *Revelation*, p. 384.
127. Karl Heinrich Rengstorf, "ποταμοφόρητος," *TDNT*, 6:607-8.
128. Bruce M. Metzger, *A Textual Commentary on the Greek New Testament* (New York: United Bible Societies, 1971), p. 748.

17
Background Concluded and Introductory Episodes for the Seven Bowls

b. The Beast Out of the Sea (13:1-10)

Translation

¹And I saw a beast coming up out of the sea, having ten horns and seven heads, and upon his horns were ten diadems, and upon his heads names of blasphemy. ²And the beast which I saw was like a leopard, and his feet [were] as [those] of a bear, and his mouth [was] as the mouth of a lion. And the dragon gave to him his power and his throne and great authority. ³And [I saw] one of his heads as slain unto death, and the wound of his death was healed. And the whole earth marveled after the beast, ⁴and worshiped the dragon—because he gave the authority to the beast—and worshiped the beast saying, "Who is like the beast, and who can make war with him?"

⁵And a mouth speaking great things, even blasphemies against God, was given to him and authority to continue forty-two months was given to him. ⁶And he opened his mouth for blasphemies against God, to blaspheme His name and His tabernacle, those who tabernacle in heaven. ⁷And it was given to him to make war with the saints and to overcome them, and authority over every tribe and people and tongue and nation was given to him. ⁸And all those who dwell upon the earth will worship him, whose names are not written from the foundation of the world in the book of life of the Lamb slain.

⁹**If anyone has an ear, let him hear:**
¹⁰**If anyone is for captivity,**
　into captivity he departs;
If anyone is to be killed by the sword,
　[it is necessary for] him to be killed by the sword.
Here is the endurance and the faithfulness of the saints.

Exegesis and Exposition

Characteristics of the beast. The first four verses of chapter 13 tell some the aspects of the beast's appearance.

13:1 With the dragon in position (12:18), καὶ εἶδον (*kai eidon*, "and I saw") introduces a new scene which tells the way the dragon moves in his effort to wage war with the seed of the woman (12:17):[1] Καὶ εἶδον ἐκ τῆς θαλάσσης θηρίον ἀναβαῖνον, ἔχον κέρατα δέκα καὶ κεφαλὰς ἑπτά, καὶ ἐπὶ τῶν κεράτων αὐτοῦ δέκα διαδήματα, καὶ ἐπὶ τὰς κεφαλὰς αὐτοῦ ὄνομα[τα]* βλασφημίας (*Kai eidon ek tēs thalassēs thērion anabainon, echon kerata deka kai kephalas hepta, kai epi tōn keratōn autou deka diadēmata, kai epi tas kephalas autou onoma[ta] blasphēmias,* [2] "And I saw a beast coming up out of the sea, having ten horns and seven heads, and upon his horns were ten diadems, and upon his heads names of blasphemy"). This is a continuation of John's vision of the woman clothed in the sun and the dragon, but at this point it enters a new phase in a description of the resultant warfare between the beast out of the sea and the seed of the woman whom this section calls "the saints" (cf. 13:7).

The preposition ἐκ (*ek*, "out of") tells the source of this θηρίον (*thērion*, "beast") as it does for the beast in 13:11. The source is τῆς θαλάσσης (*tēs thalassēs*, "the sea") as the vision draws upon the imagery of Dan. 7:3 here and at several points in this section.[3] Various understandings of "the sea" have surfaced. Is it the sea as a symbol of the great mass of humanity, particularly the Gentiles? This finds support in Rev. 17:15[4] and in this apparent figurative meaning in Dan. 7:2-3 where the four winds of heaven make the sea turbulent.[5] Yet if the sea is a figure for the mass of humanity, what do the sands of the

---

1. Alan F. Johnson, "Revelation," in *EBC*, ed. Frank E. Gaebelein (Grand Rapids: Zondervan, 1981), 12:520.
2. See 12:18 for what is the opening clause of 13:1 in English translations.
3. Archibald Thomas Robertson, *Word Pictures in the New Testament* (Nashville: Broadman, 1933), 6:398.
4. Henry Barclay Swete, *The Apocalypse of St. John* (London: Macmillan, 1906), p. 161; William Lee, "The Revelation of St. John," in *The Holy Bible,* ed. F. C. Cook (London: John Murray, 1881), 4:672.
5. Henry Alford, *The Greek Testament* (London: Longmans, Green, 1903), 4:674.

sea on which the dragon stands (12:18) symbolize? Then too, this explanation leaves no corresponding meaning for the beast out of the earth in 13:11.[6] For these reasons, this symbolic meaning is unsatisfactory.

Is the sea a reference to the Mediterranean Sea? Rome is the opponent of primary concern in John's immediate situation and would be the power that would come to mind as John looked westward from the coast of Asia Minor.[7] But this identification is too restricted. In the apocalyptic visions, the focus of attention is not localized, but takes in the whole world. Does John have the actual sea, not just the Mediterranean, in mind? The ocean or the abyss is the traditional origin of such a beast.[8] The order of describing various parts of the beast's body is what would be expected as an eyewitness watches the creature ascend from the water (Mounce). In the ancient thought, the sea was commonly the reservoir of evil.[9] This understanding leaves room for a comparable understanding of ἐκ τῆς γῆς (*ek tēs gēs*, "out of the earth") in 13:11. This view also agrees with the plain language of the text.[10]

To say the beast ascended out of the *actual* sea, however, would contradict 11:7 and 17:8 which say he ascended from the abyss (Mounce). Rev. 11:7 has him ascending from the abyss, the source of demonic powers opposed to God. To say that the sea stands for the abyss carries on the OT concept of the sea, that it is the source of satanic sea monsters (cf. Job 26:12-13; Pss. 74:13-14; 87:4; 89:9-10; Isa. 27:1; 51:9-10) (Johnson). Also, Paul equates the sea with the abyss in his Rom. 10:7 citation of Deut. 30:13.[11] One hesitates to attach such a figurative meaning to the sea, but related texts in the Apocalypse furnish grounds for doing so. In his prophetic state of being "in the spirit," what met John's spiritual eyes was the sea, but this was a representation to him of what he calls the abyss in 11:7 and 17:8.

As noted earlier in connection with 11:7, the noun θηρίον (*thērion*,

---

6. Friedrich Düsterdieck, *Critical and Exegetical Handbook to the Revelation of John*, in Meyer's Commentary, trans. and ed. Henry E. Jacobs (New York: Funk & Wagnalls, 1887), pp. 364-65; R. C. H. Lenski, *The Interpretation of St. John's Revelation* (Columbus, Ohio: Lutheran Book Concern, 1935), p. 389.
7. Isbon T. Beckwith, *The Apocalypse of John* (New York: Macmillan, 1919), p. 633.
8. Ibid., p. 633; Robert H. Mounce, *The Book of Revelation*, NICNT (Grand Rapids: Eerdmans, 1977), p. 250.
9. Leon Morris, *The Revelation of St. John*, TNTC (Grand Rapids: Eerdmans, 1969), p. 165; Mounce, *Revelation*, pp. 249-50.
10. Düsterdieck, *Revelation*, p. 364.
11. G. V. Caird, *A Commentary on the Revelation of St. John the Divine*, HNTC (New York: Harper & Row, 1966), p. 161.

"beast") denotes a bestially ferocious nature.[12] Etymologically, it is the diminutive of θήρ (*thēr*), but it often carries the same sense as the source noun. Just as βιβλίον (*biblion*) means "scroll" and not "little scroll," so θηρίον (*thērion*) means "beast" and not "little beast." As contrasted with the Lamb of God, he stands for chaos against order, evil against good, and death against life. The symbolic connotation of *thērion* is in question, as noted in the discussion of 11:7. To make him an inhuman entity being like the incarnation of evil (Morris), is too general to satisfy the details of the text. Identifying him as the aggregate of empires of the world under satanic power in opposition to Christ (Alford, Bullinger), is little better. Yet the unified personal qualities of the beast do not lend themselves to an aggregate figure. The beast must be a personal figure as well as the head of an empire.[13] A satanic force operative in the empire or empires must have its embodiment in a malevolent person.[14]

The view that sees the beast as picturing the Roman Empire rests to some degree on identifying Nero Caesar as the wounded head of the beast (13:3).[15] Also figuring into the supporting evidence is the mention of the seven hills in 17:9.[16] The obvious affinity of the beast's description with the fourth kingdom of Dan. 7:7 is another pointer to Rome.[17] Also, a corroborating consideration is the appropriation of the blasphemous titles to themselves by the Roman emperors during the first and second centuries.[18] Rome, of course, was the immediate oppressor in John's personal situation.[19]

But taking the beast as the Roman Empire also has its obstacles. No historical situation, including John's own, can fully satisfy all the

---

12. E. W. Bullinger, *The Apocalypse* or *"The Day of the Lord"* (London: Eyre & Spottiswoode, n.d.), p. 421; John Peter Lange, *The Revelation of John*, Lange's Commentary, ed. E. R. Craven (Grand Rapids: Zondervan, 1968), p. 265.
13. John F. Walvoord, *The Revelation of Jesus Christ* (Chicago: Moody, 1966), p. 200.
14. Philip Edgcumbe Hughes, *The Book of Revelation* (Grand Rapids: Eerdmans, 1990), p. 145.
15. Morris, *Revelation*, p. 167; David Chilton, *The Days of Vengeance* (Fort Worth, Tex.: Dominion, 1987), p. 329.
16. Norman B. Harrison, *The End* (Minneapolis: Harrison Service, 1948), p. 135; David A. Desilva, "The 'Image of the Beast' and the Christians in Asia Minor: Escalation of Sectarian Tension in Revelation 13," *TrinJ* 12NS, no. 2 (Fall 1991): 202-4.
17. R. H. Charles, *The Revelation of St. John*, ICC (New York: Scribner's Sons, 1920), 1:345-46; Homer Hailey, *Revelation, an Introduction and Commentary* (Grand Rapids: Baker, 1979), pp. 284-85.
18. Robertson, *Word Pictures*, 6:398.
19. Düsterdieck, *Revelation*, p. 368.

criteria regarding the beast.[20] Though the beast may represent the empire in part, a transition to the ruler of the empire comes no later than the last clause of v. 3.[21] Further, the dominion of this empire exceeds the limit of what the Roman Empire has ever been or ever will be; it is worldwide.[22] Then too, the dragon is a created being, and so is the false prophet (the beast out of the earth). This beast must be a created being too.[23]

To satisfy the obvious relation of this beast to the future climax of history, some see him as typical of the revived Roman Empire in the future Great Tribulation.[24] This certainly has an element of truth in it, because the last of Daniel's four world empires, the one that the Messiah crushes in the end (cf. Dan. 2:40-45; 7:23-25; 8:22), is Rome. The stage of the empire represented by the beast is the period after the emergence of the little horn of Dan. 7:8 (Walvoord). This would have been evident to John's readers familiar with Dan. 7:2-8.[25] Yet this view is too simplistic and makes inadequate allowance for the personal qualities of the beast in Rev. 13:3 ff. (Morris).

So a fifth view that the beast is the false Christ of the last times personalizes the beast.[26] The parallelism between 13:8 and 17:8 points to such an identification[27] as does the fact that the beast's number is the number of a man (13:18). The beast is identified with one of its heads (13:3*a* = 13:6) who is a travesty of the slain Lamb.[28] Other parallels between the beast and Christ include both wielding swords, both having followers on whose foreheads were inscribed their names (cf. 13:16-17; 14:1), both having horns (5:6; 13:1), both being slain (σφάζω [*sphazō*], 13:3, 8), both rising to new life and authority, and both having power over the whole world (cf. 1:5; 7:9; 13:7; 17:12)

---

20. Walvoord, *Revelation*, p. 198; George E. Ladd, *A Commentary on the Revelation of John* (Grand Rapids: Eerdmans, 1972), p. 177; Mounce, *Revelation*, p. 251.
21. G. R. Beasley-Murray, *The Book of Revelation*, NCB (Grand Rapids: Eerdmans, 1978), p. 209.
22. Bullinger, *Apocalypse*, pp. 422-23.
23. J. B. Smith, *A Revelation of Jesus Christ* (Scottdale, Pa.: Herald, 1961), p. 197.
24. H. A. Ironside, *Lectures on the Book of Revelation* (New York: Loizeaux, n.d.), p. 230; Walvoord, *Revelation*, p. 199.
25. Martin Kiddle, *The Revelation of St. John*, HNTC (New York: Harper, 1940), p. 242.
26. Swete, *Apocalypse*, p. 161; Lee, "Revelation," 4:689-90; Johnson, "Revelation," 12:521.
27. Beckwith, *Apocalypse*, p. 636.
28. James Moffatt, "The Revelation of St. John the Divine," in *The Expositor's Greek Testament*, ed. W. Robertson Nicoll (Grand Rapids: Eerdmans, n.d.), 5:430.

(Johnson). This must be a person (Lee). The obvious problem with this view, however, is that it does not do justice to the kingdom aspects of the beast.

Since the fourth beast of Daniel 7 is a composite of the other three, this beast must be a panoramic representation of dominant world empires of all time, but in Rev. 13:1-10, John's vision focuses on that series of empires as they come to their climactic end. First-century Rome was one of those empires, and the world empire of the end times will bear some relationship to Rome. The keys to the chronological location of the beast lie in its heads and crowned horns. The best solution to the problem appears to be a combination of the view that this is the revived Roman Empire and the view that this is the end-time false Christ. This final world empire will embody a satanically empowered individual who will present himself as a counterfeit Christ in order to deceive the earth-dwellers.

The beast's ten horns and seven heads show his close affinity to the dragon (12:3), but here the κέρατα δέκα (*kerata deka*, "ten horns") are more prominent because of their naming prior to the κεφαλὰς ἑπτά (*kephalas hepta*, "seven heads"). Placement of the διαδήματα (*diadēmata*, "diadems") on the horns rather than the heads as in 12:3 also accents the horns' importance in this picture of the beast. The horns, an emblem of power in Scripture,[29] represent ten kings or kingdoms of which the final of the seven world empires (i.e., the seven heads) will consist,[30] so the shift of the diadems from the seven heads to the ten horns—necessitating a change from seven to ten diadems—represents a shift in perspective from 12:3 to 13:1. The conflict of 12:1-5 transpires while the seven world empires are running their course, but at 13:1 the focus has shifted to the last of these kingdoms when the beast will enjoy his supremacy over the ten kings who act as subrulers under his authority (cf. 17:12).[31] The imagery here fits that of Dan. 7:7, 24 where the fourth beast has ten horns (Alford). The horns and the heads are not just part of the pictorial effect (contra Moffatt, Beasley-Murray). They both represent kingdoms, because 17:10 and 12 say that both are "kings," i.e., kingdoms whose personal leaders the heads and horns picture.

But they do not represent kingdoms in the same extensive sense as the beast himself. An analysis of 17:10 will reveal that the seven heads

---

29. Moses Stuart, *A Commentary on the Apocalypse* (Edinburgh: Maclachlan, Stewart, 1847), p. 636.
30. See the discussion at 17:9-10 for an amplified explanation of the symbolism of the seven heads.
31. Walter Scott, *Exposition of the Revelation of Jesus Christ* (Swengel, Pa.: Bible Truth Depot, n.d.), p. 270; Smith, *Revelation*, p. 193.

stand for seven successive world monarchies: Egypt, Assyria, Babylon, Medo-Persia, Greece, Rome, and the regime represented by the ten simultaneous kingdoms—i.e., the ten horns (cf. Dan 7:16, 17, 23, 24) (Lee). This pattern follows the pattern of Daniel's visions where a horn "represents either a king (see vii. 24, viii.5, 8*a*, 9, 21) or a dynasty of kings (viii. 3, 6, 7, 8*b*, 20, 22) rising up in, or out of, the empire symbolized by the creature to which the horn belongs."[32] The explanation that sees the ten horns as ten Roman emperors of the past (i.e., Augustus, Tiberius, Caligula, Claudius, Nero, Galba, Otho, Vitellius, Vespasian, and Titus) and the seven heads as seven of these less the three usurpers (i.e., Galba, Otho, and Vitellius), is so arbitrary that it has little to commend it (Lee). The horns are here a symbol for a number of kings who will aid Satan's deputy in the end (cf. 17:10 ff.) (Beckwith). The beast can have only one head at a time (cf. 17:9-10), so the heads must be successive. In contrast, the ten horns live and rule at the same time (Dan. 7:24; Rev. 17:12) (Smith). It appears that one head designates the entire existence of the beast at some given time, because the wounded head (13:3) equates with the whole beast in 13:12, 14 (Lee, Charles, Beckwith).

A διάδημα (*diadema*, "diadem") was a mark of kingly rank (cf. 19:12). Στέφανος (*Stephanos*, "Crown") perhaps carried the same connotation at times (cf. 4:4: 14:14), but more often it denoted victory (Beckwith). Here the diadems mark the regal state of the subordinate kings, as verified by 17:12, 18 which declare both their regal status and their subordination.[33]

The "names of blasphemy" (ὄνομα βλασφημίας [*onomata blasphēmias*]) on the beast's heads are names that amounted to words or conduct injurious to God's honor and holiness. Specifically, they involved the assumption of deity by the beast which is tantamount to arrogant blasphemy. An expansion of what the blasphemy is comes in 13:5-6 (Mounce, Beckwith). Roman emperors from the time of Augustus onward illustrate in a lesser way what this blasphemy will be. The use of divine titles applied to these emperors and found in the imperial letters among the inscriptions at Ephesus amounted to blasphemy against God. The magnification of this practice will characterize the activities of the false Christ of the future (cf. 2 Thess. 2:4).[34]

13:2 The likening of the beast to a leopard, bear, and lion recalls

32. Samuel Rolles Driver, *The Book of Daniel* (Cambridge: Cambridge Univ., 1905), p. 84.
33. Stuart, *Apocalypse*, p. 637.
34. Swete, *Apocalypse*, pp. 161-62; Charles, *Revelation*, 1:348; Moffatt, "Revelation," 5:429; Beckwith, *Apocalypse*, p. 635; Robertson, *Word Pictures*, 6:398; Caird, *Revelation*, p. 163.

the fourth beast of Dan. 7:3-7, because he is a composite of the first three and their characteristics (Beckwith): καὶ τὸ θηρίον ὃ εἶδον ἦν ὅμοιον παρδάλει, καὶ οἱ πόδες αὐτοῦ ὡς ἄρκου, καὶ τὸ στόμα αὐτοῦ ὡς στόμα λέοντος (kai to thērion ho eidon ēn homoion pardalei, kai hoi podes autou hōs arkou, kai to stoma autou hōs stoma leontos, "and the beast which I saw was like a leopard, and his feet [were] as [those] of a bear, and his mouth [was] as the mouth of a lion"). The combined strength and brutality of historical Babylon, Medo-Persia, and Greece is what will comprise the total character of this beast. Rome had and in its restored form will have the agility, the catlike vigilance and craft, and fierce cruelty of a leopard, the feet of a bear to crush her enemies, and the roar of a lion. This is what the saints will face in the last days (Swete).

Παρδάλει (Pardalei, "Leopard") is an associative instrumental case following ὅμοιον (homoion, "like").[35] Occurring only here in the NT, the word depicts a cross between a panther and a lioness (Walvoord). This part of the picture derives from Dan. 7:6. The bruising force of a bear's feet in crushing its prey is proverbial.[36] Ἄρκου (Arkou, "Of a bear") is genitive, because it presupposes a repetition of οἱ πόδες (hoi podes, "feet") from earlier in the verse.[37] This part of the description is from Dan. 7:5. It is probably the last of the heads, the one that is yet to come (17:10), that has τὸ στόμα (to stoma, "the mouth"). The lion's mouth was large, exhibiting menacing teeth and having not only the terror of a loud roar but also fearful devouring capabilities.[38] The repetition of (stoma) between ὡς (hōs, "as") and λέοντος (leontos, "lion") matches constructions in 9:8, 9, but in 1:10; 4:1, 7 no noun comes between hōs and the following genitives (Charles). This part of the picture of the beast comes from Dan. 7:4. The picture of all three animals combines qualities of all of Israel's former oppressors (cf. Hos. 13:7-8): craft, lust for blood, and vicious energy (Moffatt).

The dragon is the source of the beast's power and authority: καὶ ἔδωκεν αὐτῷ ὁ δράκων τὴν δύναμιν αὐτοῦ καὶ τὸν θρόνον αὐτοῦ καὶ ἐξουσίαν μεγάλην (kai edōken autō ho drakōn tēn dynamin autou kai ton thronon autou kai exousian megalēn, "and the dragon gave to him his power and his throne and great authority"). The dragon works through the beast. The war is of Satan's making, but the ruler and his empire is his tool for waging it. Satan claimed such power when tempting Christ (cf. Matt. 4:9; Luke 4:6), but never does he exercise it in such a direct

---

35. Robertson, Word Pictures, 6:398.
36. Stuart, Apocalypse, p. 639; James Glasgow, The Apocalypse (Edinburgh: T. & T. Clark, 1872), p. 350.
37. Robertson, Word Pictures, 6:398.
38. Stuart, Apocalypse, p. 639; Glasgow, Apocalypse, p. 351.

and blatant way as he will when his champion, the beast, emerges as the world leader.[39]

"His power" refers to that of the dragon as granted to his vice-regent (Beckwith). It includes power over freedom and life (13:10) and the entire business of mankind (13:17),[40] summed up in the occupancy of a throne that grants to the beast a βασιλεία (*basileia*, "kingdom") (cf. 16:10). As Jesus is one with the Father and shares His throne (cf. 3:21), so this beast shares the throne of the dragon (cf. 2:13).[41] "Great authority" (ἐξουσίαν μεγάλην [*exousian megalēn*]) is widely extended control that covers the whole world, because Satan is the god of this world (cf. 2 Cor. 4:4).[42]

13:3 Another καί (*kai*, "and") continues the narrative of v. 1 (Swete): καὶ μίαν ἐκ τῶν κεφαλῶν αὐτοῦ ὡς ἐσφαγμένην εἰς θάνατον, καὶ ἡ πληγὴ τοῦ θανάτου αὐτοῦ ἐθεραπεύθη (*kai mian ek tōn kephalōn autou hōs esphagmenēn eis thanaton, kai hē plēgē tou thanatou autou etherapeuthē*, "and [I saw] one of his heads as slain unto death, and the wound of his death was healed"). A finite verb εἶδον (*eidon*, "I saw") is not in the text, but the force of the (*eidon*) in v. 1 continues into v. 3, requiring an accusative case μίαν (*mian*, "one") as its direct object.[43]

The phrase ὡς ἐσφαγμένην εἰς θάνατον (*hōs esphagmenēn eis thanaton*, "as slain unto death") parallels ὡς ἐσφαγμένον (*hōs esphagmenon*, "as slain") in 5:6 where the Lamb carried the scars of death (cf. 13:8), so this head, like the Lamb, has sustained a mortal wound (Swete). The fact that he was "slain" points to the violent death of the head, but the likeness indicated in "*as* slain" indicates a restoration to life (Charles). This is all part of the dragon's attempt to counterfeit the death and resurrection of Christ.

An identification of this death-to-life sequence has been a question. A suggested reference to the repeated demise and recovery of the pagan state throughout history[44] is not an ultimate solution, because it does not account for the placement of the event at the end of history. A referral of the description to Caligula, a first-century Roman emperor who had a serious illness and recovered (cited by Charles, Mounce, Morris) suffers from the same objection. Besides, Caligula never returned and never will (Lenski).

---

39. Swete, *Apocalypse*, pp. 162-63; Moffatt, "Revelation," 5:429; Robertson, *Word Pictures*, 6:398.
40. Düsterdieck, *Revelation*, p. 369.
41. Ibid.
42. Stuart, *Apocalypse*, p. 639.
43. Düsterdieck, *Revelation*, p. 369; Swete, *Apocalypse*, p. 163; Beckwith, *Apocalypse*, p. 635; Robertson, *Word Pictures*, 6:399.
44. Mounce, *Revelation*, p. 253; J. P. M. Sweet, *Revelation* (Philadelphia: Westminster, Pelican, 1979), p. 208.

A widely held view attaches these words to Nero whose restoration to life after committing suicide in A.D. 68, was a belief current at the end of the first century A.D. (Beckwith, Morris). Since he was notorious as a persecutor of Christians, some would not believe he was dead for a while, but when the belief that he was still alive faded, by the end of the century the expectation that he would rise from the dead to resume his persecution replaced that belief.[45] The other side of the issue is strong in opposing the Nero view, though. It is doubtful that John or other Christians believed the Nero-*redivivus* myth.[46] Nero has never returned from the dead and never will (Lenski). The facts of the case simply do not fit the details of Revelation 13 and 17.[47] In Nero's case, a wound to the emperor was not a wound to the empire as 13:12, 14 would require. Ancient tradition reflected by Irenaeus had no knowledge of a Nero-*redivivus* myth.[48] Another detail that does not fit is the use of πληγή (*plēgē*, "wound") and ἐσφαγμένην (*esphagmenēn*, "slain") in 13:3, both of which require a violent death such as would not fit the suicide of Nero. Though Nero may be a kind of preview of the future false Christ, the unveiling of the real figure is yet to come (Kiddle). Interestingly, the Nero view was unknown to the earliest fathers of the church, being first suggested by Victorinus and made explicit by Augustine.[49]

Connecting this death-to-life sequence with the terrible convulsions of the Roman Empire in A.D. 69 and its restoration shortly thereafter by Vespasian is another proposed identification (Moffatt, Walvoord). The big weakness of this proposal is its failure to recognize that the pronoun αὐτοῦ (*autou*, "his") in the expression τοῦ θανάτου αὐτοῦ (*tou thanatou autou*, "of his death") limits the wounding and healing to one of the heads, a king, and cannot apply to the whole kingdom (Charles). Revelation 13:12, 14 with v. 3 require the equivalence of the head to the beast and vice versa. The healing of the head is the healing of the beast, and the healing of the beast is the healing of the head. Besides, the healing is a future, not a past, happening.

It is best to identify this restoration to life with an end-time satanically controlled king who will come to the world as a false Christ. This allows for the interchangeability of the head with the whole beast—i.e., the king with his kingdom—as vv. 12, 14 require.[50] It co-

---

45. Paul S. Minear, *I Saw a New Earth* (Washington: Corpus, 1968), pp. 248-49; Caird, *Revelation*, pp. 164-65; Mounce, *Revelation*, pp. 252-53.
46. Düsterdieck, *Apocalypse*, pp. 371-74; Lenski, *Revelation*, p. 394.
47. Minear, *I Saw*, p. 247.
48. B. M. Newman, "The Fallacy of the Domitian Hypothesis," *NTS* 10 (1963): 136.
49. Düsterdieck, *Apocalypse*, pp. 371, 373.
50. Robertson, *Word Pictures*, 6:399.

incides with further details to come in 17:8. It agrees with a final climactic appearance of the beast in history as a person, in concert with the vision's focus on the future (Kiddle). This means a future sequence that will be a close counterfeiting of Christ's death and resurrection. The climax of history will include a healing (ἐθεραπεύθη [*etherapeuthē*]) of an individual that closely approximates the resurrection of Christ from the dead. The question of whether Satan has the power to restore a dead person to life (Walvoord) requires no answer here. Whether the beast performs this marvelous feat through deception or through power permitted by God, it still brings him into the limelight as never before.

That is why the healing will attract such wide attention: καὶ ἐθαυμάσθη ὅλη ἡ γῆ ὀπίσω τοῦ θηρίου (*kai ethaumasthē holē hē gē opisō tou thēriou*, "and the whole earth marveled after the beast"). His feat in overcoming the fatal wound will win for him worldwide admiration.[51] Ὅλη ἡ γῆ (*Holē hē gē*, "The whole earth") does not lend itself to the limitation of meaning the "land" or apostate Israel.[52] The language of the context (e.g., v. 7*b*) extends the reference to a universal application. This will be the final embodiment of the false Christ (Beckwith).

13:4 The wonder of the world over the healing of the beast's death-wound evolves into worship of the dragon and the beast: καὶ προσεκύνησαν τῷ δράκοντι ὅτι ἔδωκεν τὴν ἐξουσίαν τῷ θηρίῳ, καὶ προσεκύνησαν τῷ θηρίῳ λέγοντες, Τίς ὅμοιος τῷ θηρίῳ, καὶ τίς δύναται πολεμῆσαι μετ᾽ αὐτοῦ (*kai prosekynēsan tō drakonti hoti edōken tēn exousian tō thēriō, kai prosekynēsan tō thēriō legontes, Tis homoios tō thēriō, kai tis dynatai polemēsai met' autou*, "and worshiped the dragon—because he gave the authority to the beast—and worshiped the beast saying, 'Who is like the beast, and who can make war with him'"). Worship of the dragon—explicitly mentioned only here in Revelation—who empowers the beast is one and the same with worship of the beast. Both will be associated with image worship (13:14-15), which, like all idolatry, is devil worship (cf. 1 Cor. 10:19-21). Revelation mentions worship of the beast several other times (cf. 13:8, 12; 14:9, 11; 20:4) and worship of his image several times (cf. 13:15; 14:9, 11; 16:2; 19:20).

The incomparability of the beast is what provokes people to worship him. "Who is like the beast" (Τίς ὅμοιος τῷ θηρίῳ [*Tis homoios tō thēriō*]) is a parody on the name "Michael" (מִיכָאֵל [*mîkā'ēl*]), which in Hebrew means, "Who is like God?" It also echoes, perhaps even mocks, similar language about God in the OT (cf. Ex. 15:11; Pss. 35:10; 113:5;

---

51. Hughes, *Revelation*, p. 147.
52. Contra Chilton, *Days of Vengeance*, p. 331.

Isa. 40:18, 25; 46:5; Jer. 49:19; Mic. 7:18). The similarity of this blasphemy of the beast worshipers to that mentioned in 2 Thess. 2:4 is unmistakable. The backdrop of Revelation is a diversion of attention away from God to the worship of the civil power and the figure who heads it up (Charles). The implied answer to the question, "Who is like the beast?" is no one.

The worshipers of the beast somehow relate his alleged power over the grave to his ability to wage war victoriously. When they ask, "Who can make war with him?" the implied answer is no one. His brute force derived from the dragon is more than anyone else can muster. The rhetorical question remains unanswered for the moment, but later answers come in 14:1-5; 17:14; 19:11-21 (Sweet). The Lamb is more than up to the task of facing the beast on the battlefield.

Activities of the beast (13:5-8). Verses 5-8 of chapter 13 speak of some of the activities in which the beast engages. He blends two types of endeavor: insolent blasphemy toward God and almost irresistible powers of seduction over men. Both resemble the activities of the little horn in Daniel (cf. Dan. 7:8, 11, 20, 25; 12:7), sometimes identified as Antiochus Epiphanes, the prototype of anti-God forces who climax world history (Moffatt).

13:5 The beast is a persuasive speaker and has authority to continue in operation for forty-two months: Καὶ ἐδόθη αὐτῷ στόμα λαλοῦν μεγάλα καὶ βλασφημίας, καὶ ἐδόθη αὐτῷ ἐξουσία ποιῆσαι μῆνας τεσσαράκοντα [καὶ] δύο (*Kai edothē autǭ stoma laloun megala kai blasphēmias, kai edothē autǭ exousia poiēsai mēnas tesserakonta [kai] dyo,* "And a mouth speaking great things, even blasphemies against God, was given to him and authority to continue forty-two months was given to him"). A significant question is whether his ability is God-given or not. It relates to both occurrences of ἐδόθη (*edothē,* "was given") in v. 5. One opinion relates the verb to ἔδωκεν (*edōken,* "gave") in vv. 2, 4, and concludes that it comes from the dragon.[53] It reasons that the use of the same form in v. 7a could not say that God gives the beast the ability to overcome the saints (Smith). This rationale does not appear valid, however, because vv. 5-8 have a different perspective from vv. 1-4. The new perspective notes the providence of God that allows the beast his degree of authority so that the saints will be able to endure it for a while (Kiddle). Furthermore, if this were the provision of the dragon, he would hardly limit the operation of the beast to forty-two months (Beasley-Murray). He would have him continue indefinitely.

---

53. Swete, *Apocalypse,* p. 165; Robertson, *Word Pictures,* 6:400.

The better opinion is that *edothē* carries the connotation "granted by God" as it does throughout the rest of the book (cf. 6:4, 8; 7:2; 9:5) (Alford, Swete, Lenski). God allows the beast to blaspheme for a limited time, but will still hold him accountable. One of the great lessons in Daniel from which John draws so heavily is the sovereignty of God over the world's governments (cf. Dan. 4:17, 25, 32) (Caird). The future will be no different.

The στόμα λαλοῦν μεγάλα (*stoma laloun megala*, "a mouth speaking great things") granted to the beast has a durative force, "a mouth that continues speaking great things." This is like Daniel's description of the little horn of the last days (cf. Dan. 7:8, 11, 20, 25) (Swete, Walvoord). He will presumably appropriate the name and attributes of God to himself.[54] The καὶ (*kai*) following μεγάλα (*megala*, "great things") probably has its ascensive meaning, "even" (Beckwith). The "great things" consist of the blasphemies against God.

God also grants him authority ποιῆσαι μῆνας τεσσαράκοντα [καὶ] δύο (*poiēsai mēnas tesserakonta [kai] dyo*, "to continue for forty-two months"). Ποιῆσαι (*Poiēsai*) may also have the sense of "work," in which case the meaning would be "to work [signs] for forty-two months" (cf. Dan. 8:12, 14; 11:28, 30, 32). In any case, μῆνας τεσσαράκοντα [καὶ] δύο (*mēnas tesserakonta [kai] dyo*) is an accusative of the duration of time. It seems preferable to understand ποιέω (*poieō*) to have the meaning of "continue," however, as it does in Matt. 20:12; Acts 20:3; James 4:13.[55] In any event, frantic activity will mark the behavior of the beast as it does that of Daniel's little horn (Sweet). It will be allowed to continue for the last half of Daniel's seventieth week, after the beast has emerged from the abyss to exercise his direct satanic power (cf. 11:2-3; 12:6, 13; Dan. 7:25-27; 12:7) (Scott, Walvoord).

13:6 Verse 6 is an amplification of v. 5a, i.e., the blasphemous speech of the beast (Beckwith): καὶ ἤνοιξεν τὸ στόμα αὐτοῦ εἰς[56] βλασφημίας πρὸς τὸν θεόν, βλασφημῆσαι τὸ ὄνομα αὐτοῦ καὶ τὴν σκηνὴν αὐτοῦ,* τοὺς ἐν τῷ οὐρανῷ σκηνοῦντας (*kai ēnoixen to stoma autou eis blasphēmias pros ton theon, blasphēmēsai to onoma autou kai tēn skēnēn autou, tous en tō ouranō skēnountas*, "and he opened his mouth for blasphemies against God, to blaspheme His name and His tabernacle, those who tabernacle in heaven"). The aorist tense ἤνοιξεν (*ēnoixen*, "he opened") is constative, viewing the whole career of the beast.[57]

---

54. Stuart, *Apocalypse*, p. 642.
55. Beckwith, *Apocalypse*, pp. 636-37; Robertson, *Word Pictures*, 6:400.
56. The preposition εἰς expresses the intention of the beast's speech. He opened his mouth *for the purpose of* blasphemies against God (Robertson, *Word Pictures*, 6:400-401).
57. Robertson, *Word Pictures*, 6:401.

Obviously, blasphemy is not an incidental feature of the beast's kingdom, but one of its continuing characteristics. As Satan's mouthpiece, he utters the ultimate in unbelief and disrespect for God as he magnifies himself above all, claiming to be the sovereign. In this, he resembles the man in Dan. 11:36-45 (Walvoord). Lev. 24:16 tells the serious consequences of this sin (Lee).

Βλασφημίας πρὸς τὸν θεόν (*Blasphēmias pros ton theon*, "Blasphemies against God") are an elaboration of the "names of blasphemy" on the heads of the beast (v. 1). They in turn receive a further elaboration in βλασφημῆσαι τὸ ὄνομα αὐτοῦ καὶ τὴν σκηνὴν αὐτοῦ, τοὺς ἐν τῷ οὐρανῷ σκηνοῦντας (*blasphēmēsai to onoma autou kai tēn skēnēn autou, tous en tō ouranō skēnountas*, "to blaspheme His name and His tabernacle, those who tabernacle in heaven"). Blaspheming the name of God is to demean it directly or appropriate it for oneself. Blaspheming "the tabernacle" (τὴν σκηνὴν [*tēn skēnēn*]) of God is derogatory speech about His heavenly dwelling place (cf. 7:15; 12:12; 21:3).[58]

With no καί (*kai*, "and") preceding τοὺς ἐν τῷ οὐρανῷ σκηνοῦντας (*tous en tō ouranō skēnountas*, "those who tabernacle in heaven") (see Additional Notes), the meaning of the phrase is problematic. Two options, that it refers to the faithful still alive on earth or to the holy angels who inhabit heaven, are not viable in light of the textual decision to omit an introductory καί (*kai*). Another possibility sees the phrase as furnishing the location of ὄνομα (*onoma*, "name") and σκηνήν (*skēnēn*, "tabernacle") (Alford). The negation of this arrangement is grammatical in that the participle τοὺς . . . σκηνοῦντας (*tous . . . skēnountas*) agrees in gender with neither of the two nouns. A further drawback would be the strange combination "the tabernacle which tabernacles in heaven." A fourth possibility interprets this to refer to the saints who have died and gone to heaven (Smith). This view has particularly in mind "those coming out of the great tribulation" (7:14) who are now in heaven, having sustained a close association with the male child of chapter 12, thereby intensifying the enmity of the dragon against them (Smith). This view has difficulty in explaining why the beast is still so bitter against the dead, some of whose deaths were of his doing. Why should he continue to slander them?

The probable answer to the dilemma is to understand τοὺς ἐν τῷ οὐρανῷ σκηνοῦντας (*tous en tō ouranō skēnountas*) as in apposition to τὴν σκηνὴν (*tēn skēnēn*) alone and explaining the place name in terms of those who occupy that place: "His tabernacle, that is, those who tabernacle in heaven" (Beckwith). This satisfies the cognate rela-

---

58. Beckwith, *Apocalypse*, p. 637; Charles, *Revelation*, 1:352; Robertson, *Word Pictures*, 6:401; Caird, *Revelation*, p. 166.

tionship between σκηνόω (*skēnoō*) and σκηνή (*skēnē*) and provides a reason for the special animosity of the beast against heaven's inhabitants. They are members of the angelic army who joined their leader Michael in expelling the dragon from heaven (12:7-9, 12). The dragon in turn passed on his frustration and anger to the beast. The masculine plural σκηνοῦντας (*skēnountas*) in apposition with a feminine singular σκηνὴν (*skēnēn*) is explainable as agreement according to sense rather than natural agreement. The masculine agrees with an implied τοὺς ἀγγέλους (*tous angelous*).

So the beast's blasphemous words direct themselves toward heaven where God and the holy angels reside.

13:7 The beast's rule over other humans becomes explicit: καὶ ἐδόθη αὐτῷ ποιῆσαι πόλεμον μετὰ τῶν ἁγίων καὶ νικῆσαι αὐτούς,* καὶ ἐδόθη αὐτῷ ἐξουσία ἐπὶ πᾶσαν φυλὴν καὶ λαὸν καὶ γλῶσσαν καὶ ἔθνος (*kai edothē autǭ poiēsai polemon meta tōn hagiōn kai nikēsai autous, kai edothē autǭ exousia epi pasan phylēn kai laon kai glōssan kai ethnos*, "and it was given to him to make war with the saints and to overcome them, and authority over every tribe and people and tongue and nation was given to him"). Repetition of the earlier statement about the beast's conflict with the two witnesses (11:7) tells of his conflict with the saints (or the rest of the woman's seed, 12:17), the ones not escaping the dragon's reach into the wilderness (cf. Matt. 24:16; Rev. 13:14) (Lee, Smith). Making war and overcoming the saints are the same concepts as in Dan. 7:21, 23 where the dismal prospect is counterbalanced with the consolation of Dan. 7:22. Overcoming the saints in this case is a termination of their physical lives (cf. 13:15) (Johnson). The use of νικάω (*nikaō*) is ironic here, because in the end it is the martyrs who are the victors (cf. 12:11; 14:1-5; 17:14).

The beast's God-permitted authority (ἐδόθη . . . ἐξουσία [*edothē . . . exousia*, "authority . . . was given"]) over every lineage, nation, language group, and racial group (ἐπὶ πᾶσαν φυλὴν καὶ λαὸν καὶ γλῶσσαν καὶ ἔθνος [*epi pasan phylēn kai laon kai glōssan kai ethnos*]) is explicitly worldwide in its extent (cf. "the whole earth," Dan. 7:23). The Lamb died to redeem people from the same four groups as this ruler will dominate politically (cf. 5:9). This last ruler will have accomplished what every ruler has ever dreamed about. That is to have total world domination (Beckwith, Walvoord). This was his commission from the dragon (v. 2*b*). The all-inclusive scope of this statement prohibits an application of it to any past ruler or empire (Morris).

13:8 The prophet's perspective changes as he shifts from the use of past tenses to the future προσκυνήσουσιν (*proskynēsousin*): καὶ προσκυνήσουσιν αὐτὸν πάντες οἱ κατοικοῦντες ἐπὶ τῆς γῆς, οὗ οὐ γέγραπται τὸ ὄνομα αὐτοῦ ἐν τῷ βιβλίῳ τῆς ζωῆς τοῦ ἀρνίου τοῦ ἐσφαγμένου ἀπὸ καταβολῆς κόσμου (*kai proskynēsousin auton pantes hoi katoikountes* *epi tēs gēs, hou ou gegraptai to onoma autou en tō bibliō tēs zōes tou arniou tou esphagmenou apo katabolēs kosmou,* "and all those who dwell upon the earth will worship him, whose names are not written from the foundation of the world in the Book of Life of the Lamb slain"). The prophecy anticipates the almost universal success the beast will have in attracting worshipers. The only limiting factor will be the refusal of the elect to comply (cf. Matt. 24:24) (Moffatt). Hand in hand with an enthusiastic antagonism against anything Christian will develop a conscious bowing of the knee before Satan's representative and his principles on which the beast will base his kingdom.[59] Universal worship of the beast will be the ultimate achievement of those seeking one worldwide religion as they withhold from the true God His central place.

The masculine pronoun αὐτόν (*auton,* "him") confirms an earlier conclusion that the beast must be a person as well as a kingdom.[60] With the neuter θηρίον (*thērion,* "beast") as its antecedent, grammatical agreement would have called for a neuter pronoun, but the writer chose the masculine because this agent of the dragon is a living king (Alford, Lee). Referral of *auton* to the dragon as the object of worship, as in v. 4,[61] is not probable because that possible antecedent is too far removed from v. 8. A masculine relative pronoun ὅς (*hos,* "who") in 13:14, referring to this same beast, is additional verification of his humanity.

Πάντες οἱ κατοικοῦντες ἐπὶ τῆς γῆς (*Pantes hoi katoikountes epi tēs gēs,* "All those who dwell upon the earth") reintroduces the earth-dwellers into the scene. They have appeared earlier (cf. 3:10; 6:10; 8:13; 11:10 [twice]) and will yet play a role in earth's last days (cf. 13:14 [twice]; 17:8). Their hardness against God has been apparent already, but here their allegiance to and worship of the beast receives affirmation. The addition of πάντες (*pantes,* "all") to the usual technical expression brings out the universality of beast worship in that future time (Smith).

A further characteristic of the earth-dwellers is the absence of their names from the Lamb's Book of Life. The negation of the perfect tense γέγραπται (*gegraptai,* "are . . . written") emphasizes a permanent state of affairs: "the name does not stand (or remain) written."[62] This is the permanent incapacity for life in those who have chosen to lay up treasure on earth and worship the beast (Sweet). The current non-appearance of their names in the Book of Life could be because they

---

59. Lange, *Revelation*, p. 268.
60. See the discussion of θήριον in 13:1.
61. Düsterdieck, *Revelation*, p. 377.
62. Robertson, *Word Pictures*, 6:401.

have never been there or because they were there at one time, but have been removed because of disbelief and consequent disobedience. The discussion of removal of names from the Book of Life at 3:5 opts for the latter of these alternatives.[63] Because of the Lamb's death for all men, the simplest explanation appears to be that the names of all were originally in the book (Walvoord). The idea of such a book as this has deep scriptural roots, extending back into the OT (cf. Ex. 32:32; Ps. 69:28) and the rest of the NT (Phil. 4:3). It appears quite often in Revelation (cf. 3:5; 17:8; 20:12, 15; 21:27).

This book is the Lamb's (ἀρνίου [arniou]) (cf. 21:27 also) and the earth-dwellers have chosen to worship the beast instead of the Lamb. This is why their names have been permanently removed from the book. In chapter 5, He is the only one qualified to open the seals (5:6, 8, 12) and is the Lamb slain to redeem men to God (5:9). In chapter 6, men hide themselves from His wrath (6:16). In chapter 7, His blood has cleansing power (7:14) and He receives worship as God (7:10). In chapter 19, it is His marriage supper that is celebrated (19:7, 9), and in chapter 21, He illumines the city of God (21:14, 23).[64] Τοῦ ἐσφαγμένου (*Tou esphagmenou*, "Slain") identifies this with the slain Lamb of 5:6.

The remainder of v. 8, ἀπὸ καταβολῆς κόσμου (*apo katabolēs kosmou*, "from the foundation of the world"), occurs six other times in the NT: Matt. 13:35; 25:34; Luke 11:50; Heb. 4:3; 9:26; Rev. 17:8. As in a similar expression, πρὸ καταβολῆς κόσμου (*pro katabolēs kosmou*, "before the foundation of the world") (cf. John 17:24; Eph. 1:4; 1 Peter 1:20), κόσμος (*kosmos*, "world") cannot be limited to the beginning of human history, but must refer to the founding of the whole visible order (Swete, Walvoord, Mounce). The connection of the phrase ἀπὸ καταβολῆς κόσμου (*apo katabolēs kosmou*) with what precedes it is in question, however. Is it connected directly with γέγραπται (*gegraptai*), "the book of life written from the foundation of the world," or with ἐσφαγμένου (*esphagmenou*), "the Lamb slain from the foundation of the world"?

The chief support for connecting it with *esphagmenou* is the verse's word order. The phrase follows immediately after the participle.[65] This compares with a twelve-word separation between the phrase and *gegraptai* (Mounce). On the other side, the chief argument for connecting the phrase with *gegraptai* is a parallel in 17:8 where that is the only connection possible. The same finite verb and the same phrase in that

---

63. Robert L. Thomas, *Revelation 1-7, An Exegetical Commentary* (Chicago: Moody, 1992), pp. 260-64.
64. J. Gess, "Lamb, Sheep," *NIDNTT*, 2:411-12.
65. Alford, *Greek Testament*, 4:677; Walvoord, *Revelation*, p. 202; Robertson, *Word Pictures*, 6:402.

verse must have a direct connection because the verse has no word about the Lamb or His being slain (Swete, Lenski). Of course, in 13:8 John may be supplementing the thought of 17:8 with something different (Alford, Caird, Johnson), but 17:8 offers a rejoinder to the principal objection to the *gegraptai* connection. It has a seven-word separation between the phrase and *gegraptai*, thus showing that a contextual separation is no serious obstacle to its connection with *gegraptai*. Consistency of usage by the same author is the stronger consideration, so the sense "the book of life written from the foundation of the world" is the best solution. This sense fits into the immediate context better too. It advances the argument that continues through 13:10 by implying that the elect are predestined to refrain from beast-worship and therefore suffer persecution. This reassures them in the midst of their powerlessness against the beast, they are still in the keeping providence of God, having been there since the foundation of the world (Ladd).

Submission to the beast's persecution and divine providence (13:9-10). How are the persecuted saints to respond to their persecution?

13:9 The prophecy at this point turns aside for a direct word to the faithful regarding their response to these future troublous times: Εἴ τις ἔχει οὖς ἀκουσάτω (*Ei tis echei ous akousatō*, "If anyone has an ear, let him hear"). This charge to hear may refer more closely to what precedes it in vv. 1-8 (cf. Matt. 11:15; 13:9, 43; Mark 4:9, 23; 7:16; Luke 8:8; 14:35) (Lenski, Walvoord) or what follows it in v. 10 (Swete, Lee, Smith). This appears to be a call to hear what follows in v. 10 because of the proverbial nature of v. 10. In other words, it is prospective rather than retrospective.[66]

This call to hear differs slightly from those in chapters 2-3 of Revelation (cf. 2:7, 11, 17, 29; 3:6, 13, 22). There the call is to hear "what the Spirit says to the churches," but the omission of "to the churches" here accords with the promise of 3:10 that Christians will be preserved away from the scene of all this misery. The call in v. 9 addresses a different group of the faithful, telling them what their response should be to the awful treatment at the hands of the beast (Bullinger, Walvoord). The call is to endure in their faith and not give in to the oppressor.[67]

13:10 Several very difficult textual issues complicate an understanding of the meaning of v. 10, but the best estimates of the original text result in the following: εἴ τις εἰς αἰχμαλωσίαν, εἰς αἰχμαλωσίαν ὑπάγει*· εἴ τις ἐν μαχαίρῃ ἀποκτανθῆναι, αὐτὸν* ἐν μαχαίρῃ ἀπο-

---

66. Swete, *Apocalypse*, p. 167; Robertson, *Word Pictures*, 6:402.
67. Anne-Marit Enroth, "The Hearing Formula of the Book of Revelation," *NTS* 36, no. 4 (October 1990): 606-7.

κταυθῆναι (*ei tis eis aichmalōsian, eis aichmalōsian hypagei; ei tis en machairē apoktanthēnai, auton en machairē apoktanthēnai*, "if anyone is for captivity, into captivity he departs; if anyone is to be killed by the sword, [it is necessary for] him to be killed by the sword"). The "Additional Notes" for this section have a brief discussion of the major textual issues.

Some try to understand v. 10 as a warning of divine punishment to persecutors. This has the indirect effect of providing encouragement to the saints because of eventual divine retaliation.[68] This view, which agrees with the reading that inserts ἀπάγει (*apagei*, "goes away") into the protasis of v. 10a (Beckwith), draws evidence from the general truth of divine retribution. God will ultimately triumph and punish the wicked. This furnishes a basis for the patience and faithfulness of the saints in the hour of their persecution (cf. Gen. 9:6; Matt. 5:38; 26:52; Rom. 12:19; Gal. 6:7) (Alford, Charles, Scott, Smith, Walvoord). This also serves to warn the persecutors (cf. Rev. 13:5; 16:6; 18:2-3, 5-8, 20; 19:20) (Walvoord). The problem with this line of thought is that it does not harmonize with the immediate context. The tone in this part is the beast's victorious war against the saints (Alford), with no reference to the saints' eventual victory until 14:1-5. Furthermore, the words are addressed to saints, not to the persecutors as the view proposes. Verse 9 would hardly be the way to introduce a threat (Sweet). The best support for the view is in the OT passages John alludes to, such as Jer. 15:2 and 43:11, passages that teach the eventual downfall of the sinful,[69] but John's license as a NT writer is to assign Jeremiah's words a different sense from what Jeremiah meant.

A second interpretation of v. 10 sees it as addressed to the saints, encouraging readiness for destined sufferings and warning them not to take action against the beast. The warning, however, rests on a reading, ἀποκτενεῖ (*apoktenei*, "will kill") instead of ἀποκτανθῆναι (*apoktanthēnai*, "to be killed") in the protasis of v. 10a, which does not have substantial textual evidence (see "Additional Notes"). Reasons given to support this reading include the appropriateness of addressing such words to the saints rather than to beast worshipers; similar calls to hear in chapters 2-3 that address saints; the threat of captivity has meaning for prospective martyrs, but not for worshipers of the monster; and the call for endurance and faithfulness at the end of v. 10 has no meaning for the ungodly awaiting retribution (Caird). But these

---

68. Alford, *Greek Testament*, 4:678; Ironside, *Revelation*, pp. 234-35; Walvoord, *Revelation*, p. 204.
69. Mounce, *Revelation*, p. 257; Sweet, *Revelation*, p. 213; Chilton, *Days of Vengeance*, pp. 334-35; M. Robert Mulholland, *Revelation, Holy Living in an Unholy World* (Grand Rapids: Zondervan, 1990), p. 227.

reasons apply equally to a third view discussed below. The only distinctive support for this second view derives from Jesus' words in Matt. 26:52, advocating refraining from the use of the sword (Moffatt, Caird), a context different from this one. The logical deficiencies of this view are its explanations of the first protasis-apodosis of v. 10 as supporting the duty of resignation and of the last protasis-apodosis as suggesting the law of human requital (Charles). These bring the two parts of the verse into conflict with each other.

A third view, resting on the Greek text as printed above, has v. 10 warning the saints of the impending persecution by the beast and urging them to submit to divine providence (Swete). The verse contains no reference to their use of force. It stresses the inevitability of persecution and death for the faithful (Alford, Mounce). This interpretation agrees with the invitation to hear in v. 9. It also fits with the reference to endurance at the end of v. 10. It invites the faithful to recognize that the actions of this false Christ have been decreed by God, as indicated in the fourfold use of ἐδόθη (edothē) (13:5, 7, 14, 15) (Kiddle). This meaning also coincides with the emphasis on divine providence in the Jeremiah passages to which John alludes in v. 10 (Jer. 15:2; 43:11).[70] The emphasis in the immediate context on the victory of the beast over the saints leaves little room for any other meaning except an encouragement to accept this as the sovereign will of God.

The close of v. 10 names the personal qualities needed to sustain believers in the face of harsh treatment: Ὧδέ ἐστιν ἡ ὑπομονὴ καὶ ἡ πίστις τῶν ἁγίων (Hōde estin hē hypomonē kai hē pistis tōn hagiōn, "Here is the endurance and the faithfulness of the saints"). The adverb ὧδέ (hōde, "here") focuses on the attitude of submission to the inevitable.[71] Here and in 14:12 the term focuses attention on endurance, but in 13:18 and 17:9 the same word points out wisdom. The suggestion of inevitability implies the supremacy of God's will which always promotes the ultimate good and blessing of the redeemed community,[72] though it may include times of temporary hardship.

"Endurance" (Ὑπομονή [Hypomonē]) characterized the outlook of John and his contemporaries in their persecutions (Rev. 1:9). The churches at Ephesus, Thyatira, and Philadelphia received commendation for their perseverance too (Rev. 2:2, 3, 19; 3:10). Πίστις (Pistis, "Faithfulness") is a word translated "faith" most often in the NT, but in certain contexts such as this it requires the connotation of "faithfulness" or "fidelity" (Charles, Beckwith). The pressures of the times will

---

70. Robertson, Word Pictures, 6:402.
71. Ibid.
72. Hughes, Revelation, p. 150.

require endurance because of the persecuting hand of the tyrant and faithfulness through dark times until his eventual doom.[73] Remembrance that God is sovereign over all that happens and that the dragon and the beast have only a short time, will provide fuel to sustain these two spiritual qualities.

Additional Notes

13:1 The genitive case follows ἐπὶ when the horns are in view (τῶν κεράτων), but the accusative case τὰς κεφαλὰς follows the same preposition when designating the heads. The position of the crowns *upon* the horns as distinct from the names *inscribed on* the heads probably accounts for the difference (Alford).

Some MSS such as p⁴⁷, Sinaiticus, and Ephraemi read the singular ὄνομα here. Others such as Alexandrinus, 046, 051, and 2053 have the plural ὀνόματα. The external evidence for the plural reading is a bit stronger, but internal considerations appear to favor the singular, with copyists tending to alter the singular to a plural after the plural κεφαλὰς. In a close decision, the plural is probably correct.[74] In a similar context, ὀνόματα βλασφημίας occurs in 17:3.[75] No matter which reading is correct, the apparent meaning is that each head had a name of blasphemy on it (Alford).

13:3 The preposition ὀπίσω has a pregnant force here: "wondered *at and followed after* the beast." It carries such a meaning in John 12:19; Acts 5:37; 20:30; 1 Tim. 5:15.[76]

13:4 Τῷ θηρίῳ is an associative instrumental case following ὅμοιος.[77]

13:6 A number of the better MSS, including p⁴⁷, Alexandrinus, and Ephraemi, omit καί just between τὴν σκηνὴν αὐτοῦ and τοὺς ἐν τῷ οὐρανῷ σκηνοῦντας. The inclusion of the καί makes for a strange sense by adding a third object of blasphemy, that is, blasphemy against God, His tabernacle, *and those who dwell in heaven.* Omission of the καί enhances the enormity of the blasphemy by emphasizing the lofty nature of God's holy name and dwelling place. The omission has the disadvantage, however, of being a type of asyndeton not found elsewhere in the Apocalypse (Alford). The inclusion of καί has widespread versional support, but lacks substantial evidence from the Greek MSS.

---

73. Stuart, *Apocalypse*, p. 644.
74. Bruce M. Metzger, *A Textual Commentary on the Greek New Testament* (New York: United Bible Societies, 1971), p. 748.
75. Robertson, *Word Pictures*, 6:398.
76. Alford, *Greek Testament*, 4:676; Robertson, *Word Pictures*, 6:399; BDF, par. 196.
77. Lee, "Revelation," 4:678; Robertson, *Word Pictures*, 6:400.

169

Internal criteria lend their support to the omission as the reading that best explains the origin of the others, so the omission is the choice.[78]

13:7 Of several variant readings in v. 7a, the most significant is the one that omits καὶ ἐδόθη . . . νικῆσαι αὐτούς. The stronger MSS, including p⁴⁷, Alexandrinus, Ephraemi, and 2053, omit this first half of the verse completely. The omission probably resulted through the unintentional copyist error called *homoeoteleuton*, the eye of an early scribe looking away from the first ἐδόθη and picking up the second ἐδόθη upon returning to the page.[79] Inclusion of the words has the support of Sinaiticus, 046, and 051 among other MS sources.

13:8 The direct object of προσκυνήσουσιν is the accusative αὐτόν, though in v. 4 the same verb had a dative as object. Revelation has both usages.[80]

The singular relative pronoun οὗ with the plural antecedent πάντες has the effect of separating the πάντες into its component individuals.[81] A ἕκαστος after the collective πάντες is implied (Beckwith). This perspective carries with it a singular number for ὄνομα and αὐτοῦ too. ῎Ονομα referring to a plurality is a Hebraism (cf. Num. 26:33; 32:38; Deut. 12:3; 1 Sam. 14:49) (Charles, Beckwith). Early copyists were disturbed by this apparent inconcinnity, so they changed οὗ to ὄν. This affected the readings in p⁴⁷, Sinaiticus, and a number of other MSS. Some of these also have αὐτῶν instead of αὐτοῦ and ὀνόματα rather than ὄνομα. The singular relative, singular ὄνομα, and singular αὐτοῦ have the support of Alexandrinus and Ephraemi, however, and being the harder readings, they most probably are original.[82]

13:10 The terseness of εἰς αἰχμαλωσίαν, εἰς αἰχμαλωσίαν ὑπάγει, supported by Alexandrinus and a few other MSS, apparently caused a rash of attempted improvements by copyists such as the insertion of ἀπάγει or συνάγει in the first part of the statement. The only other reading with significant MS support omits one of the εἰς αἰχμαλωσίαν phrases altogether, resulting in an impossible reading: εἰς αἰχμαλωσίαν ὑπάγει has the support of p⁴⁷, Sinaiticus, Ephraemi, and 2053. Yet this reading gives the appearance of being an unintentional omission of one of the duplicate phrases. The reading of Alexandrinus best accounts for the origin of the others.[83]

---

78. Metzger, *Textual Commentary*, pp. 748-49.
79. Swete, *Apocalypse*, p. 166; Robertson, *Word Pictures*, 6:401; Metzger, *Textual Commentary*, p. 749.
80. Robertson, *Word Pictures*, 6:401.
81. Alford, *Greek Testament*, 4:677; Archibald Thomas Robertson, *A Grammar of the Greek New Testament in the Light of Historical Research* (Nashville: Broadman, 1934), p. 722; idem, *Word Pictures*, 6:401.
82. Metzger, *Textual Commentary*, p. 749.
83. Ibid., pp. 749-50.

In place of the ἀποκτανθῆναι, αὐτόν in Alexandrinus, a number of sources have used ἀποκτενεῖ, δεῖ αὐτόν (e.g., Ephraemi) or ἀποκτείνει, δεῖ αὐτόν (e.g., Sinaiticus). Most of the substitutions introduce the idea of retribution for the duty of endurance and the fulfillment of the will of God. Alexandrinus is the least unsatisfactory among the many variants.[84]

Though no δεῖ occurs before αὐτόν in what is construed as the original text, the construction still justifies understanding the sense of the particle: "[it is necessary for] him to be killed . . ." or "he [is to be] killed. . . ."

c. The Beast Out of the Earth (or Land) (13:11-18)

Translation

[11]And I saw another beast coming up out of the earth, and he had two horns like a lamb's, and he spoke like a dragon, [12]and he exercises all the authority of the first beast before him. And he causes the earth and those who dwell in it that they should worship the first beast, whose wound of death was healed. [13]And he does great signs, that he even makes fire come down out of heaven into the earth before men. [14]And he deceives those who dwell upon the earth because of the signs which it is granted him to do before the beast, saying to those who dwell upon the earth to make an image for the beast who has the wound of the sword and came to life. [15]And it was given to him to give breath to the image of the beast, that the image of the beast might both speak and cause that as many as do not worship the image of the beast be killed. [16]And he causes all, the small and the great, and the rich and the poor, and the free and the slaves, that they give to them a mark upon their right hand or upon their forehead, [17]and that no one may buy or sell except the one who has the mark, the name of the beast or the number of his name. [18]Here is wisdom: let the one who has understanding count the number of the beast, for it is the number of man; and his number is six hundred sixty-six.

Exegesis and Exposition

13:11 The introductory καὶ εἶδον (*kai eidon*, "and I saw") marks this as a new scene of the vision in progress since 12:1, one that brings a new beast to John's attention: Καὶ εἶδον ἄλλο θηρίον ἀναβαῖνον ἐκ τῆς γῆς, καὶ εἶχεν κέρατα δύο ὅμοια ἀρνίῳ, καὶ ἐλάλει ὡς δράκων (*Kai eidon allo thērion anabainon ek tēs gēs, kai eichen kerata dyo homoia arniǭ, kai elalei hōs drakōn*, "And I saw another beast coming up out of the

---

84. Ibid., p. 750.

earth, and he had two horns like a lamb's, and he spoke like a dragon"). This beast ascends out of the earth rather than the sea and plays a secondary role in support of the beast from the sea (Walvoord). In the minds of the ancients, none of the terrestrial animals could compare in magnitude with monsters from the deep, so coming out of the earth in itself indicated a degree of inferiority in power of the second beast to the first.[85] He is just as ferocious as the first because he appears in the form of a ἄλλο θηρίον (*allo thērion*, "another beast"), the ἄλλο (*allo*) hinting that he is another of the same kind. His supporting role is of a religious nature as his title of "false prophet" later in the book indicates (16:13; 19:20; 20:10) (Swete). His likening to a lamb gives the same impression (Walvoord) as does his role in worship (13:12) (Mounce).

A quest for a closer identification of this new beast has led in a number of different directions. A common Protestant interpretation has seen him as papal Rome.[86] This does not jibe with his title "false prophet," however, nor does it harmonize with his eventual fate in the lake of fire (19:20; 20:10).[87] Only individual persons, not institutions, will meet that fate. Preterist interpreters of Revelation have seen the beast as the embodiment of the priests of the Caesar-cult in the provinces of first-century Rome. These had charge of implementing the emperor's program at the local level and were opposite counterparts of true Christian prophets (Charles, Moffatt, Kiddle). Yet these priests did not match the signs performed by this beast (Johnson). Neither can the pagan priesthood as an institution qualify as a singular "false prophet" whose destiny is the lake of fire (Seiss). The contemporary sacerdotal system of John's time cannot exhaust the transhistorical character of the beast's description. It looks to a future situation that will be far more comprehensive (Ladd, Hailey, Johnson).

Another suggestion does look to the future and says the beast is the false prophet Jesus spoke about in His Olivet Discourse (Matt. 24:24; Mark 13:22) (Johnson). This allows for a worldwide anti-God system sponsored by Satan that manifests itself in periodic human antichrists (ibid.). The glaring deficiency in this approach, though, is the difference between the "prophets" that Jesus spoke of and this "prophet." He is a single individual, not many, and must be so to meet an ultimate fate in the lake of fire (Seiss). The view also fails to allow that "anti-Christian prophecy" will in the last times converge into one personal agent (Lee).

---

85. Stuart, *Apocalypse*, p. 645.
86. Robertson, *Word Pictures*, 6:403; Hughes, *Revelation*, p. 151.
87. J. A. Seiss, *The Apocalypse* (New York: Charles C. Cook, 1909), 2:420-21.

A view that goes all the way back to Irenaeus, Hippolytus, and Victorinus is that this beast is the main religious assistant or henchman of the first beast or the end-time false Christ (Swete, Morris). All of chapter 13 is a parody of the Christian era, with a counterfeit trinity, a death and resurrection, and a universal church with its mark of membership (Seiss, Sweet). So the beast has an outwardly Christian image. This agrees with his role as false prophet in contrast to the two true prophets of chapter 11. Like them, he performs great signs, stands before the one he represents (11:4; 13:12), has special power over fire (11:5; 13:13), has a connection with resurrection (11:11; 13:14-15), convinces men of their superior's supreme power (11:5-6; 13:17), and directs men to worship the one they designate (11:13; 13:15) (Kiddle). It is apparent that the second beast captures organized religion in the service of the first beast (Ladd). To fulfill this role, he will possibly be of Jewish lineage whose principal domain will be Palestine (cf. Dan. 11:37; 2 Thess. 2:4) and who will receive his accreditation through the signs and wonders Satan enables him to perform (2 Thess. 2:9),[88] but dogmatism on this detail is impossible.

The Lamb in 5:6 has seven horns, but this second beast has only two horns of a little lamb in contrast with the ten horns of the first beast (Beckwith). The lesser number is indicative of lesser power.[89] The likeness to a lamb points to this beast's counterfeiting of the milder nature of the Lamb introduced in chapter 5 and seen again in chapter 14, though a direct contrast with the Lamb of 14:1 is not intended. The absence of an article with ἀρνίῳ (*arniō*, "lamb") forbids a direct comparison (Alford), as does the difference in the number of horns.

Δράκων (*Drakōn*, "Dragon"), though anarthrous, undoubtedly refers to the dragon of chapter 12 and 13:2 (Swete). Though the beast's mannerisms appear so gentle, his words are satanic (cf. Matt. 7:15) (Alford). What he lacks in power, he compensates for in cunning and corrupting influence.[90] This type of persuasiveness contrasts with the first beast's loud blasphemy against all heavenly things (13:6) (Beckwith). This is not blustering fierceness (Kiddle), but deceptive, subtle, seductive speech to lure people away from faith in Christ and into the dragon's trap.[91]

13:12 The second beast is the implementer of the first beast's agenda: καὶ τὴν ἐξουσίαν τοῦ πρώτου θηρίου πᾶσαν ποιεῖ ἐνώπιον αὐτοῦ. καὶ ποιεῖ τὴν γῆν καὶ τοὺς ἐν αὐτῇ κατοικοῦντας ἵνα προσκυνήσουσιν τὸ θηρίον τὸ πρῶτον, οὗ ἐθεραπεύθη ἡ πληγὴ τοῦ θανάτου αὐτοῦ (*kai tēn*

---

88. Scott, *Revelation*, pp. 279, 281-82.
89. Stuart, *Apocalypse*, p. 646.
90. Ibid.
91. Chilton, *Days of Vengeance*, p. 337.

exousian tou prōtou thēriou pasan poiei enōpion autou. kai poiei tēn gēn kai tous en autę katoikountas hina proskynēsousin to thērion to prōton, hou etherapeuthē hē plēgē tou thanatou autou, "and he exercises all the authority of the first beast before him. And he causes the earth and those who dwell in it that they should worship the first beast, whose wound of death was healed"). He is the effective agent of much of the satanic persecution on behalf of the first beast.[92] The verb ποιέω (*poieō*, "I exercise," "I cause," "I do") occurs five times in vv. 12, 13, and 16 to speak of his actions. He exercises authority, forces worship, produces great signs, brings fire down from heaven, and causes people to receive the mark of the first beast (Lenski, Walvoord). Four of the five uses of *poieō* (vv. 12a, 12b, 13a, 16) are "dramatic" uses of the present tense to point out vividly the habitual practice of the beast in doing these things.[93] This is a satanic imitation of the ministry of the Holy Spirit in pointing people to Christ.

The first beast has full confidence in the second and has entrusted him with all his authority. The first beast fights the dragon's battles, and the second supports the first in his own peculiar ways (Swete). The first beast has general oversight of the second's activities, as ἐνώπιον αὐτοῦ (*enōpion autou*, "before him") implies. It is comparable to the relationship between Moses and Aaron (cf. Ex. 4:16; 7:9) and between the LORD and Elijah (cf. 1 Kings 17:1).[94] The association between the two is intimate.[95]

A specific exercise of authority is to bring men to worship the first beast, to practice gross idolatry by worshiping a man as God.[96] The objects of the persuasive action are τὴν γῆν καὶ τοὺς ἐν αὐτῇ (*tēn gēn kai tous en autę*, "the earth and those who dwell in it"). This, a Hebrew figure of speech, is a pleonasm or redundancy to speak of all the earth's inhabitants (Bullinger). It differs slightly from τοὺς κατοικοῦντας ἐπὶ τῆς γῆς (*tous oikountas epi tēs gēs*, "those who dwell upon the earth") of v. 14. The latter is Revelation's technical expression for those in rebellion against God, but the expression here speaks more broadly of all earth's inhabitants. It includes the people of Israel who have escaped to the wilderness and are exempt from this campaign of worship (12:13-16) (Smith), and also includes the rest of the woman's seed who are not exempt but must face directly the antagonistic pressure to worship the beast (12:17; 13:7, 17).

---

92. Robertson, *Word Pictures*, 6:403.
93. Ibid.
94. Alford, *Greek Testament*, 4:680; Swete, *Apocalypse*, p. 169; William Henry Simcox, *The Revelation of St. John the Divine* (Cambridge: Cambridge Univ., 1893), p. 82; Lenski, *Revelation*, p. 404.
95. Glasgow, *Apocalypse*, p. 360.
96. Stuart, *Apocalypse*, p. 646; Mounce, *Revelation*, p. 259.

As it does also in v. 14, the relative pronoun οὗ (*hou*) has a secondary causal tone in introducing a reason for worshiping the first beast, his miraculous healing. This counterfeits the reason Christians have for worshiping the Lamb, His resurrection (cf. Acts 17:30-31).[97] An explanation of the beast's healing that interprets that the beast himself recovered but one of his heads with the mortal wound did not, seeks fulfillment of the phenomenon in the restoration of order in the Roman Empire by Vespasian (A.D. 69-79) after a bloody revolution. The chaotic times followed the death of Nero two years earlier (Mounce). This explanation gives inadequate attention to the equation between the head (v. 3) and the beast himself (vv. 12, 14). The death-stroke comes to both, so the head and the beast are interchangeable.[98] The healing of the beast is the healing of the head, so the fulfillment of this healing must await the future reign of the false Christ, who after receiving a death-wound, rises to live again and exercise his world dominion (Beckwith).

13:13 Exploits of the second beast include σημεῖα μεγάλα (*sēmeia megala*): καὶ ποιεῖ σημεῖα μεγάλα, ἵνα καὶ πῦρ ποιῇ ἐκ τοῦ οὐρανοῦ καταβαίνειν εἰς τὴν γῆν ἐνώπιον τῶν ἀνθρώπων (*kai poiei sēmeia megala, hina kai pyr poiȩ̄ ek tou ouranou katabainein eis tēn gēn enōpion tōn anthrōpōn*, "and he does great signs, that he even makes fire come down out of heaven into the earth before men"). In his gospel, John generally employs the combination ποιέω σημεῖον (*poieō sēmeion*, "I do a sign") to designate the miracles of Christ, but Christ warned that counterfeit signs would indicate the arrival of false Christs (Matt. 24:24-25). These counterfeit signs parody the true ones as a part of the dragon's overall plan to verify the claims of his false prophet (cf. 16:14; 19:20; Mark 13:22; 2 Thess. 2:9). The pseudo-prophet will perform these to obscure the truth, to confuse people, and to win the wrong orientation for their inner allegiance.[99] His effort will far outdo what the Egyptian magicians could do (e.g., Ex. 7:10-12)[100] and the efforts of Simon Magus who reputedly brought statues to life (Caird). These will be genuine miracles, supernatural accomplishments, not mere trickery or skill in pyrotechnics.[101] They will almost deceive the elect

---

97. Beckwith, *Apocalypse*, p. 640; Sweet, *Revelation*, p. 216; Chilton, *Days of Vengeance*, p. 338.
98. Robertson, *Word Pictures*, 6:403.
99. Bullinger, *Apocalypse*, p. 436; Lange, *Revelation*, p. 270; Morris, *Revelation*, p. 171; Caird, *Revelation*, p. 172; Kiddle, *Revelation*, pp. 255-56; Sweet, *Revelation*, p. 216; Johnson, "Revelation," 12:512, 530.
100. Swete, *Apocalypse*, p. 170; Seiss, *Apocalypse*, 2:443; Hughes, *Revelation*, p. 152.
101. Contra Stuart, *Apocalypse*, p. 647, and Steven J. Scherrer, "Signs and Wonders in the Imperial Cult: A New Look at a Roman Religious Institution in the Light of Rev 13:13-15," *JBL* 103, no. 4 (December 1984): 610.

(Matt. 24:24), but the faithful will recognize them for what they are because of the purpose for which they are performed and the doctrine that they seek to prove (Seiss).

The beast's sign-producing power extends even to the point of John's wildest dreams of calling down fire from heaven. John and his brother James had asked Jesus' permission to wield this power (Luke 9:54; cf. 1 Kings 18:38; 2 Kings 1:10-12), but had been denied. A reference to the tongues of fire at Pentecost (Acts 2:2-3) is possible, but the resemblance to Elijah and the two witnesses (11:5) is stronger (Alford, Swete, Morris, Walvoord).

13:14 The very thing Jesus said would happen, deception (Matt. 24:24), will happen by the hand of the second beast: καὶ πλανᾷ τοὺς κατοικοῦντας ἐπὶ τῆς γῆς διὰ τὰ σημεῖα ἃ ἐδόθη αὐτῷ ποιῆσαι ἐνώπιον τοῦ θηρίου, λέγων τοῖς κατοικοῦσιν ἐπὶ τῆς γῆς ποιῆσαι εἰκόνα τῷ θηρίῳ ὃς ἔχει τὴν πληγὴν τῆς μαχαίρης καὶ ἔζησεν (kai planą tous katoikountas epi tēs gēs dia ta sēmeia ha edothē autǭ poiēsai enōpion tou thēriou, legōn tois katoikousin epi tēs gēs poiēsai eikona tǭ thēriǭ hos echei tēn plēgēn tēs machairēs kai ezēsen, "and he deceives those who dwell upon the earth because of the signs which it is granted him to do before the beast, saying to those who dwell upon the earth to make an image for the beast who has the wound of the sword and came to life"). The signs performed by the beast will serve to lead people astray and bring them to the worship of a false god. Πλανᾷ (Planą, "He deceives") is frequent in John's writings to speak of pointing victims to the worship of false gods (2:20; 12:9; 18:23; 19:20; 20:3, 8, 10; 1 John 2:26; 3:7; cf. Matt. 24:11, 24) (Johnson).

Planą is a dramatic present to portray the same repetitive action as the uses of *poiei* discussed in v. 12. This man will keep on fooling people into believing lies as though they were God's truth. He will parody the Holy Spirit who promotes God's truth by drawing people to Christ (cf. John 16:13-14).[102] Deception is a characteristic trait of Satan (Rev. 12:9), so this beast comes about his ability naturally (Swete). It is particularly the persuasive power of the signs performed (διὰ τὰ σημεῖα ἃ ἐδόθη αὐτῷ ποιῆσαι [dia ta sēmeia ha edothē autǭ poiēsai, "because of the signs which it is granted him to do"]) that accomplish the ulterior designs of the false prophet and his superior.[103] The victims of the deception compose the entire body of unregenerate humanity, designated by the semitechnical phrase τοῖς κατοικοῦσιν ἐπὶ τῆς γῆς (tois katoikousin epi tēs gēs, "those who dwell upon the earth") (Charles, Mounce). The doing of the signs ἐνώπιον τοῦ θηρίου (enōpion

---

102. Robert Wall, *Revelation*, New International Biblical Commentary, ed. W. Ward Gasque (Peabody, Mass.: Hendrickson, 1991), pp. 171-72.
103. Stuart, *Apocalypse*, p. 648.

tou thēriou, "before the beast") means that the second beast has the approval of and is the constant and willing servant of the first beast (Swete, Kiddle). A command to the deceived accompanies the beast's deceptive actions. Λέγων (*Legōn*, "Saying") is practically equivalent to κελεύων (*keleuōn*, "commanding") in this setting.[104] The substance of the command, conveyed in ποιῆσαι (*poiēsai*, "to make") (cf. Acts 21:21),[105] is to construct an image to the first beast. Here is the first of ten references to this image in Revelation (cf. 13:15 [thrice]; 14:9, 11; 15:2; 16:2; 19:20; 20:4). Following this anarthrous εἰκόνα (*eikona*), the rest of the references have the article pointing back to this first mention (Smith). Whether this is an image of an emperor on a coin as that of Caesar in Christ's time (Matt. 22:20)[106] or a statue to which people must bow down, such as that of Nebuchadnezzar in Daniel 3 (Scott) is not clear. Since the pattern of this demand for worship comes from Daniel (Dan. 3:4-6), the latter appears more probable. In John's day, the cities of Asia, Pergamum in particular, had temples erected for the worship of emperors (Thomas, *Revelation 1-7*, pp. 179-80). Why should this great ruler of the future not have at least a full-blown statue toward which people could direct their worship? (Seiss).

The secondary causal force of the relative (ὅς [*hos*, "who"]) once again calls special attention to the beast's recovery from death as the reason for worshiping him (Lenski). The οὗ (*hou*, "whose") of 13:12 does the same. This time, instead of being spoken of as a healing, his recovery is called a return to life. The aorist tense ἔζησεν (*ezēsen*, "came to life") looks at the time when the beast first began to live again.[107] This is the verb and form used to speak of Christ's resurrection earlier (2:8). When one of the heads receives a death-wound (v. 3), the beast along with the head dies (v. 12). The beast along with the head lives again after his resuscitation (Beckwith). This is the final emperor spoken of as the eighth in 17:10-11 (Sweet). The resurrection terminology here is an inspired interpretation of the healing mentioned in vv. 3, 12 (Smith).

13:15 By divine permission, the second beast exercises remarkable powers on behalf of the first beast's image: καὶ ἐδόθη αὐτῷ δοῦναι πνεῦμα τῇ εἰκόνι τοῦ θηρίου, ἵνα καὶ λαλήσῃ ἡ εἰκὼν τοῦ θηρίου καὶ ποιήσῃ [ἵνα]* ὅσοι ἐὰν μὴ προσκυνήσωσιν τῇ εἰκόνι* τοῦ θηρίου ἀπο-κτανθῶσιν (*kai edothē autō dounai pneuma tē eikoni tou thēriou, hina kai lalēsē hē eikōn tou thēriou kai poiēsē [hina] hosoi ean mē pros-*

---

104. BDF, par. 409[2].
105. Robertson, *Word Pictures*, 6:404.
106. Alford, *Greek Testament*, 4:681; Hughes, *Revelation*, p. 152.
107. Beckwith, *Apocalypse*, pp. 640-41; Robertson, *Word Pictures*, 6:404.

kynēsōsin tē eikoni tou thēriou apoktanthōsin, "and it was given to him to give breath to the image of the beast, that the image of the beast might both speak and cause that as many as do not worship the image of the beast be killed"). Though God alone can give life, the ἐδόθη (*edothē*, "it was given") indicates that He permits the beast to do it in this instance. Πνεῦμα (*Pneuma*, "Breath") is not the same as ζωή (*zōē*, "life"), so some feel that the beast made the image only appear to be breathing (Smith, Walvoord). But the remainder of v. 15 indicates that the image spoke and caused the execution of those who refused to worship the image. The *pneuma* is therefore the equivalent of πνεῦμα ζωῆς (*pneuma zōēs*, "the breath of life") so recently encountered in connection with the two witnesses (11:11). So this beast exceeds all earlier idolaters in blaspheming God and usurping His power to bestow life (Kiddle).

The suggested explanation of the speaking capability of the image as resulting from ventriloquism draws an analogy with a similar trick of contemporary magic practiced during the first century (Moffatt). Magic no doubt had a place in emperor worship of the time, as in the cases of Elymas (Acts 13:6-12), the young woman in Philippi (Acts 16:16), and the practitioners in Ephesus (Acts 19:13-20), all of whom had a connection with evil spirits (Sweet). Even if these early examples used trickery to make their feats appear to be supernatural, however, that need not apply to this end-time false prophet. John's language in no way implies a sleight-of-hand deceptiveness. The signs are genuine, but they fool people into following false gods (Kiddle). So his works should not be in the category of "magic." As one of the beast's signs (13:13), he gave life to the image so that it actually spoke.

Not only did it speak, but it also caused the execution of non-worshipers. Ποιήσῃ (*Poiēsē*, "Cause") is parallel with λαλήσῃ (*lalēsē*, "might . . . speak"), both being part of the ἵνα (*hina*) clause that tells the purpose of the breath bestowed on the image. The subject of both verbs is the same (Alford, Lee, Mounce). The image performs both actions, the second possibly resulting from commands spoken in the first.[108] The image causes as many as do not worship the image of the beast to be killed. In this clause the description passes on to the future of nonworshipers as he in v. 8 spoke about the future of worshipers of the beast (Charles). The requirement placed on these future citizens resembles the demand made of Daniel and his friends when Nebuchadnezzar made his image (Dan. 3:1-11). The lesson to the readers is that temporizing is an impossibility for followers of the Lamb (Kiddle, Sweet, Johnson). Worship of the beast and his image is always

---

108. Stuart, *Apocalypse*, p. 649; Mounce, *Revelation*, p. 261.

associated with receiving his mark as v. 16 will indicate. Receiving the mark is impossible without the act of worship (cf. 14:9, 11; 16:2; 19:20; 20:4) (Charles).

A question is whether ἀποκτανθῶσιν (apoktanthōsin, "be killed") means that nonworshipers will only be sentenced to die or will actually be killed. The major impetus for saying the verb refers to sentencing only is the need to have some saints remaining to populate the Millennium at the end of the Great Tribulation (Kiddle, Smith, Walvoord). This forces an unnatural understanding of the language, however. The explicit statement is that the image causes the death of those refusing to worship. John speaks of actual killing in v. 15 (Smith), and his allusion to Dan. 3:5-6 is confirmation of this plain sense (Caird).

Earlier contexts of Revelation indicate that this is not a complete denuding of the righteous from the earth. The woman's escape and protection from the dragon (12:13-16) show that the Messianic community as a whole will survive unharmed. They are out of the beast's reach, because they are out of the dragon's reach. The embargo of 13:17-18 will not affect those protected in the wilderness. The rest of the woman's seed (12:17) will bear the brunt of this massacre. They are the ones who must resign themselves to this act of divine providence (13:9-10). They are the martyrs who receive major attention from this point on. They are the 144,000 who are destined for the greater glory associated with martyrdom (14:1-5). They are the exceptions to the hyperbolic designation "the whole earth" that wonders after the beast (13:3), because they remain loyal to the Lamb through it all (Kiddle).

13:16 The second beast adds the obligation of receiving a visible mark of the first beast to that of worshiping his image: καὶ ποιεῖ πάντας, τοὺς μικροὺς καὶ τοὺς μεγάλους, καὶ τοὺς πλουσίους καὶ τοὺς πτωχούς, καὶ τοὺς ἐλευθέρους καὶ τοὺς δούλους, ἵνα δῶσιν αὐτοῖς χάραγμα ἐπὶ τῆς χειρὸς αὐτῶν τῆς δεξιᾶς ἢ ἐπὶ τὸ μέτωπον αὐτῶν (kai poiei pantas, tous mikrous kai tous megalous, kai tous plousious kai tous ptōchous, kai tous eleutherous kai tous doulous, hina dōsin autois charagma epi tēs cheiros autōn tēs dexias ē epi to metōpon autōn, "and he causes all, the small and the great, and the rich and the poor, and the free and the slaves, that they give to them a mark upon their right hand or upon their forehead"). The natural sense carrying over from the αὐτῷ (autō) of v. 15 is to understand the second beast as the subject of ποιεῖ (poiei, "he causes").

"All" (Πάντας [Pantas]) receive orders from the supreme command to accept an identification emblem. This mandate extends to all people of every civic rank, "the small and the great" (τοὺς μικροὺς καὶ τοὺς μεγάλους [tous mikrous kai tous megalous]) (cf. 11:18; 19:5; 20:15). It includes all classes ranked according to wealth, "the rich and the poor" (τοὺς πλουσίους καὶ τοὺς πτωχούς [tous plousious kai tous ptōchous]). It

179

covers every cultural category, "the free and the slaves" (τοὺς ἐλευ-θέρους καὶ τοὺς δούλους [*tous eleutherous kai tous doulous*]) (cf. 6:15; 19:18). The three expressions are a formula for universality. Pressure will come on the entire population to receive the symbol of allegiance to the first beast.[109]

The ἵνα (*hina*) clause defines the object of that pressure. It is to put the beast's mark either on the right hand or on the forehead of every individual. This movement parodies the sealing of the slaves of God in chapter 7. Just as the elect receive a seal to protect them from the coming of the wrath of God, so the followers of the beast receive his mark to escape his wrath against followers of the Lamb (Mounce). The conferral of the beast's mark will probably begin shortly after the sealing of the 144,000, i.e., early in the last half of the seventieth week. Those who receive the mark will receive it willingly.[110]

Suggestions regarding the nature of the mark have included an official stamp, a wearing of phylacteries, the letter X (*CH*) that begins Christ's name, an invisible mark, and a branding imprint. The use of χάραγμα (*charagma*, "mark") to designate the seals put on commercial documents and stamped with the name and date of the emperor is evidence to support the reference to an official stamp.[111] Papyrus documents from the general period of Revelation that use *charagma* abound with references to the emperor and show the need for imperial approval to buy and sell (Bullinger). The problem with this explanation is that these marks were on certificates or, in the case of references to the forehead, involved only the general reputation of an individual's devotion to the emperor.[112] This hardly satisfies the use of ἐπὶ (*epi*, "upon") to specify the location of the mark "upon their right hand or upon their forehead."

Neither will an analogy to Jewish phylacteries suffice to satisfy the data (cf. Charles, Mounce). The powers of a false Christ would not utilize portions of the law or prayer scrolls as its insignia. Besides, phylacteries were on the left hand, not the right. The use of the first letter of Christ's name[113] is an implausible way to explain the mark too. Though customarily practiced among Christians at a later time, it was not well enough known by the time John wrote Revelation to

---

109. Stuart, *Apocalypse*, p. 649; Beckwith, *Apocalypse*, p. 641; Charles, *Revelation*, 1:362.
110. Düsterdieck, *Revelation*, p. 381.
111. Mounce, *Revelation*, p. 262; J. Massyngberde Ford, *Revelation*, vol. 38 of AB (Garden City, N.Y.: Doubleday, 1975), p. 215.
112. Cf. W. M. Ramsay, *The Letters to the Seven Churches of Asia* (New York: A. C. Armstrong, 1904), pp. 110-11.
113. R. H. Preston and A. T. Hanson, *The Revelation of Saint John the Divine* (London: SCM, 1949), p. 99.

qualify for such a prominent purpose. The theory of inscription with an invisible mark rests on the assumption that the sealing of the 144,000 in chapter 7 was invisible too (Alford, Swete, Kiddle, Ladd). Yet in his vision, the mark was visible to John (Mounce). The locations of the hand and forehead, places most conspicuous to the observer, also attest that the mark's purpose is its visibility.[114]

The mark must be some sort of branding similar to that given soldiers, slaves, and temple devotees in John's day. In Asia Minor, devotees of pagan religions delighted in the display of such a tatoo as an emblem of ownership by a certain god (Kiddle, Sweet). In Egypt, Ptolemy Philopator I branded Jews, who submitted to registration, with an ivy leaf in recognition of their Dionysian worship (cf. *3 Macc.* 2:29).[115] This meaning resembles the long-time practice of carrying signs to advertise religious loyalties (cf. Isa. 44:5) (Kiddle) and follows the habit of branding slaves with the name or special mark of their owners (cf. Gal. 6:17).[116] *Charagma* ("Mark") was a term for the images or names of emperors on Roman coins, so it fittingly could apply to the beast's emblem put on people.

The question of why *charagma* instead of the customary σφράγις (*sphragis*, "seal") designates the mark, if this is the meaning (Johnson), is interesting, but does not negate the viewpoint. The objection that branding on the forehead was a sign of disgrace (Caird) is debatable. Slavery in these early times was not degrading as it has come to be in modern times. It could just as well denote loyalty, ownership, and protection, just as the seal given the slaves of God. The verb χαράσσω (*charassō*, "I engrave") is the source of *charagma* (cf. Acts 17:29). It will be visible and the point of recognition for all in subjugation to the beast (cf. 13:7; 14:9; 16:2; 19:20; 20:4).[117] In v. 16 the right hand and the forehead are given as alternative locations of the mark, being connected by ἤ (*ē*, "or"), but in 20:4 a καί (*kai*, "and") connects the two positions because that verse speaks of those who received the mark in neither place.

13:17 A second decree of the beast dictates the impossibility of transacting commerce without the mark: καὶ* ἵνα μή τις δύνηται ἀγοράσαι ἢ πωλῆσαι εἰ μὴ ὁ ἔχων τὸ χάραγμα, τὸ ὄνομα* τοῦ θηρίου ἢ τὸν ἀριθμὸν τοῦ ὀνόματος αὐτοῦ (*kai hina mē tis dynētai agorasai ē*

---

114. Düsterdieck, *Revelation*, p. 382.
115. Alford, *Greek Testament*, 4:682; Moffatt, "Revelation," 5:433; Robertson, *Word Pictures*, 6:405-406; Mounce, *Revelation*, p. 262.
116. Alford, *Greek Testament*, 4:682; Scott, *Revelation*, p. 284; Robertson, *Word Pictures*, 6:405; Edwin A. Judge, "The Mark of the Beast, Revelation 13:16," *TynBul* 42 (May 1991): 159-60.
117. Wall, *Revelation*, p. 173.

pōlēsai ei mē ho echōn to charagma, to onoma tou thēriou ē ton arith-mon tou onomatos autou, "and that no one may buy or sell except the one who has the mark, the name of the beast or the number of his name"). No one could engage in trade without the mark of the beast (Morris). Conditions of hardship imposed on those suspected of dis-loyalty to Domitian during John's time[118] may illustrate what will be in the future, but they were nowhere near the severity of the regime of the future false Christ. Under the third seal, the world as a whole had difficulty obtaining the necessities of life (6:5-6), but here deprivation of the necessities of life is a tool of the false prophet to punish the faithful for their loyalty to the Lamb. Until the appointed time of their execution (13:15), they must undergo this nagging harassment at the hands of the dragon-sponsored regime. This is constant pressure to become a worshiper of the beast, because receiving the mark and worshiping the beast are inseparable commitments.

Τὸ ὄνομα (*To onoma*, "The name") is in apposition with τὸ χάραγμα (*to charagma*, "the mark"). The mark consists of the name. The num-ber of the beast's name is one and the same with the name, since ἤ (*ē*, "or") has in this usage the sense of τοῦτ᾽ ἐστιν (*tout' estin*, "that is"). It is "the name, or, which is the same thing, the number of the name" (Swete). The equivalence means that as a name, it is written in letters, but as a number, the name's equivalent is in numbers.[119] The number will receive further elaboration in v. 18.

13:18 The writer now momentarily drops his role as a seer and becomes, in a manner of speaking, a hierophant or cabalist by speak-ing in riddles (Moffatt): Ὧδε ἡ σοφία ἐστίν· ὁ ἔχων νοῦν ψηφισάτω τὸν ἀριθμὸν τοῦ θηρίου, ἀριθμὸς γὰρ ἀνθρώπου ἐστίν· καὶ ὁ ἀριθμὸς αὐτοῦ ἑξακόσιοι ἑξήκοντα* ἕξ (*Hōde hē sophia estin; ho echōn noun psē-phisatō ton arithmon tou thēriou, arithmos gar anthrōpou estin; kai ho arithmos autou exakosioi hexēkonta hex*, "Here is wisdom: let the one who has understanding count the number of the beast, for it is the number of man; and his number is six hundred sixty-six"). Verse 10 has a similar use of ὧδε (*hōde*, "here"), and 17:9 has a similar formula to the one opening v. 18. Here and in 17:9, the adverb anticipates what follows, but in 13:10 and 14:12, it refers to what precedes it (Charles, Smith).

The verse provides a means by which the intelligent reader can compute the first beast's number (Morris). The term σοφία (*sophia*, "wisdom") is the understanding and skill necessary to solve the prob-lem of the number (cf. Dan 9:22) (Beckwith). This is probably not the

---

118. Ramsay, *Seven Churches*, pp. 106-7.
119. Charles, *Revelation*, 1:364; Robertson, *Word Pictures*, 6:406.

same as the spiritual gift of wisdom through which early Christians received enablement to apprehend and interpret direct revelations from God (cf. 1 Cor. 12:8; Eph. 1:17) (contra Swete), but is along with the voῦν (*noun*, "understanding") the special intelligence to be given believers alive during the days of the false Christ's reign. Through the God-given ability, they will be able to unravel the mystery of the number. Daniel 12:10 speaks of this special understanding also.[120]

Whatever the solution, the way to reach it is by counting. Ψηφισά-τω (*Psēphisatō*, "Let [him] count") is a verb coming from ψῆφος (*psēphos*, "pebble") (cf. Luke 14:28).[121] The ancients used pebbles for counting. The more precise meaning of ψηφισάτω τὸν ἀριθμόν (*psēphisatō ton arithmon*, "let [him] count the number") is a significant issue. To affix the phrase with a general meaning involving no arithmetic complexities and with a simple call to discern the identity of the beast from a broad symbolism, is one proposal. The triple six has each digit falling short of the perfect number seven and so is the number of a man. The number, then, limits the beast to man's level which is far short of the deity of Christ.[122] This solution, however, falls short on two counts. It ignores the command to "count," and it overlooks the writer's intention that the number be understood well enough to identify an individual from it (Alford). General numerical symbolism cannot yield the identity of a specific person.

So the calculation technique called *gematria* or something comparable must come into play. In ancient times, letters of the alphabet served as numbers. The first nine letters stood for the numbers one through nine, and the next nine for the numbers ten through ninety, and so on. In Greek, the current alphabet did not have enough letters, so certain obsolete letters and signs supplemented the system. Every name yielded a number, the deciphering of which proved to be a fascinating riddle. An example of this practice occurs in the *Sibylline Oracles* 1.324-29 where the number of the name Ἰησοῦς (*Iēsous*, "Jesus") is eight hundred eighty-eight (Walvoord, Mounce).

In applying *gematria*, however, a precaution offered long ago by Irenaeus is necessary. The identity of the person represented by the number 666 should not be a subject of speculation until that person

---

120. Gregory K. Beale ("The Danielic Background for Revelation 13:18 and 17:9," *TynBul* 31 [1980]: 165) sees Daniel 2, 9, 11, and 12 as the background of the "eschatological insight" spoken of in v. 18.
121. G. Abbott-Smith, *A Manual Greek Lexicon of the New Testament* (Edinburgh: T. & T. Clark, 1950), p. 488.
122. Minear, *I Saw*, p. 258; Ladd, *Revelation*, p. 187; William Hendriksen, *More Than Conquerors* (Grand Rapids: Baker, 1944), p. 182; Thomas F. Torrance, *The Apocalypse Today* (Grand Rapids: Eerdmans, 1959), p. 86; Walvoord, *Revelation*, p. 210.

arrives on the earthly scene.[123] This precaution answers the objection based on the unreliable and imaginative speculations resulting from the use of *gematria* (cf. Walvoord). It is true that 666 has a secondary implication regarding human limitation, but its primary meaning will be to help Christians of the future recognize the false Christ when he becomes a public figure.

The conjunction γὰρ (*gar*, "for") offers the reason that the calculation should be made. It is because it is the number of a man. Ἀριθμὸς ἀνθρώπου ἐστίν (*Arithmos anthrōpou estin*, "It is the number of man") has two possible meanings. It can mean that it is a humanly intelligible number or that it is the number of a certain individual. The former possibility takes ἀνθρώπου (*anthrōpou*, "human") as an adjectival genitive to mean that the number is easily understandable by anyone with a fair measure of wisdom. This same word, *anthrōpou*, has this meaning in Rev. 21:17 in speaking of "a human measure" (Lenski). Yet it is not valid to use 21:17 as a criterion, because in that verse an angel is the measurer, creating the need for the sense of "a humanly understood measure." To say something is humanly understood here is pointless (Charles). It raises the unanswerable question, what is a nonhuman number? (Moffatt, Mounce).

The inescapable conclusion is that the expression means this is a mysterious hint about a man whose name gives the number 666 (Beckwith, Charles). It is the name of the beast as well as that of one of the beast's heads. He is a king or emperor who at times in the narrative is emblematic of the empire he rules.

If 666 is the number of a future individual, attempts to identify past entities through the number are futile. One such attempt has said that the number combines the common character of the rulers of the former pagan Roman Empire with the rules of later papal Rome (Alford). This errs in making it the number of an empire instead the number of a man. Another attempt has referred the number to specific historic Roman emperors such as Nero Caesar, Domitian, or Caligula, one who personifies the future false Christ.[124] Nero Caesar and Caligula supposedly have names that calculate to 666 or 616 (see "Additional Notes") (Lee, Moffatt, Charles, Beckwith, Mounce, Ford), and Domitian was the apex among first-century Roman emperors in requiring his subjects to worship him (Beasley-Murray, Ford). The Neronic calculation requires using a Hebrew transliteration of the

---

123. Irenaeus, *Contra Haereses* v. 30. 3.
124. Lange, *Revelation*, p. 272; Moffatt, "Revelation," 5:434; Charles, *Revelation*, 1:365.

Greek form of a Latin name for a readership who knew no Hebrew. It also involves a defective spelling.[125] The only sensible conclusion is to agree with the ancient commentators that it does not refer to Nero (Lee, Morris, Mounce). Caligula and Domitian have evidence even weaker than that for Nero.

Another view of 666 sees it as a symbolic reference to the future person of the false Christ (Walvoord, Ladd, Bullinger) but resorts to excess symbolism to identify him. It compares 666, the penultimate claiming ultimacy, with 888, the number of *Iēsous* ("Jesus").[126] This fails to use *gematria* to point to a particular individual and so is not specific enough.

A further attempt to decipher 666 settles on it as a symbolic representation of the whole anti-Christian international power in the whole world of the NT era. It is the epitome of blasphemy and wickedness (Johnson). This is true, but it does not identify a specific individual who heads up the system. Another proposal, by Irenaeus who had close ties with John, refers the number to the Latin Empire.[127] The *gematria* calculations work out better here than in any other proposal (Alford, Johnson). It also bases its calculation on the Greek alphabet, which makes sense for the first readers of Revelation (Lee). Yet this view still fails in that it does not identify an individual, but an empire.[128]

The better part of wisdom is to be content that the identification is not yet available, but will be when the future false Christ ascends to his throne.[129] The person to whom 666 applies must have been future to John's time, because John clearly meant the number to be recognizable to someone. If it was not discernible to his generation and those immediately following him—and it was not—the generation to whom it will be discernible must have lain (and still lies) in the future. Past generations have provided many illustrations of this future personage, but all past candidates have proven inadequate as fulfillments. Christians from generation to generation may manifest the same curiosity as the prophets of old regarding their own prophecies (cf. 1 Pet. 1:10-11), but their curiosity will remain unsatisfied until the time of fulfillment arrives.

---

125. Mounce, *Revelation*, p. 264; Wall, *Revelation*, p. 174.
126. Austin M. Farrer, *The Revelation of St. John the Divine* (Oxford: Clarendon, 1964), pp. 158-59; Caird, *Revelation*, p. 176; Beasley-Murray, *Revelation*, pp. 220-21; Ford, *Revelation*, p. 216.
127. Irenaeus, v. 30. 3; Johnson, "Revelation," 12:533.
128. Stuart, *Apocalypse*, p. 788.
129. Alford, *Greek Testament*, 4:683; Ladd, *Revelation*, p. 187.

Additional Notes

13:11 Through a mode of expression called "breviloquence," ὅμοια ἀρνίῳ stands for a lengthened expression ὅμοια κέρασιν ἀρνίῳ. Thought moves more rapidly than expression of the thought permits, so the words crowd together in a compressed way that is terse and, at first, obscure.[130]

13:12 The ἵνα clause is a sub-final or noun clause (cf. John 11:37; Col. 4:16; Rev. 3:9). This type usually has a subjunctive verb, but its verb here προσκυνήσουσιν is future indicative. This is the construction in 3:9 also.[131]

The direct object τὸ θηρίον is an accusative case following προσκυνέω as it is in 13:8. It contrasts with the dative case following this verb in 13:4.

The relative pronoun οὗ points forward to the αὐτοῦ later in the clause. This is the same Semiticism as found in v. 8 (Beckwith).

13:13 The ἵνα is a rare ecbatic use (i.e., consecutive, introducing result) (cf. John 9:2; 1 John 1:9). The result of the great signs performed is that the beast even goes so far as to call down fire from heaven.[132]

The καὶ immediately after ἵνα has its ascensive force: "even." The second beast's power is so great that he can even duplicate the miracle of Elijah (2 Kings 1:10-12) (Swete).

13:14 At least one has taken τῷ θηρίῳ as a dative of possession, with the sense that the image belongs to the beast, is like him and is consequently his property.[133] A preferable understanding is that it is a dative of advantage, however, "an image for the sake of the beast" (Alford, Ford). In the remaining nine uses of the noun εἰκών in Revelation, it has a genitive, not a dative, referring to the beast to show possession.

The masculine relative ὅς agrees with the natural gender of the person pictured by the neuter τῷ θηρίῳ. The masculine αὐτόν in 13:8 does the same.

13:15 The textual issue of whether to include the bracketed ἵνα is quite difficult. The inclusion has the support of Alexandrinus and a number of other witnesses, but is missing in Sinaiticus and a few other sources. The evidence is further complicated by the conjunction's appearance at other locations in still other sources. The omission may result from what copyists thought was a change of subject from the

---

130. Stuart, *Apocalypse*, pp. 645-46; Robertson, *Grammar*, p. 1203.
131. Beckwith, *Apocalypse*, p. 640; Robertson, *Word Pictures*, 6:403.
132. Alford, *Greek Testament*, 4:680; Stuart, *Apocalypse*, p. 647; Beckwith, *Apocalypse*, p. 640; Robertson, *Grammar*, p. 998.
133. Glasgow, *Apocalypse*, p. 361.

image speaking (λαλήσῃ) to the second beast causing (ποιήσῃ) people to be killed. It must be accidental instead of intentional, however, so the reading supported by Alexandrinus and others must be correct.[134]

The direct object following προσκυνέω is in this instance dative as it is in v. 4, but Alexandrinus and a few other MSS have the accusative τὴν εἰκόνα instead of the dative τῇ εἰκόνι here.

13:16 Though the subject of δῶσιν could be the agents of the beast (Alford, Lenski), the verb is best taken as an indefinite plural, a Hebraism. It replaces a passive voice. Verbs of this nature occur in 10:11; 12:6; 16:15 also.[135] The textual variations that read "that they should receive a mark" and "that he should give them a mark" have only insignificant external support.[136]

The genitive τῆς χειρός following ἐπί emphasizes the visibility of the mark, but the accusative τὸ μέτωπον after the same preposition suggests more the act of making an impression on the hand (Alford). In 7:3 and 9:4, the genitive after ἐπί spoke of the seal on the foreheads of God's slaves.[137]

13:17 Significant MS support, including Sinaiticus and Ephraemi, omits καί at the beginning of v. 17. This takes the ἵνα clause of the verse as dependent on δῶσιν of v. 16. But equally strong witnesses, including p[47] and Alexandrinus, have the conjunction to open the verse, in which case the ἵνα clause of v. 17 is parallel to the one of v. 16. The omission seems to have arisen because of a misunderstanding that v. 17 was dependent on v. 16 rather than parallel to it. The presence of the καί is genuine.[138]

Other readings with significant MS support include "the mark of the name of the beast or the number of his name" (Ephraemi), "the mark or the name of the beast or the number of his name" (p[47]), and "the mark of the beast or his name or the number of his name" (Sinaiticus) (Ford). The reading of Alexandrinus's τὸ χάραγμα, τὸ ὄνομα τοῦ θηρίου ἢ τὸν ἀριθμὸν τοῦ ὀνόματος αὐτοῦ is the one that best explains the origin of the others.

13:18 Instead of ἑξήκοντα which has very strong external support, Ephraemi and a few others read δέκα. This results in the number 616 rather than 666. With Greek letters as numerals, this only involves a change from ξ to ι (666 = χξς and 616 = χις). Perhaps the later change to 616 tried to make the Neronic identification more specific. Neron Caesar in Hebrew (נרון קסר) equaled 666, but required the addition of *n*

---

134. Metzger, *Textual Commentary*, pp. 750-51.
135. Charles, *Apocalypse*, 1:336; Robertson, *Word Pictures*, 6:405.
136. Glasgow, *Apocalypse*, p. 364.
137. Robertson, *Word Pictures*, 6:406.
138. Metzger, *Textual Commentary*, p. 751; Mounce, *Revelation*, p. 263.

at the end of the first name. "Nero Caesar" in Latin equaled 616, necessitating no alteration in spelling.[139]

d. The Victorious Followers of the Lamb (14:1-5)

Translation

[1]And I looked, and behold, the Lamb standing on Mount Zion, and with Him one hundred forty-four thousand having His name and the name of His Father written on their foreheads. [2]And I heard a voice from heaven like a voice of many waters and like a sound of great thunder, and the voice which I heard was like harpers playing on their harps. [3]And they sing [something] [like] a new song before the throne and before the four living beings and the elders; and no one was able to learn the song except the one hundred forty-four thousand, who were redeemed from the earth. [4]And these are those who have not been defiled with women, for they are virgins. These are the ones who follow the Lamb wherever He goes. These were redeemed from men, a contribution to God and to the Lamb, [5]and in their mouth a lie was not found; they are blameless.

Exegesis and Exposition

14:1 Καὶ εἶδον, (*Kai eidon*, "And I looked") introduces each of the three scenes of chapter 14 as it did the two scenes of chapter 13: Καὶ εἶδον, καὶ ἰδοὺ τὸ ἀρνίον* ἑστὸς ἐπὶ τὸ ὄρος Σιών, καὶ μετ' αὐτοῦ ἑκατὸν τεσσαράκοντα τέσσαρες χιλιάδες ἔχουσαι τὸ ὄνομα αὐτοῦ καὶ τὸ ὄνομα τοῦ πατρὸς αὐτοῦ γεγραμμένον ἐπι τῶν μετώπων αὐτῶν (*Kai eidon, kai idou to arnion hestos epi to oros Siōn, kai met' autou hekaton tesserakonta tessares chiliades echousai to onoma autou kai to onoma tou patros autou gegrammenon epi tōn metōpōn autōn*, "And I looked, and behold, the Lamb standing on Mount Zion, and with Him one hundred forty-four thousand having His name and the name of His Father written on their foreheads"). The three scenes consist of the Lamb on Mount Zion with the 144,000 (vv. 1-5), four climactic announcements about the coming prophesied period (vv. 6-13), and the harvest and the vintage (vv. 14-20) (Lee, Lenski, Hailey). Like the third of the three scenes in chapter 14, this one has an addition of καὶ ἰδοὺ (*kai idou*) added to its introduction to call special attention to the greatness of the sight and the striking quality of the vision thus introduced (Lenski). This signals an unexpected and forceful contrast to the visions of chapter 13.[140] It is the opposite side of the picture, a victorious

---

139. Metzger, *Textual Commentary*, pp. 751-52.
140. Düsterdieck, *Revelation*, p. 390; Mounce, *Revelation*, p. 267; Beasley-Murray, *Revelation*, p. 221.

stance of the Lamb and His followers after their temporary setbacks portrayed in chapter 13.[141]

The whole of chapter 14 is proleptic. As a summary of the Millennium (20:4-6), the first five verses feature the Lamb in place of the beast, the Lamb's followers with His and the Father's seal in place of the beast's followers with the mark of the beast, and the divinely controlled Mount Zion in place of the pagan-controlled earth (Alford, Moffatt, Kiddle). The remainder of the chapter furnishes a proleptic outline of the catastrophes and the bliss that receives a chronological and more detailed treatment in 16:17–22:5. In this fashion, the chapter is a sort of *intermezzo* to provide encouragement by telling the ultimate triumph for those who refuse the beast's mark and to predict the doom of those who do receive it.[142]

The center of attention in the first scene is τὸ ἀρνίον (*to arnion*, "the Lamb") who began the whole revelatory process by breaking the seals of the scroll (5:6). Besides suggesting the meekness and sacrificial death of Christ, the figure of a lamb also denotes His resurrection and ultimate victory.[143] His shed blood is the means through which His victory and that of the faithful comes (cf. 5:9; 7:14; 12:11)[144] The contrast of the gentleness of the Lamb to the ferocity of the δράκων (*drakōn*, "dragon") and the θήρια (*thēria*, "beasts") is striking. He is a direct opposite of the beast with two horns like those of a lamb in 13:11.[145] The beasts arise from the sea or the earth (13:1, 11), but He has His feet firmly planted, as the perfect tense of ἑστός (*hestos*, "standing") suggests (Ford). He also contrasts with the dragon who "stood" (ἐστάθη [*estathē*]) on the sands of the sea in 12:18. He is on the rock of Mount Zion instead of the unstable sand (Swete). His pose is no longer that of a slain Lamb, but now that of a militant victor with His feet solidly fixed on the Mount of Olives (cf. Zech. 14:3-4) (Moffatt).

The mention of Mount Zion recalls the vision beginning at 11:1, because the temple was on that mount.[146] It also connects with John's allusions to Psalm 2 and victory over the nations through this middle portion of Revelation (Ps. 2:6; cf. Rev. 11:18; 12:5) (Caird). Major efforts have sought to demonstrate that this is a heavenly Mount Zion. A large consideration in favor of a heavenly scene is the singing that occurs before the throne and the living beings and the elders in

141. Elisabeth Schüssler Fiorenza, in "The Followers of the Lamb: Visionary Rhetoric and Social-Political Situation," *Semeia* 36 (1986): 124, 131.
142. Düsterdieck, *Revelation*, pp. 394-95; Charles, *Revelation*, 2:1; Ladd, *Revelation*, p. 189.
143. Swete, *Apocalypse*, pp. 78, 176; Lee, "Revelation," 4:700; Beckwith, *Apocalypse*, p. 315; Mounce, *Revelation*, p. 145.
144. Düsterdieck, *Revelation*, p. 390.
145. Charles, *Apocalypse*, 2:4; Robertson, *Word Pictures*, 6:408.
146. Alford, *Greek Testament*, 4:684; Mulholland, *Revelation*, p. 240.

14:2-3.[147] The use of Mount Zion as a figure for heaven in Heb. 12:22 is also possible support for this location (cf. Gal. 4:26).[148] This latter evidence is inconclusive, however, because the heavenly Jerusalem of Heb. 12:22 and the Jerusalem that is above of Gal. 4:26 are the perfect archetype of the Jerusalem that will exist in the new creation (cf. 20:9; 21:9–22:5) (Beckwith). Without some special qualification, Scripture never uses Mount Zion to denote a celestial abode of God or His people. The text does not say that the 144,000 are in the same place as the singers, only that they hear the singers. Through a proleptic projection, the martyr victims of 13:15 receive this advance picture of their ultimate victory and stance on earth with the returning Lamb. The 144,000 are a distinctive group with a physical connection to the Jewish nation and the throne of David that requires an earthly location (Seiss).

Another proposal has Mount Zion as the new city of God that will come down from heaven and become the seat of the eschatological kingdom (Ladd, Mounce). The fact that the vision describes the final state of the 144,000, after their trial has passed, makes this explanation appealing (Beckwith). This view has the heavenly Zion of Heb. 12:22 descending to earth in the eschatological framework (Ladd). The difficulty with this view is its assignment of Mount Zion to the new creation rather than the old, thereby distinguishing it from the Zion of history. "Zion" appears 162 times in the Bible and refers practically every time to a locality related to the city of Jerusalem of the old creation. Since the focus of this scene is immediately after the storm of persecution has passed, this must be the millennial kingdom of 20:4-6, not the eternal kingdom of 21:1–22:5. This view also necessitates an equating of the 144,000 with the total body of the redeemed (Beckwith), a questionable equation as subsequent discussion will show.

Another way of handling the name "Mount Zion" is simply to make it a figure for strength (Swete). It is true that this is often the connotation in the OT (Pss. 2:6; 48:2; 78:68; 87:2; 125:1; Isa. 28:16; 59:20; Obad. 17, 21; Mic. 4:7) (Swete), but this explanation does not satisfy the particulars of the text. A place name can have a physical locality and still symbolize safety and security.

The dominant biblical connotation of the name fits here too. Jewish tradition expected a rallying of the faithful remnant at Mount Zion (Ps. 48:1-2; Isa. 11:9-12; 24:23; Joel 2:32) after the difficulties of the latter days (Moffatt, Charles, Johnson). Of the possible meanings,

---

147. Lee, "Revelation," 4:701; Bullinger, *Apocalypse*, p. 443; Kiddle, *Revelation*, pp. 264-65; Mounce, *Revelation*, p. 267; Charles Caldwell Ryrie, *Revelation*, Everyman's Bible Commentary (Chicago: Moody, 1968), p. 88.
148. Robertson, *Word Pictures*, 6:408; Lenski, *Revelation*, p. 419.

whether the hilly area of southeast Jerusalem, the temple mount, the whole city of Jerusalem, or the whole land of Judah and the whole Israelite nation,[149] any one would amount to a literal understanding of the earthly Zion. Since John has Psalm 2 in mind in this larger context (cf. 11:18; 12:5), a reference to earthly Zion is probable. This locality also corresponds to the prophecy of Zech. 14:4-5. So this advance projection pictures the Warrior-King of 19:11-16 as having already returned to earth bringing with Him that select number who have suffered martyrdom at the hand of the beast (13:15).

In the company of the Lamb in Jerusalem are 144,000 sealed individuals. Several factors indicate that these are a special group within a larger body. Besides the assignment of a finite number, the application of ἀπαρχὴ (*aparchē*, "contribution") and certain distinguished moral qualities to them (v. 4) marks them out as a select group from the larger body of the redeemed. They are celibates as v. 4*a* indicates and so cannot include all the faithful. Efforts to explain away their distinctives (Beckwith, Mounce) are to no avail as the discussion of v. 4 will reflect. The fact that the group is redeemed (οἱ ἠγορασμένοι (*hoi ēgorasmenoi*, "who were redeemed," v. 3) does not demand that they constitute *all* the redeemed.

The effort to identify this group as spiritual Israel rather than national Israel faces the same obstacles as it did in connection with the comparable number of Israelites in 7:1-8 (Thomas, pp. 473-78). It lacks exegetical substance and rests on an assumption that is at the same time the point to be proven. The earlier account of the 144,000 related them to national Israel by naming the individual tribes. Here that same connection comes through the placement of the scene in Jerusalem and by the relationship of the group to the woman of chapter 12 (cf. 12:17). A suggestion that this group is not the same as in 7:1-8 rests on the absence of the article from ἑκατὸν τεσσαράκοντα τέσσαρες χιλιάδες (*hekaton tesserakonta tessares chiliades*, "one hundred forty-four thousand") in 14:1,[150] on an alleged difference between the seal of God in 7:2 and the seal with the name of the Lamb and His Father in 14:1 (Scott), and on the absence of a tribe-by-tribe listing in 14:1-5 (Swete). The first and third reasons are not determinative, being explainable in other ways. Neither is the second reason, because the two seals are not different. The latter account in 14:1 simply supplies more detail about the seal than 7:2 does (Walvoord). If this group were different from the earlier one, the writer would have used the word

---

149. A. A. MacRae, "Zion," in *The Zondervan Pictorial Encyclopedia of the Bible*, ed. Merrill C. Tenney (Grand Rapids: Zondervan, 1975), 5:1063-65.
150. Mulholland, *Revelation*, p. 240.

"another" as he does so often (e.g., "another beast," "another angel," "another sign," "another voice") (Smith). The sameness of number and the sealing on the forehead in each case shows that the two groups are the same (Alford).

The view that identifies this with the slaves of God in chapter 7 is correct (Walvoord), but not in its assertion that they receive physical protection from the persecution of the beast. The sealing they received protects them only from the wrath of God, not from the wrath of the dragon and the beast (cf. 12:12). These are the same 144,000 as in chapter 7, but they are also the same as the rest of the woman's seed in 12:17, the witnesses to whom the dragon has access through the beast and who will experience martyrdom because of their refusal to worship the beast (13:15). They are a special group as 14:4 indicates. They are the vanguard who bear the brunt of the struggle against the beast and pay the price of their own lives. They enjoy a special bliss because they faced martyrdom bravely in anticipation of their ultimate triumph that is pictured here (Moffatt). In this scene, they have returned to earth to share in Christ's millennial reign (Charles).

Their emblem of recognition distinguishes them from the worshipers of the beast (13:16). They bear the name of the Lamb and of His Father because they belong to the Father and the Son, not to the dragon and the beast. This is the same seal as is mentioned in 7:3 and is the mark of ultimate victory (cf. 22:4) (Beckwith).

14:2 After viewing the triumphant multitude with the Lamb, John heard a triumphant voice: καὶ ἤκουσα φωνὴν ἐκ τοῦ οὐρανοῦ ὡς φωνὴν ὑδάτων πολλῶν καὶ ὡς φωνὴν βροντῆς μεγάλης, καὶ ἡ φωνὴ ἣν ἤκουσα ὡς κιθαρῳδῶν κιθαριζόντων ἐν ταῖς κιθάραις αὐτῶν (kai ēkousa phōnēn ek tou ouranou hōs phōnēn hydatōn pollōn kai hōs phōnēn brontēs megalēs, kai hē phōnē hēn ēkousa hōs kitharōdōn kitharizontōn en tais kitharais autōn, "and I heard a voice from heaven like a voice of many waters and like a sound of great thunder, and the voice which I heard was like harpers playing on their harps"). This is not the voice of the martyred saints in heaven (contra Smith and Walvoord). The 144,000 are learners of the new song, not the singers. The description of the voice is impressive, likening it to many waters, thunder, and harpers playing their harps (Mounce). It is comparable to the voices from heaven at 10:4, 8; 14:13; 18:4, but has characteristics of the voice of Christ in 1:10, 15. The singers are probably a loud angelic chorus such as the one in 5:11 (Johnson).

A comparison to many waters occurs also at 1:15 and 19:6. In Ezek. 1:24 and 43:2, the simile describes the voice of God, and in Dan. 10:6, the voice of an angel. A comparison to thunder occurs also in 6:1 where one of the living beings speaks, but 19:6 likens the voice to that of a great multitude and to "strong thunder," with ἰσχυρῶν (ischurōn, "strong") replacing the μεγάλης (*megalēs*, "great") of this verse. The author, as one of the "sons of thunder" (Mark 3:17), refers to thunder once in John 12:29 and twelve times in Revelation.[151] Harps appear in 5:8 and 15:2 also. These were the traditional instruments of Psalmody (e.g., Pss. 33:2; 92:3). The voice was not only full and loud, it had the likeness of a melodious strain.

14:3 The song is not just melody, however. It has lyrics to be sung too: καὶ ᾄδουσιν [ὡς]* ᾠδὴν καινὴν ἐνώπιον τοῦ θρόνου καὶ ἐνώπιον τῶν τεσσάρων ζῴων καὶ τῶν πρεσβυτέρων· καὶ οὐδεὶς ἐδύνατο μαθεῖν τὴν ᾠδὴν εἰ μὴ αἱ ἑκατὸν τεσσαράκοντα τέσσαρες χιλιάδες, οἱ ἠγορασμένοι ἀπὸ τῆς γῆς (*kai ǎdousin [hōs] ōdēn kainēn enōpion tou thronou kai enōpion tōn tessarōn zōōn kai tōn presbyterōn; kai oudeis edynato mathein tēn ōdēn ei mē hai hekaton tesserakonta tessares chiliades, hoi ēgorasmenoi apo tēs gēs*, "and they sing [something] like a new song before the throne and before the four living beings and the elders; and no one was able to learn the song except the one hundred forty-four thousand, who were redeemed from the earth"). The plural ᾄδουσιν (*ǎdousin*, "they sing") shows that the singular φωνήν (*phōnēn*, "voice") first heard in 14:2 is actually a chorus of voices (Mounce).

The harpers sang what sounded like (ὡς [*hōs*, "(something) like"]) a song never heard before. In 5:9, the living beings and elders sang a new song, but here they are the audience for the singing.[152] Like the earlier new song, this one depicts joy in heaven over the redemption of the saints (7:11; cf. Luke 15:10) (Beckwith). The song is new because it has a new subject, but also because the singers are new (Bullinger).

Some want to identify the singers as the redeemed ones themselves.[153] The reasons for assigning this identity are the inability of anyone else to learn the song (v. 3) (Kiddle) and the analogy of 15:2 where the overcomers have harps (Beasley-Murray). This cannot be, however, because the song is sung in heaven and the 144,000 redeemed ones are on the earthly Mount Zion (Alford, Beckwith). The song is intelligible to the 144,000, but they are not the singers (Moffatt). The singers are apparently an innumerable angelic company of angels as at 5:11 and 7:11, though their identity is left indefinite as at 11:15; 12:10; 19:16. They do not include the living beings and elders (Beckwith). They cannot experience redemption, but they are deeply interested in everything pertaining to man's salvation (cf. Luke 15:7; Eph. 3:10; 1 Pet. 1:12), so they join in praising the Lamb (Swete). The idea that it is theologically inappropriate for angels to sing of salvation

---

151. Robertson, *Word Pictures*, 6:339.
152. Alford, *Greek Testament*, 4:684; Robertson, *Word Pictures*, 6:408-9.
153. Robertson, *Word Pictures*, 6:408-9; Kiddle, *Revelation*, p. 266; Morris, *Revelation*, p. 176.

(Mounce) is not well taken, because the living beings and elders sing about redemption in 5:9-10. It may seem strange that those who have not experienced redemption can teach such a song to a throng who are among the redeemed (cf. Morris), but that is the probable meaning of the text. The assumption that the singers are martyred saints in heaven who are familiar with the trials faced by the surviving 144,000 (Walvoord) rests on the further assumption that the 144,000 do not suffer martyrdom. The 144,000 are themselves the martyrs who have been raised to stand with the Lamb on Mount Zion, so they cannot be the singers.

In the OT, the "new song" was one of praise to God for new mercies (cf. Pss. 33:3; 40:3; 96:1; 98:1; 144:9; 149:1; Isa. 42:10; see Thomas, p. 399). It resembles the one sung by the Israelites when delivered from Egypt (Ex. 15:1-18) (Ford). Such a song celebrates a mighty deed of God that furnishes a new impulse of gratitude and joy. The new song in Revelation is in celebration of the new age about to be ushered in, a victory based on the sacrificial work of the Lamb.[154] As the 144,000 stand on Mount Zion, the future reign of the redeemed on earth is about to begin (cf. 5:9) (Johnson). This is the occasion of their ultimate victory.[155]

The place of the singing is before God's throne which is the focal point for all the activity beginning in chapter 4. It is also before the living beings and elders, indicating that they are not among the singers this time (cf. 5:9).

The only ones able to learn the song are the 144,000 who have been redeemed from the earth. Their spiritual achievement reflects their spiritual growth, which is the measure of their spiritual apprehension or ability to appreciate the new song deeply (Swete, Charles, Beckwith, Mounce). In 15:2, the ones who have overcome the beast sing the song of Moses and of the Lamb. This appears to be the same company who learn the new song here. The theme of their new song and the song in 15:2 probably relates to the dangers through which they have come (Bullinger). Their redemption (ἠγορασμένοι [*ēgorasmenoi*, "who were redeemed"]) came through the blood of the Lamb, according to 5:9. They now enjoy liberation from the tyranny of the beast and the earth-dwellers (Ford).

14:4 Three appearances of the demonstrative pronoun οὗτοι (*houtoi*, "these") in v. 4, each time in an emphatic position, single out the 144,000 as worthy of high honor for maintaining very high standards in the midst of a corrupt religious, social, and cultural environ-

---

154. Charles, *Revelation*, 1:146; Beckwith, *Apocalypse*, p. 642; Ladd, *Revelation*, p. 190; Robertson, *Word Pictures*, 6:335-36; Mounce, *Revelation*, p. 268.
155. Düsterdieck, *Revelation*, p. 392.

ment (Smith): οὗτοί εἰσιν οἳ μετὰ γυναικῶν οὐκ ἐμολύνθησαν, παρθένοι γάρ εἰσιν. οὗτοι οἱ ἀκολουθοῦντες τῷ ἀρνίῳ ὅπου ἂν ὑπάγει*. οὗτοι ἠγοράσθησαν ἀπὸ τῶν ἀνθρώπων ἀπαρχὴ τῷ θεῷ καὶ τῷ ἀρνίῳ (*houtoi eisin hoi meta gynaikōn ouk emolynthēsan, parthenoi gar eisin. houtoi hoi akolouthountes tǭ arniǭ hopou an hypagei. houtoi ēgorasthēsan apo tōn anthrōpōn aparchē tǭ theǭ kai tǭ arniǭ*, "these are those who have not been defiled with women, for they are virgins. These are the ones who follow the Lamb wherever He goes. These were redeemed from men, a contribution to God and to the Lamb"). The change from the imperfect tense of ἐδύνατο (*edynato*, "was able") of v. 3 to the present tense εἰσιν (*eisin*, "are" [both occurrences]) shows the permanence of their fixed essential character as those who have been undefiled with women and who are virgins. This is how they escaped the pollution of living on earth under the reign of the beast (Alford, Lee, Beckwith).

The aorist tense of ἐμολύνθησαν (*emolynthēsan*, "been defiled") looks back to their lives as a thing of the past, because as they stand on Mount Zion with the Lamb, their earthly sojourn has now ended (note also the aorist εὑρέθη (*heurethē*, "found," v. 5).[156] Whether the term has a figurative meaning or not has been a point of discussion. Favoring a figurative thrust is the logical consideration that a literal meaning to include intercourse within marriage, according to Scripture, does not constitute sinful behavior, whereas a figurative meaning of involvement with pagan immorality is always sinful (cf. Heb. 13:4) (Johnson). This is restraint from intercourse of the wicked type practiced by non-Christian religions, so the term refers ultimately to spiritual purity or the avoidance of idolatry. Yet the position of the phrase μετὰ γυναικῶν (*meta gynaikōn*, "with women") is emphatic, and even if it were not emphatic, it would still exclude a figurative interpretation (Alford; Beckwith). One of the special criteria for these slaves of God was that they have no intercourse with women. The Tribulation will be a very special time in history, requiring an especially high degree of dedication. Paul taught in 1 Corinthians 7 the desirability of the unmarried state because of the nature of the times (1 Cor. 7:26). The single can best render undistracted service for the Lord. So in the future Great Tribulation, virginity will be requisite for this special group.[157] Marriage is the norm for the Christian life during relative tranquil times, but this future reign of the beast will be anything but tranquil for the faithful.

It is not too strange that the 144,000 include men only. The exigencies of the times, including imprisonment and death, are such as re-

---

156. Ibid.; Alford, *Greek Testament*, 4:685.
157. Alford, *Greek Testament*, 4:685-86; William R. Newell, *The Book of Revelation* (Chicago: Moody, 1971), pp. 215-16.

quire males to meet them. If Paul could forbid a woman to teach in the local church assembly (1 Tim. 2:12), John could just as well judge that resistance to the beast require a masculine constitution (Kiddle).

The reason for the group's freedom from defilement (γάρ [*gar*, "for"]) is their fixed principle of character that makes them παρθένοι (*parthenoi*, "virgins"). Like the English word "virgin," the Greek term can apply to any person who has had no sexual intercourse, whether male or female.[158] In Matt. 25:1 and 2 Cor. 11:2, as a figurative term it includes men.[159] The question here is its precise meaning, whether literal or figurative and whether corporate or individual. The case for a figurative meaning leans heavily on references to Israel (2 Kings 19:21; Isa. 23:12; 37:22; Jer. 14:17; 18:13; 31:4, 21; Lam. 1:15; 2:13; Amos 5:2)[160] and the church as a virgin (2 Cor. 11:2) (Lenski). This does not mean that every Israelite or every Christian is a virgin in a literal sense, of course. The problem with this evidence, though, is that all the passages cited refer to a corporate people of God, not to the use of *parthenoi* to speak of individual purity. The other main argument to support a figurative meaning assumes that "virgin" is a symbol for the opposite of spiritual impurity or idolatry which equates with spiritual adultery (Ladd, Morris, Hailey). In other words, it says that these servants of God have refused to join in the religious system of the false Christ (Bullinger). But the assumption of this equation finds no justification in the text, not even in the following statement about their being followers of the Lamb (contra Walvoord).

The passage contains no clues that *parthenoi* is intended to be figurative or metaphorical. Sexual immorality outside the bonds of marriage condemns one to the lake of fire (21:8; 22:15), but John here speaks of standards higher than moral purity. He says that sexual intercourse of any type defiles in the sense that it detracts from the purity of the sacrifice necessary in these times of special stress (Kiddle).

Another explanation of *parthenoi* has related it to the Deuteronomic regulations regarding soldiers going into battle (Deut. 20; 23:9-10; cf. 1 Sam. 21:5; 2 Sam. 11:11) (Caird). These preparations for battle bear some similarity to the dedication required of the 144,000, but 14:1-5 is hardly a battle scene. The very opposite posture of nonresistance is the proper attitude for the martyrs-to-be (13:9-10).

The most probable meaning of *parthenoi* is that it refers to celibates, i.e., it excludes married men (Beckwith). The peculiar demands

---

158. Swete, *Apocalypse*, p. 179; Beckwith, *Apocalypse*, p. 650; Robertson, *Word Pictures*, 6:409.
159. Smith, *Revelation*, p. 210; Ryrie, *Revelation*, p. 89.
160. Walvoord, *Revelation*, p. 216; Chilton, *Days of Vengeance*, p. 356.

of the times require celibacy.[161] This is the basic meaning of the word (Ladd), and it also agrees with the meaning of defilement reached earlier in v. 4. Jesus spoke approvingly of eunuchs (Matt. 19:12), and Paul wished all men to have the gift of continence (1 Cor. 7:1, 32) (Mounce). This is a special holiness of the 144,000 that dictates an entire abstinence because of the nature of the last times (cf. Lev. 15:18).[162] This in no way degrades the institution of marriage, but is in special recognition of the critical times through which this group must pass.

A further special quality of the 144,000 is their persistence in following the Lamb. The words οἱ ἀκολουθοῦντες (*hoi akolouthountes,* "who follow") can refer either to the past habit of life that has led to their present position with the Lamb or to their present state of bliss and privilege as inseparable from the Lamb.[163] The latter meaning is improbable because grammatically the present participle can hardly refer to their present habit of continually following the Lamb. It simply calls them "followers of the Lamb" and refers to their earthly loyalty that earned them their special privilege. The repeated admonition of Christ was for people to follow Him (e.g., Matt. 9:9; 10:38; 16:24; 19:21; Mark 8:34; 9:38; 10:21; Luke 5:27; 9:23; John 8:12; 10:4, 5, 27; 12:26; 21:22) (Charles, Beckwith, Hailey). These obeyed, adding their faithfulness to the Lamb as another past characteristic that puts them in this special company with the Lamb on Mount Zion. They followed Him wherever His leading took them, even to the point of giving up their lives as He did (Smith).

Verse 4 closes by referring to their consecration to God that resulted from their redemption (Beckwith, Mounce). The aorist indicative ἠγοράσθησαν (*ēgorasthēsan,* "were redeemed") is not a mere repetition of the perfect participle ἠγορασμένοι (*ēgorasmenoi,* "redeemed") (v. 3). It advances to a focus upon ἀπαρχή (*aparchē,* "contribution"). The redemption enjoyed by all the faithful (5:9) applies in a special sense to the 144,000, because they are the firstfruits or a contribution.[164]

A common understanding of *aparchē* takes it in the sense of the first portion of a great harvest about to occur, a sense the word has in Rom. 8:23; 16:15; 1 Cor. 15:20, 23; 16:15; James 1:18 (Swete, Beckwith, Bullinger, Walvoord, Beasley-Murray). This could portray the 144,000 as the token godly remnant who will repopulate the millennial earth, including Jews converted during the Tribulation and saints born dur-

---

161. Newell, *Revelation,* p. 216.
162. Düsterdieck, *Revelation,* p. 393.
163. Ibid., p. 394; Lee, "Revelation," 4:702; Moffatt, "Revelation," 5:436.
164. Düsterdieck, *Revelation,* p. 394.

ing the Millennium.[165] They are the earnest of the blessings about to come to the earth.[166] But the serious issue this interpretation must face is who is the larger group to follow. To be of the same kind as the 144,000, they must face the fiercest persecution imaginable at the hands of the beast, a condition that will not exist during the Millennium. The purpose of the snapshot of the 144,000 in 14:4-5 is to show why this group is so special and their singular qualifications that have enabled them to fulfil their special mission. No hint of another group to follow is present.

A preferable meaning of *aparchē* sees the primary idea of these people being offered to God as a one-time contribution (Charles, Mounce, Johnson). In two out of every three of its sixty-six occurrences in the LXX, the word refers simply to a contribution without the connotation of a larger harvest to follow (e.g., Num. 5:9; Deut. 18:4; 26:2; Ezek. 48:8, 10, 20) (Charles, Johnson, Mounce). The use of ἄμωμοι (*amōmoi*, "blameless") in the next verse enhances the sacrificial tone of the passage and enforces this meaning for *aparchē* (Charles, Moffatt). These are the elite who have a prestige all their own, a factor that distinguishes this use of *aparchē* from the use of the term in Rom. 11:16. The idea of priority grows into one of superiority (Moffatt). The emphasis is less on chronological sequence and more on quality.[167] Their being an offering "to God and to the Lamb" shows their special consecration to divine service. No other group of their kind is to follow.

14:5 Truthfulness is another of this group's special qualities: καὶ ἐν τῷ στόματι αὐτῶν οὐχ εὑρέθη ψεῦδος· *ἄμωμοί εἰσιν* (*kai en tō stomati autōn ouch heurethē pseudos; amōmoi eisin*, "and in their mouth a lie was not found; they are blameless"). Particularly commendable is their refraining from the falsity represented by the religion of worshiping the beast (Rev. 13:14; cf. 2 Thess. 2:11) (Bullinger, Lenski).

The absence of lying from their mouths could refer to the general quality of honesty, but this is a quality that belongs to all who will enter the new Jerusalem, not just to this special group (cf. 21:8, 27; 22:15) (Moffatt). The special distinction of these is their separateness from those who participate in the lies and infamies of the beast (Seiss). The condition of lying—note the anarthrous ψεῦδος (*pseudos*, "lie") to emphasize quality—will prevail during the reign of the false Christ,

---

165. Smith, *Revelation*, pp. 210-11; Walvoord, *Revelation*, p. 216; Ryrie, *Revelation*, p. 89.
166. Newell, *Revelation*, p. 217; Scott, *Revelation*, p. 294; Mounce, *Revelation*, p. 271.
167. BAGD, p. 81.

but these have overcome the prevailing pressure to worship the image of the beast.

Verse 5 alludes to statements about the faithful remnant of Israel in Zeph. 3:13 and the suffering servant of the LORD in Isa. 53:9 (cf. John 8:44; 1 Pet. 2:22) (Swete, Charles, Beckwith). Truthfulness and purity receive special attention because of the prevalence of untruth and impurity in the surrounding society.

With an abrupt explanation, the writer states their continuing state[168] of purity to account for their truthfulness: ἄμωμοί εἰσιν (amōmoi eisin, "they are blameless"). Ἄμωμος (Amōmos) refers to the blamelessness of Christ in 1 Pet. 1:19 and Heb. 9:14 and to the blamelessness of Christians in Phil. 2:15 and Jude 24. Behind all these usages lies the OT Levitical term for sacrifices without flaw and therefore fit to be offered. These were sacrificially perfect.[169] They lacked any insincerity or duplicity that would make their self-consecration unacceptable to God (Swete).

Additional Notes

14:1 The noun ἀρνίον is arthrous in most MSS of 14:1 except in p[47] and a few other MSS. Evidence for the article's inclusion is strong. This contrasts to the anarthrous use of the noun in 13:11. The latter reference is the only place in Revelation where the noun does not refer to the Lamb of God (Beckwith, Mounce). See Thomas, pp. 390-91, for a suggestion why the diminutive ἀρνίον was chosen over ἀμνός in Revelation.

14:2 A direct object of ἀκούω is usually in the genitive case, because verbs of hearing generally govern that case. Here the object φωνὴν is accusative.

The combination κιθαριζόντων . . . ᾄδουσιν in vv. 2-3 is a Greek reproduction of a Hebraism, the likeness of which has already appeared in 1:5-6; 2:2, 9, 20; 7:14 and will appear again in 15:2. Ἀιδόντων would have been expected rather than ᾄδουσιν, resulting in the meaning "harping (or playing) . . . singing" (Charles). The combination of three cognates, κιθαρῳδῶν, κιθαριζόντων, and κιθάραις, is impressive in its emphasis on the type of instrument furnishing the musical accompaniment for the singing.[170] The combination φωνὴ κιθαρῳδῶν occurs again in 18:22.

---

168. Note another present tense of εἰσιν as found twice in v. 4 (Swete, *Apocalypse*, p. 181; Moffatt, "Revelation," 5:437; Mounce, *Revelation*, p. 271).

169. Swete, *Apocalypse*, p. 181; Charles, *Revelation*, 2:10; Moffatt, "Revelation," 5:437; Robertson, *Word Pictures*, 6:410; Mounce, *Revelation*, p. 271.

170. Bullinger, *Apocalypse*, p. 444; Robertson, *Word Pictures*, 6:408.

This use of ἐν has been called the ἐν of investiture. It expresses the vehicle in which the action of the verb is carried out (Alford).

14:3 External evidence supporting the inclusion of ὡς includes Alexandrinus, Ephraemi, and other MSS. It is about equal to that omitting the comparative particle, including p⁴⁷, Sinaiticus, and other MSS. The word was either introduced mechanically by copyists as an echo of v. 2 where it occurs three times, or was dropped by copyists accidentally or in imitation of 5:9 where ᾄδουσιν ᾠδὴν καινὴν appears without a ὡς.[171] It appears that the inclusion is the harder reading because it differs from 5:9, so ὡς is probably original.

The masculine οἱ ἠγορασμένοι modifies the feminine χιλιάδες, the difference in gender being explained by natural agreement rather than grammatical agreement. Natural agreement explains a difference in gender in 5:13; 7:5, 8, but in 14:1 grammatical agreement prevails.[172]

The preposition ἀπό does not denote separation, but extraction as with the ἐκ of 5:9 (Swete, Mounce). They already had a relation with God before leaving the earth through martyrdom. While in that state they enjoyed protection from earth's tyranny and pernicious philosophies. This phrase is similar to ἀπὸ τῶν ἀνθρώπων in 14:4, which tells of their being redeemed "from among" men (cf. John 7:15).

14:4 Alexandrinus, Ephraemi, and a few other MSS support the indicative ὑπάγει rather than the subjunctive ὑπάγῃ recommended by the UBS 3d Edition text. Beckwith considers the indicative as totally irregular, but Alford says that it is a matter of the ἄν simply losing its force. Swete applies the force of the ἄν to ὅπου only: the direction is uncertain, but the movement of ὑπάγει is actual. Though well-supported, the subjunctive reading is the easier reading and so is not the preferable one. The indicative has sufficient MS support. It depicts action of an indefinite frequency in its rare appearances with ἄν in the NT.[173]

14:5 Several MSS, including p⁴⁷ and Sinaiticus, have the connective γάρ to introduce ἄμωμοί εἰσιν. This was a natural addition for copyists to make, especially in light of the explanatory γάρ in v. 4. On the other hand, it is difficult to see why a copyist would have deleted the conjunction. The text that omits γάρ has the support of Alexandrinus and Ephraemi among other sources, so it is probably original.[174]

The addition of ἐνώπιον τοῦ θρόνου τοῦ θεοῦ follows the precedent

---

171. Metzger, *Textual Commentary*, p. 752.
172. Alford, *Greek Testament*, 4:685; Robertson, *Word Pictures*, 6:409.
173. Robertson, *Grammar*, p. 958; Nigel Turner, *Syntax*, vol. 3 of *A Grammar of New Testament Greek* (Edinburgh: T. & T. Clark, 1963), p. 110.
174. Charles, *Revelation*, 2:10; Metzger, *Textual Commentary*, pp. 752-53.

of the other occurrences of ἄμωμος in the NT (cf. Eph. 1:4; Col. 1:22; Jude 24) (Smith), but MS support for the addition is extremely weak.[175]

e. Four Climactic Announcements (14:6-13)

Καὶ εἶδον (*Kai eidon,* "And I saw") introduces the next scene of John's vision that begins in 12:1. The scene consists of three angelic announcements regarding the everlasting gospel (14:6-7), the fall of Babylon (14:8), and the torment awaiting beast worshipers (14:9-12). A final announcement by a voice from heaven promises blessedness to the faithful (14:13). All four announcements furnish incentives to give glory to God by remaining faithful to the Lamb and resisting the overtures of the beast.

(1) THE EVERLASTING GOSPEL (14:6-7)

Translation

⁶And I saw another angel flying in midheaven, having an eternal gospel to preach to those who sit upon the earth, even to every nation and tribe and tongue and people, ⁷saying with a loud voice, "Fear God and give Him glory, because the hour of His judgment has come, and worship the one who made the heaven and the earth and sea and fountains of waters."

Exegesis and Exposition

14:6 "Another angel" marks a new turn in the drama as "another angel" did at 7:2; 8:3; 10:1:[176] Καὶ εἶδον ἄλλον ἄγγελον πετόμενον ἐν μεσουρανήματι, ἔχοντα εὐαγγέλιον αἰώνιον εὐαγγελίσαι ἐπὶ τοὺς καθημένους ἐπὶ τῆς γῆς καὶ ἐπὶ πᾶν ἔθνος καὶ φυλὴν καὶ γλῶσσαν καὶ λαόν (*Kai eidon allon angelon petomenon en mesouranēmati, echonta euangelion aiōnion euangelisai epi tous kathēmenous epi tēs gēs kai epi pan ethnos kai phylēn kai glōssan kai laon,* "And I saw another angel flying in midheaven, having an eternal gospel to preach to those who sit upon the earth, even to every nation and tribe and tongue and people"). The angel is the first of six to participate in the announcements and enactments of this chapter (cf. vv. 8, 9, 15, 17, 18).

The entrance of this angel has evoked considerable discussion since no angel has taken part in the narrative since 11:15. The proposal that the ἄλλον (*allon,* "another") distinguishes the angel from the ones in vv. 8 and 9 (Lenski) is contrary to the normal usage of the adjective

---

175. Metzger, *Textual Commentary,* p. 753.
176. Robertson, *Word Pictures,* 6:410.

to refer back to something previously mentioned.[177] To explain "another" as meaning in addition to the angels singing in 14:2-3 (Beckwith, Ladd) is inadequate because the identity of the singers there is too uncertain. Another alternative is to omit the adjective on the basis of its absence from p[47], Sinaiticus, and other MSS,[178] but there is no way of accounting for a copyist's insertion later on because of the difficulty it creates.[179] Inclusion of *allon* is the harder reading, and it has the support of Alexandrinus, Ephraemi, and a good number of other authorities.[180]

A further suggestion is to treat the adjective as having no significance (Mounce), but it is hermeneutically irresponsible simply to relegate a word to insignificance just because of the difficulty it creates. Another possibility takes "another" as meaning in addition to the Lamb, i.e., "another, an angel" (Beckwith), but the word order dictates the naturalness of "another angel." A similar suggestion uses the eagle of 8:13 as the point of reference (Scott), but it suffers from the same difficulty as taking the Lamb thus.

Having *allon* refer back to the angels in chapters 8, 9, and 10 is another possibility (Charles, Walvoord). This answers a similar problem arising in 10:1 (Walvoord). The difference between this and 10:1 is that in 10:1, it had been only six verses since the last mention of an angel, but since 10:1 refers to "another *strong* angel" with the closest previous reference to such a being in 5:2, the cases are somewhat parallel. Another good possibility is that *allon* distinguishes this angel from the seventh trumpet-angel in 11:15 (Swete). The objection that the distance is a problem (Mounce) has the same answer as the one just given regarding "another *strong* angel" in 10:1. Another possibility, and probably the best one, is that the adjective refers back to the mention of Michael and his angels in 12:7. This is part of the same three-chapter unit of the book and is the closest to 14:6, so "another" probably means "another besides Michael."

John saw the angel "flying in midheaven" (πετόμενον ἐν μεσουρανήματι [*petomenon en mesouranēmati*]) where he was in the sight of all and his announcement was audible to all (Beckwith, Lenski). The angel is in flight the same as the eagle of 8:13 and not stationary as the angel in 19:17. He had in his possession (ἔχοντα [*echonta*, "having"]) an eternal gospel to preach "to those who sit upon the earth and to every nation and tribe and tongue and people." This is not the usual phrase for the earth-dwellers because καθημένους (*kathēmenous*, "sit")

---

177. BAGD, pp. 39-40.
178. Lange, *Revelation*, p. 285.
179. Beckwith, *Apocalypse*, p. 655.
180. Metzger, *Textual Commentary*, p. 753.

takes the place of κατοικοῦντας (katoikountas, "dwell").[181] The result is an expression identical with one occurring in Jer. 32:29 [LXX] (25:29, Eng.) (Swete). The total expression, including καὶ ἐπὶ πᾶν ἔθνος καὶ φυλὴν καὶ γλῶσσαν καὶ λαόν (kai epi pan ethnos kai phylēn kai glōssan kai laon, "even to every nation and tribe and tongue and people") (cf. 5:9; 7:9; 11:9; 13:7) depicts the worldwide population.[182] The καὶ (kai, "even") introducing the latter part is ascensive because the phrase it introduces is an emphatic repetition of the immediately preceding ἐπὶ (epi, "to") phrase (Alford, Beckwith, Charles, Mounce). No barrier will hinder the transmission of this angel's gospel to all.

14:7 The substance of this gospel is to give God glory and worship Him as Creator of the material universe: λέγων ἐν φωνῇ μεγάλῃ, Φοβήθητε τὸν θεὸν καὶ δότε αὐτῷ δόξαν, ὅτι ἦλθεν ἡ ὥρα τῆς κρίσεως αὐτοῦ, καὶ προσκυνήσατε τῷ ποιήσαντι τὸν οὐρανὸν καὶ τὴν γῆν καὶ θάλασσαν καὶ πηγὰς ὑδάτων (legōn en phōnē megalē, Phobēthēte ton theon kai dote autō doxan, hoti ēlthen hē hōra tēs kriseōs autou, kai proskynēsate tō poiēsanti ton ouranon kai tēn gēn kai thalassan kai pēgas hydatōn, "saying with a loud voice, 'Fear God and give Him glory, because the hour of His judgment has come, and worship the one who made the heaven and the earth and sea and fountains of waters'"). The "loud voice" (φωνῇ μεγάλῃ [phōnē megalē]) of the announcement assures that all will hear, but the loudness also connotes urgency and concern (Smith, Mounce).

The gospel has no invitation to believe, but only a command to fear God who is bringing impending judgment. Its appeal is specially to pagans who are incapable of understanding anything else about God except their accountability to Him (cf. Rom. 1:32).[183] To fear God requires self-humiliation and self-surrender to Him (Charles). It is the same command as penned by the writer of Ecclesiastes (12:13) and recalls the one of Christ's advice in Luke 12:5. This is the inner state of those who are faithful to Christ.[184]

To give God glory is an idiom of repentance, acknowledging His attributes (Swete, Beckwith, Lenski). This is to recognize Him as God and to refuse that is concession to the dragon and the false Christ. This is a command to reverse the prevailing state of chapter 13 (Alford). The

---

181. The theory of Charles that a copyist changed κατοικοῦντας to καθημένους to avoid the wicked connotations of the former (Revelation, 2:12-13) has the support of Alexandrinus which reads κατοικοῦντας, but otherwise, external evidence for κατοικοῦντας is quite weak.
182. Hughes, Revelation, p. 161.
183. Swete, Apocalypse, pp. 182-83; Mounce, Revelation, p. 273; Robertson, Word Pictures, 6:411.
184. Mulholland, Revelation, p. 245.

song of 15:4 illustrates a positive response to this command, but the responses of 16:9, 11, 21 are instances of a negative response (Sweet).

῞Οτι ἦλθεν ἡ ὥρα τῆς κρίσεως αὐτοῦ (Hoti ēlthen hē hōra tēs kriseōs autou, "Because the hour of His judgment has come") assigns the reason for fearing God and giving Him glory. The form and diction of this phrase are common in the fourth gospel (cf. John 2:4; 4:21, 23; 5:25, 28; 7:30; 8:20; 12:23; 13:1; 16:2, 4, 21, 25, 32; 17:1) (Swete, Beckwith, Charles). ῞Ωρα (Hōra) points to the *fixed* moment as compared with καιρός (kairos, "season"), which would have referred to the *fit* moment (Moffatt). The verb ἦλθεν (ēlthen, "has come") is a dramatic aorist expressing a state that is on the point of being realized.[185] This is the very last chance to change allegiance to the God of heaven. Κρίσις (Krisis, "Judgment") occurs here for the first time in the book. It will appear later at 16:7; 18:10; 19:2. It is almost synonymous with ὀργή (orgē, "wrath") and θυμός (thymos, "anger") (cf. 6:16-17; 11:18; 14:8, 10; 15:1; 16:1; 18:3; 19:15) (Johnson). This is the right decision of a holy God against an unrepentant world.

The final command of this angelic gospel calls for the worship of the Creator. He who created all things has the right to expect worship as He has the right to judge what He has created (4:10; 10:6; cf. Acts 4:24; 14:15-17). This description of the Creator alludes to Neh. 9:6 and Ps. 33:6-9 (cf. Ps. 146:6) and is an appropriate appeal to natural theology with a worldwide audience that includes the heathen (Swete, Moffatt, Beckwith, Charles, Lenski).

The four categories τὸν οὐρανὸν καὶ τὴν γῆν καὶ θάλασσαν καὶ πηγὰς ὑδάτων (ton ouranon kai tēn gēn kai thalassan kai pēgas hydatōn, "the heaven and the earth and sea and fountains of waters") encompass the entirety of creation. The distinction between the last two continues as marking a difference between the second and third bowl judgments (16:3-4) (Alford). The fourth expression receives separate attention because of the life-sustaining importance of such springs in the dry climate of Palestine (cf. Ex. 15:27; Lev. 11:36; Num. 33:9; 1 Kings 18:5; 2 Kings 3:19, 25) (Swete, Charles, Lenski, Ford).

Additional Notes

14:7 Like ἔχοντα in v. 6, λέγων modifies the accusative ἄγγελον even though it is a nominative case. As at 4:1, the author handles participles with a rather free use of the nominative (Robertson, *Word*

---

185. Bullinger, *Apocalypse*, p. 452; Robert Govett, *Govett on Revelation*, 2 vols. (1981 reprint; Miami Springs, Fla.: Conley & Schoettle, 1861), 2:289; H. E. Dana and Julius R. Mantey, *A Manual Grammar of the Greek New Testament* (New York: Macmillan, 1927), p. 198.

Pictures, 6:410). See the discussion of λέγων at 4:1 (Thomas, p. 336 n. 20).

A comparison of the dative of τῷ ποιήσαντι with the accusative τὸ θηρίον in 14:9 shows that προσκυνέω may govern either case as its object.

(2) THE FALL OF BABYLON (14:8)

Translation

⁸And another angel, a second one, followed saying, "Babylon the great has fallen, has fallen, who made all nations drink of the wine of the anger of her fornication."

Exegesis and Exposition

14:8 The second of the six angels announces briefly but with emphasis the fall of Babylon: Καὶ ἄλλος ἄγγελος δεύτερος* ἠκολούθησεν λέγων, Ἔπεσεν, ἔπεσεν Βαβυλὼν ἡ μεγάλη, ἥ ἐκ τοῦ οἴνου τοῦ θυμοῦ τῆς πορνείας αὐτῆς πεπότικεν πάντα τὰ ἔθνη (*Kai allos angelos deuteros ēkolouthēsen legōn, Epesen, epesen Babylōn hē megalē, hē ek tou oinou tou thymou tēs porneias autēs pepotiken panta ta ethnē*, "And another angel, a second one, followed saying, 'Babylon the great has fallen, has fallen, who made all nations drink of the wine of the anger of her fornication'"). The committing of each new announcement to a new angel increases the dramatic animation of the scene (Alford, Lee). The announcement of each angel builds upon the message of his predecessor, implying a consequence of that message. In this instance, the declaration of the fall of Babylon intimates a rejection of the everlasting gospel just preached (Swete, Mounce).

The second angel "followed" (ἠκολούθησεν [*ēkolouthēsen*]) the first one, not only sequentially, but also in the sense of delivering a follow-up message to his. In his double announcement[186] of the fall of Babylon —i.e., ἔπεσεν, ἔπεσεν (*epesen, epesen*, "has fallen, has fallen")—his words are a sort of dirge that carries a tragic emphasis (cf. Isa. 21:9).[187] The proleptic use of the aorist tense of *epesen* implies the imminence and certainty of the fall (Morris) as the announcement anticipates the climax of the plagues against the earth precipitated by the reign of the beast (Kiddle). This tense use, sometimes called the "prophetic pre-

---

186. The repetitiveness of the verb ἔπεσεν is called an "epanadiplosis," which is a repetition of an important word for the sake of emphasis (BDF, par. 493).
187. Robertson, *Word Pictures*, 6:411; Lenski, *Revelation*, p. 432; Walvoord, *Revelation*, p. 218.

terit," views a future event as so certain that it is as though it were already accomplished (cf. 10:7; 11:18; 18:2).[188]

As with the anticipatory announcement of the beast in 11:7 before his fuller description in 13:1-8, this is an anticipatory word about the fate of Βαβυλὼν ἡ μεγάλη (Babylōn hē megalē, "Babylon the great") before the extended word about this city that will be the object of the last bowl judgment (16:17-18:24). The angelic announcement assumes that his readers have some preliminary knowledge about the city before he gets to the details describing it (Swete, Lee). A few preliminary remarks at this point regarding what the proper name signifies will facilitate an understanding of the progress this series of announcements.

The view that Babylon is a code name for Jerusalem[189] derives from a worldview that requires the writing and fulfillment of the Apocalypse before A.D. 70. Besides an impossible date for the book's writing, this view goes against the historical fact that Jerusalem is related to the people of God and Babylon to the world at large (Lee). The viewpoint cannot be valid. Another view takes the city name as symbolic of those who worship the beast (Lenski, Johnson). This idea has an element of truth, but it leaves no room for a literal reference in the term. Symbolism and a literal connotation are not mutually exclusive.

The most popular explanation of Babylon has it as a way Christians had of disguising their mentions of Rome (Swete, Beckwith). Allegedly, 1 Pet. 5:13 uses Babylon in this way, and others adopted the same practice.[190] In the OT, Babylon was the great enemy of God's people (cf. Isa. 21:9; Jer. 50:2; 51:8) and thus is a fitting symbol for the capital of the final apostate civilization, which will be a revived form of Rome (Walvoord, Ladd). A questioning of this interpretation of 1 Pet. 5:13 which notes that the verse refers to Babylon on the Euphrates rather than Rome, greatly weakens this line of reasoning, however. John has used city names literally in Revelation 1-3, and when he has departed from a literal meaning, as in 11:8, he has made very evident that he intended a figurative sense. Often supporters of the symbolic view use the *Sibylline Oracles* (V. 143, 159, 434) and the *Apocalypse of Baruch* (11:1; 67:7) to prove that Babylon was a code name for Rome (Swete, Charles, Ladd), but the composition of these two works came in the second century, quite a while after John wrote Revelation.[191]

---

188. Lee, "Revelation," 4:704; Lange, *Revelation*, p. 285; Lenski, *Revelation*, p. 432; Ladd, *Revelation*, p. 194.
189. Chilton, *Days of Vengeance*, p. 362; Joseph R. Balyeat, *Babylon, the Great City of Revelation* (Sevierville, Tenn.: Onward, 1991), pp. 69-142.
190. Robertson, *Word Pictures*, 6:411; Walvoord, *Revelation*, p. 218; Ladd, *Revelation*, p. 194.
191. J. J. Collins, "Sibylline Oracles," in *The Old Testament Pseudepigrapha*, ed. James H. Charlesworth (Garden City, N.Y.: Doubleday, 1983), 1:390;

Making Babylon a direct reference to the papacy (Alford) also has an element of truth in it, but it is too narrow to limit its meaning just to apostate Christianity. Babylon symbolizes the world as a whole (Lee). The best solution is to assign Babylon its literal significance of the city on the Euphrates by that name. Mentions of the Euphrates River at other points (9:14; 16:12) corroborate this which is the natural way to understand it. Place names have their literal significance in 1:9; 2:1, 8, 12, 18; 3:1, 7, 14, and the writer is very clear to point it out when he intends a figurative meaning as in 11:8. A reference to the literal city does not exclude further implications regarding political and religious systems connected with the city (Walvoord). What the literal city stands for will become more conspicuous in John's further discussion of it in chapters 17-18. Taking its cue from the words of Nebuchadnezzar in Dan. 4:30, this book always refers to the city as "the great" (ἡ μεγάλη [hē megalē]) (16:19; 17:5; 18:2, 10, 21) (Swete, Charles). Its imposing influence on world affairs is a constant major factor in the period just before Christ returns to judge her.

The relative pronoun ἥ (hē, "who") has a secondary causal meaning in assigning a reason for Babylon's fall: her corruption of the nations (cf. 17:2, 4) (Beckwith). She "made all nations drink" (πεπότικεν πάντα τὰ ἔθνη [pepotiken panta ta ethnē]) is another way of saying she exercised coercive power over earth's inhabitants in causing them to choose a path that they in no way would have chosen without her influence.[192] The expression τοῦ οἴνου τοῦ θυμοῦ τῆς πορνείας αὐτῆς (tou oinou tou thymou tēs porneias autēs, "the wine of the anger of her fornication") in telling what that path is contains two distinct ideas that receive a separate development elsewhere: (1) the wine that the courtesan gives to intoxicate in seducing someone to fornication (cf. 17:2, 4) and (2) the cup of God's wrath that He gives to those whom He will severely punish (cf. 14:10). Acceptance of Babylon's wine of fornication entails the drinking of God's wine of wrath. They are inseparable (Beckwith, Beasley-Murray). The imagery here corresponds to that of Jer. 51:6-7 (cf. 25:15). Far from incapacitating God's power, the orgy of rebellion against Him activates His judgment as v. 10 will show.[193]

The wine of Babylon is a symbol for not only sexual licentiousness, but every kind of excess that expresses unfaithfulness to God,[194] but it

---

A. F. J. Klijn, "2 (Syriac Apocalypse of) Baruch," in *The Old Testament Pseudepigrapha*, 1:616-17; Larry Kreitzer, "Hadrian and the Nero Redivivus Myth," *ZNW* 79 (1988): 97.
192. Wall, *Revelation*, p. 185.
193. Hughes, *Revelation*, p. 162.
194. Ibid.

eventually turns into the wine of God's wrath (cf. Pss. 60:3; 75:8; Isa. 51:17, 22) (Alford; Lee). The "anger" (θυμοῦ [*thymou*]) is God's passionate indignation about to be poured out on Babylon because of her sins (Swete, Charles, Moffatt). "Fornication" (Πορνείας [*Porneias*]) is a sin repeatedly attributed to Babylon (cf. 17:1, 2, 5, 15, 16; 18:3, 9; 19:2).[195]

Additional Notes

14:8 The reading ἄλλος ἄγγελος δεύτερος appears to be the one that best explains the origin of the other readings. The others include ἄλλος δεύτερος ἄγγελος (supported by Alexandrinus and other MSS), ἄλλος ἄγγελος (supported by a number of minuscules), and ἄλλος δεύτερος (supported by p[47], Sinaiticus, and others). Ἄλλος ἄγγελος δεύτερος has the support of Ephraemi, the third reviser of Sinaiticus, 2053, and other authorities, and agrees with the sequence ἄλλος ἄγγελος τρίτος in v. 9. This sequence is the author's style in 6:4; 10:1; 15:1 also, and so is most probably original.[196]

The concatenation of genitives involved in τοῦ οἴνου τοῦ θυμοῦ τῆς πορνείας αὐτῆς is more common in Paul, but Revelation has its share (16:19; 18:3; 19:15). Here as in most cases the governing genitive precedes the dependent genitive with the last in the series being possessive.[197]

(3) THE TORMENT OF THE BEAST WORSHIPERS (14:9-12)

Translation

⁹And another angel, a third one, followed them saying with a loud voice, "If anyone worships the beast and his image, and receives the mark upon his forehead or upon his hand, ¹⁰even he himself will drink of the wine of the anger of God which is mixed unmixed in the cup of His wrath, and he shall be tormented in fire and brimstone before the holy angels and before the Lamb. ¹¹And the smoke of their torment ascends forever and ever, and they do not have rest day and night, who worship the beast and his image, and if anyone receives the mark of his name. ¹²Here is the endurance of the saints, who keep the commandments of God and the faith of Jesus."

Exegesis and Exposition

14:9 The third of the six angels advances with a special warning to beast worshipers: Καὶ ἄλλος ἄγγελος τρίτος ἠκολούθησεν αὐτοῖς λέγων

---

195. Mulholland, *Revelation*, p. 247.
196. Metzger, *Textual Commentary*, p. 753.
197. BDF, par. 168[2]; Turner, *Syntax*, p. 218.

ἐν φωνῇ μεγάλῃ, Εἴ τις προσκυνεῖ τὸ θηρίον καὶ τὴν εἰκόνα αὐτοῦ, καὶ λαμβάνει χάραγμα ἐπὶ τοῦ μετώπου αὐτοῦ ἢ ἐπὶ τὴν χεῖρα αὐτοῦ (*Kai allos angelos tritos ēkolouthēsen autois legōn en phōnē megalē, Ei tis proskynei to thērion kai tēn eikona autou, kai lambanei charagma epi tou metōpou autou ē epi tēn cheira autou,* "And another angel, a third one, followed them saying with a loud voice, 'If anyone worships the beast and his image, and receives the mark upon his forehead or upon his hand'"). These words begin what is in vv. 9-12 a counter-proclamation warning to those tempted to yield to the threats of the second beast regarding boycott and death (13:11-17).[198] The goal of the warning is to frighten potential beast worshipers into believing and to encourage the faithful to remain faithful (Moffatt, Mounce). In other words, "Waverer, beware! The suffering you may avoid under the rule of the beast is immeasurably smaller than the eternal punishment you will otherwise incur" (cf. Matt. 10:28) (Kiddle).

The third angel "followed" (ἠκολούθησεν [*ēkolouthēsen*]) the second, again indicating a connection of his message with the preceding. The progression of the first three announcements is from the compulsory fear and worship of God to the fall of Babylon that prompts that fear and worship to the eternal punishment decreed for those who repudiate the truth (Kiddle). The third angel uses "a loud voice" (φωνῇ μεγάλῃ [*phōnē megalē*]) as did the first, to emphasize the importance of his warning (Lenski).

The protasis of a conditional sentence in v. 9b sets the stage for the warning in v. 10. The "if" clause (εἴ τις προσκυνεῖ τὸ θηρίον καὶ τὴν εἰκόνα αὐτοῦ, καὶ λαμβάνει χάραγμα ἐπὶ τοῦ μετώπου αὐτοῦ ἢ ἐπὶ τὴν χεῖρα αὐτοῦ [*ei tis proskynei to thērion kai tēn eikona autou, kai lambanei charagma epi tou metōpou autou ē epi tēn cheira autou,* "if anyone worships the beast and his image, and receives the mark upon his forehead or upon his hand") specifies that the warning has beast worshipers as its object. The first beast of chapter 13 required the whole world to worship him or else. Worship of his animated image amounts to worshiping the beast himself, as did the acceptance of his mark on the forehead or the hand. He expected undistracted loyalty from everyone with the threat of death to anyone who did not comply. All the pressure was to do as he said.

14:10 Yet for a person to comply is disastrous: καὶ αὐτὸς πίεται ἐκ τοῦ οἴνου τοῦ θυμοῦ τοῦ θεοῦ τοῦ κεκερασμένου ἀκράτου ἐν τῷ ποτηρίῳ τῆς ὀργῆς αὐτοῦ, καὶ βασανισθήσεται ἐν πυρὶ καὶ θείῳ ἐνώπιον ἀγγέλων ἁγίων καὶ ἐνώπιον τοῦ ἀρνίου (*kai autos pietai ek tou oinou tou thymou tou theou tou kekerasmenou akratou en tō potēriō tēs orgēs autou, kai*

---

198. Swete, *Apocalypse*, p. 184; Robertson, *Word Pictures*, 6:412.

basanisthēsetai en pyri kai theiǭ enōpion angelōn hagiōn kai enōpion tou arniou, "even he himself will drink of the wine of the anger of God which is mixed unmixed in the cup of His wrath, and he shall be tormented in fire and brimstone before the holy angels and before the Lamb"). This apodosis constitutes the warning of the consequences to the worshipers of the false Christ. Αὐτός (*Autos,* "Himself") individualizes the responsibility and, along with καί (*kai,* "even"), puts emphasis on the very person who chooses to go along with the beast's program.[199]

Instead of the aorist to dramatize or fix the certainty of a future happening (cf. ἔπεσεν [*epesen*], v. 8), the third angel uses future tenses to predict the lasting anguish of those who are weak or wavering regarding whom to worship. Πίεται (*Pietai,* "He will drink") and βασανισθήσεται (*basanisthēsetai,* "he will be tormented") tell the fate of the beast worshipers, who are also the paramours of Babylon. Their future is a far cry from what the redeemed will face (14:1-5) (Kiddle). They must drink of the wine of God's "anger" (θυμοῦ [*thymou*]) in the cup of His "wrath" (ὀργῆς [*orgēs*]). Θυμός (*Thymos*) and ὀργῆς (*orgēs*) are in the same series of genitives, "the anger of the wrath of God," in 16:19 and 19:15. The former word is vehement fury and the latter a settled indignation. Used together, they intensify the reality of God's anger. He will unleash the white heat of His wrath that has been restrained for so long.[200] *Thymos* refers to God's wrath only once in the NT outside of Revelation (Rom. 2:8), but in Revelation both it and *orgē* frequently do so (6:16, 17; 14:10, 19; 15:1, 7; 16:1, 19; 19:15) (Swete, Beckwith). They are the counterparts of the OT expression "the anger of the LORD (or God)" (cf. Num. 12:9; 22:22). A bold and powerful oxymoron strengthens the picture of *thymou.*

It is "mixed unmixed" or "mixed undiluted" (κεκερασμένου ἀκράτου [*kekerasmenou akratou*]). The common practice was to mix wine with water to weaken its concentration, but this wine has its concentration strengthened through the addition of spices. Its intoxicating effect is thereby greater. Eschatological judgment will be without any mercy or grace. This is an OT way of picturing the awfulness of future judgment by God (cf. Ps. 75:8; Jer. 25:15).[201]

To imbibe from this cup is tantamount to eternal torment in fire and brimstone. With the angels and the Lamb whom they have

---

199. Lange, *Revelation,* p. 286; Beckwith, *Apocalypse,* p. 657; Scott, *Revelation,* p. 301.
200. Robertson, *Word Pictures,* 6:412; Ladd, *Revelation,* p. 195.
201. Lee, "Revelation," 4:705; Moffatt, "Revelation," 5:438; Beckwith, *Apocalypse,* p. 657; Robertson, *Word Pictures,* 6:412; Walvoord, *Revelation,* p. 219; Beasley-Murray, *Revelation,* p. 226; Johnson, "Revelation," 12:541.

spurned observing, worshipers of the false Christ will experience unbearable pain at the hand of unnamed agents. Their destiny recalls the fate of Sodom and Gomorrah (Gen. 19:24) and Edom (Isa. 34:8-10; cf. Isa. 30:33; Ezek. 38:22) and is an indirect allusion to the lake of fire that becomes prominent later in Revelation (19:20; 20:10; 21:8) (Swete, Charles, Beckwith, Johnson). The holy environment of the holy angels and the Lamb enhances the misery of punishment for the wicked, just as the public persecution of the faithful before their fellow men increased their humiliation (cf. Luke 12:8-9). The opposite case is that of the overcomer who will receive open recognition in the presence of the Father and His angels (3:5) (Swete, Beckwith, Smith, Beasley-Murray). A question about the appropriateness of this anguish in such a holy presence (Ford) has its answer in recognizing this is only temporary. Eventually those in endless misery will have no place in these surroundings (21:27; 22:14-15; cf. Matt. 25:41; Mark 9:43; 2 Thess. 1:8-9).[202]

14:11 A constant reminder of the permanence of their misery is the endless trail of smoke that keeps on ascending: καὶ ὁ καπνὸς τοῦ βασανισμοῦ αὐτῶν εἰς αἰῶνας αἰώνων ἀναβαίνει, καὶ οὐκ ἔχουσιν ἀνάπαυσιν ἡμέρας καὶ νυκτός, οἱ προσκυνοῦντες τὸ θηρίον καὶ τὴν εἰκόνα αὐτοῦ, καὶ εἴ τις λαμβάνει τὸ χάραγμα τοῦ ὀνόματος αὐτοῦ (*kai ho kapnos tou basanismou autōn eis aiōnas aiōnōn anabainei, kai ouk echousin anapausin hēmeras kai nyktos, hoi proskynountes to thērion and tēn eikona autou, kai ei tis lambanei to charagma tou onomatos autou,* "and the smoke of their torment ascends forever and ever, and they do not have rest day and night, who worship the beast and his image, and if anyone receives the mark of his name"). Abraham saw the smoke from Sodom and Gomorrah as a sign of God's punishment on the cities of the valley (Gen. 19:28). Smoke is also a token of God's future punishment of the wicked (cf. Rev. 19:3) (Beckwith, Mounce).

It comes from torment (βασανισμοῦ [*basanismou*]) that is unending and unlike the five-month torment under the fifth trumpet (9:5). The fate of the individual is the same as that of the city that led him astray (cf. 19:2-3) (Sweet), but now the individual (τις [*tis*, "anyone"]) of v. 9 becomes a group made up of such individuals. This is the smoke of "their" (αὐτῶν [*autōn*]) torment. The noun βασανισμός (*basanismos,* "torment") has an active meaning in 9:5, but here and in 18:7, 10, 15, it has a passive force, referring to being tormented (cf. Luke 16:23, 28) (Charles).

The expression εἰς αἰῶνας αἰώνων (*eis aiōnas aiōnōn*) occurs without articles only here in Revelation, but εἰς τὰς αἰῶνας τῶν αἰώνων (*eis tas aiōnas tōn aiōnōn*) occurs eleven times in the book. It expresses the

---

202. Hughes, *Revelation*, p. 163.

eternal existence of God (4:9, 10; 7:12; 10:6; 15:7) and of Christ (1:18), God's eternal reign (11:15), the eternal glory of the Lamb (5:13), the eternal reign of believers (22:5), the eternal doom of the devil (20:10), and the eternal torment of the lost (here and 19:3) (Scott). This torment will never end. The absence of the articles enhances the notion of endless duration in this case (Lee). The temporal punishments have now given way to an ultimate sentence that has no time restrictions (Swete). This doctrine is repugnant to human sensitivity. Nevertheless, it stands, not just on the word of one NT writer, but of Jesus and other writers (e.g., Matt. 25:46; Rom. 2:3-9; 2 Thess. 1:6-9). This truth is not appealing, but it communicates sober reality (Johnson). No kind of semantic manipulation or recourse to symbolic language can erase the fact of eternal punishment conveyed in this announcement (Mounce). This is the most horrible picture of eternal punishment in the entirety of Revelation (Sweet).

The present tenses of ἀναβαίνει . . . ἔχουσιν ἀνάπαυσιν (anabainei . . . echousin, "ascends . . . have rest') reinforces the contextual emphasis on uninterrupted continuity of the ascending smoke and torment (Smith). The wording οὐκ ἔχουσιν ἀνάπαυσιν ἡμέρας καὶ νυκτός (ouk echousin anapausin hēmeras kai nyktos, "they do not have rest day and night"), except for the word order, is exactly the same in 4:8 to describe the ceaseless worship by the living beings. That is voluntary, but this is involuntary. The renegade must pay a different kind of tribute to the one whose power he once ignored (Swete, Lee, Charles, Kiddle, Smith, Johnson).

To avoid any misunderstanding about the identity of the victims of God's wrath, the angel at the end of v. 11 repeats from v. 9 their characteristics: οἱ προσκυνοῦντες τὸ θηρίον καὶ τὴν εἰκόνα αὐτοῦ, καὶ εἴ τις λαμβάνει τὸ χάραγμα τοῦ ὀνόματος αὐτοῦ (hoi proskynountes to thērion kai tēn eikona autou, kai ei tis lambanei to charagma tou onomatos autou, "who worship the beast and his image, and if anyone receives the mark of his name").

14:12 John adds a closing word of warning and encouragement to the third angelic announcement: Ὧδε ἡ ὑπομονὴ τῶν ἁγίων ἐστίν, οἱ τηροῦντες τὰς ἐντολὰς τοῦ θεοῦ καὶ τὴν πίστιν Ἰησοῦ (Hōde hē hypomonē tōn hagiōn estin, hoi tērountes tas entolas tou theou kai tēn pistin Iēsou, "Here is the endurance of the saints, who keep the commandments of God and the faith of Jesus"). This is comparable to the writer's injected comments at 13:10, 18; 17:9. This one is an admonition to steadfastness and comes as a warning to the weak who may contemplate defecting to beast-worship and as an encouragement to the faithful to persevere.[203] The struggle with the beast provides the saints an

---

203. Beckwith, *Apocalypse*, p. 658; Moffatt, "Revelation," 5:439; Robertson, *Word Pictures*, 6:413.

opportunity to work out their salvation through perseverance (Swete, Beckwith, Lenski). Since the fate of the beast worshipers is so dreadful, how important it is for Christ's followers to endure and keep God's commandments. It is better to be killed by the beast than to suffer eternal torment with him. Ὑπομονή (*Hypomonē*, "Endurance") is the key to enablement for sustained and persistent faithfulness under persecution (cf. 1:9; 2:2, 9; 3:10) (Swete, Charles, Lenski).

These faithful ones are related to and probably the same as "the rest" of the woman's seed in 12:17, because they too keep the commandments of God. This, in turn, connects them with the 144,000 of chapters 7 and 14 and with those who experience execution under the beast (13:15). Refusal to worship the beast will make them martyrs (Smith). The connection of the commandments with τὴν πίστιν (*tēn pistin*, "the faith") shows that obedience is not a requirement for sonship, but the result of it (Swete, Moffatt). The genitive Ἰησοῦ (*Iēsou*, "of Jesus") following πίστιν (*pistin*) shows that here *pistin* means "faith" as in 2:13, not "faithfulness" as in 13:10 (Beckwith, Mounce). The genitive is objective and means that the people of God must have a living faith in Jesus to keep them obedient and sustain them under the severe pressures of persecution (Alford, Swete, Beckwith, Ladd).

Additional Notes

14:9 Here the verb προσκυνέω has an accusative object, τὸ θηρίον καὶ τὴν εἰκόνα. The contrast to the dative τῷ ποιήσαντι in 14:7 is notable, perhaps as an indication of the distinction between one worthy of worship and one not worthy.[204]

The difference between the genitive μετώπου and the accusative χεῖρα has no great significance. With the preposition ἐπί, such changes seem relatively inconsequential.[205] In 7:3; 9:4; 14:1; 22:4, the genitive plural μετώπων occurs, but in 13:16; 17:5; 20:4, it is the accusative singular μέτωπον. Χείρ is a genitive in 13:16, but an accusative in 20:1, 4 (Beckwith).

14:10 The καὶ before αὐτός is intensive or "quasi-redundant." It emphasizes that *the very same people* who worship the beast will be the recipients of this cup of punishment (Alford, Swete, Lee, Beckwith, Lenski, Ford).

14:12 Οἱ τηροῦντες is a nominative case rather than a genitive even though it modifies the genitive τῶν ἁγίων. It is loosely added like ἡ καταβαίνουσα in 3:12. Solecisms of this type are common in Revelation (cf. 2:20).[206]

---

204. Robertson, *Word Pictures*, 6:412.
205. Beckwith, *Apocalypse*, p. 657; Robertson, *Grammar*, p. 565; idem, *Word Pictures*, 6:412; Turner, *Syntax*, p. 272.
206. Robertson, *Word Pictures*, 6:413; BDF, par. 136.

(4) THE BLESSEDNESS OF THOSE DYING IN THE LORD (14:13)

Translation

13And I heard a voice from heaven saying, "Write: Blessed are the dead who die in the Lord from now." "Yes," says the Spirit, "that they shall rest from their labors; for their works follow with them."

Exegesis and Exposition

14:13 Loyalty to Christ under the beast's reign will mean inevitable death for many (13:15), so John moves immediately from his exhortation to loyalty to speak of the blessedness of those who experience a martyr's death: Καὶ ἤκουσα φωνῆς ἐκ τοῦ οὐρανοῦ λεγούσης, Γράψον· Μακάριοι οἱ νεκροὶ οἱ ἐν κυρίῳ ἀποθνήσκοντες ἀπ' ἄρτι (*Kai ēkousa phōnēs ek tou ouranou legousēs, Grapson: Makarioi hoi nekroi hoi en kyriō apothnēskontes ap' arti*, "And I heard a voice from heaven saying, 'Write: Blessed are the dead who die in the Lord from now'"). This pause to promise blessedness provides a positive incentive for loyalty to complement the negative one just given (Beckwith, Kiddle).

A voice from heaven heard four times earlier (10:4, 8; 11:12; 14:2) and to be heard twice later (18:4; 21:3) is a divine pronouncement here as at 10:4, 8; 11:12, not a message through an intermediate agent (Smith, Walvoord). John's first two commands to write (1:11, 19) came from the lips of Jesus. The command here emphasizes the importance of what follows (Smith, Mounce). Telling John to do what he probably was doing all along anyway—i.e., writing down what he saw and heard—is an additional way of reflecting God's concern for His people.

He is to write the second of seven beatitudes (or "macarisms") in Revelation (cf. 1:3; 16:15; 19:9; 20:6; 22:7, 14). Μακάριος (*Makarios*) here as often assures a future reward for present obedience to God.[207] The proclamation of blessedness in the future regularly comes in contrast to a painful present reality and hence can be deeply emotional.[208] This beatitude goes further than Paul's similar words regarding the dead at the time of the Parousia (1 Cor. 15:51-53; 1 Thess. 4:14-16). Far from being at a disadvantage to the living, the dead receive a special blessing not pronounced for anyone else.[209] This adds a further motive for endurance to that of the judgment of the wicked (vv. 10-11) (Lee). The episodes in 14:1-5 and 15:1-4 picture the eventual outcome of this blessing (Bullinger).

---

207. Beckwith, *Apocalypse*, p. 422; U. Becker, "Blessing, Blessed, Happy," *NIDNTT*, 1:216-17.
208. F. Hauck, "μακάριος, μακαρίζω, μακαρισμός," *TDNT*, 4:363.
209. Moffatt, "Revelation," 5:439; Robertson, *Word Pictures*, 6:413.

Οἱ νεκροὶ (*Hoi nekroi*, "The dead") refers to the victims executed at the prompting of the beast (13:15). They follow the example of the faithful martyr Antipas (2:13) (Kiddle). Theirs is also a death in union with the Lord, as οἱ ἐν κυρίῳ ἀποθνῄσκοντες (*hoi en kyriō apothnēskontes*, "who die in the Lord") attests. Some have equated the ἐν κυρίῳ (*en kyriō*, "in the Lord") with Paul's ἐν Χριστῷ (*en Christō*, "in Christ") formula (e.g., 1 Cor. 15:18; 1 Thess. 4:16) (e.g., Beckwith), but a slightly different word order here makes this more an expression of a union-in-death with the Lord than of a personal union with Christ. They die in faith, their loyalty to their Lord being the cause of death (Moffatt). They did not love their lives, even to the point of death (12:11). With their promotion to a higher life, the number of martyrs alluded to in 6:11 attains completion (Charles).

The temporal indicator ἀπ' ἄρτι (*ap' arti*, "from now") connects with "who die in the Lord" in sense rather than with "blessed" or with the Spirit's promise that immediately follows it.[210] Relating the words to those facing persecution and death does not deny blessedness to all other saints when they die. It simply means that death for those who remain faithful in the face of more active persecution is a greater relief (Mounce). When violent treatment and cruelty issuing in execution are the consequences of living for the truth, the sooner one dies, the better off he is (Seiss).

Three proposals regarding the placement of the period implied by *ap' arti* have been all periods of the church (Alford), the period from John's writing onward (Johnson), and the period of the death of the martyrs under the rule of the future false Christ. The suggested reference to all periods of the church requires connecting the phrase with *makarioi* ("blessed") and ignores the contextual reference of the words to the last days. Referral to the period of John's writing onward has the advantage of recognizing John's perspective of an imminent beginning of the period of persecution under the beast (Kiddle, Johnson), but this meaning also gives too general an application to the words (Beckwith) and gives too great a prominence to martyrdom in light of the relatively small number of martyrs during the centuries since John's time. It is better to limit this particular blessing to those whom the beast executes.[211] This satisfies the special condition of taking place after the dragon has been banished from heaven (12:9).[212] It also agrees

---

210. Swete, *Apocalypse*, p. 187; Beckwith, *Apocalypse*, p. 659; Robertson, *Word Pictures*, 6:413; Mounce, *Revelation*, p. 277.
211. Contra Virgil P. Cruz, "The Beatitudes of the Apocalypse: Eschatology and Ethics," in *Perspectives on Christology*, ed. Marguerite Shuster and Richard Muller (Grand Rapids: Zondervan, 1991), p. 275.
212. Wall, *Revelation*, p. 187.

with the timing of the next scene of the harvest and the vintage (14:14-20) (Alford) and with the timing of the three angelic announcements (14:1-12) (Beckwith). Without saying anything about conditions before their time, this beatitude comforts those who will face the coming persecution (Swete).

The Spirit adds His affirmation in response to the blessing just pronounced: ναί*, λέγει τὸ πνεῦμα, ἵνα ἀναπαήσονται ἐκ τῶν κόπων αὐτῶν· τὰ γὰρ ἔργα αὐτῶν ἀκολουθεῖ μετ᾽ αὐτῶν (nai, legei to pneuma, hina anapaēsontai ek tōn kopōn autōn; ta gar erga autōn akolouthei met' autōn, "'Yes,' says the Spirit, 'that they shall rest from their labors; for their works follow with them'"). This is the only direct utterance of the Spirit in the Apocalypse except for 22:17 (Johnson). It resembles the affirmation of the beatitude in 19:9, but the wording is different (Lee). As with the invitation in the seven messages (2:7, 11, 17, 29; 3:6, 13, 22), the Spirit identifies with the speaker of the preceding words, whether God or Christ (Beckwith).

The ἵνα (hina, "that") clause has the same force as a ὅτι (hoti, "that") clause would have: "in that" (Swete, Smith). It can hardly express the purpose of the blessedness or the dying just mentioned.[213] It says rather that dying in the Lord consists of resting from one's labors. Herein lies the rationale behind the blessedness. Revelation 22:14 has another hina clause that tells the substance of and the reason for a blessing just pronounced (Beckwith). The future indicative of ἀναπαήσονται (anapaēsontai, "they shall rest") lends itself to the emphasis that their rest is assured and is the providential design of their dying (Simcox). This is the state enjoyed by the martyrs under the fifth seal (6:11) and alludes to God's rest after His labors in creation (Gen. 2:2; cf. Heb. 4:4, 9) (Moffatt). Here is the direct opposite of the beast worshipers who will have no rest day or night.[214] To be sure, those opposing God will not endure the "labors" (κόπων [kopōn]) or violent death caused by a saintly life, because they will comply with the beast's demands, but beyond the grave the story will be different. The saints will rest from their troubles and harsh treatment, but at death, the troubles of their antagonists will begin and never end.

In explanation of the future-life prosperity of the blessed (γὰρ [gar, "for"]), the Spirit adds a word about the continuance of the result of good works. Before martyrdom, these included not just deeds, but spiritual attitude, steadfastness of faith, obedience to the commands of God, and firm resistance to the pressures of the false Christ (Swete,

---

213. Contra Düsterdieck, Revelation, pp. 399-400; Robertson, Word Pictures, 6:413.
214. Chilton, Days of Vengeance, p. 370.

Beckwith, Moffatt, Ladd, Mounce). The attitude is primarily in view because what one is inwardly inevitably determines what he does (Beckwith, Mounce). No one can separate a person from what he has done, even after death. Their works will not be in vain, because the Lord will remember and reward them (cf. 1 Tim. 5:24-25; Heb. 6:10) (Moffatt, Johnson).

Additional Notes

14:13 A shorter reading in which the Καί is absent has respectable support from p⁴⁷, Sinaiticus, and other authorities and is possibly original, with the other readings resulting from expansions of it. But the inclusion of Καί has strong external support in Alexandrinus, Ephraemi, and others, and matches the style of the Apocalypse elsewhere (1:7; 16:7; 22:20), so it is the preferred reading.[215]

The future indicative with ἵνα makes this clause a mixture between "that they may rest" and "in that they shall rest" (cf. 9:20).[216] Such epexegetical clauses are frequent in John's writings (cf. John 8:56).[217]

f. The Harvest and the Vintage (14:14-20)

Translation

¹⁴And I looked, and behold, a white cloud, and upon the cloud one sitting like the Son of Man, having upon his head a golden crown and in his hand a sharp sickle. ¹⁵And another angel came out of the temple, crying with a loud voice to the one sitting upon the cloud, "Send your sickle and reap, because the hour to reap has come, because the harvest of the earth has become ripe." ¹⁶And the one sitting upon the cloud cast his sickle upon the earth, and the earth was reaped. ¹⁷And another angel came out from the temple which is in heaven, himself having also a sharp sickle. ¹⁸And another angel [came out] from the altar, [who] had authority over the fire, and he called with a loud voice to the one who had the sharp sickle, saying, "Send your sharp sickle and gather in the clusters of the vineyard of the earth, because her bunches of grapes are ripe." ¹⁹And the angel cast his sickle into the earth, and gathered the vineyard of the earth and cast [it] into the great winepress of the anger of God. ²⁰And the winepress was trodden down outside the city, and blood came out from the winepress up to the bridles of the horses from [a distance of] a thousand six hundred stadia.

---

215. Metzger, *Textual Commentary*, p. 754.
216. Alford, *Greek Testament*, 4:690; BDF, par. 369[2]; Turner, *Syntax*, p. 102.
217. Burton, *Moods and Tenses*, pars. 215-17; Beckwith, *Apocalypse*, p. 660.

Exegesis and Exposition

14:14 One more scene remains in the section furnishing information as a background for the seven bowls. Its introductory formula, the familiar Καὶ εἶδον, καὶ ἰδοὺ (*Kai eidon, kai idou*, "And I looked, and behold"), marks another major advance to a particularly important subject (Swete, Walvoord): Καὶ εἶδον, καὶ ἰδοὺ νεφέλη λευκή, καὶ ἐπὶ τὴν νεφέλην καθήμενον ὅμοιον υἱὸν ἀνθρώπου, ἔχων ἐπὶ τῆς κεφαλῆς αὐτοῦ στέφανον χρυσοῦν καὶ ἐν τῇ χειρὶ αὐτοῦ δρέπανον ὀξύ (*Kai eidon, kai idou nephelē leukē, kai epi tēn nephelēn kathēmenon homoion hyion anthrōpou, echōn epi tēs kephalēs autou stephanon chrysoun kai en tē cheiri autou drepanon oxy*, "And I looked, and behold, a white cloud, and upon the cloud one sitting like the Son of Man, having upon his head a golden crown and in his hand a sharp sickle"). The scene is in two parts, the first of which alludes to Joel 3:13 in picturing future judgment as a harvest. This is a return to the theme of divine judgment, so recently in view in 14:9-11. It follows a pause designed to encourage the faithful in 14:12-13. The total scene in 14:14-20 closes the section on coming judgment (14:6-20) with a proleptic summary in anticipation of the more detailed account of the same in chapters 15-20 (Beckwith, Moffatt, Johnson).

A white cloud (νεφέλη λευκή [*nephelē leukē*]) is the first thing to catch John's eye. The cloud is an allusion to Dan. 7:13-14 as the one that accompanies the Messiah at His Second Advent (Matt. 24:30; 26:64; Acts 1:9, 11; cf. Matt. 17:5) (Beckwith, Walvoord, Ladd, Mounce). Daniel 7:13 also accounts for ὅμοιον υἱὸν ἀνθρώπου (*homoion hyion anthrōpou*, "like the Son of Man") (cf. Rev. 1:13). Efforts to prove this figure to be an angel rather than the Messiah point to references to "*another* angel" in vv. 15, 17 below and to the similar role of this being to those angels in v. 19 (Morris). They also cite the "rather peremptory" command given this person by another angel in v. 15 (ibid.). Yet identical terminology in 1:13 definitely refers Christ (cf. 1:7 also) (Beckwith). Also, the background passage in Daniel 7 has the Messiah in view (Swete, Charles, Mounce). "Son of Man" is a title for Christ used often in the gospels in connection with Jesus' suffering, the glory of His Second Advent, and His right to judge the world (e.g., Matt. 24:30; 26:64; John 5:27) (Beckwith, Johnson). For Him to receive divine instructions through an angel (14:15) is no stranger than His need to communicate with men through an angel (1:1) (Moffatt). He does not respond to angelic authority in thrusting in His sickle, but receives divine notification through an angel that the proper time to do so has arrived (Acts 1:7; cf. Matt. 24:36; Mark 13:32).[218]

---

218. Alford, *Greek Testament*, 4:691; Lee, "Revelation," 4:708; Beckwith, *Apocalypse*, p. 663; Wall, *Revelation*, p. 188.

The Son's golden crown—a στέφανον (*stephanon*, "crown") as a symbol of victory—is emblematic of His coming conquest over His enemies (Alford, Swete, Mounce). Once He has prevailed, He will wear a "diadem" (διάδημα [*diadēma*], 19:12) as a sign of His royalty.[219] His possession of a δρέπανον ὀξύ (*drepanon oxy*, "sharp sickle") fits His role as reaper in the harvest of the end of the age (Mounce). Seven of the eight NT uses of *drepanon* are in this scene of the harvest and the vintage (cf. Mark 4:29). As in Mark 4:29, this implement introduces the image of a harvest and tells what the Son is about to do in the world. It is sharp and so will do its job swiftly and completely (Lenski).

14:15 Another angel, this one from the heavenly temple, comes out with the signal that the time for harvest has arrived: καὶ ἄλλος ἄγγελος ἐξῆλθεν ἐκ τοῦ ναοῦ, κράζων ἐν φωνῇ μεγάλῃ τῷ καθημένῳ ἐπὶ τῆς νεφέλης, Πέμψον τὸ δρέπανόν σου καὶ θέρισον, ὅτι ἦλθεν ἡ ὥρα θερίσαι*, ὅτι ἐξηράνθη ὁ θερισμὸς τῆς γῆς (*kai allos angelos exēlthen ek tou naou, krazōn en phonē megalē tō kathēmenō epi tēs nephelēs, Pempson to drepanon sou kai therison, hoti ēlthen hē hōra therisai, hoti exēranthē ho therismos tēs gēs*, "and another angel came out of the temple, crying with a loud voice to the one sitting upon the cloud, 'Send your sickle and reap, because the hour to reap has come, because the harvest of the earth has become ripe'"). Ἄλλος (*Allos*, "Another") refers back to v. 9 and marks this as the fourth angel in the series of six in chapter 14. The first three have proclaimed the coming judgment; this one conveys the command to execute it (Swete, Beckwith, Lenski).

Heaven is a ναός (*naos*, "temple"), "sanctuary," or "holy place" whence proceeds the initiative to cleanse earth of its unholiness (Kiddle). It is the dwelling place of God after which the earthly tabernacle and temple were patterned (Beckwith, Charles, Mounce). By this time it is open (11:19; 15:5) to allow the angels with the seven last plagues to exit and perform their bidden task (15:6) (Lee). This is an appropriate point of origin for the angel with this kind of instruction (cf. v. 17 also).

Πέμψον (*Pempson*, "Send") replaces the ἀποστέλλω (*apostellō*, "I send") of Mark 4:29 and the ἐξαποστέλλω (*exapostellō*, "I send out") of Joel 3:13 [LXX] (Beckwith). As an aorist imperative, it stresses the urgency of the directive, just as does the aorist imperative θέρισον (*therison*, "reap").[220] Both aorists are inceptive (i.e., ingressive) (Beckwith). Harvesting is an OT figure for divine judgment (Joel 3:13; cf. Matt. 13:30, 39), especially that of Babylon (Jer. 51:33).

An interesting possibility is that this could refer to the harvest of the elect (Alford). This figure of harvest speaks of the gathering of the

---

219. Robertson, *Word Pictures*, 6:414.
220. Charles, *Apocalypse*, 2:23; Robertson, *Word Pictures*, 6:414.

elect in Isa. 21:12; Matt. 9:37-38; Luke 10:2; John 4:35-38, and includes the elect in Matt. 3:12.[221] This interpretation would explain why the scene has both a harvest and a vintage, without the second being a duplication of the first (Alford). Yet even if usage elsewhere in Scripture were determinative of the meaning here, it would be better to explain this as a mixed harvest rather than one of the elect only (cf. Matt. 13:30, 39) (Lee, Beckwith, Mounce). The present context of Revelation must provide the key. The prevailing tone of this section is one of judgment, not salvation. Glimpses of the gathering of the elect have already come in 14:1-5, 12-13, but the general tone of 14:6-20 is one of punishment for the wicked (Beckwith, Kiddle, Walvoord, Mounce, Johnson). Then too, like the vintage in vv. 17-20, this harvest has its roots in Joel 3:13 which is a judgment of the heathen in the Day of the Lord (Seiss, Beasley-Murray, Sweet). Harvest and vintage are too closely associated for one to apply to the righteous and the other to the wicked (Kiddle).

So this must be the harvest of the condemned spoken of in 19:11-21 (Mounce). The "sharp sickle" speaks of the severity of that judgment (cf. 2:12; 19:15) (Seiss, Smith). Following the pattern of Joel 3:13, the scene furnishes two pictures of the same judgment for the same reason that Joel does, i.e., to emphasize the terror of it. Differences between the pictures such as the absence of something comparable to a winepress in the first picture and the differences in agency in the two, pose no serious obstacle to seeing this as picturing the judgment of earth's rebels. As a preview of 19:11-21, only this meaning does justice to the harvest.

The words ἦλθεν ἡ ὥρα (*ēlthen hē hōra*, "the hour . . . has come") duplicate what the announcement of v. 7 said about the hour of judgment, furnishing further evidence that the hour to reap applies to the nonrepentant. The verb ἐξηράνθη (*exēranthē*, "has become ripe") states the reason for (ὅτι [*hoti*, "because"]) the timing of the harvest. Whether it refers to overripeness (Beckwith) or simply ripeness (Swete), it signals a readiness for the harvest. The word ξηραίνω (*xērainō*, "I am dry") has a negative connotation in the LXX (e.g., Joel 1:17) and in the NT (Matt. 21:19-20; Mark 3:1, 3; 11:20; Luke 8:6; James 1:11; Rev. 16:12) (Charles, Smith, Walvoord). This use too is anything but positive. The harvest, under the control of God's sovereignty and according to His timetable, has reached its appointed state for reaping (Ladd).

14:16 Responding to the angelic signal, the Son of Man cast His sickle into the earth and reaped it: καὶ ἔβαλεν ὁ καθήμενος ἐπὶ τῆς νεφέλης τὸ δρέπανον αὐτοῦ ἐπὶ τὴν γῆν, καὶ ἐθερίσθη ἡ γῆ (*kai ebalen ho*

---

221. Mulholland, *Revelation*, pp. 252-53.

kathēmenos epi tēs nephelēs to drepanon autou epi tēn gēn, kai etheristhē
hē gē, "and the one sitting upon the cloud cast his sickle upon the earth,
and the earth was reaped"). As the duly authorized judge (John 5:27),
He pronounces His verdict in setting His sickle to work (Swete, Lenski,
Ladd). The aorists ἔβαλεν (*ebalen*, "cast") and ἐθερίσθη (*etheristhē*,
"was reaped") are further instances of the prophetic (or proleptic) use
of that tense, pointing forward to what will yet transpire in the book's
sequential unfolding.[222] Two references to "the earth" (τὴν γῆν [*tēn
gēn*] and ἡ γῆ [*hē gē*]) in such a short statement emphasize the beings
with whom the judgment will deal (Bullinger). The brevity of the statement dramatizes the suddenness of the judgment.

14:17 The second part of this last scene of background data is a
picture of the future judgment as a vintage: Καὶ ἄλλος ἄγγελος ἐξῆλθεν
ἐκ τοῦ ναοῦ τοῦ ἐν τῷ οὐρανῷ, ἔχων καὶ αὐτὸς δρέπανον ὀξύ (*Kai allos
angelos exēlthen ek tou naou tou en tō ouranō, echōn kai autos drepanon
oxy*, "And another angel came out from the temple which is in heaven,
himself having also himself a sharp sickle"). This is the fifth in the
series of angels, and like the fourth, he comes from the heavenly temple. This angel comes to gather the vintage as Christ did the harvest.
The vintage is more vivid than the harvest, climaxing in the treading of
the winepress (v. 20), not just in the gathering of the grapes (v. 19)
(Beckwith). The function of angels as punishers of the wicked is a
theme in Matt. 13:41-42, 49-50 also (ibid.).

This angel like the Son of Man (ἔχων καὶ αὐτὸς [*echōn kai autos*,
"himself having also"]) has a sharp sickle (cf. v. 14). Pruning the vine
required the same tool as gathering the harvest (Beckwith).

14:18 A sixth angel, this one from the heavenly altar, then came
forth indicating the arrival of the appointed time to gather in the
grapes: Καὶ ἄλλος ἄγγελος *ἐκ τοῦ θυσιαστηρίου, [ὁ] ἔχων ἐξουσίαν ἐπὶ
τοῦ πυρός, καὶ ἐφώνησεν φωνῇ μεγάλῃ τῷ ἔχοντι τὸ δρέπανον τὸ ὀξὺ
λέγων, Πέμψον σου τὸ δρέπανον τὸ ὀξὺ καὶ τρύγησον τοὺς βότρυας τῆς
ἀμπέλου τῆς γῆς, ὅτι ἤκμασαν αἱ σταφυλαὶ αὐτῆς (*Kai allos angelos ek
tou thysiastēriou, [ho] echōn exousian epi tou pyros, kai ephōnēsen
phōnē megalē tō echonti to drepanon to oxy legōn, Pempson sou to
drepanon to oxy kai trygēson tous botryas tēs ampelou tēs gēs, hoti ēkmasan hai staphylai autēs*, "And another angel [came out] from the
altar, [who] had authority over the fire, and he called with a loud voice
to the one who had the sharp sickle, saying, 'Send your sharp sickle
and gather in the clusters of the vineyard of the earth, because her
bunches of grapes are ripe'"). The altar from which the angel exits
must be the only altar in heaven, the golden altar of incense (cf. 8:3).

---

222. Robertson, *Word Pictures*, 6:415.

This is appropriate because that altar is the one from which God's judgments against the earth have proceeded all along (cf. 6:9; 8:3; 16:17) (Alford).

If this were the altar of burnt offering, as some allege, in 6:9 and 11:1, the angel's authority over fire would apply to that altar and his appearance would recall the blood of the martyrs.[223] Yet there is no good case for an altar of burnt offering in heaven in Revelation. The authority of this angel over fire is rather an allusion to 8:3 ff. where an angel took a censer full of fire and threw it into the earth. So the implications of this reference to fire suggest the figure of a minister of wrath responding to the prayers of the saints. This is probably the same angel who cast fire to the earth earlier, and here as there, the connection of the imprecatory prayers of the saints for vengeance is conspicuous.[224]

The angel "called with a loud voice" (ἐφώνησεν φωνῇ μεγάλῃ [ephōnēsen phōnē megalē]) to convey his instructions to the angel with the sharp sickle. This is the only occurrence of φωνέω (phōneō, "I call") in Revelation. The combination φωνῇ μεγάλῃ (phōneō phōnē megalē, "I call with a loud voice") appears in Mark 1:26 and Acts 16:28 also (Charles). His two-part command, πέμψον (pempson, "send") (cf. v. 15) and τρύγησον (trygēson, "gather in"), indicates that it is time for the vintage to begin. "The clusters" (τοὺς βότρυας [tous botryas]) to be gathered are further defined by "the vineyard" (τῆς ἀμπέλου [tēs ampelou], genitive of apposition), which has as its source "the earth" (τῆς γῆς [tēs gēs], ablative of source). Just as God's people are His vineyard to produce the fruit of righteousness, the earth's people are another vineyard that produces evil fruit (Walvoord).

This fruit of evil has now reached the point of ripeness, "because her bunches of grapes are ripe" (ὅτι ἤκμασαν αἱ σταφυλαὶ αὐτῆς [hoti ēkmasan hai staphylai autēs]). It has reached its prime and is fully ripe (Swete). The picture of the verb ἤκμασαν (ēkmasan) differs from that of ἐξηράνθη (exēranthē) (v. 15), but the point is the same: the time for the harvest has come (Walvoord). It is time to extract the effects of the growth process. Σταφυλαὶ (Staphylai, "Bunches of grapes") depicts ripe grapes in contrast with ὄμφαξ (omphax) which refers to unripe ones (cf. Gen. 40:10 [LXX]), and the grapes themselves as opposed to βότρυς (botrys) which refers to the clusters in which they grow (Swete).

14:19 The angel with the sharp sickle responds by casting his sickle into the earth: καὶ ἔβαλεν ὁ ἄγγελος τὸ δρέπανον αὐτοῦ εἰς τὴν γῆν, καὶ ἐτρύγησεν τὴν ἄμπελον τῆς γῆς καὶ ἔβαλεν εἰς τὴν ληνὸν τοῦ

---

223. E.g., Robertson, *Word Pictures*, 6:415.
224. Beckwith, *Apocalypse*, p. 664; Chilton, *Days of Vengeance*, p. 374. See Excursus 2, "The Imprecatory Prayers of the Apocalypse," Thomas, pp. 517-22.

θυμοῦ τοῦ θεοῦ τὸν μέγαν* (*kai ebalen ho angelos to drepanon autou eis tēn gēn, kai etrygēsen tēn ampelon tēs gēs kai ebalen eis tēn lēnon tou thymou tou theou ton megan*, "and the angel cast his sickle into the earth, and gathered in the vineyard of the earth and cast [it] into the great winepress of the anger of God"). A vineyard in Scripture sometimes represents Israel (e.g., Isa. 5:1-7), but in this context it is specifically the enemies of God.

The "vineyard" (ἄμπελον [*ampelon*]) has produced the wrong kind of fruit and must be trodden in the great winepress (ληνὸν [*lēnon*]) which is the anger of God (τοῦ θυμοῦ τοῦ θεοῦ [*tou thymou tou theou*], τοῦ θυμοῦ [*tou thymou*] being a genitive of apposition). Isaiah 63:1-6, Lam. 1:15, and Joel 3:13 bring out the OT imagery utilized here. The winepress in ancient times consisted of two bowls hewn out of solid rock. One was higher than the other and contained the grapes which someone walked on to squeeze the juice from them. The juice flowed through a duct into the lower basin where it collected until being removed for consumption. The redness of the juice and the staining of the feet and garments of the treaders made this an apt picture of divine judgment (cf. Gen. 49:11).[225] This is God's judgment against the rebels (Johnson), not a picture of the deaths of martyrs (contra Caird). The same imagery will arise again in 19:15 (Lee).

14:20 The vineyard account goes further than that of the harvest to picture the gruesome outcome of the judgment process: καὶ ἐπατήθη ἡ ληνὸς ἔξωθεν τῆς πόλεως, καὶ ἐξῆλθεν αἷμα ἐκ τῆς ληνοῦ ἄχρι τῶν χαλινῶν τῶν ἵππων ἀπὸ σταδίων χιλίων* ἑξακοσίων (*kai epatēthē hē lēnos exōthen tēs poleōs, kai exēlthen haima ek tēs lēnou achri tōn chalinōn tōn hippōn apo stadiōn chiliōn exakosiōn*, "and the winepress was trodden down outside the city, and blood came out from the winepress up to the bridles of the horses from [a distance of] a thousand six hundred stadia"). The passive voice ἐπατήθη (*epatēthē*, "was trodden") leaves unstated the agent of treading, but the location of the treading is fixed as being "outside the city" (ἔξωθεν τῆς πόλεως [*exōthen tēs poleōs*]).

The proposal of leaving the city unidentified so that it can have a symbolic meaning (Johnson) shirks the responsibility of interpreting something the author intended to be understood. The suggestion that the city is Babylon because of the city's prominence in this part of Revelation (Kiddle) misses the point that Babylon does not escape God's judgment the way this city does.[226] Jerusalem is the obvious answer to which city this is. The OT predicts that the final battle will happen near there, in the valley of Jehoshaphat which is traditionally

---

225. Beckwith, *Apocalypse*, p. 663; Mounce, *Revelation*, p. 282; Robertson, *Word Pictures*, 6:416; Sweet, *Revelation*, p. 232.
226. Wall, *Revelation*, p. 189.

located in the area of the Kidron Valley (cf. Joel 3:12-14; Zech. 14:4) (Beckwith, Walvoord, Mounce). This identification also agrees roughly with the wording of 11:2 and the location where 14:1 has tacitly set the scene of the current action (Alford). The objection to seeing this as Jerusalem is that Rev. 16:16 fixes the final battle at Armageddon which is nowhere near Jerusalem (Johnson). This is not insuperable, however, if the battle is a widespread one covering a large part of Palestine.

The nauseous result of the judgment is the flow of blood from the winepress. Red blood, resembling the color of the juice of the grape (cf. Gen. 49:11), flows excessively from the treading of the vine of the earth (cf. 19:15) (Alford, Swete, Beckwith). What is possibly a hyperbole, ἄχρι τῶν χαλινῶν τῶν ἵππων ἀπὸ σταδίων χιλίων ἑξακοσίων (*achri tōn chalinōn tōn hippōn apo stadiōn chiliōn exakosiōn*, "up to the bridles of the horses from [a distance of] a thousand six hundred stadia"), tells the sad truth of massive failure under the scrutinizing judgment of God. The terminology suggests a sea of blood resulting from a direct confrontation on the field of battle (Johnson). The depth of the blood and the land area covered are both indicative of a massive slaughter and loss of human life.

Assigning 1,600 a purely symbolic meaning as the square of forty, the traditional number of punishment (Beasley-Murray) is possible, but this view exhibits an inclination toward excessive symbolism in interpreting the book. The number could be just a symbol for completeness (Swete, Beckwith, Charles, Mounce), a hyperbole for a field inconceivably vast. But a literal meaning is not out of the question. This distance is the length of Palestine, approximately 184 miles (Ladd). Also, the valley of Megiddo where the war will occur (16:16) is in the northern part of Palestine and drains into the Jordan system. This allows the necessary distance for the prophecy to have a literal fulfillment.[227] The objection that Palestine is only 1,280 stadia or 160 miles in length (Alford) is invalid if one measures from Tyre to El Arish (Beasley-Murray, Ford) or from Bozra in the southeast to Megiddo (Seiss). Either way, the distance is 200 miles or 1,600 stadia. The literal meaning of the 1,600 stadia receives a slight preference in interpretation, but this is a preference unsupported by strong argumentation.

So the extended section preliminary to the seven bowls comes to its end on the somber note of judgment. This sets a sad but necessary tone for the entrance of the seven bowls of God's anger.

Additional Notes

14:14 The εἶδον accounts for the accusative case of καθήμενον (direct object), and since the ἰδού is an interjection, not a verb, the nominative of νεφέλη is explainable (Simcox, Lenski).

---

227. Ryrie, *Revelation*, p. 93.

The accusative υἱόν following ὅμοιον is a solecism, because normally a dative follows ὅμοιον (cf. 1:13).[228] The anarthrous υἱὸν ἀνθρώπου is rare in the NT, the only other occurrence being at John 5:27. It is attributable here to the influence of the LXX of Dan. 7:13, which in turn was influenced by the construct state of the Hebrew expression.[229]

The nominative ἔχων modifying the accusative καθήμενον is probably one of the many illustrations of this author's freedom in his use of participles, though it may be a nominative following ἰδού, the same as νεφέλη.[230]

14:15 As objects of ἐπὶ, the change from the accusative τὴν νεφέλην in v. 14 to the genitive τῆς νεφέλης in vv. 15 and 16 entails a change of meaning so slight that it is almost imperceptible (Swete). The position is a kind of pose in the first case and a directional pose in the last two.

Sinaiticus and a few other MSS replace θερίσαι with τοῦ θερισμοῦ, while p[47] has simply ὁ θερισμὸς in place of ἡ ὥρα θερίσαι. Neither variant has sufficient external support to merit serious consideration as the original reading. The infinitive θερίσαι is epexegetical, telling that with reference to which the hour pertains.[231]

14:18 The presence of ἐξῆλθεν in v. 18 is doubtful, because it is missing from p[47], Alexandrinus, 2053, and other MSS. Its presence in Sinaiticus, Ephraemi, and many other sources raises the possibility that copyists may have added it on the basis of its appearance in v. 17. The other possibility is that an accidental or deliberate omission accounts for its absence from some texts. Repetition as an authorial characteristic favors its inclusion.[232] Preference for the shorter and harder reading are on the side of the omission being original. The sense of the verse is not affected, however, because the force of the ἐξῆλθεν in v. 17 carries over into v. 18.

14:19 Some magnify the importance of the difference between εἰς here and ἐπὶ in v. 16 to the point of making the prepositions distinguish between the punishment of the rebels here and the gathering of the elect there.[233] This is too heavy an exegetical load for the prepositions to bear in light of the strong contextual indications that both verses portray the judgment of the wicked.

14:19 The postponement of τὸν μέγαν as a modifier of τὴν ληνόν

---

228. Robertson, *Grammar*, p. 136; BDF, par. 182[4].
229. Charles, *Revelation*, 2:19; C. F. D. Moule, *An Idiom Book of New Testament Greek* (Cambridge: Cambridge Univ., 1960), p. 177.
230. Robertson, *Word Pictures*, 6:414.
231. Ibid.
232. Metzger, *Textual Commentary*, p. 754.
233. E.g., Mulholland, *Revelation*, pp. 254-55.

until after the genitive τοῦ θυμοῦ τοῦ θεοῦ puts more emphasis on the greatness of the winepress. The masculine τὸν μέγαν modifying the feminine τὴν ληνόν is one of the frequently cited solecisms in Revelation.[234] Ληνός can be either feminine as it is in 14:20 and 19:15 or masculine as it sometimes was in ancient Greek (cf. Gen. 30:38, 41 [LXX]).[235] Perhaps the severity of the judgment symbolized by the press prompted a change to the masculine adjective (Beckwith).

Instead of τὸν μέγαν, Sinaiticus and the Textus Receptus read τὴν μεγάλην to bring the adjective into gender agreement with ληνὸν, and p[47] and a few witnesses have τοῦ μεγάλου making the adjective a modifier of τοῦ θεοῦ. Both variants are obviously efforts to "correct" the harder reading τὸν μέγαν that Alexandrinus, Ephraemi, and other authorities ably support.[236]

14:20 Ἔξωθεν is usually an adverb, but functions here as a preposition. The only other two places in the NT where this happens are Rev. 11:2 and Mark 7:15.[237]

This use of the preposition ἀπὸ measures distance from the distant point to the beholder, and not as commonly done, from the beholder to the distant point (Lenski). It is a common construction meaning "at a distance of" in late Greek, but occurs with this meaning only here and in John 11:18 and 21:8 in the NT (Simcox).

Sinaiticus and a few other MSS read χιλίων διακοσίων, probably because 1,200 lends itself better to symbolic interpretation. The χιλίων ἑξακοσίων reading has strong external support in Alexandrinus, Ephraemi, and others and is most probably the original reading.[238]

---

234. BDF, par. 136[3].
235. Alford, *Greek Testament*, 4:692-93; Swete, *Apocalypse*, p. 192; Robertson, *Word Pictures*, 6:415-16.
236. Metzger, *Textual Commentary*, pp. 754-55.
237. Robertson, *Word Pictures*, 6:416; Moule, *Idiom Book*, p. 84.
238. Metzger, *Textual Commentary*, p. 755.

18
The Seven Bowls
or the Seven Last Plagues

With the background data for the seven bowls in place in chapters 12-14, John's visional experience continues in his encounter with seven new angels whose responsibility it is to dispense the seven bowl judgments, otherwise known as the seven last plagues.

2. THE REJOICING OVER THE SEVEN LAST PLAGUES (15:1-4)

Translation

¹And I saw another sign in heaven, a great and marvelous one, seven angels having seven plagues, the last ones, because in them the anger of God was completed.

²And I saw [something] like a sea of glass mixed with fire, and [I saw] those who overcame from the beast and from his image and from the number of his name, standing upon the sea of glass, having harps of God, ³and they sang the song of Moses the slave of God and the song of the Lamb, saying,

"Great and marvelous are Your works,
    Lord God Almighty;
righteous and true are Your ways,
    King of the nations.
⁴Who will not fear [You], Lord,
    and glorify Your name?

because [You] only [are] holy,
because all the nations will come
and worship before You,
because Your righteous acts have been manifest."

Exegesis and Exposition

A scene in heaven precedes the bowl series as happened with the seals (chaps. 4-5) and the trumpets (8:2-6) too. Chapter 15 is a sort of celestial interlude to introduce the pouring out of the seven bowls of wrath in chapter 16. The former facilitates an understanding of the latter. It is time for what has been anticipated in the cup of wine (14:10), the harvest (14:14-16), and the vintage (14:17-20) to be delineated in its chronological fulfillment. Correspondences between chapter 14 and chapters 15-16 reflect how the visions have prepared the way up to now—15:2-4 = 14:1-5; 15:1, 5 and 16:1-21 = 14:6-11, 14-20.[1]

Following the sign of the seven angels with the seven last plagues, the fifteenth chapter has two visions, the first one picturing the victors fresh from their triumph and the second describing the white-and-gold clad angels who hold the seven bowls (Johnson).

15:1 The first verse of chapter 15 is a superscription for chapters 15-16 and perhaps for the remainder of the visional portion of the book: Καὶ εἶδον ἄλλο σημεῖον ἐν τῷ οὐρανῷ μέγα καὶ θαυμαστόν, ἀγγέλους ἑπτὰ ἔχοντας πληγὰς ἑπτὰ τὰς ἐσχάτας, ὅτι ἐν αὐταῖς ἐτελέσθη ὁ θυμὸς τοῦ θεοῦ (*Kai eidon allo sēmeion en tō ouranō mega kai thaumaston, angelous hepta echontas plēgas hepta tas eschatas, hoti en autais etelesthē ho thymos tou theou,* "And I saw another sign in heaven, a great and marvelous one, seven angels having seven plagues, the last ones, because in them the anger of God was completed"). To view the verse as a superscription touches on the question of whether it relates more closely to what precedes or to what follows. Arguments for grouping it with the preceding include the observation that καὶ εἶδον (*kai eidon,* "and I saw") is the customary way of introducing a new vision in Revelation, but not a new section.[2] Also, the opening of the temple in 15:5 is the way that, according to some, a new section began

1. James Moffatt, "The Revelation of St. John the Divine," in *The Expositor's Greek Testament,* ed. W. Robertson Nicoll (Grand Rapids: Eerdmans, n.d.), 5:442; R. C. H. Lenski, *The Interpretation of St. John's Revelation* (Columbus, Ohio: Lutheran Book Concern, 1935), p. 453; Martin Kiddle, *The Revelation of St. John,* HNTC (New York: Harper, 1940), p. 229; Alan F. Johnson, "Revelation," in *EBC,* ed. Frank E. Gaebelein (Grand Rapids: Zondervan, 1981), 12:544.
2. Michael Wilcock, *The Message of Revelation* (Downers Grove, Ill.: InterVarsity, 1975), p. 137.

in 11:19. A serious deficiency of this viewpoint, however, is the appearance of the plague angels in v. 1, a factor that places the verse squarely in relationship with what follows this verse. To answer that their appearance is anticipatory like that of Babylon (cf. 14:18 and 16:19 with chaps. 17-18) and Jerusalem (cf. 19:7 with 21:2)[3] misses the distinction between sections of intercalation and sections involving numbered series. Only events of the numbered series are sequential, and to term the appearance of the angels in v. 1 as anticipatory of their appearance in v. 6 overlooks the characteristic that intercalations such as chapter 15 is are not sequential (see Excursus 3).

Viewing the section 15:1-4 as part of what follows does face the task of explaining why there is no change of scenery as occurs at other points,[4] but this is not the first time a simple *kai eidon* has made such a transition (e.g., 8:2). Grouping the words with what comes later also faces the question of why the song of triumph (15:2-4) occupies a slot between John's first sight of the plague angels (15:1) and their actual emergence (15:5-7).[5] A suitable answer is available, however, in the comparison with the appearance of the trumpet angels in 8:2, followed by a picture of activity connected with the prayers of the saints (8:3-5) before the angels ready themselves to sound (8:6). The tone of finality that prevails in the ἐσχάτας (*eschatas*, "last") and ἐτελέσθη (*etelesthē*, "was completed") (15:1) and in the πάντα τὰ ἔθνη ἥξουσιν (*panta ta ethnē hēxousin*, "all the nations will come") (15:4) shows that it is only appropriate that this section be a part of the visions where the angels play the major role (15:5-7; 16:1 ff.).

The seven angels comprise ἄλλο σημεῖον ἐν τῷ οὐρανῷ μέγα καὶ θαυμαστόν (*allo sēmeion en tọ ouranọ mega kai thaumaston*, "another sign in heaven, a great and marvelous one"), with the allusion being to the first two signs that appeared to John in heaven (12:1, 3)—the woman clothed in the sun and the great fiery-red dragon.[6] This vision is in heaven, but it looks beyond to the theological meaning couched in end-time history on earth.[7] The mission of these angels has forebodings for mankind regarding the end of this creation. The sign of the woman in 12:1 was "great," but this one is "great and marvelous." Μέγας (*Megas*, "Great") and θαυμαστός (*thaumastos*, "marvelous") oc-

---

3. Ibid., pp. 139-40.
4. Ibid., p. 137.
5. Ibid.
6. Isbon T. Beckwith, *The Apocalypse of John* (New York: Macmillan, 1919), p. 673; Lenski, *Revelation*, p. 453; Kiddle, *Revelation*, p. 300; John F. Walvoord, *The Revelation of Jesus Christ* (Chicago: Moody, 1966), p. 255.
7. Robert H. Mounce, *The Book of Revelation*, NICNT (Grand Rapids: Eerdmans, 1977), p. 285.

cur together only here and in 15:3 in the NT.[8] *Thaumastos* usually speaks of God and His works (cf. Ps. 93:4[LXX]; Matt. 21:42), so its use here strikes a note of divine awe.[9] The awesomeness of the angels stems from the goal of their mission, which is the completion of God's wrath (Johnson). The plagues are great and evoke fear through their effects on nature, mankind, and the unholy trinity of the dragon, the beast, and the false prophet (Mounce).

The sign consists of "seven angels having seven plagues, the last ones" (ἀγγέλους ἑπτὰ ἔχοντας πληγὰς ἑπτὰ τὰς ἐσχάτας [*angelous hepta echontas plēgas hepta tas eschatas*]). Ἔχοντας (*Echontas*, "Having") carries the sense of "having the duty of inflicting," as does a participle from the same verb in 15:6 (Beckwith). Πληγάς (*Plēgas*, "Plagues") is used fifteen times in Revelation, always in an eschatological sense. In the NT outside Revelation, it never has an eschatological sense (Ford). This is the first reference in Revelation to these seven angels, as the absence of an article with ἀγγέλους (*angelous*, "angels") indicates (Lee). They appear seven times as a group in the remainder of the book (15:1, 6, 7, 8; 16:1; 17:1; 21:9), and nine times individual representatives of the group involve themselves in the activities (16:2, 3, 4, 8, 10, 12, 17; 17:7; 21:9). It is customary for angels to be agents of God in carrying out His purposes (cf. Ps. 103:20) (Lenski). This verse does not announce the actual entrance of the angels to undertake their task. That comes later in 15:5-6. This early mention accords with the writer's habit of giving a general or comprehensive statement that he later develops in greater detail (cf. 8:2; 12:6; 21:2) (Beckwith).

Their duty is to inflict "seven plagues, the last ones" (πληγὰς ἑπτὰ τὰς ἐσχάτας [*plēgas hepta tas eschatas*]). Five of the plagues recall five of the ten Egyptian plagues in Exodus 7-10. The first and third bowl-plagues are particularly reminiscent of what God did to punish the Egyptians and to deliver His people Israel. Besides the plagues, other features of this context that resemble God's previous deliverance are the crossing of the sea (16:12), the song of Moses (15:3), the giving of the Law amid the smoke of Sinai (15:8), and the erection of the tent of testimony (15:5).[10] These similarities hint that the seven bowls have a similar purpose, that of punishing the world as a whole and delivering the faithful into their promised bliss.

---

8. J. B. Smith, *A Revelation of Jesus Christ* (Scottdale, Pa.: Herald, 1961), p. 222; Walvoord, *Revelation*, p. 226.
9. J. Massyngberde Ford, *Revelation*, vol. 38 of AB (Garden City, N.Y.: Doubleday, 1975), p. 254.
10. E. W. Bullinger, *The Apocalypse* or *"The Day of the Lord,"* (London: Eyre and Spottiswoode, n.d.), p. 475; Beckwith, *Apocalypse*, pp. 671-73; Moffatt, "Revelation," 5:442; G. V. Caird, *A Commentary on the Revelation of St. John the Divine*, HNTC (New York: Harper & Row, 1966), p. 297.

The first six seals and the first six trumpets were also plagues (e.g., 9:20), but these seven have the distinction of being the last ones.[11] The earlier series were temporal punishments to warn people of the severity of God's wrath, but these are the climax of them all, coming at the end of the Great Tribulation (Alford, Kiddle). These also comprise the third woe announced as early as 11:14, but only now developed in its external effects. No announcement that the third woe has passed is in the offing, because by the time it has passed, human history will have reached its culmination.[12] No amount of rationalization—such as some theonomists practice to soften the tone of ultimacy, absoluteness, and universality in finding a fulfillment of these plagues in the A.D. 70 events surrounding the destruction of Jerusalem[13]—can mitigate the force of this language regarding the finality of these plagues.

The conjunction ὅτι (*hoti*, "because") assigns the reason for the emphatic "lastness" of these plagues: ἐν αὐταῖς ἐτελέσθη ὁ θυμὸς τοῦ θεοῦ (*en autais etelesthē ho thymos tou theou*, "in them the anger of God was completed"). The form ἐτελέσθη (*etelesthē*, "was completed") is identical with one already discussed in 10:7. It is a proleptic (or prophetic) use of the aorist tense.[14] In other words, in them the anger of God "will have been completed" or "will have reached its ultimate goal," when the seven plagues are over. Though future from a human perspective, God sees it as already done, making a past tense the appropriate way to speak of it (Lee). The plagues encompass the casting of the dragon, the beast, and the false prophet into the lake of fire (19:20; 20:10) and the judgment and consignment of rebellious mankind to that same lake (20:12-15). "The anger of God" (ὁ θυμὸς τοῦ θεοῦ [*ho thymos tou theou*]) must overtake all sin as 14:8, 10 (cf. 14:19) have already forewarned and as 16:19 and 19:15 (cf. 15:7; 16:1) will develop more fully (Swete, Charles). *Thymos* is the venting of God's anger based on ὀργή (*orgē*, "wrath") which is God's attitude toward sin (cf. 16:19). The two words occur together in 16:19 and 19:15 (Smith, Walvoord). The wrath of God and of the Lamb begun under the seal judgments reaches its concluding apex with these seven last plagues.

---

11. Henry Barclay Swete, *The Apocalypse of St. John* (London: Macmillan, 1906), p. 193; Smith, *Revelation*, pp. 222-23.
12. Beckwith, *Apocalypse*, pp. 669-71; Robert W. Wall, *Revelation*, New International Biblical Commentary, ed. W. Ward Gasque (Peabody, Mass.: Hendrickson, 1991), p. 192. See Excursus 5 at the conclusion of this volume for an analysis of the seventh bowl.
13. E.g., David Chilton, *The Days of Vengeance* (Fort Worth, Tex.: Dominion, 1987), pp. 383-84.
14. Archibald Thomas Robertson, *Word Pictures in the New Testament*, 6 vols. (Nashville: Broadman, 1933), 6:417; Smith, *Revelation*, p. 223; Charles Caldwell Ryrie, *Revelation*, Everyman's Bible Commentary (Chicago: Moody, 1968), p. 94.

15:2 In the scene of 15:2-4 the seer's eye comes to rest for a moment on the martyrs in their bliss, a sharp contrast to the prospects of coming doom under the seven last plagues: Καὶ εἶδον ὡς θάλασσαν ὑαλίνην μεμιγμένην πυρί, καὶ τοὺς νικῶντας ἐκ τοῦ θηρίου καὶ ἐκ τῆς εἰκόνος αὐτοῦ καὶ ἐκ τοῦ ἀριθμοῦ τοῦ ὀνόματος αὐτοῦ ἑστῶτας ἐπὶ τὴν θάλασσαν τὴν ὑαλίνην, ἔχοντας κιθάρας τοῦ θεοῦ (*Kai eidon hōs thalassan hyalinēn memigmenēn pyri, kai tous nikōntas ek tou thēriou kai ek tēs eikonos autou kai ek tou arithmou tou onomatos autou hestōtas epi tēn thalassan tēn hyalinēn, echontas kitharas tou theou*, "And I saw [something] like a sea of glass mixed with fire, and [I saw] those who overcame from the beast and from his image and from the number of his name, standing upon the sea of glass, having harps of God"). This is a scene of victory, peace, and tranquillity (Swete, Johnson).

The surrounding focus on divine judgment evokes reverence from the saints (15:4), a reaction in sharp contrast to the response of others to that judgment (16:9, 11) (Moffatt). This is at least the third time that songs have celebrated the promised and imminent accomplishment of God's decrees (cf. 11:15-18; 14:1-5) (Lee). The bowl plagues about to begin are the occasion of the current song (Beckwith).

A sea of glass, probably the one already encountered in 4:6 even though no article appears, is the first thing to meet John's eye. The four living beings are here (15:7) just as they were in the earlier picture of heaven. As stated earlier, this sea of glass is an emblem of "the splendor and majesty of God on His throne that set Him apart from all His creation, a separation stemming from His purity and absolute holiness, which He shares with no one else."[15]

Unlike the picture of 4:6, the sea of glass here is "mixed with fire" (μεμιγμένην πυρί [*memigmenēn pyri*]). In 4:6, the sea is limpid and untroubled, making it look like crystal, but here the intermingling of fire suggests the punitive providence to materialize shortly as the seven angels pour out the terrible contents of their bowls. The sea is a mighty reservoir of just judgments about to become realities. The overcomers have forded the new "Red Sea" (cf. 12:15-16) which will shortly engulf their foes (Alford, Lee, Lenski, Kiddle, Smith, Walvoord). It is insufficient in this context to see fire as a mere picturesque detail (contra Mounce) or a symbol for the trials through which the martyrs

---

15. Robert L. Thomas, *Revelation 1-7, An Exegetical Commentary* (Chicago: Moody, 1992), p. 353; cf. Henry Alford, *The Greek Testament*, 4 vols. (London: Longmans, Green 1903), 4:693-94; Kiddle, *Revelation*, p. 300; Walvoord, *Revelation*, p. 226; Philip Edgcumbe Hughes, *The Book of the Revelation, A Commentary* (Grand Rapids: Eerdmans, 1990), pp. 170-71.

have passed (contra Hailey). The fire has a specific meaning related to the mission of the seven angels.

"Those who overcame" (τοὺς νικῶντας [*tous nikōntas*]) are at least like and are probably identical with the martyrs of 12:11. They did not love their lives all the way to death. The beast overcame them during the Great Tribulation (13:7), but now roles are reversed. Having been martyred, they are now victors on high (Scott). This picture of the martyrs differs markedly from that in 6:9-11, because now the avenging of their blood must wait no longer (Swete). Because membership in the eschatological community of God requires faithfulness, not necessarily martyrdom, some interpret these overcomers to include all the faithful, not just martyrs.[16] But those given refuge from the beast (12:13-17) have not directly encountered him and had no need of overcoming him as these singers have. The special interest of this section is in those who have remained faithful to death instead of yielding to the blasphemous demands of the false Christ (cf. 13:15). Here as at 12:11, a comparison to the tremendous odds against which they had to contend enhances their triumph. A later portion describes their resurrection and special rewards (20:4-6).[17] This is the group especially in mind in 14:1-5 and 14:13 also.

Three occurrences of ἐκ (*ek*, "from") list the specific obstacles overcome by this throng of singers. They are the beast, his image, and the number of his name. These three are covert references to the murderous persecution of the second beast in 13:11-18 (Beasley-Murray). "The number of his name" (Τοῦ ἀριθμοῦ τοῦ ὀνόματος αὐτοῦ [*Tou arithmou tou onomatos*]) replaces the receipt of the mark of the beast (13:17) in this list (Johnson). A number of the weaker MSS add ἐκ τοῦ χαράγματος αὐτοῦ καί (*ek tou charagmatos autou kai*, "from his mark and") before "the number of his name," not realizing that this takes its place (Mounce). The combination of the verb νικάω (*nikaō*, "I overcome") and ἐκ (*ek*, "from") gives the dual concept of victory over and deliverance from the temptation to worship the beast's image and receive his mark.[18] They prevailed over the coercion to which others acquiesced (cf. 13:4, 14, 15, 16, 17; 14:9, 11; 19:20) and so will receive the appropriate reward (cf. 20:4).[19]

---

16. Wall, *Revelation*, p. 193.
17. Moffatt, "Revelation," 5:443; Walvoord, *Revelation*, p. 227; George E. Ladd, *A Commentary on the Revelation of John* (Grand Rapids: Eerdmans, 1972), p. 204.
18. David E. Aune, ("A Latinism in Revelation," *JBL* 110, no. 4 [Winter 1991]: 691-92) construes the expression to be a Latinism meaning "victors over," but the rarity of Latinisms in Revelation renders this highly improbable.
19. Alford, *Greek Testament*, 4:694; William Lee, "The Revelation of St. John," in *The Holy Bible*, ed. F. C. Cook (London: John Murray, 1981), 4:712;

On the basis of the analogy with the children of Israel who stood *beside* the sea when they sang the song of Moses, some want to locate the overcomers beside the sea of glass (Alford, Lee), but this is not what the text says. They are standing on the solid pavement that comprises the final approach to the throne (4:6) (Swete, Beckwith). The case of the Israelites cannot be determinative in this context. The conquerors have harps that are for the purpose of worshiping God (τοῦ θεοῦ [*tou theou*, "of God"] being an objective genitive).[20] Earlier harps have been in the hands of the living beings and elders (5:8) and of the heavenly singers (14:2). These are instruments that speak of dedication to the service of God (cf. 1 Chron. 16:42). The harp and the trumpet are the only musical instruments mentioned in Revelation.[21]

15:3 The overcomers sing in celebration of the momentous occasion that has arrived: καὶ ᾄδουσιν τὴν ᾠδὴν Μωϋσέως τοῦ δούλου τοῦ θεοῦ καὶ τὴν ᾠδὴν τοῦ ἀρνίου λέγοντες (*kai ādousin tēn ōdēn Mōyseōs tou doulou tou theou kai tēn ōdēn tou arniou legontes*, "and they sang the song of Moses the slave of God and the song of the Lamb, saying"). "The song of Moses" looks back to either Exodus 15 or Deuteronomy 32. In the former case, Moses praised God for delivering the Israelites from the Egyptians who had just drowned in the Red Sea. In the latter case, the song is one Moses personally wrote and spoke to Israel at the close of his career. The Deuteronomy song is not entirely unrelated to the events of the seven last plagues, in that the words "just and true" in 15:3 are part of the central theme of the song (cf. Deut. 32:3-4).[22] It also predicts the ultimate subjugation of all nations to God (Deut. 31:1-8; 32:44–33:29), which is the hope of this song too.[23] Specific points of similarity to the Deuteronomy song include Rev. 15:4*a* with Deut. 32:3; 15:3*b* with 32:4; 15:4*b* with 32:4*b*; the fire of God's anger with 32:22; and plagues of hunger, burning heat, pestilence, wild beasts, vermin, the sword with 32:23-27 (Ford). Also, Deut. 32:42 bears a striking similarity to what will happen at Armageddon according to 14:20 and 19:18-21 (Smith).

The similarities to Deuteronomy 32 are real, but a marked difference separates this OT passage from the present song. That song treated Israel's unfaithfulness and God's punishment of her because of this, before He eventually brings her back and gives her victory over her enemies. This "last plague" context has nothing to say about the

---

Beckwith, *Apocalypse*, p. 674; Moffatt, "Revelation," 5:443; Robertson, *Word Pictures*, 6:417-18.
20. Robertson, *Word Pictures*, 6:418.
21. Smith, *Revelation*, p. 195; Walvoord, *Revelation*, p. 227; Hughes, *Revelation*, p. 170.
22. Wall, *Revelation*, p. 193.
23. Ibid., pp. 193-94.

overcomers' being disobedient. It rather dwells on their faithfulness, and the persistent sovereign power of God in eventually overcoming their unfaithfulness which is unmentioned explicitly in the song.

The Exodus 15 background has a better footing because that was a song of victory just as this is a song of victory over the beast, his image, and his number (Johnson). Another tie-in is in the Passover lamb that commemorated the Egyptian deliverance. Now the greater Lamb has come through with the ultimate deliverance of His people. John's dependence on the Exodus typology elsewhere in Revelation leads in the direction of the Exodus song too. Lines 1 and 2 of the overcomers' song echo the theme of Exodus 15 (Beasley-Murray), and Rev. 15:4 is quite similar to Ex. 15:11 (Mounce). The consciousness of triumph by the singers in both cases, the use of the term "plague" in both songs as well as the similarity of the plagues there and here, and the apocalyptic-type judgments on both Egypt and the beast add to the reasons for seeing a relationship between the two songs (Scott). It is true that the verbal recollections of Exodus 15 are not as specific, but the thematic resemblances are definitely there. The reason why the overcomers do not sing of their own personal deliverance as Moses and the Israelites did is that the martyrs are so absorbed with the wonders around them and the larger picture of what God is doing, that their personal sufferings and victory are infinitesimally small in comparison (Swete).

It is not clear whether the song of Moses and the song of the Lamb constitute one song or two. The one-song option notes the similarity of vv. 3-4 to Moses' song and looks upon it as a renewal of that earlier song (Alford, Lee). But if this meaning had been the intention, the text would have said "the song of Moses and of the Lamb" (Swete). The notes of the two songs are different, but they are in harmony with each other. An underlying motive for identifying the two songs as one apparently has been theological rather than exegetical, i.e., a desire to fuel the case for identifying Israel with the church (cf. Alford, Ladd).

There is no clearer way of designating two songs than the twofold occurrence of τὴν ᾠδήν (*tēn ōdēn*, "the song") (Bullinger). One recounts the faithfulness of God to Israel in recognition of the large number of Israelites that are among the overcomers, and the song of the Lamb celebrates the ultimate victory over sin and the forces of the dragon that is based on the sacrifice of the Lamb of God (Smith, Walvoord). The view that these are two songs makes a distinction between the two, but does not separate them. Both rejoice in the same theme, that of deliverance. The earlier one was a real historical deliverance that pointed forward to the latter song, which celebrates another deliverance that will be not only real and historical, but also ultimate. John only cites the song of the Lamb in 15:3-4, however, leaving it to the reader's memory to recall the song of Moses from Exodus 15.

235

One way of understanding the genitives Μωϋσέως (*Mōyseōs*, "of Moses") and τοῦ ἀρνίου (*tou arniou*, "of the Lamb") is to take them both as objective genitives: "the song about Moses' accomplishments with God's help and the song about the Lamb's accomplishment with God's help" (Moffatt, Lenski, Johnson). This hypothesis cannot explain why Moses and the Lamb are not mentioned in the songs (Beckwith), however, neither does it agree with the clear fact that Moses was the composer and singer of his song. Another way of interpreting is to consider the former genitive as subjective and the latter as objective: "the song Moses sang and the song about the Lamb."[24] Yet the song does not mention the Lamb, so this proposal falters (Beckwith). The best analysis takes both genitives as subjective: "the song by Moses and the song for which the Lamb is responsible." It is the song of Moses because its thought and language came from Moses. It is the song of the Lamb because He composed it, not in words but in actions that are the essential focus of this whole revelation of last things (Beckwith). The actions of the Lamb have dominated throughout the process of deliverance that reaches its climax at this point (cf. 5:5), so in that sense He is responsible for the overcomers' ability to sing as they do.

The first part of the song of the Lamb extols the works and ways of God: Μεγάλα καὶ θαυμαστὰ τὰ ἔργα σου, κύριε ὁ θεὸς ὁ παντοκράτωρ· δίκαιαι καὶ ἀληθιναὶ αἱ ὁδοί σου, ὁ βασιλεὺς τῶν ἐθνῶν* (*Megala kai thaumasta ta erga sou, kyrie ho theos ho pantokratōr; dikaiai kai alēthinai hai hodoi sou, ho basileus tōn ethnōn,* "Great and marvelous are Your works, Lord God Almighty; righteous and true are Your ways, King of the nations"). The works of God create impressions of greatness and amazement as did the sign just seen in v. 1. Μεγάλα (*Megala,* "Great") comes from Ps. 111:2 and θαυμαστά (*thaumasta,* "marvelous") from Ps. 139:14.[25] Just as His works were great and wonderful in judging the Egyptians at the Red Sea, they also are and will be great and will cause astonishment in punishing the world through the seven last plagues (Lenski, Walvoord).

"The Lord God Almighty" (κύριε ὁ θεὸς ὁ παντοκράτωρ [*kyrie ho theos ho pantokratōr*]) harks back to the title for God in a song of the four living beings (4:8) and one by the twenty-four elders (11:17). A song from the altar will yet use the same title (16:7). Παντοκράτωρ (*Pantokratōr,* "Almighty") speaks of His omnipotence (1:8; cf. Amos 4:13) and is especially appropriate in this context speaking of God's great works of judgment leading to ultimate victory (Beckwith, Mounce).

---

24. Hughes, *Revelation*, p. 170.
25. Robertson, *Word Pictures*, 6:418.

Δίκαιαι καὶ ἀληθιναί (*Dikaiai kai alēthinai,* "Righteous and true") comes from Deut. 32:4.[26] The combination of the two qualities comes again at 16:7 and 19:2 in reference to the judgments of God. The tone of the present context indicates that ὁδοί (*hodoi,* "ways") refers to the ways of God's judgment. His ways are absolutely just and completely in accord with truth (Mounce). Δίκαιος (*Dikaios,* "Righteous") applies to the rectitude of God as judge and His judgment again in 16:5 (cf. John 5:30) (Lee). God is true in keeping His promises of judgment against an unrepentant world (Walvoord).

The title ὁ βασιλεὺς τῶν ἐθνῶν (*ho basileus tōn ethnōn,* "King of the nations") reasserts God's rulership over the nations (cf. Pss. 22:28; 47:2, 7-8; 82:8). It especially highlights His role in this book (cf. 1:5; 19:16).

15:4 The song continues by noticing the inevitability of fearing God and giving Him glory: τίς οὐ μὴ φοβηθῇ*, κύριε, καὶ δοξάσει τὸ ὄνομά σοῦ; ὅτι μόνος ὅσιος, ὅτι πάντα τὰ ἔθνη ἥξουσιν καὶ προσκυνήσουσιν ἐνώπιόν σου, ὅτι τὰ δικαιώματά σου ἐφανερώθησαν (*tis ou mē phobēthē, kyrie, kai doxasei to onoma sou; hoti monos hosios, hoti panta ta ethnē hēxousin kai proskynēsousin enōpion sou, hoti ta dikaiōmata sou ephanerōthēsan,* "who will not fear [You], Lord, and glorify Your name? Because [You] only [are] holy, because all the nations will come and worship before You, because Your righteous acts have been manifest"). A two-part rhetorical question implies the answer "no one." Eventually, after the last plagues are over, everyone will willingly reverence and glorify the name of God. The question resembles the one in 13:4 that brings out the incomparability of the beast, the rival object of worship that the majority in their delusion will choose prior to the Lord's ultimate conquest.

After the purging of the earth through the plagues, the survivors will respond positively to God. Universal fear of God will replace a blatant unwillingness to repent and defiant blasphemy (cf. 16:9, 11, 21) and a repudiation of His "everlasting gospel" (14:7) as responses to the "King of the nations" (Beckwith, Moffatt). In the Messianic age all nations will worship the God of Israel and glorify Him as the OT anticipates (Ps. 86:8-10; Jer. 10:7) (Beasley-Murray, Mounce). To construe this language to mean that the majority of all men in the present age will come to salvation[27] is to miss the figure of speech and the future expectation that extends the fulfillment into the future kingdom (cf. Phil. 2:9-11).

The object of fear and glorification is "the name" (τὸ ὄνομά [*to*

---

26. Ibid.; Mounce, *Revelation,* p. 287.
27. Chilton, *Days of Vengeance,* pp. 387-88.

onoma]) of God. This is not a particular title or name that He bears, but the total revelation of who He is. To glorify His name is to praise Him for all that He is, has accomplished, and will accomplish (Mounce).

Two reasons expressed in the first and second ὅτι (hoti, "because") clauses support the anticipated universal fear and attribution of glory to God's name. The first grounds it in His exclusive holiness, a sort of an inner foundation for His ultimate recognition.[28] The adjective ὅσιος (hosios, "holy") is not the usual word for holiness in the NT, being applied to God elsewhere only in 16:5 (Alford, Lenski). Its basic meaning of "sacred" means that God's sacred character is one reason for universal worship of Him. It is not so much God's holiness in the sense of His sinlessness as it is His unapproachable majesty that this word brings out (Beckwith). The word applies to Christ in Acts 2:27; 13:35; Heb. 7:26 (Lee). Μόνος (Monos, "Only") makes the uniqueness of His holiness explicit (Moffatt).

The second reason for universal recognition of God comes in the next ὅτι (hoti, "because") clause which is a positive expression of what the rhetorical question beginning v. 4 implies (Lee, Beckwith). It specifies the essence of the OT prophecies regarding the coming of the nations to God.[29] This is a familiar theme in the Psalms and prophets (Pss. 2:8-9; 24:1-10; 66:1-4; 72:8-11; 86:9; Isa. 2:2-4; 9:6-7; 66:18-23; Dan. 7:14; Zeph. 2:11; Zech. 14:9; Mal. 1:11) (Walvoord, Mounce). Recognition that this will happen only when Christ returns is a confirmation of the futurist interpretation of Revelation (Lee). Then will come more than an awed submission to a superior power. It will be voluntary worship (Caird).

The cheerful certainty that "all the nations will come and worship before You" (πάντα τὰ ἔθνη ἥξουσιν καὶ προσκυνήσουσιν ἐνώπιόν σου [panta ta ethnē hēxousin kai proskynēsousin enōpion sou]) does not result from God's judgment on Israel in the destruction of Jerusalem[30] nor from a worldwide martyrdom (contra Caird), but from the personal return of Christ (chaps. 19-22). An initial increase in universal worship of God will come during the millennial kingdom, but that will be marred by the revolt of the nations at the Millennium's end (20:8). The full realization of this ideal will characterize the eternal state that follows the Millennium (Ladd).

A third hoti clause in v. 4 gives the reason why the nations will

---

28. Friedrich Düsterdieck, Critical and Exegetical Handbook to the Revelation of John, in Meyer's Commentary, trans. and ed. Henry E. Jacobs (New York: Funk & Wagnalls, 1887), pp. 410-11.
29. Ibid., pp. 410-11.

come and worship before God: the manifestation of His judgments (Alford, Lee). The term δικαιώματα (*dikaiōmata*, "righteous acts") depicts God's deeds of righteousness toward the nations. These include His righteous verdicts (Alford, Lenski, Mounce). These are His judicial sentences of condemnation against the world (Ex. 6:6; 7:4; 12:12; Dan. 9:14-15) (Moffatt), not His victorious activity in bring deliverance for His people (contra Caird, Ford, Mounce, Sweet). That deliverance is a secondary effect, but the thing that brings Him universal worship from the nations is His activity in purging the earth. The aorist ἐφανερ-ώθησαν (*ephanerōthēsan*, "have been manifest") is prophetic of the demonstration of God's acts of judgment in the last plagues about to begin. It is instructive that the overcomers do not sing about their own victory over the beast, but about the sovereignty, justice, and glory of God (Ladd).

Additional Notes

15:2 The accusative τοὺς νικῶντας is a second direct object of the εἶδον that begins v. 2.[31] The articular present participle is timeless and merely characterizes the conquerors. It does not state the fact of their conquest, but is roughly equivalent to "the conquerors."[32]

15:3 The OT calls Moses the servant or slave of the Lord often (Ex. 14:31; Num. 12:7; Josh. 14:7; 22:5; 1 Chron. 6:49; Ps. 105:26; Dan. 9:11; Mal. 4:4) (Alford, Lee). In most cases, the LXX renders the Hebrew by θεράπων or παῖς rather than by δοῦλος, however (cf. Heb. 3:5) (Alford, Lee).

The reading ἐθνῶν has slightly weaker external support (i.e., first reviser of Sinaiticus, Alexandrinus, 2053, and others) than the variant αἰώνων (i.e., p[47], original hand and third reviser of Sinaiticus, Ephraemi, and others). Since copyists could have introduced the latter variant from 1 Tim. 1:17 and since this context supports a reference to ἐθνῶν (v. 4), ἐθνῶν is the preferred reading. The *Textus Receptus* reading of ἁγίων has very weak support from the Greek witnesses.[33]

15:4 Different MSS have σε either in place of μή or in addition to it (Lee, Ford). Alexandrinus, Ephraemi, 2053, and others omit the pronoun, but some copyists, feeling the need of a direct object for φοβηθῇ, added it either before οὐ (p[47], Sinaiticus, and others) or after it (051,

---

30. Contra Chilton, *Days of Vengeance*, p. 388.
31. Robertson, *Word Pictures*, 6:417.
32. Düsterdieck, *Revelation*, p. 410; Alford, *Greek Testament*, 4:694; Swete, *Apocalypse*, p. 194; Beckwith, *Apocalypse*, p. 674; Smith, *Revelation*, p. 224.
33. Bruce M. Metzger, *A Textual Commentary on the Greek New Testament* (New York: United Bible Societies, 1971), pp. 755-56.

Textus Receptus, and others). Sinaiticus reads οὖ instead of οὐ μή. The reading that omits the pronoun is most probably original.[34]

The construction of v. 4*a* is a mixed one, a combination of τίς οὐ μή φοβηθῇ and τίς οὐ δοξάσει. Φοβηθῇ is an aorist subjunctive and δο-ξάσει is a future indicative. Both have a future meaning, but the subjunctive carries a shade of meaning, "come to fear," that the future indicative does not convey.[35]

The verb φανερόω occurs here and in 3:18 in the Apocalypse. It is a frequent word in John's other writings, occurring nine times in his gospel and nine times in his first epistle (e.g., John 1:31; 3:21; 1 John 2:19) (Lee).

3. THE PREPARATION FOR THE SEVEN LAST PLAGUES (15:5-8)

Translation

5And after these things I looked, and the temple of the tabernacle of testimony was opened in heaven, 6and the seven angels having the seven plagues went out of the temple, clothed in clean bright linen and girded about the breasts with golden girdles. 7And one of the four living beings gave to the seven angels seven golden bowls filled with the anger of God who lives forever and ever. 8And the temple was filled with smoke from the glory of God and from His power, and no one could enter the temple until the seven plagues of the seven angels were finished.

Exegesis and Exposition

15:5 It is now time for the main actors introduced in v. 1 to receive their tools of misery and that in a very dramatic setting: Καὶ μετὰ ταῦτα εἶδον, καὶ ἠνοίγη ὁ ναὸς τῆς σκηνῆς τοῦ μαρτυρίου ἐν τῷ οὐρανῷ (*Kai meta tauta eidon, kai ēnoigē ho naos tēs skēnēs tou martyriou en tō ouranō*, "And after these things I looked, and the temple of the tabernacle of testimony was opened in heaven"). In this book μετὰ ταῦτα εἶδον (*meta tauta eidon*, "after these things I looked") is a transition to a new vision and an important new subject, because the bowl plagues are in a category all their own (Scott, Kiddle, Walvoord, Hailey; see Thomas, *Revelation 1-7*, p. 333). The new vision obviously relates to the next to the last scene of the previous one, where John saw the angels who had the seven last plagues (15:1). They are the main actors in this new vision. The subject of 15:5–16:1 is the immediate preparation for the seven last plagues (Beckwith).

---

34. Ibid., p. 756.
35. Alford, *Greek Testament*, 4:694; Lenski, *Revelation*, p. 458; Robertson, *Word Pictures*, 6:418.

The form ἠνοίγη (*ēnoigē*, "was opened") occurred in 11:19 too. There the temple of God was opened to reveal the ark of the covenant. Here "the temple of the tabernacle of testimony" (ὁ ναὸς τῆς σκηνῆς τοῦ μαρτυρίου [*ho naos tēs skēnēs tou martyriou*]) is opened to allow the seven angels to exit from the presence of God. Both passages tell the source of the last plagues, with this one being a further development of the former.[36] Emphasis falls on the presence of God as the source from which come the troubles about to transpire (Swete, Beckwith, Mounce).

Some discussion of this temple has fallen into the habit (earlier seen in 11:1-2) of equating the temple with the church.[37] NT references to the church as God's temple are usually cited as precedent for this interpretation (cf. 1 Cor. 3:16; 2 Cor. 6:16; Eph. 2:21; 1 Pet. 2:5). Such a spiritual understanding of ναὸς (*naos*, "temple") has no grounds in this context, however. With the setting of the vision in heaven in the very presence of God, it makes no sense for this to be the church. Also, the timing of this vision during the last half of Daniel's seventieth week means that the focus of attention is back on God's earthly people, Israel, and not on the church (Walvoord).

Another view wants to make this a literal temple on earth representing the inner holy place in heaven. During the Tribulation it will be a restored place of worship for the reestablishment of the ancient sacrificial system, but after being desecrated, will become a place of worship for the false Christ (cf. Dan. 9:27; 12:11; 2 Thess. 2:4; Rev. 13:14-15) (Walvoord). This explanation provides for an adequate representation of the judicial revelation and the immediate presence of God. "The tabernacle of the testimony" was evidence of His covenant with His people (Moffatt; Kiddle). The pattern John witnessed in heaven was doubtless along the same lines as the earthly tabernacle (cf. Ex. 25:16, 21; Heb. 8:5) (Lee). As required by the Mosaic standards, the *naos* contained "the tabernacle of the testimony" (τῆς σκηνῆς τοῦ μαρτυρίου [*tēs skēnēs tou martyriou*]), including the golden furniture and the tables of stone on which Moses had written God's moral requirements for man (Ex. 25:16, 21; cf. Ex. 38:21; Num. 1:50; 9:15; 17:7; Acts 7:44).[38] "The testimony" refers to what was written on the stones,

---

36. Kiddle, *Revelation*, pp. 310, 312.
37. Albert Barnes, *The Book of Revelation* (New York: Harper, 1851), p. 269; Swete, *Apocalypse*, p. 130; R. H. Charles, *The Revelation of St. John*, ICC (New York: Scribner's Sons, 1920), 2:276-77; Lenski, *Revelation*, p. 328; Homer Hailey, *Revelation, an Introduction and Commentary* (Grand Rapids: Baker, 1979), p. 250; Chilton, *Days of Vengeance*, p. 389.
38. Düsterdieck, *Revelation*, p. 411; Walter Scott, *Exposition of the Revelation of Jesus Christ* (Swengel, Pa.: Bible Truth Depot, n.d.), p. 319; G. R. Beasley-Murray, *The Book of Revelation*, NCB (Grand Rapids: Eerdmans, 1978), p. 237.

which "testified" against sin. Τῆς σκηνῆς (*tēs skēnēs*, "the tabernacle") is a genitive of apposition defining the *naos*, because this compartment housed the sacred record of laws from the One who is about to execute His judgments against all lawbreakers (Lee, Beckwith, Kiddle). Along with the writer of Hebrews, the apostle John here chooses the tabernacle in the wilderness rather than the temple in Jerusalem as the counterpart of the heavenly presence-chamber. The tabernacle that Moses constructed according to a divinely given plan was the archetype of the later temple (Ex. 25:40; Heb. 8:5) (Swete).

John defines the heavenly temple in terms of the tabernacle of the testimony in this context, because that particular room was the location of the tablets of God's law so blatantly disregarded by the earth-dwellers (9:20-21). God is about to enforce these standards on a rebellious earth through the judgments of the seven last plagues. The expression actually makes no reference to a rebuilt temple on earth as suggested above, but refers exclusively to the temple "in heaven." The earthly temple only provides a frame of reference pointing to the one in heaven.

15:6 From the temple come the seven angels of v. 1: καὶ ἐξῆλθον οἱ ἑπτὰ ἄγγελοι [οἱ]* ἔχοντες τὰς ἑπτὰ πληγὰς ἐκ τοῦ ναοῦ, ἐνδεδυμένοι λίνον* καθαρὸν λαμπρὸν καὶ περιεζωσμένοι περὶ τὰ στήθη ζώνας χρυσᾶς (*kai exēlthon hoi hepta angeloi [hoi] echontes tas hepta plēgas ek tou naou, endedymenoi linon katharon lampron kai periezōsmenoi peri ta stēthē zōnas chrysas*, "and the seven angels having the seven plagues went out of the temple, clothed in clean bright linen and girded about the breasts with golden girdles"). The οἱ (*hoi*) with ἄγγελοι (*angeloi*, "the angels") and the τὰς (*tas*) with πληγὰς (*plēgas*, "the plagues") point back to the first mention of these two anarthrous nouns in 15:1 (Lee, Beckwith).

The perfect participles ἐνδεδυμένοι (*endedymenoi*, "clothed") and περιεζωσμένοι (*periezōsmenoi*, "girded") are the same as the two perfect participles describing the Son of Man in John's vision of 1:13. The "linen" (λίνον [*linon*]) worn by the angels represents righteousness in action as it does with the wife of the Lamb, though βύσσινον (*byssinon*) is the word in 19:8 for the latter's garments. *Linon* is a product from which linen is made (i.e., flax), and *byssinon* is the material itself (i.e., linen).[39] Both καθαρόν (*katharon*, "clean") and λαμπρόν (*lampron*, "bright") appear again to describe the garments of the bride of Christ (19:8) who composes His army that is so clothed when they return with Him (19:14). The purity of their clothing befits the purpose of

---

39. Lee, "Revelation," 4:716; M. Robert Mulholland, *Revelation, Holy Living in an Unholy World* (Grand Rapids: Zondervan, 1990), p. 262.

their mission which is purification. "Bright" or "glistening" is a way to describe angelic clothing (cf. Acts 10:30) (Alford, Swete). The golden girdles with which the angels were girded are positioned the same as Christ's in 1:18 and apparently carry the same symbolism. They mark those who are on a punitive mission (Beckwith, Kiddle; see Thomas, p. 100).

15:7 Having left the temple, the angels are positioned to receive the seven bowls of God's anger: καὶ ἕν* ἐκ τῶν τεσσάρων ζῴων ἔδωκεν τοῖς ἑπτὰ ἀγγέλοις ἑπτὰ φιάλας χρυσᾶς γεμούσας τοῦ θυμοῦ τοῦ θεοῦ τοῦ ζῶντος εἰς τοὺς αἰῶνας τῶν αἰώνων (*kai hen ek tōn tessarōn zōōn edōken tois hepta angelois hepta phialas chrysas gemousas tou thymou tou theou tou zōntos eis tous aiōnas tōn aiōnōn*, "and one of the four living beings gave to the seven angels seven golden bowls filled with the anger of God who lives forever and ever"). The part of one of the living beings in imparting the last plagues recalls the roles of the four in the imposition of the first four seals (6:1-8) (Kiddle). They also held an unstated number of golden bowls in 5:8, which connected them with the prayers of the saints for vindication (cf. 8:3-5).[40] Those are not necessarily the same bowls that he gives to the angels here, however.

The bowls in 5:8 were full of incense, but these are full of the wrath of God. They portend dreadful events ahead for the earth.[41] The term φιάλας (*phialas*) designates shallow bowls or saucers. Unlike the ones in 8:4, they do not exhale the smoke of gratefulness to God, but are full of poisonous, hot, bitter wine, from which emanates the divine majesty whose intense holiness breaks forth in judgment against human sin (Moffatt). Perhaps they resemble the cups or goblets in Isa. 55:17, 22, which are full of the wrath of God (Beasley-Murray). Golden bowls were associated with the earthly temple (1 Kings 7:50; 2 Kings 12:13; 25:15) (Johnson). The heavenly temple is the source of these bowls that the living being gives to the seven angels.

The bowls are full to the brim (γεμούσας [*gemousas*]) with the hot anger of God. The fullness speaks of the devastating character as well as the finality of the coming divine judgment (cf. 14:8, 10). The phrase τοῦ ζῶντος εἰς τοὺς αἰῶνας τῶν αἰώνων (*tou zōntos eis tous aiōnas tōn aiōnōn*, "who lives forever and ever") differentiates God from the image of the beast and all other lifeless idols. It adds solemnity to the scene as in 10:6 (cf. Deut. 32:40) (Alford, Lee, Lenski) and gives a solemn cast to the wrath about to be inflicted forever and ever on those who perish (Walvoord). "It is a fearful thing to fall into the hands of the living God" (Heb. 10:31).

---

40. Wall, *Revelation*, p. 195.
41. Robertson, *Word Pictures*, 6:419.

15:8 With the bowls in the hands of the angels, the heavenly temple undergoes an awe-inspiring transformation into an environment accessible only to God: καὶ ἐγεμίσθη ὁ ναὸς καπνοῦ ἐκ τῆς δόξης τοῦ θεοῦ καὶ ἐκ τῆς δυνάμεως αὐτοῦ, καὶ οὐδεὶς ἐδύνατο εἰσελθεῖν εἰς τὸν ναὸν ἄχρι τελεσθῶσιν αἱ ἑπτὰ πληγαὶ τῶν ἑπτὰ ἀγγέλων (*kai egemisthē ho naos kapnou ek tēs doxēs tou theou kai ek tēs dynameōs autou, kai oudeis edynato eiselthein eis ton naon achri telesthōsin hai hepta plēgai tōn hepta angelōn*, "and the temple was filled with smoke from the glory of God and from His power, and no one could enter the temple until the seven plagues of the seven angels were finished"). "Smoke" (Καπνοῦ [*Kapnou*]) is a symbol of God's presence to emphasize His role in originating the judgments about to come (cf. Ex. 19:18; 40:34 ff.; 1 Kings 8:10-11; 2 Chron. 5:11-14; 7:1-3; Ezek. 11:23; 44:4). It recalls the Shekinah that first filled the tabernacle and later the temple. In this case it arises "from the glory of God and from His power" (ἐκ τῆς δόξης τοῦ θεοῦ καὶ ἐκ τῆς δυνάμεως αὐτοῦ [*ek tēs doxēs tou theou kai ek tēs dynameōs autou*]) that are on display in the seven bowls of anger about to come (cf. Ps. 18:8-9; Isa. 65:5) (Alford, Swete, Bullinger, Scott, Mounce, Johnson).

The smoke from God's glory and power is so intense that "no one could enter the temple" (οὐδεὶς ἐδύνατο εἰσελθεῖν εἰς τὸν ναὸν [*oudeis edynato eiselthein eis ton naon*]). Smoldering fires of indignation are here at the point of erupting into punishment issuing from an arsenal of divine wrath (Moffatt). God is unapproachable when He is immediately present and working in this way (Alford, Lee).

God's unapproachableness continues only for the duration of the plagues, however. The clause ἄχρι τελεσθῶσιν αἱ ἑπτὰ πληγαὶ τῶν ἑπτὰ ἀγγέλων (*achri telesthōsin hai hepta plēgai tōn hepta angelōn*, "until the seven plagues of the seven angels were finished") sets the period of an unapproachable heavenly temple as simultaneous with the outpouring of the seven bowls. As Excursus 5 later shows, this carries through to the replacing of the old order with the New Jerusalem (21:1-2).[42] Then a new heaven and new earth in which the glory of God is the light (21:23) will replace the old ones which have passed away (20:11).

Additional Notes

15:6 A number of MSS, including p[47], Sinaiticus, and 2053, omit the article οἱ before ἔχοντες. Alexandrinus, Ephraemi, and others include it. The harder reading is the omission because articles which did not appear in v. 1 occur with ἀγγέλους and πληγὰς. A copyist probably felt the need to add one here. The difference in meaning is slight. The

---

42. Wall, *Revelation*, p. 195.

article might suggest that they already had the plagues, which they did not yet. The anarthrous participle suggests that possession of the seven last plagues was their office (Alford).

Instead of λίνον, some respected witnesses, including Alexandrinus, Ephraemi, and 2053, attest to the reading λίθον. Except for support from a superficial parallel in Ezek. 28:13, it is hard make sense out of what a "clean" (καθαρὸν) stone for clothing would be other than a garment studded with precious stones.[43] What is probably the correct reading, λίνον, has weak external support, except for the secondary evidence supplied by the λινοῦν found in p[47] and a few others and the λίνους found in Sinaiticus. "Made of linen" (λινοῦν) is an impossible reading because it leaves the expression with no noun, and λίνους is grammatically incorrect, being a masculine plural ending on a neuter noun.[44]

Στήθη is different from the word used in 1:13 to speak of Christ's breast. There it was μαστός. Στῆθος occurs four other times in the NT (Luke 18:13; 23:48; John 13:27; 21:20).

15:7 Two principal MSS, p[47] and Sinaiticus, omit ἕν (Ford), but stronger textual support is for the adjective's inclusion. The omission does not affect the sense appreciably, since the partitive ἐκ itself implies the sense of ἕν.

15:8 The noun καπνοῦ is an ablative, expressing the means by which the temple was filled with smoke.

4. THE FIRST BOWL: INCURABLE SORES ON THE BEAST WORSHIPERS (16:1-2)

Translation

1And I heard a loud voice from the temple saying to the seven angels, "Depart and pour out the seven bowls of the anger of God into the earth." 2And the first went away and poured out his bowl into the earth; and a bad and malignant sore came upon men who had the mark of the beast and who worshiped his image.

Exegesis and Exposition

16:1 Καὶ ἤκουσα (*Kai ēkousa*, "And I heard") introduces a chapter in which the seven angels with the seven bowls receive and implement their instructions to dispense the contents of their bowls: Καὶ ἤκουσα μεγάλης φωνῆς ἐκ τοῦ ναοῦ* λεγούσης τοῖς ἑπτὰ ἀγγέλοις, Ὑπάγετε καὶ

---

43. Swete, *Apocalypse*, p. 198; contra Düsterdieck, *Revelation*, p. 411 and Lee, "Revelation," 4:714.
44. Lenski, *Revelation*, p. 460; Metzger, *Textual Commentary*, p. 756; Mounce, *Revelation*, p. 289.

ἐκχέετε τὰς ἑπτὰ φιάλας τοῦ θυμοῦ τοῦ θεοῦ εἰς τὴν γῆν (*Kai ēkousa megalēs phōnēs ek tou naou legousēs tois hepta angelois, Hypagete kai ekcheete tas hepta phialas tou thymou tou theou eis tēn gēn,* "And I heard a loud voice from the temple saying to the seven angels, 'Depart and pour out the seven bowls of the anger of God into the earth'"). The bowls occur in rapid succession, pausing only briefly between the third and fourth for a dialogue between the angel of the waters and the altar (Walvoord, Johnson).

The "loud voice" (μεγάλης φωνῆς [*megalēs phōnēs*]) is not the voice of an angel, but that of God, as 15:8 shows. God's mention of His own name in the command (i.e., τοῦ θεοῦ [*tou theou*, "God"]) is no obstacle to this identification. No one else has access to the heavenly temple (cf. Matt. 3:17; 17:5; John 12:28; 2 Pet. 1:17-18) (Alford, Swete). Isaiah 66:6 also tells of a voice from the temple initiating recompense to the Lord's enemies. This is the same "loud voice" that in 16:17 accompanies the pouring out of the seventh bowl. Μέγας (*Megas,* "Loud" or "Great") is unusually frequent in this chapter, being applied to great heat (v. 9), the great river Euphrates (v. 12), that great day of God Almighty (v. 14), a great earthquake ("so mighty an earthquake so great," v. 18), the great city (v. 19), great Babylon (v. 19), great hail (v. 21), and the "exceedingly great" plague (v. 21). This adjective occurs eleven times in this chapter, more than in any other chapter of the NT (Smith). The chapter that ranks second is Revelation 18 where it appears nine times, an interesting characteristic since chapter 18 is an elaboration on the seventh bowl of 16:17-21. The accent is on greatness because this series leads up to the final assault on the infernal trio composed of the dragon, the beast, and the false prophet. This is "the great and terrible day of the Lord" (Bullinger).

God commands all seven angels at once to carry out their mission. Each of the seven complies in sequence without further direction (Swete, Hailey). The former command ὑπάγετε (*hypagete,* "depart") is a present imperative, in effect telling the angels, "Go your way" (cf. Mark 6:38; 14:13; 16:7; James 2:16). The latter command ἐκχέετε (*ekcheete,* "pour out") is an aorist imperative telling them to tip their bowls over and empty their contents. The aorist imperative expresses urgency to which the angels respond by emptying their bowls in rapid succession and cumulatively. The plagues pile upon one another until the end (cf. 16:9) (Lenski). Ἐκχέω (*Ekcheō,* "I pour out") occurs repeatedly in this chapter, but not elsewhere in Revelation. It is a bit of irony that the same verb tells of the pouring out of God's Spirit on His servants on the Day of Pentecost and following and in the last days in conjunction with Christ's second advent (Joel 2:28-29, LXX; Acts 2:17, 18, 33; Titus 3:5-6).

The contents of the seven bowls bear some resemblances to the earlier series of seals and trumpets, but they are not just a recapitulation by way of enlargement.[45] Some have opted for a recapitulatory model, based on superficial similarities of the bowls to the others.[46] Close scrutiny and comparison reflect numerous differences, particularly in the degree of finality of the bowl series. For example, the fourth bowl is entirely new, and no personal suffering comes with the first four trumpets, but with the bowls, people are in agony from the very beginning.[47] Also, this can hardly be recapitulation because the effect is total rather than partial as with the other series.[48] The bowls are universal and far more intense, showing beyond reasonable doubt that this whole series deals with the time of the end (Alford, Walvoord). The very fact that the plagues are called τὰς ἐσχάτας (*tas eschatas*, "the last") shows that they do not go back in time to retrace the same period as the seals and trumpets (Alford).

16:2 In response to the divine command, the first angel departs to pour out his bowl: Καὶ ἀπῆλθεν ὁ πρῶτος καὶ ἐξέχεεν τὴν φιάλην αὐτοῦ εἰς τὴν γῆν· καὶ ἐγένετο ἕλκος κακὸν καὶ πονηρὸν ἐπὶ τοὺς ἀνθρώπους τοὺς ἔχοντας τὸ χάραγμα τοῦ θηρίου καὶ τοὺς προσκυνοῦντας τῇ εἰκόνι αὐτοῦ (*Kai apēlthen ho prōtos kai execheen tēn phialēn autou eis tēn gēn; kai egeneto helkos kakon kai poneron epi tous anthrōpous tous echontas to charagma tou thēriou kai tous proskynountas tē eikoni autou,* "And the first went away and poured out his bowl into the earth; and a pernicious and malignant sore came upon men who had the mark of the beast and who worshiped his image"). The formula ἀπῆλθεν . . . καὶ ἐξέχεεν (*apēlthen . . . kai execheen,* "went away . . . and poured out") appears only with the first angel, but it is doubtlessly implied with the other six (vv. 3, 4, 8, 10, 12, 17). After each angel discharges his duty, he vanishes rather than returning to his place in the procession (Swete, Morris).[49] One or two of the angels reappear at 17:1 and 22:9, but it is impossible to tell which one or ones carry out the revelatory tasks there. The brevity of style whereby ὁ πρῶτος (*ho prōtos,* "the

---

45. See Excursus 3 at the end of this volume.
46. Lee, "Revelation," 4:717; Moffatt, "Revelation," 5:446; Wilcock, *Revelation,* p. 146; J. Stuart Russell, *The Parousia: A Critical Inquiry into the New Testament Doctrine of Our Lord's Second Coming* (Grand Rapids: Baker, 1983), p. 476.
47. Düsterdieck, *Revelation,* p. 415; Swete, *Apocalypse,* p. 200; Mounce, *Revelation,* pp. 291-92; J. P. M. Sweet, *Revelation* (Philadelphia: Westminster, Pelican, 1979), pp. 242-43.
48. Hughes, *Revelation,* p. 173.
49. Swete, *Apocalypse,* p. 200; Leon Morris, *The Revelation of St. John,* TNTC (Grand Rapids: Eerdmans, 1969), p. 193.

first") stands for "the first angel" contrasts with the trumpet series which used ἄγγελος (angelos, "angel") with each part of the series except the first (8:8, 10, 12; 9:1, 13; 11:15).

The destination of the first bowl is εἰς τὴν γῆν (eis tēn gēn, "into the earth"). Several divide the bowls into two groups of the first three which use εἰς (eis, "into") to express destination and the last four which express ἐπί (epi, "upon") for the same (Lee, Beckwith). A better arrangement is into groups of the first four and the last three, a system that has characterized the two earlier series (Moffatt, Scott). The first four affect individuals directly either through personal affliction or through objects of nature, and the last three are on more of an international scale, leading the way to a final major confrontation.

The γῆν (gēn, "earth") in v. 2 is more particular than the gēn of v. 1 which is general in inclusion of the objects of all the bowls—i.e., the sea (v. 3), the rivers (v. 4), etc. (Alford). Whatever poured upon, the plague eventually strikes against "those who dwell on the earth" (Beckwith). "The earth" is the first of the four divisions of nature hit by the first four plagues. The other three are the sea, the rivers, and the sky. The four become media used to torture mankind (Moffatt, Johnson).

The "sore" (ἕλκος [helkos]) inflicted by the first bowl is "an ulcer, a wound, especially a suppurated wound" (cf. Ex. 9:9-11; Lev. 13:18-27; Job 2:7, all in the LXX).[50] The language resembles that of Deut. 28:35 (Beasley-Murray). This is an inflamed and running sore that refuses to be healed (Lenski). This recalls the sixth Egyptian plague where the Egyptian magicians were the victims (Ex. 9:9-11). Here, the followers of the beast receive the harm. Job responded positively and repented when similarly afflicted (Job 42:1-6), but not these worshipers of the false Christ (Rev. 16:9, 11, 21).

A proposal to understand the sores in a less literal fashion in referring to them as the incapacitating problems resulting from persistent sin[51] or mental suffering coming from moral failures (Scott) is out of keeping with the common understanding of the last three bowls which are clearly literal in depicting political judgments. If these were only localized and repeatable maladies, the unparalleled excitement in heaven to prepare for them would be inexplicable.[52] The sixth Egyptian plague imposed physical maladies on the Egyptians, so why should these sores be any different? (Bullinger, Seiss). Happenings on such a catastrophic scale stretch the capacity of human comprehen-

---

50. Joseph Henry Thayer, *A Greek-English Lexicon of the New Testament* (New York: American Book, 1889), p. 204; G. Abbott-Smith, *A Manual Greek Lexicon of the New Testament* (Edinburgh: T. & T. Clark, 1950), p. 146.
51. Hughes, *Revelation*, p. 173.
52. J. A. Seiss, *The Apocalypse* (New York: Charles C. Cook, 1909), 3:69.

sion. No precedent in human history can measure up to the future supernatural intervention of God, but man's inability to grasp the magnitude of it is no reason to deny its literal meaning. He must simply believe what God says will happen (Bullinger).

The sores are κακὸν καὶ πονηρὸν (*kakon kai ponēron*, "pernicious and malignant"). The former adjective is something evil in itself and the latter denotes pain to the sufferers (Alford). These are bad, unpleasant, agonizing ulcers that refuse to go away after they have broken out on τοὺς ἀνθρώπους τοὺς ἔχοντας τὸ χάραγμα τοῦ θηρίου καὶ τοὺς προσκυνοῦντας τῇ εἰκόνι αὐτοῦ (*tous anthrōpous tous echontas to charagma tou thēriou kai tous proskynountas tē eikoni autou*, "men who had the mark of the beast and who worshiped his image"). Since beast worship will be universal except for the followers of the Lamb (13:3-4, 15-17), so will the plague be (Smith, Ladd, Walvoord). Presumably by this time the 144,000 witnesses will have suffered martyrdom, leaving only the faithful who are in a place of refuge (12:13-17) untouched by this awful affliction (Moffatt). This exceptional group recalls the Israelites who remained untouched by the Egyptian plagues (Lenski).

Additional Notes

16:1 The position of μεγάλης before φωνῆς stresses the impressiveness of the voice. Elsewhere in the chapter the adjective follows its noun in customary Johannine fashion. Also, elsewhere in the Apocalypse when used with φωνή, it always follows it (cf. 1:10; 5:2, 12; 6:10; 7:2, 10; 8:13; 10:3; 11:12, 15; 12:10; 14:7, 9, 15, 18; 16:7; 19:1, 17; 21:3) (Charles, Morris, Mounce).

The inclusion of the phrase ἐκ τοῦ ναοῦ has adequate external support, but is omitted from p[47vid], 046, and a large number of minuscules. The omission occurred probably when a copyist viewed the words as inappropriate in the context.[53]

5. THE SECOND BOWL: DEATH TO ALL SEA LIFE (16:3)

Translation

3And the second poured out his bowl into the sea; and it became blood like [that of] a dead person, and every living soul which lives in the sea died.

Exegesis and Exposition

16:3 The pouring of the second bowl into the sea is reminiscent of the first Egyptian plague, except it affects the sea rather than the fresh

---

53. Metzger, *Textual Commentary*, pp. 756-57; Mounce, *Revelation*, p. 293; Ford, *Revelation*, p. 260.

waters (cf. Ex. 7:19-21): Καὶ ὁ δεύτερος ἐξέχεεν τὴν φιάλην αὐτοῦ εἰς τὴν θάλασσαν· καὶ ἐγένετο αἷμα ὡς νεκροῦ, καὶ πᾶσα ψυχὴ ζωῆς* ἀπέθανεν, τὰ* ἐν τῇ θαλάσσῃ (*Kai ho deuteros execheen tēn phialēn autou eis tēn thalassan; kai egeneto haima hōs nekrou, kai pasa psychē zōēs apethanen, ta en tē thalassē*, "And the second poured out his bowl into the sea; and it became blood like [that of] a dead person, and every living soul which lives in the sea died"). To John, "the sea" was the Mediterranean Sea (Beasley-Murray), but the universality of the language extends the reference throughout the world. Water covers most of the earth's surface, so this affliction will be extremely widespread (Walvoord).

The issue of literal versus nonliteral interpretation arises once again. The latter sees a use of the sea as an emblem for the nations (Lee) and the masses of humanity who die in the plague (Scott), but the sea is no more symbolic than the waters of Egypt smitten by Moses or the waters of the Euphrates mentioned later in this chapter (16:12). The precedent of the first Egyptian plague and the analogy of the other plagues in the bowl series make a literal understanding most probable. The literal meaning of θάλασσαν (*thalassan*, "sea") in 14:7 should govern the present passage too.

The bowl's contents turn the sea into αἷμα ὡς νεκροῦ (*haima hōs nekrou*, "blood like [that of] a dead person"). The third trumpet brought bitterness to the water, causing the deaths of many, but here the change is into coagulated blood or a bloodlike substance similar to it (Swete, Moffatt). The substance will be decayed and have a foul odor that makes it loathsome (Alford). It will be no longer fluid, but thickened and congealed (Lee). In the first Egyptian plague, all the fish in the Nile died (Ex. 7:21). Here death will come to πᾶσα ψυχὴ ζωῆς (*pasa psychē zōēs*, "every living soul") in the sea. This will amount to a reversal of Gen. 1:21 when God gave life to all sea creatures (Johnson). This is a complete destruction of all marine life, not a partial one as under the second trumpet.[54]

Additional Notes

16:3 The genitive ζωῆς is one of quality, otherwise known as a descriptive genitive. It refers to every soul "marked by life."[55] Some MSS, including p[47], Sinaiticus, 2053, and others, read ζῶσα rather than ζωῆς, but Alexandrinus, Ephraemi, and others supply ample external support for the genitive ζωῆς, which is also a slightly more difficult variant (Mounce).

---

54. Düsterdieck, *Revelation*, p. 416; Swete, *Apocalypse*, p. 201; Robertson, *Word Pictures*, 6:420-21.
55. Beckwith, *Apocalypse*, p. 680; Robertson, *Word Pictures*, 6:420.

A number of MSS do not have τά, resulting in the meaning that all living souls die in the sea. The omission occurs in p⁴⁷ and Sinaiticus, but Alexandrinus and Ephraemi include the article, which changes the meaning to refer to the deaths only of those living souls which are in the sea. The omission is too difficult to be correct, because it would have impossible repercussions for the remainder of chapter 16 (Mounce). The neuter plural τά in apposition to the feminine singular ψυχή is explainable by noting the implied neuter plural κτίσματα for which the ψυχή stands (cf. 8:9) (Lee).

6. THE THIRD BOWL: TRANSFORMING OF ALL FRESH WATER INTO BLOOD (16:4-7)

Translation

⁴And the third poured out his bowl into the rivers and the fountains of waters; and they became blood. ⁵And I heard the angel of the waters, saying,
    "You are righteous, who is and who was, the holy one,
        because You have judged these things,
        ⁶because they have poured out the blood of saints and prophets,
        and You have given them blood to drink;
    they are worthy."
⁷And I heard the altar saying,
    "Yes, Lord God Almighty,
        Your judgments are true and righteous."

Exegesis and Exposition

16:4 The contamination of the fresh waters follows that of the sea as was the sequence with the second and third trumpets (8:8-10): Καὶ ὁ τρίτος ἐξέχεεν τὴν φιάλην αὐτοῦ εἰς τοὺς ποταμοὺς καὶ τὰς πηγὰς τῶν ὑδάτων· καὶ ἐγένετο* αἷμα (*Kai ho tritos execheen tēn phialēn autou eis tous potamous kai tas pēgas tōn hydatōn; kai egeneto haima*, "And the third poured out his bowl into the rivers and the fountains of waters; and they became blood"). The wording telling the destination of the third bowl's contents is practically identical with that of the falling star's destination under the third trumpet (8:10). The first Egyptian plague affected the Nile River principally, but this third bowl will affect all rivers, and to keep the earth-dwellers from doing the same thing as the Egyptians did to find drinking water (Ex. 7:24; cf. Ps. 78:43-44), it will turn the fountains or springs into blood too. It affects all sources of fresh water.

Τὰς πηγὰς τῶν ὑδάτων (*Tas pēgas tōn hydatōn*, "The fountains of waters") is literal in meaning as is the comparable πηγὰς ὑδάτων (*pēgas hydatōn*, "fountains of waters") in 14:7. So is the αἷμα (*haima*, "blood")

251

into which the water turns. The blood is just as literal as the blood of the saints which parallels the blood God gives the earth-dwellers to drink in the song of the angel of the waters in 16:6 (Alford). The havoc caused throughout the world by this absence of drinking water is unimaginable and is part of the price that the majority must pay for choosing the beast instead of the Lamb as their object of worship.

16:5 In conjunction with this visitation of misery, John heard another song: καὶ ἤκουσα τοῦ ἀγγέλου τῶν ὑδάτων λέγοντος, Δίκαιος εἶ, ὁ ὢν καὶ ὁ* ἦν, ὁ ὅσιος, ὅτι ταῦτα ἔκρινας (*kai ēkousa tou angelou tōn hydatōn legontos, Dikaios ei, ho ōn kai ho ēn, ho hosios, hoti tauta ekrinas*, "and I heard the angel of the waters, saying, 'You are righteous, who is and who was, the holy one, because You have judged these things'"). The singer this time is the angel who controls the sea and freshwater bodies, a different one from the angel who poured out the third bowl. Revelation 7:1 has four angels in charge of the winds, and in 9:11, an angel has authority over the abyss. In 14:18 is the angel with power over fire. The angel of the waters is of the same order as these others.[56] Angelic ministry connects with the elemental forces of nature elsewhere in Scripture (cf. Ps. 104:4; Heb. 1:7).[57] The same outlook characterized Jewish thought in general. In *1 Enoch* 66:1-3, Enoch saw angels of punishment with powers over the waters to loose them and bring destruction on people who dwell upon the earth (Ford).

This angel's song is somewhat of an echo of the one sung by the overcomers in 15:3-4 (Beckwith). The justice of God as recognized in δίκαιος (*dikaios*, "righteous") is one of those echoes (15:3; cf. 19:2). His holiness and majesty (6:10; 15:4) assert themselves on behalf of His people and in self-vindication, resulting in righteous activity (Moffatt). Rather than complain to God for what He has done to the waters, the angel of the waters confirms the justice of the punishment inflicted thereby (Swete, Lee).

The expression ὁ ὢν καὶ ὁ ἦν (*ho ōn kai ho ēn*, "who is and who was") addresses God the same way as the song of 11:17 addressed Him (cf. 1:4, 8; 4:8). This is a title recalling God's eternality which was expressed in similar terms in Ex. 3:14 when God revealed Himself to Moses in the burning bush. Shortly after this, God used Moses to apply the principle of *lex talionis* in delivering His people from Egypt (Ford). The bowls are in process of applying the same principle in a more far-reaching and ultimate situation.

A second address calls God by the title ὁ ὅσιος (*ho hosios*, "holy

---

56. Swete, *Apocalypse*, p. 202; Robertson, *Word Pictures*, 6:421.
57. Wilcock, *Revelation*, p. 145; Walvoord, *Revelation*, p. 233; Hughes, *Revelation*, p. 174.

one"), another echo of 15:4. Δίκαιος (*Dikaios*, "Righteous") and ὅσιος (*hosios*) together apply to God in 15:3-4 as they do here (cf. Titus 1:8). "The sacred one" here maintains His sacredness by sending judgment on all those who trample on His sacred things. It would be impossible for such a one ever to judge unrighteously or unjustly (Lenski).

The ὅτι (*hoti*, "because") clause gives the reason for calling God "righteous": He judged "these things" (ταῦτα [*tauta*]). The antecedent of *tauta* is the judgment of v. 4 (Alford), not the judgments of vv. 2-4 (Lee). It excludes the earlier judgments of the first two bowls because the subject is the shortage of drinking water (cf. v. 6), not sea water.[58]

16:6 The angel's song continues from v. 5 with an elaboration of the appropriateness of the judgment: ὅτι αἷμα ἁγίων καὶ προφητῶν ἐξέχεαν, καὶ αἷμα αὐτοῖς δέδωκας* πιεῖν· ἄξιοί εἰσιν (*kai haima hagiōn kai prophētōn exechean, kai haima autois dedōkas piein; axioi eisin*, "because they have poured out the blood of saints and prophets, and You have given them blood to drink; they are worthy"). Some want to begin a new sentence with the ὅτι (*hoti*, "because") clause that opens v. 6: "Because they poured out the blood of saints and prophets, You have also given them blood to drink" (Swete, Mounce). To punctuate the verse this way, though, breaks the continuity in emphasis on the theme of the song, which is the righteousness and holiness of God. This leaves the thought of v. 5 somewhat incomplete. In addition, the position of the καὶ (*kai*) before αἷμα (*haima*, "blood") also argues against the meaning "also" in this case (Alford).

It is better to see this *hoti* clause as parallel to or epexegetical of the *hoti* clause of v. 5 (Lenski). Parallelism is perhaps not the best way to express the relationship, though this is the way the first two *hoti* clauses of 15:4 are taken. Actually, the second clause explains the first: "God's judging these things is defined as God's giving the persecutors blood to drink in response to their pouring out the blood of the saints and prophets."

The double appearance of αἷμα (*haima*, "blood") as direct objects in the forward emphatic positions highlights the correspondence between the crime and its punishment (cf. Isa. 49:26). This illustrates the principle of *lex talionis* according to which God deals with the enemies of His people (Lenski, Ford). It is the blood of "saints and prophets" (ἁγίων καὶ προφητῶν [*hagiōn kai prophētōn*]) that the oppressors poured out (cf. 11:18; 18:24). All the prophets are saints, but not all the saints are prophets (Moffatt). The former group are Christians in general, and the latter a particular class among them (cf. Mark 16:7; Acts 1:14, for this use of καὶ [*kai*, "and"]) (Beckwith, Mounce). The entity

---

58. Düsterdieck, *Revelation*, p. 417.

known as Babylon is the guilty party according to 17:6, as is the system controlled by the beast and the false prophet according to 13:15. The two are either one and the same or else are united in their effort to rid the world of the faithful. God "pours out" (ἐξέχεεν [execheen]) the third bowl in response to their "pouring out" (ἐξέχεαν [exechean]) of the blood of His people. His action deprives them of drinking water and gives them instead the very element they have been guilty of shedding (cf. Gen. 4:10-11; 9:6) (Ford). Here is the correlation between sin and sin's punishment (cf. 18:7) (Moffatt).

The angel ends his song in a rather abrupt manner by adding the blunt assertion ἄξιοί εἰσιν (axioi eisin, "they are worthy"). These two emphatic words are a "terrible antithesis" to the axioi eisin of 3:4 where worthiness is of the exact opposite type (Swete). Those loyal to the beast deserve exactly what they receive. This is the principle that goes by other names besides lex talionis. It is the inexorable law of retribution, the law of retaliation, eye for eye, reaping what you sow, being paid in one's own coin, falling in the ditch you dig for another, hanging on Haman's gallows, and the punishment fitting the crime (cf. Obad. 15-16) (Smith, Morris, Hailey).

The subject of εἰσιν (eisin, "they are") is not the saints and the prophets as sometimes construed.[59] The subject supplied from the nearest pronoun αὐτοῖς (autois, "them") is those guilty of taking the lives of saints and prophets. This grammatical necessity keeps the focus of the song on God's righteous judgment in returning to the guilty their due reward. They are the worthy ones.

16:7 The next voice John heard was that of the altar: Καὶ ἤκουσα *τοῦ θυσιαστηρίου λέγοντος, Ναί, κύριε ὁ θεὸς ὁ παντοκράτωρ, ἀληθιναὶ καὶ δίκαιαι αἱ κρίσεις σου (Kai ēkousa tou thysiastēriou legontos, Nai, kyrie ho theos ho pantokratōr, alēthinai kai dikaiai hai kriseis sou, "And I heard the altar saying, 'Yes, Lord God Almighty, Your judgments are true and righteous'"). The altar throughout Revelation relates to judgment except in 11:1 (6:9; 8:3-5; 9:13; 14:18).[60] So when it is personified as speaking here, it carries an association with the prayers of the saints for vengeance (Alford). The altar concurs with the song of the angel just concluded that these prayers have now received their answer. A voice from the four horns of the golden altar in 9:13 has prepared for a personification of the altar such as this. Other illustrations of speech from inanimate objects are Gen. 4:10; Luke 19:40; Heb. 12:24.[61]

---

59. Contra Hughes, Revelation, p. 174.
60. Mounce, Revelation, p. 296; Thomas, Revelation 1-7, pp. 517-22: Excursus 2.
61. Düsterdieck, Revelation, p. 417; Moffatt, "Revelation," 5:446; Beckwith, Apocalypse, p. 680; Wilcock, Revelation, p. 262; Ford, Revelation, p. 262.

In another remarkable echo from 15:3-4, the altar addresses God by His title κύριε ὁ θεὸς ὁ παντοκράτωρ (*kyrie ho theos ho pantokratōr*, "Lord God Almighty") (cf. 15:3). It then voices agreement with the words of the angel in 16:5-6 through a "yes" (ναί [*nai*]) (Lee). The altar adopts the tone of ascription of praise to God for His just judgment (Beckwith). His judgments are "true and righteous" (ἀληθιναὶ καὶ δίκαιαι [*alēthinai kai dikaiai*]). They are never vengeful or capricious like those of pagan deities. They agree with His just nature (Ps. 119:137; cf. Ps. 19:9).[62] In v. 7, κρίσεις (*kriseis*, "judgments") replaces the ὁδοί (*hodoi*, "ways") in 15:3, and the order of the adjectives describing the judgments is the reverse of that in 15:3. His "acts of judgment" are an integral part of His "ways."

Additional Notes

16:4 To reconcile the singular verb with the plural subject implied by τοὺς ποταμούς and τὰς πηγάς, p47, Alexandrinus, 2053, and other MSS have ἐγένοντο instead of ἐγένετο. The more difficult reading ἐγένετο has adequate support from Sinaiticus, Ephraemi, and other MSS.[63] Quite possibly the explanation for the singular verb is an implied neuter plural ὕδατα carried over from the ὑδάτων at the end of the previous clause (Lee, Beckwith).

16:5 Τοῦ ἀγγέλου is a genitive as the direct object of a verb of sensation, and τῶν ὑδάτων is an objective genitive because the angel has jurisdiction over the waters, both the sea and fresh water affected by the plagues just described.[64]

A number of variants cloud what the original reading was for ὁ ἦν, ὁ ὅσιος. Instead of this, a number of MSS, including p47, support the reading ὃς ἦν [καὶ] ὅσιος ("who was [also] holy"). This makes ὅσιος parallel with δίκαιος, being predicated as a result of God's manifested acts just as δίκαιος is: "You are righteous, who are, and who was, holy."[65] Another reading, supported by Alexandrinus, Ephraemi, and others, has ὁ ἦν ὅσιος ("the one who was holy"). This reading too indicates a parallelism with δίκαιος (Charles), though it may mean that ὅσιος is a predicate with ὁ ὢν καὶ ὁ ἦν instead of with εἶ (Alford). In this case, ὅσιος would be an essential attribute assigned to God alone (ibid.). Taking ὅσιος as parallel with δίκαιος creates an intolerable harshness, however, and taking the adjective as a predicate adjective

---

62. Swete, *Apocalypse*, p. 203; Mounce, *Revelation*, p. 295; Wall, *Revelation*, p. 198.
63. Metzger, *Textual Commentary*, p. 757.
64. Alford, *Greek Testament*, 4:698; Robertson, *Word Pictures*, 6:421; Sweet, *Revelation*, p. 244.
65. Düsterdieck, *Revelation*, pp. 416-17.

with ὁ ὢν καὶ ὁ ἦν breaks the pattern of the Apocalypse in not assigning the expression a predicate nominative or adjective (Swete). The remaining option, ὁ ἦν, ὁ ὅσιος, taking ὁ ὅσιος as a vocative addressed to God, has the support of Sinaiticus, 051, and other authorities and agrees with the position of the words (Charles) and the presence of the article with the adjective (Charles). This offers the best alternative from both textual and syntactical perspectives (Beckwith).

16:6 On the basis of slightly stronger external evidence, especially Alexandrinus and Ephraemi, the reading of the perfect tense δέδωκας is preferred over the aorist ἔδωκας, which has the support of p[47] and Sinaiticus. This refers the verb to punishment that is permanent as well as just.[66]

16:7 A few of the weaker MSS supply an ἐκ before τοῦ θυσιαστηρίου to avoid difficulty in explaining how an altar can speak. The shorter reading that omits the preposition is obviously original, having overwhelmingly strong external support.

7. THE FOURTH BOWL: SCORCHING OF ALL THROUGH THE SUN'S INTENSITY (16:8-9)

Translation

8And the fourth poured out his bowl upon the sun; and [power] was given to it to burn the men with fire. 9And the men were burned with great heat, and they blasphemed the name of God who had the authority over these plagues, and they did not repent to give Him glory.

Exegesis and Exposition

16:8 The role of the fourth angel was to direct his bowl upon the sun: Καὶ ὁ τέταρτος ἐξέχεεν τὴν φιάλην αὐτοῦ ἐπὶ τὸν ἥλιον· καὶ ἐδόθη αὐτῷ καυματίσαι τοὺς ἀνθρώπους ἐν πυρί (*Kai ho tetartos execheen tēn phialēn autou epi ton hēlion; kai edothē autǭ kaumatisai tous anthrōpous en pyri*, "And the fourth poured out his bowl upon the sun; and [power] was given to it to burn the men with fire"). The preposition ἐπὶ (*epi*, "upon") instead of εἰς (*eis*, "into") as in vv. 2, 3, 4, indicates the destination of this bowl. The fourth trumpet also had the sun as its object of judgment, but that former affliction was a darkening. This, by contrast, increases rather than decreases the sun's intensity (Walvoord).

The form ἐδόθη (*edothē*, "there was given") shows God's sovereign power to be behind the widespread scorching men received. He over-

---

66. Robertson, *Word Pictures*, 6:421; Mounce, *Revelation*, p. 295; Johnson, "Revelation," 12:549.

ruled the processes of nature to bring this torment upon them. They fully knew who was responsible as evidenced by their blasphemous response to the heat (v. 9) (Lee, Ladd, Sweet). The immediate agent of burning was the sun, the antecedent of αὐτῷ (*autǭ*, "to it"), but it was not the sun's inherent power to do this sort of thing (Alford). Καυματίσαι (*Kaumatisai*, "To burn") dramatizes the theme of horrible punishment by itself, but the addition of ἐν πυρί (*en pyri*, "with fire") intensifies the picture.[67] The victims of this scorching are τοὺς ἀνθρώπους (*tous anthrōpous*, "the men"). The article τοὺς (*tous*) is possibly generic (Alford), but the repetition of οἱ ἄνθρωποι (*hoi anthrōpoi*, "the men") in v. 9 raises the likelihood that it refers to a previous mention of "the men," the one in v. 2 (Smith, Walvoord). The sufferers under this bowl are those who have received the mark of the beast and worshiped his image. The faithful are clearly exempt from this type of affliction as the promise of an opposite future for them in 7:16 shows (Lee).

16:9 A relentless stress accents the severity of the scorching that rebellious men will receive: καὶ ἐκαυματίσθησαν οἱ ἄνθρωποι καῦμα μέγα, καὶ ἐβλασφήμησαν τὸ ὄνομα τοῦ θεοῦ τοῦ ἔχοντος τὴν ἐξουσίαν ἐπὶ τὰς πληγὰς ταύτας, καὶ οὐ μετενόησαν δοῦναι αὐτῷ δόξαν (*kai ekaumatisthēsan hoi anthrōpoi kauma mega, kai eblasphēmēsan to onoma tou theou tou echontos tēn exousian epi tas plēgas tautas, kai ou metenoēsan dounai autǭ doxan*, "and the men were burned with great heat, and they blasphemed the name of God who had the authority over these plagues, and they did not repent to give Him glory"). A cognate accusative καῦμα (*kauma*, "heat") with ἐκαυματίσθησαν (*ekaumatisthēsan*, "were burned") is part of the intensification of the punishment. The adjective μέγα (*mega*, "great") strengthens the effect even more. These features together with the addition of ἐν πυρί (*en pyri*, "with fire") in v. 8 have the effect of heaping up the terrible agony of the torment.[68]

The human response is blasphemy against the God who is directly responsible for all this human misery. "They blasphemed the name of God" (ἐβλασφήμησαν τὸ ὄνομα τοῦ θεοῦ [*eblasphēmēsan to onoma tou theou*]) in token of their hardness of heart. The same response comes in vv. 11 and 21 too. This is the only chapter in the visional portion of the book that speaks of widespread human blasphemy, the other references being to blasphemy from the beast (13:1, 5-6; 17:3). These men have now taken on the character of the god whom they serve (Caird, Ford). They blame God for the first four plagues, rather than blaming their own sinfulness.

They are right in recognizing Him as the one "who had the authori-

---

67. Robertson, *Word Pictures*, 6:422.
68. Morris, *Revelation*, p. 196; BDF, par. 153[1].

ty over these plagues" (τοῦ ἔχοντος τὴν ἐξουσίαν ἐπὶ τὰς πληγὰς ταύτας [*tou echontos tēn exousian epi tas plēgas tautas*]). God is sovereign and in control of everything that happens (Charles), but their unwillingness to honor Him as sovereign is the typical heathen spirit (Rom. 1:28; cf. Rom. 2:24; 1 Tim. 6:1; James 2:7) (Moffatt).

"They did not repent" (Οὐ μετενόησαν [*Ou metenoēsan*]) is a refrain like a funeral dirge (9:20-21; 16:11). In 11:13 some did repent because of the earthquake in Jerusalem, but not here. Deserved punishment hardens the callous heart even more.[69] Since this is one of the *last* plagues, this impenitence represents a hopeless case.[70] The ἀποτομία (*apotomia*, "severity") (Rom. 11:22) of God no less than His χρηστότης (*chrēstotēs*, "kindness") (Rom. 2:4) calls people to repentance, but earth's inhabitants, like Pharaoh, harden their hearts in the face of God's judgments (Swete).

The expression δοῦναι[71] αὐτῷ δόξαν (*dounai autō doxan*, "to give Him glory") tells what the result would have been had they repented. "Giving God glory" is a goal in 11:13; 14:7; 19:7 also.

8. THE FIFTH BOWL: DARKENING OF THE BEAST'S KINGDOM (16:10-11)

Translation

10And the fifth poured out his bowl upon the throne of the beast; and his kingdom became darkened, and they gnawed their tongues because of the pain, 11and they blasphemed the God of heaven because of their pains and because of their sores and they did not repent of their works.

Exegesis and Exposition

16:10 As with the fifth member of the two previous series, so it is here that God "gives the screw an extra turn." He not only punishes man by land, sea, water, and fire, but through bowl five He throws the entire human system into disarray:[72] Καὶ ὁ πέμπτος ἐξέχεεν τὴν φιάλην αὐτοῦ ἐπὶ τὸν θρόνον τοῦ θηρίου· καὶ ἐγένετο ἡ βασιλεία αὐτοῦ ἐσκοτωμένη, καὶ ἐμασῶντο τὰς γλώσσας αὐτῶν ἐκ τοῦ πόνου (*Kai ho pemptos execheen tēn phialēn autou epi ton thronon tou thēriou; kai egeneto hē basileia autou eskotōmenē, kai emasōnto tas glōssas autōn ek tou ponou*, "And the fifth poured out his bowl upon the throne of the

---

69. Robertson, *Word Pictures*, 6:422; Ford, *Revelation*, p. 262.
70. Hughes, *Revelation*, p. 175.
71. Δοῦναι is an infinitive of result, sometimes called an epexegetic infinitive (Beckwith, *Apocalypse*, p. 681; Robertson, *Word Pictures*, 6:422; BDF, par. 291[4]).
72. Wilcock, *Revelation*, p. 146.

beast; and his kingdom became darkened, and they gnawed their tongues because of the pain"). This bowl along with the sixth and seventh have more of a political orientation than any plague encountered heretofore (Sweet).

The destination of this bowl is τὸν θρόνον (*ton thronon*, "the throne") of the beast, i.e., the one spot where his power and presence reside or the seat of his rule, authority, and dominion (Alford, Lenski). The earliest mention of the throne is in 13:2 which notes the dragon's gift of that throne to the beast. So long untouched, that throne through which the dragon has perverted all of human society into a demonic civilization is now the focal point of God's anger.[73] The beast will be just as helpless against this plague as Pharaoh was against the comparable ninth plague against Egypt (Ex. 10:21-23) (Bullinger).

"His kingdom" ('H βασιλεία αὐτοῦ [*Hē basileia autou*]), an obvious corollary of "the throne of the beast" (τὸν θρόνον τοῦ θηρίου [*ton thronon tou thēriou*]), receives the consequences of this bowl. This is the first mention of the beast's kingdom. It obviously refers to a concrete kingdom with geographical extent, not to an abstract rulership of the beast.[74] The plague puts the realm in a lasting condition of darkness. This is like the ninth Egyptian plague (Ex. 10:21-22), but worse because it aggravates the continuing effects of the previous plagues.[75] Since the beast's kingdom is worldwide, this amounts to a darkness that covers the whole earth. It may be assumed, however, that the faithful remnant in its place of refuge is untouched by the plague, just as were the children of Israel during the Egyptian darkness (Ex. 10:23) (Beasley-Murray). A view that this darkness will be only moral and spiritual, not physical,[76] gives inadequate consideration to the parallel with conditions under the ninth Egyptian plague and those under the fifth trumpet judgment where a physical darkness prevailed (9:2) (Charles).

The subject of ἐμασῶντο (*emasōnto*, "they gnawed") is unstated, but is assumed to be the subjects of the beast's kingdom. The verb's imperfect tense shows that they "kept on chewing" their tongues (Lenski). This expresses a most agonizing and excruciating kind of pain. 'Εκ τοῦ πόνου (*Ek tou ponou*, "Because of the pain") has the idea of "out of distress." Πόνος (*Ponos*, "Pain") is from πένομαι (*penomai*, "I

---

73. Lenski, *Revelation*, p. 473; Ladd, *Revelation*, p. 212; Wilcock, *Revelation*, p. 147.
74. Düsterdieck, *Revelation*, p. 418.
75. Moffatt, "Revelation," 5:447; Robertson, *Word Pictures*, 6:422; Mounce, *Revelation*, p. 291.
76. Kiddle, *Revelation*, pp. 321-22; Johnson, "Revelation," 12:550; Hughes, *Revelation*, p. 175.

work for a living"), "pain" being a result of the toil expended.[77] The text does not tell precisely how darkness can create such agony. One suggestion is that this is the darkness of the fifth trumpet and the pain is that associated with the locust plague (Charles), but this is a visitation distinct from that earlier one. Another posits that this is the pain from the first four bowls aggravated by the pitch black condition that covers the earth (Alford). But the plural πόνων (ponōn, "pains") in v. 11 sums up those cumulative pains and implies that this singular ponou is a particular distress caused by the darkness (Beckwith). Perhaps the difficulty in explaining the source of pain relates to the fact that the world has never experienced such a widespread and extended darkness. Conceivably, this will create all sorts of physical havoc.

16:11 In token of their continuing allegiance to the beast, his subjects once again opt to blaspheme God (cf. 13:6) (Lee): καὶ ἐβλασφήμησαν τὸν θεὸν τοῦ οὐρανοῦ ἐκ τῶν πόνων αὐτῶν καὶ ἐκ τῶν ἑλκῶν αὐτῶν, καὶ οὐ μετενόησαν ἐκ τῶν ἔργων αὐτῶν (kai eblasphēmēsan ton theon tou ouranou ek tōn ponōn autōn kai ek tōn helkōn autōn, kai ou metenoēsan ek tōn ergōn autōn, "and they blasphemed the God of heaven because of their pains and because of their sores and they did not repent of their works"). Their reaction once again refutes the notion that wicked men will repent when faced with catastrophic conditions. Instead of repenting, they plunge more deeply into blasphemy (cf. v. 9) (Walvoord). "The God of heaven" (Τὸν θεὸν τοῦ οὐρανοῦ [Ton theon tou ouranou]) occurs one other place in Revelation, in 11:13 where victims of the earthquake responded in a radically different manner to God's judgment. This title for God recalls the pride of Nebuchadnezzar and the rulers after him (cf. Dan. 2:44) (Swete).

This time, the blasphemy stems from the cumulative effect of the first four plagues, as the plural "pains" (πόνων [ponōn]) implies. But specifically the lingering effects of the first plague cause their disrespect for God (ἐκ τῶν ἑλκῶν αὐτῶν [ek tōn helkōn autōn, "because of their sores"]). The plagues come so fast that each one finds its victims still suffering from all that have preceded.[78] This differs from the seal and trumpet series, in which each plague concluded before the next one began (see Excursus 3). One can imagine the conditions of panic that already existed until now, when the darkness comes and compounds the hysteria.

Once again, earth's inhabitants refuse to repent of their works, as noted already at the conclusion of the fifth trumpet (9:20-21). They choose to cling to their idolatries and their immoralities (Swete).

---

77. Robertson, *Word Pictures*, 6:422-23.
78. Chilton, *Days of Vengeance*, p. 407.

Additional Notes

16:10 The compound tense ἐγένετο . . . ἐσκοτωμένη is a periphrastic pluperfect.[79] As usual in a periphrastic pluperfect, the tense has an intensive emphasis, i.e., it focuses on the existing results of a completed process. The resulting darkness is continuous.

As it does occasionally, the preposition ἐκ expresses cause in this instance and in 16:11 (cf. 8:13).[80]

9. THE SIXTH BOWL: PREPARATION FOR THE DOOM OF EARTH'S KINGS (16:12-16)

Translation

12And the sixth poured out his bowl upon the great river Euphrates; and its water was dried up, that the way of the kings who were from the rising of the sun might be prepared. 13And I saw [coming] from the mouth of the dragon and from the mouth of the beast and from the mouth of the false prophet three unclean spirits like frogs 14—for they are spirits of demons performing signs— which go out to the kings of the whole inhabited world, to gather them to the battle of the great day of God Almighty. 15("Behold I come as a thief. Blessed is the one who watches and keeps his garments, that he not walk naked and they see his shame.") 16And they gathered them into the place which is called in Hebrew "Harmagedon."

Exegesis and Exposition

16:12 The sixth bowl, like the fifth seal, has no immediate visitation against mankind. It simply looks forward and prepares for a coming battle (Beckwith, Ladd). The theory that it entails a mutual destruction by armies from the east and those from the rest of the world[81] is insupportable with valid exegetical data. Also, the idea that it represents the various forces that cause the social and political machinery of the Roman Empire to crumble, thus rendering it defenseless before the barbarian invasion (Ford), is also difficult to sustain.

The destination of this bowl's contents is the great river Euphrates: Καὶ ὁ ἕκτος ἐξέχεεν τὴν φιάλην αὐτοῦ ἐπὶ τὸν ποταμὸν τὸν μέγαν τὸν Εὐφράτην· καὶ ἐξηράνθη τὸ ὕδωρ αὐτοῦ, ἵνα ἑτοιμασθῇ ἡ ὁδὸς τῶν βα-

---

79. Robertson, *Word Pictures*, 6:422; Nigel Turner, *Syntax*, vol. 3 of *A Grammar of New Testament Greek* (Edinburgh: T. & T. Clark, 1963), p. 89.
80. BDF, par. 212; C. F. D. Moule, *An Idiom Book of New Testament Greek* (Cambridge: Cambridge Univ., 1960), p. 73; Turner, *Syntax*, pp. 259-60.
81. Wilcock, *Revelation*, p. 148-49.

σιλέων τῶν ἀπὸ ἀνατολῆς ἡλίου (*Kai ho hektos execheen tēn phialēn autou epi ton potamon ton megan ton Euphratēn; kai exēranthē to hydōr autou, hina hetoimasthȩ̄ hē hodos tōn basileōn tōn apo anatolēs hēliou*, "And the sixth poured out his bowl upon the great river Euphrates; and its water was dried up, so that the way of the kings who were from the rising of the sun might be prepared"). This is one of the great rivers of the world that constituted the eastern boundary of both the ancient Roman Empire and the land God promised to the seed of Abraham (Gen. 15:18; Deut. 1:7; 11:24; Josh. 1:4). The city of Babylon was also beside this river (Johnson). The first mention up of this river in the Bible is in Gen. 2:14, and its last mention is here. Revelation 9:14 mentions the river in connection with the origin of the sixth trumpet judgment also, where it posed a similar temporary barrier to check the progress of events.

This mention occasions the same question discussed there: Is this proper name symbolic or literal? A suggested symbolism is that it represents a barrier that impedes the progress of the ungodly world-power in assaulting the church (Lee). But the unmistakable geographic usage of the river's name in Scripture is a staunch refutation against any symbolic meaning (Walvoord). The drying up of the river is to provide access for the kings from the east, so it must have a geographical and literal connotation. If the battle for which the kings gather in 19:18-21 is literal, the drying up of this river to give them access to the battle site must be literal too (Bullinger). A comparable episode in the OT, the drying up of the Red Sea to allow Israel passage, was literal. So must this one be (Seiss). Everything else in chapter 16 is literal, so the Euphrates should have the same connotation (Bullinger, Seiss).

Isaiah 11:15-16 prophesies the drying up of the Euphrates to facilitate the return of scattered Israelites from the east. The Jordan River also became dry before the Israelites as they entered Canaan (Josh. 3:13-17; 4:23). Elijah parted the waters of the Jordan to allow passage for himself and Elisha (2 Kings 2:8). The miracle at the Red Sea is the closest counterpart to this sixth bowl, however (Ex. 14:21-22; cf. Isa. 11:16) (Beckwith). According to the historian Herodotus, Cyrus walked across the drained bed of the Euphrates in his conquest of Babylon, a conquest in fulfillment of prophecy (Jer. 50:38; 51:36).[82] On the occasion of the sixth bowl judgment, the stoppage of the river's flow appears to be a favor for the kings from the east, but it eventually becomes a trap for them just as the parted Red Sea proved to be a trap for the pursuing Egyptians (Seiss).

---

82. Herodotus 1. 191; cf. Swete, *Apocalypse*, p. 205; Moffatt, "Revelation," 5:447; Mounce, *Revelation*, p. 398; Ford, *Revelation*, p. 263; Chilton, *Days of Vengeance*, p. 407.

The result of this miraculous act is explicit, "the way of the kings who were from the rising of the sun might be prepared" (ἑτοιμασθῇ ἡ ὁδὸς τῶν βασιλέων τῶν ἀπὸ ἀνατολῆς ἡλίου [*hetoimasthē hē hodos tōn basileōn tōn apo anatolēs hēliou*]). A more immediate suggested identification of the kings from the east (i.e., "the rising of the sun") could be the Parthian rulers who were a continual threat to Rome during John's day,[83] but this was hardly a factor in preparation for the battle of Harmagedon in 16:16. This bowl looks to the future and the last conflict of world empires against God and His Messianic people (Joel 3:2; Zeph. 3:8). This is the historical program yet to come anticipated in 17:12-14 also (Swete, Moffatt, Beckwith, Mounce, Johnson).

A mention of the kings from the east separate from the kings of the whole earth has suggested to some an enmity between the two groups (Charles, Beasley-Murray, Mounce). This opinion rests largely on an identification of the kings from the east with the Parthian invaders of ancient times and on an association of them with the internal strife noted in Rev. 17:16 (Beasley-Murray). John does not involve them in this strife within the beast's kingdom, however. The direct import of this passage is that they join with the kings of the whole earth in a warfare against believers, not against Babylon.[84] They appear to be oriental kings who invade Palestine in connection with the final great conflict (Walvoord). Their reason for invading this territory is not explicit, but it may very well have some connection with the revival in Jerusalem at the end of the second half of the seventieth week (cf. 11:13). Conceivably, they cross the dried-up river bed on their way to put down this new center of disloyalty to the beast, who himself has his headquarters in Babylon on the Euphrates and can participate with others in this invasion.

16:13 Verses 13-16 are not an interlude between the sixth and seventh bowls as have appeared between the sixth and seventh members of the two previous series. The section is rather a topical expansion of or a commentary on v. 12 (Walvoord, Mounce). It shows that the kings of the whole earth will join the kings from the east in the final great conflict (Smith).

Verse 13 begins the explanation of the means used to muster such a large fighting force: Καὶ εἶδον ἐκ τοῦ στόματος τοῦ δράκοντος καὶ ἐκ τοῦ στόματος τοῦ θηρίου καὶ ἐκ τοῦ στόματος τοῦ ψευδοπροφήτου πνεύματα τρία ἀκάθαρτα ὡς βάτραχοι (*Kai eidon ek tou stomatos tou drakontos kai ek tou stomatos tou thēriou kai ek tou stomatos tou pseudoprophētou pneumata tria akatharta hōs batrachoi*, "And I saw [com-

---

83. See *Sibylline Oracles*, 4. 115-39.
84. Düsterdieck, *Revelation*, p. 419.

ing] from the mouth of the dragon and from the mouth of the beast and from the mouth of the false prophet three unclean spirits like frogs"). The three uses of στόματος (*stomatos*, "mouth") is indicative of a propaganda campaign through which the unholy trinity will lead most to an unconditional commitment to evil in the last days. The influence of the mouth can hardly be overstated, especially in the activity of these three (12:15; 13:6, 12-15; cf. 1:16; 2:16; 11:5; 19:15, 21; Isa. 11:4).[85]

This lining up of the infernal trio is a helpful confirmation to the interpretation already advanced in chapters 12-13 (Smith). The dragon, who entered the visional activity at 12:3, 9, has been behind the scenes empowering the beast all along (13:2). The beast is his featured proponent of evil, in the picture since 11:7 but more fully described in 13:1 ff. This is the first use of the name ψευδοπροφήτου (*pseudoprophētou*, "false prophet"), but it refers to the beast from the earth, met in 13:11 ff. This designation will go with him through the remainder of the book (19:20; 20:10). It expresses his deceptiveness as the lying prophet who is in league with Satan's political front man (13:14). The NT warns continually about avoiding false prophets (Matt. 7:15; Mark 13:22; Acts 13:6; 2 Pet. 2:1; 1 John 2:22; 4:1, 3; 2 John 7). This is the false prophet to end all false prophets, however. In light of his role as the climax of all others, the words of Jesus in Mark 13:22 suggest that his companion in error, the beast, is well designated the false Christ (Caird).

From these three mouths come "three unclean spirits" (πνεύματα τρία ἀκάθαρτα [*pneumata tria akatharta*]). Another meaning for πνεῦμα (*pneuma*) is "breath" (cf. 2 Thess. 2:8), so the figure is quite appropriate (Swete). "Unclean spirits" is a common way the NT has for referring to fallen angels or demons (cf. Matt. 10:1; Mark 1:23-24; 3:11; 5:2, 13; Acts 5:16; 8:7), as v. 14 will explain (Lee, Charles). Jesus engaged in freeing people from the power of such beings, but this unholy trinity uses them to perform their destructive work (Swete), which is at this point that of gathering the kings of the entire earth to the climactic battle. The appearance of these spirits resembles that of "frogs" (βάτραχοι [*batrachoi*]). The Levitical standards declared frogs to be unclean animals and an abomination to God's people (Lev. 11:10-11, 41). Frogs recall the second Egyptian plague (Ex. 8:5; Pss. 78:45; 105:30) (Swete), but no pestilence arises in this case, which distinguishes this from the plague in Egypt.[86] Frogs were unclean and loathsome to the Persians and Egyptians too (Johnson).

---

85. Swete, *Apocalypse*, p. 207; Robertson, *Word Pictures*, 6:424; Scott, *Revelation*, p. 333; Caird, *Revelation*, p. 206; Mounce, *Revelation*, p. 299.
86. Düsterdieck, *Revelation*, p. 420; Bullinger, *Apocalypse*, p. 488.

16:14 Verse 14 clarifies the power and mission of the unclean spirits: εἰσὶν γὰρ πνεύματα δαιμονίων ποιοῦντα σημεῖα, ἃ ἐκπορεύεται ἐπὶ τοὺς βασιλεῖς τῆς οἰκουμένης ὅλης, συναγαγεῖν αὐτοὺς εἰς τὸν πόλεμον τῆς μεγάλης ἡμέρας τοῦ θεοῦ τοῦ παντοκράτορος (*eisin gar pneumata daimoniōn poiounta sēmeia, ha ekporeuetai epi tous basileis tēs oikoumenēs holēs, synagagein autous eis ton polemon tēs hēmeras tēs megalēs tou theou tou pantokratoros*, "—for they are spirits of demons performing signs—which go out to the kings of the whole inhabited world, to gather them to the battle of the great day of God Almighty"). A parenthetical explanation indicated by γὰρ (*gar*, "for") extends through σημεῖα (*sēmeia*, "signs") and explains the power of the three unclean spirits. As unclean spirits, they have the same miraculous powers that the second beast had in deceiving people into worshiping the beast (13:13-14; cf. 2 Thess. 2:9-10). Their deceptive work with the kings is reminiscent of the deceiving spirit that lured Ahab into battle in 1 Kings 22:19-22. The immediate agents of persuasion are the three demons, but the ultimate disposition of the kings to give their authority to the beast comes from God (Rev. 17:17) (Bullinger, Beckwith).

The words ἃ ἐκπορεύεται ἐπὶ τοὺς βασιλεῖς τῆς οἰκουμένης ὅλης, συναγαγεῖν αὐτοὺς εἰς τὸν πόλεμον τῆς μεγάλης ἡμέρας τοῦ θεοῦ τοῦ παντοκράτορος (*ha ekporeuetai epi tous basileis tēs oikoumenēs holēs, synagagein autous eis ton polemon tēs hēmeras tēs megalēs tou theou tou pantokratoros*, "which go out to the kings of the whole inhabited world, to gather them to the battle of the great day of God Almighty") resume and complete the statement of v. 13, following the parenthesis. The mission of the three unclean spirits is to contact the world's kings and assemble them for a major world war. The already assembled kings from the east supply an impetus that helps them spur on the rest of the rulers.[87] The expression "the whole inhabited world" (τῆς οἰκουμένης ὅλης [*tēs oikoumenēs holēs*]) appears in 3:10 and 12:9 with the same meaning it has here. Combined with the kings from the east, this will be a worldwide fighting force allied with the beast for a great battle. Ἡ οἰκουμένη ὅλη (*Hē oikoumenē holē*, "The whole inhabited world") is probably intended as more extensive that ἡ οἰκουμένη (*hē oikoumenē*, "the inhabited world") (Luke 2:1; Acts 17:6; 19:27; 24:5). It is not just the empire, but the whole planet (Swete, Mounce). According to 17:12-14, ten kings will lend their resources to this battle (Moffatt, Beckwith).

The infinitive συναγαγεῖν (*synagagein*) expresses the purpose of this demonic expedition, which is "to gather." Under this sixth bowl,

---

87. Moffatt, "Revelation," 5:447; Robertson, *Word Pictures*, 6:424.

only the gathering occurs. The battle comes under the final of the seven last plagues. Whether to translate πόλεμον (*polemon*) "battle" or "war" is probably only a decision of semantics (cf. Smith, Walvoord). Whether it will be a series of conflicts or one major confrontation, depends on how one views the events of the seventh bowl in 19:19-21 (cf. 14:16, 18-20; 17:14). For now, however, this is only the preparation.

This gathering of world forces is in line with OT teaching that Israel's enemies would gather against her in the last days (Joel 2:11; 3:2; Zech. 14:2-3) (Moffatt, Mounce). This is the ultimate battle predicted in Ps. 2:1-3.[88] The prophet terms it τὸν πόλεμον τῆς μεγάλης ἡμέρας τοῦ θεοῦ τοῦ παντοκράτορος (*ton polemon tēs hēmeras tēs megalēs tou theou tou pantokratoros,* "the battle of the great day of God Almighty"), with "great" distinguishing the day from all lesser days, "of God" showing it is not man's or the false Christ's day, and "Almighty" reasserting that God's power is supreme (Morris). His omnipotence and sovereignty will fully demonstrate itself on this occasion. This is the day of the Lord's coming to do battle with the beast (Alford, Beckwith), the climax of human history when God assumes His great power and begins to reign (11:17). It is "the great and terrible day of the LORD" (Joel 2:31), the time of Christ's personal return within the larger period including also the seventieth week of Daniel's prophecy before His personal return (cf. 6:17) and His reign on earth following that return.[89] This is not a battle between nations such as the invasion of Rome by the Parthians, but the nations at war against God (Ps. 2:2). This is God's final reckoning with them on the field of conflict.[90]

16:15 Abruptly, in the middle of the sixth-bowl description, an ejaculatory parenthesis interrupts the recounting of the sixth bowl: Ἰδοὺ ἔρχομαι ὡς κλέπτης· μακάριος ὁ γρηγορῶν καὶ τηρῶν τὰ ἱμάτια αὐτοῦ, ἵνα μὴ γυμνὸς περιπατῇ καὶ βλέπωσιν τὴν ἀσχημοσύνην αὐτοῦ (*Idou erchomai hōs kleptēs. makarios ho grēgorōn kai tērōn ta himatia autou, hina mē gymnos peripatȩ kai blepōsin tēn aschēmosynēn autou,* "Behold I come as a thief. Blessed is the one who watches and keeps his garments, that he not walk naked and they see his shame"). The tendency toward this sudden form of utterance is characteristic of the Apocalypse (cf. 1:8; 8:13; 9:12; 11:14; 13:9-10, 18; 14:12-13; 16:5, 7; 18:20; 20:6) (Beckwith). The voice is unidentified, but the saying so resembles two earlier sayings that there is little doubt that it is the voice of the same glorified Son of Man who appeared to John in chap-

---

88. Hughes, *Revelation,* p. 177.
89. For a discussion of "the day of the Lord," see Thomas, *Revelation 1-7,* p. 458.
90. Robertson, *Word Pictures,* 6:424-25.

ter 1. The words are a reiteration of those by Christ to the church of Sardis in 3:3 and to the church of Laodicea in 3:18 (Swete). Who are the addressees in this warning? Are they the followers of the Lamb suffering persecution under the regime of the beast, or are they the professing Christians in the churches of chapters 2-3? The two groups cannot be the same because Christ promised to preserve the overcomers in the churches in a setting away from the scene of "the hour of trial," which period includes the beast's oppression of the saints (3:10).[91] If the warning is an encouragement to the persecuted remnant under the beast, Christ's promised coming is the one in 19:11-16, which by the time of the sixth bowl follows almost immediately (Alford). If the warning is to people in the churches, it returns to the theme of chapters 2-3, the imminence of the hour of trial as an incentive for the book's recipients to make their calling and election sure so they can escape this coming dreaded period. The close similarity to 3:3, 18 and the parenthetical nature of the announcement favor the latter alternative. Unparalleled misery and utter hopelessness face anyone allied with the beast against God. Here the Son of Man repeats His earlier plea because of things "that must happen soon" (1:1; 22:6), "for the time is at hand" (1:3; 22:10). The other possibility of this being an encouragement to the faithful to persevere could serve no useful purpose at this point. By the time of the sixth bowl, those not in a place of refuge (12:13-17) have suffered martyrdom (13:15; 14:1-5, 13; 15:2).[92] The beast's oppression of the saints has run its course. Therefore this announcement is a repetition of excerpts from the two earlier messages to Sardis and Laodicea; it is a call to genuineness of faith.

After re-announcing His coming as a thief, Jesus pronounces the third of seven beatitudes in the book (cf. 1:3; 14:13; 19:9; 20:6; 22:7, 14). "The one who watches and keeps his garments" (ὁ γρηγορῶν καὶ τηρῶν τὰ ἱμάτια αὐτοῦ [*ho grēgorōn kai tērōn ta himatia autou*]) contrasts with the one who is not awake or alert and hence suffers loss when Christ comes to initiate "the hour of trial." The overcomer will maintain his vigil and guard his garments so that he will have them at hand in case of need (Beckwith). This is the essence of the warning to Laodicea in 3:18, to guard against spiritual nakedness when the moment of truth arrives. The negative purpose of the ἵνα (*hina*, "that") clause is to avoid walking naked and the consequent shame of having one's disgraceful sin exposed to the eyes of all (cf. Isa. 47:3; Ezek. 16:37; 23:24-29; Hos. 2:10; Nah. 3:5) (Lee, Lenski). This is a figura-

---

91. See Thomas, *Revelation 1-7*, pp. 283-90, for a full discussion of 3:10.
92. Cf. Charles, *Revelation*, 2:49.

tive way of speaking of spiritual destitution. The subject of βλέπωσιν (*blepōsin*, "they see") is men in general (Alford). The verb is impersonal and practically equivalent to a passive (Morris). Ἀσχημοσύνην (*Aschēmosynēn*, "Shame") is most likely a euphemism for "private parts" as in the OT (Ex. 20:26; Lev. 18:6 ff.; Deut. 23:14, all in the LXX).[93]

16:16 The connective καί (*kai*, "and") resumes the main account of the sixth bowl following the brief aside of v. 15: καὶ συνήγαγεν αὐτοὺς εἰς τὸν τόπον τὸν καλούμενον Ἑβραϊστὶ Ἁρμαγεδών (*kai synēgagen autous eis ton topon ton kaloumenon Hebraisti Harmagedōn*, "and they gathered them into the place which is called in Hebrew 'Harmagedon'"). Like ἐκπορεύεται (*ekporeuetai*, "go out") in v. 14, the verb συνήγαγεν (*synēgagen*, "they gathered") is singular as is customary with a neuter plural subject, which in this case is understood as the πνεύματα (*pneumata*, "spirits") of v. 13. The subject is demons, not God.[94] In the Apocalypse, neuter plural subjects have singular verbs in a number of places (e.g., 8:3; 13:14; 14:13; 16:14), but most of the time they follow the koine Greek pattern of using plural verbs (Charles). The antecedent of the plural αὐτοὺς (*autous*, "them") is the kings of the whole earth who are named in v. 14.[95]

For most of Revelation's immediate readers who were Gentiles in Asia Minor, a Hebrew word had to be translated or transliterated. They would have been unable to connect it with a particular location of Palestinian geography or with a particular etymological significance (Beckwith). So John clarifies the Hebrew connotation of the name with the preceding Ἑβραϊστί (*Hebraisti*, "in Hebrew"). He does this also in 9:11, but that passage differs from this one in giving the etymological significance of the Hebrew word in Greek (cf. John 5:2; 19:13, 17) (Alford, Lee).

The transliteration Ἁρμαγεδών (*Harmagedōn*, "Harmagedon") more precisely written is Ἁρ Μαγεδών (*Har Magedōn*, "the Mount of Megiddo"), most commonly referred to in English as "Armageddon." It has been a puzzle to exegetes, because Megiddo is in the valley of Esdraelon (i.e., the plain of Jezreel) and is not the name of a mountain in the OT. It was by the waters of Megiddo (the Kishon River) that Barak gained a decisive victory over Sisera that is celebrated in the song of Deborah and Barak (Judg. 5:19; cf. Judg. 4).[96] The plain of Jezreel was also the scene of Gideon's great victory over the Midianites (Judg. 7; cf. Judg. 6:33).

Suggested solutions to the puzzle of *Harmagedōn* have been many

---

93. BAGD, p. 119.
94. Contra Smith, *Revelation*, p. 235, and Walvoord, *Revelation*, p. 238.
95. Robertson, *Word Pictures*, 6:425; Mulholland, *Revelation*, p. 271.
96. Robertson, *Word Pictures*, 6:425.

and varied. One proposal is that it is another name for Mount Carmel which is located near Megiddo, but this name for Mount Carmel appears nowhere else. Besides, the geographical proximity of Mount Carmel to Meggido would have been unknown to John's Asian readers because the territory of Palestine was quite a distance form them (Johnson). The derivation of the name from הַר מוֹעֵד (*har môʿēd*, "the mount of the assembly") is another possibility. This is where the throne of God stands, a mountain that the king of Babylon tried to climb (Isa. 14:12-15).[97] However, this view rests on emending the Greek text to make the transliteration fit (Johnson). Then too, this takes the term as symbolic in the midst of a context which has a literal river, the Euphrates, and a literal geographical direction, east. This occasion, however, involves real people and a real point in future history.

Another etymological explanation traces *Magedōn* to the Hebrew גָּדַד (*gādad*), which means "cut, attack, maraud." Combined with הַר (*har*), it means "marauding mountain" (Caird). This then is an alternate name for Jeremiah's "destroying mountain," another name for Babylon (Jer. 51:25) (Kiddle). This is very improbable, though, because it makes the term figurative instead of a real place in the midst of a context of realities and because it presupposes a knowledge of the Hebrew language that the Christians of Ephesus and the other Asian cities did not have. Another etymological proposal that falters for the same two reasons is a derivation of the term from גָּדַד (*gādad*), which means "gather in troops." This results in the combined meaning of "his place of gathering in troops" (Johnson). Such a figurative connotation for a proper name will not satisfy the criteria of the present context, however. The suggestion that this is an imaginary name for the place of the great battle between the false Christ and the Messiah (Beckwith) is also lacking. If "Euphrates" is a real place, so is *Harmagedōn*.

Another interpretation sees "Megiddo" as symbolic because Josiah was overthrown there. The argument is that Ἑβραϊστί (*Hebraisti*, "in Hebrew") indicated a symbolic meaning in 9:11, so it must do the same here (Kiddle, Johnson). This view also uses the failure of other proposed solutions and the absence of the name from all other literature as corroborative evidence (Lee). Responses that nullify proof for this view include elements already cited, i.e., the real place name "Euphrates" in 16:12 and the realities of the people and the time of this great battle. Besides, John would hardly have included the words τὸν τόπον

---

97. Joachim Jeremias, "Ἁρ Μαγεδών," *TDNT*, 1:468; Roland E. Loasby, "'Har Magedon' according to the Setting of the Seven Last Plagues in Revelation 16," *AUSS* 27, no. 2 (Summer 1989): 129-32.

τὸν καλούμενον (*ton topon ton kaloumenon*, "the place which is called") if he were not referring to a real place (Alford). Then, too, a comparison with 9:11 shows that if he had intended a symbolic meaning, he doubtless would have given his Greek-speaking readers the interpretation in Greek.[98] Another figurative interpretation uses the etymology based on הַר מִגְדּוֹ (*har migĕdô*, "His fruitful mountain") and applies it to Jerusalem, because this would place the battle scene near Jerusalem, the place where the OT said it would be (Joel 3:2; Zech. 14:12 ff.) (Charles). This etymology would have escaped Greek-speaking readers, however. Even if Jerusalem is the place of slaughter, *Harmagedōn* is the place they assemble before the slaughter (Scott).

A literal and geographical understanding of *Harmagedōn* is certainly preferable if it does not face insuperable obstacles. The Hebrew הַר (*har*) can mean "hill-country,"[99] so *Har Megidōn* can refer to the "hill-country of Megiddo." מְגִדּוֹן (*Mĕgiddôn*, "Megiddon") is the name of a Canaanite fortress in the Plain of Jezreel that the Israelites under Deborah and Barak captured later (Josh. 12:21; Judg. 5:19). It was the scene of Josiah's defeat (2 Chron. 35:22). Zechariah mentions the sadness connected with Megiddo in the same context as that cited by John in the theme verse of the Apocalypse (Zech. 12:10-11; Rev. 1:7) (Caird). From OT times this was a renowned battleground and is a fit location for Christ's final victory (Alford). Armies from the east would have to cross the Euphrates to get here, as 16:12 indicates. The main obstacle to this identification is that nowhere else is an explicit reference to such a place found.[100] A "tell" or small mound covering earlier ruins is there, but no mountain. But the writer may have in mind "the mountains of Israel" that are so prominent in Ezekiel's prophecy alluded to in Rev. 19:17-21 (Ezek. 38:8, 21; 39:2, 4) and may have connected them with the name "Megiddo" that is so famous in Israel's history.[101] The plain of Megiddo is admittedly not large enough to contain armies from all over the world, so this must be the assembly area for a much larger deployment that covers a two hundred mile distance from north to south and the width of Palestine from east to west (cf. 14:20). Some

---

98. Düsterdieck, *Revelation*, p. 71.
99. BDB, pp. 250-51.
100. Beckwith, *Apocalypse*, p. 685; Kiddle, *Revelation*, p. 330; Mounce, *Revelation*, p. 301; Johnson, "Revelation," 12:551; M. Eugene Boring, *Revelation*, in Interpretation, A Bible Commentary for Teaching and Preaching (Louisville: John Knox, 1989), pp. 176-77; Hans K. LaRondelle, "The Etymology of *Har-Magedon* (Rev. 16:16)," *AUSS* 27, no. 1 (Summer 1989): 73.
101. Charles, *Revelation*, 2:50; Ford, *Revelation*, p. 262; Hans K. LaRondelle, "The Biblical Concept of Armageddon," *JETS* 28, no. 1 (March 1985): 30-31; William Sanford Lasor, *The Truth about Armageddon* (Grand Rapids: Baker, 1982), pp. 137-40.

decisive battles against this massive force will probably occur around Jerusalem (Zech. 14:1-3).[102]

The preparations of the sixth bowl look forward toward the battle of 19:11-21, and *Harmagedōn* is the place where the kings and their armies will meet the returning Warrior-King and His armies.

Additional Notes

16:12 In 9:14 ἐπὶ has the great river Euphrates as its object too, but there it is the locative case, compared to the accusative case of τὸν ποταμὸν τὸν μέγαν τὸν Εὐφράτην here. Also, the earlier passage has a double use of the article with the river title, but here it is a triple use: τὸν . . . τὸν . . . τὸν.[103]

16:13 Though no participle such as ἐρχόμενα or ἐξερχόμενα occurs with the three uses of ἐκ, the preposition alone conveys the force of "coming out of." The verb ἐκπορεύεται in v. 14 also shows that this is the meaning of the preposition.[104]

16:14 The parenthetical γὰρ clause is not to justify the βάτραχοι (contra Alford) which is only a subordinate element in the preceding clause. Nor does it explain the πνεύματα τρία ἀκάθαρτα in themselves (contra Swete, Mounce), because their equivalency to "spirits of demons" requires no explanation (Beckwith). The parenthetical clause clarifies the power of the unclean spirits by means of the ποιοῦντα σημεῖα with which it closes (ibid.). Like the second beast in 13:13-14, they work miracles and thereby influence the kings in furthering the cause of the beast. The relative clause ἃ ἐκπορεύεται κ.τ.λ. resumes and completes the main line of thought regarding πνεύματα τρία ἀκάθαρτα of v. 13.

The genitive δαιμονίων is one of apposition. The spirits and the demons are one and the same.[105]

10. THE SEVENTH BOWL: THE DESTRUCTION OF BABYLON (16:17–18:24)

a. The Bowl Summarized (16:17-21)

Translation

17And the seventh poured out his bowl upon the air; and a loud voice went forth out of the temple from the throne, saying, "It is done." 18And [flashes of] lightning and voices and [peals of] thunder came, and a great earthquake such as has not happened

---

102. Walvoord, *Revelation*, pp. 238-39; Lasor, *The Truth*, p. 146.
103. Robertson, *Word Pictures*, 6:423.
104. Ibid.
105. Ibid., 6:424.

since man came upon the earth, so mighty an earthquake so great, came. ¹⁹And the great city became three parts, and the cities of the Gentiles fell. And Babylon the great was remembered before God to give to her the cup of the wine of the anger of His wrath. ²⁰And every island fled, and the mountains were not found. ²¹And great hail about a talent's weight descended from heaven upon men. And men blasphemed God because of the plague of the hail, because its plague was exceedingly great.

Exegesis and Exposition

The vastness of the phenomena of the seventh bowl and the fullness of the style used to describe it match this bowl's place as the last in the series of seven (Beckwith). Excursus 5 at the end of this volume discusses in some detail the extent of the seventh bowl, so it is only necessary at this point to observe that the account of the bowl beginning at this point carries all the way through 22:5.

16:17 The opening part of that extended section is an introductory summary in vv. 17-21 that sets the stage for the remainder: Καὶ ὁ ἕβδομος ἐξέχεεν τὴν φιάλην αὐτοῦ ἐπὶ τὸν ἀέρα· καὶ ἐξῆλθεν φωνὴ μεγάλη ἐκ τοῦ ναοῦ ἀπὸ τοῦ θρόνου λέγουσα, Γέγονεν (*Kai ho hebdomos execheen tēn phialēn autou epi ton aera; kai exēlthen phōnē megalē ek tou naou apo tou thronou legousa, Gegonen*, "And the seventh poured out his bowl upon the air; and a loud voice went forth out of the temple from the throne, saying, 'It is done'"). The destination of this last bowl is "the air" (τὸν ἀέρα [*ton aera*]). This is the most pervasive of all the bowls, more so than the ones poured on the earth (16:2), the sea (16:3), the fresh waters (16:4), and the sun (16:8). Air is what people breathe, so this plague is of an even wider impact than the others (Swete). Evidence is slight that the air is intended to picture the laboratory of thunder, lightning, and hail, all of which have occurred in connection with previous plagues. Nor can one view the air as the region of the power of evil, based on Eph. 2:2 (contra Lee). This context contains no hint of that significance.

The "loud voice" (φωνὴ μεγάλη [*phōnē megalē*]) is once again the voice of God as in 16:1. The phrase ἀπὸ τοῦ θρόνου (*apo tou thronou*, "from the throne") confirms this. It is altogether appropriate that the One who sits upon that throne should speak in the administering of the very last of the last plagues (cf. 21:3) and that the voice should come out of His heavenly temple (Swete). Only one other verse in Revelation mentions the heavenly temple and throne together; that is 7:15. The adjective μέγας (*megas*, "great," "loud") appears seven times in this introductory summary of this bowl, indicating the bowl's climactic nature.

The voice from the throne delivers its climactic message in one word, γέγονεν (*gegonen*, "it is done"). The singular verb *gegonen* refers to the divine decree that has set the series of last plagues in motion (Swete). The perfect tense of the verb indicates that what has been developing through a long period in the past has now occurred in the final outpouring (Lenski). It is proleptic or anticipatory in the sense that it covers the following happenings down to and including the final event of the seventh bowl (Alford, Ladd), and moves closer to the culmination spoken of in 10:7 (Smith). In other words, it extends to the comparable declaration in 21:6, the perfect tense verb γέγοναν (*gegonan*, "they are done"), which looks back over the completed outpouring of the seventh bowl. This bowl results in the opening of heaven and the proceeding forth of the Son of God for the final great battle (19:11-21). This last plague culminates the description of the dark side of how the new creation will come into existence (Sweet). Efforts to undermine the finality of this announcement through a "now/not yet" analogy[106] or through its referral to the finished work of Christ (John 19:30) (Lee) are all off target. This is the *last* of the seven last plagues.

16:18 As on earlier occasions in connection with the seventh members of series and allusions to the temple setting in heaven (8:3-5; 11:19; cf. 4:5), a recurrence of the storm theophany comes: καὶ ἐγένοντο ἀστραπαὶ καὶ φωναὶ καὶ βρονταί, καὶ σεισμὸς ἐγένετο μέγας οἷος οὐκ ἐγένετο ἀφ' οὗ ἄνθρωπος ἐγένετο* ἐπὶ τῆς γῆς τηλικοῦτος σεισμὸς οὕτω μέγας (*kai egenonto astrapai kai phōnai kai brontai, kai seismos egeneto megas hoios ouk egeneto aph' hou anthrōpos egeneto epi tēs gēs tēlikoutos seismos houtō megas*, "and [flashes of] lightning and voices and [peals of] thunder came, and a great earthquake such as has not happened since man came upon the earth, so mighty an earthquake so great, came"). These phenomena are signs of God's punishment (Isa. 29:6). This time the earthquake is of far greater proportions than ever before (cf. 6:12; 11:13). This time the storm theophany comes after rather than before the seventh member of a series, and it only begins the consequences of the seventh bowl (Alford). These disturbances signal that the end has arrived, not just the end of the bowl series, but also the end of the seal and trumpet series too.[107]

The judgmental aspect of the seventh bowl goes far beyond the effect of the earthquake on the world.[108] That earthquake and even the hail that follows in v. 21 have their devastating impact, but people continue to blaspheme God after these afflictions. This negative re-

---

106. E.g., Mulholland, *Revelation*, p. 272.
107. See Excursus 3 at the end of this volume for an explanation of how all three series end at the same time.
108. Contra Walvoord, *Revelation*, p. 240.

sponse shows that these are not final.[109] A case for seeing chapters 18 and 19 as further developments of the earthquake and hailstorm (Kiddle) is questionable, but it has merit in extending the seventh bowl at least through chapter 19. The case for extending the seventh bowl, or "chalice" as some choose to call it, into chapter 22 has the most in its favor.[110] The seventh bowl sweeps away time and history, and so must be more than just an earthquake and hail.[111]

At this point in the visional narrative, the earthquake is the notable item. This is not an attempt of John to portray eschatological truth in apocalyptic language, but a report of what he actually saw in an authentic vision (Mounce). Writing in an area of the world especially noted for earthquakes, John carefully distinguishes this final shaking from the greatest previously known up to that time (Swete). Just as Daniel and Christ spoke about an unparalleled time of trouble (Dan. 12:1; Mark 13:19) (Beasley-Murray, Ford), John's vision now reveals σεισμὸς ἐγένετο μέγας οἷος οὐκ ἐγένετο ἀφ᾽ οὗ ἄνθρωπος ἐγένετο ἐπὶ τῆς γῆς τηλικοῦτος σεισμὸς οὕτω μέγας (*seismos egeneto megas hoios ouk egeneto aph' hou anthrōpos egeneto epi tēs gēs tēlikoutos seismos houtō megas*, "a great earthquake such as has not happened since man came upon the earth, so mighty an earthquake so great"). As Joel wrote about the locust plague (Joel 2:2) and Moses about the plagues of hail and locusts (Ex. 9:18; 10:6, 14; 11:6), this will be a calamity unprecedented in human history (Kiddle, Beasley-Murray). It will be the final great shaking predicted in Hag. 2:6 and Heb. 12:26-27.[112] The present expression gains additional emphasis through the adjective μέγας (*megas*, "great"), through the quantitative correlative τηλικοῦτος (*tēlikoutos*, "so mighty"), and finally through the repetition (redundantly) of the pleonastic *tēlikoutos* in the οὕτω μέγας (*houtō megas*, "so great").[113] A second occurrence of ἐγένετο (*egeneto*, "came") in consecutive clauses further enhances the focus of attention on this massive earthquake (Lenski, Ford).

16:19 A third *egeneto* in close sequence tells the instantaneous result of the earthquake: καὶ ἐγένετο ἡ πόλις ἡ μεγάλη εἰς τρία μέρη, καὶ αἱ πόλεις τῶν ἐθνῶν ἔπεσαν (*kai egeneto hē polis hē megalē eis tria merē, kai hai poleis tōn ethnōn epesan*, "and the great city became three parts, and the cities of the Gentiles fell"). Verse 19 turns aside in a parenthetical observation regarding "the great city," "the cities of the Gentiles,"

---

109. Mulholland, *Revelation*, p. 274.
110. Chilton, *Days of Vengeance*, p. 418.
111. Wilcock, *Revelation*, p. 150.
112. Swete, *Apocalypse*, p. 210; Bullinger, *Apocalypse*, p. 491; Wilcock, *Revelation*, p. 150.
113. Swete, *Apocalypse*, p. 210; Beckwith, *Apocalypse*, p. 686; Robertson, *Word Pictures*, 6:426.

and "Babylon the great" (Swete). In the OT, earthquakes and invasions sometimes come together (cf. Isa. 13:13-14; Hag. 2:21-22). Whether that is intended at this point or not is hard to tell (Moffatt, Kiddle), but the invasion will come shortly (19:11-21) even if it is not simultaneous with the earthquake.

Two quite different explications have sought to clarify what "the great city" (ἡ πόλις ἡ μεγάλη [*hē polis hē megalē*]) is. One says it is Babylon, and the other says Jerusalem. The principal support for Babylon is the application of "the great" to that city in 14:8 and in 17:18 (Beckwith). The consideration that makes this view very questionable is the separate mention of Babylon in 16:19*b*. Despite the coming emphasis on Babylon in chapters 17-18, nothing within v. 19 identifies "Babylon the great" of the last half of the verse with "the great city" of the first half. On the contrary, the likelihood of Babylon's being named twice (or even three times if "the cities of the nations" refers to Babylon) in the same verse is quite remote. Revelation 11:8 has a clear identification of Jerusalem as "the great city" (Moffatt, Ford). Furthermore, its separation from "the cities of the Gentiles (or nations)" in the next phrase indicates that Jerusalem is in view.[114] This interpretation that does justice to this context also concurs with predicted topographical changes that will take place around Jerusalem in conjunction with the second advent (Zech. 14:4) (Seiss). Jerusalem experienced a fairly severe earthquake earlier (11:13), but that was only partial. This earthquake will divide the city into three parts. What these three will be is not a subject of the revelation, but it is rather clear that it is geophysical rather than a division into people groups.[115]

The cities of the Gentiles will receive greater damage than Jerusalem, however. The earthquake will be worldwide and wreak devastation in all the major population centers (Swete). This havoc may very well happen in conjunction with the defeat of the beast and his allies by the Lamb (17:12-14) (Ladd).

In particular, the headquarters city of the beast, Babylon the great, will come under siege. Discussion in connection with 14:8 has already given Babylon on the Euphrates as the identity of this city. Further data about Babylon in chapters 17-18 will reflect the influence of this city on world affairs, even to the extent that it represents a vast political, religious, and commercial system controlling the lives of men and nations. The final bowl will not overlook this city and system. Far from it! Καὶ Βαβυλὼν ἡ μεγάλη ἐμνήσθη ἐνώπιον τοῦ θεοῦ δοῦναι αὐτῇ τὸ

---

114. Moffatt, "Revelation," 5:449; Smith, *Revelation*, p. 237; Ford, *Revelation*, p. 264; J. Massyngberde Ford, "The Structure and Meaning of Revelation 16," *ExpTim* 98, no. 11 (August 1987): 329.

115. Contra Lee, "Revelation," 4:727.

ποτήριον τοῦ οἴνου τοῦ θυμοῦ τῆς ὀργῆς αὐτοῦ (*Kai Babylōn hē megalē emnēsthē enōpion tou theou dounai autȩ to potērion tou oinou tou thymou tēs orgēs autou*, "And Babylon the great was remembered before God to give to her the cup of the wine of the anger of His wrath"). The passive ἐμνήσθη (*emnēsthē*, "was remembered") carries the import of "remembered by God" (cf. Acts 10:31). The subsequent words in 17:1-5 confirm explicitly this implied reference to God's memory of Babylon (Lee). The fall of Babylon is the central teaching of the seventh bowl. It is an event already announced in 14:8 and prefigured in the harvest and vintage of 14:14-20. God remembers the oppressors of His people, though at times He may seem to have forgotten (Ladd).

The epexegetic infinitive δοῦναι (*dounai*, "to give") reveals His memory-based action against Babylon. He will give her τὸ ποτήριον τοῦ οἴνου τοῦ θυμοῦ τῆς ὀργῆς αὐτοῦ (*to potērion tou oinou tou thymou tēs orgēs autou*, "the cup of the wine of the anger of His wrath"). This expression contains both θυμός (*thymos*, "anger") and ὀργή (*orgē*, "wrath"), each of the synonyms intensifying the other. Similar expressions have occurred in 14:8, 10. In this string of genitives, τοῦ οἴνου (*tou oinou*, "of the wine") is a genitive of contents telling what is in the cup. The τοῦ θυμοῦ τῆς ὀργῆς (*tou thymou tēs orgēs*, "of the anger of His wrath") is a double appositional genitive: "the wine = the anger that is hot with wrath" (Lenski). The monstrous earthquake was only preliminary. Babylon's drinking of God's wrath is yet to come (Alford). This terminology indicates the extremity of punishment that is reserved for Babylon. Stages in Babylon's downfall come in 17:16 and 18:8 (Beckwith), but her ultimate collapse is in 19:18-21.

16:20 The twentieth verse resumes a description of the earthquake's effect: καὶ πᾶσα νῆσος ἔφυγεν, καὶ ὄρη οὐχ εὑρέθησαν (*kai pasa nēsos ephygen, kai orē ouch heurethēsan*, "and every island fled, and the mountains were not found"). "Fled" (Ἔφυγεν [*Ephygen*]) apparently refers to what sometimes happens to islands during earthquakes; they sink into the sea. "Were not found" (Εὑρέθησαν [*Heurethēsan*]) appears to echo the Hebrew לֹא נִמְצָאוּ (*lō' nimsĕ'û*) (cf. 1 Sam. 13:22; Ps. 37:36; Ezek. 26:21; Zeph. 3:13).[116] Φεύγω (*Pheugō*, "I flee") and εὑρίσκω (*heuriskō*, "I find") are used nowhere else together in Revelation in this manner except in 20:11, where radical topographical changes signal the disappearance of the old creation. Very probably this detail is a foreshadowing of the recreation of 20:11 and 21:1-2 (Ladd). Other apocalyptic writings note similar topographical changes in conjunction with end-time activities (cf. *1 Enoch* 1:6; *Assumption of Moses* 10:4).

---

116. Swete, *Apocalypse*, p. 211; Robertson, *Word Pictures*, 6:426.

These words speak of literal topographical changes, not figuratively of political turmoil.[117] A literal understanding is no obstacle to having the earth as the scene of Christ's future kingdom.[118]

16:21 The final element in the preliminary overview of the seventh bowl is a storm of huge hailstones: καὶ χάλαζα μεγάλη ὡς ταλαντιαία καταβαίνει ἐκ τοῦ οὐρανοῦ ἐπὶ τοὺς ἀνθρώπους· καὶ ἐβλασφήμησαν οἱ ἄνθρωποι τὸν θεὸν ἐκ τῆς πληγῆς τῆς χαλάζης, ὅτι μεγάλη ἐστὶν ἡ πληγὴ αὐτῆς σφόδρα (*kai chalaza megalē hōs talantiaia katabainei ek tou ouranou epi tous anthrōpous; kai eblasphēmēsan hoi anthrōpoi ton theon ek tēs plēgēs tēs chalazēs, hoti megalē estin hē plēgē autēs sphodra*, "and great hail about a talent's weight descended from heaven upon men. And men blasphemed God because of the plague of the hail, because its plague was exceedingly great"). This hail recalls the seventh Egyptian plague (Ex. 9:23-24) and the first trumpet judgment (Rev. 8:7).

The weight of each hailstone, given in the term ταλαντιαία (*talantiaia*, "a talent's weight"), was between 108 and 130 pounds, heavy enough to kill anyone on whom one landed (Swete, Ford). Hailstones are indicative of divine judgment all through the Bible (cf. Josh. 10:11; Job 38:22-23; Isa. 28:2, 17; Ezek. 13:11-13; 38:22-23).[119] The theory that the hail is only symbolic (Kiddle) is faulty, however. The text has no hint to support this. Besides, it is doubtful that men would blaspheme God because of something symbolic only. The Egyptian plague of hail was literal, so this one must be too.

The articles in τοὺς ἀνθρώπους (*tous anthrōpous*, "men") and οἱ ἄνθρωποι (*hoi anthrōpoi*, "men") may again be taken as generic (Alford), as in v. 8, but they probably refer back to the same men loyal to the beast as in v. 2 (Lee). The hailstones did not kill all of them. Otherwise, they could not continue their blasphemy against God). Ἐβλασφήμησαν (*Eblasphēmēsan*, "They blasphemed") marks a continuation of the defiance already in progress at least since the fourth and fifth bowls (16:9, 11). The positions of μεγάλη (*megalē*, "great") and σφόδρα (*sphodra*, "exceedingly") in their clause are very emphatic. The followers of the beast knew exactly the source of these huge stones, and responded by shaking their fist in the face of God.

This hailstorm and its response obviously does not mark the end of the seventh bowl. Chronological sequence resumes in 19:11, after an intercalation (17:1–19:10) expanding upon Babylon, her history, and what has made her what she is up to this point in history.

---

117. Contra Caird, *Revelation*, p. 209.
118. Smith, *Revelation*, p. 238; contra Beasley-Murray, *Revelation*, p. 247.
119. Lee, "Revelation," 4:728; Hughes, *Revelation*, p. 180.

Additional Notes

16:18 Instead of singular ἄνθρωπος ἐγένετο which is in Alexandrinus and partially in p⁴⁷ (ἄνθρωπος ἐγένοντο), Sinaiticus, 2053, and others have the plural ἄνθρωποι ἐγένοντο. Though the external evidence in support of the latter variant is a bit stronger, the former has internal considerations to swing the balance in its favor. The plural appears to have been introduced to avoid the repetition of ἐγένετο from the clause just before (Metzger, pp. 757-58).

16:19 For comparable examples of the epexegetic infinitive (i.e., the infinitive to express result) δοῦναι, see 11:18 and 16:9.[120]

---

120. Beckwith, *Apocalypse*, p. 687; Robertson, *Word Pictures*, 4:426.

19
The History and Fall of Babylon

The section 17:1–19:10 is a unit, with introductory and concluding formulas (17:1-3*a*; 19:9-10).[1] Whether referred to as an appendix[2] or as an extended footnote,[3] it is an expansion and explanation of the seventh bowl judgment. An angel proclaimed Babylon's doom as early as 14:8, and the introductory overview of the seventh bowl has told of the city's drinking of "the cup of the wine of the anger of God's wrath" (16:17). Yet the account has given no information about the city's religious and commercial outreach and about what events have led up to her final spiritual and material devastation. Chapters 17-18 fill this void. On the order of a comparable intercalation in 21:9–22:5, it pictures Babylon under the figure of an immoral woman, the very opposite of a comparable picture of the New Jerusalem in the later intercalation. Excursus 5 at the end of this volume elaborates on aspects of the parallelism between these two parenthetical sections.

---

1. G. R. Beasley-Murray, *The Book of Revelation*, NCB (Grand Rapids: Eerdmans, 1978), p. 248; M. Robert Mulholland, *Revelation, Holy Living in an Unholy World* (Grand Rapids: Zondervan, 1990), pp. 26-30.
2. Alan F. Johnson, "Revelation," in *EBC*, ed. Frank E. Gaebelein (Grand Rapids: Zondervan, 1981), 12:554.
3. Robert W. Wall, *Revelation*, in New International Biblical Commentary, ed. W. Ward Gasque (Peabody, Mass.: Hendrickson, 1991), p. 204.

b. Religious Babylon Destroyed (17:1-18)

Chapter 17 focuses on the religious factor in the Babylonian system. It falls into three parts: the harlot and the beast (vv. 1-6a), the significance of the symbolism (vv. 6b-14), and the judgment of the great harlot (vv. 15-18).[4]

Translation

[1]**And one of the seven angels who had the seven bowls came and spoke with me, saying, "Come, I will show you the judgment of the great harlot who sits beside many waters,** [2]**with whom the kings of the earth have committed fornication, and those who dwell in the earth have become drunk from the wine of her fornication."** [3]**And he carried me away into the wilderness in the spirit. And I saw a woman sitting upon a scarlet beast, full of names of blasphemy, having seven heads and ten horns.** [4]**And the woman was clothed with purple and scarlet, and adorned with gold and precious stones and pearls, having a golden cup in her hand filled with abominations, even the unclean things of her fornication,** [5]**and upon her forehead [was] a name written, a mystery, "Babylon the great, the mother of harlots and of the abominations of the earth."** [6]**And I saw the woman drunken from the blood of the saints and from the blood of the witnesses of Jesus.**

And I marveled with great amazement, seeing her. [7]**And the angel said to me, "Why do you marvel? I will tell you the mystery of the woman and of the beast which bears her, who has the seven heads and ten horns;** [8]**the beast which you saw was and is not, and is about to ascend out of the abyss, and he departs into perdition; and those who dwell upon the earth will marvel, whose names are not written upon the book of life from the foundation of the world, seeing the beast, that he was and is not and will be present.** [9]**Here is the mind which has wisdom. The seven heads are seven mountains, on which the woman sits.** [10]**And they are seven kings; five have fallen, one is, the other has not yet come, and when it comes, it is necessary for it to remain a little [time].** [11]**And the beast which was and is not, even he himself is an eighth and is [one] of the seven, and he departs into perdition.** [12]**And the ten horns which you saw are ten kings, who are such ones as have not yet received a kingdom, but they receive authority with the beast for one hour.** [13]**These have one purpose, and they give their power and authority to the beast.** [14]**These will make war with the Lamb, and the Lamb will overcome them, because He is Lord of lords**

---

4. William Lee, "The Revelation of St. John," in *The Holy Bible*, ed. F. C. Cook (London: John Murray, 1881), 4:735.

and King of kings, and the called and elect and faithful who are with Him [will overcome them]." 15And he says to me, "The waters which you saw, where the harlot sits, are peoples and multitudes and nations and tongues. 16And the ten horns which you saw and the beast, these will hate the harlot, and will make her desolated and naked, and will devour her flesh, and will burn her up with fire. 17For God has put into their hearts to put into practice His purpose, and to put into practice one purpose and to give their kingdom to the beast, until the words of God will be fulfilled. 18And the woman whom you saw is the great city which has a kingdom over the kings of the earth."

Exegesis and Exposition

The harlot and the beast (17:1-6a). Chapter 17 features two figures whom its first section introduces and describes, the harlot and the beast.

17:1 The appointed angelic guide for this "excursion" through Babylon is appropriately one of the seven angels who have administered the bowl judgments: Καὶ ἦλθεν εἷς ἐκ τῶν ἑπτὰ ἀγγέλων τῶν ἐχόντων τὰς ἑπτὰ φιάλας, καὶ ἐλάλησεν μετ' ἐμοῦ λέγων, Δεῦρο, δείξω σοι τὸ κρίμα τῆς πόρνης τῆς μεγάλης τῆς καθημένης ἐπὶ ὑδάτων πολλῶν (*Kai ēlthen heis ek tōn hepta angelōn tōn echontōn tas hepta phialas, kai elalēsen met' emou legōn, Deuro, deixō soi to krima tēs pornēs tēs megalēs tēs kathēmenēs epi hydatōn pollōn,* "And one of the seven angels who had the seven bowls came and spoke with me, saying, 'Come, I will show you the judgment of the great harlot who sits beside many waters'"). This is an amplification of Babylon's judgment announced in conjunction with the last of these bowls, so an angel connected with them provides the enlightening explanation (Johnson). The involvement of a member of the same group shows the connection of 21:9–22:5 with these bowls too (cf. 21:9).[5] It is pure conjecture to specify which of the seven angels this is. It may have been the seventh since it is under his bowl that the announcement of Babylon's judgment comes, but this is uncertain because the text only stipulates εἷς ἐκ τῶν ἑπτὰ ἀγγέλων τῶν ἐχόντων τὰς ἑπτὰ φιάλας (*heis ek tōn hepta angelōn tōn echontōn tas hepta phialas,* "one of the seven angels who had the seven bowls").[6] It does not say the *last* of the seven angels. This is the

---

5. Mulholland, *Revelation*, p. 276.
6. Friedrich Düsterdieck, *Critical and Exegetical Handbook to the Revelation of John*, in Meyer's Commentary, trans. and ed. Henry E. Jacobs (New York: Funk & Wagnalls, 1887), p. 428; Henry Alford, *The Greek Testament* (London: Longmans, Green, 1903), 4:704.

first appearance of an interpretive angel in Revelation,[7] unless one considers one of the twenty-four elders who assumed this role in 7:13 to be an interpretive angel (cf. 5:5 also). The angel initiates the conversation with John by his invitation to witness a judgment. His words are δεῦρο, δείξω σοι (*deuro, deixō soi*, "come, I will show you"), the very words he uses in 21:9 when introducing "the bride, the wife of the Lamb." This is one of a number of factors that shows the intended contrast between the Babylon here and the New Jerusalem there.[8] The angel promises to show "the judgment of the great harlot" (τὸ κρίμα τῆς πόρνης τῆς μεγάλης [*to krima tēs pornēs tēs megalēs*]). Κρίμα (*Krima*, "Judgment") is a judicial verdict as well as the implementation of that verdict.[9] The future tenses of 17:14-17 give the verdict in the form of prediction, but the implementation of that verdict comes in chapter 18 which continues the angel's revelation of the great harlot (cf. 18:3, 8, 10, 20).[10]

The term πόρνης (*pornēs*, "harlot") applied to Babylon matches the practice of πορνεία (*porneia*, "fornication") attributed to her in 14:8.[11] It is indicative of her spiritual harlotry and representative of an ecclesiastical or religious facet that is a counterfeit of the real. In prophetic language, prostitution, fornication, or adultery is equivalent to idolatry or religious apostasy (Isa. 23:15-17; Jer. 2:20-31; 13:27; Ezek. 16:17-19; Hos. 2:5; Nah. 3:4).[12] The OT prophets charged Nineveh (Nah. 3:1, 4), Tyre (Isa. 23:15-17), and Babylon (Jer. 23:17) with harlotry. Even Jerusalem acted the part of a harlot through her spiritual whoredom and religious apostasy (Isa. 1:21; Jer. 3:8-9). With this background, it is beyond dispute that this woman of Rev. 17:1 is the epitome of spiritual fornication or idolatry.[13] She leads the world in the pursuit of false religion whether it be paganism or perverted revealed religion. She is the symbol for a system that reaches back to the tower of Babel (Gen. 10:9-10; 11:1-9) and extends into the future when it will peak under the

---

7. Isbon T. Beckwith, *The Apocalypse of John* (New York: Macmillan, 1919), p. 691.
8. Lee, "Revelation," 4:735; Wall, *Revelation*, p. 205.
9. J. Massyngberde Ford, *Revelation*, vol. 38 of AB (Garden City, N.Y.: Doubleday, 1975), p. 277; Homer Hailey, *Revelation, an Introduction and Commentary* (Grand Rapids: Baker, 1979), p. 342.
10. Düsterdieck, *Revelation*, p. 428; Lee, "Revelation," 4:735; R. H. Charles, *The Revelation of St. John*, ICC (New York: Scribner's Sons, 1920), 2:62.
11. Henry Barclay Swete, *The Apocalypse of St. John* (London: Macmillan, 1906), p. 213.
12. Ford, *Revelation*, p. 277; Wall, *Revelation*, p. 205; contra Thomas R. Edgar, "Babylon: Ecclesiastical, Political, or What?" *JETS* 25, no. 3 (September 1982): 336-38.
13. Johnson, "Revelation," 12:555; Hailey, *Revelation*, p. 343; Philip Edgcumbe Hughes, *The Book of Revelation* (Grand Rapids: Eerdmans, 1990), p. 182.

regime of the beast.[14] Since the angel never uses the term "adultery" (μοιχεία [*moicheia*])—a more restricted term implying a previous marital relationship—in connection with the woman, she need not be representative of apostate Israel or the apostate church.[15] *Pornēs* can include *moicheia*, because it is broader. So this woman represents all false religion of all time, including those who apostatize from the revealed religion of Christianity.

This harlot will be the object of future judgment—*pornēs* is an objective genitive following *krima*. Her religious corruption comes into view repeatedly in ἐπόρνευσαν (*eporneusan*) (v. 2), πορνείας (*porneias*) (v. 2), πορνείας (*porneias*) (v. 4), τῶν πορνῶν (*tōn pornōn*) (v. 5), πόρνη (*pornē*) (v. 15), and πόρνην (*pornēn*) (v. 16). Seven times this chapter uses words from this family that denote whoredom. The emphasis continues in chapters 18 and 19 too (18:3, twice; 18:9; 19:2). Her existence is a travesty of the worship of the true God.

The harlot's position as one "who sits beside many waters" (τῆς καθημένης ἐπὶ ὑδάτων πολλῶν [*tēs kathēmenēs epi hydatōn pollōn*]) raises the question of how she can sit "upon many waters" and upon the scarlet beast (17:3) at the same time. It is unnecessary to attribute this to the fluidity of apocalyptic language and John's inconsistency with himself.[16] In his vision, he saw the woman sitting beside the waters—ἐπί (*epi*) can mean "on the shore of" (cf. John 21:1) (Beckwith) —and upon the beast. In other words, he saw the woman sitting in both positions. The "many waters" represent "peoples and multitudes and nations and tongues," according to 17:15. These groups represent the world's population over whom she has control.[17] Verse 3 will picture her control over the beast who rules these people, a control that is of limited duration, however (cf. 17:16-17).

The "many waters" (ὑδάτων πολλῶν [*hydatōn pollōn*]) interestingly corresponds to Babylon's situation on the Euphrates, with its canals, irrigation trenches, dikes, and marshes surrounding the city and contributing to its protection and wealth.[18] Jeremiah addressed Babylon as "you who dwell beside many waters" (Jer. 51:13). This geograph-

---

14. J. A. Seiss, *The Apocalypse* (New York: Charles C. Cook, 1909), 3:114-15.
15. Lee, "Revelation," 4:735-36; Leon Morris, *The Revelation of St. John*, TNTC (Grand Rapids: Eerdmans, 1969), p. 204.
16. Contra George E. Ladd, *A Commentary on the Revelation of John* (Grand Rapids: Eerdmans, 1972), p. 223; Morris, *Revelation*, p. 205; Robert H. Mounce, *The Book of Revelation*, NICNT (Grand Rapids: Eerdmans, 1977), pp. 308-309; cf. Robert L. Thomas, *Revelation 1-7, An Exegetical Commentary* (Chicago: Moody, 1992), pp. 33-34.
17. John F. Walvoord, *The Revelation of Jesus Christ* (Chicago: Moody, 1966), p. 243.
18. Hailey, *Revelation*, pp. 342-43.

ical feature of the city doubtless came to John's mind as the angel spoke and provides a good metaphor for the city's preeminent position in world affairs, but his first meaning must be the one clarified in v. 15.

17:2 The harlot has committed fornication with all levels of society, from the kings of the earth to the rest of earth's inhabitants: μεθ' ἧς ἐπόρνευσαν οἱ βασιλεῖς τῆς γῆς, καὶ ἐμεθύσθησαν οἱ κατοικοῦντες τὴν γῆν ἐκ τοῦ οἴνου τῆς πορνείας αὐτῆς (*meth' hēs eporneusan hoi basileis tēs gēs, kai emethysthēsan hoi katoikountes tēn gēn ek tou oinou tēs porneias autēs*, "with whom the kings of the earth have committed fornication, and those who dwell in the earth have become drunk from the wine of her fornication"). The diction of this accusation against her reappears in 18:3, 9.[19] Religious prostitution occupies the forefront in this chapter and the closely related economic harlotry in chapter 18. The Babylonian system gains international influence and even domination in both realms through its cooperation with the beast in his political domination.[20] Religious compromise necessitated in this kind of association is totally incompatible with the worship of the one true God, and so amounts to spiritual prostitution.

The title for human rulers contrasted with the παντοκράτωρ (*pantokratōr*) is οἱ βασιλεῖς τῆς γῆς (*hoi basileis tēs gēs*, "the kings of the earth") (cf. 1:5; 6:15; 16:14; 17:18; 18:3, 9; 19:19; 21:24) (Swete). These leaders join the Babylonian system at the sacrifice of whatever spiritual principles are necessary. This has always been the case as with Assyria, Babylon, and others in the past. It was the case with Rome in John's day, and will be especially true in the final days just before Christ returns (Lenski, Ford). Pragmatic considerations will dictate cooperation with the powers that be in an atmosphere that is strongly anti-God and eventually boils down to worshiping the beast.[21] Included in this compromising alliance are now, but even more so in the future, the apostate church which has eagerly sought and solicited an adulterous relationship with world political powers (Walvoord).

The alliance thus forged by the leaders inevitably induces drunkenness in all earth's inhabitants. Since in 14:8 Babylon "made all nations drink," the peoples of the earth "have become drunk from the wine of her fornication" (ἐμεθύσθησαν . . . ἐκ τοῦ οἴνου τῆς πορνείας αὐτῆς [*emethysthēsan . . . ek tou oinou tēs porneias autēs*]). The designation οἱ κατοικοῦντες τὴν γῆν (*hoi katoikountes tēn gēn*, "those who dwell in the earth") differs slightly from the usual designation in this book, οἱ

---

19. Charles, *Revelation*, 2:63.
20. Swete, *Apocalypse*, p. 213.
21. Ladd, *Revelation*, p. 222.

κατοικοῦντες ἐπὶ τῆς γῆς (*hoi katoikountes epi tēs gēs*, "those who dwell upon the earth") (cf. 3:10, etc.). They appear to be the same people, however. Their "marriage" to the harlot is so binding that they marvel at the beast and have no place on the roster of the Lamb's Book of Life (17:8; cf. 13:14-18). Their allegiance to the false Christ is so strong that it intoxicates them and creates in them a lust to go after false gods.

17:3 After his initial speech, the angelic guide removed John to a different vantage point to give him a perspective of the harlot: καὶ ἀπήνεγκέν με εἰς ἔρημον ἐν πνεύματι (*kai apēnegken me eis erēmon en pneumati*, "and he carried me away into the wilderness in the spirit"). Very similar terminology describes John's prophetic trance in 21:10. This is the third of four uses of ἐν πνεύματι (*en pneumati*, "in the spirit"). In the other three, John finds himself on earth (1:10), in heaven (4:1), and on a mountain top (21:10). This time the angel takes him to a place of desolation, a solitary wasteland (εἰς ἔρημον [*eis erēmon*, "into the wilderness"]).

A wilderness was a place of refuge for the woman in 12:14, but this has no relationship to that wilderness. This wilderness alludes to Isaiah's "oracle concerning the wilderness" (Isa. 21:1) which includes the prophecy "fallen, fallen is Babylon" (cf. 14:8; 18:2; Jer. 51:8). This may refer to the desert outside of Babylon of the Euphrates as John's vantage point for his vision,[22] or it may anticipate the harlot's desolate condition in the end (17:16).[23]

From his new perspective, John saw a woman sitting on a scarlet beast: καὶ εἶδον γυναῖκα καθημένην ἐπὶ θηρίον κόκκινον, γέμον[τα] ὀνόματα βλασφημίας, ἔχων κεφαλὰς ἑπτὰ καὶ κέρατα δέκα (*kai eidon gynaika kathēmenēn epi thērion kokkinon, gemon[ta] onomata blasphēmias, echōn kephalas hepta kai kerata deka*, "and I saw a woman sitting upon a scarlet beast, full of names of blasphemy, having seven heads and ten horns"). Her position atop the beast is quite fitting to picture the influence of the religious power over the secular leader.[24] The scarlet beast is the same one who emerged out of the sea in 13:1. The earlier passage does not give his color, but it does note his seven heads and ten horns and names of blasphemy. The second and third angelic announcements in chapter 14 implied a close association of this beast with Babylon (14:8-11) in that the doom of Babylon entailed the doom of those who worship the beast. Here that relationship becomes explicit.

22. James Moffatt, "The Revelation of St. John the Divine," in *The Expositor's Greek Testament*, ed. W. Robertson Nicoll (Grand Rapids: Eerdmans, n.d.), 5:451; Archibald Thomas Robertson, *Word Pictures in the New Testament*, 6 vols. (Nashville: Broadman, 1933), 6:429.
23. Düsterdieck, *Revelation*, p. 429; Lee, "Revelation," 4:737.
24. Alford, *Greek Testament*, 4:706.

The beast is the empire, or more particularly, the ruler who perfectly embodies the spirit of the empire.[25] He controls the system politically, but the woman represents the false religion that gives spiritual cohesion to the system. Even though θηρίον (*thērion*, "beast") has no article here, Rev. 19:19-20 fully establish that this beast is the same as the one in 13:1 (Alford, Swete).

The beast's scarlet (κόκκινον [*kokkinon*]) color matches part of the woman's clothing (17:4) and is a possible ironic allusion to the symbolism of atonement or purification under the law (cf. Lev. 14:4, 6, 49, 51, 52; Num. 19:6) (Ford). Luxurious textile materials were often this color (18:12, 16; cf. Num. 4:8; 2 Sam. 1:24; Jer. 4:30). Scarlet blended with dark blue (ὑακίνθινον [*hyakinthinon*], Isa. 3:23, LXX) and red-blue (πορφύρα [*porphyra*], "purple," Ex. 39:1[39:13, LXX]; 2 Chron. 2:7[2:6, LXX]) (Swete). The color symbolized luxury and splendor, which are its apparent connotations here and in v. 4. They mockingly put a scarlet robe on Jesus just before His crucifixion (Matt. 27:28-29). But scarlet is also the color of sin (Isa. 1:18) and contrasts with the whiteness of righteousness and purity (Moffatt, Hailey). A little later a rider on a white horse will come with His armies all dressed in white (19:11, 14) (Johnson).

The names of blasphemy were on the seven heads in 13:1, but here they cover the beast's whole body. The masculine participle γέμοντα (*gemonto*, "full") understands the neuter noun θηρίον (*thērion*, "beast") to represent a person, an agreement according to sense rather than a grammatical one (Beckwith). Here is a secular power that blatantly and profusely profanes the name of the true God, but the ecclesiastical and religious authorities have no qualms about forging a close alliance with such a ruler and kingdom. This shows the depth to which apostasy can sink (Walvoord). In its ultimate form the blasphemous names on the beast refer to the self-deification of the false Christ and his demands that his subjects worship him (Ladd).

As tentatively suggested at 13:1, the seven heads of the beast are seven consecutive world empires throughout history, and the ten horns on the last of the heads are ten kingdoms contemporaneous with the final false Christ (17:12). The relationship between the harlot and the beast has existed throughout human history, but will reach its ultimate closeness in the days just before Christ returns. She controls him, but she also is dependent on him as the friction between the two later in chapter 17 will show (17:16).

17:4 The woman's clothing and adornment is elegant, but repulsive to the pious mind: καὶ ἡ γυνὴ ἦν περιβεβλημένη πορφυροῦν καὶ

---

25. Beasley-Murray, *Revelation*, pp. 252, 254, 255-56.

κόκκινον, καὶ κεχρυσωμένη χρυσίῳ καὶ λίθῳ τιμίῳ καὶ μαργαρίταις, ἔχουσα ποτήριον χρυσοῦν ἐν τῇ χειρὶ αὐτῆς γέμον βδελυγμάτων καὶ τὰ
ἀκάθαρτα τῆς πορνείας αὐτῆς (*kai hē gynē ēn peribeblēmenē porphyroun
kai kokkinon, kai kechrysōmenē chrysiō kai lithō timiō kai margaritais,
echousa potērion chrysoun en tē cheiri autēs gemon bdelygmatōn kai ta
akatharta tēs porneias autēs,* "and the woman was clothed with purple
and scarlet, and decked with gold and precious stones and pearls,
having a golden cup in her hand filled with abominations, even the
unclean things of her fornication"). A description of "the great city" in
18:16 resembles this one very closely (Charles).

"Purple and scarlet" (πορφυροῦν καὶ κόκκινον [*porphyroun kai kokkinon*]) are the two colors used to describe the robe they tauntingly
put on Christ. Because the two colors are so close to each other, one
gospel writer calls the robe scarlet (Matt. 27:28) and two others say it
was purple (Mark 15:17, 20; John 19:2, 5) (Alford, Swete, Lee, Charles).
Yet they were two distinct colors (cf. Ex. 26:1) (Swete). The Tyrian
purple dye was produced from two shellfish on the Phoenician coast
(Lee). Κόκκινον (*Kokkinon*, "Scarlet") is a word derived from the *coc-
cus* or *Kermas berry*, though the *Kermas* was a little worm instead of a
berry, from which the dye was made.[26] The former color denoted
royalty and the latter luxury and splendor as outlined above in connection with the color of the beast (v. 3).

The woman's adornment with gold stands out because of the expression combining two cognate words with the same idea (cf. Ex.
26:37, LXX). She was "decked (lit., made gold) with gold." She was
excessively bedizened with the richest ornaments. Precious stones and
pearls enhanced her attire even more. Her appearance was like the
greatest queen in order to impress and allure her paramours.[27] This
flashy adornment may have recalled to John the finery of the temple
prostitutes in Asia Minor, though prostitutes of all times and in all
places adopt this kind of appearance (cf. Jer. 4:30) (Alford, Swete,
Moffatt). This description is in sharp contrast to the appearance of the
bride of the Lamb whose apparel consists of "fine linen, bright and
clean" (19:8).[28]

The last part of the woman's paraphernalia is the golden cup in her
hand, which adds to her royal appearance but whose contents epito-

---

26. Lee, "Revelation," 4:738; G. Abbott-Smith, *A Manual Greek Lexicon of the
    New Testament* (Edinburgh: T. & T. Clark, 1950), p. 251.
27. Swete, *Apocalypse*, p. 216; Robertson, *Word Pictures*, 6:430; R. C. H. Lenski,
    The Interpretation of St. John's Revelation (Columbus, Ohio: Lutheran Book
    Concern, 1935), pp. 494-95.
28. J. P. M. Sweet, *Revelation* (Philadelphia: Westminster, Pelican, 1979),
    p. 254; Wall, *Revelation*, p. 206.

mize the depths of her degeneration. Jeremiah used a golden cup to picture the degrading influence Babylon on those around her (Jer. 51:7). From her perspective, the cup's contents represent her own glory and grandeur, but in reality they are her self-destruction as the consequences of her sins turn upon her (Hailey). God sees the true picture and calls them βδελυγμάτων καὶ τὰ ἀκάθαρτα τῆς πορνείας αὐτῆς (*bdelygmatōn kai ta akatharta tēs porneias autēs*, "abominations, even the unclean things of her fornication"). "Abominations" was a characteristic term for idols in the OT (Beasley-Murray), where it denotes ceremonial and moral impurity, but especially idolatrous rites (cf. Deut. 18:9; 29:17; 32:16; 1 Kings 14:24; 2 Kings 16:3; 21:2; 23:24; Ezek. 8:6, 9, 13, 15, 17; 11:18; 14:6; 16:2; 20:7, 8).[29] These are blasphemous activities that God detests, and the harlot's cup is full of them!

"The unclean things of her fornication" (τὰ ἀκάθαρτα τῆς πορνείας αὐτῆς [*ta akatharta tēs porneias autēs*]) further defines those abominations. The adjective ἀκάθαρτος (*akathartos*) in the NT has associations with idolatry (2 Cor. 6:17) and perhaps cult prostitution (Eph. 5:5) (Johnson). So the harlot thrives on spreading her filthy vices and corruptions by allowing earth's inhabitants to drink from her beautiful, but contaminated cup.

17:5 John also saw a label on the woman's forehead which divulged her identity: καὶ ἐπὶ τὸ μέτωπον αὐτῆς ὄνομα γεγραμμένον, μυστήριον, Βαβυλὼν ἡ μεγάλη, ἡ μήτηρ τῶν πορνῶν καὶ τῶν βδελυγμάτων τῆς γῆς (*kai epi to metōpon autēs onoma gegrammenon, mystērion, Babylōn hē megalē, hē mētēr tōn pornōn kai tōn bdelygmatōn tēs gēs*, "and upon her forehead [was] a name written, a mystery, 'Babylon the great, the mother of harlots and of the abominations of the earth'"). John does not tell whether the label was directly on the skin as with the mark of the beast (13:16-18) or the seal of the slaves of God (7:3; 9:4; 14:1) or was on a band such as the ones worn by Roman prostitutes (cf. Jer. 3:3) (Swete). Either way, the name written on her forehead was a mark of identification.

Some have used the first word of her name, μυστήριον (*mystērion*, "mystery"), to argue for a nonliteral understanding of the name "Babylon."[30] They compare the adverb πνευματικῶς (*pneumatikōs*, "spiritually") in 11:8 that the writer allegedly uses the same way and refer to the use of *mystērion* in 1:20 as a precedent. But *mystērion* used again in

---

29. Swete, *Apocalypse*, p. 216; E. W. Bullinger, *The Apocalypse or "The Day of the Lord"* (London: Eyre and Spottiswoode, n.d.), p. 501.

30. Moffatt, "Revelation," 5:452; Robertson, *Word Pictures*, 6:430; Martin Kiddle, *The Revelation of St. John*, HNTC (New York: Harper, 1940), p. 343; Johnson, "Revelation," 12:556.

v. 7 certainly does not furnish a license for allegorical interpretation, nor is its usage in 1:20 any ground for a spiritualized interpretation here. *Mystērion* is a noun, not an adverb like *pneumatikōs*, and it comes from a different root. The frequently cited arguments from the use of "Babylon" as a code word for Rome in the *Sibylline Oracles* and *2 Baruch* do not give adequate consideration to the second-century dating of these two books.[31] Apparently Tertullian late in the second century is the first church father to use "Babylon" as a name for Rome.[32] The "seven hills" mentioned in 17:9 and the reference to the great world-city in 17:18 and throughout the chapter also serve as proof that "Babylon" means Rome, but the "seven hills" can and probably does have a nonliteral meaning as the end of v. 9 shows. The woman sits upon seven kings or kingdoms, as subsequent discussion will explain. The rest of the alleged evidence for a Roman reference is too general to be decisive. The references to "many waters" in v. 1 and to the "wilderness" or "desert" in v. 3 are inapplicable to Rome, but fit quite well with Babylon on the Euphrates (Johnson).

Mystērion in the NT is usually a mystery to be revealed. So here the true character and identity of the woman, previously kept concealed, are now objects of clear revelation (Hailey). The word implies a new revelation, not something to be kept hidden. In this case it is the exposing of what is evil about Babylon (Lenski). Subsequent revelation will show her to be a great city (17:18), but also a vast system of idolatry through the centuries that the great city represents (Bullinger). The system had its beginning on the plains of Shinar through the work of Nimrod and will reach its pinnacle there just before the second advent (Bullinger, Seiss). Reports of Babylon's present utter desolation and impossible restoration[33] are radically overstated.

The other question about the syntactical role of *mystērion*, whether it is in apposition to ὄνομα (*onoma*, "name") or part of the inscription on the woman's head is resolvable through a comparison with 14:8 and 18:2. The woman's name is "Babylon the Great," not "Mystery Babylon the Great" (Smith, Walvoord). This along with the fact that *mystērion* seems to have a parenthetical independence here brings a decision favoring the appositional relationship.[34] This gives the sense, "a name written, which is a mystery" (Johnson).

"Babylon the great, the mother of harlots and of the abominations of the earth" (Βαβυλὼν ἡ μεγάλη, ἡ μήτηρ τῶν πορνῶν καὶ τῶν βδελυγ-

---

31. See discussion at 14:8.
32. *Adv. Marc.* iii. 13.
33. J. B. Smith, *A Revelation of Jesus Christ* (Scottdale, Pa.: Herald, 1961), p. 242.
34. Düsterdieck, *Revelation*, p. 431.

μάτων τῆς γῆς [Babylōn hē megalē, hē mētēr tōn pornōn kai tōn bdelygmatōn tēs gēs]) is the name that constitutes the mystery. Babylon is a theme in Scripture beginning in Gen. 10:9-10 with its first mention and continuing into these closing chapters of the last book of the Bible. It was a city where false religion began (Gen. 11:1-9) that has continually plagued Israel, the church, and the world (Walvoord). It will once again become the world's leading city religiously as well as commercially and politically as the end draws near. Her role as "the mother of harlots and of the abominations of the earth" makes her the progenitress of everything anti-Christian.[35] This includes all false religions, not just those that are Christian in name only, but also everything that is pagan and idolatrous under Satan's control (Seiss). The Genesis 11 passage tells where it all began, with the building of a tower that became a forerunner of the world's idolatrous practices throughout history (Seiss, Walvoord). So the metropolis that functions as headquarters for the beast's empire has a long reputation for its anti-God stance. It is a city, but it is also a vast religious system that stands for everything God does not tolerate.

17:6a The anti-Christian posture of the woman is visible in her treatment of the faithful: καὶ εἶδον τὴν γυναῖκα μεθύουσαν ἐκ τοῦ αἵματος τῶν ἁγίων καὶ ἐκ τοῦ αἵματος τῶν μαρτύρων Ἰησοῦ (kai eidon tēn gynaika methyousan ek tou haimatos tōn hagiōn kai ek tou haimatos tōn martyrōn Iēsou, "and I saw the woman drunken from the blood of the saints and from the blood of the witnesses of Jesus"). Not only does she entice others to intoxication through the enticements of her lust; she herself gets drunk from the blood of the saints and witnesses of Jesus (cf. 18:24).

"The saints" (τῶν ἁγίων [tōn hagiōn]) and "the witnesses of Jesus" (τῶν μαρτύρων Ἰησοῦ [tōn martyrōn Iēsou]) are two names for the same persons, the repetition of ἐκ τοῦ αἵματος (ek tou haimatos) being for emphasis, not to distinguish one from the other (Swete, Beckwith, Moffatt, Lenski). The designation "saints" indicates they have kept themselves pure, and "witnesses" shows they have faithfully preached the gospel about Jesus (Kiddle). Christians should do both, and this is why the woman is against them (Lee). This persecution and martyrdom of the faithful is a chief reason for God's indictment of the woman (Beckwith). It is not just what she promotes; it is also what she opposes that makes her an object of judgment. Among the ancients, being drunk with blood spoke of a lust for violence, vastness of slaughter, and their maddening effect on one who was inclined to initiate savag-

---

35. Alford, Greek Testament, 4:707; Walter Scott, Exposition of the Revelation of Jesus Christ (Swengel, Pa.: Bible Truth Depot, n.d.), p. 342.

ery (Beckwith, Charles). This was the reaction of the earth-dwellers over the deaths of the two witnesses in Jerusalem (11:10). The past has witnessed isolated examples of this degree of persecution, but nothing like what it will be in the future. The reign of the beast will create an environment in which the harlot will martyr saints and witnesses on a universal scale (cf. 13:7, 15) (Bullinger, Ladd).

The significance of the symbolism (17:6b-14). A few words of explanation from the angel will clarify matters more.

17:6b John's amazement at what he had seen provides a natural transition to his explanation: Καὶ ἐθαύμασα ἰδὼν αὐτὴν θαῦμα μέγα (*Kai ethaumasa idōn autēn thauma mega,* "And I marveled with great amazement, seeing her"). "Complete astonishment" is not too strong to express John's reaction to the sight of the woman on the beast. The cognate construction ἐθαύμασα . . . θαῦμα (*ethaumasa . . . thauma*) is literally, "I marveled a marvel." With the addition of μέγα (*mega*), an already emphatic statement attains greater strength.

The reason for his great amazement is unstated. It may have been the sight of such unrestrained wickedness in the true nature of the woman and God's permitting her to exist (Kiddle). It may have been his inability to grasp the symbolic meaning of what he saw.[36] It may have been the contrast between the splendidly attired woman and beast on the one hand and a city in ruins that he had expected to see (Swete, Ladd). It could have been some combination of these, but whatever it was, it was different from the marveling of the earth-dwellers over the beast in 13:3, because he was not about to become a follower of the beast.[37]

17:7 Seeing his astonishment, the angel asks him rhetorically the reason for his reaction, and then proceeds to explain the meaning of the symbols: καὶ εἶπέν μοι ὁ ἄγγελος, Διὰ τί ἐθαύμασας; ἐγὼ ἐρῶ σοι τὸ μυστήριον τῆς γυναικὸς καὶ τοῦ θηρίου τοῦ βαστάζοντος αὐτήν, τοῦ ἔχοντος τὰς ἑπτὰ κεφαλὰς καὶ τὰ δέκα κέρατα (*kai eipen moi ho angelos, Dia ti ethaumasas; egō erō soi to mystērion tēs gynaikos kai tou thēriou tou bastazontos autēn, tou echontos tas hepta kephalas kai ta deka kerata,* "and the angel said to me, 'Why do you marvel? I will tell you the mystery of the woman and of the beast which bears her, who has the seven heads and ten horns'"). He proceeds with an extensive explanation of the beast (vv. 8-17) and a less extensive one of the woman (v. 18).[38] What has been hidden will now be revealed about the two

---

36. Hughes, *Revelation*, p. 184.
37. Michael Wilcock, *The Message of Revelation*, The Bible Speaks Today, ed. John R. W. Stott (Downers Grove, Ill.: InterVarsity, 1975), p. 160.
38. Bullinger, *Apocalypse*, p. 514; Robertson, *Word Pictures*, 6:431.

(i.e., *mystērion*). They are one mystery not two because of the close relations between them (Lee). The fate of one is inextricably tied to that of the other. The revelation concerning the beast has several parts: the beast himself (v. 8), his heads (vv. 9-11), his horns (vv. 12-14), the waters (v. 15), and the horns again (vv. 16-17) (Moffatt). The change from καθημένην (*kathēmenēn*, "sitting") in v. 3 to βαστάζοντος (*bastazontos*, "which bears") in this verse is significant. The verb that here portrays the beast's relationship to the woman indicates that he supplies her motive force and purpose (Kiddle).

17:8 In explaining the beast, the angel uses several details from chapters 11 and 13 and adds new information: τὸ θηρίον ὃ εἶδες ἦν καὶ οὐκ ἔστιν, καὶ μέλλει ἀναβαίνειν ἐκ τῆς ἀβύσσου, καὶ εἰς ἀπώλειαν ὑπάγει*· καὶ θαυμασθήσονται οἱ κατοικοῦντες ἐπὶ τῆς γῆς, ὧν οὐ γέγραπται τὸ ὄνομα ἐπὶ τὸ βιβλίον τῆς ζωῆς ἀπὸ καταβολῆς κόσμου, βλεπόντων τὸ θηρίον ὅτι ἦν καὶ οὐκ ἔστιν καὶ παρέσται (*to thērion ho eides ēn kai ouk estin, kai mellei anabainein ek tēs abyssou, kai eis apōleian hypagei; kai thaumasthēsontai hoi katoikountes epi tēs gēs, hōn ou gegraptai to onoma epi to biblion tēs zōēs apo katabolēs kosmou, blepontōn to thērion hoti ēn kai ouk estin kai parestai*, "the beast whom you saw was and is not, and is about to ascend out of the abyss, and he departs into perdition; and those who dwell upon the earth will marvel, whose names are not written upon the book of life from the foundation of the world, seeing the beast, that he was and is not and will be present"). In each of his appearances in this book, the beast is either an empire or the ruler of that empire. Each head of the beast is a partial incarnation of satanic power that rules for a given period, so the beast can exist on earth without interruption in the form of seven consecutive kingdoms, but he can also be nonexistent at a given moment in the form of one of an empire's kings. The nonexistent beast in v. 8 must therefore be a temporarily absent king over the empire that will exist in the future (Moffatt, Kiddle).

The designation of the beast as the one who "was and is not, and is about to ascend out of the abyss" (ἦν καὶ οὐκ ἔστιν, καὶ μέλλει ἀναβαίνειν ἐκ τῆς ἀβύσσου [*ēn kai ouk estin, kai mellei anabainein ek tēs abyssou*]) ties him to the beast with the death-wound who was healed in 13:3, 12, 14. Both there and here the earth-dwellers express amazement (Johnson). The words "is not" refer to the beast's death, and his ascent from the abyss means he will come to life again (cf. 13:14). This is the same as his reappearance as an eighth king in 17:11.[39] His departure to perdition (εἰς ἀπώλειαν ὑπάγει [*eis apōleian hypagei*, "he

---

39. Lee, "Revelation," 4:741; Robertson, *Word Pictures*, 6:431.

departs into perdition"]) is his future assignment to the lake of fire (19:20) (Lenski).

An understanding of the past-present-future description of the beast requires the establishing of a point of reference for the designation. When is "now," the point of the beast's "not being"? One opinion is that it is the entirety of the present era, since the defeat of the beast by the Lamb at Calvary (Johnson). This views the point of John's writing in the last decade of the first century as a natural understanding of the "now" (Lee, Smith). It is a confusion of the beast with the dragon, however, if one takes 20:1-3 and the binding of Satan to be this "is-not" condition of the beast. Christ wounded the head of the serpent, not the beast, at Calvary. The beast cannot in any sense be in the abyss throughout this age so as to allow him to arise therefrom at the end of the age. In the form described in chapters 13 and 17, he had no existence before Calvary and will not exist until the future.

Another explanation for the "is-not" condition takes it as the recurring cycle of the waning of world conquests that are antagonistic to God.[40] Nazi Germany and the Soviet Union are examples from the past.[41] Yet this view coincides with an idealistic view of the Apocalypse and does not account for the details and events that connect this beast's activity with the return of Christ.

It is better to locate the "is-not" state of the beast entirely in the future and make that the point of reference for the total description. That state must coincide with the death wound of the beast in 13:3, 12, 14. This is his career midpoint, i.e., a time at the very beginning of chapter 13 when he comes up out of the sea (Bullinger, Smith, Ladd). This is most probably a point at the very middle of the seventieth week, between the beast's human and superhuman careers (Walvoord). Whenever it is, it must have a relationship to the period just before Christ's return in order to be relevant to the last of the seven last plagues to which this intercalation attaches. How the reference point for "is-not" can differ from that in 17:10 where the sixth kingdom that "is" dates during John's lifetime is a legitimate question to raise. The answer lies in a literary difference between the two passages. Verse 8 is a part of the chapter that is purely prophetic, but vv. 9-11 are an injected explanation to help in understanding the prophecy. All these considerations lead to the conclusion that the perspective of this description of the beast is entirely future, at a point just before the beast from the sea begins his three and a half year reign.

---

40. Hughes, *Revelation*, p. 184.
41. Mulholland, *Revelation*, p. 279.

The discussion at 13:1 identified the beast's future ascension from the abyss (μέλλει ἀναβαίνειν ἐκ τῆς ἀβύσσου [*mellei anabainein ek tēs abyssou*]) with his coming up from the sea. After his death he will come to life again.[42] When he does, he will come back in a demonic rather than a purely human form to establish his world domination (Beckwith). This explains why the abyss, the abode of demons (Luke 8:31; Rev. 9:1, 2, 11), is his origin. As concluded at 13:3, John had no knowledge of and hence could not use this terminology to refer to a Nero *redivivus* expectancy.

Even though ὑπάγει (*hypagei*) is a present indicative, it takes on a futuristic force because of the μέλλει (*mellei*) in the previous clause. Revelation 19:20 is the commentary on the beast's future departure to perdition (Lee). He will depart only after he has deceived everyone but the elect (Matt. 24:24; Mark 13:22) (Moffatt). His destiny will be the second death rather than eternal life, eternal separation from God rather than an everlasting fellowship with God.

The angel's continuing explanation of the beast picks up a theme from 13:3 and places it in the future instead of the past. The marveling over the beast in 13:3 was an aorist tense, ἐθαυμάσθη (*ethaumasthē*, "marveled"), but here the future θαυμασθήσονται (*thaumasthēsontai*, "will marvel") looks ahead of the beast's "is-not" condition to his coming resurrection. The earth-bound, God-rejecting earth-dwellers will be struck with an amazement of horrible surprise and admiration (Swete), not realizing that he will shortly be on his way to perdition (Morris). These are the very ones "whose names are not written upon the book of life from the foundation of the world" (ὧν οὐ γέγραπται τὸ ὄνομα ἐπὶ τὸ βιβλίον τῆς ζωῆς ἀπὸ καταβολῆς κόσμου [*hōn ou gegraptai to onoma epi to biblion tēs zōēs apo katabolēs kosmou*]). This reiterates the earlier exclusion of the earth-dwellers from that book of the Lamb (13:8). They cannot be in that book and still marvel at the beast.

The cause of their amazement comes in the causal participle βλεπόντων (*blepontōn*, "seeing" or "because they see") (cf. 13:3). Their knowledge of his miraculous recovery from his death-wound convince them of his invulnerability. The expression ἦν καὶ οὐκ ἔστιν καὶ παρέσται (*ēn kai ouk estin kai parestai*, "he was and is not and will be present") restates the past-present-future phenomenon from earlier in the verse in a slightly different form, with παρέσται (*parestai*, "will be present") replacing μέλλει ἀναβαίνειν (*mellei anabainein*, "about to ascend"). This makes the beast's description a parody on the name of God in 1:4 and several other times in Revelation, the name ὁ ὢν καὶ ὁ ἦν καὶ ὁ ἐρχόμενος (*ho ōn kai ho ēn kai ho erchomenos*, "the one who is

---

42. Robertson, *Word Pictures*, 6:431.

and who was and who is coming") (Charles). The change to *parestai* also reflects that the observers of this miracle of healing are unaware of the beast's origin—the abyss—and his destiny, perdition.

17:9 The angel continues with an invitation to John and others to listen carefully and think clearly: ὧδε ὁ νοῦς ὁ ἔχων σοφίαν (*hōde ho nous ho echōn sophian*, "here is the mind which has wisdom"). Verses 9-11 are not in the form of a vision. They are rather an explanation or exposition (Moffatt). This kind of clarification anticipates the difficulty and complexity of the vision of v. 8 (Kiddle, Walvoord). These words closely resemble the ὧδε ἡ σοφία ἐστίν· ὁ ἔχων νοῦν . . . (*hōde hē sophia estin; ho echōn noun . . .*) in the very difficult 13:18. Special spiritual wisdom is necessary to grasp the meaning.

The beast's seven heads receive first attention: αἱ ἑπτὰ κεφαλαὶ ἑπτὰ ὄρη εἰσίν, ὅπου ἡ γυνὴ κάθηται ἐπ᾽ αὐτῶν (*hai hepta kephalai hepta orē eisin, hopou hē gynē kathētai ep' autōn*, "the seven heads are seven mountains, on which the woman sits"). The seven mountains or hills on which the woman sits have been the subject of much debate. The view that the seven heads and mountains refer to seven literal emperors of ancient Rome[43] is too restricted. It limits the scope of the vision to Europe, the Roman Empire, and its Caesars, but its scope is worldwide (Lenski). Also, the seven hills belong to the beast, not the woman who sits upon the heads. Obviously the woman did not exercise controlling influence over seven successive emperors of that nation (Johnson). The view encounters further difficulty in that no matter which emperor is the starting point, counting to a total of seven leads to problems without satisfactory answers.[44] A discussion in the next verse of "five have fallen . . ." will furnish further details on this view's weakness.

A similar view that they are all kings, but not necessarily Roman kings (Bullinger) is weak because nothing in the passage points to a relevance of these miscellaneous kings to this passage and the beast. The view that finds a geographical significance in the seven hills relating them to Rome, the city of seven hills, has had a wide appeal. Seven hills were the nucleus of the city on the left bank of the river Tiber (Walvoord). Roman coinage and literature has made much of this feature of the city's topography (Alford, Swete, Hailey). An annual festival, *septimontium*, received its name because of this (Beasley-Murray). Hence, it is easy to see how the mention of seven hills could suggest Rome in the minds of John's readers (Mounce, Hailey). An

---

43. Beckwith, *Apocalypse*, pp. 699, 704-11.
44. G. V. Caird, *A Commentary on the Revelation of St. John the Divine*, HNTC (New York: Harper & Row, 1966), pp. 217-18.

apparent failure of this view, however, is its inability to show how an identification of geographical features of a city could call for the special theological and symbolic insight invited as a preface to this explanation (Lee, Johnson). Then, too, the fact that vv. 9-10 tell of the scope and nature of the beast's power forbids limitation to just one city that is geographically identified (Kiddle). Also, what connection is there between seven hills in Rome and seven Roman emperors in the next verse? (Ladd). The view is implausible because it gives the heads a double meaning, one geographical and the other political, but its most obvious flaw is its failure to maintain a distinction between the beast and the woman, "Babylon the Great." The seven heads connect with the secular anti-Christian power, not with the religious anti-Christian power (Alford, Johnson).

A preferable view of the seven heads and mountains is that they are seven successive empires, with the seven kings of v. 10 as heads and personifications of those empires (Seiss, Ladd). This view agrees with a common meaning of "mountain" or "hill" in the Bible (e.g., Pss. 30:7; 68:15-16; Isa. 2:2; 41:15; Jer. 51:25; Dan. 2:35; Hab. 3:6, 10; Zech. 4:7) (Lee, Bullinger, Seiss, Ladd, Johnson). This is sensible because the next phrase says the heads are also seven kings (v. 10). This double identification is probable especially in light of Daniel 7 where at one point Daniel identifies the four beast-kingdoms as four kings (v. 17) (Ladd). The principal weakness of this viewpoint is that it involves a double symbolism, a rare if not impossible hermeneutical principle.[45] Yet the view that identifies the seven hills with the city of Rome entails double symbolism of a different and an even more unusual type. This view gives the heads a geographical and political meaning, which is probably unprecedented. Giving the mountains the double meaning of kingdoms and kings is a much better choice. The call for special wisdom in v. 9*a* probably has in view the ability to grasp this double meaning of the mountains. Rome as one of the seven world empires is indirectly in view. It is probably the sixth empire, referred to as "one is," in v. 10, but the seven mountains or hills is not a reference to the city's topography.

The final clause of v. 9 ὅπου ἡ γυνὴ κάθηται ἐπ᾽ αὐτῶν (*hopou hē gynē kathētai ep' autōn*, "on which the woman sits") indicates once again that the woman is separate from the beast. Verse 3 places her on the beast, but this verse is more precise and places her on the beast's seven heads. She rides upon the seven empires, but is not one of them. She influences them, not by governing, but by imposing her false religious standards upon them (Seiss, Ladd, Lenski). Just as the woman

---

45. Düsterdieck, *Revelation*, pp. 433-34.

sits "on" or "beside" many waters that are symbolic (17:1, 15), so she sits "on" the seven mountains whose symbolism receives clarification in the next clause.

17:10 The first clause of v. 10 gives the second meaning of the seven heads and tells what the seven mountains symbolize: καὶ βασιλεῖς ἑπτά εἰσιν (*kai basileis hepta eisin*, "and they are seven kings"). The view that takes these "head-kings" as the thoughts, plans, and designs that usurp the holy thoughts of God understands the number seven as symbolic of a complete number of emperors with no exact historical reference.[46] This position raises unanswerable questions, however. For example, how can five of the seven have fallen if the number is symbolic? The assumption that numbers in the Apocalypse are symbolic is completely unwarranted. This type of analysis is vulnerable to all the weaknesses of the idealist approach to the book, already seen to be inadequate (Thomas, *Revelation 1-7*, pp. 31-32).

It has been popular to take the seven kings as literal kings or emperors of Rome (e.g., Beckwith, Sweet). The view is promising only until one tries to apply it to specific kings. Does one begin counting with Julius Caesar or with Caesar Augustus? The answer to this is purely arbitrary (Johnson, Sweet). Are all the emperors counted or just the ones that emphasized emperor worship? This, too, is arbitrary (Caird, Johnson). Are Galba, Otho, and Vitellius excluded because of the shortness of their reigns? If so, this is quite arbitrary (Kiddle, Johnson). For those who resort to counting emperors, the text is enigmatic beyond hope.[47] If John wrote Revelation during Nero's reign, the Roman emperors are too few. If he wrote it during Domitian's reign, they are too many (Johnson, Hailey). This method of identification cannot be the answer.

The best solution is that the seven kings represent seven literal Gentile kingdoms that follow one another in succession (Walvoord). In Dan. 7:17, 23 kings and kingdoms are interchangeable, showing that a king can stand for the kingdom ruled by that king (Swete, Lee). The seven kingdoms are the seven that dominate world scene throughout human history: Egypt (or Neo-Babylonia, Gen. 10:8-11), Assyria, Babylon, Persia, Greece, Rome, and the future kingdom of the beast (Seiss, Hailey).

The matching of this sequence with the rest of v. 10 provides confirmation of this conclusion: οἱ πέντε ἔπεσαν, ὁ εἷς ἐστιν, ὁ ἄλλος οὔπω

---

46. Alford, *Greek Testament*, 4:710-11; Lenski, *Revelation*, p. 505; Mulholland, *Revelation*, p. 280; Hughes, *Revelation*, pp. 185-86.
47. Kiddle, *Revelation*, p. 350; Wilcock, *Revelation*, p. 163; Charles H. Dyer, "The Identity of Babylon in Revelation 17-18," *BSac* 144, no. 576 (October-December 1987): 439.

ἦλθεν, καὶ ὅταν ἔλθῃ ὀλίγον αὐτὸν δεῖ μεῖναι (*hoi pente epesan, ho heis estin, ho allos oupō ēlthen, kai hotan elthē oligon auton dei meinai*, "five have fallen, one is, the other has not yet come, and when it comes, it is necessary for it to remain for a little [time]"). What appears in chapter 13 as though they existed simultaneously is actually a succession of kings or kingdoms, according to these words (Beckwith).

Trying to reconcile this five, one, and one to the symbolic number theory by simply saying this threefold division of the number seven is meaningless (Beckwith, Lenski, Mounce, Sweet) evades dealing with the exegetical data. This timeless-symbolic approach does hermeneutical injustice to the details of the text. A book of prophecy deserves precise interpretation when applied to history.[48]

Another attempt to explain the five, one, and one, the aligning of first-century Roman emperors with the number seven, has evidenced its lack of substance in the earlier discussion of v. 10.[49] The following is a sample attempt at this listing of Roman emperors of this period: the emperors are Tiberius, Caligula, Caludius, Nero, Galba, Otho, Vitellius, Vespasian, Titus, Domitian, Nerva, and Trajan. Dispensing with Galba, Otho, and Vitellius, who ruled only briefly, leaves Vespasian, who ruled from A.D. 69 to 79, as the sixth, and Titus (79-81) as the one still to come (Charles). This alignment contradicts either possible dating of the Apocalypse, and simply does not satisfy the data of the text.

The remaining solution sees the five which have fallen as five forms of Gentile world power which had already existed by the time John wrote this book: Egypt, Assyria, Babylon, Persia, and Greece. The "one which is" is the Roman empire which was in power at the time of writing (Walvoord). The "one which has not yet come" will be the future kingdom of the beast.[50] The five kingdoms of the past are the ones who have persecuted God's people (Egypt, Ezek. 29-30; Nineveh or Assyria, Nah. 3:1-19; Babylon, Isa. 21:9 and Jer. 50-51; Persia, Dan. 10:13 and 11:2; Greece, Dan. 11:3-4).[51] The persecutor of God's people during John's lifetime was Rome. Adding to the case for identifying these as kingdoms is the appropriateness of the verb ἔπεσαν (*epesan*) to speak of a kingdom's fall (e.g., Rev. 14:8; 18:2) (Alford). So the angel's clarifying word to John about the seven heads spans essentially the entire history of Gentile world empires.

---

48. Contra Beasley-Murray, *Revelation*, p. 257.
49. Cf. Robertson, *Word Pictures*, 6:432; Ladd, *Revelation*, pp. 228-29; Mounce, *Revelation*, p. 315.
50. Seiss, *Apocalypse*, 3:129-30; William Kelly, *Lectures on the Revelation* (London: H. Morrish, n.d.), pp. 364-68.
51. Alford, *Greek Testament*, 4:710; William Hendriksen, *More Than Conquerors* (Grand Rapids: Baker, 1944), pp. 60, 204.

The future leader and his empire will have a short life according to the words, ὅταν ἔλθῃ ὀλίγον αὐτὸν δεῖ μεῖναι (*hotan elthē oligon auton dei meinai*, "when it comes, it is necessary for it to remain for a little [time]"). The adjective ὀλίγον (*oligon*, "little") has the idea of brevity as it does in Rev. 12:12. This is a limitation of God's will (Lenski) and indicates among other things that its time will be shorter than the six previous empires (Seiss). This factor alone would eliminate the possibility of the seven kings being first-century Roman emperors.

17:11 In some mysterious way, the beast is one of the seven heads and is at the same time the eighth head: καὶ τὸ θηρίον ὃ ἦν καὶ οὐκ ἔστιν, καὶ αὐτὸς ὄγδοός ἐστιν καὶ ἐκ τῶν ἑπτά ἐστιν, καὶ εἰς ἀπώλειαν ὑπάγει (*kai to thērion ho ēn kai ouk estin, kai autos ogdoos estin kai ek tōn hepta estin, kai eis apōleian hypagei*, "and the beast which was and is not, even he himself is an eighth and is [one] of the seven, and he departs into perdition"). Chapter 13 has indicated the interchangeability of the beast with its wounded head (13:3, 12, 14). Sometimes it is the same as its heads and sometimes different from them (Ladd). In v. 11, it is one of the heads, the seventh and then the eighth.

Before exploring how he can be two heads in the sequence, one must establish whether the beast is the kingdom or the king. Discussion of the first part of v. 10 has shown the use of βασιλεῖς (*basileis*, "kings") to stand for "kingdoms," a sense that carries through the rest of v. 10. In v. 11, however, the kingdom correlation alone is unsatisfactory, because a kingdom cannot sustain a death-wound and be healed. That can happen only to the kingdom's representative king. So as one of the seven, the beast is a kingdom, but as an eighth, he is the king of that kingdom who sustains the wound and ascends from the abyss after his wound (cf. v. 8) (Lee). When this occurs, he is king over an eighth kingdom because his reign following his ascent from the abyss will be far more dynamic and dominant than before. This is the sense in which he is one of the seven, but also an eighth.

Identification of the eighth head as Domitian depends on the theory that John has the Nero *redivivus* legend in mind and that Domitian is the revived Nero.[52] As already seen, however, the theory is of doubtful validity. Other weaknesses of saying it was Domitian include the manner in which Nero died, which does not match the account of the beast's death (13:3, 12, 14), and the unlikely conclusion that the seven heads are emperors instead of kingdoms. Another theory says that the raised Nero himself is the eighth (Swete), but the Neronic identification of the beast is without merit, as earlier discussion has shown. The obscure suggestion that the heads represent plans and designs to over-

---

52. Robertson, *Word Pictures*, 6:433.

throw God (Lenski) misses the concrete nature of the heads, i.e., they represent kingdoms, not abstract ideas. It is clear that the eighth is an eighth king or world ruler, and not a distinctly different kingdom from the seventh head (Alford, Beckwith, Ladd). He is distinct from his predecessors in that he subsequently has received supernatural powers from Satan at his resuscitation. Yet he is also one of the seven, the seventh which has not yet come (v. 10), in that he takes the shape of an emperor in charge of an empire (Kiddle). Making the eighth a fusion of the raised beast and the empire over which he rules is the only way to meet all the criteria of this passage.

In another echo from v. 8, the words εἰς ἀπώλειαν ὑπάγει (*eis apōleian hypagei*, "he departs into perdition") remind the reader that this king does not "fall" like the kingdoms before him, but meets his destiny at the hands of the Lord Himself (Alford).

17:12 The angel guide next offers a few words of explanation about the beast's ten horns (vv. 12-14): καὶ τὰ δέκα κέρατα ἃ εἶδες δέκα βασιλεῖς εἰσιν, οἵτινες βασιλείαν οὔπω* ἔλαβον, ἀλλὰ ἐξουσίαν ὡς βασιλεῖς μίαν ὥραν λαμβάνουσιν μετὰ τοῦ θηρίου (*kai to deka kerata ha eides deka basileis eisin, hoitines basileian oupō elabon, alla exousian hōs basileis mian hōran lambanousin meta tou thēriou*, "and the ten horns which you saw are ten kings, who are such ones as have not yet received a kingdom, but they receive authority with the beast for one hour"). The seven heads are kingdoms, but the ten horns are kings without kingdoms at the time John wrote.

The suggestion that these are ten Parthian satraps who were to return with Nero to seize control of the Roman Empire does not fit, because the text says that they had not yet received a kingdom (Ladd). Their implied receipt of kingdoms subsequent to John's time locates them in the future when they will rule all the earth in submission to the false Christ (Beckwith). But this along with the assumption that the number ten is symbolic of the sum total of anti-Christian power (Lenski) is not as specific as it might be. A symbolic ten is usually justification for finding a reference to an indefinite number of Roman governors in John's day.[53] But a symbolic number is a suspect conclusion in a context where one of the numbers is a seven that is divided three ways. The number ten must be quantitative, not qualitative. The way this can work out is to interpret these as ten kings who with their kingdoms will join in a confederacy under the leadership of the beast in the final Gentile world empire. They will rule simultaneously with one another and with the beast.[54] According to Dan. 7:7, 24, these are

---

53. Moffatt, "Revelation," 5:454; David Chilton, *The Days of Vengeance* (Fort Worth, Tex.: Dominion, 1987), p. 437.
54. Bullinger, *Apocalypse*, pp. 545-48; Walvoord, *Revelation*, p. 255; Kelly, *Lectures*, pp. 368-76.

rulers who will receive their dominions in the last days (Beckwith, Smith). This is the form which the final world empire will take (Walvoord). As the angel speaks to John, they have no kingdoms (βασιλείαν οὔπω ἔλαβον [*basileian oupō elabon*, "(they) have not yet received a kingdom"]), but they will receive them in time to give them to the beast (v. 17) and to do battle with the Lamb at Armageddon (v. 14).

The "one hour" (μίαν ὥραν [*mian hōran*], an adverbial accusative of time) indicates a very short time (Beckwith), much shorter than the beast himself (cf. 13:5).[55] Some time after he begins his three and a half year superhuman reign, he will invest these kings with their power to rule, and will reign until their war with the Lamb at His return (17:14) (Walvoord).

17:13 The support of the ten kings for the beast is unanimous: οὗτοι μίαν γνώμην ἔχουσιν, καὶ τὴν δύναμιν καὶ ἐξουσίαν αὐτῶν τῷ θηρίῳ διδόασιν (*houtoi mian gnōmēn echousin, kai tēn dynamin kai exousian autōn tō thēriō didoasin*, "these have one purpose, and they give their power and authority to the beast"). This verse enlarges on the words "with the beast" of v. 12. Their unity of purpose here relates to warfare with the Lamb (v. 14) (Beckwith). They have the same unity regarding hatred toward and opposition to the harlot in v. 16 (Lee). The present tense of ἔχουσιν (*echousin*) anticipates the time in the future when they will receive their kingdoms (Alford). The word for "purpose" (γνώμη [*gnōmē*]) occurs at 1 Cor. 1:10 where Paul exhorts the Corinthian church to unity.

Their unity in giving their τὴν δύναμιν καὶ ἐξουσίαν (*tēn dynamin kai exousian*, "power and authority") to the beast is part of God's sovereign plan (17:17). The dragon had given power and authority to the beast (13:2), but in quite a different way these kings will do the same. Again, a present tense διδόασιν (*didoasin*, "they give") points to future when they will receive their kingdoms and therefore have power and authority to give.

17:14 The angel uses a brief digression to illustrate the enmity of the ten kings toward God and His people: οὗτοι μετὰ τοῦ ἀρνίου πολεμήσουσιν, καὶ τὸ ἀρνίον νικήσει αὐτούς, ὅτι κύριος κυρίων ἐστὶν καὶ βασιλεὺς βασιλέων, καὶ οἱ μετ' αὐτοῦ κλητοὶ καὶ ἐκλεκτοὶ καὶ πιστοί (*houtoi meta tou arniou polemēsousin, kai to arnion nikēsei autous, hoti kyrios kyriōn estin kai basileus basileōn, kai hoi met' autou klētoi kai eklektoi kai pistoi*, "these will make war with the Lamb, and the Lamb will overcome them, because He is Lord of lords and King of kings, and the called and elect and faithful who are with Him [will overcome them]"). The single-mindedness of the ten is ultimately anti-God in character (Kiddle, Beasley-Murray). In expressing their ani-

---

55. Robertson, *Word Pictures*, 6:433; Kiddle, *Revelation*, p. 352.

mosity against the Lamb, they will suffer a crushing defeat. This will be a great boost to the morale of the faithful in the midst of severe trials (Beckwith).

The conflict anticipated in this parenthetical statement is "the battle of the great day of God Almighty" (16:14). As supporters of the beast, they must wage war with the Lamb as He returns to earth. This is the same battle that 19:19-21 describes in its chronological setting in the prophecy (Alford, Kiddle). It is the occasion of the rout of the beast and his forces, so the ten kings must be among or else identical with "the kings of the earth" in 19:19 who go down in defeat with him. The future tense of νικήσει (nikēsei, "will overcome") predicts that future triumph by the Lamb.

The ὅτι (hoti, "because") clause assigns the reason for His triumph. He is κύριος κυρίων . . . καὶ βασιλεὺς βασιλέων (kyrios kyriōn . . . kai basileus basileōn, "Lord of lords and King of kings"), the sovereign over all others who rule in the earth. Paul applies the title ὁ βασιλεὺς τῶν βασιλευόντων καὶ κύριος τῶν κυριευόντων (ho basileus tōn basileuontōn kai kyrios tōn kyrieuontōn) to God the Father in 1 Tim. 6:15, but in Revelation the Son frequently has the same titles as the Father (Swete). The title "Lord of lords" occurs earliest in Deut. 10:17 as a title for God. Daniel 2:47 quotes Nebuchadnezzar as calling Daniel's God "a Lord of kings" (cf. Ps. 136:3; Rev. 1:5).[56] These two titles marking the Lamb as supreme over all earthly power recur in 19:16 where at His return to earth in triumph the name appears on the part of His cloak that covers His thigh.

He will not be alone in His triumph. "The called and elect and faithful who are with Him [will overcome them]" (οἱ μετ' αὐτοῦ κλητοὶ καὶ ἐκλεκτοὶ καὶ πιστοί [hoi met' autou klētoi kai eklektoi kai pistoi]) too. Contextual considerations imply the sense of νικήσουσιν (nikēsousin, "they will overcome") with this last clause of v. 14. Otherwise, the words have no relevance to the subject of the rest of the sentence.[57] Those described by the three adjectives must be the same as τὰ στρατεύματα [τὰ] ἐν τῷ οὐρανῷ (ta strateumata [ta] en tō ouranō, "the armies which are in heaven") that return with the triumphant warrior-king in 19:14 (cf. Jude 14) (Charles, Scott, Smith). This agrees with the promise

---

56. G. K. Beale ("The Origin of the Title 'King of Kings and Lord of Lords' in Revelation 17:14," NTS 31, no. 4 [October 1985]: 618-20) cites Dan. 4:37 in the LXX as the probable source of the combined titles. John's independence in his use of both the MT and the LXX raises the question of whether he would have dependend on a single verse as a source for so significant a title.

57. Düsterdieck, Revelation, p. 438; Alford, Greek Testament, 4:712; Charles, Revelation, 2:75; Beckwith, Apocalypse, pp. 701-2; Robertson, Word Pictures, 6:434.

to the overcomers in Thyatira, that the saints will share in this victory (Moffatt).

"Called," "elect," and "faithful" can apply only to saints, not to angels (Scott). Κλητοί (*Klētoi*, "Called") and ἐκλεκτοί (*eklektoi*, "elect") occur together in Matt. 22:14, where Jesus' statement is, "Many are called, but few are chosen." To be chosen by God is more than being called by Him. In order of time *klētoi* comes first, but in order of moral significance *eklektoi* precedes *klētoi* (Swete). Not all who are called are chosen, but all the chosen are first called (cf. 2 Pet. 1:10) (Alford). In Paul's writings, however, the call of God is always effectual. It amounts to an effectual call in this verse too, because "elect" applies to all the "called" in this triple designation. "Faithful" (Πιστοί [*Pistoi*]) indicates the fulfillment of the human response by this select group. The faithfulness of the saints climaxes the calling and election by God. It is their inevitable response to His initiative. Such a choice group will be fitting associates of the Lamb in His great victory.

The judgment of the great harlot (17:15-18). The angel now leaves his detailed discussion of the beast to tell how the harlot will meet her end.

17:15 In changing the subject slightly, the angel reverts to v. 1 to explain the meaning of "the waters": Καὶ λέγει μοι, Τὰ ὕδατα ἃ εἶδες, οὗ ἡ πόρνη κάθηται, λαοὶ καὶ ὄχλοι εἰσὶν καὶ ἔθνη καὶ γλῶσσαι (*Kai legei moi, Ta hydata ha eides, hou hē pornē kathētai, laoi kai ochloi eisin kai ethnē kai glōssai*, "And he says to me, 'The waters which you saw, where the harlot sits, are peoples and multitudes and nations and tongues'"). Usually "water" in Revelation means literal water. This is an exceptional case, occasioning a special explanation of the water's figurative meaning (Walvoord). In the OT, water is a common symbol for people (e.g., Pss. 18:4, 16; 124:4; Isa. 8:7; Jer. 47:2) (Lee, Beckwith).

The reference, of course, is to 17:1 which earlier mentioned the harlot's position atop the waters. She controls the lifestyle of the mixed populations of the world through their voluntary submission to her. The categories of humanity match those over whom the beast had authority in 13:7, except ὄχλοι (*ochloi*, "multitudes") replaces the more usual φυλαί (*phylai*, "tribes") in the comparable list of 11:9. Perhaps her widespread recruitment of victims as in Ezek. 16:15, 25, 31 influenced the change (Moffatt). Similar fourfold listings apply both to the faithful (cf. 5:9; 7:9) and to the rebels of earth (cf. 10:11; 11:9; 13:7; 14:6; 17:15) (Mounce).

17:16 Eventually it is against such a dominant religious system that the ten horns and the beast will suddenly turn: καὶ τὰ δέκα κέρατα ἃ εἶδες καὶ* τὸ θηρίον, οὗτοι μισήσουσιν τὴν πόρνην, καὶ ἠρημωμένην ποιήσουσιν αὐτὴν καὶ γυμνήν, καὶ τὰς σάρκας αὐτῆς φάγονται, καὶ αὐτὴν κατακαύσουσιν ἐν πυρί (*kai ta deka kerata ha eides kai to thērion, houtoi misēsousin tēn pornēn, kai ērēmōmenēn poiēsousin autēn kai gymnēn, kai tas sarkas autēs phagontai, kai autēn katakausousin en pyri*, "and the ten horns which you saw and the beast, these will hate the harlot, and will make her desolated and naked, and will devour her flesh, and will burn her up with fire"). False religion has used its hold on the beast to gain a greatness all her own, but suddenly the charm disappears and the attraction for the harlot turns to hatred toward her. Changes from love to bitter hatred are familiar enough in history (e.g. 2 Sam. 13:15) (Swete). In the end, Satan's kingdom will divide against itself, signaling that its demise is near (cf. Mark 3:23-26).[58] The future tense μισήσουσιν (*misēsousin*, "will hate") marks a return to pure prophecy by John's angelic revealer (cf. 14). The revelation goes beyond anything seen by John in the vision (Alford). The angel does not tell the immediate cause of the hatred, but the world-city Babylon will become the object of enmity to those whom she formerly controlled (cf. Ezek. 16:37; 23:22) (Lee).

The first act of hatred against Babylon will be a plundering of her wealth, the apparent meaning of ἠρημωμένην (*ērēmōmenēn*, "desolated"). Then they will make her "naked" (γυμνήν [*gymnēn*]), that is, expose her moral corruption to public view. This aspect of Babylon's description alludes to a similar fate predicted for Jerusalem in Ezek. 16:39-40; 23:25-27 (Kiddle). She will lose her rich adornment (17:4) and former spiritual power over her lovers (Alford). Following this, the ten horns and the beast "will devour her flesh" (τὰς σάρκας αὐτῆς φάγονται [*tas sarkas autēs phagontai*]). The figure recalls the eating of Jezebel's flesh by dogs (1 Kings 21:23-24; 2 Kings 9:30-37). This is what wild beasts do to corpses, and so it became a vivid way of describing the utter destruction of man by other men (cf. Ps. 27:2; Jer. 10:25; Mic. 3:3; Zeph. 3:3) (Beckwith). It expresses extreme vengeance with keen hostility (Alford).

The city's ultimate fate at the hands of her former lovers is to be burned up with fire (αὐτὴν κατακαύσουσιν ἐν πυρί [*autēn katakausousin en pyri*, "will burn her up with fire"]). The wording of this destiny comes from a legal formula condemning those who had committed detestable fornications (cf. Lev. 20:14; 21:9; Josh. 7:15, 25) (Alford, Swete). It speaks the utter destruction of a system of false religion that will have reached its peak in the days just before its destruction.

17:17 The sovereign purpose of God is behind this internal strife within the kingdom of evil: ὁ γὰρ θεὸς ἔδωκεν εἰς τὰς καρδίας αὐτῶν ποιῆσαι τὴν γνώμην αὐτοῦ, καὶ ποιῆσαι μίαν γνώμην καὶ δοῦναι τὴν βα-

---

58. Wilcock, *Revelation*, p. 165; Johnson, "Revelation," 12:562.

σιλείαν αὐτῶν τῷ θηρίῳ, ἄχρι τελεσθήσονται οἱ λόγοι τοῦ θεοῦ (*ho gar theos edōken eis tas kardias autōn poiēsai tēn gnōmēn autou, kai poiēsai mian gnōmēn kai dounai tēn basileian autōn tō thēriō, archri telesthēsontai hoi logoi tou theou*, "for God has put into their hearts to put into practice His purpose, and to put into practice one purpose and to give their kingdom to the beast, until the words of God will be fulfilled"). The immediate cause of the devastating friction among former allies is unknown, but the ultimate cause is known. God has put into the hearts and minds[59] of the ten kings and their leader to turn against the religious structure which they feel no longer serves a useful purpose for them. The words ἔδωκεν εἰς τὰς καρδίας αὐτῶν (*edōken eis tas kardias*, "has put into [their] hearts") follows a Hebrew idiom נתן אל-לבב (*ntn 'l-lbb*) (cf. Neh. 7:5; Jer. 32:40; Heb. 8:10) (Charles). His sovereign power is behind this breakup of anti-Christian power. Because of the future mold created by the predictions of v. 16, the aorist ἔδωκεν (*edōken*, "has put") is proleptic, adopting a perspective after the predicted events take place (Alford, Beckwith).

This is not the only time when God uses the forces of evil for His purposes of judgment. He used Babylon to judge Israel (Jer. 25:9-11). He also uses enemies to destroy themselves (cf. Judg. 7:22; 2 Chron. 20:23; 1 Sam. 14:20; Ezek. 38:21; Hag. 2:2; Zech. 14:14) (Mounce, Hailey). A divine overruling controls the fate of the world's political powers, so that at times Satan is an instrument in serving a providential purpose (Moffatt). A case in point is Rev. 16:13-14, 16 where he sends the spirits of demons to assemble a massive army to a battle scene where God wants them to be (Lee).

The same word for "purpose" (γνώμην [*gnōmēn*]) occurs in v. 13. There it is the entertainment of that purpose (ἔχουσιν [*echousin*, "they have"]), but here it is the execution of that purpose (ποιῆσαι [*poiēsai*, "to put into practice"]). The ten kings and the beast are unconscious that they are carrying out God's design.[60] They think they are fulfilling their own plans, but in reality they are blindly fulfilling the divine counsel (Lee, Bullinger).

The point on which God gives them the closest agreement with one another is in giving their kingdom to the beast (ποιῆσαι μίαν γνώμην καὶ δοῦναι τὴν βασιλείαν αὐτῶν τῷ θηρίῳ [*poiēsai mian gnōmēn kai dounai tēn basileian autōn tō thēriō*, "to put into practice one purpose and to give their kingdom to the beast"]). It is obviously sinful for these

---

59. In Hebrew and Greek, the heart (καρδία) is the seat of the mind and will (Sweet, *Revelation*, p. 262).
60. The antecedent of the pronoun αὐτοῦ is God, not the beast. Θηρίον is too far removed in the context to be the antecedent (Beckwith, *Apocalypse*, pp. 702-3; contra Düsterdieck, *Revelation*, p. 439).

kings to give their kingdom to the beast for the purpose of making war with the Lamb (vv. 13-14), so this creates a theological problem for the human mind. How can a God who is absolutely righteous in all His ways (Ps. 145:17) be a party to this sinful activity? The seeming contradiction of this verse to the character of God is irresolvable to finite minds.[61] In the outworking of His plan for this creation God allowed the existence of evil, but He is not in any sense the author of evil (James 1:13). He does not put it into the hearts of the kings to make war with the Lamb, but to give their kingdom to the beast. He now allows that evil to run its course in bringing this creation to its inevitable end as the kings decide on their own to make war with the Lamb.

This unity of mind in joining with the beast will continue "until the words of God will be fulfilled" (ἄχρι τελεσθήσονται οἱ λόγοι τοῦ θεοῦ [*archri telesthēsontai hoi logoi tou theou*]). "The words of God" pertain to more than just the overthrow of the city. They are all the prophecies of last events until the overthrow of the false Christ. This statement recalls the sweeping words of the angel in 10:7 regarding the fulfillment of the mystery of God (Lee). The prophecies will reach their goal as God permits wickedness to continue until the cup of iniquity overflows (Walvoord). God's will and God's words dictate that the kingdom of this world be under the control of the beast until the end of the age. Unification of evil will mark the very end according to the prophetic word.

17:18 After the sobering words about the decimation of the harlot and the divinely intentioned unity of the evil forces that destroy her, the angel states in simple terms the identity of the woman riding on the beast: καὶ ἡ γυνὴ ἣν εἶδες ἔστιν ἡ πόλις ἡ μεγάλη ἡ ἔχουσα βασιλείαν ἐπὶ τῶν βασιλέων τῆς γῆς (*kai hē gynē hēn eides estin hē polis hē megalē hē echousa basileian epi tōn basileōn tēs gēs*, "and the woman whom you saw is the great city which has a kingdom over the kings of the earth"). Some take this statement as the crowning evidence that John thinks the woman is Rome (e.g., Swete, Moffatt). Another opinion is that John thought this, but was wrong in his application of the prophecy to his own generation (Beasley-Murray). Neither of these is correct, however. John nowhere indicates a direct association of the harlot with Rome, not even in the widely cited v. 9 of this chapter. Besides this, the historical dissolution of the Roman Empire does not match the description of the city's destruction just given in vv. 16-17.[62]

It is better to see the woman to be the whole anti-Christian religious system of the future that will be bent on seducing the world's

61. Chilton, *Days of Vengeance*, pp. 441-42.
62. Wall, *Revelation*, p. 211.

population away from true religion (Walvoord). The many OT allusions to Babylon in Revelation 17-18 indicate her tie to a certain geographical city, yet her primary function is not political, but religious. She stands for an ideology associated with the political institution of the beast.[63] Of the many connections between Revelation 17-18 and OT passages on Babylon, the following are typical: Jer. 51:13 w/ Rev. 17:1; Jer. 51:7 w/ 17:2, 4; Jer. 51:29 w/ 17:16 and 18:8; Isa. 47:5, 7 w/ 17:17 and 18:7, 8; Jer. 51:8 [Isa. 21:9] and Isa. 13:21 w/ 18:2; Jer. 50:8 and 51:6, 45 w/ 18:4; Jer. 51:9 w/ 18:5; Jer. 50:15 and 51:24-49 w/ 18:6; Jer. 51:25 w/ 18:8; Jer. 51:63, 64 w/ 18:21. John's angel-guide quite clearly alludes repeatedly to Babylon on the Euphrates throughout chapters 17-18. So the woman will be a religious system connected with that city.

When the angel uses the present tense ἔστιν (*estin*, "is"), it is not from the perspective of John's own time, but of the time when the false Christ will have attained his ascendancy (Lee). "The great city" (ἡ πόλις ἡ μεγάλη [*hē polis hē megalē*]) is Babylon in its religious sense (Walvoord). Referral of this expression to Jerusalem[64] is flawed because Jerusalem never had a kingdom over all the kings of the earth. To refer the name "Babylon" to Jerusalem is unprecedented. Jerusalem cannot possibly fit the picture of this final Babylon (Seiss). Rome was a city with a kingdom over the kings of the earth,[65] but it was never the great city of commerce described in chapter 18 (Seiss). The suggestion that "the great city" is an ideal city without geographical location (Lenski) falls short of the text's requirement that this be a real city at a certain spot on the earth (Seiss).

The only viable identification remaining is the conclusion already reached; it is Babylon on the Euphrates. The OT prophecies of Babylon's destruction in Isaiah 13 and Jeremiah 51 are yet unfulfilled and are awaiting the future Day of the Lord for that fulfillment (Isa. 13:6) (Seiss). Furthermore, Babylon on the Euphrates has a location that fits this description politically, geographically, and in all the qualities of accessibility, commercial facilities, remoteness of interferences of church and state, and yet centrality in regard to the trade of the whole world (Seiss).

In the future day anticipated in the pages of this prophecy, this city will become the focal point for a religious system staunchly opposed to the truth of Christianity. The system will thrive for a time in gaining influence over the commercial and political entities of its time, until

---

63. Wilcock, *Revelation*, p. 165.
64. Chilton, *Days of Vengeance*, p. 442.
65. Robertson, *Word Pictures*, 6:435.

the beast and the ten kings determine that it no longer has a usefulness for their purposes. They will then dismantle it.

Additional Notes

17:2 The combination κατοικέω with an accusative direct object occurs in Acts 19:10, 17, but nowhere else in Revelation. The usual combination in this book is κατοικέω followed by the preposition ἐπί (3:10; 6:10; 8:13; 11:10; 12:14; 13:8; 17:8).

17:3 The verb γέμω almost always has the genitive case after it in the Apocalypse (4:6, 8; 5:8; 17:4, 7; 21:9) and in the rest of the NT (Matt. 23:27; Luke 11:39; Rom. 3:14), but here and in 17:4 (τὰ ἀκάθαρτα) the accusative follows the verb.

Some MSS, including Sinaiticus, read ἔχοντα rather than ἔχων to bring the participle into agreement with γέμοντα which it parallels. The nominative ἔχων has the support of Alexandrinus and others, however, and as the harder reading, appears to be the reading that best explains the origin of the others. This is another of the irregularities in syntax similar to the ones occurring at 2:20; 3:12; 9:14; 14:20.

17:4 The compound tense ἦν περιβεβλημένη is a periphrastic pluperfect, with the meaning "had been and thus still was clothed (with)."[66] A second perfect participle κεχρυσωμένη extends the periphrastic tense: "had been and thus still was gilded with gold."[67]

Λίθῳ and μαργαρίταις constitute a *zeugma* when used with the verb κεχρυσωμένη. A person can hardly be "made gold" with precious stones and pearls. Some verb such as κεκοσμημένη would be the normal one to use with these nouns. Λίθῳ is collective, standing for a group of stones as in 18:12, 16.[68]

It is possible that τὰ ἀκάθαρτα is part of a compound direct object of ἔχουσα and therefore parallel with ποτήριον, but the greater probability is that the καὶ immediately preceding it is ascensive and that "the unclean things" are a further definition of "abominations" (Charles, Lenski). Thus the accusative τὰ ἀκάθαρτα replaces the genitive βδελυγμάτων following γέμον, because the "abominations" are more abstract and "the unclean things" more concrete (Alford).

17:6 The genitive Ἰησοῦ is an objective genitive. They are those who witness about Jesus (cf. 2:13). They did so to the point of death (16:6; 18:24), and so became "martyrs" in the modern sense.[69]

17:8 Some read into the present infinitive ἀναβαίνειν that ascend-

---

66. Ibid., 6:429; Lenski, *Revelation*, p. 494.
67. Robertson, *Word Pictures*, 6:430.
68. Alford, *Greek Testament*, 4:707; Swete, *Apocalypse*, p. 216; Moffatt, "Revelation," 5:451; Robertson, *Word Pictures*, 6:430.
69. Robertson, *Word Pictures*, 6:431.

ing out of the abyss is an essential characteristic of the beast because of the durative force of the tense (Caird, Mounce, Johnson). This conclusion fails to account for the infinitive's use with μέλλει, however. The combination of the two is a periphrasis to express simple futurity. Instead of the indicative ὑπάγει which has the support of Alexandrinus, 2053, and other MSS, Sinaiticus and others read the infinitive ὑπάγειν. The indicative is the harder reading, because a copyist would have been more inclined to think of a second infinitive after μέλλει. This internal consideration along with its significant external support make ὑπάγει the preferred reading.

17:9 The two uses of εἰσίν, one in v. 9 and the other in v. 10, carry the sense of "represent" or "signify" as the same form does in 1:20 (Lee).

The ὅπου implies an ἐφ᾽ ὧν, which in combination with ἐπ᾽ αὐτῶν is the well-known Hebraistic redundancy (Alford). It is a pleonasm like ὅπου . . . ἐκεῖ in 12:6.[70]

17:11 Some take ἐκ in the sense of "a successor to the seven" (Alford) rather than taking it partitively, "one of the seven." Citing the former sense as typical Johannine usage (cf. John 15:19; 17:14; 1 John 3:12) (Lee) is only partially true, because John uses the preposition frequently in the partitive sense too (Thomas, pp. 410-11). The partitive sense is better in this verse (Beckwith).

17:12 Alexandrinus and a few Latin MSS read οὐ instead of οὔπω, resulting in the meaning that they had not received a kingdom because they had given it to the beast. External support for οὐ is so weak, however, that the reading does not merit serious attention.

17:15 The relative adverb οὗ refers to the waters as the location where the harlot sits. Another adverb ὅπου has the same function of telling where the woman sits in 17:9.[71]

17:16 The nouns κέρατα and θηρίον are nominative absolutes, since οὗτοι is the subject of μισήσουσιν. The pronoun οὗτοι is masculine with these two neuter nouns as its antecedent. Κέρατα and θηρίον represent persons, so this is agreement according to sense rather than strict grammatical agreement (Lee). The construction is a figure of speech sometimes called *syllepsis* acccording to which the pronoun agrees with its antecedent logically rather than grammatically (Bullinger).

The *Textus Receptus* reads ἐπί instead of καί before θηρίον, but the variant is lacking in MS support. It possibly arose when Erasmus compiled his Greek NT in the sixteenth century. The καί has the support of Sinaiticus, Alexandrinus, the Vulgate, and the Syriac, so it is

---

70. Ibid., 6:432.
71. Alford, *Greek Testament*, 4:712; Robertson, *Word Pictures*, 6:434.

obviously the original reading.[72] Both the ten horns and the beast combine in this action against the harlot (Walvoord).

17:17 The infinitive ποιῆσαι is epexegetic to define what it is that God has put into the hearts of the ten horns and the beast.[73]

c. Commercial Babylon Destroyed (18:1-24)

Translation

¹After these things I saw another angel coming down out of heaven, having great authority, and the earth was illuminated by his glory. ²And he cried out with a strong voice saying,
"Babylon the great has fallen, has fallen,
    and has become the habitation of demons
and a prison of every unclean spirit
    and a prison of every unclean bird
    and a prison of every unclean and hated beast,
³because of the wine of the anger of her fornication
    all the nations have drunk,
and the kings of the earth have committed fornication with
        her,
    and the merchants of the earth have become rich because
        of the power of her wantonness."
⁴And I heard another voice out of heaven saying,
"Come out of her, My people,
    that you not share with her sins,
and that you might not receive of her plagues.
⁵Because her sins have joined unto heaven,
    and God has remembered her unrighteous acts.
⁶Give back to her as even she has given back,
    and double the double things according to her works;
    in the cup which she has mixed, mix for her double;
⁷in as many things as she has glorified herself and become
        wanton,
    give so much torment and sorrow to her.
Because in her heart she says,
    'I sit a queen,
and am not a widow,
    and I will in no way see sorrow';
⁸on account of this in one day her plagues will come,
    death and sorrow and famine,

---

72. Zane C. Hodges and Arthur L. Farstad, *The Greek Testament according to the Majority Text* (Nashville: Thomas Nelson, 1982), p. 778.
73. Robertson, *Word Pictures*, 6:435.

and she shall be burned up with fire;
because the Lord God who judges her is strong."
⁹"And the kings of the earth who committed fornication with her and became wanton will cry and mourn over her, when they see the smoke of her burning, ¹⁰standing at a distance because of the fear of her torment, saying,
'Woe woe, the great city,
Babylon the strong city,
because in one hour your judgment has come.'
¹¹"And the merchants of the earth weep and grieve over her, because none buys their merchandise any longer, ¹²merchandise of gold and silver and precious stones and pearls and fine linen and purple and silk and scarlet, and all thyine wood and every vessel of ivory and every vessel of most precious wood and brass and iron and marble, ¹³and cinnamon and spice and incense and perfume and frankincense and wine and olive oil and fine flour and wheat and cattle and sheep, and of horses and chariots and slaves, even souls of men.
¹⁴'And your ripe autumn fruit of the lust of your soul
has departed from you,
and all the luxurious and splendid things
have perished from you,
and they will in no way find them any longer.'
¹⁵"The merchants of these things, who have become rich from her, will stand at a distance because of the fear of her torment, weeping and mourning, ¹⁶saying,
'Woe woe, the great city,
which was clothed in fine linen and purple and scarlet,
and adorned with gold and precious stones and pearls,
¹⁷because in one hour such wealth has become desolate.'
"And every helmsman and everyone who sails from place to place and the sailors and as many as work the sea stood at a distance. ¹⁸And they were crying out when they saw the smoke of her burning, saying, 'What [city] is like the great city?' ¹⁹And they threw dust on their heads and were crying out weeping and mourning, saying,
'Woe woe, the great city,
by which all who have ships in the sea
have become rich because of her treasures,
because in one hour she has become desolate.'
²⁰Make merry over her, heaven,
and saints, even apostles and prophets,
because God has judged your judgment on her."

²¹And a strong angel lifted a stone like a great millstone and threw it into the sea saying,
"Thus with a rush will be cast down
    Babylon the great city,
    and she will in no way be found any longer.
²²And the sound of harpists and musicians and flutists and
       trumpeters
    will in no way be heard in you any longer,
and no craftsman of any craft
    will in any way be found in you any longer,
and the sound of a mill
    will in no way be heard in you any longer,
²³and the light of a lamp
    will in no way shine in you any longer,
and the voice of the bridegroom and of the bride
    will in no way be heard in you any longer;
because your merchants were the great men of the earth,
    because by your sorcery all the nations have been
       deceived,
²⁴and in her was found the blood of the prophets and saints
    and all those slain upon the earth."

As John with his angel-guide turns to a new aspect of Babylon's decline and fall, he focuses on the departure of Babylon's economic prosperity (18:9-19), but also notes that her place on earth becomes a desolate waste and a haunt of demons and foul creatures (18:2) and that all signs of her social and domestic life vanish (18:21-23) (Beckwith). The main divisions of the discussion are three in number: a first angelic pronouncement of judgment on Babylon (18:1-3), prediction of a voice from heaven that Babylon will fall (18:4-20), and a second angelic pronouncement of judgment on Babylon (18:21-24).[74] A fourth division that comes in chapter 19 and will receive attention in the next chapter of this commentary deals with praise to God by voices in heaven over the fall of Babylon (19:1-8).[75]

First angelic pronouncement of judgment on Babylon (18:1-3). An angel different from the "last-plague" angel that began this lengthy

---

74. Richard Bauckham, "The Economnic Critique of Rome in Revelation 18," in *Images of Empire*, ed. Loveday Alexander (Sheffield, England: JSOT, 1991), pp. 48-49. The same material found in this essay is available in idem, *The Climax of Prophecy* (Edinburgh: T. & T. Clark, 1993), pp. 338-83.
75. Ibid.

excursus on Babylon (17:1) enters the picture to describe and dramatize the downfall of the city's great commercial system.

18:1 Μετὰ ταῦτα (*Meta tauta*, "After these things") in this instance indicates what came next in the sequence of visions John received: Μετὰ ταῦτα εἶδον ἄλλον ἄγγελον καταβαίνοντα ἐκ τοῦ οὐρανοῦ, ἔχοντα ἐξουσίαν μεγάλην, καὶ ἡ γῆ ἐφωτίσθη ἐκ τῆς δόξης αὐτοῦ (*Meta tauta eidon allon angelon katabainonta ek tou ouranou, echonta exousian megalēn, kai hē gē ephōtisthē ek tēs doxēs autou*, "After these things I saw another angel coming down out of heaven, having great authority, and the earth was illuminated by his glory"). Μετὰ ταῦτα (*Meta tauta*) in Revelation generally introduces something new (cf. 4:1, 2), denoting a new commencement and a new set of circumstances. The question is, how different from the Babylon of chapter 17 is the Babylon of chapter 18?

Undoubtedly the city is the same in both instances. Both have the name "Babylon the great" (17:5; 18:2). Both are guilty of fornication (17:1, 2, 4, 5, 16; 18:3) and of causing the kings of the earth and the earth-dwellers to imbibe of the wine (of the anger) of the city's fornication (17:2; 18:3). The destiny of both is to be burned with fire (17:16; 18:8, 9, 18) and to become an utter desolation (17:16; 18:17, 19). In both chapters Babylon is "the great city" (17:18; 18:10, 16, 18, 19, 21) and wears the apparel and adornment of a harlot (17:4; 18:16). Both are responsible for the martyrdom of the faithful (17:6; 18:20, 24 [cf. 19:2]).[76]

Yet a different aspect of the city is in view in chapter 18. The major guilt in chapter 17 stems from the city's abominations (βδελυγμάτων [*bdelygmatōn*], 17:4, 5), but in chapter 18 it is her sensuality associated with luxury (στρήνους [*strēnous*, "wantonness"], 18:3, cf. vv. 7, 9). Heavy interaction with the merchants of the earth (18:3, 11, 15, 23) and those connected with the sea (18:17) characterizes the Babylon of chapter 18, but is missing from chapter 17. Chapter 18 attributes to Babylon a distinctive attitude of arrogance that is missing from chapter 17 (18:7). The deep lamentation of uninvolved witnesses of her destruction in chapter 18 (18:9-11, 15-16, 19) contrasts strongly with the absence of such witnesses and lamentations at the destruction of Babylon in chapter 17 (17:16). The economic prosperity and luxury of the latter Babylon (18:11-14, 19) is a marked difference from anything said about the earlier Babylon.

The distinction between the two chapters is that between two systems or networks that have the same geographical headquarters. In

---

76. Edgar, "Babylon," 333-35.

chapter 17 it is a religious system that operates independently of and in opposition to the true God, but in chapter 18 it is an economic system that does the same. The collapse of the city leaves an unspeakably large void in both areas. The two chapters tell how two aspects of the city's function will come to a dramatic end and how this will affect other world entities at the time. Whether they will fall simultaneously or consecutively is yet to be determined, but they both will mark the internal deterioration of the beast's empire prior to the defeat of his political structure by the returning warrior-king (19:11-21).

The angel who pronounces judgment on Babylon is different from the one who served as John's guide (17:1, 7, 15). His function is to announce Babylon's doom in conjunction with the vision granted through the agency of the earlier guide, one of the angels with the seven bowls. This new angelic agent resembles those who descend from heaven to fulfil special missions in 10:1 and 20:1. His resemblance to the angel in 10:1 is especially close.[77] This has provoked discussion of the same issue that arose in 10:1, whether the angel is Christ or not.

For those who identify this angel as Christ, the glory of his presence—ἡ γῆ ἐφωτίσθη ἐκ τῆς δόξης αὐτοῦ (*hē gē ephōtisthē ek tēs doxēs autou*, "the earth was illuminated by his glory")—that brings illumination to the earth serves as proof of who the angel is.[78] This theory also cites his "great authority" (ἐξουσίαν μεγάλην [*exousian megalēn*]) and heavenly origin (καταβαίνοντα ἐκ τοῦ οὐρανοῦ [*katabainonta ek tou ouranou*, "coming down out of heaven"]) as proof.[79] Yet it is demeaning to the deity of Christ to speak of Him as ἄλλον ἄγγελον (*allon angelon*, "another angel"), especially when the angel most recently mentioned was a mere creature (17:1) (Smith). This angel carries the same basic message as the "second angel" in 14:8 and so is not any more the same as Christ than that one (Mounce). The adjective ἄλλον (*allon*, "another") probably means that this is another of the same kind as the angel-guide of chapter 17,[80] conceivably it could refer back to the last angel who descended from heaven in 10:1 (Alford). Contextual distance makes the latter less probable.

The angel has ἐξουσίαν μεγάλην (*exousian megalēn*, "great authority") which some have related to his role as executor of the judgment he is to announce (e.g., Swete). Since the subsequent description has no hint of his administering that judgment, the authority more probably

77. Swete, *Apocalypse*, p. 226; Robertson, *Word Pictures*, 6:436; Kiddle, *Revelation*, p. 360.
78. Mulholland, *Revelation*, p. 284.
79. Ibid.; Chilton, *Days of Vengeance*, pp. 445-46.
80. Düsterdieck, *Revelation*, p. 442; Beckwith, *Apocalypse*, p. 712.

has to do with his capability of making himself heard through his ἰσχυρᾷ φωνῇ (ischyrą phōnę, "strong voice") (v. 2; cf. 5:2; 10:1). This voice of great authority is necessary to break the spell of Babylon and her allurements.[81] The use of ἐξουσία (exousia) in 9:3, 10, 19 illustrates angelic authority used in the opposite way (Beckwith, Mounce).

The angel's impact on the earth was not minimal, but ἡ γῆ ἐφωτίσθη ἐκ τῆς δόξης αὐτοῦ (hē gē ephōtisthē ek tēs doxēs autou, "the earth was illuminated by his glory"). Having come so recently from the heavenly presence, he reflects a broad belt of light over a darkened earth (Swete), very similar to the countenance of Moses after he had been in God's presence (Ex. 34:29-35) (Mounce). The verb φωτίζω (phōtizō, "I illuminate") also occurs in 21:23 and 22:5 to depict the light-giving impact of the glory of God's presence in the new Jerusalem. The news of the coming pronouncement is so extraordinary that an angel with resplendent glory is the one to convey it. His impact on the earth is so great that it is comparable to the return of the divine glory to the restored temple (Ezek. 43:2; cf. 11:23) (Kiddle, Johnson).

18:2 The "strong voice" (ἰσχυρᾷ φωνῇ [ischyrą phōnę]) of this angel recalls the "great voices" of the angels that made the dramatic announcements just before and just after the pronouncement of Babylon's fall in 14:8: καὶ ἔκραξεν ἐν ἰσχυρᾷ φωνῇ λέγων, Ἔπεσεν, ἔπεσεν Βαβυλὼν ἡ μεγάλη, καὶ ἐγένετο κατοικητήριον δαιμονίων καὶ φυλακὴ παντὸς πνεύματος ἀκαθάρτου καὶ φυλακὴ παντὸς ὀρνέου ἀκαθάρτου [καὶ φυλακὴ παντὸς θηρίου ἀκαθάρτου]* καὶ μεμισημένου (kai ekraxen en ischyrą phōnę legōn, Epesen, epesen Babylōn hē megalē, kai egeneto katoikētērion daimoniōn kai phylakē pantos pneumatos akathartou kai phylakē pantos orneou akathartou [kai phylakē pantos thēriou akathartou] kai memisēmenou, "and he cried out with a strong voice saying, 'Babylon the great has fallen, has fallen, and has become the habitation of demons and a prison of every unclean spirit and a prison of every unclean bird and a prison of every unclean and hated beast'"). The strength of the angel's voice makes it impossible for anyone to ignore what he has to say (Kiddle).

The participle λέγων (legōn, "saying") introduces the substance of the angel's cry. It is the first of a series of voices that draw heavily from OT descriptions of Babylon (Isa. 13:21; 34:14; 47:7-9; Jer. 50-51), Tyre (Ezek. 26-28), and Nineveh (Nah. 3; Zeph. 2:15). The chapter combines a song of triumph (18:20) with the wailing strains of lamentation (Moffatt, Johnson). The prelude (vv. 1-3) and finale (vv. 21-24) of the chapter tell two fundamental reasons for God's judgment of the city: political self-interest and materialism (18:3, 23).[82]

---

81. Wilcock, *Revelation*, p. 166.
82. Wall, *Revelation*, p. 213.

This pronouncement begins with words identical with the announcement of 14:8, ἔπεσεν, ἔπεσεν Βαβυλὼν ἡ μεγάλη (*epesen, epesen Babylōn hē megalē*, "Babylon the great has fallen, has fallen"). Both passages hark back to Isa. 21:9 and perhaps Jer. 51:8. Prophetic (or proleptic) aorists of πίπτω (*piptō*, "I fall") express the certainty of the future fall and are part of this solemn dirge over the condemned city. Throughout this chapter John varies his tenses from present to future to preterit, a symptom of his journeys from the visionary future to the present and back again. The present statement of Babylon's fall is a picture of established ruin. As he has described God only through the hymns of worship up to this point, he now pictures the fall of Babylon only through the laments of heavenly and earthly onlookers.[83] He does not see the act of destruction itself, because it is still impending at the end of the chapter (vv. 21-24) as it is through the central body of the chapter (vv. 9-20).[84] These words are a reminiscence of the judgment pronounced against ancient Babylon (Isa. 13:19-22; 14:11; 47:1-15; Jer. 50:39; 51:1-58). Ancient Babylon fell in 539 B.C., but this was not the ultimate fulfillment of OT prophecies. For John this awaited a future consummation at the end of world history.[85]

A question similar to the one faced in discussing 14:8 is how literally "Babylon" should be understood. One proposal has been to avoid taking it as a literal city and to understand this chapter to speak of God's judgment of the great satanic system of evil that has corrupted the world's history (Johnson). In other words, Babylon is the world-city throughout all time (Lee). Though the characteristics of this city display problems of materialism recurring throughout history, as this view notes, the destruction foretold in this chapter lies in John's future and so cannot speak directly of just any city of this type (Bullinger). A comparison of 18:16 with 17:4 shows that this is Babylon of the last times (Lee).

Until the present, Babylon has never undergone the destruction prophesied for her in the OT (Isa. 47:11; 51:8). The present devastation of the region is the result of slow decay, not of sudden destruction.[86] In fact, the site of Babylon of old has been the location of a city of one type or another until very recent times.[87] The sea-traffic of the city,

---

83. Swete, *Apocalypse*, pp. 226-27; Lee, "Revelation," 4:766; Beckwith, *Apocalypse*, p. 712; Robertson, *Word Pictures*, 6:436; Kiddle, *Revelation*, p. 361; Caird, *Revelation*, p. 227; Mounce, *Revelation*, p. 323; Sweet, *Revelation*, p. 267.
84. Düsterdieck, *Revelation*, p. 441; Alford, *Greek Testament*, 4:714.
85. Kiddle, *Revelation*, pp. 359-60; Wilcock, *Revelation*, p. 168.
86. Bullinger, *Apocalypse*, p. 553.
87. B. W. Newton, *Babylon: Its Future History and Doom* (London: Wertheimer, Lea and Company, 1890), pp. 31-41; Charles H. Dyer, *The Rise of Babylon: Sign of the End Times* (Wheaton: Tyndale House, 1991), pp. 25-27;

indicated in 18:17, suits this location since the Euphrates in ancient times was navigable for ships for some five hundred miles from its mouth (Bullinger). The prophecy thus indicates that before the advent of the warrior-king in 19:11-16, Babylon will rise to its greatest heights, not only of idolatry (chap. 17), but also of luxury (chap. 18).[88] John's allusions in chapter 18 to OT passages dealing with other cities such as Tyre and Jerusalem is not a convincing argument against limiting this chapter to Babylon of the future, because John in his use of the OT freely adapts it to his own purposes without regard for the meaning of passages in their original setting. Babylon of the future, therefore, will be the center for both false religion and world economic prosperity.

Evidence of the city's fall is its transition into "the habitation of demons" (κατοικητήριον δαιμονίων [*katoikētērion daimoniōn*]). To become a den of demons is to have the desert return to stake an irrevocable claim on its own, in other words, to utterly vanish (Caird). Demons or fallen angels come into view at Rev. 9:20 and 16:14 in connection with the practice of idolatry. This connection probably came to John's mind as the angel made his pronouncement (Swete, Kiddle, Johnson, Sweet). Isaiah and Jeremiah prophesied this kind of desolation for Babylon (Isa. 13:21-22; 34:11-17; Jer. 51:37). Jeremiah and Zephaniah did the same regarding the city of Nineveh (Jer. 50:39; Zeph. 2:14-15). The LXX of Isa. 13:21 uses δαιμόνια (*daimonia*, "demons") in place of the "satyrs" or "shaggy goats" at the end of the verse.

A further indication of desolation is the site's function as φυλακὴ παντὸς πνεύματος ἀκαθάρτου (*phylakē pantos pneumatos akathartou*, "a prison of every unclean spirit"). Unclean spirits are, of course, synonymous with demons, as indicated by 16:13-14, but the notion of φυλακή (*phylakē*, "prison") adds the implication of their being in the place involuntarily. Some want to assign *phylakē* the meaning of "garrison" or "watch-tower" instead of "prison," because they question the appropriateness of the latter for the birds listed later.[89] Yet the idea of a watching place for the unclean spirits seems inappropriate too. A probable meaning is that *phylakē* refers to a place where the unclean spirits and birds are kept safe (Beckwith), with the added implication that they are there against their wills.[90]

---

idem, "The Biblical Argument for the Rebuilding of Babylon" (unpublished paper presented to Pre-Tribulation Study Group, Dallas, Tex.; December 15, 1993), pp. 5-18.

88. Walvoord, *Revelation*, p. 263; Bullinger, *Apocalypse*, p. 560; contra Walvoord, *Revelation*, p. 257.

89. Swete, *Apocalypse*, p. 227; Beckwith, *Apocalypse*, pp. 712-13; Robertson, *Word Pictures*, 6:436.

90. Düsterdieck, *Revelation*, p. 442.

The expression φυλακὴ παντὸς ὀρνέου ἀκαθάρτου (*phylakē pantos orneou akathartou*, "a prison of every unclean bird") is another symbol for desolation (cf. Isa. 34:11). In Jer. 50:39, it refers to the desolation of Babylon, and in Zeph. 2:13-14, to that of Nineveh (Lee). Isaiah 34:11*a*, 13*b* mention the pelican or hawk, the owl, the raven, and the ostrich, together with unclean animals, the jackals. Jeremiah 50:39 mentions ostriches with unclean animals, the hyenas. Most of the species listed are scavengers (Ford). The evil spirits hover over the fallen city like night-birds waiting for their prey. The former thriving metropolis has become a wilderness (Swete, Johnson). The closing expression of v. 2 adds "every unclean and hated beast" (παντὸς ὀρνέου ἀκαθάρτου καὶ μεμισημένου [*pantos thēriou akathartou kai memisēmenou*]) to the creatures imprisoned in what used to be Babylon. These are mentioned along with the unclean birds in the OT passages cited earlier in this paragraph. This completes the forecast of the city's utter desolation after its predicted fall.

18:3 The conjunction ὅτι (*hoti*, "because") focuses on the cause of the city's fall: her prostitution with the kings of the earth and luxurious immorality with the merchants of the earth: ὅτι ἐκ τοῦ οἴνου τοῦ θυμοῦ τῆς πορνείας* αὐτῆς πέπωκαν* πάντα τὰ ἔθνη, καὶ οἱ βασιλεῖς τῆς γῆς μετ᾽ αὐτῆς ἐπόρνευσαν, καὶ οἱ ἔμποροι τῆς γῆς ἐκ τῆς δυνάμεως τοῦ στρήνους αὐτῆς ἐπλούτησαν (*hoti ek tou oinou tou thymou tēs porneias autēs pepōkan panta ta ethnē, kai hoi basileis tēs gēs met' autēs eporneusan, kai hoi emporoi tēs gēs ek tēs dynameōs tou strēnous autēs eploutēsan,* "because of the wine of the anger of her fornication all the nations have drunk, and the kings of the earth have committed fornication with her, and the merchants of the earth have become rich because of the power of her wantonness"). The phrase ἐκ τοῦ οἴνου τοῦ θυμοῦ τῆς πορνείας (*ek tou oinou tou thymou tēs porneias*, "of the wine of the anger of her fornication") indicates the source from which the kings have drunk. Surprisingly, "the wine of her fornication" in 17:2 has become divine anger toward herself through the inclusion of τοῦ θυμοῦ (*tou thymou*, "of the anger") to the earlier expression (Alford). The passionate luxury and materialism of the great city have intoxicated all the nations.

The three groups πάντα τὰ ἔθνη . . . οἱ βασιλεῖς τῆς γῆς . . . οἱ ἔμποροι (*panta ta ethnē . . . hoi basileis tēs gēs . . . hoi emporoi tēs gēs,* "all the nations . . . the kings of the earth . . . the merchants of the earth") encompass the entire gamut of the world's population. Everyone has united in an ungodly union with the great city, so mankind is universally morally bankrupt and God has chosen this time to act (Kiddle). The words τῆς γῆς (*tēs gēs*, "of the earth") with the last two groupings denotes the mass of mankind as it does so often in this book (Lee). The merchants will suffer more than the kings with the fall of the city, because the kings will have their political power left. They have only lost a partner in fornication, but the merchants will have lost everything. Commerce and trade is the major subject of the remainder of the chapter. The NT has frequent references to trade (Matt. 13:45; 22:5; 25:14; James 4:13), but none comes near portraying the vast world traffic of this chapter (Swete).

The fornication of all the nations (πορνείας [*porneias*]) and of the kings (ἐπόρνευσαν [*eporneusan*]) is of the nature set forth in the final clause of the verse. The city has promoted herself by instilling an unquestioning faith in her supposedly inexhaustible resources, thereby discouraging any sense of a deeper need for God (Caird). The word for merchants, ἔμποροι (*emporoi*), comes from combining ἐν (*en*, "in") and πόρος (*poros*, "journey"). A merchant is one on a journey to conduct business. The word occurs only here, in 18:11, 15, 23, and in Matt. 13:45 in the NT.

The shade of meaning of δυνάμεως (*dynameōs*, "power") implies that the luxury of Babylon is actual power that has worked to enrich the traders (Beckwith). Other suggested meanings in this context for the term are "quantity" (Alford) and "wealth" (Charles). That power, quantity, or wealth receives closer definition in τοῦ στρήνους (*tou strēnous*, "wantonness"). The noun appears in the NT only here, but the cognate verb στρηνιάω (*strēniaō*) is in 18:7, 9. The idea of the term is that of insolent luxury, self-indulgence with accompanying arrogance and vicious exercise of strength, exuberance of strength which is the flower of pride, or the impudence of wealth, wantonness, and unruliness arising from the fullness of bread (cf. 1 Tim. 5:11; Deut. 32:15). Στρῆνος (*Strēnos*, "Wantonness") is closer to ὕβρις (*hybris*, "outrage") than it is to lewdness.[91] The connection of fornication and luxury in this verse indicates that Babylon's fornication consists not only of idolatry, but also includes her pride in excessive wealth (Johnson). False religion often has gone hand in hand with the accumulation and abusive use of luxury.

Prediction of a voice from heaven that Babylon will fall (18:4-20). This extended prediction is in three parts: a call for God's people to come out of Babylon (vv. 4-8), laments by the kings of the earth, the

---

91. Alford, *Greek Testament*, 4:715; Swete, *Apocalypse*, p. 228; Richard Chenevix Trench, *Synonyms of the New Testament* (Grand Rapids: Eerdmans, 1953), pp. 200-201; Beckwith, *Apocalypse*, p. 713; Robertson, *Word Pictures*, 6:437; Wall, *Revelation*, p. 214; Christopher R. Smith, "Reclaiming the Social Justice Message of Revelation: Materialism, Imperialism and Divine Judgment in Revelation 18," *Transformation* 7, no. 4 (October/December 1990): 29.

merchants, and the sea people (vv. 9-19), and a note of heavenly rejoicing (v. 20).

18:4 After an introduction in v. 4*a*, the call for God's people to exit the city follows in v. 4*b*: Καὶ ἤκουσα ἄλλην φωνὴν ἐκ τοῦ οὐρανοῦ λέγουσαν, 'Εξέλθατε, ὁ λαός μου, ἐξ αὐτῆς, ἵνα μὴ συγκοινωνήσητε ταῖς ἁμαρτίαις αὐτῆς, καὶ ἐκ τῶν πληγῶν αὐτῆς ἵνα μὴ λάβητε (*Kai ēkousa allēn phōnēn ek tou ouranou legousan, Exelthate, ho laos mou, ex autēs, hina mē sygkoinōnēsēte tais hamartiais autēs, kai ek tōn plēgōn autēs hina mē labēte*, "And I heard another voice out of heaven saying, 'Come out of her, My people, that you not share with her sins, and that you might not receive of her plagues'"). John heard "another voice out of heaven" (ἄλλην φωνὴν ἐκ τοῦ οὐρανοῦ [*allēn phōnēn ek tou ouranou*]) issuing this call to God's people. It is not the voice of God or of Christ, because the long poetic lamentation that follows would violate prophetic decorum if it were a divine voice. It is rather an angel speaking in the name of God as in 11:3 and 22:7-8. In this connection note the first person pronoun μου (*mou*, "my") (v. 4) and the third person reference to ὁ θεὸς (*ho theos*, "God") (v. 5) included in this call.[92]

The aorist imperative form of ἐξέλθατε (*exelthate*, "come out") expresses the urgency of the call. This summons resembles the ones to leave Babylon in Isa. 48:20; 52:11; Jer. 50:8; 51:6, 9, 45; Zech. 2:6-7). A call of a different kind came to Abraham (Gen. 12:1), but Lot received a similar one (Gen. 19:12) (Swete). The calls in Isaiah were invitations to a joyful exit, but this is a cautionary call and more closely approximates the ones in Gen. 19:15-22; Num. 16:23-26; Matt. 24:16. This allusion is probably to Jer. 50:8; 51:6-9, 45 (Alford). This is a call to leave a literal city (Mounce), but beyond that it is also a call to shun the enticements represented by the system of which that city is the embodiment (Beasley-Murray). It is a call to leave the enticements of idolatry, self-sufficiency, reliance on luxury, and violence against human life (Johnson).

The vocative ὁ λαός (*ho laos*, "people") with the personal pronoun μου (*mou*, "My") indicates that the first part of this statement (vv. 4-5) addresses the faithful (Moffatt). They are primarily those alive at the apex of the beast's kingdom and the yet-to-come climax of the Babylonian system. A legitimate inference from this call is that saints will inhabit the beast's kingdom to the very end, with the danger of being deluded through a lingering fondness for Babylon and a consequent involvement in her remaining judgments. The illustration of the linger-

---

92. Düsterdieck, *Revelation*, p. 443; Alford, *Greek Testament*, 4:715; Swete, *Apocalypse*, p. 228; Bullinger, *Apocalypse*, p. 561; Lee, "Revelation," 4:767.

ing fondness of Lot's wife for Sodom is an appropriate analogy for what this call tries to preclude (cf. Alford, Caird).

The purpose of the call comes in the words ἵνα μὴ συγκοινωνήσητε ταῖς ἁμαρτίαις αὐτῆς, καὶ ἐκ τῶν πληγῶν αὐτῆς ἵνα μὴ λάβητε (*hina mē sygkoinōnēsēte tais hamartiais autēs, kai ek tōn plēgōn autēs hina mē labete*, "that you not share with her sins, and that you might not receive of her plagues"). The words ταῖς ἁμαρτίαις (*tais hamartiais*, "with her sins") is associative instrumental, prompted by the συγ- (*syg-*, "with") prefix of the verb συγκοινωνήσητε (*sygkoinōnēsēte*).[93] The precaution is not against having fellowship with the *punishments* of Babylon's sins, but against having fellowship with the sins themselves.[94]

The position of ἐκ τῶν πληγῶν αὐτῆς (*ek tōn plēgōn autēs*, "of her plagues") is proleptic and therefore emphatic.[95] Failure to separate from Babylon will involve the disobedient in the plagues to fall on the city and all who fellowship with her sins (Johnson). For John to place the plagues in the future after having spoken of the city's destruction as past (18:2) is no problem, because this is a poetic intercalation in which chronological sequence is not a governing consideration.[96] This is a call to separate from the evil system and receive protection from the remaining plagues of God's wrath (Smith, Walvoord).

18:5 A continuation of the call assigns an additional reason (ὅτι [*hoti*], "because") for God's people to depart from Babylon: ὅτι ἐκολλήθησαν αὐτῆς αἱ ἁμαρτίαι ἄχρι τοῦ οὐρανοῦ, καὶ ἐμνημόνευσεν ὁ θεὸς τὰ ἀδικήματα αὐτῆς (*hoti ekollēthēsan autēs hai hamartiai achri tou ouranou, kai emnēmoneusen ho theos ta adikēmata autēs*, "because her sins have joined unto heaven, and God has remembered her unrighteous acts"). The picture presented by the aorist passive deponent verb ἐκολλήθησαν (*ekollēthēsan*, "have joined") is an unusual one. The verb κολλάω (*kollaō*, "I glue together") is from the noun κόλλα (*kolla*, "glue"). The passive form means "cleave to," "to join one another in a mass," or "to grow together into a mass."[97] The idea is not that Babylon's sins cling to heaven, because this does injustice to the reflexive note in the word, but that they cling to each other steadily until the cumulative "structure" of which they are a part has finally reached to heaven (Beckwith). The allusion is possibly to the use of bricks in building the tower of Babel where the destitute career of ancient Babylon began (Gen. 11:3-4) (Walvoord). The phrase ἄχρι τοῦ οὐρανοῦ

---

93. Robertson, *Word Pictures*, 6:437.
94. Düsterdieck, *Revelation*, p. 443.
95. Robertson, *Word Pictures*, 6:437.
96. Wall, *Revelation*, p. 215.
97. Charles, *Revelation*, 2:97-98; Robertson, *Word Pictures*, 6:437-38.

(*achri tou ouranou*, "unto heaven") (cf. Jer. 51:9) paints the picture of a combined stack of bricks (i.e., sins) so high that it elevates the roof of heaven (cf. Gen. 18:20-21).[98]

Like ἐκολλήθησαν (*ekollēthēsan*), the aorist ἐμνημόνευσεν (*emnē-moneusen*, "has remembered") is also prophetic. God will not forget the crimes of Babylon (16:19). The noun ἀδικήματα (*adikēmata*, "un-righteous acts") refers to crimes in the legal sense as it does in Acts 18:14; 24:20 (Ford). The massive misdeeds of the Babylonian system have indelibly impressed themselves on the memory of a God of justice. He must do the right thing by punishing Babylon for her iniquities, so it behooves God's people to distance themselves from the city as far as they can.

18:6 The call continues with words directed to the executioners of God's judgment: ἀπόδοτε αὐτῇ ὡς καὶ αὐτὴ ἀπέδωκεν, καὶ διπλώσατε [τὰ] διπλᾶ κατὰ τὰ ἔργα αἰτῆς· ἐν τῷ ποτηρίῳ ᾧ ἐκέρασεν κεράσατε αὐτῇ διπλοῦν (*apodote autē hōs kai autē apedōken, kai diplōsate [ta] dipla kata ta erga autēs; en tō potēriō hō ekerasen kerasate autē diploun*, "give back to her as even she has given back, and double the double things according to her works; in the cup which she has mixed, mix for her double"). The aorist imperative ἀπόδοτε (*apodote*, "give back") and the aorist indicative ἀπέδωκεν (*apedōken*, "she has given back") are forms of ἀποδίδωμι (*apodidōmi*, "I give back"), a verb for requital. This is an echo of the *lex talionis* of the OT (Jer. 50:15, 29; 51:24, 56; cf. Pss. 28:4; 137:8) and the words of Christ (Matt. 7:2; cf. Gal. 6:7-8).

In contrast, a kindly disposition toward one's enemies is a mark of the disciple of Jesus. The Christian should bless his persecutors (Matt. 5:43) and never repay evil for evil (Rom. 12:14, 17; 1 Thess. 5:15; 2 Tim. 4:14; 1 Pet. 3:9). Yet this does not cancel out God's final vindication of Himself and His own (Rom. 12:19). He alone can judge human motives. The verb ἀπέδωκεν (*apedōken*) is not used with strict propriety, since Babylon's was a giving, not a giving back. A desired correspondence with the ἀπόδοτε (*apodote*, "give back") is the reason for its use here. God alone can implement the law of retaliation. It appears that particular reference in this case is to the persecutions and martyrdom of the saints by Babylon (18:24; 19:2b) rather than to her corruption of the nations. Otherwise, the "paying back" notion in the verb *apodote* would not be quite as appropriate (Alford, Beckwith, Ladd, Johnson).

This is not a prayer for personal vengeance by the persecuted saints, but a heavenly interpretation of the divine response to cruelty committed by wicked persons who have passed the point of no return in their moral choices. The last hour has now struck, and it is too late

---

98. Moffatt, "Revelation," 5:457; Robertson, *Word Pictures*, 6:437-38.

for repentance. This is a judicial pronouncement against a sinful civilization that has reached the ultimate limit of evil.[99]

A natural question to ask is to whom is v. 6 addressed? Or, in other words, who are God's executioners? One suggestion has been that it is a prayer to God by the heavenly voice, i.e., the prophetic voice, a view that has support in the passage to which the verse alludes, Jer. 50:29, where Jeremiah the prophet is the one offering the prayer (Kiddle). This explanation fails to distinguish the prophet's voice from that of the angel who began speaking in v. 4 and continues to do so in this verse, however. Another proposal says the executioners are unidentified because the passage is rhetorical in form (Beckwith). Persuasively, it argues that this is simply a rhetorical device to emphasize the cause and certainty of God's vengeance against the city (Beckwith, Scott). The vagueness of the view is a strong consideration against it, however, as is a comparison with 17:16, which names the ten kings and the beast as the destroyers of the city.

So the best way is to identify the executioners as God's enemies whom He uses to execute His vengeance (Moffatt). According to 17:16-17, it is the false Christ and his allies who will destroy Babylon in compliance with the overarching purpose of God.[100] Further confirmation of this conclusion surfaces in noting that the result of the judgment is the same in both chapters: the burning of the city (17:16; 18:8, 9, 18). Even though vengeance is the prerogative of God alone (Deut. 32:35; Rom. 12:19; Heb. 10:30) (Caird), God may choose His enemies to implement it. He used Cyrus to carry out judgment (Isa. 44:28; 45:1). He has chosen in a number of conspicuous instances to collaborate with man in the execution of His will: the use of Moses' rod and the word of the Lord in destroying the Egyptians (Ex. 14:26-27), the part of Aaron and Hur in holding Moses' hands up in the destroying of the Amalekites (Ex. 17:12-13), the maneuvers of Deborah and Barak and the divine ordering of the stars in the fight against Sisera (Judg. 4-5), and Gideon's three hundred in breaking their pitchers and the Lord's setting everyone's sword against his fellow (Judg. 7) (Smith). Added to these, one could note Amos 3:6; Ezek. 24:7-8; and other examples (Beckwith). The plea that the judgment of chapter 18 goes beyond that in chapter 17, connecting directly with the return of Christ (Scott, Seiss) is not without merit. Yet God puts into the hearts of these enemies to do what they do, so it appears wisest to connect the city's burning in chapter 18 with that in chapter 17. The beast and his

---

99. Kiddle, *Revelation*, pp. 366-67; Hughes, *Revelation*, p. 190.
100. Lee, "Revelation," 4:768; Moffatt, "Revelation," 5:456-57; Smith, *Revelation*, p. 251; Wall, *Revelation*, p. 215.

accomplices move suddenly and unexpectedly to destroy the city and its commercial (as well as its religious) preeminence.

A cognate accusative emphatically highlights the command to the executioners, διπλώσατε [τὰ] διπλᾶ (*diplōsate ta dipla*, "double the double things"). To requite in double measure meant to requite in full (cf. Ex. 22:4, 7, 9; Isa. 40:2; 61:7; Jer. 16:18; 17:18; Zech. 9:12). It does not mean retribution double in severity to the seriousness of the sin.[101] "Double" has the sense that the punishment should be the exact equivalent of the offence in the same way that a person who looks exactly like someone else is called his "double." The guideline in meting out the exact equivalent is κατὰ τὰ ἔργα αὐτῆς (*kata ta erga autēs*, "according to her works"). This is consistently the basis for God's future judgment of mankind (Pss. 28:4; 62:12; Prov. 24:12; Isa. 59:18; Jer. 17:10; Rom. 2:6; 1 Cor. 3:8; 2 Cor. 11:15; 2 Tim. 4:14; 1 Pet. 1:17; Rev. 2:23; 20:12, 13; 22:12).

"The cup" (τῷ ποτηρίῳ [*tǭ potēriǭ*]) is the same one mentioned earlier in 14:8, 10; 17:4; 18:3. The vessel Babylon used to seduce others has now become the instrument of her own punishment (Lee). The instructions to her executioners are to "mix for her double" (κεράσατε αὐτῇ διπλοῦν [*kerasate autę diploun*]) in that cup. This is a reemphasis on doubling to ensure that she receives back every bit of the deserved punishment for her wrongdoings. The same verb κεράννυμι (*kerannumi*, "I mix") tells of the mixing of undiluted divine anger in 14:10.

18:7 The angel continues his directions to the executioners in v. 7 by furnishing further insights into reasons why judgment is necessary: ὅσα ἐδόξασεν αὐτὴν* καὶ ἐστρηνίασεν, τοσοῦτον δότε αὐτῇ βασανισμὸν καὶ πένθος. ὅτι ἐν τῇ καρδίᾳ αὐτῆς λέγει ὅτι Κάθημαι βασίλισσα, καὶ χήρα οὐκ εἰμί, καὶ πένθος οὐ μὴ ἴδω (*hosa edoxasen autēn kai estrēniasen, tosouton dote autę basanismon kai penthos. hoti en tę kardią autēs legei hoti Kathēmai basilissa, kai chēra ouk eimi, kai penthos ou mē idō*, "in as many things as she has glorified herself and become wanton, give so much torment and sorrow to her. Because in her heart she says, 'I sit a queen, and am not a widow, and I will in no way see sorrow'"). The relative pronoun ὅσα (*hosa*, "as many things") could be called an accusative of kindred meaning (Beckwith). It is a quantitative relative and functions as a cognate accusative with ἐδόξασεν (*edoxasen*, "she has glorified"). The pronoun also has a secondary causal force, "because she has glorified herself in many things."

---

101. Hailey, *Revelation*, pp. 361-62; Chilton, *Days of Vengeance*, p. 450; Hughes, *Revelation*, p. 191; contra Walvoord, *Revelation*, p. 261, and Smith, *Revelation*, p. 251.

102. Swete, *Apocalypse*, p. 230; Hughes, *Revelation*, p. 191.

If the first sin of Babylon is self-glorification (*edoxasen*), the second one is that of finding satisfaction in luxury (Johnson). The verb ἐστρηνίασεν (*estrēniasen*, "become wanton") is a cognate of the noun στρῆνους (*strēnous*) in v. 3. Another form of the same verb is in v. 9. It denotes a luxurious lifestyle with the accompanying trappings of discourtesy, arrogance, self-indulgence, ruthless exercise of strength, and unruliness.

Just like διπλώσατε (*diplōsate*), the correlative pronoun τοσοῦτον (*tosouton*, "so much") is a way of saying that the torment and sorrow should correspond exactly with the self-glorification and wantonness of Babylon. The principle of matching the punishment to the crime is a constantly affirmed scriptural principle (e.g., Isa. 3:16 ff.; Prov. 29:23; Luke 1:51; 14:11).[102] "Torment" (βασανισμὸν [*basanismon*]) as temporal punishment has appeared earlier in 9:5, but in 14:11 it indicates eternal punishment. Πένθος (*Penthos*) is elsewhere in the NT only at James 4:9; Rev. 18:7 ff.; 21:4. It is akin to πάθος (*pathos*, "passion") and πένομαι (*penomai*, "I am poor").[103] It is the usual word for mourning over the dead (cf. LXX of Gen. 27:41; Amos 8:10) (Lee). The noun occurs again later in vv. 7 and 8, and the cognate verb in v. 11. So acute suffering will replace the easy life of luxury, and the gloom of bereavement will supplant luxury's lighthearted laugh (Swete).

The scrutinizer of motives has detected a self-centeredness that is tantamount to self-deification. Meditations of τῇ καρδίᾳ (*tē kardia*, "the heart") are an open book to Him, so He knows Babylon's attitude that is essentially, "There is no other God but me." This is the extremity of wickedness (Pss. 10:4, 11, 13; 14:1; 53:1; Ezek. 28:2-9).[104] For her to say to herself, "I sit a queen" (κάθημαι βασίλισσα [*kathēmai basilissa*]), puts her into the class of Babylon, Tyre, and Nineveh who were noted for such boasting in the OT (Isa. 47:7-9; Ezek. 27:3; 28:2; Zeph. 2:15).[105] This, the third sin of Babylon in v. 7, is a haughty self-confidence (cf. Isa. 47:5, 7, 8). It is a self-sufficiency that puts one beyond the reach of any punishment. Such an overweening presumption is bound to draw the wrath of heaven upon itself (Lee, Moffatt, Kiddle).

The fourth sin of Babylon in v. 7 is the avoidance of suffering (Johnson). She rejects the possibility of widowhood and sorrow: καὶ χήρα οὐκ εἰμί, καὶ πένθος οὐ μὴ ἴδω (*kai chēra ouk eimi, kai penthos ou mē idō*, "and am not a widow, and I will in no way see sorrow"). Two grammatical features accentuate her confident boast of security: the

---

103. Robertson, *Word Pictures*, 6:439.
104. Hughes, *Revelation*, p. 192.
105. Beckwith, *Apocalypse*, p. 715; Robertson, *Word Pictures*, 6:439.

emphatic position of πένθος (*penthos*, "sorrow") and the expression of future emphatic negation by οὐ μὴ (*ou mē*, "in no way").[106] The claim of self-sufficiency that this claim climaxes is a vivid reminder of the attitude of the church in Laodicea (3:17).

18:8 This brazen attitude will add to the intensity and speed of Babylon's judgment: διὰ τοῦτο ἐν μιᾷ ἡμέρᾳ ἥξουσιν αἱ πληγαὶ αὐτῆς, θάνατος καὶ πένθος καὶ λιμός, καὶ ἐν πυρὶ κατακαυθήσεται· ὅτι ἰσχυρὸς κύριος ὁ θεὸς* ὁ κρίνας αὐτήν (*dia touto en miᾳ hēmerᾳ hēxousin hai plēgai autēs, thanatos kai penthos kai limos, kai en pyri katakauthēsetai; hoti ischuros kyrios ho theos ho krinas autēn*, "on account of this in one day her plagues will come, death and sorrow and famine, and she shall be burned up with fire; because the Lord God who judges her is strong"). As frequently used in prophetic literature to show cause and effect (cf. in LXX, Amos 3:11; Mic. 3:12), διὰ τοῦτο (*dia touto*, "on account of this") looks back to Babylon's blatant boast and presumptuousness as the cause of her sudden and utter ruin.[107]

The phrase ἐν μιᾷ ἡμέρᾳ (*en miᾳ hēmerᾳ*, "in one day") is a symbol for suddenness the same as the expression μιᾷ ὥρᾳ (*miᾳ hōrᾳ*, "in one hour") is in 18:10, 16, 19. John continues alluding to Isa. 47:7-9.[108] The locative case does not express duration of time, but is a figurative way of expressing abruptness (Beckwith, Beasley-Murray). The phrase's forward position in its clause emphasizes how quickly Babylon will experience what she sought to avoid through her luxury: death, mourning, and famine (Smith, Walvoord, Johnson). These are her three "plagues" (πληγαὶ [*plēgai*]). "Death" (Θάνατος [*Thanatos*]) comes in response to her scorn of the prospect of widowhood, "sorrow" (πένθος [*penthos*]) in return for her reveling, and "famine" (λιμός [*limos*]) in response to her abundance (Alford).

The prophet does not predict a gradual decline of the city, but a sudden collapse (cf. vv. 10, 16, 19). "She shall be burned up with fire" (ἐν πυρὶ κατακαυθήσεται [*en pyri katakauthēsetai*]) corresponds closely to the κατακαύσουσιν ἐν πυρί (*katakausousin en pyri*) of 17:16 and must be the same destruction.[109] The same dual representation of destruction appears in the OT source, Isa. 34:8 ff., a picture of desolation (18:2) and one of burning (Beasley-Murray).

A causal ὅτι (*hoti*, "because") introduces a further reason for this visitation on Babylon. The predicate adjective ἰσχυρός (*ischuros*, "strong") is at the head of its clause to emphasize what that reason is,

---

106. Robertson, *Word Pictures*, 6:439.
107. Swete, *Apocalypse*, p. 230; Lee, "Revelation," 4:769; Robertson, *Word Pictures*, 6:439; Smith, *Revelation*, p. 252.
108. Robertson, *Word Pictures*, 6:439.
109. Lee, "Revelation," 4:769; Robertson, *Word Pictures*, 6:439.

the strength of the Lord God who judges her. His work of creation (cf. 4:11; 5:13) and other interventions in human history have demonstrated His strength, so that "the strong city" (18:10) is no match for the might of God. His overruling control has created the alliance that destroys her (17:17; cf. Amos 3:6) (Lee). His strength is the ground for the suddenness and severity of the judgment to come upon Babylon (Alford).

The words "who judges her" (ὁ κρίνας αὐτήν [*ho krinas autēn*]) are a constantly needed reminder that the Lord God is the ultimate judge. He may use agents to inflict that punishment, as in 17:16-17, but the divine side of it is the ultimate reality (Moffatt). The allusion is to Jer. 50:34 where the strength of Babylon's judge is also the subject.

18:9 After completing his call for God's people to remove themselves from Babylon, the revealing angel describes the laments of the kings of the earth (vv. 9-10), the merchants (vv. 11-13, 15-17*a*), and the sea people (vv. 17*b*-19). An interjection addressed to Babylon interrupts the mourning of the merchants (v. 14).[110] The kings sob openly (κλαύσουσιν[111] [*klausousin*], "cry") first: Καὶ κλαύσουσιν καὶ κόψονται ἐπ' αὐτὴν οἱ βασιλεῖς τῆς γῆς οἱ μετ' αὐτῆς πορνεύσαντες καὶ στρηνιάσαντες, ὅταν βλέπωσιν τὸν καπνὸν τῆς πυρώσεως αὐτῆς (*Kai klausousin kai kopsontai ep' autēn hoi basileis tēs gēs hoi met' autēs porneusantes kai strēniasantes, hotan blepōsin ton kapnon tēs pyrōseōs autēs*, "And the kings of the earth who committed fornication with her and became wanton will cry and mourn over her, when they see the smoke of her burning"). The angel uses a predictive future tense, κλαύσουσιν καὶ κόψονται (*klausousin kai kopsontai*, "will cry and mourn"), to speak of this first lament. In the second one he uses the present tense (vv. 11-14) and in the third one the past tense (vv. 17-19) (Lee). Κόψονται (*Kopsontai*, "Mourn") is the form used in 1:7 to describe the mourning of despair of an unrepentant world at the sight of the returning Christ. Here it is a mourning over a smoldering city. The two verbs κλαίω (*klaiō*) and κόπτω (*koptō*) combine again in Luke 8:52.

"The kings of the earth" (Οἱ βασιλεῖς τῆς γῆς [*Hoi basileis tēs gēs*]) whose connection with Babylon has already been apparent (17:2, 18) are the first of the three groups to express their lamentation. The same three groups have roles relating to Tyre in Ezekiel 26-28 (the kings in 26:15-18, the traders very briefly and indirectly in 27:36, and the mariners in 27:29-36). Reasons for the sadness vary. The kings regret having lost their power so suddenly (Rev. 18:10). The merchants have lost

---

110. Bauckham, "Economic Critique," p. 50.
111. The verb κλαίω means "sob openly" and is different from δακρύω, the shedding of tears. So this is a loud expression of pain (Mounce, *Revelation*, p. 328 n. 21).

their most profitable market (18:11, 16), and the severe crippling of the shipping trade has hurt the sea-people (18:19) (Moffatt). The inclusion of the kings in the lament has occasioned an accusation of inconsistency against John in light of the kings that joined in causing Babylon's destruction (Beckwith). Yet these are not the same kings as in 17:16. Whoever these are, they make no effort to save the city. They keep their distance, perhaps because of political expediency. They realize that Babylon's doom is inevitable.[112] Just as the ten kings are always in company with the beast, these kings are always in the company of Babylon until her destruction. It is the ten kings that destroy Babylon (Bullinger). This is a larger circle of rulers than the harlot has attracted (Ladd).

Their sin is the double mistake that they "committed fornication with her and became wanton" (οἱ μετ' αὐτῆς πορνεύσαντες καὶ στρηνιά-σαντες [hoi met' autēs porneusantes kai strēniasantes]). In 18:3 it is the kings who commit fornication with the harlot and the merchants who are enriched by her luxury. Here the kings do both. Apparently sharing in Babylon's luxury is a part of committing fornication with her (Johnson).

"The smoke of her burning" (τὸν καπνὸν τῆς πυρώσεως αὐτῆς [ton kapnon tēs pyrōseōs autēs]) is the sight that provokes the misery of the kings. The expression looks back to the destruction of Sodom (Gen. 19:28), the destruction of Tyre (Ezek. 28:18), and later to the fall of Edom (Isa. 34:10). Other plagues contribute to Babylon's downfall (cf. 18:8), but fire is the main cause of the city's ruin (14:11; 17:16; 18:8, 18; 19:3) (Beckwith).

18:10 The kings are careful to distance themselves from the grim sight as they witness Babylon's burning: ἀπὸ μακρόθεν ἑστηκότες διὰ τὸν φόβον τοῦ βασανισμοῦ αὐτῆς, λέγοντες, Οὐαὶ οὐαί, ἡ πόλις ἡ μεγάλη, Βαβυλὼν ἡ πόλις ἡ ἰσχυρά, ὅτι μιᾷ ὥρᾳ* ἦλθεν ἡ κρίσις σου (apo makrothen hestēkotes dia ton phobon tou basanismou autēs, legontes, Ouai ouai, hē polis hē megalē, Babylōn hē polis hē ischyra, hoti mią hōrą ēlthen hē krisis sou, "standing at a distance because of the fear of her torment, saying, 'Woe woe, the great city, Babylon the strong city, because in one hour your judgment has come'"). As most would be, the kings of the earth are fascinated by the horrifying blaze. Yet they fear to come close, so they keep a safe distance. They are helpless to do anything to help the city and are probably afraid that the same thing will happen to them (Swete, Lee). This demonstrates that the burning of Babylon is not the ultimate end of history (Caird). The great fire does not hurt this group directly.[113] Why they have assembled to witness this conflagration is

---

112. Wall, *Revelation*, p. 216.
113. Mulholland, *Revelation*, p. 286.

unknown, but it could have been any number of motives. This precedes their assemblage for the final great conflict with the returning Warrior-King (16:14; 19:19).

The participle λέγοντες (*legontes*, "saying") introduces the dirge of the kings as it does the one for the merchants (v. 16) and sea-people (v. 19). Their lament begins with a miserable οὐαὶ οὐαί (*ouai ouai*, "woe woe"). A slight grammatical variation distinguishes these and the woes of 18:16, 19 from the woes earlier in the book. The accusative case follows the earlier uses (8:13; 12:12), but the nominative case follows the three uses in chapter 18. These are an exclamation of sorrow, but the earlier ones are a denunciation of woe.[114] The doubling of the woe expresses the depth of their sorrow occasioned by the suddenness of Babylon's fall and the emptiness of life without her (Lee, Johnson). The illusion was that Babylon could defy God, martyr His saints, and get away with it, but now that misconception has disappeared (Ladd). They call her "the strong city" (ἡ πόλις ἡ ἰσχυρά [*hē polis hē ischyra*]), but in reality she only seemed to be so strong (contra Isa. 26:1) (Swete).

The temporal μιᾷ ὥρᾳ (*mia hōra*, "in one hour") indicates the suddenness of judgment on the harlot. The merchants (18:17) and the sea-people (18:19) use the exact expression in their laments too. The notion of immediate demise comes from Jer. 51:8, but Jeremiah expresses it differently.[115]

18:11 The merchants take up their dirge in v. 11: Καὶ οἱ ἔμποροι τῆς γῆς κλαίουσιν καὶ πενθοῦσιν ἐπ' αὐτήν*, ὅτι τὸν γόμον αὐτῶν οὐδεὶς ἀγοράζει οὐκέτι (*Kai hoi emporoi tēs gēs klaiousin kai penthousin ep' autēn, hoti ton gomon autōn oudeis agorazei ouketi*, "And the merchants of the earth weep and grieve over her, because none buys their merchandise any longer"). Babylon is the epitome of luxury, so with her gone, no one remained to buy their commodities (Johnson). They had made money their god, using unscrupulous means to accumulate material goods and placing their whole confidence on this center of commerce. Primarily they bemoan the loss of profits and customers, but they also grieve over the disappearance of so great a treasure as this city represents (vv. 16-17a). This recalls the situation with ancient Tyre (Ezek. 27:25-31).[116] The wail of the merchants is more extended than that of the kings or the sea-people because their loss is greater. The dirge centers on trade because the wealth it generates is generally

---

114. Lee, "Revelation," 4:770; Robertson, *Word Pictures*, 6:440.
115. Lee, "Revelation," 4:770; Robertson, *Word Pictures*, 6:440.
116. Beasley-Murray, *Revelation*, p. 267; Wall, *Revelation*, p. 216; Hughes, *Revelation*, p. 189.

associated with a sense of false security that keeps people from seeing greed, cruelty, injustice, etc., in their true light (Sweet).

The description becomes more graphic at this point as the verb tenses change to the present, κλαίουσιν καὶ πενθοῦσιν (*klaiousin kai penthousin*, "weep and grieve"). At v. 15, however, it reverts to the future tense to describe the same thing (Alford). An analogous shift in tenses occurs in the description of the two witnesses in 11:9-10 (Lee). The two verbs occur together at 18:15, 19 also (cf. Luke 6:25; James 4:9). It is a picture of overwhelming sadness.

The cause of the deep sorrow of the merchants comes in the causal clause introduced by ὅτι (*hoti*, "because"). The complaint of the traders is that no one buys their merchandise. This is ironic because these merchants belonged to a system that denied the right to buy or sell to anyone who refused to accept the mark of the beast (13:17). Now the merchants themselves are denied that right to buy (Lee). Derived from γέμω (*gemō*, "be full"), γόμος (*gomos*, "merchandise") sometimes refers to a ship's cargo (Acts 21:3) and sometimes to any merchandise (here and in v. 12). It can be a load carried by a horse, camel, or donkey (cf. Ex. 23:5, LXX), but more often it is a ship's cargo. Many of the items in the following list of merchandise appear in the description of Tyre's destruction in Ezekiel 26-27 (esp. Ezek. 27:12-24 where fifteen of the items occur; cf. Isa. 23; Ezek. 16:9-13). The list gives twenty-eight or twenty-nine items—along with twenty-eight uses of καί (*kai*, "and," "even"), possibly more than any other passage in extant literature.[117] These traders profited from the enormous supply of materials required to satisfy Babylon's demands, things which the world holds dear and for which the ungodly are willing to sell their souls.[118]

The range of items include ornaments, apparel, furniture, perfumes (for personal and religious use), food, and social requirements (Moffatt). The articles divide themselves into seven categories: (1) precious wares (gold, silver, precious stones, pearls); (2) materials of rich attire (fine linen, purple, silk, scarlet); (3) materials for costly furniture (all thyine wood, every vessel of ivory, of most precious wood, brass, iron, marble); (4) precious spices (cinnamon, spice, incense, ointment, frankincense); (5) articles of food (wine, oil, fine flour, wheat); (6) merchandise for agricultural and domestic uses (cattle, sheep, horses, chariots); (7) traffic in men (bodies, the souls of men) (Lee).

John drew the list from items known in his day, not from the future time depicted in the prophecy (Alford), but it is a matter of

---

117. Swete, *Apocalypse*, p. 232; Robertson, *Word Pictures*, 6:440; Smith, *Revelation*, p. 254; Mounce, *Revelation*, p. 328.
118. Moffatt, "Revelation," 5:456; Hughes, *Revelation*, p. 193.

disagreement as to whether the list better suits the city of Rome[119] or Asia Minor where John wrote the Apocalypse.[120] Probability is on the side of the latter in light of the earlier identification of Babylon as the city on the Euphrates. Yet this list also has a timeless quality as evidenced by the large number of the items in this list that also appear in OT descriptions, particularly of Tyre.

18:12 The twelfth verse lists articles in the first three of the above categories: γόμον χρυσοῦ καὶ ἀργύρου καὶ λίθου τιμίου καὶ μαργαριτῶν* καὶ βυσσίνου* καὶ πορφύρας καὶ σιρικοῦ καὶ κοκκίνου, καὶ πᾶν ξύλον θύϊνον καὶ πᾶν σκεῦος ἐλεφάντινον καὶ πᾶν σκεῦος ἐκ ξύλου τιμιωτάτου καὶ χαλκοῦ καὶ σιδήρου καὶ μαρμάρου (*gomon chrysou kai argyrou kai lithou timiou kai margaritōn kai byssinou kai porphyras kai sirikou kai kokkinou, kai pan xylon thyinon kai pan skeuos elephantinon kai pan skeuos ek xylou timiōtatou kai chalkou kai sidērou kai marmarou*, "merchandise of gold and silver and precious stones and pearls and fine linen and purple and silk and scarlet, and all thyine wood and every vessel of ivory and every vessel of most precious wood and brass and iron and marble").

Items in the first category, gold and silver, occur in Ezekiel's description of Jerusalem's extravagance (Ezek. 16:13). Gold and precious stones are in the items of wealth in Tyre also (Ezek. 27:22). Pearls are unmentioned in OT lists, but Job 28:18 indicates its existence as a precious stone. In the first century A.D. Rome imported its gold especially from Spain, and its use was a frequently cited indicator in ancient writers of the growth of extravagant luxury in the empire.[121] Most silver came from Spain too. Like gold, silver typified luxury through its common use for silver-plated couches, baths made of silver, its customary use to make implements for serving food, and the like.[122] The precious stones already mentioned as part of the adornment of the harlot originated in India. Rome had the wealth to import them, and love for them grew to a violent passion during the first century. Women wore them in large quantities and men had them set in rings for themselves to wear.[123] Low-grade pearls came from the Red Sea and the highest quality from the Persian Gulf, but the largest number were from India. By the end of the first century, they may have constituted the majority of oriental trade. Citizens of Rome valued pearls below diamonds, but were willing to pay more for very large,

---

119. Bauckham, "Economic Critique," pp. 59-60.
120. Hanns Lilje, *The Last Book of the Bible*, trans. Olive Wyon (Philadelphia: Muhlenberg, 1955), p. 236.
121. Bauckham, "Economic Critique," p. 60.
122. Ibid., p. 61.
123. Ibid., pp. 61-62.

high quality pearls. Pearls epitomized Rome's increasing turn to extravagant luxury.[124]

Fine linen begins the second category of merchandise in the list of the merchants. Βυσσίνου (*Byssinou*, "Fine linen") refers to a garment made from Egyptian flax. It was quite expensive and delicate (Moffatt). Egypt was the main source, but some also came from Spain and Asia Minor.[125] Fine linen and purple are among the items of wealth in OT Tyre too (Ezek. 27:16). Scarlet (Jer. 4:30) and silk (Ezek. 16:10) are among the items of Jerusalem's extravagance which the OT prophet's decry. "Purple," a fabric treated with purple dye extracted from a shellfish one drop at a time, was synonymous with extreme luxury. The Caesars' distinctive mark was their military or imperial robe of purple (Lee, Mounce). Because it took so many of the small fish to make a noticeable quantity of dye, the dye was much more expensive than the materials of silk, linen, and wool it was used to dye. Purple clothing was another item for which Rome developed an insane craze. Some of Rome's purple cloth probably came from the clothing and dyeing industries of Miletus, Thyatira (cf. Acts 16:14), Laodicea, and Hierapolis, located in the province of Asia to which John sent Revelation.[126] Silk came from China, the name being derived from the Indian or Chinese people—οἱ Σῆρες (*hoi Sēres*)—from whom Alexander obtained the fabric when he invaded India.[127] For a while, Roman law forbade the wearing of silk by men, but it eventually developed into use in the manufacture of male and female garments.[128] "Scarlet" (κοκκίνου [*kokkinou*]) is the color of the beast (17:3) and of the harlot's clothing (17:4). As noted earlier, it came from the kermes oaks that grew in various parts of Asia Minor.[129]

The third category of materials marks a grammatical change from items in the genitive case dependent on γόμον (*gomon*, "merchandise") to items in the accusative case no longer dependent on *gomon*. These accusatives are direct objects of ἀγοράζει (*agorazei*) (v. 11).[130] "Thyine wood" is a sweet-smelling North African citrus tree valued because of its coloring. Its use in costly doors and dining tables colored the items like the eyes of a peacock's tail, the stripes of a tiger, or the spots of a panther (Alford, Swete, Lee, Charles, Ford). The price paid for one

---

124. Ibid., p. 62.
125. Ibid.
126. Ibid., pp. 62-63.
127. Lee, "Revelation," 4:771; Robertson, *Word Pictures*, 6:441.
128. Bauckham, "Economic Critique," p. 64.
129. Ibid., pp. 64-65.
130. Alford, *Greek Testament*, 4:718; Charles, *Revelation*, 2:103; Robertson, *Word Pictures*, 6:441.

table made of this wood could have purchased a large estate. As the feminine mark of extravagance was pearls, that of men was their mania for citrus wood tables.[131] Ivory was a mark of Ezekiel's description of Tyre (Ezek. 27:15). Because Roman use of ivory had produced a shortage of elephants in accessible areas of Africa, supplies of ivory from India increased to make up the difference. Romans used ivory for all sorts of purposes, e.g., chairs, beds, scabbards, chariots, dice. It was a mark of luxury that ivory had replaced wood in making images of the gods and table legs.[132] The ἐκ (*ek*, "of") before ξύλου (*xylou*, "wood") carries the sense of "made from" and governs the last four genitives in v. 12 (Lee). "Most precious wood" included maple, cedar, and cypress and possibly ebony from Africa and India. They made these woods into furniture, doors, and the like, and also used them for veneering.[133] Corinthian bronze was the material of expensive works of art. Perhaps they did the same with Spanish bronze.[134] Bronze was one of the rich materials of Tyre too (Ezek. 27:13). Iron was the material of cutlery, swords, and other implements of warfare. Spain and Pontus were the sources of this material.[135] Iron was another of Tyre's precious commodities (Ezek. 27:12, 19). Marble was part of the rich royal surroundings of the palace in Susa (Esth. 1:6). Rome's imported marble came mainly from Africa, Egypt, and Greece. The reign of Augustus marked the beginning of the lavish use of marble in Rome.[136]

18:13 Verse 13 lists the last four categories of goods: καὶ κιννάμωμον καὶ ἄμωμον* καὶ θυμιάματα καὶ μύρον καὶ λίβανον καὶ οἶνον καὶ ἔλαιον καὶ σεμίδαλιν καὶ σῖτον καὶ κτήνη καὶ πρόβατα, καὶ ἵππων καὶ ῥεδῶν καὶ σωμάτων, καὶ ψυχὰς ἀνθρώπων (*kai kinnamōmon kai amōmon kai thymiamata kai myron kai libanon kai oinon kai elaion kai semidalin kai siton kai ktēnē kai probata, kai hippōn kai hredōn kai sōmatōn, kai psychas anthrōpōn*, "and cinnamon and spice and incense and perfume and frankincense and wine and olive oil and fine flour and wheat and cattle and sheep, and of horses and chariots and slaves, even souls of men"). Among the precious spices, κιννάμωμον (*kinnamōmon*, "cinnamon") corresponds to the Hebrew term קִנָּמוֹן (*qinnāmôn*). The name is of Phoenician origin, but the substance, made from the bark of a tree, originated in East Asia or South China. The Phoenicians and Arabians brought it to Judea. Among the Romans, it was one of the cosmetics of the banquet, used for incense, medicine, perfume, and as

---

131. Bauckham, "Economic Critique," pp. 65-66.
132. Ibid., p. 66.
133. Ibid., p. 67.
134. Ibid.
135. Ibid., pp. 67-68.
136. Ibid., pp. 68.

a condiment in wines.[137] In the OT, it is an ingredient in the holy oil for anointing (Ex. 30:23), and one of the perfumes on the bed of an adulteress (Prov. 7:17). "Spice" was from the seeds of a fragrant shrub from the hot regions of India and Africa. Its main uses were as a valuable perfume and an aromatic balsam for the hair.[138] The ingredients used to make "incense" were expensive aromatic spices and gums. When burned, this mixture produced a perfumed smoke that was used not only for religious purposes, but also for perfuming the rooms and the funerals of the rich.[139] One of Ezekiel's charges against Jerusalem is her misuse of expensive incense (Ezek. 16:18). Μύρον (*Myron*, "Perfume") is a general term for sweet-smelling ointment, not just that made from myrrh (σμύρνα [*smyrna*]). Myrrh imported from Yemen and Somolia at great expense was one of the most desired types of perfume, but it was also one of a number of ingredients combined in other types.[140] Myrrh was one of the precious commodities known in Solomon's day too (Prov. 7:17; Song 1:13; 3:6; 4:6, 14; 5:1, 5, 13). "Frankincense" (cf. Song 3:6; 4:6, 14) was a fragrant gum-resin imported from South Arabia (cf. Isa. 60:6; Jer. 6:20). It found use as perfume for the body, as one of the ingredients of incense (cf. Ex. 30:34-37), and as an additive to wine at banquets.[141]

The first item in the articles-of-food category is "wine." Producing wine was very profitable in first-century Rome. In fact the wealthy landowners quit planting grain and corn and cultivated vines for this reason.[142] Wine was one of the precious commodities connected with Tyre too (Ezek. 27:18). Africa and Spain were the chief sources of the vast quantities of "olive oil" used in the Roman Empire.[143] It was part of a symbol for a life of plenty in the OT (Deut. 8:8). "Fine flour" refers to the finest grade of wheaten flour. Not only did the Jews put it to use with wine and incense in their sacrifices (Lev. 2:1-2), but Jerusalem also misused it as a delicacy in luxurious living (Ezek. 16:14). Rome imported wheat from Alexandria for the use of her rich.[144] Egypt was

---

137. Alford, *Greek Testament*, 4:718-19; Swete, *Apocalypse*, p. 234; Moffatt, "Revelation," 5:458; Robertson, *Word Pictures*, 6:441; Bauckham, "Economic Critique," pp. 68-69.
138. Alford, *Greek Testament*, 4:719; Lee, "Revelation," 4:771; Moffatt, "Revelation," 5:458; Robertson, *Word Pictures*, 6:441.
139. Lee, "Revelation," 4:771; Moffatt, "Revelation," 5:458; Bauckham, "Economic Critique," p. 69.
140. Bauckham, "Economic Critique," p. 69.
141. Beckwith, *Apocalypse*, p. 716; Moffatt, "Revelation," 5:458; Bauckham, "Economic Critique," pp. 69-70.
142. Bauckham, "Economic Critique," pp. 70-71.
143. Ibid., p. 71.
144. Swete, *Apocalypse*, p. 234; Lee, "Revelation," 4:771; Moffatt, "Revelation," 5:458; Robertson, *Word Pictures*, 6:441; Bauckham, "Economic Critique," p. 71.

the granary for Rome's wheat (Charles). This area along with other areas of Africa supplied the bulk of Rome's need through an armada of what must have been thousands of ships. Not only did private parties purchase the wheat thus imported, but the government did too so as to distribute it to the poor of the city. This apparently aroused resentment in the rest of the empire where it was not done.[145]

The sixth category, merchandise for agricultural and domestic uses, begins with "cattle." Cattle were used primarily as working animals and for the supply of milk. Beef was not an important part of the diet, even of the rich. The Roman aristocracy had acquired large sheep and cattle ranches both in Italy and in the provinces through conquest and confiscation.[146] The OT sees cattle as a sign of wealth too (Ps. 50:10). The import of sheep was probably not for food but for breeding purposes, to improve the quality of Roman wool.[147] The OT background connects sheep with wealth (1 Sam. 25:2). With the next animal, ἵππων (hippōn, "horses"), the writer returns to the genitive case dependent on the γόμον (gomon, "merchandise") of v. 12. This is perhaps to relieve the monotony of the string of accusatives, or perhaps to put greater emphasis on the very last expression ψυχὰς ἀνθρώπων (psychas anthrōpōn) where he returns to the genitive once again (Swete). Merchants brought horses from Africa, Spain, Sicily, Cappadocia, and parts of Greece,[148] as well as from Armenia (Ford). Spain and Cappadocia had stud farms maintained to supply horses for chariot racing in the circuses.[149] Tyre must have been very familiar with the importance of horses and chariots in warfare, because this was the means Nebuchadnezzar used to conquer their city (Ezek. 26:7, 10). "Chariots" were four-wheeled carriages that furnished transportation for the well-to-do. Roman senators rode in chariots decorated with silver ornamentation, perhaps imported from Gaul.[150]

The final category of merchandise is human beings. The noun σωμάτων (sōmatōn, "bodies") continues the series of genitives of which it is the last member and the expression psychas anthrōpōn returns to the accusative case, directly dependent on ἀγοράζει (agorazei, "buys") of v. 11. Some have cited the difference in case as a reason for understanding two groups of human merchandise: slaves connected with the horses and chariots just mentioned (somatōn) and slaves in general

---

145. Bauckham, "Economic Critique," pp. 71-72.
146. Ibid., pp. 72-73.
147. Ibid., p. 73.
148. Ibid., p. 74.
149. Ibid.
150. Lee, "Revelation," 4:772; Moffatt, "Revelation," 5:458; Bauckham, "Economic Critique," p. 74.

(*psychas anthrōpōn*).[151] This is hardly a probable distinction in a list such as this, however. The effort to refer *psychas anthrōpōn* to the corrupting effect of wealth on the inner man is futile too, because *psychas* can mean refer to the whole being with a meaning "persons" (cf. Acts 27:37) (Beckwith). It is hard to see how the souls of men could be a part of the city's merchandise except as slaves (Sweet).

So the καὶ (*kai*) separating the two expressions is ascensive, meaning "even," as frequently in this book, and the second expression is a restatement of *sōmatōn*. In Ezek. 27:13, the "souls of men" are part of Tyre's trade too. The LXX of that verse uses *psychais anthrōpōn* with the meaning of "slaves" as here (Beckwith). The term *sōmatōn* is a shortened way of writing σωμάτων δούλων (*sōmatōn doulōn*) or σωμάτων οἰκετικῶν (*sōmatōn oiketikōn*). In Gen. 34:29 of the LXX *sōmatōn* refers to slaves.[152] The slave merchant bore the title σωματέμ-πορος (*sōmatemporos*). He viewed slaves as "human livestock," so references to slaves climax the long list of the follies and vices of commercial Babylon. Slaves staffed the large households of the rich, filled their brothels, and provided entertainment of a brutal nature in the amphitheaters (Swete, Sweet). They were a means for great financial gain (Moffatt). Their emphatic position at the end of the list is a comment on the whole list regarding the inhuman brutality and contempt for human life on which the city's prosperity rests.[153]

The unparalleled list of goods given John by the angel has abundant illustrations from John's own time and from OT times, but the materialism of the future times of which this prophecy speaks will far outdo anything that has preceded it. When that system collapses, those whose lives have been built around it will find nothing but grief and sorrow because of their great loss.

18:14 The shift from third to second person and from present tense to aorist tense in v. 14 signals a change from the complaints of the merchants to a continuation of their lamentation. Though the speakers are unidentified, they are probably the merchants continued from v. 11 and renamed in v. 15:[154] καὶ ἡ ὀπώρα σου τῆς ἐπιθυμίας τῆς ψυχῆς ἀπῆλθεν ἀπὸ σοῦ, καὶ πάντα τὰ λιπαρὰ καὶ τὰ λαμπρὰ ἀπώλετο ἀπὸ σοῦ, καὶ οὐκέτι οὐ μὴ αὐτὰ εὑρήσουσιν (*kai hē opōra sou tēs epithymias tēs psychēs apēlthen apo sou, kai panta ta lipara kai to lampra apōleto apo sou, kai ouketi ou mē auta heurēsousin*, "and your ripe autumn

---

151. Düsterdieck, *Revelation*, p. 445; Alford, *Greek Testament*, 4:719; Lee, "Revelation," 4:772.
152. Alford, *Greek Testament*, 4:719; Moffatt, "Revelation," 5:458; Robertson, *Word Pictures*, 6:441-42.
153. Bauckham, "Economic Critique," p. 79.
154. Alford, *Greek Testament*, 4:718; Wall, *Revelation*, p. 216.

fruit of the lust of your soul has departed from you, and all the luxurious and splendid things have perished from you, and they will in no way find them any longer"). Because connecting this verse with its context is not easy, some have proposed relocating it to a position between vv. 23 and 24 (e.g., Kiddle). A change of persons is not out of the ordinary in a setting such as this, however (cf. vv. 21-22), so it is best to accept the verse in its present position (Beasley-Murray). It typifies John's freedom of expression (Mounce).

The noun ὀπώρα (*opōra*, "ripe autumn fruit") appears in the NT only here. Its derivation is uncertain, but perhaps it is a combination of ὀπός (*opos*, "sap") and ὥρα (*hōra*, "hour"), conveying the idea "the hour (or time) for juicy sap." It has a kinship to the "summer fruit" of Jer. 40:10, 12 and to a related expression, δένδρα φθινοπωρινά (*dendra phthinopōrina*, "autumn trees") of Jude 12.[155] Both genitives τῆς ἐπιθυμίας τῆς ψυχῆς (*tēs epithymias tēs psychēs*, "the lust of your soul") are subjective: the fruit is the object of the lust and the lust is carried out by the soul. The departure (ἀπῆλθεν [*apēlthen*, "has departed"]) of this deeply desired fruit is the cause of great anguish.

Λιπαρά (*Lipara*, "Luxurious") is an adjective from λίπος (*lipos*, "grease") that also means "fat." It conveys the idea of "oily" and hence "splendid." Found nowhere else in the NT, it occurs in the LXX of Isa. 30:23 where it translates שָׁמֵן (*šāmēn*, "plenteous"). In Prov. 21:17 and Ezek. 16:13, the Hebrew word is a sign of luxury. Here *lipara* refers to food, and λαμπρά (*lampra*, "splendid things") refers to clothing.[156] The proleptic aorist ἀπώλετο (*apōleto*, "have perished") conveys the shocking announcement of the unavailability of these highly cherished items. The doubled double negative οὐκέτι οὐ μὴ (*ouketi ou mē*, "in no way . . . any longer") says in as emphatic a way as the Greek language is capable of that they will not return.[157] With the verb εὑρήσουσιν (*heurēsousin*, "they will . . . find") the person changes abruptly once again, this time to an impersonal third person (Beckwith).

18:15 The deep lament of the merchants comes into view once again: οἱ ἔμποροι τούτων, οἱ πλουτήσαντες ἀπ᾽ αὐτῆς, ἀπὸ μακρόθεν στήσονται διὰ τὸν φόβον τοῦ βασανισμοῦ αὐτῆς, κλαίοντες καὶ πενθοῦντες (*hoi emporoi toutōn, hoi ploutēsantes ap' autēs, apo makrothen stēsontai dia ton phobon tou basanismou autēs, klaiontes kai penthountes*, "the merchants of these things, who have become rich from her, will stand at a distance because of the fear of her torment, weeping and mourning"). The antecedent of τούτων (*toutōn*, "these things") is the

---

155. Robertson, *Word Pictures*, 6:442.
156. Swete, *Apocalypse*, p. 235; Lee, "Revelation," 4:772; Charles, *Revelation*, 2:108; Robertson, *Word Pictures*, 6:442.
157. Robertson, *Word Pictures*, 6:442.

listed items of vv. 12-13, but particularly the summarization of them in "the luxurious and splendid things" of v. 14.[158] The enrichment of the merchants derived from their trade with Babylon (οἱ πλουτήσαντες ἀπ' αὐτῆς [*hoi ploutēsantes ap' autēs*, "who have become rich from her"]) is the implied reason for their mourning (cf. 18:3).

Their position "at a distance" (ἀπὸ μακρόθεν [*apo makrothen*]) resembles that of the kings earlier (18:10) and of the sea-people later (18:17). The angel's description now reverts back to the future tense, στήσονται (*stēsontai*, "will stand"), as he predicts the prolonged lamentation of the merchants. They distance themselves from the scene of destruction rather than rushing in to try to stop it, however, because they fear the same thing might happen to them (διὰ τὸν φόβον τοῦ βασανισμοῦ αὐτῆς [*dia ton phobon tou basanismou autēs*, "because of the fear of her torment"]). The same two verbs, κλαίοντες καὶ πενθοῦντες (*klaiontes kai penthountes*, "crying and mourning"), describe the grieving in v. 11.

18:16 The dirge of the merchants combines the harlot image of 17:4 with the city image of chapter 18 (Johnson): λέγοντες, Οὐαὶ οὐαί, ἡ πόλις ἡ μεγάλη, ἡ περιβεβλημένη βύσσινον καὶ πορφυροῦν καὶ κόκκινον, καὶ κεχρυσωμένη [ἐν] χρυσίῳ καὶ λίθῳ τιμίῳ καὶ μαργαρίτῃ (*legontes, Ouai ouai, hē polis hē megalē, hē peribeblēmenē byssinon kai porphyroun kai kokkinon, kai kechrysōmenē [en] chrysiǭ kai lithǭ timiǭ kai margaritǭ*, "saying, 'Woe woe, the great city, which was clothed in fine linen and purple and scarlet, and adorned with gold and precious stones and pearls'"). This dirge begins and ends (v. 17a) the same way as that of the kings in v. 10. In the middle they differ, however, with the appreciation of the merchants for the city's opulence and splendor replacing the kings' reference to her strength (Swete). Each group evaluates the disaster in terms of its own self-interest (Mounce).

The figurative description of the city's clothing and adornment in this dirge is almost the same as that of the harlot who symbolizes the city in 17:4 (Lee), with the addition of *bussinon* to the picture here. The fine linen and the gold, jewels, and pearls are part of the wardrobe and adornment of the saints (19:8) and the holy city later on (21:10 ff.), but not the purple and scarlet. These two have associations too close to the beast (Sweet). The fine linen, purple, scarlet, gold, precious stones, and pearls are all items from the list of merchandise in vv. 12-13.

18:17 The first clause of v. 17 concludes the dirge of the merchants: ὅτι μιᾷ ὥρᾳ ἠρημώθη ὁ τοσοῦτος πλοῦτος (*hoti miǡ hōrǡ erēmōthē ho tosoutos ploutos*, "because in one hour such wealth has become deso-

---

158. Düsterdieck, *Revelation*, p. 446; Alford, *Greek Testament*, 4:719-20; Lee, "Revelation," 4:773; Robertson, *Word Pictures*, 6:442.

late"). The ὅτι (*hoti*, "because") gives the reason for the woes expressed in v. 16 (Alford, Lee). The words μιᾷ ὥρᾳ (*mią hōrą*, "in one hour") tells of the brevity of the process of Babylon's destruction as in v. 10. The proleptic aorist ἠρημώθη (*ērēmōthē*, "has become desolate") anticipates the future desolation also spoken of in 17:16 and 18:19.

The remainder of v. 17 begins a description of a new set of mourners, the sea-people: Καὶ πᾶς κυβερνήτης καὶ πᾶς ὁ ἐπὶ τόπον* πλέων καὶ ναῦται καὶ ὅσοι τὴν θάλασσαν ἐργάζονται ἀπὸ μακρόθεν ἔστησαν (*Kai pas kybernētēs kai pas ho epi topon pleōn kai nautai kai hosoi tēn thalassan ergazontai apo makrothen estēsan*, "And every helmsman and everyone who sails from place to place and the sailors and as many as work the sea stood at a distance"). This lament better suits Babylon or Tyre, cities with their own seaports, than it does a city such as Rome which had no port of its own (Swete, Bullinger, Johnson). The words of vv. 17b-19 clearly allude to Ezek. 27:29-36 where the seafarers express their grief over the loss of Tyre.

A "helmsman" (κυβερνήτης [*kybernētēs*]) was the pilot of a ship. The noun occurs only here and in Acts 27:11 in the NT. In rank, the helmsman or "sailing master" was subordinate to the ναύκληρος (*nauklēros*), the "supreme commander" of the ship.[159] Πᾶς ὁ ἐπὶ τόπον πλέων (*Pas ho epi topon pleōn*, "Everyone who sails from place to place" or, more literally, "Everyone who sails to a place") is an idiom similar to μέλλοντι πλεῖν τοὺς κατὰ τὴν Ἀσίαν τόπους (*mellonti plein tous kata tēn Asian topous*, "those sailing to the regions down along Asia") in Acts 27:2. It could refer to the ship's captain,[160] but it more probably refers to the ship's passengers (Bullinger, Mounce). The term ναῦται (*nautai*, "sailors") is part of the number who "work the sea" (τὴν θάλασσαν ἐργάζονται [*tēn thalassan ergazontai*]), but the latter group includes others such as fishermen and divers for pearls who also make their living from the sea (cf. Ps. 107:23). The corresponding Greek expression for "work the ground" occurs in the LXX of Gen. 2:5, 15; 3:23; 4:2 (Charles).

The picture of these sea-people closely resembles that of the kings (v. 10) and the merchants (v. 15): they "stood at a distance" (ἀπὸ μακρόθεν ἔστησαν [*apo makrothen estēsan*]). The only difference is the past tenses of vv. 17-19 have replaced the future tenses of vv. 8-9 and the present tense in v. 11. The animated nature of the description accounts for this change (Lee).

18:18 The grandeur of the city is once again a cause for awe

---

159. Lee, "Revelation," 4:773; Beckwith, *Apocalypse*, p. 717; Robertson, *Word Pictures*, 6:443.
160. Alford, *Greek Testament*, 4:720; Swete, *Apocalypse*, pp. 236-37; Lee, "Revelation," 4:773; Robertson, *Word Pictures*, 6:443.

(cf. vv. 10, 16): καὶ ἔκραζον βλέποντες τὸν καπνὸν τῆς πυρώσεως αὐτῆς λέγοντες, Τίς ὁμοία τῇ πόλει τῇ μεγάλῃ (*kai ekrazon blepontes ton kapnon tēs pyrōseōs autēs legontes, Tis homoia tǭ polei tǭ megalǭ*, "and they were crying out when they saw the smoke of her burning, saying, 'What [city] is like the great city?'"). The occasion of their dirge comes in the βλέποντες (*blepontes*, "when they saw") phrase, that recalls the ὅταν βλέπωσιν (*hotan blepōsin*, "when they saw") clause of v. 9 (Charles). The smoke of the city's burning provokes deepest regrets among the sea-people.

The question implies an unexpressed πόλις (*polis*, "city") after τίς (*tis*, "what"). This is an echo of the question asked about Tyre in Ezek. 27:32.[161] An association of this question with the one asked in 13:4 is also inevitable: "Who is like the beast?" The implied answer to the question here is "no city." Babylon that represents all that a city can be in the realm of materialism is no more!

18:19 With a symbolic act to express their anxiety, the sea-people utter their brief lament: καὶ ἔβαλον χοῦν ἐπὶ τὰς κεφαλὰς αὐτῶν καὶ ἔκραζον κλαίοντες καὶ πενθοῦντες, λέγοντες, Οὐαὶ οὐαί, ἡ πόλις ἡ μεγάλη, ἐν ᾗ ἐπλούτησαν πάντες οἱ ἔχοντες τὰ πλοῖα ἐν τῇ θαλάσσῃ ἐκ τῆς τιμιότητος αὐτῆς, ὅτι μιᾷ ὥρᾳ ἠρημώθη (*kai ebalon choun epi tas kephalas autōn kai ekrazon klaiontes kai penthountes, legontes, Ouai ouai, hē polis hē megalē, en hǭ eploutēsan pantes hoi echontes ta ploia en tǭ thalassǭ ek tēs timiotētos autēs, hoti miǫ hōrǫ ērēmōthē*, "and they threw dust on their heads and were crying out weeping and mourning, saying, 'Woe woe, the great city, by which all who have ships in the sea have become rich of her treasures, because in one hour she has become desolate'"). Casting dust on one's head is a symbol for grief throughout the OT (Josh. 7:6; 1 Sam. 4:12; 2 Sam. 1:2; 13:19; 15:32; Job 2:12; Lam. 2:10). This is in imitation of the grief over Tyre's demise (Ezek. 27:30).

Along with this, they kept on crying out (imperfect tense of ἔκραζον [*ekrazon*, "crying out"]), weeping and mourning (κλαίοντες καὶ πενθοῦντες [*klaiontes kai penthountes*]) like the merchants in v. 15. The double woe begins their lament as in vv. 10, 16, and a nominative absolute, ἡ πόλις ἡ μεγάλη (*hē polis hē megalē*, "the great city"), immediately follows. They bewail the loss of the city by which (ἐν ᾗ [*en hǭ*], an instrumental *en*) those who have ships have become rich. Her treasures are the reason (a causal use of ἐκ [*ek*]) in the phrase ἐκ τῆς τιμιότητος αὐτῆς [*ek tēs timiotētos autēs*, "because of her treasures"]) the sea-people were able to accumulate such riches. The wealth of

---

161. Lee, "Revelation," 4:774; Wall, *Revelation*, p. 217.

Babylon represents great spending power and so is a welcome resource for seafarers who use her port (cf. Ezek. 27:33). But this will be no more. The sea-people speak of the desolation of Babylon in almost the same terms as the merchants in v. 17*a*. They are in deep mourning because their source of wealth has gone up in flames.

18:20 As vv. 9-19 have told of the sorrow of three groups over the occurrence of the catastrophe proclaimed in vv. 1-8, v. 20 speaks of the exultation of the faithful over the same event (Beckwith): Εὐφραίνου ἐπ' αὐτῇ, οὐρανέ, καὶ οἱ ἅγιοι καὶ οἱ ἀπόστολοι καὶ οἱ προφῆται, ὅτι ἔκρινεν ὁ θεὸς τὸ κρίμα ὑμῶν ἐξ αὐτῆς (*Euphrainou ep' autę, ourane, kai hoi hagioi kai hoi apostoloi kai hoi prophētai, hoti ekrinen ho theos to krima hymōn ex autēs*, "Make merry over her, heaven, and saints, even apostles and prophets, because God has judged your judgment on her"). Some have supposed that John is the singer of this brief song of joy over the doom of Babylon (Charles, Beckwith). But since no break in the sequence begun at v. 4 is discernible, the voice must be that of the angel who continues his words by turning John's attention to heaven.[162] The analogy of this verse with 12:12 is against John's being the singer, as is the consideration that it is hardly fitting for an earthly figure to call on heaven to rejoice.

The angel calls on heaven to "make merry" (εὐφραίνου [*euphrainou*]). This is the same verb as is used in 11:10 to describe the joy of the wicked over the deaths of the two witnesses. The rejoicing is on the opposite side this time (Swete). It is quite conceivable that the heavenly songs of 19:1-5 are in response to this invitation (Lee, Bullinger, Beasley-Murray).

The involvement of heaven in this song is reminiscent of Jer. 51:48-49, another song of joy over the demise of Babylon.[163] The vocative οὐρανέ (*ourane*, "heaven") changes the mood of singing from lamentation to that of gaiety. The same thing that causes deep sorrow on earth brings great jubilation to heaven.

Without explicitly saying whether they are living or dead, the angel broadens his appeal to include οἱ ἅγιοι καὶ οἱ ἀπόστολοι καὶ οἱ προφῆται (*hoi hagioi kai hoi apostoloi kai hoi prophētai*, "saints, even apostles and prophets"). "Saints" is a general term for all the faithful. Apostles and prophets are special classes of saints (cf. 11:18), the καὶ (*kai*, "even") following ἅγιοι (*hagioi*) being ascensive (Beckwith). A similar

162. Alford, *Greek Testament*, 4:721; Lee, "Revelation," 4:774, 777; Wall, *Revelation*, p. 217.
163. Hughes, *Revelation*, p. 194.

call in 12:12 with its following expansion would imply that the saints appealed to are in heaven (Mounce). Also, if 19:1-5 is a response to this call to rejoice, this too would probably exclude its being addressed to anyone still on earth.

The noun ἀπόστολοι (*apostoloi*, "apostles") occurs here, in 2:2, and in 21:14 in Revelation. The word's use in 2:2 and 21:14 argues strongly that it should have its technical sense here, according to which it refers to Christ's authoritative representatives who were witnesses of His resurrection. The bulk of NT uses of ἀπόστολος (*apostolos*) are in this sense. If 18:20, 24 refers to the martyrdom of the apostles, John may have in mind the death of his brother James at the hand of Herod Agrippa I in the early forties (Acts 12:1-2) and of Peter and Paul in Rome in the late sixties. They indeed were victims of a false religious system that had its origin at the tower of Babel. Yet the perspective of this song is not John's own time, but the future era when Babylon will have reached its peak of world influence and receive its consummating destructive blow from the hand of God. By this time, all the apostles, including John, will be in heaven readying themselves to return to earth with Christ.

The prophets singled out are not representatives of the old covenant, but are those who have been persecuted for Jesus' sake. They are therefore NT prophets (Beasley-Murray).

The reason given for the invitation to make merry (ὅτι [*hoti*, "because"]) is, "God has judged your judgment on her" (ἔκρινεν ὁ θεὸς τὸ κρίμα ὑμῶν ἐξ αὐτῆς [*ekrinen ho theos to krima hymōn ex autēs*]). Two rather distinct meanings for κρίμα (*krima*) are possible. It can speak of a case for trial or of a sentence pronounced. The former meaning would give the clause the sense of "the Judge has pronounced in your favor" or "decided the case in your favor" (Swete). The idea of the saints' being vindicated agrees with the thrust of the song of 19:2-3 (Moffatt). Further support within the book comes from the imprecatory prayers of the saints that cry out for God's avengement of His people throughout the book (Thomas, pp. 517-24, Excursus 2). In essence, the song would say, "God has done what you thought was right." The fact that *krima* never has this meaning elsewhere in Revelation and rarely does in the rest of the NT and the LXX (Caird), is enough to cause hesitation, but not to reject the view out of hand. The noun does appear to have this meaning in 1 Cor. 6:7.

To assign the meaning of "sentence pronounced" to *krima* results in the meaning, "God has imposed on her the sentence she passed on you" (Caird). This allows *krima* to have the same meaning it has in 17:1. Also, of the noun's possible meanings, the sentence passed by a judge is the most probable (Caird). Since God is the Judge, it must refer to the sentence passed *on* you rather than the sentence passed *by* you. This view also agrees with the principle of reciprocation expressed in 16:6 (Moffatt) and with the law of malicious witness in Deut. 19:16-19 (Caird, Sweet). Yet the view is too indirect. Too many thoughts have to be supplied that are not in the context. For example, neither the verse nor the context refers to Babylon's judgment of the saints. It refers to her martyring of the saints, but not to a sentence she pronounced.

The merit of both viewpoints is unquestionable, but the weight of evidence is on the side of seeing *krima* as a reference to a case for trial. This means that the genitive ὑμῶν (*hymōn*, "your") is subjective rather than objective, i.e., the sentence that you thought was right. The thought of avenging the blood of the saints comes up repeatedly (e.g., 18:24; 19:2).

Second angelic pronouncement of judgment on Babylon (18:21-24). With the completion of the long discourse of 18:4-20, the writer turns to a second announcement in predicting the city's fall.

18:21 With all the lamentation and rejoicing over the demise of Babylon, one might expect the sequel to the catastrophe to come next, but it does not. Instead, returning to the time of vv. 4-8, the text predicts the city's destruction again, first in symbolic act and then in explicit terms (Beckwith): Καὶ ἦρεν εἷς ἄγγελος ἰσχυρὸς λίθον ὡς μύλινον μέγαν καὶ ἔβαλεν εἰς τὴν θάλασσαν λέγων, Οὕτως ὁρμήματι βληθήσεται Βαβυλὼν ἡ μεγάλη πόλις, καὶ οὐ μὴ εὑρεθῇ ἔτι (*Kai ēren heis angelos ischyros lithon hōs mylinon megan kai ebalen eis tēn thalassan legōn, Houtōs hormēmati blēthēsetai Babylōn hē megalē polis, kai ou mē heurethē̦ eti*, "And a strong angel lifted a stone like a great millstone and threw it into the sea saying, 'Thus with a rush will be cast down Babylon the great city, and she will in no way be found any longer'"). This is the third angel to participate in the revelation of this chapter. The task he is to perform requires that he be "strong" (ἰσχυρός [*ischyros*]). Strong angels have participated earlier in the book (5:2; 10:1), but this one is not called "another" strong angel. The two earlier strong angels had duties connected with the great scroll and the little scroll. This raises the possibility that this new strong angel has something to do with the consummation of what those two scrolls represent (Caird, Mounce).

The stone picked up by the angel was so large that it *appeared* to John (ὡς [*hōs*, "like"]) to be a "great millstone" (μύλινον μέγαν [*mylinon megan*]). Μύλινος (*Mylinos*) is an adjective used only here in the NT. A related word, μυλικός (*mylikos*, "belonging to a mill") is in Luke 17:2. That word speaks of the fitness of the stone for the use it is to have (cf. Matt. 18:6; Mark 9:42). *Mylinos*, however, stresses the purpose for which the stone is to be used. This is not a small millstone turned by women (cf. Matt. 24:41), but one turned by a donkey (cf. Mark 9:42) and therefore "great," four to five feet in diameter and twelve inches thick and weighing thousands of pounds.[164]

After picking it up, the angel threw it into the sea, graphically portraying the doom of Babylon. With one swift motion, Babylon the great is gone. The symbolic act derives partly from Jer. 51:63-64 (cf. Ezek. 26:21) (Moffatt). Prophets often portrayed symbolically the events about which they prophesied (cf. Isa. 20; Jer. 13; Ezek. 4; Acts 21:11) (Beckwith), but this time it is an angel doing so.

The angel accompanies his symbolic act with an explanation of what he is typifying. Οὕτως ὁρμήματι (*Houtōs hormēmati*, "Thus with a rush") portrays the manner of Babylon's demise as sudden and violent. Ὅρμημα (*Hormēma*, "A rush") comes from ὁρμάω (*hormaō*, "I rush"). It speaks of something like an attacking army coming "with mighty force."[165] This is the sudden and complete elimination of "Babylon the great city" from the earth. Nor will the disappearance be just temporary. "She will in no way be found any longer" (οὐ μὴ εὑρεθῇ ἔτι [*ou mē heurethē eti*]). The emphatic negation of οὐ μὴ (*ou mē*, "in no way") tells the completeness of the disappearance, and the adverb ἔτι (*eti*, "any longer") indicates its permanence. This is a total vanishing as when a large stone sinks beneath the water's surface, never to be seen again (cf. Ex. 15:5; Neh. 9:11) (Lee).

So begins the account of Babylon's internal deterioration in vv. 21-23. Verses 9-19 have told of the city's ruin from the standpoint of outsiders. It remains now to tell of the extinction of its internal state (Beckwith).

18:22 The city will be marked by the absence of music, trades, and industry: καὶ φωνὴ κιθαρῳδῶν καὶ μουσικῶν καὶ αὐλητῶν καὶ σαλπιστῶν οὐ μὴ ἀκουσθῇ ἐν σοὶ ἔτι, καὶ πᾶς τεχνίτης πάσης τέχνης* οὐ μὴ εὑρεθῇ ἐν σοὶ ἔτι, καὶ φωνὴ μύλου οὐ μὴ ἀκουσθῇ ἐν σοὶ ἔτι (*kai phōnē kitharōdōn kai mousikōn kai aulētōn kai salpistōn ou mē akousthē en soi eti, kai pas technitēs pasēs technēs ou mē heurethē en soi eti, kai phōnē mylou ou mē akousthē en soi eti,* "and the sound of harpists and musicians and flutists and trumpeters will in no way be heard in you any longer, and no craftsman of any craft will in any way be found in you any longer, and the sound of a mill will in no way be heard in you any longer"). The angel's song alludes to Jer. 25:10 where Nebuchadnezzar, king of Babylon, is God's instrument for punishing Jerusalem.[166] Another angel represented Babylon's desolation through the

---

164. Swete, *Apocalypse*, pp. 238-39; Lee, "Revelation," 4:775; Robertson, *Word Pictures*, 6:444; Johnson, "Revelation," 12:568.
165. Beckwith, *Apocalypse*, p. 719; Robertson, *Word Pictures*, 6:444.
166. Alford, *Greek Testament*, 4:722; Robertson, *Word Pictures*, 6:444.

presence of strange and repulsive creatures in 18:2, but silence that will dominate its location is the means used by this angel (Beasley-Murray).

The city will be void of music from "harpists" (κιθαρῳδῶν [*kitharǭdōn*]), "musicians" (μουσικῶν [*mousikōn*]), "flutists" (αὐλητῶν [*aulētōn*]), and "trumpeters" (σαλπιστῶν [*salpistōn*]). Harpists (14:2) and trumpeters (e.g., 8:6) appear elsewhere in Revelation. Flutists often performed with the harpists at special events among the Hebrews (cf. Isa. 5:12; 30:29) (Swete). Matthew 9:23 has the only other NT use of the word. *Mousikōn* is a general word for musicians playing all kinds of instruments. Since it occurs in connection with three specific types of musicians, some have wanted to refer it to "singers" instead of giving it a general meaning. This meaning is unjustifiable both on the basis of this context and of the word's usage elsewhere, however (Charles, Moffatt).

The words οὐ μὴ ἀκουσθῇ ἐν σοὶ ἔτι (*ou mē akousthę̄ en soi eti*) emphasize the complete and permanent disappearance of all types of music from the city. The sixfold use of *ou mē . . . eti* in vv. 21-23 increases the forcefulness of expression of cessation in various realms. The angel turns abruptly to the second person σοί (*soi*, "you") in addressing Babylon, making the words even more pointed (cf. vv. 11-13). Such changes as this are common in the prophets (e.g., Pss. 52:4-6; 62:3-4; 81:10-12; Ezek. 32:11-12; Amos 6:3-7) (Beckwith).

The angel also notes the absence of every "craftsman" (τεχνίτης [*technitēs*]). Among other trades, craftsmen included silversmiths (Acts 19:24; cf. Deut. 27:15; Song 7:1, both in LXX), stone-workers (1 Chron. 22:15, LXX), and architects (Heb. 11:10).[167] All these were destined to disappear permanently from Babylon (*ou mē heurethę̄ en soi eti*, cf. v. 21). "The sound of a mill" (Φωνὴ μύλου [*Phōnē mylou*]) was commonplace in every inhabited area in those days. In Babylon's desolation, however, the sound of the promising stir of business will be absent (*ou mē akousthę̄ en soi eti*, cf. v. 22a) (Swete, Moffatt).

18:23 Illumination and marriage festivities will also be missing from the city: καὶ φῶς λύχνου οὐ μὴ φάνῃ ἐν σοὶ ἔτι, καὶ φωνὴ νυμφίου καὶ νύμφης οὐ μὴ ἀκουσθῇ ἐν σοὶ ἔτι· ὅτι οἱ ἔμποροί σου ἦσαν οἱ μεγιστᾶνες τῆς γῆς, ὅτι ἐν τῇ φαρμακείᾳ σου ἐπλανήθησαν πάντα τὰ ἔθνη (*kai phōs lychnou ou mē phanę̄ en soi eti, kai phōnē nymphiou kai nymphēs ou mē akousthę̄ en soi eti; hoti hoi emporoi sou ēsan hoi megistanes tēs gēs, hoti en tę̄ pharmakeią sou eplanēthēsan panta ta ethnē*, "and the light of a lamp will in no way shine in you any longer, and the voice of the bridegroom and of the bride will in no way be

---

167. Swete, *Apocalypse*, p. 240; Robertson, *Word Pictures*, 6:445.

heard in you any longer; because your merchants were the great men of the earth, because by your sorcery all the nations have been deceived"). Streetlights to illumine the thoroughfares in the evenings were apparently nonexistent in first-century cities, even in Rome, but torchlight provided illumination for various types of processions at night. The wealthy had ample means for brightening their houses, but φῶς λύχνου (*phos lychnou*, "the light of a lamp") probably refers to even the smallest of lights. The decimation of the city will mean the extinguishing of even these (Swete, Charles).

The words φωνὴ νυμφίου καὶ νύμφης (*phōnē nymphiou kai nymphēs*, "the voice of the bridegroom") recall the language of Jer. 7:34; 16:9; 25:10-11 (cf. John 3:29). The language of the prophet there tells of coming judgment against Jerusalem through the coming of foreign invaders, but Jeremiah also records the restoration of that very place in language of this same type. He tells the renewal of the voice of the bridegroom and the bride in the city because of God's everlasting lovingkindness toward His people Israel (Jer. 33:10-11).[168] For Babylon, however, no such renewal will happen. The city's conflagration will be final. All work and play and marrying and giving in marriage will come to an abrupt halt as they did in the days of Lot (Luke 17:28-30) (Sweet).

Two occurrences of ὅτι (*hoti*, "because") introduce reasons for the complete demise just predicted: Babylon's raising up of earthly magnates who wantonly exalt themselves (cf. vv. 3, 7, 11 ff.) and her leading astray of the nations through her seductions (cf. vv. 3, 6-7, 9; 17:2). Verse 24 gives a third reason: the martyring of the saints (cf. vv. 6-7).[169] The language of the first reason, οἱ ἔμποροί σου ἦσαν οἱ μεγιστᾶνες τῆς γῆς (*hoi emporoi sou ēsan hoi megistanes tēs gēs*, "your merchants were the great men of the earth"), alludes to Isa. 23:8 where the prophet describes Tyre (cf. Ezek. 27:21). These merchants are not themselves Babylonians, but they have gained riches through Babylon's luxurious lifestyle (cf. v. 15) (Lee). Οἱ μεγιστᾶνες τῆς γῆς (*Hoi megistanes tēs gēs*, "The great men of the earth") conveys a tone of arrogance. The merchants had not only gained wealth, but had also imbibed of Babylon's wanton pride (cf. v. 7) (Beckwith). In light of Babylon's infectious influence, it is no wonder that God will judge Babylon so severely. The change to an imperfect tense ἦσαν (*ēsan*, "were") from the future thrust earlier in the verse adopts the perspective of fulfilled prophecy, as is so often done in this book (Beckwith).

The second ὅτι (*hoti*) clause supplies the reason for the enrichment

---

168. Robertson, *Word Pictures*, 6:445; Kiddle, *Revelation*, p. 372; Hughes, *Revelation*, p. 195.
169. Düsterdieck, *Revelation*, p. 448; Beckwith, *Apocalypse*, p. 719.

and noble standing of those trading with Babylon: she has allured all the nations through her deceptive seductions (Lee). This subordination of the second *hoti* clause to the first makes better sense than coordinating the two. The submerging of Babylon because of her contribution in elevating her merchants has come about from her achievement of greatness through bewitching and misleading the world (Swete). It is true that Babylon's harlotry has occasioned her judgment (17:2, 4), but it is also true that the harlotry is responsible for promoting the city's merchants to prominence. The latter is the primary reason for judgment cited here, and the former the secondary one.

In the OT φαρμακείᾳ (*pharmakeią*, "sorcery") has connections with Jezebel (2 Kings 9:22), Babylon (Isa. 47:12), and Nineveh (Nah. 3:4). A cognate of φαρμάκων (*pharmakōn*, "sorceries") in Rev. 9:21, it refers to sorcery and magical arts. Jews and early Christians had an aversion to magic and sorcery. Since Rome allowed these practices to flourish and since they usually had a connection with religion, it was natural for this prophecy to relate them to the existing world power. Revelation 21:8 and 22:15 note the exclusion of sorcerers from the heavenly city. Babylon will use some form of this quackery to deceive (ἐπλανήθησαν [*eplanēthēsan*, "have been deceived"]) all the nations and to allure them into a spiritually immoral relationship with herself (cf. Nah. 3:4).

18:24 The force of the second *hoti* in v. 23 carries over into v. 24, making it a further reason for Babylon's overthrow—her bloodguiltiness (Swete): καὶ ἐν αὐτῇ αἷμα προφητῶν καὶ ἁγίων εὑρέθη καὶ πάντων τῶν ἐσφαγμένων ἐπὶ τῆς γῆς (*kai en autę̄ haima prophētōn kai hagiōn heurethē kai pantōn tōn esphagmenōn epi tēs gēs*, "and in her was found the blood of the prophets and saints and all those slain upon the earth"). To emphasize this third point of the guilt, the angel switches from the second person to the third, dropping his direct address to the city and telling the last great cause of her overthrow as a general fact (Alford, Lee).

Jerusalem has a long history in shedding righteous blood (Matt. 23:35; cf. Ezek. 24:6, 9; Luke 13:33). Babylon too is a city of bloodshed in the OT (Jer. 51:35, 36, 49) as it is in Revelation (17:6; 19:2). Others in Revelation who bear the responsibility for martyrdom are the earth-dwellers (6:10), the beast from the abyss (11:7; 13:7), and the beast from the earth (13:15).[170] Blood violently shed cries out for vengeance until it is rewarded by the punishment of the murderers. The destruction of Babylon answers to that punishment.

"The prophets and saints" (Προφητῶν καὶ ἁγίων [*Prophētōn kai hagiōn*]) has the meaning of "the prophets and the *other* saints," the

---

170. Robertson, *Word Pictures*, 6:446; Johnson, "Revelation," 12:568-69.

first group being a special class included in the second (Beckwith, Mounce). "All those slain upon the earth" (Πάντων τῶν ἐσφαγμένων ἐπὶ τῆς γῆς [*Pantōn tōn esphagmenōn epi tēs gēs*]) includes all those slain for the sake of Christ and His word (Alford). The city of Babylon is not the only scene of martyrdom, but it is through her example that antagonists have killed saints around the world. So ultimately the guilt for this worldwide slaughter rests on her shoulders. Nothing of this scope has heretofore transpired. The prophecy looks to the future and a massive system that will encompass the globe in its animosity against Christianity (Ladd).

Additional Notes

18:1 The preposition ἐκ in the phrase ἐκ τῆς δόξης αὐτοῦ may have a causal sense, "by reason of" or "because of" (Robertson, 6:436), or it may tell the source of the illumination, "from" (Alford). The latter usage differs only slightly from an expression of the means of the illumination, "by," which seems to fit best with the passive ἐφωτίσθη. Means seems to fit this context best.

18:2 The bracketed words καὶ φυλακὴ παντὸς θηρίου ἀκαθάρτου are missing from an important group of MSS, including Sinaiticus and 2053, but probably an unintentional scribal error is responsible for this omission, when a scribe's eye jumped from the second ἀκαθάρτου in the verse to the third one. Inclusion of the words is necessary to complete the three elements alluding to Isa. 13:21; 34:11.[171]

18:3 Various MSS offer a number of options for the words τοῦ οἴνου τοῦ θυμοῦ τῆς πορνείας. Alexandrinus and 2053 omit τοῦ οἴνου. Ephraemi omits τοῦ οἴνου and reverses the order of τοῦ θυμοῦ τῆς πορνείας. Other MSS reverse the positions of τοῦ οἴνου and τοῦ θυμοῦ. Probably the difficulty in explaining the expression in the sequence that appears initially in this paragraph accounts for the variety of scribal changes that resulted in the other readings. The preferable reading τοῦ οἴνου τοῦ θυμοῦ τῆς πορνείας is the one that appears in Sinaiticus, 046, and other authorities.[172]

The reading πέπωκεν is from πίνω, but another primary variant is πέπτωκαν, which is from πίπτω and is in place of the more usual third person plural πεπτώκασι.[173] Either by accident or intentionally, various scribes made this verb conform to the two occurrences of ἔπεσεν in 18:2. Neither πέπτωκαν nor other forms of πίπτω supported by different MSS fit the sense of this passage or the OT prophetic imagery on

---

171. Bruce M. Metzger, *A Textual Commentary on the Greek New Testament* (New York: United Bible Societies, 1971), pp. 758-59.
172. Ibid., p. 759.
173. Robertson, *Word Pictures*, 6:437.

which this passage is based (cf. Jer 25:15; 51:7, 39) even though they have the support of Sinaiticus, Alexandrinus, and Ephraemi. Both the context and the OT foundation require some form of the verb πίνω. The form πέπωκαν is preferable to πεπτώκασι and πέπωκεν which improve the grammar of πέπωκαν.[174]

The preposition ἐκ in the phrase ἐκ τῆς δυνάμεως carries the force of "by reason of" or "because of" as it does also in 8:13; 16:11; 18:1 (Swete, Lee, Charles).

18:5 As sometimes happens, the verb ἐμνημόνευσεν governs an accusative case, τὰ ἀδικήματα, rather than the usual genitive. The same happens in Matt. 16:9; 1 Thess. 2:9.[175]

18:6 The relative pronoun ᾧ is the same case as its antecedent ποτηρίῳ by attraction. If attracation had not occurred, it would have been an accusative case instead of a locative.

18:7 The pronoun αὐτήν is sometimes pointed αὑτήν to make its reflexive force perfectly clear.[176] It is not altogether clear whether the rough breathing is necessary, however, because the intensive pronoun αὐτός in the oblique cases often does duty for a reflexive in Hellenistic Greek.[177] A small number of insignificant MSS have the usual reflexive pronoun ἑαυτήν.

The masculine singular τοσοῦτον agrees with βασανισμὸν. By extension, it also governs the neuter πένθος.[178]

18:8 Alexandrinus has ὁ θεός in place of κύριος ὁ θεός, apparently an accidental omission of κύριος following the similar ending ἰσχυρός. The sequence ὁ θεὸς ὁ κύριος found in Sinaiticus is apparently a copyist's blunder, because this sequence occurs nowhere else in Revelation. The title κύριος ὁ θεός occurs nine other times in the book (1:8; 4:8; 11:17; 15:3; 16:7; 19:6; 21:22; 22:5, 6) and never in the sequence Sinaiticus gives. Among the probable choices for correct reading, κύριος ὁ θεός has the best MS support, including C, P, 046, and others.[179]

18:10 Alexandrinus and a few other MSS have μίαν ὥραν, an accusative of extent of time, rather than μιᾷ ὥρᾳ, a locative to show a point in time. Perhaps the accusative, which is clearly the incorrect reading, follows the pattern of the accusative in 3:3.

18:11 Various alternate readings for ἐπ᾽ αὐτήν use either a different preposition or a different form of the pronoun or a different pro-

---

174. Swete, *Apocalypse*, p. 228; Lee, "Revelation," 4:766; Beckwith, *Apocalypse*, p. 713; Metzger, *Textual Commentary*, pp. 759-60.
175. Beckwith, *Apocalypse*, p. 714; Robertson, *Word Pictures*, 6:438.
176. Robertson, *Word Pictures*, 6:438.
177. Metzger, *Textual Commentary*, pp. 615-16, 760.
178. Robertson, *Word Pictures*, 6:438-39.
179. Metzger, *Textual Commentary*, p. 760.

noun. The preferred reading stands on the basis of strong external support from Sinaiticus, Ephraemi, 046, and a goodly number of other uncials and minuscules. The other readings probably originated accidentally in some cases and with the intention of improving the reading in others.[180]

18:12 Sinaiticus is correct in reading the genitive plural μαργαριτῶν. It is a harder reading than the singular which could have been expected following the singular λίθου τιμίου. Other variants include the accusative plural in C and P, the dative plural in A, and the genitive singular in 051 and most minuscules (Lee).

Sinaiticus is alone in reading a genitive plural βυσσίνων instead of the genitive singular βυσσίνου. Alexandrinus, Ephraemi, and others combine to give much stronger support to βυσσίνου, the correct reading.

18:13 The term ἄμωμον does not appear in the *Textus Receptus*, but it is in the major uncial MSS, and therefore should be a part of the original text.

18:16 The words ἡ πόλις ἡ μεγάλη form another nominative absolute following οὐαὶ οὐαί as in 18:10 (Lee).

For a discussion of the zeugmatic construction of λίθῳ τιμίῳ καὶ μαργαρίτῃ following κεχρυσωμένη, see 17:4 (Alford).

18:17 The reading that includes τόπον has the strong external support of Sinaiticus, Alexandrinus, Ephraemi, and a large number of other MSS. The difficulty of the expression of which τόπον is a part has caused various copyists to search for other possible readings, but none of them has the earmarks of being the correct reading.[181]

18:20 The cognate accusative τὸ κρίμα with the verb ἔκρινεν is emphatic. It points to the decisiveness of God's action and His vindication as the ultimate ruler (Ladd).

The rendering of ἐξ depends on which is the correct meaning of κρίμα. If the noun refers to a case for trial, the preposition has the force of "on" (cf. 6:10; 19:2). If κρίμα speaks of the sentence pronounced, ἐξ speaks of exacting a penalty "from" someone. Since the decision favors the former meaning of the noun, the suggested translation is "on."

18:21 The adjective εἷς is not exactly the numeral "one" in this instance, but approaches the function of an indefinite article "an" (cf. 8:13).[182]

18:22 The words πάσης τέχνης are missing from Sinaiticus and Alexandrinus and the Bohairic version of the Coptic, but they have

---

180. Ibid., p. 760.
181. Ibid., p. 761.
182. Swete, *Apocalypse*, p. 238; Beckwith, *Apocalypse*, p. 719; Robertson, *Word Pictures*, 6:444.

sufficient support from C, P, 046, 051, and most minuscules and ancient versions. This omission and several others in this section seem to have arisen accidentally through homoioteleuton, i.e., several lines ending with ἐν σοὶ ἔτι.[183]

18:23 If φάνῃ were accented on the ultima, φανῇ, instead of the penult, it would be an aorist passive subjunctive ("shall be seen") instead of an aorist active subjunctive (Lee). The active form is the more probable in this context. This is the fifth of six uses of the aorist subjunctive in vv. 21-23. This very form of φαίνω occurs in 8:12 also. There it is clearly active.[184]

---

183. Metzger, *Textual Commentary*, p. 761.
184. Robertson, *Word Pictures*, 6:445.

20
Rejoicing over Babylon's Fall and Conquest of the King of Kings

The nineteenth chapter of Revelation has two main segments: songs of rejoicing triggered by the fall of Babylon (19:1-10) and the sequence of events surrounding the Lamb's return to earth (19:11-21).

D. THE CLOSING VISIONS OF JOHN (19:1–22:5)

1. REJOICING OVER THE FALL OF BABYLON (19:1-10)

Structurally speaking, 19:1-10 is the concluding part of the intercalation describing the demise of Babylon (17:1–18:24). The fourfold "hallelujahs" (19:1, 3, 4, 6) respond to the angel's invitation to the heavenly community to rejoice (18:20).[1] The formula of 19:9-10 concludes the section begun by the formula of 17:1-3, setting the intervening verses apart as a discussion of Babylon's history up to the point of the seventh bowl.[2] It is now time for the loudness of enthusiastic rejoicing to replace the silence of the ruined city (18:21-24).[3]

---

1. R. H. Charles, *The Revelation of St. John*, ICC (New York: Scribner's Sons, 1920), 2:117-18, 118-19; Robert W. Wall, *Revelation*, New International Biblical Commentary (Peabody, Mass.: Hendrickson, 1991), p. 219.
2. See Excursus 5 at the end of this volume for more details regarding the structure of the seventh-bowl section of the book.
3. Martin Kiddle, *The Revelation of St. John*, HNTC (New York: Harper, 1940), p. 375.

Translation

¹After these things I heard [something] like a loud voice of a great multitude in heaven saying,

"Hallelujah;

the salvation and the glory and the power of our God [have come]

²because His judgments are true and righteous;

because He has judged the great harlot

the very one who corrupted the earth with her fornication,

and has avenged the blood of His slaves

from her hand."

³and they said a second [time],

"Hallelujah;

and her smoke ascends forever and ever."

⁴And the twenty-four elders and the four living beings fell, and worshiped God who sits upon the throne, saying,

"Amen, Hallelujah."

⁵And a voice from the throne came forth saying,

"Praise our God,

All His slaves,

[even] those who fear Him,

small and great."

⁶And I heard [something] like a voice of a great multitude and like a sound of many waters and like a sound of loud [peals of] thunder saying,

"Hallelujah,

because our Lord God Almighty has begun to reign.

⁷Let us rejoice and exult,

and give glory to Him,

because the marriage of the Lamb has come,

and His wife has prepared herself;

⁸and it has been granted to her that she clothe herself

in bright, clean fine linen,

for the fine linen is the righteous deeds of the saints."

⁹And he says to me, "Write: Blessed are those who are invited to the marriage supper of the Lamb." And he says to me, "These words are the true [ones] of God."

¹⁰And I fell before his feet to worship him. And he says to me, "See that you do not [do this]; I am the fellow-slave of you and your brethren who have the testimony of Jesus; worship God. For the testimony of Jesus is the spirit of prophecy."

Exegesis and Exposition

The four songs of 19:1-5 look backward to the judgment of Babylon, and the song of 19:6-8 looks forward to the marriage of the Lamb. The two themes are not unrelated, as the former must occur before the latter can become reality. Taken together, the two themes comprise a response to 18:4-20. In the earlier section a voice from heaven predicts earthly mourning over the fall of Babylon, and in the latter voices from heaven praise God for this same fall.[4] The end of the harlot's regime on earth marks the beginning of the bride's enjoyment of earth's fullness.

The first part of the celebration is in four parts: a large multitude praising God for His judgment of the harlot (vv. 1-2), the same multitude celebrating Babylon's judgment (v. 3), a response of agreement and praise from the twenty-four elders and four living beings (v. 4), and a voice from the throne inviting praise to God by all His slaves (v. 5) (Johnson). Of all the heavenly songs in Revelation (cf. 4:8, 11; 5:9-10, 12-14; 7:10, 12, 15-17; 11:15, 17-18; 15:3-4; 16:5-7), this one is the most solemn and formal because of the event that occasions it: God's judgment of the enemy of His people (Alford, Lee).

19:1 The first song celebrates God's judgment of the harlot: Μετὰ ταῦτα ἤκουσα ὡς φωνὴν μεγάλην ὄχλου πολλοῦ ἐν τῷ οὐρανῷ λεγόντων, Ἁλληλουϊά· ἡ σωτηρία καὶ ἡ δόξα καὶ ἡ δύναμις τοῦ θεοῦ ἡμῶν (*Meta tauta ēkousa hōs phōnēn megalēn ochlou pollou en tō ouranō legontōn, Allēlouia; hē sōtēria kai hē doxa kai hē dynamis tou theou hēmōn*, "After these things I heard [something] like a loud voice of a great multitude in heaven saying, 'Hallelujah; the salvation and the glory and the power of our God [have come]'"). Μετὰ ταῦτα (*Meta tauta*, "After these things") often in this book indicates a change of subject, but in this instance it introduces the climax of chapter 18.[5] This is the revelation to John that followed his vision of the harlot, her seductive wiles, and her judgment.[6]

The prophet heard "[something] like a loud voice of a great multitude" (ὡς φωνὴν μεγάλην ὄχλου πολλοῦ [*hōs phōnēn megalēn ochlou pollou*]). Though John did not hear a voice as such, what he heard resembled a loud voice. Since v. 5 will invite the redeemed to voice their hallelujah, this is probably the singing of an angelic host. Elsewhere in the book, wherever songs of thanks occur, angels are usually

---

4. Richard Bauckham, "The Economic Critique of Rome in Revelation 18," in *Images of Empire*, ed. Loveday Alexander (Sheffield: JSOT, 1991), pp. 48-49.
5. Archibald Thomas Robertson, *Word Pictures in the New Testament* (Nashville: Broadman, 1933), 6:447.
6. Homer Hailey, *Revelation, an Introduction and Commentary* (Grand Rapids: Baker, 1979), p. 373.

participants, so these are probably angels. The songs of 4:8, 11, and 5:12-14 are other examples of responsive singing involving angels.[7]

The first of four NT occurrences of ἀλληλουϊά (*hallēlouia*), all in this chapter (cf. 19:3, 4, 6), begins the song. It is a transliteration of the Hebrew expression found twenty-four times in the Psalms, יָהּ הַלְלוּ (*halělû yâ*), meaning "praise the Lord." In the Hebrew text, it appears at the end of Psalms 104, 105, 115, 116, 117, at the beginning of Psalms 111 and 112, and at the beginning and end of Psalms 106, 113, 135, and 146. In the LXX, several other psalms have the Greek term where it does not appear in Hebrew. Its use in Psalms is generally in connection with the punishment of the ungodly as it is here. The feasts of Passover and of Tabernacles were the main occasions for the singing of Psalms 104-109, the "Great Hallel."[8] "The Hallel of Egypt" is the name given to Psalms 113-118 because of frequent references in them to the redemption from Egypt.

The call to praise comes first in vv. 1, 3, 6, as it usually does, but in v. 4 it is responsive as in Psalms 104, 105, 115, 116, and 117. In evoking praise to God for the ruin of sinners, Revelation 19 resembles Ps. 104:35 that includes words about both judgment and praise to the Lord.[9] The words of v. 5, αἰνεῖτε τῷ θεῷ (*ainete tǭ theǭ*, "praise God"), are almost an equivalent translation of *halělû yâ* ("praise Yah"), with "God" replacing the personal name of God in the OT, יָהּ (*yâ*, "Yah"), which is a shortened form of יהוה (*YHWH*).

"Hallelujah" is one of a number of transliterated terms with Hebrew or Aramaic background used among Christians. Others include "amen," "hosanna," "Abba," and "maranatha."[10] These show a

---

7. Henry Barclay Swete, *The Apocalypse of St. John* (London: Macmillan, 1906), p. 242; Robertson, *Word Pictures*, 6:447; Charles, *Revelation*, 2:118; Wall, *Revelation*, p. 220. Others see this as a song of the redeemed because of resemblances to the song of 7:9-10 (Walter Scott, *Exposition of the Revelation of Jesus Christ* [Swengel, Pa.: Bible Truth Depot, n.d.], p. 375; J. B. Smith, *A Revelation of Jesus Christ* [Scottdale, Pa.: Herald, 1961], p. 257; John F. Walvoord, *The Revelation of Jesus Christ* [Chicago: Moody, 1966], p. 268; Robert H. Mounce, *The Book of Revelation*, NICNT [Grand Rapids: Eerdmans, 1977], p. 337; Hailey, *Revelation*, p. 373). Yet that passage specifically labels the singers as human beings, a feature that is missing here.

8. Swete, *Apocalypse*, p. 242; William Lee, "The Revelation of St. John," in *The Holy Bible*, ed. F. C. Cook (London: John Murray, 1881), 4:778; E. W. Bullinger, *The Apocalypse* or *"The Day of the Lord"* (London: Eyre and Spottiswoode, n.d.), pp. 584-86; Robertson, *Word Pictures*, 6:447.

9. James Moffatt, "The Revelation of St. John the Divine," in *The Expositor's Greek Testament*, ed. W. Robertson Nicoll (Grand Rapids: Eerdmans, n.d.), 5:462.

10. G. R. Beasley-Murray, *The Book of Revelation*, NCB (Grand Rapids: Eerdmans, 1978), p. 271.

close connection between early Christian worship and that of the Jewish synagogue.[11]

The song first celebrates the arrival of God's salvation, glory, and power. Two earlier songs have celebrated the note of victory based on divine justice that ἡ σωτηρία (*hē sōtēria*, "the salvation") suggests (cf. 7:10; 12:10). The victory that results in God's kingdom coming on earth coincides with the removal of all that stands in its way, including the beast and Babylon (Ladd). This is the first motive for praise to the Lord.

The second motive is ἡ δόξα (*hē doxa*, "the glory"). The glory of God is awesome (cf. 15:8), so much so that evil like that connected with the city of Babylon cannot coexist with it (Kiddle). "The power" (Ἡ δύναμις [*Hē dynamis*]) earlier joins with *hē sōtēria* in 12:10 and with *hē doxa* in 4:11 and 7:12. God's power exerts itself on behalf of the loyal and the righteous. Truth and justice will in the end prevail because "the power" is God's and not Babylon's.[12] The combination of salvation, glory, and power is a vivid reminder of David's prayer in 1 Chron. 29:11.

19:2 The ὅτι (*hoti*, "because") that begins v. 2 assigns the reason for praise to God: ὅτι ἀληθιναὶ καὶ δίκαιαι αἱ κρίσεις αὐτοῦ· ὅτι ἔκρινεν τὴν πόρνην τὴν μεγάλην ἥτις ἔφθειρεν τὴν γῆν ἐν τῇ πορνείᾳ αὐτῆς, καὶ ἐξεδίκησεν τὸ αἷμα τῶν δούλων αὐτοῦ ἐκ χειρὸς αὐτῆς (*hoti alēthinai kai dikaiai hai kriseis autou; hoti ekrinen tēn pornēn tēn megalēn hētis ephtheiren tēn gēn en tē porneiạ autēs, kai exedikēsen to haima tōn doulōn autou ek cheiros autēs*, "because His judgments are true and righteous; because He has judged the great harlot, the very one who corrupted the earth with her fornication, and has avenged the blood of His slaves from her hand"). The fairness and righteousness of God's judgments furnish the reason for praise. An earlier song has celebrated this fact (16:7), and another earlier song characterized God's ways by the same two qualities (15:3).[13]

The two qualities ἀληθιναὶ καὶ δίκαιαι (*alēthinai kai dikaiai*, "true and righteous") characterize God's judgments as being in accord with factual realities and equitable in their implementation. By now all men have made their choice between God and Satan. Universal worship of the beast and universal rejoicing over the deaths of the two witnesses mark the world not only as guilty but also as irreclaimable. The earth-

---

11. Swete, *Apocalypse*, p. 242; Charles, *Revelation*, 2:119; Mounce, *Revelation*, p. 337; Alan F. Johnson, "Revelation," in *EBC*, ed. Frank E. Gaebelein (Grand Rapids: Zondervan, 1981), 12:569-70.
12. Wall, *Revelation*, pp. 220-21.
13. Lee, "Revelation," 4:779; Robertson, *Word Pictures*, 6:447.

dwellers have hardened their hearts forever to a point that precludes any possibility of repentance (Kiddle). God's judgment of those with this disposition is the special occasion of praise to God. The cause for praise in 5:12-13 was general, but here it is special as the song continues to show.

The second ὅτι (*hoti*, "because") clause of v. 2 supports the thought expressed in the first one by giving a typical example of the more general truth expressed there.[14] It is not supportive of the first because divine judgment needs no justification or human approval, but rather because the second clause gives a concrete instance of the judgment that in proleptic retrospect has just occurred.[15] That example is ἔκρινεν τὴν πόρνην τὴν μεγάλην (*ekrinen tēn pornēn tēn megalēn*, "He has judged the great harlot"). The song celebrates the fulfillment of the promise implied in the title of the lengthy excursus on Babylon: τὸ κρίμα τῆς πόρνης τῆς μεγάλης (*to krima tēs pornēs tēs megalēs*, "the judgment of the great harlot") (17:1). The aorist ἔκρινεν (*ekrinen*, "He has judged") is proleptic in anticipation of the climax of the harlot's judgment (Alford). The object of judgment, τὴν πόρνην (*tēn pornēn*, "the harlot"), has now replaced the earth-dwellers as the chief persecutor of the saints. Under the fifth seal the souls under the altar prayed for God to avenge their blood from the latter, but this is rejoicing over the avenging of the former for the same reason as in 6:10, which uses the same two verbs, κρίνω (*krinō*, "I judge") and ἐκδικέω (*ekdikeō*, "I avenge"), that occur in the last clause of this verse.

The relative pronoun ἥτις (*hētis*, "the very one who") highlights the qualitative aspect of the harlot's activities that prompted her judgment. The heart of her guilt centers in the fact that she "corrupted the earth with her fornication" (ἔφθειρεν τὴν γῆν ἐν τῇ πορνείᾳ αὐτῆς [*ephtheiren tēn gēn en tē porneia autēs*]), an unsavory influence for which the prophecy has denounced her earlier (14:8; 17:2; 18:3). A strengthened form of φθείρω (*phtheirō*, "I corrupt"), διαφθείρω (*diaphtheirō*, "I destroy"), occurs in 11:18 and is a recollection of Jer. 51:25 (LXX) where the prophet dwells on the destructive impact of Babylon. The uncompounded form used here finds frequent use in an ethical sense in the NT (1 Cor. 3:17; 15:33; Jude 10) (Swete, Mounce).

Another proleptic aorist ἐξεδίκησεν (*exedikēsen*, "has avenged") celebrates God's response to the harlot's corrupting impact. God will exact vengeance from her for the blood of His servants. The clause

---

14. Swete, *Apocalypse*, p. 243; Charles, *Revelation*, 2:119; Leon Morris, *The Revelation of St. John*, TNTC (Grand Rapids: Eerdmans, 1969), p. 224.
15. Friedrich Düsterdieck, *Critical and Exegetical Handbook to the Revelation of John*, in Meyer's Commentary, trans. and ed. Henry E. Jacobs (New York: Funk & Wagnalls, 1887), p. 451.

which speaks of this seems to be the shortened form of a larger idea: ἐρύσατο τοὺς δούλους αὐτοῦ ἐκ τῆς χειρὸς αὐτῆς, ἐκδικήσας ἐξ αὐτῆς τὸ αἷμα αὐτῶν (*erysato tous doulous autou ek tēs cheiros autēs, ekdikēsas ex autēs to haima autōn*, "He has delivered His slaves from her hand, having avenged their blood from her") (Swete). This is a note sounded earlier in the angelic pronouncement of 18:24. It is a familiar theme in the song of Moses too (Deut. 32:42-43) (Ford). The impatient cry of 6:10 has now received its answer. The wording of the present clause is very close to that of 2 Kings 9:7, which speaks of vengeance exacted from the hand of Jezebel for her killing of God's slaves. It views the vengeance as a penalty taken by force from a reluctant hand (ἐκ χειρὸς αὐτῆς [*ek cheiros autēs*, "from her hand"], cf. 6:10; 18:20) (Alford, Bullinger, Charles, Moffatt). The term δούλων (*doulōn*, "slaves") includes both saints and prophets of 18:24. This part of the song celebrates the implementation of judicial equity whereby the punishment suits the crime both in kind and in degree (cf. 16:7) (Kiddle).

19:3 Verse 3 has a heavenly encore to the first song: καὶ δεύτερον εἴρηκαν, Ἀλληλουϊά· καὶ ὁ καπνὸς αὐτῆς ἀναβαίνει εἰς τοὺς αἰῶνας τῶν αἰώνων (*kai deuteron eirēkan, Hallēlouia; kai ho kapnos autēs anabainei eis tous aiōnas tōn aiōnōn*, "and they said a second [time], 'Hallelujah; and her smoke ascends forever and ever'"). The adverbial accusative δεύτερον (*deuteron*, "a second [time]") indicates that the singers are the same as in the first song (Ford).

This second "hallelujah" is not just a formal repetition of the first one. It heightens the emphasis on the praise offered to the Lord (cf. Job 33:14; Ps. 62:11) (Swete). The reason for the praise follows the καί (*kai*) in the clause, καὶ ὁ καπνὸς αὐτῆς ἀναβαίνει εἰς τοὺς αἰῶνας τῶν αἰώνων (*kai ho kapnos autēs anabainei eis tous aiōnas tōn aiōnōn*, "and her smoke ascends forever and ever"), corresponding to the reasons introduced by ὅτι (*hoti*) in v. 2 (Alford). This is a "circumstantial" clause, a Hebraistic usage that gives the καί (*kai*) an essentially causal force. The clause states the accompanying conditions that justify the call to praise *hallelouia*, which in Hebrew is, of course, a verb הַלְלוּ (*halĕlû*) (Charles).

The reason consists of the fact that the city's destruction is final, complete, and irreversible. The terminology for permanence is somewhat the same as in God's judgments of Sodom and Gomorrah (Gen. 19:38) and Edom (Isa. 34:10). Judgments of these other cities were previews of this judgment.[16] This smoke is an allusion to the fire that will destroy Babylon (17:16; 18:8, 9, 18; cf. 14:11).[17] The continuing

---

16. Philip Edgcumbe Hughes, *The Book of Revelation* (Grand Rapids: Eerdmans, 1990), p. 197.
17. Beasley-Murray, *Revelation*, p. 272; Wall, *Revelation*, p. 221.

ascent of smoke, so vividly portrayed by the present tense of ἀναβαίνει (*anabainei*, "ascends" or "keeps on ascending"), supplies the finishing touch to the description of Babylon's collapse already set forth in 18:21-24 (Swete). It echoes what the gospels teach about unquenchable fire (Matt. 3:12; Luke 3:17; Mark 9:43) (Ford), but is in stark contrast with the continuing ascent of the incense-prayers of the saints (Rev. 8:4).[18] The rising smoke that accompanies the singing of this song demonstrates the truthfulness of the song's message (Beckwith).

The flames that destroy the physical city will, of course, burn out in due time, especially in light of the fact that the earth on which the city stands is soon to be a thing of the past (20:11). The resulting spiritual devastation will be eternal, however. Therefore, εἰς τοὺς αἰῶνας τῶν αἰώνων (*eis tous aiōnas tōn aiōnōn*, "forever and ever") must refer to the remaining period of a thousand years (20:1-10) plus, until the passing away of the old earth, insofar as the smoking or burned-out ruins of the material city is concerned (Charles, Beasley-Murray). Yet beyond this the song must view the eternal fate of individuals intimately connected with the city, because the identical expression *eis tous aiōnas tōn aiōnōn* spans the entire scope of eternity future. The comparable expression εἰς αἰῶνας αἰώνων (*eis aiōnas aiōnōn*) does the same in 14:11.

19:4 The third song comes from a different source, the twenty-four elders and the four living beings whose last mention was in 14:3: καὶ ἔπεσαν οἱ πρεσβύτεροι οἱ εἴκοσι τέσσαρες καὶ τὰ τέσσαρα ζῷα, καὶ προσεκύνησαν τῷ θεῷ τῷ καθημένῳ ἐπὶ τῷ θρόνῳ, λέγοντες, Ἀμήν, Ἀλληλουϊά (*kai epesan hoi presbyteroi hoi eikosi tessares kai ta tessara zōa, kai prosekynēsan tō theō tō kathēmenō epi tō thronō, legontes, Amēn, Hallēlouia*, "and the twenty-four elders and the four living beings fell, and worshiped God who sits upon the throne, saying, 'Amen, Hallelujah'"). These same two groups joined the rest of the angels in falling before the throne and worshiping God in 7:11, much the same as they do here. Their acts of adoration are reminiscent of what they have done in 4:9-10; 5:8, 14 also.[19] The elders and living beings, who have entered the account only incidentally in 11:16 and 14:3 after being prominent in the setting of the judgment scene (Rev. 4-5) and other earlier chapters, at this point re-enter the heavenly scene for this their last appearance to celebrate the completion of that judgment. The focus is mainly on the city of God from here on, so these heavenly beings conclude their role by joining the antiphonal chorus in positive response to the songs of praise over the demise of Babylon.

---

18. Swete, *Apocalypse*, p. 243; Robertson, *Word Pictures*, 6:448; Wall, *Revelation*, p. 221.
19. Swete, *Apocalypse*, p. 244; Robertson, *Word Pictures*, 6:448.

Τῷ θεῷ (*Tō theō*, "God") τῷ καθημένῳ ἐπὶ τῷ θρόνῳ (*tō kathēmenō epi tō thronō*, "who sits upon the throne") is the object of their worship. Only one other time in the book does the name of God, *tō theō*, appear with the appellation *tō kathēmenō epi tō thronō*. That is in 7:10. The rest of the time, "the one who sits upon the throne" functions independently as a title for the first person of the Trinity.

Each time either one or both of these two groups have sung in this book (4:8, 11; 5:9-10, 11-12, 14; 7:11; 11:17-18), their song has touched on a central theme of Revelation. So all of those themes are implicit in their brief two-word song here: ᾽Αμήν, ῾Αλληλουϊά (*Amēn, Hallēlouia*, "Amen, Hallelujah").[20] But in particular they give special assent to the praise of the heavenly voice just prior (Alford, Kiddle). The combination of "amen, hallelujah" alludes to Ps. 106:48, the doxology that closes Book IV of the Psalter (Lee, Mounce). Interestingly, the LXX (Ps. 107:48) renders that combination by γένοιτο, γένοιτο (*genoito, genoito*, "may it be, may it be") (Charles). In 7:12 the elders and living beings use "amen" to join with the angels in voicing their concurrence with the heavenly multitude's song, and in 5:14 the four living beings use "amen" to concur with the song they have just sung as a part of a larger group. Like 7:12, this is a social use of the word to indicate solemn agreement with the words of another (cf. 1 Kings 1:36) (Swete, Moffatt).

19:5 Identification of the singer of the fourth song of the chapter is no easy task: Καὶ φωνὴ ἀπὸ τοῦ θρόνου ἐξῆλθεν λέγουσα, Αἰνεῖτε τῷ θεῷ ἡμῶν, πάντες οἱ δοῦλοι αὐτοῦ, [καὶ]* οἱ φοβούμενοι αὐτόν, οἱ μικροὶ καὶ οἱ μεγάλοι (*Kai phōnē apo tou thronou exēlthen legousa, Aineite tō theō hēmōn, pantes hoi douloi autou, [kai] hoi phoboumenoi auton, hoi mikroi kai hoi megaloi*, "And a voice from the throne came forth saying, 'Praise our God, all His slaves, [even] those who fear Him, small and great'"). Even though it comes "from the throne" (ἀπὸ τοῦ θρόνου [*apo tou thronou*]), it is not the voice of God or of the Lamb, because of the first person pronoun ἡμῶν (*hēmōn*, "our") in the expression "our God." The Lamb's way of speaking of God is "my God" (θεόν μου [*theon mou*]), not "our God" (John 20:17; cf. Rev. 3:2).

The voice does not come "out of the temple" (ἐκ τοῦ ναοῦ [*ek tou naou*]) "from the throne" (ἀπὸ τοῦ θρόνου [*apo tou thronou*]) as in 16:17, but simply away from the throne. The throne is the direction from which the voice came, but not necessarily the source of the voice. Positive identification of this voice is impossible from the available information, but this is not the first time such a difficulty has arisen

---

20. M. Robert Mulholland, *Revelation, Holy Living in an Unholy World* (Grand Rapids: Zondervan, 1990), p. 292 n. 19; Wall, *Revelation*, p. 221.

(cf. 1:10; 10:4, 8; 14:2).²¹ It is impossible to rule one way or the other on the suggestion that it is one of the four living beings (cf. Beckwith, Kiddle).

Whatever its source, the voice is authoritative, however, as it commands αἰνεῖτε τῷ θεῷ ἡμῶν (*aineite tǭ theǭ hēmōn*, "praise our God"). The present imperative αἰνεῖτε (*aineite*, "praise") implies a response of continuous praise. The command alludes specifically to Ps. 135:1, 20 and refers generally to another of the Hallel psalms, Ps. 113:1 (Johnson). Allusions to these psalms demonstrate that the vindication for which the psalmists cried out so often has now occurred (Kiddle).

The potential singers addressed are πάντες οἱ δοῦλοι αὐτοῦ, [καὶ] οἱ φοβούμενοι αὐτόν (*pantes hoi douloi autou, [kai] hoi phoboumenoi auton*, "all His slaves, even those who fear Him"). This designation indicates that the slaves or servants of God are those who piously fear Him, i.e., who yield honor and obedience to Him. In 11:18 οἱ φοβούμενοι τὸ ὄνομά σου (*hoi phoboumenoi to onoma sou*) refers to the whole body of the faithful (Charles). It probably includes the saints and the prophets named in 18:14 (cf. 19:2). Preoccupied at the moment with judgment, John takes faith in God as the practical equivalent of this fear. Other NT writers emphasize the complementary element of love (e.g., Rom. 8:28) as does John elsewhere (e.g., John 5:42; 8:42), but here he places a high premium on lowly confidence rather than on warm intimacy (Swete, Moffatt).

These who are summoned to worship must be the slaves of God in heaven, because the summons of 18:20 to which this responds was addressed to heaven and because *phōnē apo tou thronou* would probably have been φωνὴ ἐκ τοῦ οὐρανοῦ (*phōnē ek tou ouranou*, "a voice out of heaven") if the call were addressed to people on earth (cf. 10:4, 8; 11:12; 14:2, 13; 18:4) (Charles).

The call extends to Christians of all levels of intellectual capacity, social standing, spiritual progress, and whatever other categories men use to group themselves (Swete). Οἱ μικροὶ καὶ οἱ μέγαλοι (*Hoi mikroi kai hoi megaloi*, "Small and great") erases all socio-economic distinctions in extending the privilege of praising God to all the faithful (Johnson). This part of the song alludes to the words of one of the Hallel psalms, Ps. 115:13 (cf. Rev. 11:18) (Kiddle, Johnson).

19:6 The last song in this series turns from retrospect and praise to God for His victory over the harlot to look to the future and praise Him for His coming reign: καὶ ἤκουσα ὡς φωνὴν ὄχλου πολλοῦ καὶ ὡς φωνὴν

---

21. Henry Alford, *The Greek Testament* (London: Longmans, Green, 1903), 4:723-24; Swete, *Apocalypse*, p. 244; Lee, "Revelation," 4:779; Isbon T. Beckwith, *The Apocalypse of John* (New York: Macmillan, 1919), p. 721; Charles, *Revelation*, 2:124; Robertson, *Word Pictures*, 6:448.

ὑδάτων πολλῶν καὶ ὡς φωνὴν βροντῶν ἰσχυρῶν λεγόντων*, 'Αλληλουϊά, ὅτι ἐβασίλευσεν κύριος ὁ θεὸς [ἡμῶν]* ὁ παντοκράτωρ (*kai ēkousa hōs phōnēn ochlou pollou kai hōs phōnēn hydatōn pollōn kai hōs phōnēn brontōn ischyrōn legontōn, Hallēlouia, hoti ebasileusen kyrios ho theos [hēmōn] ho pantokratōr*, "and I heard [something] like a voice of a great multitude and like a sound of many waters and like a sound of loud [peals of] thunder saying, 'Hallelujah, because our Lord God Almighty has begun to reign'"). This, the last song of praise in the Apocalypse, is a divine epithalamium (Moffatt). The wedding party is in place, and the marriage is about to commence. Like the songs of 19:1-5, this one celebrates the occasion of the fall of the great city, but does so by anticipating the subsequent results of that fall. Two contrasting sides of the same theme emerge pointedly in a comparison of the second ὅτι (*hoti*) clause of v. 2 and the ὅτι (*hoti*) clause of v. 7: God has judged the great harlot, and the marriage of the Lamb has come, the bride having made herself ready (Beckwith). The perspective changes, but this is not a major transition in the narrative (contra Mounce). The concluding formula of 19:9-10 is a clearer marker of the conclusion of the division of the narrative which began at 17:1.

A comparison of this voice to a large crowd of people, the roar of a mighty waterfall, and deafening peals of thunder (cf. Ezek. 1:24; 43:2; Dan. 10:6) is fittingly dramatic because of the enormous significance of its pronouncement: God has finally established His universal reign over all the earth (Mounce). John heard what resembled a great multitude only in 19:1, but the fullness of what he hears now is even more impressive. It is "[something] like a voice of a great multitude and like a sound of many waters and like a sound of loud [peals of] thunder" (ὡς φωνὴν ὄχλου πολλοῦ καὶ ὡς φωνὴν ὑδάτων πολλῶν καὶ ὡς φωνὴν βροντῶν ἰσχυρῶν [*hōs phōnēn ochlou pollou kai hōs phōnēn hydatōn pollōn kai hōs phōnēn brontōn ischyrōn*]).

Establishing the identity of the singers is once again a challenge. The fact that John heard their singing as a response to the invitation of v. 5 for the faithful to join in praising God is good reason to think that the redeemed are the singers (Lee, Charles). Yet a closer examination divulges that this is not a response to v. 5, because the specific perspective is different from that of the earlier songs in the series, even though the general theme is the same (Beckwith). Furthermore, the redeemed can hardly be the singers, because the subject of their song is partly the bride who symbolizes at least a portion, if not the total number, of the redeemed in heaven.

The better course is to see this as the singing of heavenly voices in an angelic chorus as in v. 1 (Beckwith). "The sound of many waters" compares to voices in 14:2 which were angelic. The similarity of "a sound of loud [peals of] thunder" to expressions in 6:1; 10:1-4; 14:2 is striking. In all these places the utterances had angelic sources. Identifying the singers as angels also matches with 11:15-17 where singers rejoiced in anticipation of the establishment of God's kingdom on earth just as these do.

This vast assemblage sings a fourth heavenly "hallelujah," and immediately furnishes the reason for doing so in the ὅτι (*hoti*, "because") clause: ὅτι ἐβασίλευσεν κύριος ὁ θεὸς [ἡμῶν] ὁ παντοκράτωρ (*hoti ebasileusen kyrios ho theos [hēmōn] ho pantokratōr*, "because our Lord God Almighty has begun to reign"). The kingdom of God can now replace the demolished world-power that had dominated the earth in opposition to God for so long. The aorist ἐβασίλευσεν (*ebasileusen*) is proleptic and ingressive. Looking back from the future point when the climactic battle of 19:19-21 is complete, the verb tense sees God's assumption of power in reigning over the earth.[22] This is the same use of the verb and tense as with ἐβασίλευσας (*ebasileusas*) in 11:17. This critical transition in history will accompany the marriage of the Lamb as vv. 7-8 will go on to show. In a sense, this direct divine rule will continue on into eternity in the heavenly city (20:11–21:5) (Beckwith), but first it must demonstrate itself on the old earth during the Millennium (Mounce, Johnson).

The title for God utilized by the singers is κύριος ὁ θεὸς [ἡμῶν] ὁ παντοκράτωρ (*kyrios ho theos [hēmōn] ho pantokratōr*, "our Lord God Almighty"). The same title occurs in 4:8; 11:17; 15:3; 16:7; 21:22, and nearly the same one is in 1:8; 16:14. In some of these cases, it is a vocative addressing God directly, but in others it is simply a third person designation as it is here. It took courage to use this title under the regime of the emperor Domitian who had conferred on himself the title "our lord and god" (Mounce). Angels and redeemed men have equal rights to use this mode in speaking of God (Swete).

19:7 The heavenly song continues with an exhortation to joyfulness and a recognition of God's glory: χαίρωμεν καὶ ἀγαλλιῶμεν, καὶ δώσωμεν* τὴν δόξαν αὐτῷ, ὅτι ἦλθεν ὁ γάμος τοῦ ἀρνίου, καὶ ἡ γυνὴ αὐτοῦ ἡτοίμασεν ἑαυτήν (*chairōmen kai agalliōmen, kai dōsōmen tēn doxan autō, hoti ēlthen ho gamos tou arniou, kai hē gynē autou hētoimasen heautēn*, "let us rejoice and exult, and give glory to Him, because the marriage of the Lamb has come, and His wife has prepared herself"). The two verbs χαίρω (*chairō*, "I rejoice") and ἀγαλλιόω (*agallioō*, "I exult") are together also in Matt. 5:12 where Christ calls His followers to rejoice in the face of persecution because of their great

---

22. Beckwith, *Apocalypse*, p. 726; Robertson, *Word Pictures*, 6:449; George E. Ladd, *A Commentary on the Revelation of John* (Grand Rapids: Eerdmans, 1972), p. 246.

heavenly reward. Here the two present hortatory subjunctives are a mutual invitation among the singers to keep on rejoicing and exulting because of the arrival of the Lamb's wedding.

As part of their celebration, they invite one another to "give glory" (δώσωμεν τὴν δόξαν [*dōsōmen tēn doxan*]) to God for the same reason. The work of getting the bride ready has been God's, so He deserves the credit.[23] Other mentions of giving God glory or failing to do so are in 11:13; 14:7; 16:9 (Swete). This song invites the appropriate response toward the one whose provisions for the bride have played the dominant role in her preparation (cf. Rom. 1:21; 4:20).[24]

The conjunction ὅτι (*hoti*) introduces the reason for the three exhortations in v. 7 and at the same time brings into focus a new theme, the consummation of the union between Christ and His people. This is a union that signals the end (21:1 ff.) (Alford). This is not a cause for praise that adds to the one expressed by the *hoti* clause of v. 6, because the establishment of the kingdom of God and the marriage of the Lamb are in reality one event viewed from two perspectives (Beckwith). The aorist tense of ἦλθεν (*ēlthen*, "has come") is proleptic like ἐβασίλευσεν (*ebasileusen*) in v. 6, ἡτοίμασεν (*hētoimasen*, "has prepared") in v. 7, and ἐδόθη (*edothē*, "it has been granted") in v. 8. From the perspective of the culmination of the seventh-bowl events, the marriage has come at last.[25] In one sense, the marriage-day of the Lamb and His bride is the day of His second coming (19:11-21) (Moffatt), but in another sense it does not come until the consummation of the thousand years (20:3) with the revelation of the bride (21:1 ff.). The initial phase of this wedding is now imminent (Swete), but the account cannot move immediately to a description of the wedding because the defeat of Messiah's enemies, the Millennium, the last futile effort of Satan, and the judgment that precede the wedding must come first (Moffatt, Kiddle).

In the OT, God is the bridegroom of Israel (cf. Isa. 54:6; 62:5; Jer. 31:32; Ezek. 16:7-14; Hos. 2:16, 19), and in the NT, Christ is the bridegroom of the church (cf. 2 Cor. 11:2; Eph. 5:25 ff.; Rev. 3:20; 19:9; 21:2, 9; 22:17). In the gospels, Christ is the bridegroom a number of times (cf. Matt. 9:15; Mark 2:19-20; Luke 5:34-35; John 3:29) and parables about marriage occur in Matt. 22:2-14; 25:1-13; Luke 14:15-24. The current rejoicing over "the marriage of the Lamb" (ὁ γάμος τοῦ ἀρνίου [*ho gamos tou arniou*]) sets the tone for the extended description of the

---

23. Hughes, *Revelation*, p. 201.
24. J. P. M. Sweet, *Revelation* (Philadelphia: Westminster, Pelican, 1979), p. 279.
25. Düsterdieck, *Revelation*, pp. 452-53; Alford, *Greek Testament*, 4:724; Lee, "Revelation," 4:781; Robertson, *Word Pictures*, 6:449.

Lamb's bride in 19:8 and chapters 21-22 (cf. esp. 21:2, 9). It is in accord with the writer's habit to throw out hints of a future scene some time before he begins its main description (e.g., cf. 14:8 with chaps. 17-18). The figure of marriage denotes the intimate and indissoluble union of the community of believers with the Messiah. The wedding image for the Jews was a more intimate aspect of the kingdom of God.[26]

The time and place of this marriage feast have been somewhat controversial, with one viewpoint being that it takes place in heaven and lasts throughout eternity (Mounce) and the other that it is a feast on earth and coincides with the millennial kingdom (Walvoord, Ladd, Beasley-Murray). A decision on this issue depends in part on a decision later in v. 7 regarding the identity of the bride. If she represents the church—i.e., the people of God between Pentecost and the Rapture—it is quite conceivable that the marriage takes place in heaven after the catching up of the saints to be with Christ, but before Christ returns to earth. The sequence of chapter 19 (Scott) and the location of the current scene in heaven[27] argue for this sequence and location, except for the fact that *ēlthen* in v. 7 is proleptic (Ladd), as indicated above, and this passage is part of an intercalation which is not a part of Revelation's strict chronological sequence.

The normal understanding would be that the event, coming after the destruction of Babylon and at the end of the Great Tribulation has the second coming of Christ to earth as its climax (Walvoord, Beasley-Murray). This fixes the place of the feast as on earth and the time as during the Millennium. Yet it cannot transpire on earth in a completed sense until after the Millennium when the rest of the faithful from the thousand-year period combine with the martyrs and other saints to complete the body of the redeemed (Charles). The language of 21:2, 9 is quite explicit regarding the bride in the new heaven and the new earth (Lee). The better part of wisdom is to include both the Millennium and the new heaven and the new earth as the prolonged wedding feast of the Lamb and His bride (cf. 19:9). It will commence with Christ's glorious appearance to initiate His kingdom on this present earth.

One further matter of reconciliation requires a separation of the wedding itself (19:7) from the wedding feast (19:9). It is necessary to have the marriage initiated in heaven after the Rapture of the saints, because when Christ's army of saints return with Him to earth, they

---

26. Swete, *Apocalypse*, p. 246; Lee, "Revelation," 4:731; Robertson, *Word Pictures*, 6:449; J. Massyngberde Ford, *Revelation*, vol. 38 of AB (Garden City, N.Y.: Doubleday, 1975), p. 310; Johnson, "Revelation," 12:571.
27. William R. Newell, *The Book of Revelation* (Chicago: Moody, 1935), p. 295.

will have already put on their wedding apparel (19:8, 14). So the initiation of the union happens in heaven, but the celebration of that union with a grand wedding feast ensues on earth for the span of the millennial and eternal kingdoms.

The preparedness of the bride for this wedding is a related reason for the celebration called for in the song of v. 7. The clause ἡ γυνὴ αὐτοῦ ἡτοίμασεν ἑαυτήν (*hē gynē autou hētoimasen heautēn*, "His wife has prepared herself") anticipates the ἡτοιμασμένην ὡς νύμφην (*hētoimasmenēn hōs nymphēn*, "prepared as a bride") of 21:2 and indicates a responsibility of self-preparation that rests on her shoulders (cf. 2 Cor. 7:1; 1 John 3:3; Jude 21). The ultimate preparation is that furnished by God, however, who alone deserves the glory for it (19:7*b*). This agrees with Eph. 5:25-27 where preparation of the bride is the work of Christ.[28] Two parables of Jesus illustrate the same two sides of responsibility: the parable of the talents illustrating the gracious bestowal of rewards for *service rendered* (Matt. 25:14-23) and the parable of the householder illustrating the *sovereignty* of God in giving to all alike (Matt. 20:1-16) (Scott).

"Wife" (ἡ γυνὴ [*gynē*]) is the third of three metaphors in Revelation derived from women. The mother of chapter 12 is a symbol for national Israel. The harlot of 17:1–19:3 pictures Babylon. "His wife" is a direct antithesis to the harlot, as the theme of the first song in chapter 19 is the destruction of the harlot (19:1-3) and the theme of this one is the wedding of the Lamb to His bride.[29] *Gynē* refers to a bride here as it does in a number of other places (Gen. 29:21[LXX]; Deut. 22:24[LXX]; Matt. 1:20; Rev. 21:9), but νύμφη (*nymphē*, "bride") (21:2, 9) is the more specific term. At this point the bride is the people of God, but 21:9–22:5 reapplies the figure to the new Jerusalem. The people and their city are so close to each other that the figure for one is applicable to the other (Swete).

A remaining task is to establish more specifically the identity of the bride. Does she represent the redeemed of national Israel only, the redeemed of the church only, or the redeemed of all time both from Israel and the church? Limiting the figure to the redeemed of national Israel has support when the OT speaks repeatedly of the marriage of the Lord to His people Israel (Isa. 54:5-8; 62:4-5; Jer. 3:14; Hos. 2:16, 19) (Bullinger). A major obstacle to this line of proof, however, is that in every OT context where Israel is the wife of the Lord, she is, or has been, a *faithless* wife.[30] The figure of a wife is never used to portray the

---

28. Swete, *Apocalypse*, p. 246; Robertson, *Word Pictures*, 6:449.
29. Mulholland, *Revelation*, p. 293.
30. Jan Fekkes III ("'His Bride Has Prepared Herself': Revelation 19–21 and Isaian Nuptial Imagery," *JBL* 109, no. 2 [Summer 1990]: 272-73) notes that

apostasy of the church. Besides the problem of Israel's loyalty, this viewpoint has difficulty in excluding the church from the figure of the bride, even if it does prove that Israel is the bride.

Without question, the church in the NT is Christ's bride (Eph. 5:32). She is a virgin bride (2 Cor. 11:2), not a divorced wife returning to her husband. The latter is the image of Israel (e.g., Jer. 3:14-20). She can never be a virgin again (cf. Lev. 21:13-14) (Scott). In contrast, the church is a virgin in waiting for her coming Bridegroom (Rev. 21:2, 9) (Walvoord). The place on Christ's earthly throne promised to the church in the coming kingdom (Rev. 3:21) is confirmation of her role as bride, as is Christ's anticipation of eating with her once again in the kingdom, when He instituted the Lord's Supper (Matt. 26:29; Mark 14:25; Luke 22:16, 30). More strong support for identifying the bride as the church lies in the promise to the Laodicean church of participation in the marriage supper of the Lamb (3:20). Equally strong is the consideration that the apparel of Christ's armies is the same as that of His bride (cp. 19:14 with 19:8). To come with Him at His return as His armies do presupposes their bodily resurrection prior to that time. The only ones who will have risen from the dead by then will be members of the body of Christ (1 Cor. 15:51-52; 1 Thess. 4:13-18). Only they will have had opportunity to put on the prescribed attire for a triumphant return to earth with Christ. This is substantial reason to identify the bride as the church alone.

The difficulty of including Israel along with the church as part of the bride is a chronological one. OT saints and dead saints from the period of Daniel's seventieth week will rise in time for the Millennium (Dan. 12:1-2), but not in time to join Christ in His triumphal return (19:14). It is also impossible for saints who die during the Millennium to be a part of this company, because their resurrection will not come in time (20:5-6). Yet it is incontrovertible that Israel will appear with the church in the New Jerusalem which is also Christ's bride. The city's twelve pillars and twelve foundations (21:12, 14) prove the presence of both distinctive groups. So the bride of Christ will be a growing body of people, with the church functioning as Christ's bride during that phase of the wedding feast that comes during the Millennium, but with the integration of the new order (21:1 ff.), the bride receives the enhancement of the redeemed of Israel and of all ages, including the Millennium.

With this refinement in view, the bride of 19:7 is a figure for the church, the body of Christ, which having been joined to Christ follow-

---

in the OT only Isaiah uses the marriage analogy in a consistently positive way regarding the future relationship of the Lord and His faithful remnant (cf. Isa. 54:11-12; 61:10). This is an exception to the general rule in the OT.

ing the Rapture, will return with Him for the marriage supper of the Lamb on earth during the Millennium.

19:8 Verse 8 continues with an explanation of the preparation of the bride: καὶ ἐδόθη αὐτῇ ἵνα περιβάληται βύσσινον λαμπρὸν καθαρόν, τὸ γὰρ βύσσινον τὰ δικαιώματα τῶν ἁγίων ἐστίν (*kai edothē autē hina peribalētai byssinon lampron katharon, to gar byssinon ta dikaiōmata tōn hagiōn estin*, "and it has been granted to her that she clothe herself in bright, clean fine linen, for the fine linen is the righteous deeds of the saints"). The form ἐδόθη (*edothē*, "it has been granted") occurs some twenty times in Revelation 6-20, each time signaling something granted by God.[31] Here it tells of what the bride has received through divine grace (Lee). The καί (*kai*, "and") indicates that the following words are in elaboration of the ἡτοίμασεν ἑαυτήν (*hētoimasen heautēn*, "has prepared herself") of v. 7 and could possibly mean, "*yea*, it has been granted to her . . ." (Moffatt).

This understanding of *kai* raises a related issue of whether v. 8 is a continuation of the voice of the celestial chorus or not. One opinion would end the chorus with v. 7 and have v. 8 as a resumption of John's narration, with *kai* having its common connective sense (Alford). Reasons for this interpretation include the common use of *edothē* in narrative portions, with the question of whether it is ever used in a heavenly anthem of the book (Charles), and the inappropriateness of the explanatory γάρ (*gar*, "for") clause in the middle of v. 8 if this is part of a heavenly song (Alford). In view of this latter reason, a third view would end the song in the middle of v. 8 just after βύσσινον λαμπρὸν καθαρόν (*byssinon lampron katharon*, "bright, clean fine linen") (Lee).[32] A probing consideration that opposes ending the song at the end of v. 7 or in the middle of v. 8 is the query, where did John get the information supplied in v. 8 to enable him to furnish an explanation? He is a spectator, not a narrator. The only time he is in a position to offer clarification is when he uses a καὶ εἶδον (*kai eidon*, "and I saw") or καὶ ἤκουσα (*kai ēkousa*, "and I heard") to identify his receipt of new information. Neither of these occurs here. Since v. 8 has no indication of a change in singers/speakers and v. 9 does indicate this explicitly, it is better to read v. 8 as a continuation and conclusion of the song begun in v. 6.

The combination ἐδόθη . . . ἵνα (*edothē . . . hina*, "has been granted

---

31. Swete, *Apocalypse*, p. 247; Robertson, *Word Pictures*, 6:449-50.
32. Lee, "Revelation," 4:781. An extreme of this view sees the last line of v. 8 as a gloss added by a later editor (Charles, *Revelation*, 2:127-28), but no textual sources or substantial internal data exist to show that this line came from any other hand but John's. Besides it is uncharacteristically abrupt to end the song with the particular words in the middle of this verse (Alford, *Greek Testament*, 4:724).

. . . that") appears three other times in the book (6:4; 8:3; 9:5) in stating divine provisions for various actions. What the bride has done for herself (v. 7) is in the ultimate sense a provision of God's grace. Her self-preparation (v. 7) equates to God's provision for her to clothe herself in "bright, clean fine linen" (βύσσινον λαμπρὸν καθαρόν [*byssinon lampron katharon*]). This is similar attire to that of the seven angels in 15:6 and is especially similar to that of the armies of the Word of God in 19:14. It is a glaring contrast to the gaudy clothing of the harlot already described (17:4; 18:16).[33] The adjective λαμπρὸν (*lampron*) is the color (or lack of it) that represents radiant whiteness as indicative of divine glory.[34] Καθαρόν (*Katharon*, "Clean") is the mark of purity such as will characterize the new Jerusalem (cf. 21:18, 21). This is the sober dress of a woman of dignity, not the flashy splendor of a harlot. The dazzling whiteness of the bride's garments symbolizes the inward purity of God's people collectively (cf. 7:9, 14) (Swete, Kiddle). The "fine linen" (βύσσινον [*byssinon*]) is like that of Egypt which Pharaoh put on Joseph (Gen. 41:42; cf. Dan. 10:5; 12:6-7; Rev. 18:12).

The heavenly singers explain the bridal dress with a concluding γάρ (*gar*, "for") clause, telling why the saints along with Christ have preparatory work to do.[35] The words "the fine linen is the righteous deeds of the saints" (τὸ . . . βύσσινον τὰ δικαιώματα τῶν ἁγίων ἐστίν [*to . . . byssinon ta dikaiōmata tōn hagiōn estin*]) understood in connection with the *edothē* earlier in v. 8 reflect the proper balance between the divine provision of grace and the human response of obedience (cf. Eph. 2:10). The bride receives her garments from God, but she responds to the gift by her faithfulness to Him. In the immediate sense, the moral purity and activity upon which future bliss hinges are the outcome of human effort, but ultimately they are traceable to God and Christ (cf. Matt. 21:43; 22:2, 11-14) (Moffatt). The bride receives the garment as a gift, but she must put it on.[36]

Δικαιώματα (*Dikaiōmata*, "Righteous deeds") are a manifestation of the inner life and are practically equivalent to character (cf. 14:13) (Charles). The same noun refers to the righteous acts of God in 15:4. An effort to refer it to the pure and holy state of the saints here (Alford, Morris) is fruitless because of the inability of this explanation to account for the plural number of the noun (Beckwith). The meaning "righteous deeds" agrees with the meaning of the noun in 15:4 and with the sense of the statement, "their works follow with them," in

33. Robertson, *Word Pictures*, 6:450; Johnson, "Revelation," 12:571.
34. A. Oepke, "λάμπω, ἐκλάμπω, κ. τ. λ.," *TDNT*, 4:27.
35. Robertson, *Word Pictures*, 6:450.
36. Wall, *Revelation*, pp. 222-23.

14:13 (Lee). To the question, "how can righteous deeds be given to her?" (Bullinger), the effective answer is that a transformed life is the proper response to the call of the heavenly bridegroom (Mounce).

19:9 A speaker last visible at 17:15 emerges at this point to mark the conclusion of the extended intercalation regarding Babylon: Καὶ λέγει μοι, Γράψον· Μακάριοι οἱ εἰς τὸ δεῖπνον τοῦ γάμου τοῦ γάμου τοῦ ἀρνίου κεκλημένοι. καὶ λέγει μοι, Οὗτοι οἱ λόγοι ἀληθινοὶ τοῦ θεοῦ εἰσιν (*Kai legei moi, Grapson; Makarioi hoi eis to deipnon tou gamou tou arniou keklēmenoi. kai legei moi, Houtoi hoi logoi alēthinoi tou theou eisin*, "And he says to me, 'Write: Blessed are those who are invited to the marriage supper of the Lamb.' And he says to me, 'These words are the true [ones] of God'"). This speaker is one of the angels of the seven last plagues who initiated his role as John's guide in 17:1. The material between 17:1 and this point is attributable to the same angelic mediator. Some might question this identification, but the readers would easily remain focused on one of these "last plague" angels until he clearly drops from the narrative (Beckwith, Kiddle). A comparable identification of the speaker in the parallel verse of 22:6 following an analogous intercalation in 21:9–22:5 confirms this identification.

The angel's initial command γράψον (*grapson*, "write") is the same as in 1:11, 19; 14:3. The similarity to 14:3 is particularly close because it too pertains to the writing of a beatitude (Lee). This gives the current beatitude a special emphasis (Beckwith). Μακάριοι (*Makarioi*, "Blessed") begins the fourth of the book's seven beatitudes (cf. 1:3; 14:13; 16:15; 20:6; 22:7, 14). This along with the rest of the declarations, in pronouncing blessing on the faithful, contains a subtle contrast with those who have not been faithful to Christ.[37] The present one bears a close similarity to Luke 14:15 (cf. Matt. 8:11; 26:29). John's distinctly practical purpose in writing surfaces once more in these words. He furnishes loyal Christians with added motivation to make the right choices (Kiddle).

The participial substantive οἱ . . . κεκλημένοι (*hoi . . . keklēmenoi*, "those who are invited") denotes the permanence of the invitation because of its perfect tense and the divine initiative in issuing the invitation because of its passive voice (Morris). Much discussion has revolved around the identity of these guests. One approach theorizes that two cognate figures combine in this context. One is apocalyptic as in 19:7 and one synoptic as in Matt. 22:2-3 (cf. Matt. 25:10), which when combined result in identifying both the bride and the guests as the saints (Lee, Moffatt). The other explanation separates the two figures by equating the bride with the faithful in the churches and the invited guests with the saints of other ages (Walvoord).

---

37. Robertson, *Word Pictures*, 6:450; Johnson, "Revelation," 12:572.

Decisions already reached in v. 7 regarding the time and place of the marriage and the identity of the bride leave open the door for the type of distinction represented in the second viewpoint. Since the bride in the Millennium is the church, this leaves room for the invited guests at the marriage supper to be the OT saints (Scott). Yet the fluidity of metaphorical language in Scripture is undeniable. Christ is both the Lamb and the shepherd of the sheep (cf. 7:17) and is also a conquering warrior (cf. 19:11-16). In this light, it is not unthinkable that the church is both the bride and the invited guests in this passage (Ladd). Another analogy is the woman clothed in the sun in chapter 12. She represents the people of God corporately, and her children represent the people of God individually.[38] This latter analogy is particularly close to the present passage, and commends the plausibility of the former view that sees both parabolic and apocalyptic figures in 19:7-9. So it is possible to say that this beatitude speaks of the same group of saints under two figures, one corporate and one individual.[39] Yet if this view be correct, this characteristic of figurative inconsistency is not peculiarly a characteristic of apocalyptic writings (contra Kiddle and Wilcock). It is true also of parabolic language, because in Mark 2:19 the disciples of Jesus are wedding guests, not the bride. Also, when Jesus uses the metaphor of a wedding feast to speak of the coming eschatological kingdom, the parable has no role for the bride at all, only one for the invited guests. The same is true in Matt. 25:1-13 (Ladd).

As plausible as this mixing of figures is, it still does not come across as the most probable solution. The earlier decision to limit the bride to the church leaves as the better hypothesis the view that the bride and the invited guests represent two different groups of God's people. This context confirms that distinction. It is obvious that saved people who are not of the bride of Christ will be in the Millennium, because at the very least, unresurrected mortals will be present. They too will be blessed in being part of the marriage feast. With the allowance that relationships will change somewhat at the instigation of the new heaven and new earth, the preferable viewpoint is the one that distinguishes the bride from the invited guests.

The cognate adjective χλητοί (*klētoi*, "called") (17:14) refers to those who will accompany the Lamb in His climactic encounter with the beast and ten kings (19:19-21), but that is not in the context of

---

38. G. V. Caird, *A Commentary on the Revelation of St. John the Divine*, HNTC (New York: Harper & Row, 1966), p. 234.

39. Düsterdieck, *Revelation*, p. 454; Kiddle, *Revelation*, pp. 381-82; Michael Wilcock, *The Message of Revelation* (Downers Grove, Ill.: InterVarsity, 1975), p. 173 n. 1; Wall, *Revelation*, p. 223.

invitations to a wedding feast. The invited ones here are people who validated their invitations by showing up at the wedding dressed in proper attire (cf. Matt. 22:11-14). They were not too busy to come as were the invited guests in the parables of Matt. 22:3-5 and Luke 14:16-20.

This beatitude carries the one in 14:13 one step further. The rest promised there has now ripened into high festival, called here τὸ δεῖπνον τοῦ γάμου τοῦ ἀρνίου (*to deipnon tou gamou tou arniou*, "the marriage supper of the Lamb") (cf. Isa. 25:6-8; Matt. 8:11; 26:29) (Swete, Mounce). In the culture of John's day, the wedding supper began around evening on the wedding day and lasted for many days. In Revelation, the wedding feast begins the earthly kingdom of God. The bride is the church, and the invited guests are others committed to Jesus (Johnson). Δεῖπνον (*Deipnon*, "Supper") is the same word used for the Lord's Supper that Christ instituted for the church (1 Cor. 11:20), but the Lord's Supper is not the same as the marriage supper of the Lamb which fulfills the commemorative suppers practiced by local churches and is exclusively future in connection with Christ' second advent. The Lord promised Laodicean overcomers the privilege of participation in this supper (3:20). This promise is one of the connecting links between the seven messages and the conditions of the Millennium and eternal state in chapters 20-22 (Alford, Lee).

A second occurrence of καὶ λέγει μοι (*kai legei moi*, "and he says to me") in v. 9 indicates the importance of an additional declaration of the angel-guide (cf. 22:9-10 for a similar repetition in a short space) (Alford). Beginning here and continuing through v. 10, this passage displays a great similarity to 22:6, 8-9. Both have the claim to be the words of God. Both have John falling down to worship. In both the angel refuses his worship and declares that he is a servant of God. In both the angel directs John to worship God. Both passages follow beatitudes (Ford). For a fuller discussion of the correspondences, see Excursus 5 at the end of this volume.

A natural question arises in connection with οὗτοι οἱ λόγοι (*houtoi hoi logoi*, "these words"). To what do they refer? To the beatitude just given?[40] To the words about the harlot's end (19:3) and the certainty of the wedding supper (19:7, 9)? (Johnson). To the general sense underlying the motif of all the visions thus far? (Kiddle). To all that has transpired since 17:1? (Alford). Or to the central theme of the hymn just completed, which is the coming of the kingdom and the marriage of the Lamb? (Beckwith).

To refer the phrase to the beatitude just before is the most natu-

---

40. Hughes, *Revelation*, p. 201.

ral.[41] This is the sort of statement that commonly verifies solemn statements in apocalyptic literature (cf. Dan. 8:26; 10:1; 11:2; 12:7) (Moffatt). Also, it is possible to construe the other two uses of similar statements in 21:5 and 22:6 to refer to their immediate context (Bullinger), but these other two more probably refer to more than a single statement. This last factor weakens the theory of limiting the reference to the beatitude only and broadens the purview of "these words" to a broader context.

Limiting the expression's reference to the coming of the kingdom and the marriage of the Lamb or to these plus the words about the harlot's end has in its favor the climactic nature of the song of vv. 6-8 (Beckwith) and/or the series of songs in vv. 1-8. It also has the advantage of broadening the scope of what "these words" refers to beyond a single statement (Johnson). It also indirectly captures the theme of the angel's dramatic announcement in 10:5-7 (Beckwith). Yet this antecedent of "these" falls short of encompassing all the angel-guide had just revealed to John regarding Babylon.[42]

Expanding the reference of "these words" to include the general sense of all the visions so far has support if the comparable statement in 22:6 covers all that has gone before (Sweet). That general sense would be that the loyal Christian can face his troubles with steadfastness because his persecutors are already sentenced and his own reward is assured (Kiddle). Certain contextual indicators in 22:6 that are not present here provide a ground for the broad application there, however.

In recognition that 19:9 is part of the concluding formula of the angel who became John's guide in 17:1, the best interpretation is to refer "these words" to the prophecies and revelations since then.[43] This formal and emphatic pronouncement of veracity, then, belongs not just to 19:1-8, but also to the rest of the section that it climaxes, 17:1–18:24 (Beasley-Murray). The adjective ἀληθινοί (*alēthinoi*, "true") declares the reality of the events in this narrative. These are happenings that will actually come to pass (Alford). Special methods of interpretation that tend to water down the force of this claim[44] do a serious injustice to the narrative and this statement of verification that climaxes it.

---

41. Ibid.
42. Düsterdieck, *Revelation*, p. 454; Alford, *Greek Testament*, 4:725.
43. Düsterdieck, *Revelation*, p. 454; Alford, *Greek Testament*, 4:725.
44. Swete feels compelled to state that this truth claim does not rule out nonliteral interpretation of the details of the passage (*Apocalypse*, p. 248). As consistently observed, however, literal interpretation is the normal way to understand the words unless some contextual factor warrants interpreting in another way.

19:10 John is so overwhelmed that he prostrates himself at the feet of the angel: καὶ ἔπεσα ἔμπροσθεν τῶν ποδῶν αὐτοῦ προσκυνῆσαι αὐτῷ. καὶ λέγει μοι, Ὅρα μή· σύνδουλός σού εἰμι καὶ τῶν ἀδελφῶν σου τῶν ἐχόντων τὴν μαρτυρίαν Ἰησοῦ· τῷ θεῷ προσκύνησον. ἡ γὰρ μαρτυρία Ἰησοῦ ἐστιν τὸ πνεῦμα τῆς προφητείας (*kai epesa emprosthen tōn podōn autou proskynēsai autō. kai legei moi, Hora mē; syndoulos sou eimi kai tōn adelphōn sou tōn echontōn tēn martyrian Iēsou; tō theō proskynēson. hē gar martyria Iēsou estin to pneuma tēs prophēteias,* "and I fell before his feet to worship him. And he says to me, 'See that you do not [do this]; I am the fellow-slave of you and your brethren who have the testimony of Jesus; worship God. For the testimony of Jesus is the spirit of prophecy'"). Scripture records similar responses by various individuals in Num. 22:31; Josh. 5:14; Judg. 13:20; Dan. 2:46; Acts 10:25; 16:29 (Beckwith, Morris, Sweet). All of these did not have the purpose of worship as John did, however. The combination προσκυνῆσαι αὐτῷ (*proskynēsai autō,* "to worship him") shows this to be John's intention. Clearly, the presence of one who could provide such certainty to the fulfillment of these revelations was overwhelming to John (Alford). Whether he mistakenly regarded the angel as God,[45] yielded to the temptation to worship an angel (cf. Col. 2:18), or was simply beside himself with excitement over the arrival of the consummation[46] is unknown.

Whatever the cause, he had to be corrected. The angel forbids his worship immediately with the words ὅρα μή (*hora mē,* "see that you do not [do this]") (cf. 22:9). This was a common idiom that implied an additional ποιήσεις τοῦτο (*poiēseis touto,* "do this"). This is an example of *aposiopesis* whereby there is a conscious suppression of part of a sentence under the influence of strong emotion. The full construction occurs at Matt. 8:4; 18:10; Mark 1:44; 1 Thess. 5:15.[47] No matter how well intentioned, John's attempt at worship receives a severe rebuke. The tendency toward angel worship had for some time fascinated the churches in the province of Asia (cf. Col. 2:18) and continued to linger in the area after NT times. So the writer deals decisively with the practice both here and in 22:8, even though he puts himself in a bad light in doing so. He sought to help others resist the tendency (Swete, Moffatt, Kiddle). By contrast, the beast about whom he wrote had no such compunctions about accepting human worship (13:4, 8, 12, 15) (Lee).

---

45. Düsterdieck, *Revelation*, p. 455.
46. Robertson, *Word Pictures*, 6:450.
47. Lee, "Revelation," 4:783; Archibald Thomas Robertson, *A Grammar of the Greek New Testament in the Light of Historical Research* (Nashville: Broadman, 1934), p. 1203; idem, *Word Pictures*, 6:450.

Though he uses no conjunction to connect them with his prohibition, the words σύνδουλός σού εἰμι καὶ τῶν ἀδελφῶν σου τῶν ἐχόντων τὴν μαρτυρίαν Ἰησοῦ (*syndoulos sou eimi kai tōn adelphōn sou tōn echontōn tēn martyrian Iēsou*, "I am the fellow-slave of you and your brethren who have the testimony of Jesus") are obviously the reason for his refusal to accept John's worship. His self-designation as a σύνδουλος (*syndoulos*, "fellow-slave") is insightful. It is well-established that all Christians are fellow-slaves (Matt. 18:28; 24:49; Col. 1:7; 4:7; Rev. 6:11), but mention of the similar role of angels is not that frequent. They are servants of the same Lord as Christians (Heb. 1:14) and therefore fellow-slaves too. For an angel to acknowledge his position thus is a prestigious indicator for the prophet John. So the angel's rebuke of John's attempted worship does not abase angels, but it exalts the prophet and his brethren (Moffatt, Kiddle).

The angel further identifies with John and his brethren by characterizing them as those "who have the testimony of Jesus" (τῶν ἐχόντων τὴν μαρτυρίαν Ἰησοῦ [*tōn echontōn tēn martyrian Iēsou*]). Like his human counterparts, an angel can do nothing other than bear the witness of Jesus. A parallel statement in 22:9 elaborates further by referring to being a fellow-slave "of your brothers the prophets and of those who keep the words of this book" (Lee). This does not imply that all Christians are prophets, however (cf. 1 Cor. 12:29). Believers in general do have access to the testimony of Jesus through the service of prophets such as John to convey it to them (Rev. 1:1; 22:6), but they are not themselves the immediate recipients of special revelation that would constitute them as prophets.[48]

"The testimony of Jesus" (τὴν μαρτυρίαν Ἰησοῦ [*tēn martyrian Iēsou*]) is the testimony borne by Jesus, as elsewhere in the book (1:2, 9; 6:9; 12:17; 20:4).[49] The word spoken by Christian prophets originates with the Spirit of God who is the Spirit of Christ, and so they are the testimony borne by Christ and the very words of God (Beckwith, Caird, Beasley-Murray, Johnson). They are the equivalent of Jesus' own testimony (cf. 22:20), His self-revelation that comes ultimately from His Father (1:1). Jesus is both the propagator and the subject of prophetic revelations (Moffatt). This role rests on understanding Ἰησοῦ (*Iēsou*, "of Jesus") as a subjective genitive.[50]

---

48. Düsterdieck, *Revelation*, p. 456.
49. Robertson, *Word Pictures*, 6:451.
50. See discussion at 1:1 (Robert L. Thomas, *Revelation 1-7, An Exegetical Commentary* [Chicago: Moody, 1992], pp. 51-52). A few sources vacillate on this understanding of the genitive here (Alford, *Greek Testament*, 4:726; Swete, *Apocalypse*, p. 249; Bullinger, *Apocalypse*, pp. 505-6; Ladd, *Revelation*, p. 251), but the genitive is always subjective in comparable instances in the book and in all its uses with the noun μαρτυρία.

As a corrective the angel tells John to redirect his worship: τῷ θεῷ προσκύνησον (*tō theō proskynēson*, "worship God"). John was bewildered for the moment and had lost touch with a truth that he knew quite well (cf. John 4:21-24). So the angel very succinctly reminds him of the only one deserving of worship. The aorist imperative always has a note of urgency, so προσκύνησον (*proskynēson*) politely reminds John of the importance of worshiping the proper object. Surprisingly, John needed the reminder in a comparable situation a little later (cf. 22:9).

The angel reinforces his command with a further explanation: ἡ γὰρ μαρτυρία Ἰησοῦ ἐστιν τὸ πνεῦμα τῆς προφητείας (*hē gar martyria Iēsou estin to pneuma tēs prophēteias*, "for the testimony of Jesus is the spirit of prophecy"). Some see John as the source of this explanation (e.g., Lee), but its nature requires that it come from the angel as it supplies a reason for the corrective given (Alford). In giving a reason for worshiping God, the words also clarify why "fellow-slave" can apply to both the angel and to John. Both angels and humans who convey inspired revelation do so on the basis of the divine witness of Jesus. So it is only appropriate that God alone, the ultimate source of that witness, receive the reverence of those who are impressed by that revelation (Beckwith, Moffatt). Prophecy declares the revealed message, whether delivered by an angel or a man. It is a function of servanthood. Worship does not belong to the servant, but to the one served.[51]

The sense of the explanation is, "He who has the spirit of prophecy will convey Jesus' testimony." The message attested by Jesus is "the spirit of prophecy" (τὸ πνεῦμα τῆς προφητείας [*to pneuma tēs prophēteias*]). "The spirit of prophecy" is the Spirit of God working in and through the prophet—i.e., the divinely inspired activity of the prophet (Beckwith, Sweet). The highly regarded OT prophets received revelations through the preexistent Christ (cf. 1 Pet. 1:11), but their words could not qualify as new Christian prophecy because no prophetic inspiration was genuine that did not center upon the testimony of Jesus (Moffatt). In essence, this statement means that the testimony given by Jesus is the substance of what the Spirit inspires Christian prophets to speak (Beasley-Murray). John and his fellow Christians who were gifted as prophets received prophetic inspiration to speak this testimony along with angels such as John's guide through 17:1–19:10. They were all merely vehicles of Jesus' words and did not merit the worship that belongs to God alone. John had mistakenly offered worship to the angel as the source of prophetic revelation,

---

51. Kiddle, *Revelation*, p. 383; Beasley-Murray, *Revelation*, p. 276; Hughes, *Revelation*, p. 202.

but the command to worship God directs attention to Him as the source.[52]

Additional Notes

19:1 The participle λεγόντων is plural even though it modifies a singular noun ὄχλου. An agreement in sense with the collective noun rather than a strict grammatical agreement accounts for the plural number.[53] It is remotely possible to construe it as a second dependent genitive after ὄχλου, "of people saying" (Alford), but this is improbable. A comparison with the analogous ὄχλος . . . ἑστῶτες in 7:9 argues strongly for the agreement in sense (Charles).

In the absence of a verb in the first full line of the song, English translations have rendered the genitive τοῦ θεοῦ ἡμῶν by something like "belong to our God" (cf. NASB, LB, PME, RSV, TEV, NIV, NEB). Another suggested rendering understands an implied ἦλθεν: "the salvation and the glory and the power of our God have come" (cf. Bullinger). In light of the aorist indicatives later in this song, the implied ἦλθεν is the most probable.

19:2 The form ἔφθειρεν is possibly an imperfect to express the harlot's habit of corrupting, as Alford takes it, but an aorist tense is more probable in this setting where the surrounding verbs are all aorists. The present and aorist stems of this verb are the same.

19:3 The verb εἴρηκαν is not an "aoristic" perfect, but a vivid dramatic perfect, the same with εἴληφεν as in 5:7. The third person plural again uses -αν rather than -ασιν as in 18:3; 21:6 also.[54] The plural number answers to the collective sense of the singular ὄχλου (v. 1), as does the λεγόντων of v. 1.

19:5 This is the only place in the NT where αἰνέω governs an object in the dative case. Elsewhere its objects are accusative. The LXX uses the verb with dative objects, however, in cases where the Hebrew has the preposition ל ("to") before the verb's object (e.g., 1 Chron. 16:36; 2 Chron. 20:19; Jer. 20:13) (Charles, Beckwith).

The καί before οἱ φοβούμενοι has questionable MS support. It is missing from Sinaiticus, Ephraemi, and other witnesses, but a copyist could have deleted it to avoid the possible conclusion that "those who fear Him" constituted a different group from "His slaves" named just before. The inclusion of καί does have respectable MS support, partic-

---

52. Richard Bauckham, "The Worship of Jesus in Apocalyptic Christianity," *NTS* 27, no. 3 (April 1981): 329.
53. Robertson, *Word Pictures*, 6:447.
54. Ibid., 6:447-48; H. E. Dana and Julius R. Mantey, *A Manual Grammar of the Greek New Testament* (New York: Macmillan, 1927), p. 204; Mounce, *Revelation*, p. 338 n. 6.

ularly from Alexandrinus, but a copyist possibly added it to avoid an asyndetic construction. All factors considered, it is probably better to retain the καί though the choice is a difficult one.[55]

19:6 Instead of the genitive plural λεγόντων, some MSS read an accusative plural and others have a nominative plural. The genitive plural has stronger external support, however. It refers back to the collective noun ὄχλου as the same form does in 19:1. It passes over the ὑδάτων and the βροντῶν because the roar of the waters and the roll of the thunders were inarticulate. The fourth "hallelujah" comes from [something] like this vast multitude.[56]

No other occurrences of ὁ θεὸς ὁ παντοκράτωρ in Revelation have the possessive pronoun ἡμῶν used as a part of it, so some MSS including Alexandrinus may have omitted it as inappropriate. On the other hand, some copyists may have added it because it comes following the use of θεός in vv. 1 and 5 of this chapter. The weight of MSS supporting the pronoun's presence is strong. They include Sinaiticus and strong Latin and Syriac versional support. The balance of probability favors inclusion.[57]

19:7 The active voice of ἀγαλλιῶμεν occurs only here and at Luke 1:47 in the NT, with the possibility that it appears in the active at 1 Pet. 1:8 where one of the variant readings is active. Usually it is in the middle voice.[58]

The form δώσωμεν is first aorist active subjunctive, but two other potential readings are δώσομεν (future active indicative) and δῶμεν (second aorist active subjunctive). If the future reading is correct, the sense changes from exhortation to declaration: "we shall give glory to Him."[59] The reading δῶμεν appears in Sinaiticus only and cannot easily account for how the other two arose. The future indicative δώσομεν following two hortatory verbs is too hard to be possible, even though it has the support of Alexandrinus. The difficulty with the first aorist active subjunctive δώσωμεν is the weakness of its external support. The scarcity of the first aorist of δίδωμι in the NT also makes the reading difficult to accept. This form of the verb appears only in 4:9 in Sinaiticus and six minuscules and in Mark 6:37 in Sinaiticus and D. Yet it is not impossible, and it does furnish an explanation of how each of the other readings originated, so the first aorist δώσωμεν is the preferred reading.[60]

---

55. Bruce M. Metzger, *A Textual Commentary on the Greek New Testament* (New York: United Bible Societies, 1971), pp. 761-62.
56. Robertson, *Word Pictures*, 6:448.
57. Metzger, *Textual Commentary*, p. 339.
58. Swete, *Apocalypse*, p. 246; Robertson, *Word Pictures*, 6:449.
59. Robertson, *Word Pictures*, 6:449.
60. Metzger, *Textual Commentary*, p. 762.

19:8 The aorist middle subjunctive περιβάληται is one of the rare uses of the direct middle voice in the NT. It means "clothe herself" and equates to the active voice and reflexive pronoun ἡτοίμασεν ἑαυτήν of v. 7.[61]

19:9 Various syntactical arrangements for οὗτοι οἱ λόγοι ἀληθινοὶ τοῦ θεοῦ εἰσιν are possible. Some, depending on the reading that has οἱ before ἀληθινοί, suggest, "these are the true words of God." Other suggested readings include "these words are true, [they are the words] of God," "these sayings are the true [sayings] of God," and "these true words are God's words."[62] The best choice is to understand ἀληθινοί as a substantive predicate nominative: "these are the true [ones] of God." This does not necessitate the οἱ before the adjective that has the support of only Alexandrinus and a few other MSS.

19:10 The case of αὐτῷ is dative. When this case follows προσ-κυνέω, it indicates worship with divine honor. In contrast, an accusative object with this verb means to do homage or obeisance to another. This as well as the context shows John's intention to worship this angel as God (Bullinger).

2. THE COMING OF THE KING OF KINGS (19:11-16)

Translation

11And I saw heaven opened, and behold a white horse, and the one who sat upon him was called faithful and true, and in righteousness He judges and wages war. 12And His eyes were like a flame of fire, and on His head were many diadems; He had a name written which no one knew except Himself, 13and was clothed in a garment dipped in blood, and His name was called the Word of God. 14And the armies which are in heaven were following Him upon white horses, clothed in white, clean fine linen. 15And from His mouth proceeds a sharp sword, that He might smite the nations, and He Himself will destroy them with a rod of iron; and He Himself treads the winepress of the wine of the anger of the wrath of God Almighty. 16And he has on His garment, even on His thigh, a name written: King of kings and Lord of lords.

Exegesis and Exposition

The words καὶ εἶδον (*kai eidon*, "and I saw") in v. 11 introduce the first of eight scenes that constitute the action phase of the seventh bowl.[63] The scenes that follow this one which tells of the return of

---

61. Robertson, *Word Pictures*, 6:449-50.
62. Düsterdieck, *Revelation*, p. 454; Lee, "Revelation," 4:782; Beckwith, *Apocalypse*, p. 728.
63. See Excursus 5 at the end of this volume for further discussion and the structural format of the seventh bowl segment of the Apocalypse.

Christ are the invitation to the birds of prey (19:17-18), the defeat of the beast (19:19-21), the binding of Satan (20:1-3), the Millennium and the defeat of Satan (20:4-10), the placement of the Great White Throne (20:11), the judgment of those whose names are missing from the Book of Life (20:12-15), and the new heaven and the new earth (21:1-8).[64]

This series of scenes has attracted a good bit of attention, particularly in regard to whether they are in chronological sequence or not. Among the reasons for rejecting the sequential fulfillment of these scenes is the use of terminology from Ezekiel 38-39 in both 19:17-18 and 20:8. This allegedly proves that the two scenes portray the same event (Lee). The nonsequential viewpoint represents the series as an eschatological art gallery whose seven pictures present the theme of God's victory at the end of history.[65] This understanding has weak substantive support, however. Its use of the Ezekiel passage takes no account of the principle of prophetic foreshortening that characterizes so much of biblical prophecy.

The case favoring chronological sequence in the fulfillment of these scenes is very strong. Progression from Christ's return to the invitation to the birds of prey and from that invitation to the defeat of the beast is obvious. So is the progression from the binding of Satan to the Millennium and final defeat of Satan and from that final defeat to the new heaven and the new earth with all this entails. The interpretation allowing for chronological arrangement of these eight scenes is one-sidedly strong. Excursus 5 at the end of this volume has a fuller discussion of this issue.

19:11 This series of scenes connects with the pouring out of the seventh bowl in 16:17-21 and flows naturally from the concluding part of the intercalation (17:1–19:10) that expands upon the introductory summary (16:17-21). The final song of 19:1-8 celebrates the marriage of the warrior-Messiah, but this marriage cannot happen until He returns to secure a victory on the battlefield (cf. Psalm 45). This agrees closely with traditional Jewish eschatology. The OT prophets foresaw the Lord coming in the last days as a man of war to dash his enemies in pieces and establish a kingdom over the nations (e.g., Isa. 13:4; 31:4; 42:13; Ezekiel 38-39; Joel 3; Zech. 14:3).

The present passage in 19:11-16 concerns itself with the advent leading to this last great conflict with the false Christ and his hosts in their assault on the Messiah and His people: Καὶ εἶδον τὸν οὐρανὸν

---

64. Cf. Wall, *Revelation*, p. 227, who finds seven scenes instead of eight by combining the placement of the Great White Throne and the judgment of those whose names are missing from the Book of Life.
65. M. Eugene Boring, *Revelation* (Louisville: John Knox, 1989), p. 195; Wall, *Revelation*, pp. 227-28.

ἠνεῳγμένον, καὶ ἰδοὺ ἵππος λευκός, καὶ ὁ καθήμενος ἐπ' αὐτὸν πιστὸς [καλούμενος]* καὶ ἀληθινός, καὶ ἐν δικαιοσύνῃ κρίνει καὶ πολεμεῖ (*Kai eidon ton ouranon ēneǭgmenon, kai idou hippos leukos, kai ho kathē-menos ep' auton pistos [kaloumenos] kai alēthinos, kai en dikaiosynę̄ krinei kai polemei*, "And I saw heaven opened, and behold a white horse, and the one who sat upon him was called faithful and true, and in righteousness He judges and wages war"). The Messiah returns in response to the preliminary movements of the enemy recounted briefly in 17:12, 13, 16-17 to implement the climactic war of 17:14 that culminates in a horrible Armageddon (Swete, Moffatt, Beckwith, Ford). This picture climaxes the NT emphasis on the second coming of Christ as the fulfillment and vindication of the Christian hope (e.g., Matt. 13:41-42; 25:41; Rom. 2:5; 2 Thess. 1:7-8, 9-10; 2:8) (Mounce). It answers specifically to the theme verse of Rev. 1:7 which tells of the worldwide audience this event will have (cf. Matt. 24:27-31) (Walvoord). In fact, this is the only event in Revelation that corresponds to that coming narrowly construed to refer to Christ's personal coming. This is the personal and direct exercise of His judicial power in crushing the last anti-God forces on earth (Moffatt). It also furnishes meaning to the figure of Christ as the lion of the tribe of Judah, the root of David (Rev. 5:5).

John's view of τὸν οὐρανὸν ἠνεῳγμένον (*ton ouranon ēneǭgmenon*, "heaven opened") recalls the beginning of Ezekiel's prophecy (Ezek. 1:1). Matthew and Luke describe a similar scene at the time of Jesus' baptism (Matt. 3:16; Luke 3:21). Jesus predicted that Nathaniel would see heaven opened and angels ascending and descending on the Son of Man (John 1:51). Earlier scenes in Revelation have described a door opened into heaven (4:1), the opening of the heavenly sanctuary (11:19; 15:5), the departure of angels from heaven (10:1; 14:17; 18:1), and sounds from heaven (19:1). The opening of heaven this time is on a larger scale than any of these others, however.[66] This opening purposes to reveal the Messiah, not as a Lamb or a bridegroom, but as a Warrior-King descending to do battle against the beast and his hosts (Swete, Kiddle). In essence, this is an answer to Isaiah's prayer in Isa. 64:1-2 (Smith).

The interjection ἰδού (*idou*, "behold") calls special attention to John's first sight in his visional experience, which is ἵππος λευκός (*hippos leukos*, "a white horse"). The white horse in an earlier vision had a rider who was quite different from this one (6:2). The subsequent description assures that this warrior is none other than the Messiah.[67] This time, white is a symbol of final victory, the one realized when

---

66. Swete, *Apocalypse*, p. 250; Robertson, *Word Pictures*, 6:451.
67. Robertson, *Word Pictures*, 6:451.

Christ actively exerts the authority that is rightfully His (Kiddle, Ladd). At His first coming, He sat on a donkey (Matt. 21:4-7), but in the day of His ultimate triumph He will sit on a white horse.[68]

After the white horse, John saw ὁ καθήμενος ἐπ᾽ αὐτὸν (*ho kathēmenos ep' auton*, "the one who sat upon him"). In the future Christ will come as a Warrior-Prince instead of as a Lamb (Kiddle), the commander-in-chief of the host of heaven (cf. Josh. 5:14) (Swete). "Faithful and true" (Πιστὸς . . . καὶ ἀληθινός [*Pistos . . . kai alēthinos*]) is the title applied to the rider. As indicated earlier in connection with 19:9, ἀληθινός (*alēthinos*, "true") carries the connotation of correspondence to reality though it sometimes conveys that of reliability. Some prefer the latter meaning here (Ladd, Mounce, Ford), but the idea of "real" in this instance provides a better complement to πιστὸς (*pistos*, "faithful"), which in itself carries the force of "trustworthy." He is trustworthy in fulfilling His promises and is the true Messiah announced from ancient times (cf. 3:7, 14).[69] The same two adjectives describe the words of the one on the throne in 21:5 and of the angel-guide in 22:6. This is the first of several titles in vv. 11-16, a number of which occur earlier in the book, that specify the rider's identity to be Jesus Christ.

The rider is both a judge and a warrior according to the last clause of v. 11. He discharges both responsibilities in accord with right principles: ἐν δικαιοσύνῃ κρίνει καὶ πολεμεῖ (*en dikaiosynē krinei kai polemei*, "in righteousness He judges and wages war"). This is God's way of judgment (cf. 15:3; 16:5, 7; 19:2). First, He reaches a just verdict regarding the beast, then He goes to war with him. This is the only kind of victory that can endure. The compromise kingdom offered Christ by Satan (Matt. 4:8-10) would not have lasted, because it would have sacrificed righteous principles (cf. Acts 17:31).[70] This kind of war contrasts strongly with that waged by the beast (cf. 11:7; 13:7) (Sweet). The OT allusion here is to Isa. 11:3-5 which predicts future activity for the Messiah. Earlier Christ Himself spoke of making war with the unfaithful of the church in Pergamum (Rev. 2:16) (Charles, Johnson). This war is the means of bringing about the kingdom anticipated by both Jews and Christians. For Israel, it is the earthly subjugation of her foes, but in a wider sense, it leads to an eternal and universal judgment of the dead and the living (Moffatt). The present tenses of κρίνει (*krinei*, "He judges") and πολεμεῖ (*polemei*, "makes war") are from

---

68. J. A. Seiss, *The Apocalypse* (New York: Charles C. Cook, 1909), 3:240.
69. Düsterdieck, *Revelation*, p. 457.
70. Swete, *Apocalypse*, p. 250; Robertson, *Word Pictures*, 6:451; Scott, *Revelation*, p. 386.

John's perspective as an eyewitness of the dramatization that anticipates future actualities.

The concept of Christ as a warrior has created two lines of thought
regarding the nature of the war He wages, one that says He is a military warrior and one that says He is not. The latter uses the allusion to
justice which accompanies the reference to making war to argue that
His execution of justice is His way of waging war (Johnson), but the
implementation of justice does not exclude military conflict as a
means of achieving that justice. Ruling out the military aspect of His
victory rests on conceiving of the entire character of the Apocalypse as
figurative and spiritual and seeing the final conflict as neither literal
nor visible (Lee). This assumption is unproven, however, and even
opposes the nature of the fulfillment of prophecies of Christ's first
coming. The words of Zech. 9:9 saw a literal and visible fulfillment at
His first coming (Matt. 21:4-11), so the foregone conclusion must be
that prophecy of His second coming will mean the same (cf. Zech.
9:10) (Bullinger). Reading the words of this section in a nonliteral
manner opposes the thrust of the wider context[71] and violates the
imagery of the OT passages upon which John draws in his description.
The natural way to understand the language of 19:11-21 is as a picture
of military combat. The Messiah's judicial power consists almost entirely of the external work of crushing the forces of the beast and hence
is of a military nature (Moffatt). He is a stern and militant figure intent
on securing vengeance in attacking the rebels.

Arguments denying an actual battle must resort to treating
19:11-21 as surrealistic, denying that an army of cavalry exists in heav-
en, and claiming that "the great supper of God" (19:17) is pictorial only
(Beasley-Murray, Hailey). But this confrontation must be more than a
judicial act as an ordinary historical event. The war in heaven (12:7-12)
and this war on earth belong to the same system of symbols whereby
the writer portrays a real intervention of God in history with a warfare
that transcends all ordinary historical experiences (Ladd). In other
words, the Messiah will come as a military figure of some sort.

19:12 The δέ (*de*, "and") of v. 12 marks a transition from a subjective to an objective description of the rider (Alford): οἱ δὲ ὀφθαλμοὶ
αὐτοῦ [ὡς]* φλὸξ πυρός, καὶ ἐπὶ τὴν κεφαλὴν αὐτοῦ διαδήματα πολλά,
ἔχων ὄνομα γεγραμμένον ὃ οὐδεὶς οἶδεν εἰ μὴ αὐτός (*hoi de ophthalmoi
autou [hōs] phlox pyros, kai epi tēn kephalēn autou diadēmata polla,
echōn onoma gegrammenon ho oudeis oiden ei mē autos*, "and His eyes
were like a flame of fire, and on His head were many diadems; He had
a name written which no one knew except Himself"). Various parts of
these two types of description have appeared earlier in Revelation:

---

71. Düsterdieck, *Revelation*, p. 460.

the white horse (6:2), the titles (3:14; 17:14), the eyes (1:14; 2:18), the unknown name (2:17), the sword (1:16), the rod of iron (2:27), the winepress (14:20), and the diadems (12:3; 13:1) (Lee). Not all of them applied to the person in the present paragraph, however.

In agreement with the symbolic meaning of 1:14 and 2:18, the flame-of-fire analogy indicates that nothing escapes the notice of this warrior. He is incapable of judgment by deception or fraud. His decisions accord perfectly with reality (Ford). As noted in connection with 12:3, a διάδημα (*diadēma*) differs from a στέφανος (*stephanos*) which is a victor's wreath. The dragon has a diadem on each of his seven heads (12:3) and the beast on each of his ten horns (13:1), but this warrior has διαδήματα πολλά (*diadēmata polla*, "many diadems") on His head. His multiple emblems of royalty are appropriate because He is King of kings.[72] The right to rule the world—not just Asia, Egypt, and Europe—has now passed to the Messiah (Swete, Johnson). He is infinitely more powerful than the world rulers before Him (Kiddle). His sovereignty is unassailable.[73]

The text does not disclose on what part of the rider's body was the ὄνομα γεγραμμένον ὃ οὐδεὶς οἶδεν εἰ μὴ αὐτός (*onoma gegrammenon ho oudeis oiden ei mē autos*, "name written which no one knew except Himself"). It may have been on His brow because the previous clause has focused on the head. John saw the name, but it was inscrutable to him.[74] It could have been one of the other titles assigned in this paragraph, but more probably is a name that will remain secret until the time of His return. The unknowability of the name recalls the wording of Matt. 11:27 which speaks of the limitations placed on those who can know the Son and the Father (Moffatt). Speculations about the unknown name have included references to the Tetragrammaton (יהוה [*YHWH*]), "the name that is above every name" (Phil. 2:9-11), "Jesus," and the name inscribed in the rider's thigh that is at first illegible (Mounce). Better judgment dictates against the correctness of these suggestions. It is not the prerogative of contemporary readers to have this knowledge. Neither is it proper to theorize that this is something of "inmost significance" regarding His person that is incomprehensible to the human mind.[75] The unknown new name promised to the overcomer in Pergamum (2:17; cf. 3:12) argues against this. As in Gen. 32:29 and Judg. 13:18, the one with greater authority has the privilege of withholding His name (cf. Rev. 10:4).[76]

---

72. Robertson, *Word Pictures*, 6:451-52; Caird, *Revelation*, p. 241.
73. Hughes, *Revelation*, p. 203.
74. Düsterdieck, *Revelation*, p. 457; Alford, *Greek Testament*, 4:727.
75. Contra Swete, *Apocalypse*, pp. 251-52, and Ladd, *Revelation*, p. 254.
76. Beckwith, *Apocalypse*, pp. 463, 732; Wall, *Revelation*, p. 230.

19:13 The rider's dress is the next detail: καὶ περιβεβλημένος ἱμά-τιον βεβαμμένον* αἵματι (*kai peribeblēmenos himation bebammenon haimati*, "and was clothed in a garment dipped in blood"). The ἱμάτιον (*himation*, "garment") was either a χλαμύς (*chlamys*), a rider's cloak, or a *paludamentum*, the cloak of a Roman general (Swete). Some make a case that the blood in which His garment is dipped is His own blood shed at Calvary, because elsewhere in Revelation the blood mentioned in connection with Him is His own lifeblood (1:5; 5:9; 7:14; 12:11) (Morris, Johnson). This perspective also notes the appropriateness of the verb βάπτω (*baptō*, "I dip") in speaking of His death because of parallel uses of it in Mark 10:38 and Luke 12:50 (Sweet). Yet the absence of Christ's redemptive work from this context and the writer's obvious dependence on Isa. 63:2-3 argue more strongly for a reference to the blood of others here (Alford, Swete, Charles, Bullinger). In this context Christ is a righteous Judge and Warrior.

Another suggestion has been that the blood is the blood of the saints (Caird), but this view rests on interpreting the vintage passage of 14:17-20 to speak of the blood of the saints. In earlier discussion the inadequacy of this interpretation has already been obvious. The position that the blood is that of Christ's enemies is the one with compelling support. Some have argued against this view by noting that Christ comes from heaven with His robe already dipped in blood before the battle occurs.[77] They label as ridiculous the picture of a vintager dipping his garment in grape juice as a sign of his trade before beginning to tread the winepress (Caird). The response to this line of criticism is convincing, however. The epithet of the garment dipped in blood is proleptic as is the symbolism of the white horse and the white robes of His followers. It looks forward, not backward (Beckwith, Ladd, Mounce). Also, the "many diadems" anticipate His assumption of full authority as King on earth. Both this feature of His description and that of the blood on His robe anticipate the battle about to be fought and its outcome.

A shedding of the blood of His enemies is the picture presented in Isa. 63:1-3, the source of the imagery of 19:15. Isaiah 63:1-6 is a context that prophesies how the Messiah will slaughter His enemies, with their blood splattering on His clothing during the process. It is comparable to grape juice splashing on the wine treader in the winepress. This meaning also matches the parallel scene in 14:9-11, 17-20 where John earlier alludes to Isaiah's prophecy. The two mentions of the blood of His enemies, here and in v. 15, enhance this scene's em-

---

77. Charles, *Revelation*, 2:133; Johnson, "Revelation," 12:574; Wall, *Revelation*, p. 231.

phasis on war and judgment (Hailey). The form αἵματι (*haimati*) is a locative case, telling the element in which His garment is dipped. This is a stern, militant figure wreaking vengeance upon the rebellious of earth (Moffatt).

The last part of v. 13 gives an additional name to help identify the rider: καὶ κέκληται τὸ ὄνομα αὐτοῦ ὁ λόγος τοῦ θεοῦ (*kai keklētai to onoma autou ho logos tou theou*, "and His name was called the Word of God"). The suggestion that the assignment of this name came through a later editor or copyist and is inconsistent with the unknown name of v. 12 (Moffatt) is unjustified. This like "King of kings and Lord of lords" in v. 16 is different from and in addition to the unknown name.[78]

This is the only place where the full expression ὁ λόγος τοῦ θεοῦ (*ho logos tou theou*, "the Word of God") applies to Christ, though λόγος (*logos*, "word") alone refers to Him in John 1:1, 14. The use of the same title is an important factor in linking the authorship of Revelation to that of the gospel of John.[79] In Revelation "the words (or word) of God" includes the revelation of God's purpose (1:2; 17:17; 19:9). The expression also represents the message for which antichristian forces persecute the saints (1:9; 6:9; 20:4). These words are faithful and true (19:9; 21:5; 22:6) as Christ is (19:11). So the word of God finds its full expression in His person, and appropriately He bears the name "The Word of God" (Johnson). The same *word* that brought the creation into existence (John 1:3; cf. Ps. 33:6) is powerful enough to subdue satanic powers whom the warrior-Messiah is about to confront (Kiddle). In Hebrew thought, the *word* is not a lifeless sound, but an active agent (e.g., Gen. 1:3, 6, 9; Heb. 4:12) (Mounce).

19:14 The rider on the white horse is not alone as He descends from heaven: καὶ τὰ στρατεύματα [τὰ] ἐν τῷ οὐρανῷ ἠκολούθει αὐτῷ ἐφ᾽ ἵπποις λευκοῖς, ἐνδεδυμένοι βύσσινον λευκὸν καθαρόν (*kai ta strateumata [ta] en tō ouranō ēkolouthei autō eph' hippois leukois, endedymenoi byssinon leukon katharon*, "and the armies which are in heaven were following Him upon white horses, clothed in white, clean fine linen"). This heavenly army, unlike their leader, has no swords or spears. They take no part in the action. They wear no armor because, being immortal, they are immune to injury. They are noncombatant supporters of the Messiah as He wages the war single-handedly (Lee, Beckwith, Seiss, Ladd). These are real armies and horses, not imaginary ones (Bullinger). The origin of the horses need not create a prob-

---

78. Beckwith, *Apocalypse*, p. 733; Hughes, *Revelation*, p. 204.
79. Alford, *Greek Testament*, 4:727; Robertson, *Word Pictures*, 6:453; Morris, *Revelation*, pp. 230-31.

lem as they conceivably are a special creation of "The Word of God" for the purposes of this occasion. A literal understanding of them is in order just as a literal meaning for the other features in this sequence: the opening of heaven, the descent of Christ with His heavenly armies to do battle, the destruction achieved, the victory won, and the kingdom set up (Seiss).

Attempts to identify the personnel in τὰ στρατεύματα (*ta strateumata*, "the armies") has generated some debate. Those who say angels make up the armies cite OT and NT passages that refer to angels as composing the armies of heaven (e.g., Pss. 103:21; 148:2; Luke 2:13; Acts 7:42). The association of angels with Christ at His second coming is also an established biblical teaching (e.g., Matt. 13:41; 16:27; 24:30-31; Mark 8:38; Luke 9:26; 2 Thess. 1:7) (Ladd, Beasley-Murray). A factor that causes hesitation in identifying the armies as angels, however, is the unlikelihood that they would be on white horses as their leader is (Johnson).

Two considerations that are persuasive in concluding these armies are redeemed men are their clothing and the indication of 17:14 that the elect will join Christ for this climactic event. Their clothing is βύσσινον λευκὸν καθαρόν (*byssinon leukon katharon*, "white, clean fine linen"), which closely identifies them with the Lamb's bride whose apparel is βύσσινον λαμπρὸν καθαρόν (*byssinon lampron katharon*, "bright, clean fine linen") (19:8). Seeing the armies as the company of the redeemed also corresponds with the presence of the "called and elect and faithful" at the final battle against the beast and his forces in 17:14. A confirming consideration is the promise to the overcomer in 2:27 of ruling with a rod of iron the same as Christ does here (19:15). The overcomers from the churches must be among the troops in these armies (Charles). Limiting the armies to saints is appropriate. It does not deny the presence of angels on this occasion but simply concludes that the angels are not mentioned here. The saints will have a role in judgment during this important episode.

The imperfect ἠκολούθει (*ēkolouthei*, "were following") provides a graphic picture of the celestial warrior with His armies seated on white horses following their leader into the fray.[80]

19:15 The weaponry of the warrior-Messiah consists of a sword and a rod: καὶ ἐκ τοῦ στόματος αὐτοῦ ἐκπορεύεται ῥομφαία ὀξεῖα, ἵνα ἐν αὐτῇ πατάξῃ τὰ ἔθνη, καὶ αὐτὸς ποιμανεῖ αὐτοὺς ἐν ῥάβδῳ σιδηρᾷ (*kai ek tou stomatos autou ekporeuetai hromphaia oxeia, hina en autē pataxē ta ethnē, kai autos poimanei autous en hrabdō siderą*, "and from His mouth proceeds a sharp sword, that He might smite the nations, and

---

80. Robertson, *Word Pictures*, 6:453.

He Himself will destroy them with a rod of iron"). The imagery of these words alludes to the description of the shoot from the stem of Jesse in Isa. 11:4. The first impression from these words is that the warfare this warrior comes to wage entails physical harm and death for His enemies. Physical affliction certainly characterizes the only other use of the verb πατάσσω (*patassō*, "smite") in Revelation (11:6).

Yet some try to avoid the idea of a battlefield confrontation either by claiming John changes the OT imagery by placement of the sword in Christ's mouth rather than in His hand (Johnson) or by proposing the OT sword was Isaiah's symbol for his own utterance which had a cutting edge because he had spoken the word of God (Caird). The former claim ignores Isaiah's placement of the sword in the Messiah's mouth also and his statement that He would *slay* the wicked with the breath of His lips (Isa. 11:4). The latter proposal referring to a cutting edge of spoken words assigns an overly figurative connotation to the words by divesting them of the results that Isaiah said they would have—i.e., that of taking human life.

To be sure, Christ conquers by the power of His word, but this does not exclude the actual shedding of the blood of His enemies at His second coming. Messiah's words have death-dealing power against His foes (Beckwith, Mounce). As an illustration, the rabbis applied the idea to the actions of Moses in killing an Egyptian in Ex. 2:11-12. This type of imagery also lies behind the language of 2 Thess. 2:8 (Moffatt).

The intensive pronoun αὐτός (*autos*, "Himself") highlights Christ's personal, single-handed role in the destruction of His enemies (Charles, Moffatt). The wording ποιμανεῖ αὐτοὺς ἐν ῥάβδῳ σιδηρᾷ (*poimanei autous en hrabdō siderā*, "will destroy them with a rod of iron") is identical with that in 2:27. It is almost the same as in 12:5 where the only difference is the replacement of the future ποιμανεῖ (*poimanei*, "will destroy") with μέλλει (*mellei*) and the present infinitive ποιμαίνειν (*poimainein*). Both constructions anticipate the future coming of Christ. In 2:27 the rod is in the hands of the conquerors in the seven churches (cf. Ps. 149:6-9), but in 12:5 it is in Christ's hand (Kiddle). The OT allusion is, of course, to the warrior-Messiah prophesied in Ps. 2:9.[81] The ones destroyed are τὰ ἔθνη (*ta ethnē*, "the nations"), the antecedent of the pronoun αὐτούς (*autous*, "them"). The masculine pronoun agrees in sense rather than grammatically with the neuter noun *ethnē* (Alford). Ruling with a rod of iron is to destroy, not just to govern in a stern fashion as discussed in 2:27 (Charles, Smith, Ford, Mounce).

The last part of v. 15 changes figures to repeat one similar to ones

---

81. Johnson, "Revelation," 12:575; Hughes, *Revelation*, p. 205.

used earlier in Revelation: καὶ αὐτὸς πατεῖ τὴν ληνὸν τοῦ οἴνου τοῦ θυμοῦ τῆς ὀργῆς τοῦ θεοῦ τοῦ παντοκράτορος (*kai autos patei tēn lēnon tou oinou tou thymou tēs orgēs tou theou tou pantokratoros*, "and He Himself treads the winepress of the wine of the anger of the wrath of God Almighty"). This analogy with the winepresses has OT roots in Isa. 63:1-3. Elements of the analogy have appeared earlier in 14:8, 10, 19-20; 16:19; 19:13. The repetition of καὶ αὐτὸς (*kai autos*, "and He Himself") from the immediately preceding clause adds solemnity to the description and once again emphasizes Christ's personal role in this conquest. Though already implied by the garment dipped in blood in v. 13, the identity of the agent of this terrible work of wrath is now specific (Swete).

The expression τὴν ληνὸν τοῦ οἴνου τοῦ θυμοῦ τῆς ὀργῆς τοῦ θεοῦ τοῦ παντοκράτορος (*tēn lēnon tou oinou tou thymou tēs orgēs tou theou tou pantokratoros*, "the winepress of the wine of the anger of the wrath of God Almighty") combines two ideas, one from that of the winepress (14:19) and the other from that of the cup of God's wrath (14:10). The resultant combination expresses the intense fierceness of God's wrath through the meaning that from the winepress trodden by Christ comes the wine of God's wrath that His enemies must drink.[82]

19:16 The final statement of the paragraph divulges another of the rider's descriptive titles: καὶ ἔχει ἐπὶ τὸ ἱμάτιον καὶ ἐπὶ τὸν μηρὸν αὐτοῦ ὄνομα γεγραμμένον· Βασιλεὺς βασιλέων καὶ κύριος κυρίων (*kai echei epi to himation kai epi ton mēron autou onoma gegrammenon: Basileus basileōn kai kyrios kyriōn*, "and he has on His garment, even on His thigh, a name written: King of kings and Lord of lords"). This final title is on the part of the garment that covers His thigh, "the garment" (τὸ ἱμάτιον [*to himation*]) being the same one mentioned in v. 13. This involves taking the καί (*kai*, "even") following *himation* ascensively, making the second ἐπί (*epi*, "on") a further specification of the first (Beckwith). This gives a better sense than understanding part of the name as written on the garment and part on the thigh. As He sits on His white horse, the part of the cloak covering the thigh is the most conspicuous part and is visible to all (Swete).

With a prominence all its own, the name Βασιλεὺς βασιλέων καὶ κύριος κυρίων (*Basileus basileōn kai kyrios kyriōn*, "King of kings and Lord of lords") gains even more prominence by being chosen to end the description of vv. 11-16.[83] This title, already assigned to the Lamb in reverse order (17:14), is the fourth name or title applied to the rider in this paragraph. "Faithful and true" (v. 11), "the unknown name"

---

82. Düsterdieck, *Revelation*, p. 458; Charles, *Revelation*, 2:136-37.
83. Düsterdieck, *Revelation*, p. 458.

(v. 12), and "the Word of God" (v. 13) are the other three. Paul uses almost identical wording in referring to the Father in 1 Tim. 6:15: ὁ βασιλεὺς τῶη βασιλευόντων καὶ κύριος τῶν κυριευόντων (*ho basileus tōn basileuontōn kai kyrios tōn kyrieuontōn*, "the King of the ones reigning and the Lord of the ones ruling"). Titles similar to this occur in Deut. 10:17; Ps. 136:2-3; Dan. 2:37, 47; 8:25; 11:36 (Lee).

The doubling of the name "King of kings" was a practice of the Persians and Parthians to emphasize the supremacy of their royalties (Moffatt). John courageously adopts this device in spite of comparable claims of the Roman emperor responsible for his exile. The Messiah alone has a rightful claim to the title "King of kings and Lord of lords."[84]

Additional Notes

19:11 The form ἠνεῳγμένον is from ἀνοίγω and has a triple reduplication. It is an accusative case modifying τὸν οὐρανόν, the direct object of εἶδον.[85]

Though omitted in Alexandrinus and a number of other ancient sources, the participle καλούμενος appears to be genuine because of its wide MS support. Its different location in various MSS make its presence doubtful, but the reading of Sinaiticus which puts it between πιστός and καί probably best explains the origin of the other readings. Because its presence in this location interrupted the usual sequence of πιστὸς καὶ ἀληθινός (cf. 3:14; 21:5; 22:6), various scribes either moved it or left it out.[86] Luke 6:15; 8:2; Acts 8:10 use the participle in an unusual sequence also (Swete).

19:12 External evidence for including the comparative particle ὡς is evenly balanced with that for excluding it. Its inclusion agrees with John's style and has the support of Alexandrinus and a number of other ancient witnesses. To exclude it has the support of four uncials— Sinaiticus, P, 046, 051—and many minuscules. It could have come into the text when a copyist followed the pattern of 1:14, but evidence for including it as part of the original text is a bit stronger.[87]

The nominative case of ἔχων could be an anacoluthon, the preceding αὐτοῦ that it modifies being a genitive case. But it could also be the use of the participle to function as a finite verb.[88] The latter is more probable in the setting of the surrounding clauses.

19:13 Of the many readings proposed in ancient sources, βεβαμ-

---

84. Wall, *Revelation*, p. 229.
85. Robertson, *Word Pictures*, 6:451.
86. Metzger, *Textual Commentary*, pp. 762-63.
87. Ibid., p. 763.
88. Robertson, *Word Pictures*, 6:452.

μένον was probably the one construed as the most difficult by the copyists. Among those difficulties that provoked perplexity were the absence of ἐν before αἵματι to denote the element in which the garment was dipped and a feeling that the context (including the OT source passage of Isa. 63:3) made βάπτω less appropriate. So to resolve these problems some scribes turned to a form of ῥαίνω—ἐρραμμένον in 2053 or περιρεραμμένον in Sinaiticus—or of ῥαντίζω—ἐρραντισμένον represented in the Old Latin and Vulgate versions or ῥεραντισμένον in P. So besides having the support of Alexandrinus, 046, 051, and a number of minuscules, βεβαμμένον is most probably original on the basis of internal considerations.[89]

19:14 The masculine gender of ἐνδεδυμένοι agrees grammatically with the masculine of ἵπποις, but the sense of the passage requires that it modify στρατεύματα. The agreement with a neuter noun is an agreement according to sense.

3. THE GREAT SUPPER OF GOD (19:17-21)

Translation

17And I saw an angel standing in the sun, and he cried out with a loud voice saying to all the birds which fly in midheaven, "Come, gather for the great supper of God, 18that you may eat the flesh of kings and the flesh of chiliarchs and the flesh of strong ones and the flesh of horses and of those who sit upon them and the flesh of all, both of free men and slaves and of the small and great." 19And I saw the beast and the kings of the earth and their armies gathered to make war against the one who sat upon the horse and against His army. 20And the beast and with him the false prophet who did signs before him, through which he deceived those who received the mark of the beast and who worship his image, were captured; and the two were cast living into the lake of fire that burns with brimstone. 21And the rest were killed with the sword of the one who sat upon the horse, the one which came out of His mouth, and all the birds were filled with their flesh.

Exegesis and Exposition

19:17 The second of the eight scenes that comprise the seventh-bowl judgment is the invitation to the birds of prey to the great supper of God (19:17-18): Καὶ εἶδον ἕνα ἄγγελον ἑστῶτα ἐν τῷ ἡλίῳ, καὶ ἔκραξεν [ἐν] φωνῇ μεγάλῃ λέγων πᾶσιν τοῖς ὀρνέοις τοῖς πετομένοις ἐν μεσου-

---

89. Metzger, *Textual Commentary*, p. 764.

ρανήματι, Δεῦτε συνάχθητε εἰς τὸ δεῖπνον τὸ μέγα τοῦ θεοῦ (*Kai eidon hena angelon hestōta en tō heliō, kai ekraxen [en] phōnē megalē legōn pasin tois orneois tois petomenois en mesouranēmati, Deute synachthēte eis to deipnon to mega tou theou*, "And I saw an angel standing in the sun, and he cried out with a loud voice saying to all the birds which fly in midheaven, 'Come, gather for the great supper of God'"). This further sets the stage for the brief description of the battle proper that the next scene describes (19:19-21). With the Messiah and His armies poised and ready for battle, the insertion of this brief vision adds to the suspense of this dramatic moment (Mounce).

The announcing angel positions himself so as to be conspicuous, ἑστῶτα ἐν τῷ ἡλίῳ (*hestōta en tō heliō*, "standing in the sun"). There all the birds of prey could see him and respond to his summons to the battlefield soon to be littered with the corpses of the King's enemies (Swete, Beckwith, Moffatt). The word for "birds" (ὀρνέοις [*orneois*]) appears in 18:2 in the picture of Babylon's desolation. In predicting this same battle, Jesus used the word for "eagles" (or "vultures") (οἱ ἀετοί [*hoi aetoi*]) instead of the general word for birds used here (Matt. 24:28; Luke 17:37). One of the characteristics of vultures is how incredibly swift they are in discovering and reaching a prey. Hence, this invitation implies the imminence of the doom about to come.[90]

The angel's proclamation that shows the greatness and universality of the coming slaughter builds around two words that comprise this summons to the birds (cf. 1 Sam. 17:46; Isa. 18:6; Jer. 7:33; 12:9) (Alford, Lee). Δεῦτε (*Deute*, "Come") is the adverb "hither" when addressing two or more, just as δεῦρο (*deuro*) serves the same purpose for one person (cf. 17:1; 21:9). It occurs in conjunction with imperatives also in Matt. 25:34; 28:6; John 4:29; 21:12. Συνάχθητε (*Synachthēte*, "Gather") is an aorist imperative from συνάγω (*synagō*, "I gather"). The metaphor for gathering the birds of prey is from Ezek. 39:17, with John sometimes following Ezekiel's wording and other times using his source with the freedom that characterizes his other OT allusions.[91]

The anticipated feast for the birds bears the name τὸ δεῖπνον τὸ μέγα τοῦ θεοῦ (*to deipnon to mega tou theou*, "the great supper of God"). This is stunning language describing the battlefield after the Lamb's victory, a great supper given by God. It will be a veritable feast for the vultures. Christ comments on the habits of vultures and how carrion attracts them (Matt. 24:28; Luke 17:37). Even one dead body has a magnetic attraction for the creatures, but multiplied dead will

---

90. T. W. Manson, *The Sayings of Jesus* (London: SCM, 1949), p. 147.
91. Beckwith, *Apocalypse*, p. 734; Robertson, *Word Pictures*, 6:454.

clutter this field of battle. It is a horrible picture of human carnage designed to accentuate the greatness of Christ's victory.[92] This kind of supper is a radical contrast to the wedding supper of the Lamb seen earlier (19:9) (Moffatt, Kiddle). God responds graciously to those who respond to His call, but He must deal in severe judgment with those who do not (Mounce). This is the battle at Ἁρμαγεδών (*Harmagedōn*, "Harmagedon") already anticipated in 16:16.[93]

Equating this battle with the one in 20:8-9 is another possibility. The descriptive language of 20:8-9 derives from Ezek. 39:17 ff. just as it does in 19:17-18. Yet enough differentiating features exist to show that the two are not the same. Some of these include the locations of the battles (Harmagedon vs. Jerusalem), the leader(s) (the beast and the false prophet vs. Satan himself), the enemies (the kings of the earth and their armies vs. the nations in the four corners of the earth), the means of victory (the sword from Christ's mouth vs. fire from heaven), and the results (the beast and the false prophet in the lake of fire vs. Satan himself in the lake of fire). Then too the sequential nature of the fulfillment of the eight scenes of the seventh bowl judgment argues strongly for distinguishing the two battles.[94]

John took Ezekiel's prophecies broadly enough to foreshadow both Harmagedon and the final attack on Jerusalem (20:8-9). Of the two, Harmagedon was of greater significance to him, because it was the decisive, if not the final, stroke against the forces of evil (Kiddle). Harmagedon precedes the thousand years and the other battle follows (Swete, Ford).

19:18 The ἵνα (*hina*) that begins v. 18 introduces a statement of the purpose for the gathering of birds: ἵνα φάγητε σάρκας βασιλέων καὶ σάρκας χιλιάρχων καὶ σάρκας ἰσχυρῶν καὶ σάρκας ἵππων καὶ τῶν καθημένων ἐπ᾽ αὐτῶν καὶ σάρκας πάντων ἐλευθέρων τε καὶ δούλων καὶ μικρῶν καὶ μεγάλων (*hina phagēte sarkas basileōn kai sarkas chiliarchōn kai sarkas ischyrōn kai sarkas hippōn kai tōn kathēmenōn ep᾽ autōn kai sarkas pantōn eleutherōn te kai doulōn kai mikrōn kai megalōn*, "that you may eat the flesh of kings and the flesh of chiliarchs and the flesh of strong ones and the flesh of horses and of those who sit upon them and the flesh of all, both of free men and slaves and of the small and great"). The victims of Harmagedon will be food for the birds of prey. The groups listed include all classes of mankind and every status of life. In Ezekiel's account, the vultures feed on the bodies of great men

---

92. Swete, *Apocalypse*, pp. 255-56; Johnson, "Revelation," 12:576; Hughes, *Revelation*, p. 207.
93. Robertson, *Word Pictures*, 6:454; Kiddle, *Revelation*, p. 387.
94. See Excursus 5 at the end of this volume for further discussion of this issue.

only, but here it is everyone including the rank and file (Swete). God's judgment through this battle is no respecter of persons. The indignity of having their bodies remain unburied recalls the same treatment these people meted out to the two witnesses in 11:9-10 (Ford), except there the birds of prey did not enter the picture.

Similar categorizations of humanity appear elsewhere in this book with the closest similarity being 6:15 and 13:16 (cf. 11:18; 19:5; 20:12). Some of the categories here overlap others (Beckwith). The only group not listed in one of the earlier lists are ἵππων καὶ τῶν καθημένων ἐπ' αὐτῶν (*hippōn kai tōn kathēmenōn ep' autōn*, "horses and of those who sit upon them"). The sweeping reference of πάντων (*pantōn*, "all") clearly refers to those who have accepted the mark of the beast and yielded allegiance to the false Christ (Ladd). An exclusion of some of the world's population to allow for the survival of "the nations" at the beginning of the Millennium is unnecessary and unjustified.[95] This is all-inclusive, though *pantōn* with the four genitives following refers to "all kinds of" people. The only survivors of this awful confrontation will be those loyal to Christ who have not died or suffered martyrdom. These are none other than the sheltered Israelites of 12:13-17 who will enter the kingdom as mortals and will repopulate the earth.

19:19 The third scene of the seventh bowl immediately follows the invitation to the birds of prey: Καὶ εἶδον τὸ θηρίον καὶ τοὺς βασιλεῖς τῆς γῆς καὶ τὰ στρατεύματα αὐτῶν* συνηγμένα ποιῆσαι τὸν πόλεμον μετὰ τοῦ καθημένου ἐπὶ τοῦ ἵππου καὶ μετὰ τοῦ στρατεύματος αὐτοῦ (*Kai eidon to thērion kai tous basileis tēs gēs kai ta strateumata autōn synēgmena poiēsai ton polemon meta tou kathēmenou epi tou hippou kai meta tou strateumatos autou*, "And I saw the beast and the kings of the earth and their armies gathered to make war against the one who sat upon the horse and against His army"). This is a description of the defeat of the beast (19:19-21). The Messiah meets (cf. 16:13-14, 16) and defeats (cf. 17:14) the beast (11:7; 13:1 ff.), the false prophet (13:11 ff.), and their allies (11:9, 18; 14:8; 16:14; 17:12-14) in a further description of the judgment portrayed proleptically in 14:14-20 (Moffatt). The fewness of words that here describe this battle is surprising in light of its momentous importance to world history.

"The beast" (Τὸ θηρίον [*To thērion*]) as leader of this world army is the principal focus. By this time he has achieved worldwide supremacy, so it is appropriate for him to be at the forefront. "The kings of the earth" (Τοὺς βασιλεῖς τῆς γῆς [*Tous basileis tēs gēs*]) must include the ten kings who were the beast's allies in 17:12-14 (Lee, Johnson). These are the longstanding enemies of the Lord's Anointed (cf. מַלְכֵי-אֶרֶץ

---

95. Contra Beasley-Murray, *Revelation*, pp. 282-83.

(*malĕkê-'ereṣ*, "the kings of the earth," Ps. 2:2). "Their armies" (Τὰ στρατεύματα αὐτῶν [*Ta strateumata autōn*]) consist of the entire number of earth-dwellers or their representatives (cf. 13:3-4, 8, 16).[96]

This large assembly of military strength has as its purpose ποιῆσαι τὸν πόλεμον μετὰ τοῦ καθημένου ἐπὶ τοῦ ἵππου καὶ μετὰ τοῦ στρατεύματος αὐτοῦ (*poiēsai ton polemon meta tou kathēmenou epi tou hippou kai meta tou strateumatos autou*, "to make war against the one who sat upon the horse and against His army"). It is the same gathering already portrayed under the sixth bowl judgment (16:13-16). The combination ποιῆσαι τὸν πόλεμον μετὰ (*poiēsai ton polemon meta*, "to make war against") has the same essential meaning as πολεμέω μετά (*polemeō meta*, "I make war against") in 11:7; 12:7, 17; 13:7; 17:14. The combination συνηγμένα . . . τὸν πόλεμον (*synēgmena . . . ton polemon*, "gathered for war") resembles the συνάγω εἰς πόλεμον (*synagō eis polemon*, "I gather for war") in 16:14 (cf. 20:8). The beast with his forces comes prepared for a military engagement that they hope will secure his role as world leader.

His anticipated opponent is the rider on the white horse, elsewhere called "the Lamb" (17:14). The account does not divulge the specific factors determining the occasion and scene of the battle. Quite possibly, the rider has returned to earth (19:11-16) to a spiritually revived Jerusalem (cf. 11:13), giving the beast cause for alarm. So he musters his forces as rapidly as possible and moves them to that area to try to put an end to this new threat to his leadership role. Whatever the immediate reasons, however, the wording indicates that the beast expects to encounter the warrior-King in this engagement. In Zech. 14:5 the return of Christ is with his angels to do battle with the enemies of Israel, but here He returns with His saints—the corporate singular *strateumatos* in this case replacing the plural *strateumata* of v. 14—to battle against His own enemies (Scott). The two perspectives supplement each other as descriptions of the same occasion.

19:20 The outcome of the struggle is never in doubt: καὶ ἐπιάσθη τὸ θηρίον καὶ μετ᾽ αὐτοῦ ὁ ψευδοπροφήτης ὁ ποιήσας τὰ σημεῖα ἐνώπιον αὐτοῦ, ἐν οἷς ἐπλάνησεν τοὺς λαβόντας τὸ χάραγμα τοῦ θηρίου καὶ τοὺς προσκυνοῦντας τῇ εἰκόνι* αὐτοῦ· ζῶντες ἐβλήθησαν οἱ δύο εἰς τὴν λίμνην τοῦ πυρὸς τῆς καιομένης ἐν θείῳ (*kai epiasthē to thērion kai met' autou ho pseudoprophētēs ho poiēsas ta sēmeia enōpion autou, en hois eplanēsen tous labontas to charagma tou thēriou kai tous proskynountas tē eikoni autou; zōntes eblēthēsan hoi dyo eis tēn limnēn tou pyros tēs kaiomenēs en theiō*, "and the beast and with him the false prophet who did signs before him, through which he deceived those who received

---

96. Düsterdieck, *Revelation*, p. 459.

the mark of the beast and who worship his image, were captured; and the two were cast living into the lake of fire that burns with brimstone"). The prophet includes no description of the course of the battle and no indication of any effective resistance. He simply notes that the Lamb and His forces seize the beast and the false prophet and throw them into the lake of fire (Swete, Johnson).

Some have supposed a discrepancy between the fate of these two and that of the man of lawlessness in 2 Thess. 2:8 (Beckwith), but harmonization of the two accounts of Christ's return is quite easy. The verb ἀνελεῖ (*anelei*, "destroy") used by Paul does not necessarily mean physical death. It can also refer to relegation to the lake of fire because the literal force of ἀναιρέω (*anaireō*) is "I make an end of." The agent(s) for casting the two to their fiery destiny is unnamed, but presumably it is He with whom they came to do battle.

Stern treatment of the beast requires no further justification, but in case someone has forgotten, the false prophet is the one ὁ ποιήσας τὰ σημεῖα ἐνώπιον αὐτοῦ, ἐν οἷς ἐπλάνησεν τοὺς λαβόντας τὸ χάραγμα τοῦ θηρίου καὶ τοὺς προσκυνοῦντας τῇ εἰκόνι αὐτοῦ (*ho poiēsas ta sēmeia enōpion autou, en hois eplanēsen tous labontas to charagma tou thēriou kai tous proskynountas tē eikoni autou*, "who did signs before him, through which he deceived those who received the mark of the beast and who worship his image"). His miraculous signs in promotion of beast worship explain why he receives the same treatment as the beast (Lee, Beckwith). This is language that repeats elements of 13:13-17. He could deceive only those who agreed to accept the mark of the beast (13:16; 14:9-11; 16:2; 20:4) and who worship the beast's image (13:15),[97] but this was enough to assure his destiny of doom alongside the beast.

With two prophetic aorists, ἐπιάσθη (*epiasthē*) and ἐβλήθησαν (*eblēthēsan*), John predicts the seizure and assignment of the two to τὴν λίμνην τοῦ πυρὸς τῆς καιομένης ἐν θείῳ (*tēn limnēn tou pyros tēs kaiomenēs en theiō*, "the lake of fire that burns with brimstone"). The fact that they enter this fate while alive (ζῶντες [*zōntes*, "living"]) increases the horror of the picture (cf. Num. 16:30; Ps. 55:15) (Swete). This indicates that the warrior-King has captured them alive on the field of battle and sends them off to their eternal destiny in full consciousness and that the two are more than just human, because the rest of the lost will not enter the lake until the judgment of the great white throne (20:12-15) (Alford). The beast has already undergone the healing of his death-wound (13:3, 12; 17:8, 11), a counterfeit of Christ's resurrection, so his superhuman standing is already a matter of revela-

---

97. Robertson, *Word Pictures*, 6:455.

tion. The joining of the false prophet with the beast in this doom is surprising, but not completely unexpected, though, because of his evil sign-working powers. The lake of fire is designed for punishing individuals, not corporate entities such as empires. Therefore it is clear that these two originated as created human beings (Bullinger, Scott).

Tēn limnēn tou pyros tēs kaiomenēs en theiō culminates a long series of traditions regarding the destiny of the lost (e.g., Isa. 66:24). This explains the presence of the definite articles in the Greek title for "the lake of fire" even though this is the first occurrence of the expression in the entire Bible. Τοῦ πυρὸς (*Tou pyros*, "Of fire") is a descriptive genitive characterizing the lake. The same term describes γέεννα (*geenna*) in Matt. 5:22. This lake differs from the "abyss" of Rev. 9:1; 20:1 as the final abode of Satan, the beast, the false prophet, and wicked men, not a temporary place of confinement for fallen angels.[98] "Gehenna" (sometimes translated "hell") in Matt. 10:28; Mark 9:43; James 3:6 refers to this same eternal destiny as does "eternal fire" in Matt. 25:41. This place is different from ᾅδης (*hadēs*), the temporary abode of the dead between death and resurrection (cf. Matt. 16:18; Luke 16:23; Acts 2:27) and a place sometimes synonymous with the grave (cf. Rev. 1:18; 6:8; 20:13). This is the site of punishment after judgment.[99] Consignment to the lake of fire does not mean annihilation; after the thousand years the beast and false prophet are still there when Satan is put there (20:10).

The literality of the lake of fire has been questioned on the basis of a comparison with the figurative language about heaven in chapters 4, 5, 21, and 22.[100] In spite of the frequent metaphors and symbols in the Apocalypse, the events represented in the book will be real events. The lake of fire is the same real place as that symbolized by the valley Hinnom, otherwise known as Gehenna (cf. 2 Kings 16:3; 23:10; Jer. 7:31-32; 19:6; Matt. 5:22; Mark 9:43) (Mounce). This amounts to a literal understanding of the lake of fire, because literal interpretation allows for figurative language when contextual factors favor the use of figures. Because no one has yet experienced the lake of fire, it is difficult to portray in human language the awful nature of that punishment. The figure of a burning lake is God's chosen imagery for visualizing eternity separated from Him. One should remember that figures of speech are always less than the reality, not more! "Brimstone" (Θείῳ [*Theiō*]) is a yellow sulphurous material that is combustible in air and is found in a natural state in volcanic areas such as in the

---

98. Swete, *Apocalypse*, p. 258; Lee, "Revelation," 4:789; Robertson, *Word Pictures*, 6:455.
99. Ladd, *Revelation*, p. 258; Joachim Jeremias, "γέεννα," *TDNT*, 1:657-58.
100. Robertson, *Word Pictures*, 6:456.

valley of the Dead Sea (Mounce). Along with fire, it speaks of indescribable torment (cf. 14:8; 20:10; 21:8) (Scott).

19:21 In contrast to the beast and false prophet, the kings of the
earth and their armies will lose their lives in this battle: καὶ οἱ λοιποὶ
ἀπεκτάνθησαν ἐν τῇ ῥομφαίᾳ τοῦ καθημένου ἐπὶ τοῦ ἵππου τῇ ἐξελθούσῃ
ἐκ τοῦ στόματος αὐτοῦ, καὶ πάντα τὰ ὄρνεα ἐχορτάσθησαν ἐκ τῶν σαρκῶν
αὐτῶν (*kai hoi loipoi apektanthēsan en tē hromphaia tou kathēmenou
epi tou hippou tē exelthousē ek tou stomatos autou, kai panta ta ornea
echortasthēsan ek tōn sarkōn autōn*, "and the rest were killed with the
sword of the one who sat upon the horse, the one which came out of
His mouth, and all the birds were filled with their flesh"). "The rest" (Οἱ
λοιποί [*Hoi loipoi*]) includes the defeated forces of the beast. These
were composed of men, not demons. They have received ample opportunity to repent, but refused.[101] But by extension, it must include all
the inhabitants of the earth who do not choose loyalty to the Lamb, but
have demonstrated allegiance to the beast instead. The broad coverage
of the expression is necessary in light of the exhaustive specification of
different groups in 19:18.[102]

The passive verb ἀπεκτάνθησαν (*apektanthēsan*, "were killed") tells
the fate of this vast portion of living humanity. Rather than going
immediately to the lake of fire like the beast and false prophet, their
spirits went to Hades until the judgment when they rise from the dead
(20:12) and eventually depart into the lake of fire (Charles). Some want
to make this plain reference to death in battle something different
from real military casualties. They look upon it as a stripping of power
from satanic principalities and their human puppets. Somehow they
construe this as a reference to the victory that the Lamb won at the
Cross (cf. 5:5, 9) (Johnson, Mulholland, Caird, Sweet). No one denies
the prominence of the death of Christ in Revelation, but the present
passage does not focus on that aspect of His work. The verb ἀποκτείνω
(*apokteinō*, "I kill") does not mean "to strip [someone] of power."

Another way of avoiding reference to a real military battle is to
make the word point to the conversion of the enemies, thereby remov-
ing the enmity between God and man.[103] This meaning ignores the
eschatological nature of the war, however. The text speaks of widespread bloodshed, not of people turning to Christ (Mounce). This is a
judgment scene that entails the deaths of the rebels, not their conversion (Beasley-Murray).

This must be a military confrontation. No other understanding

---

101. Wilcock, *Revelation*, pp. 186-87; Wall, *Revelation*, p. 223.
102. Düsterdieck, *Revelation*, p. 459; Lee, "Revelation," 4:789.
103. Swete, *Apocalypse*, p. 284; David Chilton, *The Days of Vengeance* (Fort
    Worth, Tex.: Dominion, 1987), p. 491.

will satisfy the plain meaning of *apektanthēsan*. Just as the beast's warfare against the saints resulted in the loss of life (e.g., 11:7; 13:7, 15), so will the warfare of the rider against the forces of the beast. The victory is not a gradual affair. It is eschatological in an absolute sense, a great historical event ending the regime of the false Christ and his forces (Ladd, Mounce). The fact that the instrument of destruction is the sword proceeding from the rider's mouth does not diminish the fact of the deadly result. Those opposing Him will probably use conventional weapons, but His weaponry will be of a different nature. The figurative way of referring to His spoken word does not change the literality of God's verbal power. The account does not specify exactly how the warrior-King accomplishes the slaughter, but the actual destruction of the armies of evil is certain (Ladd). God has used unconventional means for bringing death before (cf. Josh. 10:11-13; 2 Kings 19:35; Jer. 28:16-17; Acts 5:5, 10). The prophetic word can smite as well as heal (cf. Hos. 6:4-5) (Sweet). Whatever means the rider chooses to use, bloodshed will be rampant and many lives will be lost.

The scene closes with the fulfillment of the promise to those invited to the great supper of God: καὶ πάντα τὰ ὄρνεα ἐχορτάσθησαν ἐκ τῶν σαρκῶν αὐτῶν (*kai panta ta ornea echortasthēsan ek tōn sarkōn autōn*, "all the birds were filled with their flesh").

Additional Notes

19:17 Like the εἷς in 18:21, the adjective ἕνα is equivalent to an indefinite article.[104]

19:18 The five occurrences of the plural σάρκας point in each case to "pieces of flesh."[105]

19:19 A few authorities including Alexandrinus and the Sahidic versions read αὐτοῦ instead of αὐτῶν. Though αὐτῶν has stronger support and is the probable correct reading, the armies of the kings of the earth (i.e., αὐτῶν) are in fact the armies of the beast (i.e., αὐτοῦ) also (Charles, Mounce).

19:20 The form ἐπιάσθη is from the verb πιάζω which has a relationship with πιέζω, meaning "I press down or together."[106] Πιάζω occurs in John 7:30, 32, 44; 8:20; 10:39; 11:57; 21:3, 10; Acts 12:4; 2 Cor. 11:32. It is a characteristic Johannine word, appearing eight times in the fourth gospel and only four times in the rest of the NT (Lee, Charles). Its form is singular here because the nearest member of a compound subject, τὸ θηρίον, is singular.

---

104. Robertson, *Word Pictures*, 6:454.
105. Ibid.
106. Robertson, *Word Pictures*, 6:455; G. Abbott-Smith, *A Manual Greek Lexicon of the New Testament* (Edinburgh: T. & T. Clark, 1950), p. 360.

For the dative τῇ εἰκόνι, Sinaiticus and a few other MSS read the accusative τὴν εἰκόνα. The dative has the stronger support, however, meaning that it was divine worship that was directed toward the image.[107]

The participle τῆς καιομένης is genitive, but an accusative to agree with τὴν λίμνην would have been expected. Here, however, the participle takes its case from the intervening τοῦ πυρός. In 21:8, the agreement is as expected.[108]

---

107. Cf. Charles, *Revelation*, 2:139.
108. Robertson, *Word Pictures*, 6:455.

21
The Millennium and
the White-Throne Judgment

The twentieth chapter is most famous because of its revelation about the millennial kingdom of Christ, but the first ten verses function primarily as a two-part vision of the doom of Satan. First comes the period of his enforced restraint (20:1-3), and then his permanent assignment to the lake of fire following a desperate but unsuccessful attempt to regain power (20:4-10).[1] The chapter closes with a description of the judgment and commitment of lost human beings to that same lake (20:11-15).

4. THE BINDING OF SATAN (20:1-3)

Translation

1And I saw an angel descending from heaven, having the key of the abyss and a great chain upon his hand. 2And he seized the dragon, the serpent of old, who is the devil and Satan, and bound him for a thousand years, 3and he cast him into the abyss and shut it and sealed it above him that he might not deceive the nations any longer, until the thousand years have been completed; after these things it is necessary for him to be loosed for a little time.

---

1. James Moffatt, "The Revelation of St. John the Divine," in *The Expositor's Greek New Testament* (Grand Rapids: Eerdmans, n.d.), 5:470.

Exegesis and Exposition

20:1 With the beast, the false prophet, and their followers out of the way, the fourth scene of the seventh bowl judgment turns its attention to one who furnished their motivation and power, Satan: Καὶ εἶδον ἄγγελον καταβαίνοντα ἐκ τοῦ οὐρανοῦ, ἔχοντα τὴν κλεῖν τῆς ἀβύσσου καὶ ἅλυσιν μεγάλην ἐπὶ τὴν χεῖρα αὐτοῦ (*Kai eidon angelon katabainonta ek tou ouranou, echonta tēn klein tēs abyssou kai halysin megalēn epi tēn cheira autou*, "And I saw an angel descending from heaven, having the key of the abyss and a great chain upon his hand").

Earlier comments have established that the eight scenes of this last bowl portray events in the order of their chronological fulfillment.[2] Further reflection regarding the present paragraph confirms this conclusion. It cannot be a recapitulation of the earlier account of Satan's being cast from heaven to earth where he proceeds to deceive and persecute (12:9; 13:14; 18:23c). The account of 20:1-3 tells of a removal from the earth that keeps him from pursuing these activities any longer.[3] The only way one could view Satan as bound before a time in the future would be to construe his binding as a restriction of his activity, not a cessation of it. Confinement to the abyss, however, requires a complete termination of his activity in the sphere of the earth.[4] To date this has never happened. The uniform testimony of the NT is that Satan is not bound during the period between Christ's two advents.[5] A further problem for a view that this paragraph recapitulates the present era is its inability to explain Satan's release at the end of the Millennium. What restrictions currently placed on him will be removed at the end of this age? No credible answer to this question has ever been advanced.[6]

Even proponents of some form of recapitulation concur that their view does not rest primarily on exegesis of particular texts, but on the analogy of faith.[7] With their hermeneutical assessment of the basis of

---

2. See comments at 19:11 and Excursus 5 at the end of this volume for further discussion of these eight scenes.
3. Alan F. Johnson, "Revelation," in *EBC*, ed. Frank E. Gaebelein (Grand Rapids: Zondervan, 1981), 12:581; Jack S. Deere, "Premillennialism in Revelation 20:4-6," *BSac* 135, no. 537 (January–March 1978): 60-61.
4. E. W. Bullinger, *The Apocalypse* or *"The Day of the Lord"* (London: Eyre and Spottiswoode, n.d.), pp. 610-11.
5. John F. Walvoord, *The Revelation of Jesus Christ* (Chicago: Moody, 1966), pp. 292-93.
6. George E. Ladd, *A Commentary on the Revelation of John* (Grand Rapids: Eerdmans, 1972), p. 263.
7. William Hendriksen, *More Than Conquerors* (Grand Rapids: Baker, 1944), pp. 222-26; Michael Wilcock, *The Message of Revelation* (Downers Grove, Ill.: InterVarsity, 1975) pp. 181-82; David Chilton, *The Days of Vengeance* (Fort Worth, Tex.: Dominion, 1987), p. 493.

recapitulation, advocates of the sequential nature of these scenes agree.[8] Chronological sequence is the natural understanding of the visions.[9] Also, the OT framework that supplies the foundation for this book requires such a future period on earth to fulfill the promises of a Messianic age.[10] It is a structural necessity of Revelation that this thousand years lies in the future too. The binding of Satan and the thousand years are an element of the seventh and last of the seven bowl judgments, otherwise known as the seven last plagues. Few, if any, would dare to argue that the last of the seven last plagues is a picture of the present age prior to the second advent of Christ. So the binding of Satan and the Millennium must come in conjunction with and as a result of the second advent of Christ.[11]

This binding and imprisonment of Satan will not be limited to believers as the language of 20:1-3 makes clear. It requires an absolute stopping of his activity (Mounce, Johnson). "The nations" (20:3) who will be free from his deceptive ploys are not the same ones as Christ has destroyed at His earlier coming (19:11-21).[12] They will be a new crop of nations emerging from the faithful mortals who populate the Millennium at its beginning. The privilege of reigning with Christ will extend to those martyred by the beast, the ones who are in the forefront of 20:4, but it will also include all the faithful up to that point, both from Israel and from the church. Such a future chronologically limited kingdom on earth is necessary to allow for a rule of God in history such as the OT emphasized. It also accords with the theological framework provided by Paul in 1 Cor. 15:20-28.[13]

Various suggested identifications of the "angel" (ἄγγελον [*angelon*]) charged with the responsibility of binding Satan have been Christ, the Holy Spirit, the twelve apostles, one of the popes, and Constantine the Great.[14] None of these has convincing support, however. The better

---

8. Isbon T. Beckwith, *The Apocalypse of John* (New York: Macmillan, 1919), p. 738; Hans Lilje, *The Last Book of the Bible*, trans. Olive Wyon (Philadelphia: Muhlenberg, 1957), p. 252; R. H. Charles, *The Revelation of St. John*, ICC (New York: Scribner's Sons, 1920), 2:185.

9. Walvoord, *Revelation*, pp. 289-90; Robert H. Mounce, *The Book of Revelation*, NICNT (Grand Rapids: Eerdmans, 1977), p. 352; Johnson, "Revelation," 12:580-81.

10. See the detailed discussion of this issue in Excursus 4 at the end of this volume.

11. See Excursus 5 at the end of this volume for a further development of this rationale.

12. Contra R. Fowler White, "Reexamining the Evidence for Recapitulation in Rev. 20:1-10," *WTJ* 51, no. 2 (Fall 1989): 321-25.

13. G. R. Beasley-Murray, *The Book of Revelation*, NCB (Grand Rapids: Eerdmans, 1978), pp. 287, 290.

14. William Lee, "The Revelation of St. John," in *The Holy Bible*, ed. F. C. Cook (London: John Murray, 1881), 4:791-92.

course is to understand him to be a special angel commissioned for this particular task (Walvoord).

The expression καταβαίνοντα ἐκ τοῦ οὐρανοῦ (*katabainonta ek tou ouranou*, "descending from heaven") described angels in 10:1 and 18:1. The reason this angel must descend is that Satan's location is now on earth. He lost his place in heaven earlier according to 12:9, 12 (Lee). The beginning of the Millennium marks the end of Satan's ὀλίγον καιρὸν (*oligon kairon*, "little time") for spreading havoc on earth.

In his possession the angel has τὴν κλεῖν τῆς ἀβύσσου (*tēn klein tēs abyssou*, "the key of the abyss"), probably the same key to lock or unlock the mouth of the shaft that leads down into the abyss as in 9:1 (cf. Luke 8:31; Rom. 10:7).[15] The abyss, also mentioned earlier at 11:7 and 17:8, is different from the lake of fire in 19:20 and 20:10. The latter is more severe and is a permanent place of punishment. The picture of a locked dungeon differs from that of an open shallow pool of fire that constitutes the lake of fire. Both, however, are places and not just symbols (Swete, Lee).

The angel also carries a ἅλυσιν μεγάλην ἐπὶ τὴν χεῖρα αὐτοῦ (*halysin megalēn epi tēn cheira autou*, "a great chain upon his hand"). Paul wore a chain in Rome (2 Tim. 1:16) as Peter did during his Jerusalem imprisonment (Acts 12:6-7), but here it is not a material chain such as would bind a physical being. It is rather one that would be necessary to shackle a spiritual being such as Satan (cf. Jude 6, where a different word for "chain" appears). With this in mind, it is a literal binding of Satan, not merely a limited restraint. Just as the sickle of Rev. 14:14-15 depicts a grand and dreaded reality, so does the chain here.[16] It is stronger than the one that bound Sampson (Judg. 6:6 ff.) and stronger than "Legion" who broke the chains that restrained the Gerasene (Mark 5:3-4) (Swete). The chain was draped "over" (ἐπί [*epi*]) the angel's hand and ready for use.[17]

20:2 Swinging into action immediately, the angel seized and

---

15. Henry Barclay Swete, *The Apocalypse of St. John* (London: Macmillan, 1906), pp. 259-60; Archibald Thomas Robertson, *Word Pictures in the New Testament* (Nashville: Broadman, 1933), 6:457; Walvoord, *Revelation*, p. 290.
16. Bullinger, *Apocalypse*, pp. 608-9; J. A. Seiss, *The Apocalypse* (New York: Charles C. Cook, 1909), 3:269; Merrill C. Tenney, *Interpreting Revelation* (Grand Rapids: Eerdmans, 1957), p. 258; J. B. Smith, *A Revelation of Jesus Christ* (Scottdale, Pa.: Herald, 1961), p. 268; Walvoord, *Revelation*, p. 291.
17. Friedrich Düsterdieck, *Critical and Exegetical Handbook to the Revelation of John*, in Meyer's Commentary, trans. and ed. Henry E. Jacobs (New York: Funk & Wagnalls, 1887), p. 463; Henry Alford, *The Greek Testament* (London: Longmans, Green, 1903), 4:730.

bound the dragon: καὶ ἐκράτησεν τὸν δράκοντα, ὁ ὄφις* ὁ ἀρχαῖος, ὅς ἐστιν Διάβολος καὶ ὁ Σατανᾶς, καὶ ἔδησεν αὐτὸν χίλια ἔτη (*kai ekratēsen ton drakonta, ho ophis ho archaios, hos estin Diabolos kai ho Satanas, kai edēsen auton chilia etē*, "and he seized the dragon, the serpent of old, who is the devil and Satan, and bound him for a thousand years"). The name τὸν δράκοντα (*ton drakonta*, "the dragon"), the first of Satan's titles used here, is his most frequent title in Revelation (cf. 12:3, 4, 7, 13, 16, 17; 13:2, 4, 11; 16:13). Then follow the other names ascribed to him in 12:9.

The title ὁ ὄφις ὁ ἀρχαῖος (*ho ophis ho archaios*, "the serpent of old") receives emphasis by being in the nominative case, though in apposition with the accusative *ton drakonta* (Lee). This type of phenomenon is frequent in Revelation, and is sometimes called an anacoluthon (e.g., 1:5) and sometimes a parenthesis.[18] Διάβολος (*Diabolos*, "The devil") is the name that refers to this divine opponent in 2:10; 12:9, 12; 20:10. Ὁ Σατανᾶς (*Ho Satanas*) refers to him in 2:9, 13, 24; 3:9; 12:9.

The binding of a spiritual being such as ἔδησεν (*edēsen*, "bound") depicts is a mystery to humans accustomed to the material world only. Whatever it is, it is the same as the binding of the angels in 9:14 which prohibited their movement and activity (Swete). The idea behind this securing of the great enemy is probably the same as that in Isa. 24:22-23 (Charles).

The duration of the binding is χίλια ἔτη (*chilia etē*, "a thousand years"), an accusative expressing extent of time. The sixfold repetition of this number of years (cf. 20:3, 4, 5, 6, 7) indicates its great importance (Lee). Exegetes have expressed different understandings of this period whose duration of one thousand years was undisclosed until John wrote this (Charles). One school of thought voices concern over even discussing the issue for fear of creating strife among the saints.[19] This view emphasizes that God's clock does not follow our reckoning, so humans cannot know what "a thousand years" means. This view looks to 2 Pet. 3:8 for support, but 2 Pet. 3:8 along with Ps. 90:4 states the very opposite. "A thousand years" in these two verses refers to a literal thousand years. To say that the period with man is only one day with God, does not deny that it is actually a thousand years with God too (Walvoord). The point is that time does not limit an eternal God, not that He is ignorant of what time means with man. Another feature opposed to this agnostic approach to the meaning of "a thousand

18. Swete, *Apocalypse*, p. 260; Robertson, *Word Pictures*, 6:257.
19. Robertson, *Word Pictures*, 6:457-58.

years" is that this writer, when he wants to speak of an indefinite time, uses something like μικρὸν χρόνον (*mikron chronon*, "a little time") (20:3) rather than give an explicitly definite period of time.[20]

Another way of handling the thousand-year period has been to view it as symbolic of a relatively long age of indefinite length. This explanation looks to the pattern of using numbers symbolically throughout Revelation for support.[21] Most equate it with the period between Christ's two advents, with the binding of Satan being equal to the enlightenment of the nations through the gospel.[22] As the largest conceivable unit of time in the Bible, it represents a period absolutely long just as "half an hour" (8:1) denotes a space of time absolutely short.[23] All of this reasoning is exegetically futile, however, because it rests on preconceived theological dogma. The only semblance of exegetical support is the effort to equate the casting of the dragon from heaven in 12:7-9 with his casting into the abyss (20:3).[24] But this equation is very doubtful, as already shown.

If the writer wanted a very large symbolic number, why did he not use 144,000 (7:1 ff.; 14:1 ff.), 200,000,000 (9:16), "ten thousand times ten thousand, and thousands of thousands" (5:11), or an incalculably large number (7:9)? The fact is that no number in Revelation is verifiably a symbolic number. On the other hand, nonsymbolic usage of numbers is the rule. It requires multiplication of a literal 12,000 by a literal twelve to come up with 144,000 in 7:4-8. The churches, seals, trumpets, and bowls are all literally seven in number. The three unclean spirits of 16:13 are actually three in number. The three angels connected with the three last woes (8:13) add up to a total of three. The seven last plagues amount to exactly seven. The equivalency of 1,260 days and three and a half years necessitate a nonsymbolic understanding of both numbers. The twelve apostles and the twelve tribes of Israel are literally twelve (21:12-14). The seven churches are in seven literal

---

20. Harold W. Hoehner, "Evidence from Revelation 20," in *A Case for Premillennialism: A New Consensus*, ed. Donald K. Campbell and Jeffrey L. Townsend (Chicago: Moody, 1992), p. 249.
21. Sydney H. T. Page, "Revelation 20 and Pauline Eschatology," *JETS* 23, no. 1 (March 1980): 32; Chilton, *Days of Vengeance*, pp. 506-7; Philip Edgcumbe Hughes, *The Book of Revelation* (Grand Rapids: Eerdmans, 1990), p. 209.
22. Hughes, *Revelation*, pp. 209-10; Wilcock, *Revelation*, pp. 188-89; J. C. de Smidt, "Chiliasm: An Escape from the Present into an Extra-Biblical Apocalyptic Imagination," *Scriptura* 45 (1993): 93.
23. Lee, "Revelation," 4:792; M. Robert Mulholland, *Revelation, Holy Living in an Unholy World* (Grand Rapids: Zondervan, 1990), p. 307.
24. Hughes, *Revelation*, pp. 210-11.

cities. Yet confirmation of a single number in Revelation as symbolic is impossible.[25]

So ample good reasons exist for not taking the number symbolically, but there are many good reasons for taking one thousand to be literal (Walvoord). It is the plain statement of the text six times. It is doubtful that any symbolic number, if there be such, is ever repeated that many times. Other symbolism in Revelation is not opposed to a literal understanding of the thousand years.[26] The mention of the thousand years is not limited to the binding of Satan. John received the information by direct revelation apart from symbols also (cf. 20:4, 5, 6) (Walvoord). Alleged problems in identifying this kingdom with the one promised in the OT—such as its limited length, rather than being eternal, and its lack of the ideal conditions cited in the OT[27]— are only apparent. The kingdom will have a limited phase and will enter its eternal phase after the conclusion of the thousand years. And it will have the ideal conditions described in the OT, but John has no occasion to mention them here.

The conclusion is that the only exegetically sound answer to the issue is to understand the thousand years literally.

20:3 The angel's next action is to transfer the dragon to his place of confinement: καὶ ἔβαλεν αὐτὸν εἰς τὴν ἄβυσσον καὶ ἔκλεισεν καὶ ἐσφράγισεν ἐπάνω αὐτοῦ ἵνα μὴ πλανήσῃ ἔτι τὰ ἔθνη ἄχρι τελεσθῇ τὰ χίλια ἔτη· μετὰ ταῦτα δεῖ λυθῆναι αὐτὸν μικρὸν χρόνον (*kai ebalen auton eis tēn abysson kai ekleisen kai esphragisen epanō autou hina mē planēsē eti ta ethnē achri telesthē ta chilia etē; meta tauta dei lythēnai auton mikron chronon*, "and he cast him into the abyss and shut it and sealed it above him that he might not deceive the nations any longer, until the thousand years have been completed; after these things it is necessary for him to be loosed for a little time"). Besides being bound, the dragon must remain in the place of confinement that was at one point the prison of the demonic horde released under the fifth trumpet judgment (9:1 ff.) and the beast (11:7; 17:8) before his endowment with power from the dragon (13:4, 7) (Lee).

---

25. Cf. Smith, *Revelation*, p. 269; Walvoord, *Revelation*, p. 295; Hoehner, "Evidence," p. 249.
26. Contra Swete, *Apocalypse*, p. 266.
27. Swete, *Apocalypse*, p. 264; Martin Kiddle, *The Revelation of St. John*, HNTC (New York: Harper, 1940), pp. 393-94; Johnson, "Revelation," 12:478; cf. Robert M. Johnson, "The Eschatological Sabbath in John's Apocalypse: A Reconsideration," *AUSS* 25, no. 1 (Spring 1987): 44-46; Barbara Wooten Snyder, "How Millennial Is the Millennium? A Study in the Background of the 1000 Years in Revelation 20," *Evangelical Journal* 9, no. 2 (Fall 1991): 70-72.

The angel "shut" (ἔκλεισεν [*ekleisen*]) and "sealed" (ἐσφράγισεν [*esphragisen*]) the opening to the abyss above the dragon. The latter action was for purposes of special security as with Daniel in the lion's den (Dan. 6:17) and the tomb of Christ before His resurrection (Matt. 27:66). In normal cases, sealing prevented any attempted escape (Swete). The threefold means of incarceration—chaining, imprisonment, and sealing—is a forcible guarantee that the dragon will be helpless to deceive the nations during the thousand years. This phase of his punishment entails no specified suffering, such as will come later (Swete, Beckwith).

The purpose of the confinement comes in the words ἵνα μὴ πλανήσῃ ἔτι τὰ ἔθνη (*hina mē planēsē eti ta ethnē*, "that he might not deceive the nations any longer"). He will have been busy doing this before his confinement (cf. 13:14; 16:13-14) and will renew his deceptive tactics after his release (20:8) (Lee). In the intervening thousand years, nations on earth will be quiet and willing subjects of the warrior-King, but upon his release (v. 7) they will allow his sly trickery to lead them in rebellion against God (Alford).

Probing the origin and identity of these nations has provoked several answers. One has been that only the beast and his *demonic* armies meet their end in the battle of 19:19-21, but this violates the clear indication that those armies are composed of human fighters (Johnson). Another answer has been that not all people of the earth joined the beast in the conflict of 19:19-21, thus leaving the unaffected people alive on earth to enter the Millennium and eventually defect under the leadership of the dragon (Moffatt, Ladd). This explanation, however, questions the worldwide extent of the earlier kingdom of the beast (cf. 13:3, 7, 8) that rebelled and was eventually defeated by Christ. The suggestion that only the men of war fell during the battle of 19:19-21 (Mounce) places undue restrictions on the exhaustive categorizations of humanity upon which the birds of prey were to feast in 19:18. None but the protected faithful remnant will survive this conflict. Neither is the answer found in using this as an example of conflicting ideas that characterize Revelation.[28] The alleged conflicts lend themselves in each case to harmonization among those not bent on finding literary discrepancies. An attempt to limit the battle of 19:19-21 to political power without affecting the nations themselves[29] is also futile, because it gives inadequate attention to the military language of the battle passage.

The only viable alternative is to allow that the battle of 19:19-21

---

28. Contra Beckwith, *Apocalypse*, pp. 722-23, 739, 749.
29. G. V. Caird, *A Commentary on the Revelation of St. John the Divine*, HNTC (New York: Harper & Row, 1966), pp. 251-52.

resulted in death for all those not faithful to the Messiah. However, the redeemed but nonglorified population on earth survives the battle, enters the Millennium (cf. 11:13; 12:13-17), and reproduces offspring some of whom do not become saved as they mature. These unredeemed will comprise Satan's rebellious army at the Millennium's end. The children of the saints who survive the beast's persecution will far outnumber their parents and will quickly fill the planet.[30] The rate of population growth during this period will be far higher than ever before because physical death will be the exception rather than the rule throughout this ideal period (cf. Isa. 65:20).[31] So a new set of nations will come to exist on earth in a relatively short period. They will remain undeceived from external sources "until the thousand years have been completed" (ἄχρι τελεσθῇ τὰ χίλια ἔτη [*achri telesthē ta chilia etē*]).

It is a divine necessity (δεῖ [*dei*, "it is necessary"]), however, for the dragon to be released "after these things" (μετὰ ταῦτα [*meta tauta*])—i.e., the thousand years. The final answer as to why God sees this as a necessity with its fruition in another rebellion is hidden in the counsels of God (cf. 1:1; 4:1; Isa. 55:8; Mark 8:31; 13:7; Luke 24:26, 44) (Alford, Swete, Lee, Moffatt, Beasley-Murray, Johnson). Yet one purpose may be a partial answer. Through his release the whole universe will see that after a thousand years of his imprisonment and an ideal reign on earth, Satan is incurably wicked and men's hearts are still perverse enough to allow him to gather an army of such an immense size.[32]

The "little time" (μικρὸν χρόνον [*mikron chronon*]) allowed the dragon after the Millennium is not the same as the "little time" (ὀλίγον καιρὸν [*oligon kairon*]) (12:12) allowed him on earth before the Millennium.[33] In the earlier case he deceives through the beast and false prophet, but in this one he will deceive through personal intervention.

Additional Notes

20:2 The *Textus Receptus* and most witnesses including Sinaiticus and 046 have τὸν ὄφιν τὸν ἀρχαῖον, the accusative case rather than the nominative ὁ ὄφις ὁ ἀρχαῖος. This avoids the inconcinnity of the nominative. Besides having the support of Alexandrinus and other wit-

---

30. Walvoord, *Revelation*, p. 302; Charles Caldwell Ryrie, *Revelation*, Everyman's Bible Commentary (Chicago: Moody, 1968), p. 116.
31. Walter Scott, *Exposition of the Revelation of Jesus Christ* (Swengel, Pa.: Bible Truth Depot, n.d.), p. 407.
32. Charles, *Revelation*, 2:143; Robert Govett, *Govett on Revelation* (1981 reprint; Miami Springs, Fla.: Conley & Schoettle, 1861), 2:213-15; Ladd, *Revelation*, p. 269; Johnson, "Revelation," 12:587.
33. Homer Hailey, *Revelation, an Introduction and Commentary* (Grand Rapids: Baker, 1979), p. 392.

nesses, the nominative, however, is in accord with usage in Revelation as a whole, where a nominative case of a title or proper name is often in apposition with a noun in an oblique case.[34]

5. THE THOUSAND-YEAR KINGDOM (20:4-10)

Translation

4And I saw thrones, and they sat upon them, and judgment was given to them, and [I saw] the souls of those beheaded because of the testimony of Jesus and because of the word of God, even those who did not worship the beast nor his image and did not receive the mark upon their forehead and upon their hand; and they lived and reigned with Christ for a thousand years. 5The rest of the dead did not live until the thousand years were completed. This is the first resurrection. 6Blessed and holy is the one who has part in the first resurrection; over these the second death does not have authority, but they will be priests of God and of Christ, and they will reign with Him for the thousand years.

7And when the thousand years was finished, Satan will be loosed from his prison, 8and he will go out to deceive the nations who are in the four corners of the earth, Gog and Magog, to gather them for the battle, whose number is as the sand of the sea. 9And they ascended to the breadth of the land and surrounded the camp of the saints, even the beloved city. And fire came down from heaven and devoured them; 10and the devil who deceived them was cast into the lake of fire and brimstone, where both the beast and the false prophet are, and they will be tormented day and night forever and ever.

Exegesis and Exposition

The scene dealing with the thousand-year kingdom is in two parts, the former furnishing details about the faithful during that kingdom (vv. 4-6) and the latter giving attention to Satan's final rebellion and defeat (vv. 7-10).

20:4 This begins the fifth scene in the series started at 19:11. Its fulfillment follows chronologically the one just completed, the binding of Satan (Johnson): Καὶ εἶδον θρόνους, καὶ ἐκάθισαν ἐπ᾽ αὐτούς, καὶ κρίμα ἐδόθη αὐτοῖς, καὶ τὰς ψυχὰς τῶν πεπελεκισμένων διὰ τὴν μαρτυρίαν Ἰησοῦ καὶ διὰ τὸν λόγον τοῦ θεοῦ, καὶ οἵτινες οὐ προσεκύνησαν τὸ θηρίον οὐδὲ τὴν εἰκόνα αὐτοῦ καὶ οὐκ ἔλαβον τὸ χάραγμα ἐπὶ τὸ

---

34. Bruce M. Metzger, *A Textual Commentary on the Greek New Testament* (New York: United Bible Societies, 1971), p. 764.

μέτωπον καὶ ἐπὶ τὴν χεῖρα αὐτῶν (*Kai eidon thronous, kai ekathisan ep' autous kai krima edothē autois, kai tas psychas tōn pepelekismenōn dia tēn martyrian Iēsou kai dia ton logon tou theou, kai hoitines ou prosekynēsan to thērion oude tēn eikona autou kai ouk elabon to charagma epi to metōpon kai epi tēn cheira autōn*, "And I saw thrones, and they sat upon them, and judgment was given to them, and [I saw] the souls of those beheaded because of the testimony of Jesus and because of the word of God, even those who did not worship the beast nor his image and did not receive the mark upon their forehead and upon their hand"). The thrones that met John's eyes have a twofold function. First, the thrones are tribunal seats for the assessors of the divine Judge. This part of the picture derives from Dan. 7:9-10, 22, with the occupants of the thrones managing the judicial processes as in Dan. 7:22 (Moffatt). But the thrones are also royal thrones, as the end of v. 4 indicates. There is scarcely a doubt that both ruling and judging are entailed here (cf. Matt. 19:28) (Lee, Beckwith).

The great challenge is in identifying the occupants of these thrones indicated by the unnamed subject of the verb ἐκάθισαν (*ekathisan*, "they sat"). Because of the prominence of the twenty-four elders in connection with the saints (5:8-9; 7:13 ff.; 11:16 ff.)[35] and their connection with thrones elsewhere (4:4; 5:10; 11:16),[36] some want to identify them as the occupants, particularly as representatives of the church (Smith). The absence of this group from this context and the absence of an indication that the thrones are twenty-four in number are strong objections to this theory, however (Lee).

A widely held view is that the thrones' occupants are the martyrs seen at various points earlier in the book. The special focus of the remainder of v. 4 on the martyrs is good support for this (Alford, Beckwith, Johnson) as is the obvious special place John has for the martyrs at other points (Moffatt, Kiddle). A main purpose of his writing is to assure the steadfastness of the martyrs in the face of persecution (Bullinger, Beckwith). As feasible as this position is, however, it overlooks two contextual hurdles. The first is that the resurrection of the martyrs does not occur until later in v. 4, their reign with Christ being specified by the ἐβασίλευσαν (*ebasileusan*, "reigned") at the end of v. 4. To identify them as the subject of *ekathisan* would make that verb needlessly repetitious (Bullinger, Mounce). It is without support to write this sequential factor off as relocation[37] or as eccentric syntax.[38] The other hurdle is that John elsewhere promises that every

---

35. Düsterdieck, *Revelation*, pp. 464-65.
36. Walvoord, *Revelation*, p. 296; Chilton, *Days of Vengeance*, p. 508.
37. Contra Charles, *Revelation*, 2:182-83.
38. Caird, *Revelation*, p. 252.

faithful one, not just the martyrs, will share Christ's future reign (2:26-28; 3:12, 21; 5:10; cf. 1 Cor. 6:2-3) (Johnson).

Others on the basis of Matt. 19:28; Luke 22:30; 1 Cor. 6:2-3 want to identify the occupants of the thrones as the apostles and some of the saints,[39] with the possibility that Christ is one of them too (Bullinger). Inclusion of Christ is difficult, because He is the one giving them the right to judge in the next clause, not a recipient of that right. The absence of any reference to the apostles and other Christians in this context makes that solution too difficult also.

A little-noticed view with great plausibility is that the occupants of the thrones are all the saints who compose the armies of Christ in 19:14. It is an unvarying principle that those who win a war become the ones who assume the rulership over the conquered entity.[40] The enthroned ones must be those who have already risen from the dead and been judged.[41] The only ones who fit this description are those composing the Lamb's bride (19:7-8) and the warrior-King's armies (19:14, 19). Understanding 20:1-3 as somewhat of a parenthesis relative to this line of thought, one can see more easily how this identification is obvious.[42] This is the fifth scene of the seventh bowl, His army being last mentioned in the third scene of that sequence (19:19). Only the fourth scene has intervened since the last mention of this group, and even Christ Himself is unmentioned in that scene. This is the very promise given to members of Christ's bride earlier in the book (2:26-28; 3:12, 21). So the best solution is to identify the subject of *ekathisan* as members of the army of Christ that accompany Him at His return.

As usual in this book, ἐδόθη (*edothē*, "was given") in the clause κρίμα ἐδόθη αὐτοῖς (*krima edothē autois*, "judgment was given to them") is an action by God.[43] This is the moral judgment of living humanity spoken of by Paul in 1 Cor. 6:2. In Dan. 7:22, the source passage alluded to here, a comparable expression means that judgments rendered favor God's people Israel, but John's use of the concept in this verse refers to those given the right to judge others. In Daniel it is a judgment in the course of history, not determinative of men's eternal destinies. The same is true here. This speaks of authorization to take charge of the domain of the defeated beast (Caird).

An additional sight that met John's eyes in this scene was τὰς ψυχὰς

---

39. Swete, *Apocalypse*, p. 261; Robertson, *Word Pictures*, 6:458; Beasley-Murray, *Revelation*, p. 293.
40. Seiss, *Apocalypse*, 3:299.
41. Ibid., 3:311-12.
42. Govett, *Revelation*, 2:232.
43. J. Massyngberde Ford, *Revelation*, vol. 38 of AB (Garden City, N. Y.: Doubleday, 1975), p. 349.

τῶν πεπελεκισμένων διὰ τὴν μαρτυρίαν ᾿Ιησοῦ καὶ διὰ τὸν λόγον τοῦ θεοῦ (*tas psychas tōn pepelekismenōn dia tēn martyrian Iēsou kai dia ton logon tou theou*, "the souls of those beheaded because of the testimony of Jesus and because of the word of God"). An implied repetition of εἶδον (*eidon*, "I saw") from the beginning of the verse explains the accusative case of τὰς ψυχὰς (*tas psychas*, "the souls") (Beckwith). John does not see resurrected bodies as in v. 12, but the souls of those not yet resurrected (Lee). They are ready to be raised, however, because the full number of those to be martyred has now been completed (cf. 6:11) and their deaths have now been avenged (Swete, Beckwith).

The word πελικίζω (*pelikizō*, "I behead") derives from πέλεκυς (*pelekys*), which means "axe," the traditional weapon for execution in republican Rome. Etymologically, it means, "I cut off with an axe." The sword later replaced the axe as the instrument of execution.[44] Beheading was the ancient Roman method of capital punishment, but the word may be just a periphrasis for "put to death."[45] The prophet has referred to martyrs earlier at 6:9; 18:24; 19:2. Their martyrdom has come διὰ τὴν μαρτυρίαν ᾿Ιησοῦ καὶ διὰ τὸν λόγον τοῦ θεοῦ (*dia tēn martyrian Iēsou kai dia ton logon tou theou*, "because of the testimony of Jesus and because of the word of God"). Earlier references to martyrdom have assigned this same reason or a similar one (6:9; 12:17). The writer himself received persecution for the same reason (1:9). "The testimony of Jesus" has its customary sense of "the testimony which Jesus bore."[46]

A further description of these martyrs comes in the words καὶ οἵτινες οὐ προσεκύνησαν τὸ θηρίον οὐδὲ τὴν εἰκόνα αὐτοῦ καὶ οὐκ ἔλαβον τὸ χάραγμα ἐπὶ τὸ μέτωπον καὶ ἐπὶ τὴν χεῖρα αὐτῶν (*kai hoitines ou prosekynēsan to thērion oude tēn eikona autou kai ouk elabon to charagma epi to metōpon kai epi tēn cheira autōn*, "even those who did not worship the beast nor his image and did not receive the mark upon their forehead and upon their hand"). Using an ascensive καί (*kai*, "even"), the writer switches constructions to a relative clause. This is not bad or unusual grammar,[47] because the οἵτινες (*hoitines*, "those who") that refers back to *psychas* is nominative as the subject of its relative clause and masculine because of its agreement with masculine sense of the feminine *psychas*. These who refused allegiance to the beast of necessity gave up their lives according to 13:15. This cannot refer to the living who were loyal to Christ because this would entail an

44. Robertson, *Word Pictures*, 6:459.
45. Moffatt, "Revelation," 5:472; Leon Morris, *The Revelation of St. John*, TNTC (Grand Rapids: Eerdmans, 1969), p. 237.
46. Mounce, *Revelation*, p. 355 n. 10; contra Ladd, *Revelation*, p. 265.
47. Contra Ford, *Revelation*, p. 349.

impossible meaning for ἔζησαν (*ezēsan,* "they lived") later in v. 4, a reference to resurrection, and would conflict with the use of *psychas* earlier in v. 4. The living who enter the Millennium in their mortal state still have their bodies and have no need of resurrection at this point (Charles, Moffatt). The writer brings forward this particular class of martyrs who remained faithful during the great testing before the Millennium to assure them of the special glory awaiting them (Beckwith, Mounce).

Regarding this special group of martyrs, the prophet goes on to write, καὶ ἔζησαν καὶ ἐβασίλευσαν μετὰ τοῦ Χριστοῦ χίλια ἔτη (*kai ezēsan kai ebasileusan meta tou Christou chilia etē,* "and they lived and reigned with Christ for a thousand years"). The verb ἔζησαν (*ezēsan,* "they lived") is an ingressive aorist, conveying the force of "they came to live" or "they lived again." This is the meaning of the same form in 2:8 and in 20:5 (cf. Rom. 14:9). This second life is comparable to the second death that is the destiny of the unfaithful (cf. 2:11; 20:6, 14).[48]

Yet not all acknowledge this rather obvious meaning for the verb, because to allow this meaning is in essence to accept that the Millennium is a future period on earth. Attempts to avoid this include the following:

(1) It is a spiritual resurrection, not physical, but this ignores the obvious contextual indicator that it refers to the martyrs of the earlier part of v. 4. People who have died for Christ can hardly experience a *spiritual* resurrection. They are already spiritually alive (Seiss, Johnson). (2) It is a bodily resurrection, yet the whole section of 20:1-10 does not predict events of history but is apocalyptic language symbolizing consolation and reward for martyrs (Beckwith). This explanation questions the reality of the fulfillment of the events and individuals portrayed in this passage and does injustice to the integrity of what is written, however. (3) It is the apocalyptic unveiling of the reality of salvation in Christ as a backdrop to the reality of the suffering and martyrdom that still continue as long as Christ's kingdom remains hidden. But this view does not account for the thousand-year kingdom's being on earth and within history (Johnson). (4) It is a spiritual resurrection, meaning that martyrs have been released into the world (Caird), but this view substitutes a symbolic sense for bodily resurrection (Johnson). (5) It is spiritual resurrection referring to the new birth. This proposal cites the Christian's present possession of spiritual life as evidence (cf. John 5:24; Rom. 11:15; Eph. 2:5; 1 John 3:14).[49] But the context of John 5:24, a main passage to support this view, is

---

48. Robertson, *Word Pictures,* 6:459.
49. Lee, "Revelation," 4:796; Wilcock, *Revelation,* p. 192.

not a true analogy to this one. John 5:25-29 provides clues for the spiritual interpretation in one instance and the literal in the other, but such clues are missing from Revelation 20 (Ladd). A further rejoinder to this viewpoint compares the two occurrences of *ezēsan* in vv. 4 and 5: if there are two resurrections, the first of which has the souls of the martyrs living again and the second has the rest of the dead living again later—one spiritual, the other physical, the hermeneutical switch is arbitrary, robbing language of its normal sense and robbing Scripture of definitive meaning on any subject (Alford, Johnson).

The only hermeneutically sound theory refers *ezēsan* in v. 4 to the future bodily resurrection of the martyrs just mentioned. The same form in v. 5 refers to bodily resurrection; in fact, wherever ζάω (*zaō*, "I live") is in the context of bodily death in the NT, it always speaks of bodily resurrection (cf. John 11:25; Acts 1:3; 9:41) (Mounce, Johnson). John plainly calls this ἀνάστασις (*anastasis*, "resurrection") in 20:5, using a noun that occurs more than forty times in the NT, almost always referring to physical resurrection (Alford, Johnson). Lastly, *zaō* elsewhere in Revelation is a frequent way of referring to bodily resurrection (1:18; 2:8; 13:14; 20:5) (Ladd).

A further promise to the martyrs is that of joining Christ in His future reign. The subject of ἐβασίλευσαν (*ebasileusan*, "reigned") is still the martyrs, though the temptation might be to make it the same as the subject of *ekathisan* at the beginning of v. 4.[50] The broader teaching of the Bible on this subject might incline some to yield to the same temptation (cf. Dan. 7:9, 27; Matt. 19:28; 1 Cor. 6:2; 2 Tim. 2:12) (Alford, Ladd). Yet the occupants of the thrones represented in *ekathisan* (v. 4) have no need of resurrection from the dead as the martyrs do. They had previously been raised and returned with Christ. The martyrs are the last subject of discussion before both *ezēsan* and *ebasileusan* and furnish the natural subject for both. This conclusion does not contravene the correct anticipation of all the faithful joining Christ in His reign. It simply says that all are not in view at this point.

Some insist that this is a reign in heaven because thrones throughout the rest of the book are always in heaven, except in the cases of Satan and the beast (cf. 2:13; 13:2; 16:10),[51] but such a generalization is not decisive enough to be determinative in every single case. A number of considerations require the location of the reign on earth: 5:10 requires it (Charles); it has to be where Satan deceived the nations (20:3, 8); it has to be where Satan is (cf. 12:9; 20:1); and earth is the

---

50. Contra Beasley-Murray, *Revelation*, p. 295.
51. Hendriksen, *More Than Conquerors*, p. 230; Morris, *Revelation*, p. 236; cf. Michel Gourgues, "The Thousand Year Reign (Rev. 20:1-6): Terrestrial or Celestial?" *CBQ* 47, no. 4 (October 1985): 679-81.

location of the outworking of the seventh bowl of which this scene is a part.[52]

Significantly, the name τοῦ Χριστοῦ (*tou Christou*, "Christ") refers to the warrior-King at the end of v. 4. This name alone refers to Jesus in Revelation only here and at 11:15; 12:10; 20:6. In each of these instances it probably looks back to Ps. 2:2, referring to the Lord's Anointed (Swete). This is one of many tie-ins between the millennial reign and the OT promises of a kingdom to Israel, a feature that explodes any theories regarding the total absence of such connections.[53]

20:5 The fifth verse accounts for the ones not raised at this time and furnishes a title for this resurrection of the martyrs: οἱ λοιποὶ τῶν νεκρῶν οὐκ ἔζησαν ἄχρι τελεσθῇ τὰ χίλια ἔτη. αὕτη ἡ ἀνάστασις ἡ πρώτη (*hoi loipoi tōn nekrōn ouk ezēsan achri telesthē ta chilia etē. hautē hē anastasis hē prōtē*, "the rest of the dead did not live until the thousand years were completed. This is the first resurrection"). Except for the last five words, this verse is parenthetical, perhaps accounting for the absence of the earlier portion from Sinaiticus and a number of other MSS (Lee). Strong external support indicates that the entire verse is original, however.

Opinions vary regarding the identity of οἱ λοιποὶ τῶν νεκρῶν (*hoi loipoi tōn nekrōn*, "the rest of the dead"). A suggested reference to the "non-saints" of the old covenant[54] is far-fetched. No contextual hint even remotely suggests they are unbelievers from the old covenant who were not included at Christ's ascension when believers ascended to their heavenly throne. Another theory based on referring the *ezēsan* of v. 4 to spiritual resurrection calls this group the spiritually dead (Lee), but the theory collapses with the corrected view of *ezēsan* as bodily resurrection. A third proposal takes "the rest of the dead" to be all who are physically dead except the martyrs, including both righteous and unrighteous (Beckwith). This line of thought looks to the limitation placed on the first resurrection by the exclusive attention devoted to the martyrs in v. 4 (Beckwith, Mounce). The large difficulty facing this suggestion, though, is the indication of v. 6 that those excluded from the first resurrection will experience the second death (Johnson). This eliminates the possibility of postponing the resurrection of some of the righteous to a point after the first resurrection.

The better option is to limit "the rest of the dead" to the wicked

---

52. Excursus 4 at the end of this volume furnishes additional reasons for the earthly location of this kingdom.
53. E.g., Bruce Waltke, "A Response," in *Dispensationalism, Israel, and the Church*, ed. Craig A. Blaising and Darrell L. Bock (Grand Rapids: Zondervan, 1992), p. 353.
54. Chilton, *Days of Vengeance*, p. 515.

who are physically dead (the rest of the righteous dead, besides the martyrs, having been raised earlier to join in reigning with Christ). Previous discussion has already noted the earlier resurrection of the bride of Christ to join in this reign.[55] The possibility of "the first resurrection" having additional phases allows for inclusion of more saints than the ones explicitly specified in this prophecy.

The futility of referring *ezēsan* in v. 5 to spiritual vivification of some sort (Swete, Lee) is apparent in light of the evaluation of the same form in v. 4. It is even more evident because this would have those who have never had spiritual life coming to life after the Millennium. It is true they will experience resurrection of their bodies, but it is a strange use of *zaō* for it to speak of a resurrection to shame and contempt (cf. Dan. 12:2). The term must mean "live again" as it does in v. 4. The rest of the dead, being unbelievers, did not live again until the finish of the thousand years. In other words, they had no part in the first resurrection.

"The first resurrection" ('Η ἀνάστασις ἡ πρώτη [*Hē anastasis hē prōtē*]) applies most directly to the resurrection of the martyrs at the end of v. 4, but it does not exclude earlier phases of resurrection from its scope. For example, the resurrection of 1 Thess. 4:16 is not the same as the resurrection of the martyrs here, but by implication must be an earlier phase of the first resurrection because it too will be "first." So "the first resurrection" is inclusive and must be the same as the resurrection of the just (Luke 14:14; Acts 24:15), the resurrection from among the dead (Luke 20:34-36), the resurrection of life (John 5:29), and the resurrection to everlasting life (Dan. 12:2) (Bullinger).

Various opinions about "the first resurrection" and issues related to *ezēsan* in vv. 4 and 5 and to the identity of "the rest of the dead" earlier in v. 5 have arisen. One opinion that makes the first resurrection a return to life of the martyrs *before* the Parousia (Swete) is untenable, because it is out of accord with the sequence of the present context. In 1 Thess. 4:16, the dead are raised before the living are changed, but that is part of the first resurrection.[56] The view that makes the first resurrection equivalent to that of Christ Himself (1 Cor. 15:20-23)[57] misses the unmistakable fact that the subject of *ezēsan* (v. 4) defines the participants in the first resurrection. That subject is not Christ. To make it some form of spiritual resurrection is also out of accord with the NT usage of ἀνάστασις (*anastasis*, "resurrection"), which is practically always bodily resurrection. This rules out a refer-

---

55. See discussion of ἐκάθισαν in v. 4.
56. Robertson, *Word Pictures*, 6:460.
57. Chilton, *Days of Vengeance*, pp. 516-19; Hughes, *Revelation*, pp. 213-15.

ence to believers' participation in Christ's resurrection in a spiritual way.

Identifying the first resurrection with the "regeneration" (παλιν-γενεσία [*palingenesia*]) of Matt. 19:28 and the "restoration" (ἀποκα-τάστασις [*apokatastasis*]) of Acts 3:21[58] is also tenuous. This would necessitate beginning the Millennium with the cross and resurrection of Christ[59] and equating the new birth (John 3:3, 5) with the first resurrection (Lee). Both assumptions have already proven their inadequacy. This would require the second resurrection to be a literal rising from the grave by the same people who participated in the first resurrection that is of a spiritual nature (Beckwith). This cannot be. Nor is it sufficient to take "the first resurrection" simply to express eschatological priority.[60] This would be strange terminology for expressing the privilege of being the first to experience blessing and holiness at the return of Christ.[61]

Defining the first resurrection boils down to a choice between its being the bodily resurrection of the martyrs before the future Millennium (Charles) and the bodily resurrection of all the righteous before that Millennium (Scott). Both understandings have the support of the NT usage of *anastasis* in referring to bodily resurrection (Seiss). Limiting the event to martyrs has a clear contextual advantage in light of the emphasis of v. 4 on martyrdom (Charles, Walvoord). Three considerations in particular militate against this limitation, however. One is a consideration that Christ's resurrection has preceded this, so the resurrection of the martyrs cannot be first in an absolute and exclusive sense. Another is the necessity of earlier phases of resurrection in order to have occupants for the thrones indicated by the *ekathisan* of v. 4. The final consideration against limiting the first resurrection to martyrs is v. 6 that indicates those not included in this resurrection become victims of the second death. This could hardly happen to the righteous.

The more satisfactory delineation of "the first resurrection" equates it to the resurrection of all the just. This allows for the sequence of resurrection indicated in 1 Cor. 15:23,[62] for the resurrection

---

58. Lee, "Revelation," 4:797-98; Mulholland, *Revelation*, pp. 309-10.
59. Mulholland, *Revelation*, pp. 309-10.
60. Contra Robert W. Wall, *Revelation*, in the New International Biblical Commentary, ed. W. Ward Gasque (Peabody, Mass.: Hendrickson, 1991), p. 239.
61. The view of Meredith Kline ("The First Resurrection," *WTJ* 37 [1975]: 366-75) that the "first resurrection" is a paradoxical expression for the death of the saints reverses the meaning of the plain language of the text. See J. Ramsey Michaels, "The First Resurrection: A Response," *WTJ* 39 (1977): 100-109, for a discussion of this view's shortcomings.
62. Robertson, *Word Pictures*, 6:460.

of members of Christ's body in 1 Thess. 4:16 (Johnson), and for the resurrection of the OT saints at the time of Christ's return to earth (Dan 12:2) as well as the resurrection of the martyrs here. So the first resurrection must have at least two earlier phases than that phase which comes in conjunction with the establishment of the millennial kingdom.

20:6 Revelation's fifth beatitude (cf. 1:3; 14:13; 16:15; 19:9; 22:7, 14) declares the happy state of those participating in the first resurrection: μακάριος καὶ ἅγιος ὁ ἔχων μέρος ἐν τῇ ἀναστάσει τῇ πρώτῃ· ἐπὶ τούτων ὁ δεύτερος θάνατος οὐκ ἔχει ἐξουσίαν, ἀλλ᾽ ἔσονται ἱερεῖς τοῦ θεοῦ καὶ τοῦ Χριστοῦ, καὶ βασιλεύσουσιν μετ᾽ αὐτοῦ [τὰ]* χίλια ἔτη (*makarios kai hagios ho echōn meros en tȩ̄ anastasei tȩ̄ prōtȩ̄; epi toutōn ho deuteros thanatos ouk echei exousian, all' esontai hiereis tou theou kai tou Christou, kai basileusousin met' autou [ta] chilia etē*, "blessed and holy is the one who has part in the first resurrection; over these the second death does not have authority, but they will be priests of God and of Christ, and they will reign with Him for the thousand years"). The addition of ἅγιος (*hagios*, "holy") to μακάριος (*makarios*, "blessed") this time gives the expanded sense that bliss consists of holiness (Moffatt).

This blessed condition belongs to each one ὁ ἔχων μέρος ἐν τῇ ἀναστάσει τῇ πρώτῃ (*ho echōn meros en tȩ̄ anastasei tȩ̄ prōtȩ̄*, "who has part in the first resurrection"). The only other combination of ἔχω μέρος (*echō meros*, "I have a part") in John's writings is in John 13:8, but *meros* occurs again in Rev. 21:8 and 22:19, in both places in connection with those denied the blessings of life because of their part in the second death (Swete, Lee). By contrast, the first-resurrection participants have exemption from the power of the second death (ἐπὶ τούτων ὁ δεύτερος θάνατος οὐκ ἔχει ἐξουσίαν [*epi toutōn ho deuteros thanatos ouk echei exousian*, "over these the second death does not have authority"]). "The second death" is the spiritual death beyond physical death referred to also in 2:11; 20:14; 21:8. Since the first death is clearly the death of the body, the second death must apply to the body too. So the second death penalizes both body and soul (cf. Matt. 10:28).[63] Other notions about what the second death is will not suffice. To make the first death the death of all men with Adam and the second death the total death of all God's enemies[64] or to see the first death as the death of Christ with implications for all men and the second death as its sequel in the lake of fire[65] is simply without exegetical substan-

---

63. Ibid.
64. Hughes, *Revelation*, pp. 217-18.
65. Mulholland, *Revelation*, pp. 310-11.

tiation. Neither of these proposals acknowledges the direct impact of the first death in ending personal physical existence on the earth. Exemption from the authority of the second death means deliverance from an eternity spent in the lake of fire, a considerable privilege that partially explains the blessedness of those raised at the first resurrection.

Another aspect of their blessedness is the privilege of being priests and rulers. Guarantee of the dual role comes in the words ἔσονται ἱερεῖς τοῦ θεοῦ καὶ τοῦ Χριστοῦ, καὶ βασιλεύσουσιν μετ' αὐτοῦ [τὰ] χίλια ἔτη (esontai hiereis tou theou kai tou Christou, kai basileusousin met' autou [ta] chilia etē, "they will be priests of God and of Christ, and they will reign with Him for the thousand years"). The function of being "priests of God and of Christ," referred to also in 1:6 and 5:10, will not be primarily the impartation of knowledge to ta ethnē during the period of Satan's imprisonment, but rather will consist of the privilege of unlimited access to and intimate fellowship with God. The relationship will continue after the final departure of Satan to the lake of fire (20:10) (cf. Isa. 61:6), so it must be independent of a responsibility to mortals (Beckwith, Moffatt). Whatever ministry the resurrected saints will have to the world during this period is unrevealed in this passage (Beasley-Murray). They will join Christ in ruling the earth, but in what way this will be is not known. Priesthood and royalty are dual aspects of their future service to God (Swete).

"The thousand years" ([Τὰ] χίλια ἔτη [(Ta) chilia etē]) at the end of v. 6 indicates that the priesthood and reign are special and temporary because of the limited duration of this kingdom on earth. This is not to say, however, that both will not continue with the ushering in of the eternal phase of the kingdom. The prophecy is explicit that they will continue (22:3, 5).

20:7 The account moves quickly to the close of the Millennium and the quelling of Satan's final rebellion: Καὶ ὅταν τελεσθῇ τὰ χίλια ἔτη, λυθήσεται ὁ Σατανᾶς ἐκ τῆς φυλακῆς αὐτοῦ (Kai hotan etelesthē ta chilia etē, lythēsetai ho Satanas ek tēs phylakēs autou, "And when the thousand years was finished, Satan will be loosed from his prison"). The seventh verse recounts Satan's release that comes at the conclusion of the thousand years, but does not tell how that release comes about (Moffatt). The future tense λυθήσεται (lythēsetai, "will be loosed") predicts his future release from what is called "the abyss" in 20:1, 3, but has the name "prison" (τῆς φυλακῆς [tēs phylakēs]) here. This latter title recalls the reference to the spirits "in prison" (ἐν φυλακῇ [en phylakē]) in 1 Pet. 3:19.

The future tenses of vv. 7-8 and 10b continue the language of the predictive prophecy of esontai and basileusousin in v. 6, but in

vv. 9-10*a* John reverts to aorist tenses, using the language of a prophetic seer as in 20:1-5.[66]

20:8 Satan's incurable bent toward evil evidences itself in an immediate return to his efforts to deceive the nations: καὶ ἐξελεύσεται πλανῆσαι τὰ ἔθνη τὰ ἐν ταῖς τέσσαρσιν γωνίαις τῆς γῆς, τὸν Γὼγ καὶ Μαγώγ, συναγαγεῖν αὐτοὺς εἰς τὸν πόλεμον, ὧν ὁ ἀριθμὸς αὐτῶν ὡς ἡ ἄμμος τῆς θαλάσσης (*kai exeleusetai planēsai ta ethnē ta en tais tessarsin gōniais tēs gēs, ton Gōg kai Magōg, synagagein autous eis ton polemon, hōn ho arithmos autōn hōs hē ammos tēs thalassēs*, "and he will go out to deceive the nations who are in the four corners of the earth, Gog and Magog, to gather them for the battle, whose number is as the sand of the sea"). Deception is the Devil's special purpose, especially so after his having been cast from heaven in 12:9 (cf. 12:9; 13:14; 19:20; 20:3, 10). A suggestion has been that this particular effort at deception in recruiting a huge army is the same as the one in 16:13-14 (Lee), but this cannot be because that earlier gathering is in preparation for the battle of 19:17-21 and this one prepares for the battle of 20:9. They are two different battles (Beckwith). In Ezekiel 38 to which the present passage alludes, God is the One who brings the nations together (Ezek. 38:16). That is another perspective on the gathering that does not necessarily contradict this one.

"The nations" (Τὰ ἔθνη [*Ta ethnē*]) are not the same ones deceived into joining "the battle of the great day of God Almighty" (16:14). These are quite distinct from the earlier ones as the explanation of *ta ethnē* in 20:3 has shown. By now, the population of the millennial kingdom will have spread far and wide as the descriptive τὰ ἐν ταῖς τέσσαρσιν γωνίαις τῆς γῆς (*ta en tais tessarsin gōniais tēs gēs*, "who are in the four corners of the earth"). This is an expression for coverage of the whole earth as it is in 7:1 also (cf. Isa. 11:2) (Mounce). Sad to say, unbelievers will exist in very large numbers among the generations subsequent to the one populating the earth initially in the Millennium. These will be "fair game" for the devil's deceptive campaign.

The names "Gog and Magog" (τὸν Γὼγ καὶ Μαγώγ [*ton Gōg kai Magōg*]) furnish a further definition for these nations. Magog first occurs in the Bible at Gen. 10:2, but the allusion here is to Ezek. 38:2 where both names appear. The most that one can discern from these names is that they are emblems for the enemies of Messiah during the end times. Josephus's efforts to relate the names with districts to the north of the land of Israel by equating Magog with the Scythians and

---

66. Beckwith, *Apocalypse*, pp. 745-46; Moffatt, "Revelation," 5:473; Robertson, *Word Pictures*, 6:460-61.

Gog with their prince may have some merit in reference to the Ezekiel passage (cf. Ezek. 38:15; 39:2).[67] But the present passage differs from Ezekiel 38-39 in a number of ways that are sufficient to show this is not the specific occasion foreseen by Ezekiel (Smith). That the prophet equates Gog and Magog with "the four corners of the earth" is ample reason to refrain from limiting it to one geographical region (Walvoord, Beasley-Murray). It has been obvious throughout Revelation that John does not always cite the OT with a strictly literal interpretation of proper names and events. These two proper names are his way of referring to the nations that in the latter days will come to attack Jerusalem (Alford, Lee).

To some degree, history repeats itself. Συναγαγεῖν αὐτοὺς εἰς τὸν πόλεμον (Synagagein autous eis ton polemon, "To gather them for the battle") repeats verbatim an expression in 16:14 regarding preparations for Armageddon that occurred before the Millennium. The mustering effort is once again quite successful, judging from the number gathered for the rebellion. The troops are innumerable: ὧν ὁ ἀριθμὸς αὐτῶν ὡς ἡ ἄμμος τῆς θαλάσσης (hōn ho arithmos autōn hōs hē ammos tēs thalassēs, "whose number is as the sand of the sea"). The same hyperbole describes the number of descendants promised to Abraham (Gen. 22:17), the grain stored by Joseph in preparation for the famine (Gen. 41:49), the Canaanites conquered by Joshua (Josh. 11:4), the Midianites defeated by Gideon (Judg. 7:12), the Philistines assembled to fight against Israel (1 Sam. 13:5), the counsel given to Absalom by Hushai regarding his army (2 Sam. 17:11), and the wisdom given to Solomon (1 Kings 4:29). The vastness of the number of invaders is perhaps an allusion to the figure of "a cloud to cover the land" in Ezek. 38:16 (Lee).

20:9 The forces of Satan advance to the very heart of the Messianic empire before being destroyed: καὶ ἀνέβησαν ἐπὶ τὸ πλάτος τῆς γῆς καὶ ἐκύκλευσαν τὴν παρεμβολὴν τῶν ἁγίων καὶ τὴν πόλιν τὴν ἠγαπημένην. καὶ κατέβη πῦρ ἐκ τοῦ οὐρανοῦ* καὶ κατέφαγεν αὐτούς (kai anebēsan epi to platos tēs gēs kai ekykleusan tēn parembolēn tōn hagiōn kai tēn polin tēn ēgapēmenēn. kai katebē pyr ek tou ouranou kai katephagen autous, "and they ascended to the breadth of the land and surrounded the camp of the saints, even the beloved city. And fire came down from heaven and devoured them"). With the aorist verb ἀνέβησαν (anebēsan, "they ascended"), John returns to the manner of the seer once again, a manner seen in vv. 4-5 also.[68] The verb ἀναβαίνω (anabainō, "I ascend") is the one employed in the LXX when an army proceeds to

---

67. Josephus Ant i.6.1; cf. Lee, "Revelation," 4:800; Caird, Revelation, p. 256.
68. Robertson, Word Pictures, 6:461.

attack (e.g., Judg. 1:1; 1 Kings 22:4) (Lee), but here it more probably follows the custom of referring to the ascent to the backbone of central Palestine and the situation of Jerusalem (e.g., Luke 18:31; Acts 11:2; 15:2; 18:22; 21:12, 15) (Swete).

The destination of these armies is τὸ πλάτος τῆς γῆς (*to platos tēs gēs*, "the breadth of the land"), which conceivably could mean that Satan's forces spread over the whole earth.[69] The technical meaning of *anebēsan* in reference to approaching Jerusalem and the need for a distinction between this expression and "the four corners of the earth" (Lee) point to a more localized reference here, however. It speaks of the land of Palestine as being fully occupied by these attacking forces (Bullinger).

Then they "surrounded the camp of the saints" (ἐκύκλευσαν τὴν παρεμβολὴν τῶν ἁγίων [*ekykleusan tēn parembolēn tōn hagiōn*]). Παρεμβολή (*Parembolē*, "Camp") often referred to a military barracks (Acts 21:34, 37; 22:24; 23:10, 16, 32) or to an army in line for battle (Heb. 11:34). But since the saints have no part in repelling the attackers and have no occasion to be organized as a military unit, the meaning probably aligns more closely with usage of the noun in the LXX to speak of the camp of the Israelites (e.g., Ex. 16:13; 29:14; Deut. 23:14; Heb. 13:11, 13). It refers simply to a place of dwelling for the saints (Beckwith).

The καί (*kai*, "even") following *parembolēn* is epexegetical, because "the beloved city" (τὴν πόλιν τὴν ἠγαπημένην [*tēn polin tēn ēgapēmenēn*]) is a further definition of the camp of the saints (Alford, Smith). To understand "the beloved city" as a reference to the new Zion or as an allegory for a spiritual Jerusalem, the church (Swete, Lee), is to abandon consistent exegesis (Beckwith). "Beloved" is appropriate terminology for the earthly Jerusalem in Pss. 78:68; 87:2.[70] According to Jer. 3:17, this will be the location of the Messiah's throne during Israel's kingdom on earth (cf. Isa. 24:23; Ezek. 43:7; Mic. 4:7; Zech. 14:9-11) (Bullinger). Ezekiel 38:12 calls Jerusalem "the center of the world" and makes it the logical place for enemies to attack (Beckwith, Moffatt). The proleptic view of the 144,000 on Mount Zion in 14:1-5 verifies that Jerusalem will be the center of Messianic activity during His thousand-year reign (Moffatt). Though this city at one point was like Sodom and Gomorrah (Rev. 11:8), through the grace of God to Israel (Jer. 31:2; Zech. 12:10), it can become "beloved" during Christ's millennial reign (Smith).

Fire from heaven as an instrument of divine punishment is well-

---

69. Ibid., 6:462.
70. Ibid.

known (cf. Gen. 19:24; Lev. 10:2; Ezek. 38:22; 39:6; 2 Kings 1:10, 12; Luke 9:54).[71] It is a fitting climax to this last battle with Satan and his armies. The brief κατέφαγεν αὐτούς (*katephagen autous,* "devoured them") summarizes the fate of the rebels. Verse 10 will tell of the eternal destiny of their leader, but the destiny of the multitudes who joined with Satan remains unstated until later in the chapter (vv. 12-15).

20:10 Satan's final place is the lake of fire which he shares with the beast and false prophet: καὶ ὁ διάβολος ὁ πλανῶν αὐτοὺς ἐβλήθη εἰς τὴν λίμνην τοῦ πυρὸς καὶ θείου, ὅπου καὶ τὸ θηρίον καὶ ὁ ψευδοπροφήτης, καὶ βασανισθήσονται ἡμέρας καὶ νυκτὸς εἰς τοὺς αἰῶνας τῶν αἰώνων (*kai ho diabolos ho planōn autous eblēthē eis tēn limnēn tou pyros kai theiou, hopou kai to thērion kai ho pseudoprophētēs, kai basanisthēsontai hēmeras kai nyktos eis tous aiōnas tōn aiōnōn,* "and the devil who deceived them was cast into the lake of fire and brimstone, where both the beast and the false prophet are, and they will be tormented day and night forever and ever"). The seductive methodology of the Devil indicated by ὁ πλανῶν (*ho planōn,* "who deceived") is his most distinguishing characteristic. An unnamed agent, implied by the prophetic aorist passive ἐβλήθη (*eblēthē,* "was cast"), will cast this great deceiver "into the lake of fire and brimstone" (εἰς τὴν λίμνην τοῦ πυρὸς καὶ θείου [*eis tēn limnēn tou pyros kai theiou*]) after the fire from heaven destroys his armies.

He joins his protégés, "both the beast and the false prophet" (καὶ τὸ θηρίον καὶ ὁ ψευδοπροφήτης [*kai to thērion kai ho pseudoprophētēs*]), who have been there for a thousand years already (cf. 19:20). This is the ultimate bruising of his head (Gen. 3:15; cf. John 12:31). That this is the ultimate destiny of the Devil is not a new revelation. Jesus spoke of it during His first advent (Matt. 25:41) (Lee). He escapes the doom of his armies only to face a more awful doom (Swete).

With βασανισθήσονται (*basanisthēsontai,* "they will be tormented"), John resumes his use of the prophetic future tense as in vv. 7-8. It is hard for humans to conceive of how literal fire can bring torture to nonphysical beings, but the reality of unbearable pain inflicted on Satan is unquestionable. However the Bible may speak of that future punishment—whether as the lake of fire, outer darkness (Matt. 8:12; 22:13; 25:30), wailing and gnashing of teeth (Matt. 8:12; 13:42, 50; 22:13; 24:51; 25:30; Luke 13:28), a never-dying worm and unquenchable fire (Mark 9:48), or fire and brimstone—it presents a picture of mental agony and corporeal suffering combined in proportion to the guilt of those who have sinned (Luke 12:47-48) (Seiss, Scott, Walvoord). The continuing existence of the beast and false prophet after a

---

71. Ibid.; Johnson, "Revelation," 12:588.

thousand years already spent in this lake shows that this torment does not entail annihilation of the wicked. Their existence is eternal as they experience an eternity of torment (Walvoord).

The metaphorical expression ἡμέρας καὶ νυκτὸς (*hēmeras kai nyktos*, "day and night") expresses the unbroken continuity of their torment. This is a figure of speech based on the experience of our earthly time frame. It is used in reference to both eternal blessing when there will be no night (21:25; 22:5) and eternal punishment which is called "outer darkness" (Matt. 22:13; 25:30), which presumably means there will be no daylight (Hailey).

The phrase εἰς τοὺς αἰῶνας τῶν αἰώνων (*eis tous aiōnas tōn aiōnōn*, "forever and ever") portrays the unending nature of the torment. First cast out of heaven (12:9) and then imprisoned for a thousand years (20:2-3), he now faces a doom that is permanent torment, a doom that 14:11 pictures in a more vivid way for his followers (Lee).

Additional Notes

20:6 External evidence for the presence or absence of the article τά before χίλια ἔτη is about evenly balanced. Transcriptional and intrinsic probabilities are fairly even too.[72] Two other occurrences of the expression for the thousand years are anarthrous (20:2, 4), and three others are arthrous (20:3, 5, 7). Because one of the two anarthrous uses is the first mention in the context, the case for inclusion is slightly stronger. This leaves 20:4 as the only unexplained anarthrous use.

20:8 The relative pronoun ὧν looking forward to the possessive αὐτῶν is another example of pleonasm or the redundant pronoun that occurs frequently in this book. See 3:8 (Thomas, *Revelation 1-7*, p. 278 n. 23) for further discussion.[73]

20:9 The reading ἐκ τοῦ οὐρανοῦ has stronger external support than six other variants. The reading ἐκ τοῦ οὐρανοῦ ἀπὸ τοῦ θεοῦ is probably an expansion suggested by 21:2, 10. The rest of the variants hinge on deliberate or accidental modifications of the prepositions or of the sequence of the clauses in the expanded reading. The first editor of Sinaiticus supplied the words from πῦρ in v. 9 to λίμνην in v. 10, the lines having been omitted by the firsthand producer of the MS.[74]

6. THE WHITE-THRONE JUDGMENT (20:11-15)

Translation

[11] And I saw a great white throne and the one who sat upon it, from whose face the earth and the heaven fled, and a place was not

---

72. Metzger, *Textual Commentary*, p. 764.
73. Beckwith, *Apocalypse*, p. 746; Robertson, *Word Pictures*, 6:461.
74. Metzger, *Textual Commentary*, pp. 764-65.

found for them. [12]And I saw the dead, the great and the small, standing before the throne, and books were opened; and another book was opened, which is [the book] of life; and the dead were judged from the things written in the books according to their works. [13]And the sea gave up the dead which were in it, and death and Hades gave up the dead which were in them, and each of them was judged according to his works. [14]And death and Hades were cast into the lake of fire. This is the second death, the lake of fire. [15]And if anyone was not found written in the book of life, he was cast into the lake of fire.

Exegesis and Exposition

The sixth scene of the seventh bowl judgment furnishes a picture of a Great White Throne existing in the absence of the old earth and heaven (20:11). Then follows the seventh scene that tells of the judgment proceeding from that throne (20:12-15). Καὶ εἶδον (*Kai eidon*, "And I saw") introduces each.

20:11 Nonbiblical apocalyptic works describe in gruesome detail the judgment of the wicked, but these two scenes furnish a description that is remarkable for its simplicity and restraint (Beckwith): Καὶ εἶδον θρόνον μέγαν λευκὸν καὶ τὸν καθήμενον ἐπ᾿ αὐτόν, οὗ ἀπὸ τοῦ προσώπου ἔφυγεν ἡ γῆ καὶ ὁ οὐρανός, καὶ τόπος οὐχ εὑρέθη αὐτοῖς (*Kai eidon thronon megan leukon kai ton kathēmenon ep' auton, hou apo tou prosōpou ephygen hē gē kai ho ouranos, kai topos ouch heurethē autois*, "And I saw a great white throne and the one who sat upon it, from whose face the earth and the heaven fled, and a place was not found for them"). The two scenes together constitute the last picture connected with the present order (Swete) as evidenced by the departure of the earth and the heaven as now constituted.

The prophet's eyes fall on θρόνον μέγαν λευκόν (*thronon megan leukon*, "a great white throne") first of all. It is μέγαν (*megan*, "great") in comparison with the thrones mentioned in 20:4 because it is the throne of God Himself (Lee) and because it is the seat of the last of the judgments. It is λευκόν (*leukon*, "white") because of its purity and the holiness and righteousness of the verdicts that issue from it (cf. Ps. 97:2; Dan. 7:9).[75]

Relating this throne of judgment to the broader biblical picture has been somewhat problematic. One way of doing so has been to assume that the Bible teaches only one final judgment and this is it (cf. Matt. 25:31-46; John 5:24-29; Rom. 14:10; 2 Cor. 5:10).[76] Yet a

---

75. Robertson, *Word Pictures*, 6:463; Johnson, "Revelation," 12:589.
76. Robertson, *Word Pictures*, 6:463; cf. T. Francis Glasson, "The Last Judgment —in Rev. 20 and Related Writings," *NTS* 28, no. 4 (October 1982): 537-38.

closer examination of most passages that allegedly teach one final judgment shows that future judgment will come in several phases. The fact of two future resurrections separated by a thousand years (20:4-5) entails at least two phases of judgment. The judgment of martyrs has already taken place before the appearance of the Great White Throne (20:4-5). Then the judgment of those who sit on thrones in 20:4 precedes that of the martyrs. The judgment of Matt. 25:31-46 precedes the Millennium, but this one from the Great White Throne follows the Millennium (Scott). The judgent of 2 Cor. 5:10 takes place in heaven as it now exists, but the Great White Throne does not come until the disappearance of the present heaven (Walvoord). The inevitable conclusion is that future judgment will come in a number of phases, with this from the Great White Throne being the last of them.

The Almighty Father is undoubtedly the One seated on this throne, as He has been throughout the book (cf. 4:2-3, 9; 5:1, 7, 13; 6:16; 7:10, 15; 19:4; 21:5). He is the One on the throne in Dan. 7:9-10 from which this scene borrows. But the Son sits there with Him (3:21; 22:1, 3, 12; cf. John 5:26-27; Heb. 1:3) and works with Him (John 5:19-21; 10:30; cf. Matt. 25:31 ff.; Acts 10:42; 17:31).[77] This passage has no reference to the Son, but John elsewhere indicates His involvement in judgment (22:12). The resolution of the two lines of teaching regarding the person of the judge lies in the oneness of the Father and the Son (John 10:30; cf. John 8:16) (Swete, Beasley-Murray). What one does, the other does also.

The Great White Throne is located somewhere in limitless space (Charles) and outside human history (Scott) as the words οὗ ἀπὸ τοῦ προσώπου ἔφυγεν ἡ γῆ καὶ ὁ οὐρανός, καὶ τόπος οὐχ εὑρέθη αὐτοῖς (*hou apo tou prosōpou ephygen hē gē kai ho ouranos, kai topos ouch heurethē autois*, "from whose face the earth and the heaven fled, and a place was not found for them") make clear. Two prophetic aorists, ἔφυγεν (*ephygen*, "fled") and εὑρέθη (*heurethē*, "was . . . found"), predict the departure of the old creation. *Ephygen* pictures a sudden and violent termination of the physical universe (Kiddle) and offers another perspective of the event spoken of in 2 Pet. 3:7, 10-12 where fire is the instrument for consuming heaven and earth (Alford). This departure may be only a change of the external order of the world, not of its substance or material (Rom. 8:19-23; 2 Cor. 5:17; James 1:10; 2 Pet. 3:10, 13) (Swete, Scott, Smith), or it may be a dissolving of the old, a vanishing into nothingness, followed by an entirely new creation (Charles, Walvoord). A further discussion of these two possibilities will come at 21:1. Suffice it to notice at this point, fleeing from the face of

---

77. Alford, *Greek Testament*, 4:734; Robertson, *Word Pictures*, 6:463; Johnson, "Revelation," 12:589.

God (οὗ ἀπὸ τοῦ προσώπου [*hou apo tou prosōpou*, "from whose face"])
leaves nowhere to go because God is everywhere (Ps. 139:7) (Mounce).
This clause alludes to Ps. 114:3, 7. The exit of the old creation aligns
with the consistent teaching of the temporality of matter in both the
OT (Pss. 97:5; 102:25-26; Isa. 51:6) and the NT (Matt. 24:35; Mark
13:31; Luke 16:17; 21:33; Heb. 1:10-12; 2 Pet. 3:10).[78]

The unavailability of any "place" (τόπος [*topos*]) for the earth and
the heaven following their departure indicates that theirs is a flight
from the present existence. They will give way to the new heaven and
the new earth (Lee).

20:12 The seventh scene of the seventh bowl judgment begins with
another καὶ εἶδον (*kai eidon*, "and I saw"). It continues what has begun
with the placement of the Great White Throne: καὶ εἶδον τοὺς νεκρούς,
τοὺς μεγάλους καὶ τοὺς μικρούς, ἑστῶτας ἐνώπιον τοῦ θρόνου, καὶ βιβλία
ἠνοίχθησαν· καὶ ἄλλο βιβλίον ἠνοίχθη, ὅ ἐστιν τῆς ζωῆς· καὶ ἐκρίθησαν
οἱ νεκροὶ ἐκ τῶν γεγραμμένων ἐν τοῖς βιβλίοις κατὰ τὰ ἔργα αὐτῶν (*kai
eidon tous nekrous, tous megalous kai tous mikrous, hestōtas enōpion
tou thronou, kai biblia ēnoichthēsan; kai allo biblion ēnoichthē, ho estin
tēs zōēs; kai ekrithēsan hoi nekroi ek tōn gegrammenōn en tois bibliois
kata ta erga autōn*, "and I saw the dead, the great and the small, standing before the throne, and books were opened; and another book was
opened, which is [the book] of life; and the dead were judged from the
things written in the books according to their works").

The group that comes into the prophet's view are "the dead, the
great and the small" (τοὺς νεκρούς, τοὺς μεγάλους καὶ τοὺς μικρούς [*tous
nekrous, tous megalous kai tous mikrous*]). John saw this group of dead
persons "standing before the throne" (ἑστῶτας ἐνώπιον τοῦ θρόνου
[*hestōtas enōpion tou thronou*]). Their standing posture implies they
have risen from the dead, a feature that becomes more evident in v. 13.
By implication this is the second resurrection (cf. 20:5). These dead
have come from all classes and conditions of humanity as indicated by
τοὺς μεγάλους καὶ τοὺς μικρούς (*tous megalous kai tous mikrous*, "the
great and the small"). The writer uses the reversed order of this description earlier (11:18; 13:16; 19:5, 12, 18).[79] Jonah 3:5 uses this order, but Ps. 115:13; Jer. 6:13; 31:34 follow the other order (Charles).

No living mortals participate in this judgment, only "the dead."
These include those who joined forces with the Devil and perished in
his final rebellion after the Millennium and the rest of the dead who
had no part in the first resurrection before the Millennium (20:5).
These are the unrighteous dead from all ages, whose resurrection is a

---

78. Robertson, *Word Pictures*, 6:463.
79. Swete, *Apocalypse*, p. 272; Robertson, *Word Pictures*, 6:463.

part of universal Jewish and Christian belief (cf. Dan. 12:2) (Beckwith, Scott, Walvoord). It is groundless to view them as being the redeemed in v. 12 and the rebellious in vv. 13-14.[80] Neither is it proper to view them as "the dead" of the whole human race.[81] The raising and judgment of the martyrs came earlier (20:4), so other groups of righteous persons could have risen earlier too. If one expands "the rest of the dead" in 20:5 to include all except the martyrs, "the dead" here could include both righteous and unrighteous (Mounce), but the limitation of that earlier phrase to those who will experience the second death automatically excludes the possibility of these dead including any righteous persons among their number. This by implication is the second resurrection and includes only those who are not exempt from the second death (Johnson). The absence of any reference to the righteous at this Great White Throne judgment confirms this definition of "the dead." The Book of Life comes into the discussion only to show that the names of these dead are not written there.[82]

The question of what happens to the living just persons who are alive at the end of the Millennium does not come up in the passage. Presumably these saints will have divine protection during Satan's final rebellion and will survive the transition from the old earth and heaven to the new ones. The assumption must be that God will give them new bodies that suit them for conditions of immortality in the new heaven and the new earth.

Written records of the acts of each individual form the basis for this judgment (cf. Dan. 7:10). This is what the βιβλία (*biblia*, "books" or "scrolls") contained. The judgment is not arbitrary (Swete). The nature of the human deeds recorded in these books may be good and bad deeds or bad deeds only. Scripture makes consistent reference to a register of human actions (cf. Deut. 32:34; Ps. 56:8; Isa. 65:6; Dan. 7:10; Mal. 3:16; Matt. 12:37) (Lee). Daniel 7:10 and Mal. 3:16 seem to include both good and evil deeds in this record, but Isa. 65:6 appears to limit them to the evil only (Ford).

The greater focus of this passage, however, is on the other book, "the book of life" (βιβλίον . . . τῆς ζωῆς [*biblion* . . . *tēs zōēs*]), which apparently decides the ultimate issue (cf. 3:5; 13:8; 17:8; 21:27). This is not contradictory to a judgment according to works, however, because a person's works are an unmistakable mark of where his loyalties lie (Johnson). The other "books" are in a sense vouchers to support what is in "the book of life" (Alford). Salvation is by grace, but character in the end will be the test of the fruit of the tree (Matt. 7:16, 20; 10:32-33;

---

80. Contra Mulholland, *Revelation*, p. 312.
81. Contra Lee, "Revelation," 4:803.
82. Chilton, *Days of Vengeance*, pp. 532-33.

25:31-46; John 15:6; Rom. 2:9-10; 2 Cor. 5:10; Rev. 2:23; 22:12).[83] The Book of Life is a divine register for every loyal believer (cf. Isa. 4:3; Ps. 69:28; Dan. 12:1; Luke 10:20) (Kiddle). It originally contained the names of all for whom Christ died, i.e., the whole world, but at the judgment of the Great White Throne many blank spaces will signal the removal of many names who never believed in Christ for salvation (Walvoord).

Judgment according to works—ἐκρίθησαν οἱ νεκροὶ ἐκ τῶν γεγραμμένων ἐν τοῖς βιβλίοις κατὰ τὰ ἔργα αὐτῶν (*ekrithēsan . . . kata ta erga autōn*, "they were judged . . . according to their works")—is explicit on this decisive occasion. This is a point of emphasis at the end of v. 13 also.

20:13 The resurrection implied in v. 12*a* receives a fuller description in v. 13 as the writer returns to the event alluded to before the opening of the books and the judgment in the previous verse (Swete, Beckwith): καὶ ἔδωκεν ἡ θάλασσα τοὺς νεκροὺς τοὺς ἐν αὐτῇ, καὶ ὁ θάνατος καὶ ὁ ᾅδης ἔδωκαν τοὺς νεκροὺς τοὺς ἐν αὐτοῖς, καὶ ἐκρίθησαν* ἕκαστος κατὰ τὰ ἔργα αὐτῶν (*kai edōken hē thalassa tous nekrous tous en autē, kai ho thanatos kai ho hadēs edōkan tous nekrous tous en autois, kai ekrithēsan hekastos kata ta erga autōn*, "and the sea gave up the dead which were in it, and death and Hades gave up the dead which were in them, and each of them was judged according to his works"). Sequentially, the words of v. 13 belong in the middle of v. 12, before the opening of the books and the judgment.

The combination ἔδωκεν . . . ἔδωκαν (*edōken . . . edōkan*, "gave up . . . gave up") is another way of depicting bodily resurrection. The dead rise to receive their sentence (Moffatt; Johnson). This is a resurrection to death that corresponds to the earlier resurrection to life (cf. Dan. 12:2; John 5:29; Acts 24:15).[84] This second resurrection fulfills the implication of the first resurrection of 20:4.

The double reference to the dead who participate in this resurrection —τοὺς νεκροὺς . . . τοὺς νεκροὺς (*tous nekrous . . . tous nekrous*, "the dead . . . the dead")—involves the unsaved dead only. The passage has no sentence for those destined for life. The concept of one general resurrection and judgment for all men opposes the clear statement of 20:5, "the rest of the dead did not live until the thousand years were completed" (Scott). All those judged here will fall under the authority of the second death (20:6).

Mentioning "the sea" (ἡ θάλασσα [*hē thalassa*]) as a source of dead bodies is of course mindful of drownings or "burials at sea." The ab-

---

83. Robertson, *Word Pictures*, 6:464.
84. Ibid., 6:464-65.

horrent fate of those whose bodies were devoured by the fish accounts for the special mention of this group at the resurrection (cf. *1 Enoch* 61:5) (Beckwith, Mounce). Both Greeks and Romans attached great importance to land burial and the inviolability of the tomb. They recoiled with great horror at the thought of death by drowning or even burial at sea (Swete). The disappearance of the old earth in the prior scene (20:11) is not an inconsistency, in that the sea could have yielded its dead simultaneously with that disappearance.

The personification of "death and Hades" (ὁ θάνατος καὶ ὁ ᾅδης [*ho thanatos kai ho hạdēs*]) in 6:8 does not require that view of them here.[85] To parallel the reference to a place called "the sea," a local reference for both terms is preferable here (as in 1:18). The former word refers more to a state of death and the latter to a place of death. According to its etymology, Hades is the unseen world where all who die reside. It includes both Paradise (Luke 23:43) and Gehenna (Luke 12:5)—Abraham's bosom and the state of torment and anguish (Luke 16:22-28). The present instance involves only the latter, because the resurrection of the righteous dead has already occurred.

The ἕκαστος (*hekastos*, "each") with the plural ἐκρίθησαν (*ekrithēsan*, "was judged") individualizes the accountability at this final judgment whereas v. 12 speaks of it as judgment of the whole group with *ekrithēsan* alone. "They were judged, every one of them" conveys the constant emphasis in Christian tradition upon individual responsibility (cf. Matt. 16:27; Rom. 2:6; 14:12; 1 Cor. 3:13; 2 Cor. 5:10; 1 Pet. 1:17; Rev. 2:23) (Swete, Walvoord).

Another consistent stress of Scripture is that God's judgment is always based on works, as κατὰ τὰ ἔργα αὐτῶν (*kata ta erga autōn*, "according to his works") states.[86] The point of this passage is not to prove salvation by works, but condemnation by works. A person does not receive salvation through works, but neither does he receive it without works.[87]

20:14 This judgment marks the end of death, so death along with Hades meet their doom in the lake of fire: καὶ ὁ θάνατος καὶ ὁ ᾅδης ἐβλήθησαν εἰς τὴν λίμνην τοῦ πυρός. οὗτος ὁ θάνατος ὁ δεύτερός ἐστιν, ἡ λίμνη τοῦ πυρός (*kai ho thanatos kai ho hạdes eblēthēsan eis tēn limnēn*

---

85. Contra Johnson, "Revelation," 12:588.
86. Cf. Pss. 28:4; 62:12; Prov. 24:12; Eccl. 12:14; Isa. 59:18; Jer. 17:10; 25:14; 32:19; Ezek. 24:14; 36:19; Hos. 12:2; Matt. 16:17; 25:41 ff.; Rom. 2:6; 1 Cor. 3:13; 2 Cor. 5:10; 11:15; Eph 6:8; Col. 3:25; 2 Tim. 4:14; Heb. 4:12-13; 1 Pet. 1:17; Rev. 2:23; 18:6; 20:12; 22:12. Also cf. 2 Sam. 3:39; 22:21, 25; 1 Kings 8:32, 39; 2 Chron. 6:23, 30; 15:7; Ezra 9:13; Job 34:11; Ps. 18:20, 24; Jer. 50:29; 51:6; Lam. 3:64; Ezek. 7:3, 4, 8, 9, 27; 18:30; 39:24; Hos. 4:9; Zech. 1:6; 1 Cor. 3:8; Heb. 2:2; Rev. 11:18; 20:13.
87. Johnson, "Revelation," 12:589; Chilton, *Days of Vengeance*, p. 533.

tou pyros. Houtos ho thanatos ho deuteros estin, hē limnē tou pyros,
"and death and Hades were cast into the lake of fire. This is the second
death, the lake of fire"). The perspective now changes as "death and
Hades" come to be personified as inseparable companions, two vora-
cious and insatiable monsters who have swallowed all past generations
and now meet the same fate as the prey they have just disgorged
(Swete).

The last enemy meets his end (1 Cor. 15:26, 54-55; cf. Isa. 25:8;
Hos. 13:14). He no longer threatens the human race. Death will not be
around to disturb the tranquillity of the new heaven and the new earth
(Rev. 21:4), because it joins its victims in the lake of fire.[88]

The lake of fire is the same as the second death according to the
words οὗτος ὁ θάνατος ὁ δεύτερός ἐστιν, ἡ λίμνη τοῦ πυρός (*houtos ho
thanatos ho deuteros estin, hē limnē tou pyros,* "this is the second death,
the lake of fire"). The last words of 21:8 make the same equation. As a
second and higher life exists for the righteous, a second and deeper
death awaits the wicked (cf. 2:11; 20:6) (Alford). In the new order, the
lake of fire is the nearest analogue of death in the present creation
(Swete). The lake of fire is a figure of speech to accommodate a limited
human understanding of what eternal punishment will be, but it nevertheless corresponds to reality. Just as the rich man in Hades experienced unbearable torment in flames (Luke 16:23-24), those in the lake
of fire will have to endure punishment of the same nature. No significant difference separates the physical and the spiritual reality embodied in the lake-of-fire terminology (Walvoord). Its unending torment
makes "the second death" a suitable subtitle for it.

20:15 The short statement of v. 15 foretells the doom of all who are
outside of Christ: καὶ εἴ τις οὐχ εὑρέθη ἐν τῇ βίβλῳ τῆς ζωῆς γεγραμ-
μένος ἐβλήθη εἰς τὴν λίμνην τοῦ πυρός (*kai ei tis ouch heurethē en tē
biblō tēs zōēs gegrammenos eblēthē eis tēn limnēn tou pyros,* "and if
anyone was not found written in the book of life, he was cast into the
lake of fire"). They follow the Devil, the beast, and the false prophet
into the lake of fire. Language like this leaves no room for any form of
universalism, soul sleep, an intermediate state, a second chance, or
annihilation of the wicked.[89]

Assuming that some will not find their names written in the Book
of Life, this verse predicts their being cast into the lake of fire. The
statement is simple and does not belabor the point by assigning the
saints a role in inflicting this punishment or witnessing it (Moffatt).
This is the negation of eternal life which the lost could have received

---

88. Robertson, *Word Pictures,* 6:464; Johnson, "Revelation," 12:590.
89. Robertson, *Word Pictures,* 6:465; Ladd, *Revelation,* p. 258; Berkouwer, *The
Return of Christ* (Grand Rapids: Eerdmans, 1975), pp. 387-423.

(Swete). But it is more than that. It is a "torturous existence in the society of evil in opposition to life in the society of God" (Beasley-Murray), but it is more than that. It is the direct infliction of misery, both physical and mental, through the eternal fire spoken of by Jesus (Matt. 25:41, 46). Because of the presence of the lost in this lake, "the smoke of their torment ascends forever and ever, and they do not have rest day and night" (14:11).

Additional Notes

20:13 Sinaiticus reads κατεκρίθησαν instead of ἐκρίθησαν. This cannot be the correct reading because of the absence of further support, but it may be an enlightened interpretation of the verb if this is the resurrection of condemnation spoken of elsewhere (Bullinger).

22
The New Creation

One might expect the judgment of the Great White Throne to end the last of the seven last plagues, but it does not. One more scene remains. It may seem inappropriate to call this scene a plague or a bowl judgment, but alongside the future bliss of the saints (21:1-7) comes an indication of the exclusion of those in the lake of fire from the promised blessings of the new creation (21:8). So besides the structural features that indicate a continuation of the last plague in this section, as outlined in Excursus 5 at the end of this volume, the continuing theme of misery and punishment shows how this section belongs in the scroll of judgments first introduced in chapter 5.

7. THE NEW HEAVEN AND THE NEW EARTH (21:1-8)

Translation

¹And I saw a new heaven and a new earth; for the first heaven and the first earth passed away, and there is a sea no longer. ²And I saw the holy city, the new Jerusalem, descending out of heaven from God, prepared as a bride adorned for her husband. ³And I heard a loud voice from the throne saying, "Behold, the tabernacle of God is with men, and He will dwell with them, and they themselves will be His people, and God Himself will be with them, their God, ⁴and He will wipe away every tear from their eyes, and there will be death no longer, neither will there be sorrow or

crying or pain any longer; because the first things have passed
away."
⁵And the one sitting upon the throne said, "Behold, I make all
things new." And he says, "Write, because these words are faithful
and true." ⁶And He said to me, "They are done. I am the Alpha and
the Omega, the beginning and the end. I will give freely to the one
who thirsts [something] from the fountain of the water of life.
⁷The one who overcomes will inherit these things, and I will be to
him God and he will be to Me a son. ⁸But to the cowardly and
unfaithful and abominable and murderers and fornicators and
sorcerers and idolaters and all liars, their part will be in the lake
which burns with fire and brimstone, which is the second death."

Exegesis and Exposition

Καὶ εἶδον (*Kai eidon*) introduces the eighth and last scene of the
seventh bowl judgment. It is a picture of new beginnings, a picture of
bliss for the saints that contrasts sharply with the lake of fire so prominent in the seventh scene. Finite human beings find it difficult to grasp
what is in both scenes, but behind both pictures lie stern and glorious
realities of two possible destinies.[1] This scene is a dramatic turn-
around from the evil and miserable contents of the seven-sealed scroll
until now. It closes the direct revelations of that scroll, 21:9–22:5 being
a poetical repetition and elaboration of 21:1-8.[2]

21:1 Greeting the seer's eyes are the new heaven and the new earth
that replace the earth and the heaven that fled away in 20:11: Καὶ εἶδον
οὐρανὸν καινὸν καὶ γῆν καινήν· ὁ γὰρ πρῶτος οὐρανὸς καὶ ἡ πρώτη γῆ
ἀπῆλθαν, καὶ ἡ θάλασσα οὐκ ἔστιν ἔτι (*Kai eidon ouranon kainon kai gēn
kainēn; ho gar prōtos ouranos kai hē prōtē gē apēlthan, kai hē thalassa
ouk estin eti*, "And I saw a new heaven and a new earth; for the first
heaven and the first earth passed away, and there is a sea no longer").
The new creation will appear chronologically following the Millennium and the Great White Throne and is not a picture of the present age
of the Christian church.[3] The idea of a new heaven and a new earth

1. Archibald Thomas Robertson, *Word Pictures in the New Testament* (Nashville: Broadman, 1933), 6:466.
2. James Moffatt, "The Revelation of St. John the Divine," in *The Expositor's
   Greek Testament*, ed. J. Robertson Nicoll (Grand Rapids: Eerdmans, n.d.),
   5:478.
3. Henry Alford, *The Greek Testament* (London: Longmans, Green, 1903),
   4:736; William Lee, "The Revelation of St. John," in *The Holy Bible*, ed. F. C.
   Cook (London: John Murray, 1881), 4:815; E. W. Bullinger, *The Apocalypse
   or "The Day of the Lord"* (London: Eyre and Spottiswodde, n.d.), p. 646;
   contra David Chilton, *The Days of Vengeance* (Fort Worth, Tex.: Dominion,
   1987), pp. 538-45, and Robert H. Gundry, "The New Jerusalem: People as
   Place, not Place for People," *NovT* 29, no. 3 (July 1987): 254-64.

alludes to Isa. 65:17; 66:22; Ps. 102:25-26; and perhaps to Isa. 51:6 (cf. *1 Enoch* 45:4-5).[4]

The reason assigned (γὰρ [*gar*, "for"]) for the appearance of the new heaven and earth is the disappearance of the first heaven and earth. The entrance of sin and death spoiled the earlier creation and made it a place of rebellion and alienation, an enemy-occupied territory. Its replacement with a whole new order of life without death, mourning, crying, and pain is a necessity.[5]

The departure of the old order centers around the meaning of ἀπῆλθαν (*apēlthan*, "passed away") here and ἔφυγεν (*ephygen*, "fled") in 20:11. The question is whether they connote complete disappearance of the old before being replaced by the new or a renovation of the old resulting in the new. The renovation approach has the support of parallel passages in Rom. 8:19-22; Acts 3:21; Matt. 19:28. Paul in the Romans passage wrote about the renewal of an old creation.[6] Peter in Acts spoke of the restoration of all God spoke about through the prophets, and Jesus in Matthew about the regeneration.[7] The teaching of the OT regarding the eternality of the earth, part of which was given to Israel as their everlasting possession, also supports renovation (cf. Gen. 48:4; Ps. 119:90; Eccles. 1:4).[8] This general biblical truth also finds support in the immediate context where Rev. 21:5 says, "I make all things new," which has the most natural interpretation in referring to a renovation of the existing creation,[9] but an argument based on the use in that verse of ποιέω (*poieō*, "I make") rather than κτίζω (*ktizō*, "I create") is neutralized in that the two verbs are interchangeable in referring to a new creation in Matt. 19:4.[10]

The theory of a complete disappearance of the old before replacement by a new creation also draws heavily from other parts of the Bible. Statements like those in Ps. 102:25-26; Isa. 34:4; 51:6; Matt. 24:35; 2 Pet. 3:7, 10-13 on the surface seem to denote a discarding of

---

4. Henry Barclay Swete, *The Apocalypse of St. John* (London: Macmillan, 1906), pp. 274-75; Bullinger, *Apocalypse*, p. 647; Robertson, *Word Pictures*, 6:468.

5. Alan F. Johnson, "Revelation," in *EBC*, ed. Frank E. Gaebelein (Grand Rapids: Zondervan, 1981), 12:592.

6. J. B. Smith, *A Revelation of Jesus Christ* (Scottdale, Pa.: Herald, 1961), p. 281; Philip Edgcumbe Hughes, *The Book of Revelation* (Grand Rapids: Eerdmans, 1990), p. 221.

7. Lee, "Revelation," 4:815; Hughes, *Revelation*, p. 222.

8. J. A. Seiss, *The Apocalypse* (New York: Charles C. Cook, 1909), 3:374-75.

9. Isbon T. Beckwith, *The Apocalypse of John* (New York: Macmillan, 1919), p. 750; George E. Ladd, *A Commentary on the Revelation of John* (Grand Rapids: Eerdmans, 1972), p. 276.

10. John F. Walvoord, *The Revelation of Jesus Christ* (Chicago: Moody, 1966), pp. 315-16.

the old creation and its replacement by a new. Evidence from other Scriptures on this issue is a standoff and therefore indecisive. The language of 20:11 which depicts an entire dissolving of the old, a vanishing into nothingness followed by a new creation in 21:1 without any sea is the decisive contextual feature that determines this to be a reference to an entirely new creation.[11] It is a making of all things new, not a remaking of the old which has fallen under the curse of sin. This does not mark a failure of God's purpose for the first creation,[12] but a process that He intended from the beginning in allowing evil to have its day in the first creation before being purged.

The absence of the sea from the new creation (ἡ θάλασσα οὐκ ἔστιν ἔτι [hē thalassa ouk estin eti, "there will be a sea no longer"]) has evoked a wide variety of comments. Most justifiably see this void as representing an archetypical connotation in the sea (cf. 13:1; 20:13), a principle of disorder, violence, or unrest that marks the old creation (cf. Isa. 57:20; Ps. 107:25-28; Ezek. 28:8) (Moffatt, Beckwith, Kiddle, Johnson). It is not that the sea is evil in itself, but that its aspect is one of hostility to mankind.[13] For instance, the sea was what stood guard over John in his prison on Patmos and separated him from the churches of Asia (Swete). The sea is the first of seven evils that John says will no longer exist, the other six being death, mourning, weeping, pain (21:4), the curse (22:3), and night (21:25; 22:5).[14] The proposal that the clause about no more sea simply repeats regarding the sea what the earlier ἀπῆλθαν (apēlthan, "passed away") has stated regarding the old creation,[15] disregards the prophet's habit of joining the sea with heaven and earth in the same clause whenever he wants to convey emphatic comprehensiveness (cf. 5:13; 10:6; 14:7) (Beckwith). This

---

11. Alford, *Greek Testament*, 4:734; R. H. Charles, *The Revelation of St. John*, ICC (New York: Scribner's Sons, 1920), 2:193; Beckwith, *Apocalypse*, p. 750; Robertson, *Word Pictures*, 6:463; Martin Kiddle, *The Revelation of St. John*, HNTC (New York: Harper, 1940), p. 401; G. R. Beasley-Murray, *The Book of Revelation*, NCB (Grand Rapids: Eerdmans, 1978), p. 307. For William J. Dumbrell (*The End of the Beginning: Revelation 21-22 and the Old Testament* [Homebrush West NSW, Australia: Lancer, 1985], pp. 165-96), the new creation is the climax of the other four new entities in these last two chapters—the New Jerusalem, the new temple, the new covenant, and the new Israel.
12. Contra Hughes, *Revelation*, p. 222.
13. Hughes, *Revelation*, p. 222.
14. Leon Morris, *The Revelation of St. John*, TNTC (Grand Rapids: Eerdmans, 1969), p. 243.
15. Friedrich Düsterdieck, *Critical and Exegetical Handbook to the Revelation of John*, in Meyer's Commentary, trans. and ed. Henry E. Jacobs (New York: Funk & Wagnalls, 1887), p. 476; Seiss, *Apocalypse*, 3:380-81.

sense also would have required ἦν (*ēn*, "was") rather than ἔστιν (*estin*, "is") in the last clause of v. 1.

21:2 As a part of the new creation John saw a city descending from the new heaven to the new earth: καὶ τὴν πόλιν τὴν ἁγίαν Ἰερουσαλὴμ καινὴν εἶδον καταβαίνουσαν ἐκ τοῦ οὐρανοῦ ἀπὸ τοῦ θεοῦ, ἡτοιμασμένην ὡς νύμφην κεκοσμημένην τῷ ἀνδρὶ αὐτῆς (*kai tēn polin tēn hagian Ierousalēm kainēn eidon katabainousan ek tou ouranou apo tou theou, hētoismasmenēn hōs nymphēn kekosmēmenēn tō andri autēs*, "and I saw the holy city, the new Jerusalem, descending out of heaven from God, prepared as a bride adorned for her husband"). The inner and permanent quality of this new city of God is holiness (ἁγίαν [*hagian*, "holy"]). This feature establishes a tie-in with the old Jerusalem which the Bible also calls "holy" (Isa. 52:1; Matt. 4:5; 27:53). The naming of the city as *"new* Jerusalem" presupposes a recognition of the old Jerusalem too. The old city suffered the taint of sin and disobedience, but the hope for a renewed Jerusalem always remained. The new Jerusalem stresses the superiority of itself to anything belonging to the old creation (Smith). The city's name given in 21:10 is the same as here except for the absence of καινὴν (*kainēn*, "new") there. The Philadelphian overcomer had the promise of having the name of "the new Jerusalem" written on him in proof of his right to live in that city (3:12). Since God's throne will be in the new Jerusalem which is on the new earth, there will be an inclining of the new heaven to the new earth, the new Jerusalem providing a bond between the two (Lee).

Its coming into being does not indicate that Israel had forfeited her hope of God's dwelling among His people (Ex. 25:8; Lev. 26:11-13; Ezek. 37:26-27; Rev. 21:3). This hope comes to fruition in the millennial kingdom prior to the new creation. The old Jerusalem is good enough for the Millennium, but not for the final bliss (Moffatt). The OT does not make a clear distinction between the old and the new Jerusalems. Some passages seem to teach that the earthly Jerusalem only needs to be purified to be fit to be the final center of the Messianic reign (Isa. 54:11; 60; Ezek. 40-48). But there was also the sentiment that the old Jerusalem was too stained for such a role and so needed replacing by an unstained city. This is what comes through in the present passage. When John wrote Revelation, Jerusalem had been in ruins for about twenty-five years. Hadrian's plans for a new city had not yet come forth, but even before the old city fell, the thought of a heavenly city in a figurative sense was before the Christian church (Gal. 3:20; 4:26-27; Heb. 12:22) (Swete). These figurative references hardly prove the preexistence of the new Jerusalem in heaven, however (Walvoord), because this city is part of a new creation, not of the old.

John's privileged perspective affords him the opportunity of seeing the Holy City in the process of "descending out of heaven from God" (καταβαίνουσαν ἐκ τοῦ οὐρανοῦ ἀπὸ τοῦ θεοῦ [*katabainousan ek tou ouranou apo tou theou*]). The Greek expression describing this descent occurs in two other places, both of which describe this same event (3:12; 21:10). The preposition ἐκ (*ek*, "out of") tells the origin of the Holy City and the ἀπὸ (*apo*, "from") points to the city's originator (Beckwith, Moffatt).

The verb ἑτοιμάζω (*hetoimazō*, "I prepare") in 19:7 speaks of the bride's self-preparation, but here the passive participle ἡτοιμασμένην (*hētoismasmenēn*, "prepared") leaves the agent of preparation unnamed. In that former case the bride was the people of God, but here she is the Holy City.[16]

A more specific word for "bride" (νύμφην [*nymphēn*]) replaces the term γυνὴ (*gynē*, "wife") of 19:7. A combination of the two words designate the Lamb's wife in 21:9. The figure of a bride-city captures two characteristics of the new Jerusalem: God's personal relationship with His people (i.e., the bride) and the life of the people in communion with Him (i.e., the city, with its social connotations) (Johnson). As in common practice, the name of the material city stands for the community composed of the city's inhabitants (Alford). The bride is both the people of God and the seat of their abode, the new Jerusalem.[17]

The bride's adornment for her husband (κεκοσμημένην τῷ ἀνδρὶ αὐτῆς [*kekosmēmenēn tō andri autēs*, "adorned for her husband"]) defines the nature of her preparation. The Greek term depicting her adornment is the source of the English word for "cosmetics." The same term speaks of the adornment of the foundations of the city a little later (21:19).[18]

21:3 For about the twentieth time in Revelation, John hears a loud voice: καὶ ἤκουσα φωνῆς μεγάλης ἐκ τοῦ θρόνου* λεγούσης, Ἰδοὺ ἡ σκηνὴ τοῦ θεοῦ μετὰ τῶν ἀνθρώπων, καὶ σκηνώσει μετ' αὐτῶν, καὶ αὐτοὶ λαοὶ* αὐτοῦ ἔσονται, καὶ αὐτὸς ὁ θεὸς μετ' αὐτῶν ἔσται, [αὐτῶν θεός]* (*kai ēkousa phōnēs megalēs ek tou thronou legousēs, Idou hē skēnē tou theou meta tōn anthrōpōn, kai skēnōsei met' autōn, kai autoi laoi autou esontai, kai autos ho theos met' autōn estai, [autōn theos]*, "and I heard a loud voice from the throne saying, 'Behold, the tabernacle of God is with men, and He will dwell with them, and they themselves will be His people, and God Himself will be with them, their God'"). The loudness emphasizes the importance of the substance of the announcement by the voice (Smith, Walvoord, Morris).

The voice comes ἐκ τοῦ θρόνου (*ek tou thronou*, "from the throne")

---

16. Robertson, *Word Pictures*, 6:467.
17. Düsterdieck, *Revelation*, p. 477; Beckwith, *Apocalypse*, p. 751.
18. Robertson, *Word Pictures*, 6:467.

as in 19:5, except there the preposition is ἀπό (*apo*, "from"). As in that earlier case, it is impossible to identify whose voice this is, but it is not the voice of God who begins to speak for the first time in 21:5.[19] This is an announcement about God, not directly from Him.

Besides the loudness of the voice, the ἰδού (*idou*, "behold") calls special attention to the importance of the announcement: "the tabernacle of God is with men" (ἡ σκηνὴ τοῦ θεοῦ μετὰ τῶν ἀνθρώπων [*hē skēnē tou theou meta tōn anthrōpōn*]). Ἡ σκηνὴ (*Hē skēnē*, "The tabernacle") alludes to the tabernacle in the wilderness where God's glory dwelt with His people. His presence with them will be closer and more intimate in the new Jerusalem than ever before, however. The tabernacle has appeared in heaven earlier in John's visions (13:6; 15:5), but now it is on the new earth in the immediate presence of redeemed men. This marks a return to the condition under which God could fellowship with man before the entrance of sin with its resultant curse and estrangement (Gen. 3:8*a*). This new relationship is the supreme and immeasurable reward far surpassing all the other benefits that the new Jerusalem will afford (Ezek. 37:27; 48:35) (Kiddle). It is the fulfillment of God's promises to His people (Lev. 26:11; Jer. 24:7; 30:22; 31:1, 33; 32:38; Ezek. 37:27; 48:35; Zech. 2:10; 8:8; 2 Cor. 6:16).[20] The echo of Rev. 7:15 is unmistakable, but the substitution of μετὰ (*meta*, "with") for the ἐπί (*epi*, "over") used there suggests an even closer bond of fellowship.[21] In the earlier passage it was the temporary heavenly repose of the innumerable multitude that was in view, but here it is the permanent condition of all the saints.

The essence of v. 3 is the focal point of John's whole description of the new Jerusalem: God's immediate presence with men. The prominence of the theme is evident in v. 3 itself by virtue of a fivefold repetition of the same essential truth in that one verse. It is the principal focus again in 21:7 where the promise to the overcomer is that God would be his God and He would be God's son. The glory of God in the city in 21:11 is another indication of God's immediate presence, a presence that is also the direct emphasis of 22:3-4 which speaks of the presence of the throne of God and the Lamb in the city and immediate access to Him for His slaves, enabling them to see His face.

A number of features are indirect indicators of the same close relationship. The divine presence or glory that illumines the city (21:11, 23; 22:5) is one such indicator of God's immediate presence with His people. Another is the jasper-like appearance and the jasper

---

19. Swete, *Apocalypse*, p. 277; Robertson, *Word Pictures*, 6:467.
20. Swete, *Apocalypse*, p. 278; Hughes, *Revelation*, p. 223.
21. Walter Scott, *Exposition of the Revelation of Jesus Christ* (Swengel, Pa.: Bible Truth Depot, n.d.), p. 421.

walls of the city as emblems of the presence of the One who sits on the throne (21:11, 18; cf. 4:3). References to national Israel in naming the gates (21:12) and to the church in naming the city's twelve foundations after the apostles (21:14) are also reminders of the intimate relations of these peoples with the One who occupies the throne. The nature of the whole city as a holy place (21:22) in the shape of a cube (21:16) just like the Holy of Holies in Solomon's temple (1 Kings 6:20) is another feature emphasizing God's presence with His people in the city. A last indirect indicator is the precious stones which constitute the city's foundations (21:19-20). These recall the special privilege of access to God enjoyed by the high priest in the tabernacle of old.

So when v. 3 proceeds to predict that "He will dwell with them" (σκηνώσει μετ' αὐτῶν [skēnōsei met' autōn]), it is highlighting a relationship that dominates the thought of the whole section on the new creation (21:1–22:5). Σκηνώσει (Skēnōsei, "He will dwell"), already used in 7:15, alludes to Ezek. 37:27; Zech. 2:10; 8:8. It is a metaphor for the Shekinah glory of God in the old tabernacle. As it was before the Fall, God now dwells with men.[22]

The theme continues in αὐτοὶ λαοὶ αὐτοῦ ἔσονται (autoi laoi autou esontai, "they themselves will be His people"). A noticeable change from the singular to the plural λαοί (laoi, "peoples") marks an expansion beyond the boundaries of Israel, usually referred to by the singular λαός (laos, "people"). God promised He would make Abraham a blessing to all peoples of the earth (Gal. 3:8, 16, 26-29).[23] Many nations, not just Israel, will participate in the fulfilling experience of enjoying His presence (cf. John 10:16) (Alford, Swete, Bullinger, Charles). John updates the traditional concept of a singular people to include the many peoples represented among the redeemed (Jer. 7:23; 30:22; Hos. 2:23; Rom. 9:25).[24]

The words αὐτὸς ὁ θεὸς μετ' αὐτῶν ἔσται (autos ho theos met' autōn estai, "God Himself will be with them") further enhance the emphasis on divine fellowship. The intensification of αὐτὸς (autos, "Himself") indicates the arrival of the consummation of all things when God will be all in all (1 Cor. 15:24, 25, 28). The use of God's name five times in vv. 2-4 recalls the frequent use of His name in the account of the original creation—thirty-four times in thirty-four verses (Gen. 1:1–2:3) (Smith). The expression ὁ θεὸς μετ' αὐτῶν (ho theos met' autōn, "God with them") is a reminder of Christ's name "Emanuel" or "Immanuel"

---

22. Moffatt, "Revelation," 5:480; Bullinger, *Apocalypse*, pp. 648-49; Robertson, *Word Pictures*, 6:467.
23. Hughes, *Revelation*, p. 223.
24. Robert H. Mounce, *The Book of Revelation*, in NICNT (Grand Rapids: Eerdmans, 1977), p. 372.

—"God with us"—which will here reach its optimum meaning (Alford, Lee).

The final two words, αὐτῶν θεός (*autōn theos*, "their God"), fulfill the promises of Ex. 29:45; Lev. 26:12; Jer. 30:22; 31:33; Ezek. 11:20; 37:27 (contrast Hos. 1:9).[25]

21:4 As a follow-up to the positive incentive emphasized in v. 3, v. 4 describes conditions in the new Jerusalem in negative terms: καὶ ἐξαλείψει πᾶν δάκρυον ἐκ τῶν ὀφθαλμῶν αὐτῶν, καὶ ὁ θάνατος οὐκ ἔσται ἔτι, οὔτε πένθος οὔτε κραυγὴ οὔτε πόνος οὐκ ἔσται ἔτι· [ὅτι]* τὰ πρῶτα ἀπῆλθαν (*kai exaleipsei pan dakryon ek tōn ophthalmōn autōn, kai ho thanatos ouk estai eti, oute penthos oute kraugē oute ponos ouk estai eti; [hoti] ta prōta apēlthan,* "and He will wipe away every tear from their eyes, and there will be death no longer, neither will there be sorrow or crying or pain any longer; because the first things have passed away"). The negative description of future conditions in a sense is easier, because finite humans accustomed only to an old earth ravaged by sin are void of experience in an ideal environment such as the new creation will be (cf. 1 John 3:2) (Swete). These new conditions exceed present powers of conception (Mounce).

The singular number of πᾶν δάκρυον (*pan dakryon*, "every tear") in the statement ἐξαλείψει πᾶν δάκρυον ἐκ τῶν ὀφθαλμῶν αὐτῶν (*exaleipsei pan dakryon ek tōn ophthalmōn autōn*, "He will wipe away every tear from their eyes") focuses on God's great compassion for the individual even to the point of noticing infinitely small minutia (Smith, Morris). The same compassion has already been evidenced in connection with the earlier heavenly multitude (7:17; cf. Isa. 25:8; 65:19). These are tears caused by the grief and pain of an existence in the old creation, not tears of repentance as in Isa. 61:3-10 (Lee, Moffatt).

The absence of death presents another situation to which creatures belonging to this creation can hardly envision. All four of the ills, θάνατος . . . πένθος . . . κραυγὴ . . . πόνος (*thanatos . . . penthos . . . kraugē . . . ponos,* "death . . . sorrow . . . crying . . . pain"), entered the world in connection with the beginning of human sin in Genesis 3 (Smith), so their disappearance in the new creation represents a reversal of the curse that accompanied sin (Morris). "Sorrow" or mourning is associated with death among other things. "Crying" along with sorrow will be the lot of Babylon in the future when she falls under God's judgment for her sin (cf. 18:7, 8, 11, 15, 19), but this statement predicts the absence of mourning and crying for any reason. The "pain" that will be missing probably is physical pain of the sort

---

25. Alford, *Greek Testament*, 4:737; G. V. Caird, *A Commentary on the Revelation of St. John the Divine*, HNTC (New York: Harper & Row, 1966), pp. 264-65.

experienced under the fifth bowl judgment (16:10-11). In place of these four will be peace and bliss (cf. Isa. 35:10; 51:11).[26]

The words ὅτι τὰ πρῶτα ἀπῆλθαν (*hoti ta prōta apēlthan*, "because the first things have passed away") assign a reason for the absence of death, sorrow, crying, and pain. It lies in the passing away of the former—literally, "the first"—things, including everything that accompanied the cancerous evils of the old creation, a creation ravaged by the inestimable damage of sin (cf. Isa. 42:9; 2 Cor. 5:17; Gal. 6:15) (Swete, Kiddle). This brief word is a comprehensive summary of all contained in the announcement of v. 1 and includes the banishment of the four particular miseries listed earlier in v. 4.

21:5 John's pastoral purpose in this book is nowhere more evident than in vv. 5-8 where the personal concern of Almighty God comes into immediate view: Καὶ εἶπεν ὁ καθήμενος ἐπὶ τῷ θρόνῳ, Ἰδοὺ καινὰ ποιῶ πάντα. καὶ λέγει*, Γράψον, ὅτι οὗτοι οἱ λόγοι πιστοὶ καὶ ἀληθινοί εἰσιν (*Kai eipen ho kathēmenos epi tō thronō, Idou kaina poiō panta. kai legei, Grapson, hoti houtoi hoi logoi pistoi kai alēthinoi eisin*, "And the one sitting upon the throne said, 'Behold, I make all things new.' And he says, 'Write, because these words are faithful and true'"). John leaves the subject of the new Jerusalem for the moment to record these unique utterances of God (Kiddle). "The one sitting upon the throne" (ὁ καθήμενος ἐπὶ τῷ θρόνῳ [*ho kathēmenos epi tō thronō*]) is the same person as throughout the book, the last mention of this title being in 20:11.

This is the first direct utterance of the Father since 1:8, and is in fact the only time it is explicitly He who speaks except in 1:8. Voices have come out of the throne as in 21:3 and out of the sanctuary as in 16:1, 17 where it may be His voice, but these latter are not explicitly stated to be from Him. The ἰδοὺ (*idou*, "behold") introduces this as a special pronouncement the same as it does in 1:7, 21:3, and elsewhere. John is not the addressee of the words of this pronouncement in 21:5a as he is in 7:14; 17:7; 21:5b. They belong to the entire world of the blessed. They allude to Isa. 43:18-19[LXX]: Ἰδοὺ καινὰ ποιῶ πάντα (*Idou egō poiō kaina*, "Behold, I make things new").[27] There is a secondary sense in which this is the consummation of the revitalizing power of divine grace that during the present is active in the hearts of believers (cf. 2 Cor. 5:17),[28] but to construe the primary sense as a remaking that is always in progress even in the old order (cf. 2 Cor.

---

26. Swete, *Apocalypse*, p. 278; Beckwith, *Apocalypse*, p. 751; Robertson, *Word Pictures*, 6:467.

27. Swete, *Apocalypse*, p. 279; Moffatt, "Revelation," 5:480; Robertson, *Word Pictures*, 6:467.

28. Hughes, *Revelation*, p. 224.

3:18; 4:16-18; 5:16-17; Col. 3:1-4) (Caird) misses the chronological progression that is an integral element in John's visions in Revelation. The direct reference of these words is to God's future work of creation in bringing into being the new heaven and the new earth.

With the words καὶ λέγει (*kai legei*, "and he says") comes a change in speaker. This is why some MSS (see "Additional Notes") have added a personal pronoun, μοι (*moi*, "to me"), after the verb. The change is evident from v. 6 where καὶ εἶπέν (*kai eipen*, "and He said") resumes the speech of the one sitting on the throne.[29] The new speaker in v. 21*b* is an angel as in 14:13,[30] probably the angel-guide who last spoke to him in 19:9-10.

The angel gives John a command supported by reasoning: Γράψον, ὅτι οὗτοι οἱ λόγοι πιστοὶ καὶ ἀληθινοί εἰσιν (*Grapson, hoti houtoi hoi logoi pistoi kai alēthinoi eisin*, "Write, because these words are faithful and true"). This is the third time John receives a command to write certain words (14:13; 19:9; cf. 1:11, 19; 2:1, 8, 12, 18; 3:1, 7, 14). Possibly in the midst of all that was happening, bewilderment overcame the prophet and he forgot to write down his visions according to his original command (Morris).

The reason for the command comes in the ὅτι (*hoti*, "because") clause. It is possible that this *hoti* clause divulges the content of what he is to write (Lee), but the object of γράψον (*grapson*, "write") is the contents of vv. 1-5. With growing emphasis (cf. 19:9) the angel directs the prophet to convey the promise of supreme blessedness in the new heaven and the new earth (Beckwith).

A solemn guarantee of the truthfulness of the revelation comes in the words οὗτοι οἱ λόγοι πιστοὶ καὶ ἀληθινοί εἰσιν (*houtoi hoi logoi pistoi kai alēthinoi eisin*, "these words are faithful and true"). This is the exact statement found in 22:6 except for the addition of εἰσιν (*eisin*, "are") here. In 19:9 ἀληθινοί (*alēthinoi*, "true") again describes the words of God. Both adjectives apply to Christ in 3:14 and 19:11. The expression οὗτοι οἱ λόγοι (*houtoi hoi logoi*, "these words") refers to the information given in 21:1-5*a* (Beckwith). These great sayings rest on a secure basis. Human beings can rest assured of their reliability, that they answer to realities that will in God's time enter the experience of human life. Man's inability to grasp them or adequately express them in the present does not diminish the fact of their future realization (Swete).

21:6 The One sitting on the throne resumes His speech in v. 6: καὶ εἶπέν μοι, Γέγοναν*. ἐγώ [εἰμι]* τὸ Ἄλφα καὶ τὸ Ὦ, ἡ ἀρχὴ καὶ τὸ τέλος.

---

29. Alford, *Greek Testament*, 4:737; Swete, *Apocalypse*, p. 279; Lee, "Revelation," 4:818; contra Mounce, *Revelation*, p. 373.
30. Robertson, *Word Pictures*, 6:468.

ἐγὼ τῷ διψῶντι δώσω ἐκ τῆς πηγῆς τοῦ ὕδατος τῆς ζωῆς δωρεάν (*kai eipen moi, Gegonan. egō [eimi] to Alpha kai to ⁻O, hē archē kai to telos. egō tō dipsōnti dōsō ek tēs pēgēs tou hydatos tēs zōēs dōrean*, "and He said to me, 'They are done. I am the Alpha and the Omega, the beginning and the end. I will give freely to the one who thirsts [something] from the fountain of the water of life'"). His initial announcement γέγοναν (*gegonan*, "they are done") is almost identical with His word in 16:17, γέγονεν (*gegonen*, "it is done"). The following words ἐγὼ [εἰμι] τὸ Ἄλφα καὶ τὸ Ὦ (*egō [eimi] to Alpha kai to ⁻O*, "I am the Alpha and the Omega") match what He says about Himself in 1:8 and confirm that He is the speaker at this point.[31]

The subject of the plural *gegonan* is either οὗτοι οἱ λόγοι (*houtoi hoi logoi*, "these words") (v. 5) (Beckwith) or more probably, the πάντα (*panta*, "all things") of v. 5 (Alford). In keeping with the perfect tense of the same verb in 16:17, this perfect indicates that the action now stands accomplished. The words just spoken have been fulfilled and the state of completion is now obtained. The pronouncement of *gegonan* places the promise of v. 7 and the jeopardy of v. 8 in the setting of the whole vision: the state after the disappearance of the old world and the beginning of the new earth.[32]

The title *to Alpha kai to ⁻O* emphasizes God's absolute control over all things. His sovereign control over everything and His eternal nature guarantee His complete trustworthiness and the faithfulness and truthfulness of the words He has spoken. What He starts He is able to complete.[33] He is the unchangeable One by whom the old was and the new shall be. This agrees with His earlier assessment of Himself and with Christ's statement about Himself in 22:13 (Swete).

Something like ἡ ἀρχὴ καὶ τὸ τέλος (*hē archē kai to telos*, "the beginning and the end") occurs in Isa. 44:6 (LXX) as a self-description of God. Colossians 1:18 sees Christ's role as *hē archē* in reference to the church, and Rev. 3:14 does the same in reference to the world. Here, however, God is the first cause (*archē*) and the finality (*telos*) as in Rom. 11:36 and Eph. 4:6. The same is true of Christ according to 22:13. The use of *telos* in the NT to mean "end" or "goal" is rare, but 1 Tim. 1:5 and Rom. 10:4 approximate this meaning. Since God works through Christ, the title applies to both persons (cf. John 1:3; Col. 1:12-20; Heb. 1:2-3).[34]

The metaphor of thirst to express an earnest sense of spiritual need comes from Isa. 55:1 (cf. Pss. 42:1-2; 63:1; Isa. 12:3; 44:3). Here God

---

31. Ibid.
32. Düsterdieck, *Revelation*, p. 478; Lee, "Revelation," 4:818.
33. Hughes, *Revelation*, p. 224.
34. Swete, *Apocalypse*, p. 280; Robertson, *Word Pictures*, 6:468.

uses it in His promise to the faithful: ἐγὼ τῷ διψῶντι δώσω ἐκ τῆς πηγῆς τοῦ ὕδατος τῆς ζωῆς δωρεάν (*egō tọ dipsonti dōsō ek tēs pēgēs tou hydatos tēs zōēs dōrean*, "I will give freely to the one who thirsts [something] from the fountain of the water of life"). Three other passages contain the essence of this promise (7:17; 22:1, 17; cf. John 4:13-14; 7:37-39; contra Jer. 2:13; 17:13). The second occurrence in the verse of the personal pronoun ἐγὼ (*egō*) emphasizes that this is God's own promise: "*I and no other* will give." This is an infinitely better thirst quencher than the cup offered by the harlot Babylon (17:4; 18:3) (Ladd). God's promise implies a thirst that is ready and eager to accept the benefit that is free (δωρεάν [*dōrean*, "freely"]) and is part of the family privilege (v. 7).[35] Here God gives the water freely; in 22:17 the thirsty one receives it freely.

21:7 God's promise to the overcomer comes in the same form as the seven overcomer promises in chapters 2-3: ὁ νικῶν κληρονομήσει ταῦτα, καὶ ἔσομαι αὐτῷ θεὸς καὶ αὐτὸς ἔσται μοι υἱός (*ho nikōn klēronomēsei tauta, kai esomai autọ theos kai autos estai moi huios*, "the one who overcomes will inherit these things, and I will be to him God and he will be to Me a son"). This eighth promise to the overcomer completes and in effect includes the other seven. For the first time since 3:21, except for 16:15, the individual as opposed to the general body of the faithful receives a direct promise (Swete, Moffatt).

Revelation's only reference to an inheritance comes in the term κληρονομήσει (*klēronomēsei*, "will inherit"), though the heirship concept is quite common in Paul and elsewhere in the NT (e.g., Matt. 5:5; 19:29; 25:34; Rom. 4:13; 1 Cor. 6:9). This is one of the many indications of agreement between John and Paul (cf. Rom. 8:17; Gal. 4:7). *Klēronomēsei* here carries the general sense of "enter into possession of" or "partake of" (Swete, Lee, Moffatt). The inheritance will consist of the antecedent of ταῦτα (*tauta*, "these things") which is the πάντα (*panta*, "all things") of v. 5. The overcomer will inherit God's new creation, i.e., the glories of the new Jerusalem about to go on display (Alford).

The added promise ἔσομαι αὐτῷ θεὸς (*esomai autọ theos*, "I will be to him God") came first to Abraham and then to others (Gen. 17:7-8; Ex. 6:7; 20:2; 29:45; Lev. 26:12; Num. 15:41; Deut. 29:13; 2 Sam. 7:24; Jer. 7:23; 11:4; 24:7; 30:22; Ezek. 11:20; 34:24; 36:28; 37:23, 27; Zech. 8:8). The essence of the promise is a repetition of 21:3. The future tense looks forward to a fulfillment after the resurrection (cf. Luke 20:36; Rom. 8:23). John is not oblivious to the relationship with God that

---

35. Beckwith, *Apocalypse*, p. 752; Moffatt, "Revelation," 5:480; Robertson, *Word Pictures*, 6:468; Johnson, "Revelation," 12:594.

already exists (1 John 3:1), but he is looking forward to receiving the full inheritance and not just the ἀρραβών (*arrabōn*, "the pledge") (Eph. 1:13-14).[36]

The words αὐτὸς ἔσται μοι υἱός (*autos estai moi huios*, "he will be to Me a son") came first to David and referred to David's seed as the recipient of the promise (2 Sam. 7:14). Later they referred to Solomon and the great Son of David, his seed the Messiah (Ps. 89:26-27).[37] Elsewhere in the NT this Davidic formula has Messianic overtones in conveying the intimate relationship between the Father and Jesus. Here John transfers the Messianic formula from Christ to Christ's bride, but in so doing changes the earlier part of the saying from "Father" to "God" to reserve a unique place for Jesus as the "one and only Son of God" (cf. John 1:17-18) (Beasley-Murray). This is the only reference to sonship in Revelation. John prefers the figure of priesthood to portray the believer's closeness to God. For whatever reason, he chooses not to emphasize the relationship of sons just as he chooses to mention the love of God for His people only a few times (cf. 3:9, 19; 20:9) (Moffatt).

21:8 An adversative δὲ (*de*, "but") switches to a contrasting list of the types who are not conquerors: τοῖς δὲ δειλοῖς καὶ ἀπίστοις* καὶ ἐβδελυγμένοις καὶ φονεῦσιν καὶ πόρνοις καὶ φαρμάκοις καὶ εἰδωλολάτραις καὶ πᾶσιν τοῖς ψευδέσιν τὸ μέρος αὐτῶν ἐν τῇ λίμνῃ τῇ καιομένῃ πυρὶ καὶ θείῳ, ὅ ἐστιν ὁ θάνατος ὁ δεύτερος (*tois de deilois kai apistois kai ebdelygmenois kai phoneusin kai pornois kai pharmakois kai eidōlolatriais kai pasin tois pseudesin to meros autōn en tē limnē tē kaiomenē pyri kai theiō, ho estin ho thanatos ho deuteros*, "but to the cowardly and unfaithful and abominable and murderers and fornicators and sorcerers and idolaters and all liars, their part will be in the lake which burns with fire and brimstone, which is the second death"). This list of eight categories of vices and those who commit them differs in some points with lists in 9:20-21 and 22:15 (Moffatt). It also recalls a list in 1 Cor. 6:9-10 that includes an enumeration of those who will not inherit the kingdom of God (Lee). The kinds of sins committed are eight in number, but those who commit them unite into a single group as reflected in the single article τοῖς (*tois*, "the") that governs all eight descriptions.

The word for "cowardly" or "fearful" (δειλοῖς [*deilois*]) comes from δείδω (*deidō*, "I fear"). It refers to those who repudiate their faith in Christ when faced with persecution and opposition. Without steadfast endurance based on that faith, they are not true followers of the Lamb.

---

36. Swete, *Apocalypse*, p. 281; Robertson, *Word Pictures*, 6:468.
37. Alford, *Greek Testament*, 4:738; Robertson, *Word Pictures*, 6:469.

The word occurs elsewhere in the NT at Matt. 8:26; Mark 4:20. The cowardly one would not, of course, admit that he is timorous, but would hide his timidity by claiming his behavior stemmed from εὐλάβεια (*eulabeia*, "reverence") rather than cowardice.[38] The term describes the type "who draw back" to perdition in Heb. 10:38-39 (Lee, Bullinger). These are people who have never taken to heart the words of Jesus which said, "Whoever wishes to save his life will lose it, but whoever loses his life for My sake and the gospel's shall save it" (Mark 8:35) (Mounce). God has not given His people a spirit of cowardice (2 Tim. 1:7) (Morris).

The term ἀπίστοις (*apistois*) has a possible meaning of "unbelieving," but the meaning "unfaithful" or "untrustworthy" fits better in this series. These are a contrast to Christ, "the faithful one" (1:5; cf. 2:10, 13; 3:14; 17:14; 19:11). Disloyalty is closely related to "cowardice" (*deilois*).[39] All *deiloi* are *apistoi*, but not all *apistoi* are *deiloi*. People break their loyalty to Christ for more reasons than just cowardice (e.g., πόρνοι [*pornoi*, "fornicators"]) (Moffatt). In Paul (*apistos*) refers to non-Christians (1 Cor. 6:6; 7:12 ff.; 10:27; 14:22 ff.; 2 Cor. 6:14-15), but in this situation it applies to professing Christians who by act or word deny their faith in Christ (Swete).

The next group excluded from the Holy City are the "abominable" (ἐβδελυγμένοις [*ebdelygmenois*]). This is the perfect passive participle from βδελύσσω (*bdelyssō*, "I pollute"), a verb used only here and in Rom. 2:22 in the NT. The verb is common in the LXX, however (e.g., Ex. 5:21). In this list it refers to those who have been defiled, particularly through the worship of the beast (17:4-5; 21:27).[40] This kind of person is not simply βδελυκτοί (*bdelykti*, "detestable") as in Titus 1:16 in committing a single detestable act, but persons who have allowed their very natures to be permeated with the abominations they practiced throughout their lifetime. The context suggests that these are not just idolatrous acts (cf. 17:4), but the unthinkable and unnatural vices of heathendom (Swete).

Among those who will defect to follow the beast, the human lives of others have very little value (Rev. 9:22; cf. Mark 7:21; Rom. 1:29). By choosing the beast instead of the Lamb, they will have a part in the martyrdom of the saints and will become part of a group of "murderers" (φονεῦσιν [*phoneusin*]) (Rev. 17:6; 18:24) (Swete, Johnson). Quite often prostitution accompanies murder and the idolatry that will

---

38. Richard Chenevix Trench, *Synonyms of the New Testament* (1958 reprint; Grand Rapids: Eerdmans, 1880), pp. 34-35; Beckwith, *Apocalypse*, p. 753; Robertson, *Word Pictures*, 6:469; Johnson, "Revelation," 12:594.
39. Beckwith, *Apocalypse*, p. 753; Robertson, *Word Pictures*, 6:469.
40. Robertson, *Word Pictures*, 6:469.

characterize the popular movement of the beast. "Fornicators" (Πόρ-νοις [*Pornois*]) have often tried to pass themselves off as Christians (Rev. 2:14, 2:22; cf. 1 Cor. 5:10; 1 Tim. 1:9-10),[41] but whatever front they have put up, they cannot expect a part in the bliss of the new creation.

Also connected with idolatry are magicians or "sorcerers" (φαρ-μάκοις [*pharmakois*]). The noun *pharmakos* occurs frequently in the LXX, each time in connection with a religion that worships other than the true God (e.g., Ex. 7:11; Deut. 18:11; Dan. 2:2; Mal. 3:5). Sorcery is in the same category with idolatry in Gal. 5:20 also.[42] Sorcery will play a large part in the future delusion created by the beast (Rev. 9:21; 13:13-14; 18:23; 22:15). Already many parading themselves as Christians are "idolaters" (εἰδωλολάτραις [*eidōlolatriais*]) (1 John 5:21; cf. 1 Cor. 5:10-11; Eph. 5:5). Idolatry will be the rule rather than the exception under the reign of the beast (Rev. 9:21; 13:14-15). The new Jerusalem has no room for them (cf. 22:15).

The final group in this catalogue of sinners, πᾶσιν τοῖς ψευδέσιν (*pasin tois pseudesin*, "all liars"), comes into view in 22:15 in an individualized form πᾶς φιλῶν καὶ ποιῶν ψεῦδος (*pas philōn kai poiōn pseudos*, "everyone who loves and does a lie"). A constant stigma rests on the sin of lying (2:2; 3:9).[43] These are primarily those who lie in their denial of Christ, but include untruthful Christians who cheat (Acts 5:3) and lie to one another (Col. 3:9; contra Rev. 14:5) (Moffatt). Liars are foremost among those doomed to an eternity outside the new creation as evidenced by their appearance in each of the three lists of the ones excluded therefrom (cf. 21:27; 22:15) (Lee, Smith).

"Their part" (τὸ μέρος αὐτῶν [*to meros autōn*]) refers to the inheritance of those who have excluded themselves from the eternal city, an inheritance that contrasts boldly with that of the blessed (vv. 3-7). These whose names are missing from the Book of Life (20:15) will join Satan, the beast, and the false prophet in the lake of fire and brimstone (19:20; 20:10, 14-15), that is, the second death (2:11; 20:6, 14; cf. 14:10).[44] This statement says nothing about their nonparticipation in the new Jerusalem, but the positive statement about being in the lake of fire implies such a penalty and more (Alford). These are those who had no part in the first resurrection (20:6).

---

41. Ibid.
42. Alford, *Greek Testament*, 4:738; Moffatt, "Revelation," 5:481; Robertson, *Word Pictures*, 6:469; Johnson, "Revelation," 12:594. Magic posed a serious problem in John's day too (David E. Aune, "The Apocalypse of John and Graeco-Roman Revelatory Magic," *NTS* 33, no. 4 [October 1987]: 494.
43. Beckwith, *Apocalypse*, p. 753; Robertson, *Word Pictures*, 6:469-70.
44. Robertson, *Word Pictures*, 6:469.

Instead of placing these unforgiven sinners ἐν τῇ λίμνῃ τῇ καιομένῃ πυρὶ καὶ θείῳ (*en tẹ̄ limnẹ̄ tẹ̄ kaiomenẹ̄ pyri kai theiō̧*, "in the lake which burns with fire and brimstone"), 22:15 simply locates them ἔξω (*exō*, "outside"), meaning outside the city. The lake of fire as a picture for human penalty reverts to the judicial severity expressed in the OT (Isa. 34:10; 66:24; Dan 7:10; cf. Rev. 14:11; 19:3) (Lee). Brimstone mixed with fire is a well-known instrument of God's wrath, probably originating with the judgment of Sodom and Gomorrah (Gen. 19:24; cf. Ps. 11:6; Isa. 30:33; Ezek. 38:22; Rev. 14:10; 19:20) (Beckwith). As in 20:14, the lake of fire equates to "the second death" (ὁ θάνατος ὁ δεύτερος [*ho thanaos ho deuteros*]) (cf. 2:11; 20:6). These are the last words of the One sitting upon the throne, but yet to come from the lips of Jesus are, among other things, the sublime appeal of 21:17 and the glorious benediction of 22:21 (Lee).

Additional Notes

21:2 The spelling of the city name Ἰερουσαλήμ—sometimes with a rough breathing Ἱερουσαλήμ—is the one used uniformly in the LXX, but in the NT it alternates with Ἱεροσόλυμα, a Hellenistic mistranslation. In Mark, John, and Matthew (except 23:37) and most frequently in Luke Ἰερουσαλήμ is the spelling, but in Hebrews, Paul (except Gal. 1:17, 18; 2:1), and Revelation the name's spelling is Ἰερουσαλήμ. The NT tendency is to use Ἰερουσαλήμ which is closer to the Hebrew transliteration when the heavenly city (e.g., Gal. 4:26) is in view and Ἱεροσόλυμα to speak of the Jerusalem of this creation.[45] The use of the Hebrew form marks the new Jerusalem off from the earthly city, but by no means indicates that a less literal meaning is intended. The new heaven and the new earth are literal; so is the new city. It will be new in materials, size, shape, location, origin, and in every other way, but it will be a material city (Bullinger).

21:3 The reading θρόνου is replaced by οὐρανοῦ in P, 046, and almost all minuscules and versions. Sinaiticus, Alexandrinus, and other sources support θρόνου. The οὐρανοῦ in these other sources seems to be an assimilation to the ἐκ τοῦ οὐρανοῦ of v. 2. The variant θρόνου is preferable on both external and internal grounds.[46]

The reading λαοί has the support of Sinaiticus, Alexandrinus, 046, and other authorities, but E, P, and almost all minuscules and versions and many fathers support the reading λαός. The latter agrees better with OT prophecy which speaks of one people of God (Jer. 31:33;

---

45. Beckwith, *Apocalypse*, p. 757; G. Abbott-Smith, *A Manual Greek Lexicon of the New Testament* (Edinburgh: T. & T. Clark, 1950), p. 214.
46. Bruce M. Metzger, *A Textual Commentary on the Greek New Testament* (New York: United Bible Societies, 1971), p. 765.

Ezek. 37:27; Zech. 8:8). If the singular is correct, a scribe must have made the number conform to the plural αὐτοὶ that immediately precedes it. If the plural is correct, John intentionally altered the traditional concept by substituting the many peoples of redeemed humanity for the single elect nation. In this case an emender brought the reading into conformity with the imagery of the OT. On the basis of stronger MS support, the plural λαοὶ is preferable.[47]

A difficult textual question revolves around the bracketed words αὐτῶν θεός, as to their inclusion or noninclusion. Their inclusion in the order shown has the support of Alexandrinus and a significant number of authorities. Their inclusion in reversed order, θεὸς αὐτῶν, has the support of several other sources. Sinaiticus, 046, and most minuscules omit the two words. One suggestion is that a scribe added the words because the earlier αὐτοὶ λαοὶ αὐτοῦ ἔσονται requires such a reciprocal expression. Regarding the word order, the unemphatic position of αὐτῶν following θεός is not this author's usage elsewhere (except in 18:5), though in this instance it may have been prompted by a desire to avoid the sequence αὐτῶν ἔσται αὐτῶν. The reading αὐτῶν θεός is the best option in a very difficult choice.[48] The reading appears to have a slight edge in external support.

21:4 The reading of Sinaiticus τὰ πρόβατα is clearly wrong because it does not make sense. The reading τὰ πρῶτα has the support of A, P, 051, and a number of other authorities. If the omission of ὅτι before τὰ πρῶτα is original, it would mean that copyists added ὅτι or γάρ to avoid asyndeton. But it is more convincing that the omission of the original ὅτι was accidental, when because of the preceding ἔτι a scribe's eye skipped the ὅτι.[49] Though external evidence is a bit weak, consisting of only the first editor of Sinaiticus and 046 among the uncials, it is still preferable to see the ὅτι as original.

21:5 In the phrase ἐπὶ τῷ θρόνῳ the locative follows ἐπί as at 4:9; 7:10; 19:4, but in the rest of the book the genitive is more frequent as the object of this preposition (cf. 4:10; 5:1, 7, etc.).[50]

A number of MSS including Sinaiticus, P, 051 have the personal pronoun μοι after λέγει. External support for including the pronoun is strong, but no convincing reason explains why the pronoun should be absent from other MSS if it were original. So the reading of A, 046, about eighty minuscules, and others which omits the pronoun is preferable.[51]

---

47. Metzger, *Textual Commentary*, p. 765; contra Smith, *Revelation*, p. 283.
48. Metzger, *Textual Commentary*, pp. 765-66.
49. Ibid., p. 766.
50. Swete, *Apocalypse*, p. 279; Beckwith, *Apocalypse*, p. 751; Robertson, *Word Pictures*, 6:468.
51. Metzger, *Textual Commentary*, pp. 766-67.

21:6 Other endings for γέγοναν appear in various MSS. A number of them have γεγόνασιν which would be the normal ending for the third person plural of the perfect tense. This correction resembles the one found in Rom. 16:7. Others have γέγονε, a third person singular rather than plural, to match the reading at 16:17 apparently. A final group have γέγονα, a first person singular. Sinaiticus, P, 046, and others support this last reading, a form that is in most sources accompanied by the omission of εἰμί just after the following ἐγώ. All the alternatives appear to stumble at the aoristic ending on the perfect tense γέγοναν which has the support of Alexandrinus and other authorities.[52]

Most of the MSS that read γέγονα instead of γέγοναν lack either the εἰμί or the ἐγώ εἰμι immediately afterward. Either of these omissions is contrary to Johannine usage (cf. 1:8), and also raises the question of how God or anyone could *become* "the Alpha" or "the beginning" of all things. The pronoun ἐγώ has solid external support, but the retention of εἰμί is more questionable. If retained, it is like 1:8. If omitted, it is like 22:13. The balance of probability is on the side of retaining the verb.[53]

The use of ἐκ is partitive as it is in Matt. 25:8. In Rev. 2:17 the writer achieves the partitive function without use of the preposition.[54]

21:8 The Majority Text inserts καὶ ἁμαρτολοῖς just after ἀπίστοις, adding a ninth category of sinners to the list. The addition rests on very weak external evidence and is not admissible as original (Lee).

8. THE HOLY CITY (21:9–22:5)

Translation

⁹And one of the seven angels who had the seven bowls, which were full of the seven last plagues came, and spoke with me, saying, "Come, I will show to you the bride, the wife of the Lamb." ¹⁰And he carried me away in the spirit to a great and high mountain, and showed me the holy city, Jerusalem, descending out of heaven from God, ¹¹having the glory of God; her brilliance was like a very precious stone, as a crystal-clear jasper stone. ¹²She had a great and high wall; she had twelve gates, and at the gates twelve angels, and inscribed names which are the names of the twelve tribes of the children of Israel; ¹³from the east were three gates and from the north were three gates, and from the south were three gates and from the west were three gates; ¹⁴and the wall of the city had

---

52. Ibid., p. 767.
53. Lee, "Revelation," 4:818; Metzger, *Textual Commentary*, p. 767.
54. Robertson, *Word Pictures*, 6:468.

twelve foundations, and upon them the twelve names of the twelve apostles of the Lamb.

15And the one who spoke with me had a golden measuring rod, that he might measure the city, even her gates and her wall. 16And the city lay foursquare, and her length was like her width also. And he measured the city with the rod to the extent of twelve thousand stadia; her length and width and height are equal. 17And he measured her wall, one hundred forty-four cubits, the measure of a man, which is [that] of an angel. 18And the material of her wall was jasper, and the city was pure gold like pure glass. 19The foundations of the city were adorned with every precious stone. The first foundation was jasper, the second sapphire, the third chalcedony, the fourth emerald, 20the fifth sardonyx, the sixth sardius, the seventh chrysolite, the eighth beryl, the ninth topaz, the tenth chrysoprase, the eleventh jacinth, the twelfth amethyst. 21And the twelve gates were twelve pearls; each one of the gates was [made] from one pearl. And the street of the city was pure gold, like transparent glass.

22And I did not see a temple in her, for the Lord God Almighty is her temple, and the Lamb. 23And the city does not have need of the sun or of the moon, that they might shine in her, for the glory of God illumines her, and the Lamb is her lamp. 24And the nations will walk by her light; and the kings of the earth bring their glory into her; 25and her gates will in no way be shut by day, for there will not be night there; 26and they will bring the glory and honor of the nations into her. 27And nothing unclean and no one doing an abomination and a lie will in any way enter into her, but those written in the book of life of the Lamb [will enter into her].

1And he showed me a river of the water of life, bright as a crystal, proceeding from the throne of God and of the Lamb. 2In the middle of her street and of the river on this side and on that [was] a tree of life producing twelve fruit, yielding its fruit each month, and the leaves of the tree [were] for the healing of the nations. 3And there will be no curse any longer. And the throne of God and of the Lamb will be in her, and His slaves will serve Him, 4and they will see His face, and His name will be on their foreheads. 5And there will not be night any longer, and they have no need of the light of a lamp and the light of the sun, because the Lord God will shine upon them, and they will reign forever and ever.

Exegesis and Exposition

One of the angels with the seven bowls intervenes once again (21:9-10) to provide an extended elaboration on the Holy City Jerusa-

456

lem mentioned briefly in 21:2. First, he divulges the physical features of the city (21:11-21). Then 21:22-27 tells of the city's illumination as it impacts the nations. The concluding portion of the intercalation describes the inner life of the city as relates to the citizens of the city (22:1-5).

The angel-guide (21:9-10). In terms that bear a remarkable similarity to those of 17:1 ff., one of the angels of the seven last plagues approaches John once again to furnish him a fuller picture of the new Jerusalem.

21:9 The wording is nearly identical to the introduction of an earlier guide:[55] Καὶ ἦλθεν εἷς ἐκ τῶν ἑπτὰ ἀγγέλων τῶν ἐχόντων τὰς ἑπτὰ φιάλας, τῶν γεμόντων τῶν ἑπτὰ πληγῶν τῶν ἐσχάτων, καὶ ἐλάλησεν μετ' ἐμοῦ λέγων, Δεῦρο, δείξω σοι τὴν νύμφην τὴν γυναῖκα τοῦ ἀρνίου (*Kai elthen heis ek tōn hepta angelōn tōn echontōn tas hepta phialas, tōn gemontōn tōn hepta plēgōn tōn eschatōn, kai elalēsen met' emou legōn, Deuro, deixō soi tēn nymphēn tēn gynaika tou arniou,* "And one of the seven angels who had the seven bowls, which were full of the seven last plagues came, and spoke with me, saying, 'Come, I will show to you the bride, the wife of the Lamb'"). The closeness of these words to those that introduce the extended vision of the great harlot Babylon in 17:1 makes unmistakable the intended parallelism between this passage about the bride and that earlier one (Beckwith, Johnson). The clear point is that a person cannot inhabit both cities; he must choose between them (Morris).

This is not necessarily the same angel who guided John in 17:1 (Walvoord), though it possibly could be (Mounce). That one of the "last plague" angels should have the role of leading the prophet to a deeper understanding of the new Jerusalem is possibly a divine paradox (Swete), but the continuing attention to the denial of the joys of the city to some (21:27; 22:15; cf. 21:8) furnishes some rationale for including this as part of the account of the seven last plagues. Whatever the proper explanation, the role of this angel demonstrates the intercalation's part in the continuity of the bowl visions in 16:1–22:5 (cf. Lee).

This lengthy section about the bride-city is a development of the brief announcement of her arrival in 21:2 (Beckwith). This is a working out in detail of that earlier announcement just as 17:1–19:10 develops the announcement of Babylon's demise in 16:19.

Some have construed the description of the bride as a further description of the millennial kingdom (Lee, Charles, Beasley-Murray).

---

55. See Excursus 5 at the end of this volume for further discussion of the identical features of the language introducing and concluding the intercalations of the two women.

A main reason for this view is its allowance for a better harmonization of certain features of the city with assumed conditions in the eternal state. The position is that the nations and kings (21:24, 26), the healing of the nations (22:2), and the blessing pronounced on those who come and eat of the Tree of Life while a curse rests on those outside the city (22:14-15) are explainable in reference to the millennial kingdom, but not as characteristics of the eternal state (Charles, Beasley-Murray). The need for the city to have walls for protection also fits millennial conditions better than the eternal state (Lee).

Yet the contextual difficulty of assigning 21:1-5 to the postmillennial stage and then putting the new Jerusalem of 21:9 ff. prior to that as part of the Millennium is too great (Bullinger, Johnson). Besides being contextually unnatural, this violates the scheme of chronological progression in 19:11–20:15 that has already been evident (Johnson). The section cannot apply to the Millennium because of the absence of the curse (22:3) that will continue during the Millennium (20:8-9).[56] The absence of night (21:25) and the elimination of the sun and moon (21:23) cannot characterize the Millennium either (cp. Isa. 30:26 with 60:19). Apparently there will be a temple in Jerusalem during the Millennium (Ezek. 40-48), but in the new Jerusalem there will be none (Rev. 21:22) (Walvoord). Grounds for explaining this as a city descending like a space platform and hovering over the earth as this view sometimes proposes are nonexistent.[57]

The chronological sequence of 19:11–22:5 proves this to be a further description of the new creation mentioned in 21:1. Features of the city mentioned in 21:2 match the description in 21:9, so they must be the same (Walvoord, Johnson). It is true that the mention of nations who are not residents of the city and of kings who bring their glory to it (21:24), the leaves of the Tree of Life which are for the healing of the nations (22:2), and the picture of dogs, sorcerers, and fornicators cowering outside the city wall (22:15) do not on the surface appear to be consistent with an eternal state where perfection prevails (Charles). But these are more readily explainable in this view than in trying to make the city a part of the millennial kingdom.

The νύμφην (*numphēn*, "bride") stands in conspicuous contrast with the πόρνης (*pornēs*, "the harlot") of 17:1 (cf. 19:7; 21:2).[58] The city is also τὴν γυναῖκα (*ten gynaika*, "the wife"), but this is proleptic in

---

56. E. W. Bullinger, *Apocalypse*, p. 658; Robert Govett, *Govett on Revelation* (1981 reprint; Miami Springs, Fla.: Conley & Schoettle, 1861), 2:380.
57. Johnson, "Revelation," 12:595; contra Walvoord, *Revelation*, p. 312; Seiss, *Apocalypse*, 3:404-5.
58. Lee, "Revelation," 4:820; Robertson, *Word Pictures*, 6:470; Celia Deutsch, "Transformation of Symbols: The New Jerusalem in Rv 21₁–22₅," *ZNW* 78 (1987): 122-24.

sense. The marriage of the Lamb has not yet taken place (Beckwith). Beginning here, the next twenty-four verses refer to "the Lamb" (τοῦ ἀρνίου [*tou arniou*]) seven times. This name is increasingly prominent as the end of the book approaches.

21:10 Similarities between the language here and in 17:3 are again quite close (see Excursus 5): καὶ ἀπήνεγκέν με ἐν πνεύματι ἐπὶ ὄρος μέγα καὶ ὑψηλόν, καὶ ἔδειξέν μοι τὴν πόλιν τὴν ἁγίαν Ἰερουσαλὴμ καταβαίνουσαν ἐκ τοῦ οὐρανοῦ ἀπὸ τοῦ θεοῦ (*kai apēnegken me en pneumati epi oros mega kai hypsēlon, kai edeixen moi tēn polin tēn hagian Ierousalēm katabainousan ek tou ouranou apo tou theou*, "and he carried me away in the spirit to a great and high mountain, and showed me the Holy City, Jerusalem, descending out of heaven from God"). As in 1:10; 4:1; 17:3, ἐν πνεύματι (*en pneumati*) denotes the state of a prophetic trance. This is a fresh vision with a new transport of ecstasy (cf. Ezek. 3:14) (Moffatt).

John's destination this time is "a great and high mountain" (ὄρος μέγα καὶ ὑψηλόν [*oros mega kai hypsēlon*]) rather than the wilderness as it was in 17:3. This is not Mount Zion (14:1) because the new Jerusalem is visible from this mountain.[59] It was rather a high vantage point in John's visional experience from which he could see the site and buildings of the city (Moffatt). It is not symbolic or quasi-symbolic as a reference to Mount Zion.[60] The city was not on the mountain, but descended to a spot close to the mountain, similar to Ezekiel's vision (Ezek. 40:2) (Alford, Lee).

In fulfillment of his promise of 21:9, the angel showed John τὴν ἁγίαν Ἰερουσαλὴμ καταβαίνουσαν ἐκ τοῦ οὐρανοῦ ἀπὸ τοῦ θεοῦ (*tēn hagian Ierousalēm katabainousan ek tou ouranou apo tou theou*, "the Holy City, Jerusalem, descending out of heaven from God"). This is the exact way of naming and describing the city as in 21:2 except for the omission of καινὴν (*kainēn*, "new") here. The new Jerusalem introduced there now receives a lengthy description in a nearer and clearer vision (21:11–22:5).[61] The descent of the city is a real event within John's visional experience that previews a real future event that will usher in the eternal state (Mounce).

Physical features of the city (21:11-21). The first revelation of the angel-guide to John relates to the appearance, structures, dimensions, and construction materials of the city.

---

59. Alford, *Greek Testament*, 4:739; Robertson, *Word Pictures*, 6:470.
60. J. P. M. Sweet, *Revelation* (Philadelphia: Westminster, Pelican, 1979), p. 284; contra Kiddle, *Revelation*, p. 424, and M. Robert Mulholland, *Revelation, Holy Living in an Unholy World* (Grand Rapids: Zondervan, 1990), p. 320.
61. Swete, *Apocalypse*, p. 284; Robertson, *Word Pictures*, 6:470.

21:11 The prophet first describes the city's radiant glow: ἔχουσαν τὴν δόξαν τοῦ θεοῦ· ὁ φωστὴρ αὐτῆς ὅμοιος λίθῳ τιμιωτάτῳ, ὡς λίθῳ ἰάσπιδι κρυσταλλίζοντι (*echousan tēn doxan tou theou; ho phōstēr autēs homoios lithǭ timiōtatǭ, hōs lithǭ iaspidi krystallizonti*, "having the glory of God; her brilliance was like a very precious stone, as a crystal-clear jasper stone"). The city has "the glory of God" (τὴν δόξαν τοῦ θεοῦ [*tēn doxan tou theou*]). This is the radiance of the dazzling splendor of God as seen many places in Scripture (e.g., Ex. 40:34; Num. 9:15-23; 1 Kings 8:11; 2 Chron. 5:14; Isa. 24:23; 60:1; Ezek. 43:5; John 12:41; Acts 26:13). This is not just a divinely *caused* splendor. It is the splendor of the presence of God Himself, the Shekinah. His very presence dwells in the Holy City which is the bride of the Lamb.[62] That she possesses the glory of God is the most striking feature of this city (Ladd).

The city's "brilliance" (φωστὴρ [*phōstēr*]) results from the glory of the divine Presence (Moffatt). The noun *phōstēr* occurs along with φῶς (*phōs*, "light") in the LXX of Gen. 1:3, 14, 16 to refer to heavenly bodies of light. Here it is the effect of the divine glory shining in the city.[63] In the NT Christ is the "light" (*phōs*) of the world (John 8:12). So are His followers (Matt. 5:14) who have received the "illumination" (φωτισμός [*phōtismos*]) of God in the face of Christ (2 Cor. 4:6) and who radiate it to men (Phil. 2:15). Philippians 2:15 is the only other use of *phōstēr* besides here in the NT.

Comparison of the city's brilliance to λίθῳ τιμιωτάτῳ (*lithǭ timiō-tatǭ*, "a very precious stone") begins the extended description of the exterior of the city (vv. 11-21). The prophet speaks of the city's general appearance (v. 11), her walls with gates and foundations (vv. 12-14), her measurements (vv. 15-17), and her magnificent special features (vv. 18-21). The summary of the city's architecture fulfills the angel's promise to show John the bride[64] just as the earlier guide promised (17:1) and showed him the harlot representing the city Babylon and the Babylonian system (Lee). The bride is a figure for a material city yet to come as well as for the inhabitants of that city. The bride-figure cannot be limited to the individuals who will live in the city. It must also include the literal city with her physical characteristics (Alford).

The dimensions and layout design of the Jerusalem descending from heaven are an accommodation to finite minds, so a complete

---

62. Alford, *Greek Testament*, 4:739; Lee, "Revelation," 4:820; Moffatt, "Revela-tion," 5:482; Robertson, *Word Pictures*, 6:470-71.
63. Alford, *Greek Testament*, 4:739; Swete, *Apocalypse*, pp. 284-85; Robertson, *Word Pictures*, 6:471.
64. Robert W. Wall, *Revelation*, New International Biblical Commentary, ed. W. Ward Gasque (Peabody, Mass.: Hendrickson, 1991), p. 249.

comprehension of the new creation is not the expected result. That new heaven and new earth will exceed human understanding because it will be the handiwork of an infinite God (21:5). It will be beyond what any person has ever experienced. Yet the information conveys a picture designed for finite minds of this existence and so should not be written off as totally symbolic. It does give architectural information about the city, and is not merely theologically symbolic of the fulfillment of all God's promises. She is a real city with a material existence (Bullinger), arguments to the contrary notwithstanding.[65] To hold that "literally there never was, is not now, and never will be such a city"[66] flies in the face of the language of the text.

This is not to say that the tangible aspects of the city's architecture are without symbolic meaning. The abstractions embodied in the physical features of the city are strikingly clear.[67] John has conveyed what he saw as far as words are capable of doing so. His visional experience has taken him where his readers cannot go.[68] He actually saw what he describes accurately under the inspiration of the Holy Spirit, though some of the details—e.g., the gold that differs from anything on this present earth (21:18, 21)—are beyond present human comprehension. Because the nature of the city stretches human understanding to its limits, the wiser course is to accept the details of the description at their face value as corresponding to the physical characteristics attributed to her (Walvoord). Human words describe the indescribable and the unimaginable (Ladd). The materialistic nature of the new creation is unquestionable, but the physical transformation of the world is not the primary focus.[69] The imagery is concrete and spatial, but it has spiritual significance (Mounce). Since the corresponding city Babylon will have a material existence, so must the new Jerusalem. This is not merely an ideal and fantastic city, but a true, real, substantial, and eternal one. The presence of saints in her does not exclude her having foundations, walls, gates, streets, and edifices that make her a city (Seiss). In 22:3-5 the slaves of God inhabit the city as entities separate from the city itself, so the city cannot be purely symbolic of God's redeemed people.

"A very precious stone" has great brilliance, but "as a crystal-clear jasper stone" (ὡς λίθῳ ἰάσπιδι κρυσταλλίζοντι [*hos lithō iaspidi krystal-*

---

65. Contra Morris, *Revelation*, p. 242, Johnson, "Revelation," 12:596, and Wall, *Revelation*, pp. 243, 245.
66. Homer Hailey, *Revelation, an Introduction and Commentary* (Grand Rapids: Baker, 1979), p. 412.
67. Kiddle, *Revelation*, p. 412.
68. Ibid., p. 436.
69. Mounce, *Revelation*, p. 369.

lizonti]) is even more specific. It recalls the very similar "like in appearance to a jasper stone" (ὅμοιος ὁράσει λίθῳ ἰάσπιδι [*homoios horasei lithō iaspidi*]) that describes God Himself in 4:3. As noted at that point (Thomas, *Revelation 1-7*, p. 342), the color is in doubt, but a white diamond-like stone is not out of the question. Whatever color it is, it is "crystal-clear." It is transparent and gleaming as rock-crystal (Moffatt). The participle *krystallizonti* ("crystal-clear") requires that it have a starry, diamond-like effulgence (Lee).

21:12 The city wall with her twelve gates is the next item to catch the prophet's attention: ἔχουσα τεῖχος μέγα καὶ ὑψηλόν, ἔχουσα πυλῶνας δώδεκα, καὶ ἐπὶ τοῖς πυλῶσιν ἀγγέλους δώδεκα, καὶ ὀνόματα ἐπιγεγραμμένα ἅ ἐστιν [τὰ ὀνόματα]* τῶν δώδεκα φυλῶν υἱῶν Ἰσραήλ (*echousa teichos mega kai hypsēlon, echousa pylōnas dōdeka, kai epi tois pylōsin angelous dōdeka, kai onomata epigegrammena ha estin [ta onomata] tōn dōdeka phylōn hyiōn Israēl*, "she had a great and high wall; she had twelve gates, and at the gates twelve angels, and names were inscribed on [them], which are the names of the twelve tribes of the children of Israel"). The wall around the city is sizable, making it one of the more conspicuous features of the city. The purpose of the wall is not to help defend the city, because there is no enemy to defend against. It rather is a constant reminder of the eternal security of the city's inhabitants (Kiddle). Such a wall was a conventional feature of ancient cities (cf. Isa. 26:1; Zech. 2:5) (Swete). Verse 18 will reveal that the wall is of jasper as is her first foundation (v. 19), making it resemble the glory of God (v. 11).

The city's twelve gates are actually "gate-towers," the noun πυλών (*pylōn*) being the word for a large gateway, as in Luke 16:20, of which the smaller πυλή (*pylē*, "gate") is a part. In Revelation 21-22 it refers to the gate-towers of the city wall eleven times (21:12 [twice], 13 [four times], 15, 21 [twice], 25; 22:14). This is also the noun's meaning in 1 Kings 17:10[LXX]; Acts 14:13. Ezekiel also describes twelve gates, one for each tribe, but his are in the millennial Jerusalem (Ezek. 48:31-34).[70] In the singular the noun can designate the entrance to a palace or house (Gen. 43:19[LXX]; Matt. 26:71; Luke 16:20; Acts 10:17; 12:13, 14), but in the plural as here it designates the entrances to a city. The large number of gates are a reminder of the freedom of access to the city (Swete, Lee, Charles).

The "twelve angels" (ἀγγέλους δώδεκα [*angelous dōdeka*]) stationed at the twelve gates function as watchmen to reinforce the impression of security (Isa. 62:6; cf. 2 Chron. 8:14). The suggestion that they are there to keep all impurity from the city (cf. Gen. 3:24; Rev. 21:27) is not

---

70. Robertson, *Word Pictures*, 6:471.

without merit, but this is not to say that the city is under danger of attack from potential enemies. Evil is not a component of the new creation. The extreme of seeing the angels as simply a mark of the completeness and adornment of the city as a beautiful fortress[71] is unjustified. They have a function to perform as do all others who are part of this city.

The names of the twelve tribes of Israel inscribed on the gates is according to the plan of Ezek. 48:31-34, with one name on each gate.[72] The engraving of these names recalls the description of the high priest's breastpiece in Ex. 28:9, 29; 39:14 (Lee). It serves explicit notice of the distinct role of national Israel in this eternal city in fulfillment of their distinctive role in history throughout the centuries of their existence (cf. 7:1-8).

21:13 The four directions indicated in v. 13 show that in the new creation directions as known in the old creation will still exist: ἀπὸ ἀνατολῆς πυλῶνες τρεῖς, καὶ ἀπὸ βορρᾶ πυλῶνες τρεῖς, καὶ ἀπὸ νότου πυλῶνες τρεῖς, καὶ ἀπὸ δυσμῶν πυλῶνες τρεῖς (*apo anatolēs pylōnes treis, kai apo borra pylōnes treis, kai apo notou pylōnes treis, kai apo dysmōn pylōnes treis*, "from the east were three gates and from the north were three gates, and from the south were three gates and from the west were three gates"). The ἀπό (*apo*, "from") in each of its four usages in v. 13 signifies the direction from which the seer views the city (Beckwith). So ἀπὸ ἀνατολῆς (*apo anatolēs*, "from the east") designates the "three gates" (πυλῶνες τρεῖς [*pylōnes treis*]) facing in an easterly direction. If this follows the pattern of Ezek. 48:32, these three tribes are Joseph, Benjamin, and Dan. But the order of encampment in Num. 2:3-7 is different, with Judah, Issachar, and Zebulun having their standards on the east (Alford, Lee, Smith). The sequence of directions in Num. 2:3 ff. is east, south, west, and north. That in Ezekiel's city is north, east, south, and west. John follows the order east, north, south, and west as found in Ezek. 42:16-19 (Swete, Bullinger). In the present passage Alexandrinus and a few other MSS switch νότου (*notou*, "south") and δυσμῶν (*dysmōn*, "west") to come up with a more expected order, but the switch does not have convincing external or internal support.

The phrase ἀπὸ βορρᾶ (*apo borra*, "from the north") singles out the gates facing northward. These may be Reuben, Judah, and Levi according to Ezek. 48:31 or Dan, Asher, and Naphtali as in Num. 2:25-29 (Alford, Lee). ᾽Απὸ νότου (*Apo notou*, "from the south") designates the gates on the city's south wall. These are possibly Simeon, Issachar, and

---

71. Alford, *Greek Testament*, 4:740; Lee, "Revelation," 4:821.
72. Robertson, *Word Pictures*, 6:471.

Zebulun in agreement with Ezek. 48:33 or Reuben, Simeon, and Gad in accord with Num. 2:10-14 (Alford, Lee). The gates facing westward are last in this sequence, ἀπὸ δυσμῶν (*apo dysmōn*, "from the west"). Gad, Asher, and Naphtali complete the twelve gates on this side if Ezekiel's sequence is determinative (Ezek. 48:34) or Ephraim, Manasseh, and Benjamin following that in Num. 2:18-22 (Alford, Lee).

21:14 The wall's twelve foundations constitute one further major feature of the city's exterior: καὶ τὸ τεῖχος τῆς πόλεως ἔχων θεμελίους δώδεκα, καὶ ἐπ' αὐτῶν δώδεκα ὀνόματα τῶν δώδεκα ἀποστόλων τοῦ ἀρνίου (*kai to teichos tēs poleōs echōn themelious dōdeka, kai ep' autōn dōdeka onomata tōn dōdeka apostolōn tou arniou*, "and the wall of the city had twelve foundations, and upon them the twelve names of the twelve apostles of the Lamb"). The substantive θεμελίους (*themelious*, "foundations") is an adjective functioning as a noun. Its basic meaning is "foundational," but λίθους (*lithous*, "stones") implied by it makes it the equivalent of the noun "foundations." Sometimes it is masculine (e.g., here; 21:19; Luke 6:48-49) and sometimes neuter (e.g., Acts 16:26).[73] These foundations of the city wall strongly imply that the city will rest on the new earth and will not be suspended in the air above the earth (Walvoord).

A suggestion has been that the "twelve foundations" (θεμελίους δώδεκα [*themelious dōdeka*]) compose twelve layers of one foundation that surrounds the whole city (Lee, Smith, Walvoord). Layered foundations are hardly practical, however. Probably each portion of the wall joining two gates had a conspicuous basement made of a vast stone (Alford). The foundations were conceivably buttresses rising from an immense subbase. Looking at any of the four sides, John would have seen, in order, corner-base—gate—base—gate—base—gate—corner-base.[74] The twelve foundations bring a recollection of the city with foundations for which Abraham looked (Heb. 11:10), a city prepared by God for those who died in faith without receiving the promises (Heb. 11:13-16) (Beckwith).

The mention of "the twelve names of the twelve apostles of the Lamb" (δώδεκα ὀνόματα τῶν δώδεκα ἀποστόλων τοῦ ἀρνίου [*dōdeka onomata tōn dōdeka apostolōn tou arniou*]) written on the foundations recalls this group's mention in connection with the foundation of the church (Eph. 2:20). Various attempts to align the stones mentioned later as composing the foundations (vv. 19-20) with particular names of the twelve apostles have been fruitless. No consensus regarding

---

73. Swete, *Apocalypse*, pp. 286-87; Robertson, *Word Pictures*, 6:472.
74. Michael Wilcock, *The Message of Revelation*, The Bible Speaks Today, ed. John R. W. Stott (Downers Grove, Ill.: InterVarsity, 1975), p. 208.

which stone represents which apostle has emerged.[75] It is significant that John brings together the twelve tribes of Israel and the twelve apostles here, and makes a distinction between them. Jesus did the same earlier (Matt. 19:28; Luke 22:30). This distinction shows the wrongness of identifying the twelve tribes in 7:4-8 with the church. "Twelve" (Δώδεκα [*Dōdeka*]) represents the whole group of apostles, aside from the issue of whether the number includes Judas Iscariot, Matthias, or Paul. In John 20:24 "twelve" refers to an occasion when only ten were present. In 1 Cor. 15:5 the same number refers to a group of only eleven. The mention of the twelve apostles here shows the distinctive role of the church in the new Jerusalem, just as the mention of the twelve sons of Israel (v. 12) distinguishes the role of national Israel.

One cannot infer from this reference to the twelve apostles that the writer of Revelation was not an apostle (Alford, Lee, Beckwith). Neither is it possible to tell whether Paul or Matthias is the twelfth apostle (Lee). John does not have particular names in mind, but rather the historical and apostolic background of the group as a whole (Moffatt). Continuity from the twelve sons of Israel to the twelve apostles is not the teaching of this passage (contra Beasley-Murray, Hailey), but the dual election of Israel and the church. The words clearly show that God has an eschatological role for both peoples.[76] Beyond dispute, this description of the bride-city separates believers among Israel from believers of the church, and in a symbolic way assigns the two groups separate roles in the new creation. If the two were one merged group of believers, there would have been twenty-four gates instead of twelve or twenty-four foundations instead of twelve (Smith).

That these are apostles "of the Lamb" (τοῦ ἀρνίου [*tou arniou*]) is another reminder that this city is distinctly the city of the Lamb in His transcendent glory (Beckwith).

21:15 John's angel-guide from 21:9, here designated by ὁ λαλῶν μετ᾽ ἐμοῦ (*ho lalōn met᾽ emou*, "the one who spoke with me"), supplies him with measurements of the city in vv. 15-17. He takes the dimensions with a golden measuring rod: Καὶ ὁ λαλῶν μετ᾽ ἐμοῦ εἶχεν μέτρον κάλαμον χρυσοῦν, ἵνα μετρήσῃ τὴν πόλιν καὶ τοὺς πυλῶνας αὐτῆς καὶ τὸ τεῖχος αὐτῆς (*Kai ho lalōn met᾽ emou eichen metron kalamon chrysoun, hina metrēsē tēn polin kai tous pylōnas autēs kai to teichos autēs*, "And the one who spoke with me had a golden rod as a measure, that he might measure the city, even her gates and her wall"). The rod made

---

75. Lee, "Revelation," 4:831-33.
76. Scott, *Revelation*, pp. 433-34; M. Rissi, *The Future of the World*, Studies in Biblical Theology, 2d series, no. 25 (Naperville, Ill.: Allenson, 1972), p. 73; Walvoord, *Revelation*, pp. 322-23; Johnson, "Revelation," 12:596.

of the precious metal gold is appropriate to the dignity involved in the service of God.[77] The angel's purpose is to measure the city and to give John information he could not discern from direct vision (Caird). The measuring activity gains John's attention as does the similar pursuit in Ezek. 40:4 (Lee). Ezekiel provided measurements for his city-like temple too (Ezek. 40:2, 48; 42:16-20) (Moffatt). The measurements taken by the angel convey the holiness, perfection, absolute conformity to the ideal pattern of creation, and divine presence in the city in terms of numerical and geometrical symbols (Kiddle).

"The city" (Τὴν πόλιν [Tēn polin]) is a comprehensive one that includes "her gates and her wall" (τοὺς πυλῶνας αὐτῆς καὶ τὸ τεῖχος αὐτῆς [tous pylōnas autēs kai to teichos autēs]). This understands the καί (kai, "even") following polin to be ascensive in force. The angel never gets around to measuring the gates separately, but a description of them comes in v. 21 (Swete, Beckwith). He probably includes the gates' measurements in those of the wall.

21:16 The angel first measures the size and shape of the city: καὶ ἡ πόλις τετράγωνος κεῖται, καὶ τὸ μῆκος αὐτῆς ὅσον [καὶ]* τὸ πλάτος. καὶ ἐμέτρησεν τὴν πόλιν τῷ καλάμῳ ἐπὶ σταδίων* δώδεκα χιλιάδων· τὸ μῆκος καὶ τὸ πλάτος καὶ τὸ ὕψος αὐτῆς ἴσα ἐστίν (kai hē polis tetragōnos keitai, kai to mēkos autēs hoson [kai] to platos. kai emetrēsen tēn polin tō kalamō epi stadiōn dōdeka chiliadōn; to mēkos kai to platos kai to hypsos autēs isa estin, "and the city lay foursquare, and her length was like her width also. And he measured the city with the rod to the extent of twelve thousand stadia; her length and width and height are equal"). The predicate adjective τετράγωνος (tetragōnos, "foursquare," literally "four-cornered") indicates that the city is in the shape of a quadrangle (cf. vv. 12-13; Ezek. 48:16, 20).[78] Tetragonos was a word to depict a cube-shaped stone used for building purposes.[79] The added words τὸ μῆκος αὐτῆς ὅσον [και] τὸ πλάτος (to mēkos autēs hoson [kai] to platos, "its length was like her width also") show the city to be in the shape of a square. Ancient Babylon and Nineveh were both laid out in the shape of squares also.[80]

The angel measured the city and came up with "twelve thousand stadia" as her length, width, and height.[81] It is not clear whether twelve thousand stadia—the equivalent of fourteen or fifteen hundred miles,

---

77. Swete, *Apocalypse*, p. 287; Robertson, *Word Pictures*, 6:472.
78. Beckwith, *Apocalypse*, p. 759; Robertson, *Word Pictures*, 6:472-73.
79. BAGD, p. 821.
80. Robertson, *Word Pictures*, 6:473.
81. The preposition ἐπί with the genitive has the force of "in the matter of" in other connections. Here in the combination ἐπὶ σταδίων it carries the thrust of "to the length or extent of" (Charles, *Revelation*, 2:163; Robertson, *Word Pictures*, 6:473).

depending on the exact length of a *stadion*—is the length of each of the sides or the combined total of the four sides. Those who want to make it the combined total of the four sides usually do so with a desire to reduce the vast dimensions of the city. The words immediately following give the impression that this is the dimension in each direction, however. If this is not true, the account gives no dimension for the height. In rabbinic circles the walls of the new Jerusalem in Ezekiel were reported to reach to Damascus (cf. Zech. 9:1) and to be fifteen hundred miles high or even reach to the throne of God.[82] Another suggestion has been that a square fourteen hundred miles on each side would extend from Rome to Jerusalem on the west and east, and to the northern and southern boundaries of the Roman Empire. Patmos would be the center of this area.[83] Another comparison in land area notes that the coverage would equal the combined areas of all the states in the United States except Montana, Utah, Nevada, Arizona, Washington, Oregon, California, Alaska, and Hawaii (Smith). A further comparison likens the distance to the size of the western United States between the Pacific coast and the Mississippi River,[84] or to the distance from Adelaide to Darwin, Australia, from New York to Houston, from London to Athens, or from Delhi to Rangoon (Morris). Though staggering to the human mind (Swete), a city fifteen hundred miles high and fifteen hundred miles on each side is no more unimaginable than a pearl large enough to serve as a city-gate or gold that is as transparent as glass. The prophet is struggling to express the vastness of the city through language accommodated to this creation (Beckwith).

The same three directional indicators as in the words τὸ μῆκος καὶ τὸ πλάτος καὶ τὸ ὕψος (*to mēkos kai to platos kai to hypsos*, "the length and width and height") are expressive of Christ's love in Eph. 3:18 where a fourth dimension βάθος (*bathos*, "depth") is added to the other three. The ἴσα (*isa*, "equal") shows that the shape of the city is that of a perfect cube, just like the cube-shaped Holy of Holies in Solomon's temple (1 Kings 6:19-20). Though not expressly stated in Scripture, the Holy of Holies of the tabernacle had each of its dimensions as ten cubits according to Philo, Josephus, and all tradition (Lee). The mathematical and architectural equality of the city expresses the symmetry

---

82. Alford, *Greek Testament*, 4:741; Lee, "Revelation," 4:823; Bullinger, *Apocalypse*, p. 663; Moffatt, "Revelation," 5:483; Charles, *Apocalypse*, 2:163; Robertson, *Word Pictures*, 6:473; Johnson, "Revelation," 12:596.
83. Mulholland, *Revelation*, p. 325.
84. Smith, *Revelation*, p. 289; Charles Caldwell Ryrie, *Revelation*, in Everyman's Bible Commentary (Chicago: Moody, 1968), p. 121; cf. Michael Topham, "The Dimensions of the New Jerusalem," *ExpTim* 100, no. 11 (August 1989): 417-18.

and harmony of the divine life (Moffatt). The claim that a perfect cube is not structurally feasible (Lee) rests on a comparison with the present creation. It is impossible to impose such a limitation on the new creation.

21:17 Measurement of the city's wall is next: καὶ ἐμέτρησεν τὸ τεῖχος αὐτῆς ἑκατὸν τεσσαράκοντα τεσσάρων πηχῶν, μέτρον ἀνθρώπου, ὅ ἐστιν ἀγγέλου (*kai emetrēsen to teichos autēs hekaton tesserakonta tessarōn pēchōn, metron anthrōpou, ho estin angelou,* "and he measured her wall, one hundred forty-four cubits, the measure of a man, which is [that] of an angel"). It is not immediately clear whether "one hundred forty-four cubits" (216 feet) is the height (Deut. 3:5; 28:52) or the width (Jer. 51:58; Ezek. 41:9) of the wall. If it were the height, the measurement would be a small fraction of the 7,000,000-foot (i.e., 1,500 mile) height of the city (v. 16).[85] Yet it would be somewhat higher than Solomon's porch, the highest point in his temple, which was one hundred twenty cubits (2 Chron. 3:4). The general height of his temple was thirty cubits (1 Kings 6:2) (Alford).

Probably this one hundred forty-four cubits refers to the width of the wall as in Ezekiel's measurement of the wall around restored Jerusalem (Ezek. 40:5; 42:20) (Beckwith, Ladd). In this case the thickness would not be out of proportion to the extreme height of the wall.[86]

In the words μέτρον ἀνθρώπου, ὅ ἐστιν ἀγγέλου (*metron anthrōpou, ho estin angelou,* "the measure of a man, which is [that] of an angel"), μέτρον (*metron,* "measure") is an accusative of general reference in "lax apposition to" the verb ἐμέτρησεν (*emetrēsen,* "he measured"). The expression means that an angel did the measuring, but followed human standards in doing so. These are human measurements, figures determined by standards common among men, even though a nonhuman did the measuring (Swete, Beckwith). The proposal that the expression means that in the new Jerusalem men will be equal to angels and will measure everything by spiritual dimensions is insupportable (Lee).

21:18 The description moves on to speak of the materials which have gone into the city's construction: καὶ* ἡ ἐνδώμησις τοῦ τείχους αὐτῆς ἴασπις, καὶ ἡ πόλις χρυσίον καθαρὸν ὅμοιον ὑάλῳ καθαρῷ (*kai hē endōmēsis tou teichous autēs iaspis, kai hē polis chrysion katharon homoion hyalǭ katharǭ,* "and the material of her wall was jasper, and the city was pure gold like pure glass"). Etymologically, the noun ἐνδώμησις (*endōmēsis,* "material") means "building in," giving the impression that the wall had jasper built into it. Being cased with pre-

---

85. Lee, "Revelation," 4:824; Robertson, *Word Pictures,* 6:473.
86. Kiddle, *Revelation,* pp. 430-31; Wilcock, *Revelation,* p. 208.

cious metal, it sparkled with crystalline radiance.[87] In 4:3 the One sitting on the throne is like jasper, and in 18:11 the whole city aglow with the glory of God emits a jasper-like radiance. So the jasper wall speaks of the emission of the glory of God (Mounce).

The statement "the city was pure gold" (ἡ πόλις χρυσίον καθαρὸν [*hē polis chrysion katharon*]) means that the city shone like a mass of pure gold. This contrasts with the jasper luster of the city wall.[88] The addition ὅμοιον ὑάλῳ καθαρῷ (*homoion hyalō̦ katharō̦*, "like pure glass") pictures ideal gold so pure that it is transparent.[89] This surpasses any gold known in this present creation. The same essential feature marks the city's golden street in v. 21, with the present verse an apparent reference to the city's buildings, towers, or roofs seen from outside the city (Alford, Lee, Swete).

21:19 Attention returns to the foundations of the city wall already noticed in v. 14: *οἱ θεμέλιοι τοῦ τείχους τῆς πόλεως παντὶ λίθῳ τιμίῳ κεκοσμημένοι· ὁ θεμέλιος ὁ πρῶτος ἴασπις, ὁ δεύτερος σάπφιρος, ὁ τρίτος χαλκηδών, ὁ τέταρτος σμάραγδος* (*hoi themelioi tou teichous tēs poleōs panti lithō̦ timiō̦ kekosmēmenoi; ho themelios ho prōtos iaspis, ho deuteros sapphiros, ho tritos chalkēdōn, ho tetartos smaragdos*, "the foundations of the city were adorned with every precious stone. The first foundation was jasper, the second sapphire, the third chalcedony, the fourth emerald"). It is of interest that the twelve foundations extend above ground level enough to be visible from John's vantage point. Twelve stones in vv. 19-20 offer examples of "every precious stone" (παντὶ λίθῳ τιμίῳ [*panti lithō̦ timiō̦*]) which adorn the wall's foundations. The twelve portray "a radiant and superb structure" (Moffatt).

Eight of the twelve stones correspond to those in the breastplate of the high priest (Ex. 28:17-20; 39:10 ff.; cf. Isa. 54:11-12; Ezek. 28:13). Some uncertainty exists regarding the identification of some of the stones and their colors, the colors they represent are probably white (jasper [perhaps green, however]), blue (sapphire, jacinth, amethyst), green (chalcedony, emerald, beryl, topaz, chrysoprase), red (sardonyx, sardius), and yellow (chrysolite). A great variety in shade and brilliance of each color prevails, of course (Swete). The use of κεκοσμημένοι (*kekosmēmenoi*, "adorned") does not mean that these stones decorated the foundations, but that each of the foundations consisted of one of the twelve stones (Alford).

---

87. Beckwith, *Apocalypse*, p. 762; Robertson, *Word Pictures*, 6:474.
88. Robertson, *Word Pictures*, 6:474.
89. The noun ὑάλῳ derives from ὕει, "it rains," and hence means "raindrop." From this it took on the meaning of "glass" because of the transparency that glass has in common with a raindrop (Robertson, *Word Pictures*, 6:474; Abbott-Smith, *Manual Greek Lexicon*, p. 453).

Defining the source of the symbolism of the stones is a possibility. It is not the jewels on the apparel of the king of Tyre (Ezek. 28:11 ff.), because it would be inappropriate to use a pagan king as symbolic of the future eternal kingdom (Johnson). Besides, though the LXX has twelve stones, the Hebrew text of the Ezekiel 28 passage refers to only nine stones (Charles, Sweet). A somewhat favorable case is possible for taking the signs of the zodiac as the source of the stone symbolism (Caird, Johnson). The first zodiacal sign agrees with the twelfth foundation and the last zodiacal sign agrees with the first foundation. The whole list agrees except it is in reverse order (Caird, Johnson). The theory that the reversal in order is John's way of expressing disapproval of pagan cults and dissociating the Holy City from ethnic speculations about the city of the gods (Kiddle, Johnson) is strange, however, in light of the writer's straightforward manner in opposing everything related to paganism elsewhere in the book. Besides, major research has questioned the accuracy of assuming the sequential alignment of the stones with the signs of the zodiac.[90] Even if it were valid, the theory is somewhat irrelevant. Philo and Josephus considered the twelve stones in the high priest's breastplate to correspond to the signs of the zodiac, so the ultimate allusion must be to those stones.[91]

Eight of the stones are the same as in that breastplate, with the four remaining ones being words that are unused in the LXX: χαλκηδών, χρυσόπρασος, ὑάκινθος, σαρδόνυξ (*chalkēdōn, chrysoprasos, hyakinthos, sardonyx*, "chalcedony, chrysoprase, jacinth, sardonyx") (Swete). The symbolism is rich in meaning. The old covenant confined the privilege of direct fellowship with God to the high priest, but in the new city the privilege will belong to all the people of God (cf. v. 22) (Moffatt). A difference in the order of the stones' listing in the two situations is not a serious problem for this view.

Each one of the foundations consists of its own particular stone (Beckwith), "the first foundation was jasper" (ὁ θεμέλιος ὁ πρῶτος ἴασπις [*ho themelios ho prōtos iaspis*]). Since the whole wall standing on the foundations is of jasper (v. 18), it is appropriate that the first foundation be of jasper too (Moffatt). The OT is not specific as to which stone in the high priest's breastpiece corresponds to each tribe, but a suggestion has been that jasper corresponds to Benjamin (Ford).

---

90. T. F. Glasson, "The Order of Jewels in Rev. 21:19-20: A Theory Eliminated," *JTS* 26 (1975): 95-100.
91. Swete, *Apocalypse*, p. 291; Beckwith, *Apocalypse*, p. 762; J. Massyngberde Ford, *Revelation*, vol. 38 of AB (Garden City, N.Y.: Doubleday, 1975), p. 342; cf. William W. Reader, "The Twelve Jewels of Revelation 21:19-20: Tradition History and Modern Interpretations," *JBL* 100, no. 3 (September 1981): 435-36.

The Greek term *iaspis* appears in the LXX at Isa. 54:12, where the NASB translates the Hebrew word by "ruby."

The second foundation consisted of a large "sapphire" (σάπφιρος [*sapphiros*]), a stone in the second row of the high priestly breastplate (Ex. 28:18; 39:11) that is also referred to in Ex. 24:10 and Isa. 54:11. The Egyptians and Assyrians prized this stone very highly and used it often to decorate buildings (Moffatt). It is quite possibly the *lapis lazuli* referred to in Lam. 4:7; Ezek. 1:26; 28:13. It was either blue in color (Lee, Ford) or a sky-blue stone flecked with gold (Swete). A tie to the tribe of Issachar has been suggested for this stone (Ford).

"Chalcedony" (χαλκηδών [*chalkēdōn*]) constituted the third foundation. A precious stone referred to nowhere else in the Greek Bible, it was possibly a green silicate of copper or an agate from near Chalcedon.[92] Modern chalcedony is merely a translucent (i.e., gray) quartz with a milky tinge (Moffatt).

The green "emerald" (σμάραγδος [*smaragdos*]) is unmentioned elsewhere in the NT, though the cognate adjective σμαράγδινος (*smaragdinos*) occurs in Rev. 4:3.[93] The title "Simeon's stone" has been applied to it, but a relationship to Judah has also been a suggestion (Ford).

21:20 Verse 20 identifies the material of the remaining eight foundations: ὁ πέμπτος σαρδόνυξ, ὁ ἕκτος σάρδιον, ὁ ἕβδομος χρυσόλιθος, ὁ ἐνδέκατος ὑάκινθος, ὁ δωδέκατος ἀμέθυστος (*ho pemptos sardonyx, ho hektos sardion, ho hebdomos chrysolithos, ho ogdoos bēryllos, ho enatos topazion, ho dekatos chrysoprasos, ho hendekatos hyakinthos, ho dōdekatos amethystos*, "the fifth sardonyx, the sixth sardius, the seventh chrysolite, the eighth beryl, the ninth topaz, the tenth chrysoprase, the eleventh jacinth, the twelfth amethyst"). The fifth foundation stone was "sardonyx" (σαρδόνυξ [*sardonyx*]), a word formed by combining σάρδιον (*sardion*, "red carnelian") and ὄνυξ (*onyx*, "white"). This is a white stone with layers of red or brown in even planes.[94] The suggestion has been that this was Joseph's stone (Ford).

A σάρδιον (*sardion*, "sardius") stone comprised the sixth foundation. As noted in connection with 4:3, the sardius was a red jewel. Perhaps it was a carbuncle with a suggested relationship to Levi in the high priest's breastplate or another red stone, the ruby, related to Reuben (Ford).

The seventh foundation stone was "chrysolite" (χρυσόλιθος [*chryso-*

---

92. Swete, *Apocalypse*, pp. 291-92; Moffatt, "Revelation," 5:485; Robertson, *Word Pictures*, 6:474-75.

93. Swete, *Apocalypse*, p. 292; Robertson, *Word Pictures*, 6:475.

94. Swete, *Apocalypse*, p. 292; Robertson, *Word Pictures*, 6:475; D. R. Bowes, "Sardonyx," in *Zondervan Pictorial Encyclopedia of the Bible*, ed. Merrill C. Tenney (Grand Rapids: Zondervan, 1975), 5:278.

lithos]), a stone of golden color as the word's etymology—χρυσός (*chrysos*, "gold") plus λίθος (*lithos*, "stone")—implies. It resembles a yellow beryl or a golden jasper.[95] The modern chrysolite is merely a hard greenish mineral with no particular value (Moffatt). The suggested tie of this stone is to Asher (Ford).

The word for the eighth foundation, βήρυλλος (*bēryllos*, "beryl"), occurs only here in the NT. It also appears in the LXX of Ex. 28:20 as one of the stones in the fourth row of the high priest's breastpiece. This stone was very similar to the emerald, but was blue or sea-green in color and had a higher opacity.[96]

The "topaz" (τοπάζιον [*topazion*]) of the ninth foundation stone has a golden-greenish color. The Greek word appears only here in the NT, but is in the Greek version of Ex. 28:17 as the second stone in the first row of the breastpiece.[97] This name was thought to have come from an island in the Red Sea, thirty miles from the mainland, where its discovery occurred (Lee), but as that mineral proved to be too soft to have been topaz, the connection with that island was mistaken.[98] The suggested association of this stone is with Dan (Ford).

The noun χρυσόπρασος (*chrysoprasos*, "chrysoprase") occurs nowhere else in the NT or LXX. Its translucent golden-green color is a mark of the tenth foundation. It is somewhat similar to beryl, but of a paler green color.[99]

The "jacinth" (ὑάκινθος [*hyakinthos*]) of the eleventh foundation is violet. The bluish smoke of 9:17—ὑακινθίνους (*hyakinthinous*, "hyacinth")—has the same etymological lineage as this term.[100] The "jacinth" is one of the stones on the third row of the breastpiece, though a different Greek word refers to it in the LXX.

The final foundation is made of "amethyst" (ἀμέθυστος [*amethystos*]). The Greek word occurs only here in the NT, but the LXX has it as one of the stones in the third row of the breastpiece (Ex. 28:19). This stone has a violet and purple color that is more brilliant than the ὑάκινθος (*hyakinthos*).[101]

21:21 The final descriptive word about the city's exterior deals

---

95. Swete, *Apocalypse*, p. 292; Robertson, *Word Pictures*, 6:475.
96. Swete, *Apocalypse*, p. 292; Robertson, *Word Pictures*, 6:475; D. R. Bowes, "Beryl," in *Zondervan Pictorial Encyclopedia of the Bible*, 1:525.
97. Swete, *Apocalypse*, p. 292; Robertson, *Word Pictures*, 6:475.
98. D. R. Bowes, "Topaz," in *Zondervan Pictorial Encyclopedia of the Bible*, ed. Merrill C. Tenney (Grand Rapids: Zondervan, 1975), 5:779.
99. Swete, *Apocalypse*, p. 293; Robertson, *Word Pictures*, 6:475; D. R. Bowes, "Chrysoprase, Chrysoprasus," in *Zondervan Pictorial Encyclopedia of the Bible*, 1:845.
100. Robertson, *Word Pictures*, 6:475.
101. Swete, *Apocalypse*, p. 293; Robertson, *Word Pictures*, 6:475; D. R. Bowes, "Amethyst," in *Zondervan Pictorial Encyclopedia of the Bible*, 1:128.

with her gates and her street: καὶ οἱ δώδεκα πυλῶνες δώδεκα μαργαρῖται, ἀνὰ εἷς ἕκαστος τῶν πυλώνων ἦν ἐξ ἑνὸς μαργαρίτου. καὶ ἡ πλατεῖα τῆς πόλεως χρυσίον καθαρὸν ὡς ὕαλος διαυγής (*kai hoi dōdeka pylōnes dōdeka margaritai, ana heis hekastos tōn pylōnōn ēn ex henos margaritou. kai hē plateia tēs poleōs chrysion katharon hōs hyalos diaugēs*, "and the twelve gates were twelve pearls; each one of the gates was [made] from one pearl. And the street of the city was pure gold, like transparent glass"). "The twelve gates" (οἱ δώδεκα πυλῶνες [*hoi dōdeka pylōnes*]) are the same as the ones mentioned in vv. 12-13, each gate being inscribed with the name of a tribe of Israel. These gate-towers consisted of "twelve pearls" (δώδεκα μαργαρῖται [*dōdeka margaritai*]), each gate carved from a single large pearl (Swete; see "Additional Notes" below).

Pearls were little known in the OT (cf. Job 28:18), but were well-known among the Asiatic Greeks through their contacts with the Persians. One of the reasons Caesar tried to conquer Britain was the reports about its pearl fisheries. Among the ancients, pearls were ranked highest among precious stones, because their beauty derives entirely from nature, improvement by human workmanship being an impossibility (Lee). In NT times the dealer in good pearls was familiar on the roads of Galilee (cf. Matt. 13:46). The pearl was among the treasured ornaments of the wealthier class (cf. Matt. 7:6; 1 Tim. 2:9; Rev. 18:12) (Swete), and was one of the most valuable items in the Roman world.[102]

Both here and in 22:2 the singular πλατεῖα (*plateia*, "street") refers to the city's thoroughfare, city square, or multiple streets. *Plateia* is an adjective meaning "broad," but its use alone implies the presence of ὁδός (*hodos*, "way") with it.[103] This may be a singular to refer to all the streets of the city, or it may point to only one major artery of a typical ancient city that led from the entrance gate to the king's palace (Moffatt, Beckwith). It is more probable, however, that the term is generic, referring to the material the streets were made of. The LXX uses the substantive in this generic manner (Gen. 19:2; Est. 6:9, 11; cf. Rev. 11:8) (Alford, Caird). Because the street will be continuous, even when it changes direction or joins with avenues coming from other gate-towers, it is only one and not many.

The entire city is gold (v. 18), but in particular this is the material that the street is made of.[104] And it is not just a lower grade of gold; it is "pure" (καθαρὸν [*katharon*]), so pure that it resembles "transparent glass" (ὕαλος διαυγής [*hyalos diaugēs*]). The word διαυγής (*diaugēs*,

---

102. Hauck, "μαργαρίτης" in *TDNT*, 4:472-73.
103. Lee, "Revelation," 4:828; Robertson, *Word Pictures*, 6:475.
104. Wall, *Revelation*, p. 254.

"transparent") comes from διά (*dia*, "through") and αὐγή (*augē*, "brightness") and refers to a "brightness" or "shining through." It conveys the notion of transparency conveyed by καθαρῷ (*katharō*, "pure") in v. 18. Transparency results from purity (Swete, Lee). The old creation knows nothing of gold so pure.

The city's illumination (21:22-27). Shifting gears slightly, the author turns next to focus in particular upon how the city receives its light and how that light serves the nations (21:22-27).

21:22 The new order will require no special sanctuary for the reason explained in v. 22: Καὶ ναὸν οὐκ εἶδον ἐν αὐτῇ, ὁ γὰρ κύριος ὁ θεὸς ὁ παντοκράτωρ ναὸς αὐτῆς ἐστιν, καὶ τὸ ἀρνίον (*Kai naon ouk eidon en autē, ho gar kyrios ho theos ho pantokratōr naos autēs estin, kai to arnion*, "And I did not see a temple in her, for the Lord God Almighty is her temple, and the Lamb"). With the simple connective καί (*kai*, "and") the writer proceeds to a description of the inner life of the city. Verses 22-27 serve the special function of showing that God has brought men back into a personal relationship with Himself.[105]

John writes, "I did not see a temple in her" (ναὸν οὐκ εἶδον ἐν αὐτῇ [*naon ouk eidon en autē*]) because the whole city is, in a sense, a temple. Yet it is more than a temple even though the temple in its best days had a holy place and the Shekinah glory of God in the Holy of Holies.[106] The OT prophets foresaw the temple as the principal item in their descriptions of the glorified city (Isa. 44:28; 60:13; Ezek. 40-48). The absence of a temple from the new Jerusalem marks a significant difference from that expectation (Beckwith). A reconciliation of the two expectations notes that a restored temple as the center for future bliss belongs to the millennial kingdom, but not to the new Jerusalem where no independent temple structure will exist. In light of this absence, the promise to the overcomer in 3:12 is one of permanent citizenship in the Holy City (Swete).

The conjunction γάρ (*gar*, "for") introduces an explanation for the phenomenon of a missing temple, that in the eternal state God Himself will dwell among His people in direct unmediated communion (Ladd). In 2 Cor. 6:16 Christians are the temple of the living God, but in the words ὁ . . . κύριος ὁ θεὸς ὁ παντοκράτωρ ναὸς αὐτῆς ἐστιν, καὶ τὸ ἀρνίον (*ho . . . kyrios ho theos ho pantokratōr naos autēs estin, kai to arnion*, "the Lord God Almighty is her temple, and the Lamb"), God Himself is the temple or "sanctuary," in other words, the Holy of Holies.[107] So is the Lamb, according to the last three words. "The Lord

---

105. Wilcock, *Revelation*, p. 210.
106. Robertson, *Word Pictures*, 6:476.
107. The anarthrous ναός is predicate nominative and focuses on the quality of such a thing as the holy place.

God Almighty"—so often a descriptive title for God in this book (e.g., 1:8)—has made Himself immediately available to the entire city (Lee). What for so long was a symbol in the earthly tabernacle and temple, the presence of God with men, now gives place to reality (Kiddle).

21:23 God's presence in the city has implications for her lighting system: καὶ ἡ πόλις οὐ χρείαν ἔχει τοῦ ἡλίου οὐδὲ τῆς σελήνης, ἵνα φαίνωσιν αὐτῇ, ἡ γὰρ δόξα τοῦ θεοῦ ἐφώτισεν αὐτήν, καὶ ὁ λύχνος αὐτῆς τὸ ἀρνίον (*kai hē polis ou chreian echei tou hēliou oude tēs selēnēs, hina phainōsin autę̄, hē gar doxa tou theou ephōtisen autēn, kai ho lychnos autēs to arnion*, "and the city does not have need of the sun or of the moon, that they might shine in her, for the glory of God illumined her, and the Lamb is her lamp"). As the city will have no need of a temple, she will also not need created light because God's presence pervades the city and emits constant light in abundance (cf. 22:5). "The sun" (Τοῦ ἡλίου [*Tou hēliou*]) and "the moon" (τῆς σελήνης [*tēs selēnēs*]) of the first creation (Gen. 1:14-16) have no place in the second creation (Swete). They will not need to "shine" (φαίνωσιν [*phainōsin*]) in the city. The Shekinah glory of God provided necessary illumination for the Holy of Holies in the tabernacle and the temple. His immediate presence will do the same for the whole city that will descend from heaven (Bullinger). This element in the city's life alludes to the seed-thought regarding God's presence expressed in Isa. 60:19-20 (Charles, Ford, Mounce).

The reason why (γάρ [*gar*, "for"]) the sun and moon are unnecessary is the presence of "the glory of God" (ἡ . . . δόξα τοῦ θεοῦ [*hē . . . doxa tou theou*]) to provide the needed illumination. This is all the illumination anyone could ask or want. The sun and moon could add nothing to this radiance.[108] An earlier reference to serving God day and night in His temple (7:15-16) pertained to an epoch when "day and night" continue in cycles, but in the new Jerusalem no such alternations between light and darkness exist (Lee). It will be a condition of constant brightness and brilliance.

The words ὁ λύχνος αὐτῆς τὸ ἀρνίον (*ho lychnos autēs to arnion*, "the Lamb is her lamp") show that the Lamb will be to the city in a physical and spiritual sense what the churches (λυχνίαι [*lychniai*, "lampstands," 1:12, 20]) were in a spiritual sense to the world of their day (Swete). The Lamb is the effulgence of the Father's glory (Heb. 1:3). The glory of both persons is the same (Lee). Like the Lamb, the Father too is the lamp (22:5) (Beckwith).

21:24 The impact of this special illumination on the nations will be pronounced too: καὶ περιπατήσουσιν τὰ ἔθνη* διὰ τοῦ φωτὸς αὐτῆς· καὶ

---

108. Robertson, *Word Pictures*, 6:476.

οἱ βασιλεῖς τῆς γῆς φέρουσιν τὴν δόξαν αὐτῶν εἰς αὐτήν (*kai peri-patēsousin ta ethnē dia tou phōtos autēs; kai hoi basileis tēs gēs pher-ousin tēn doxan autōn eis autēn*, "and the nations will walk by her light; and the kings of the earth bring their glory into her"). The writer switches from the aorist ἐφώτισεν (*ephōtisen*, "illumined") of v. 23 where he reports what he saw to the future tense περιπατήσουσιν (*peri-patēsousin*) through which he predicts the fulfillment of his vision.[109] The nations will walk "by" [means of] (διά [*dia*]) the city's light, though *dia* could carry the connotation of passing "through" that light. The contextual flow affords more support to the notion of means, however. The city will be bright enough to supply illumination for the whole new creation (Alford, Lee). The allusion of this section is to Isa. 60:3, 11, 20.

The advent of nations (Isa. 2:2; 60:5; Dan. 7:14; Mic. 4:2; Zech. 2:11; 8:23) and the kings (Ps. 72:10) to Jerusalem to participate in divine blessing receives frequent attention in the OT. Isaiah 60:3 refers to both groups.[110] Yet earlier in Revelation "the nations" have been a pagan and rebellious people who trample the Holy City (11:2, 18) and become drunk with the wine of Babylon (18:3, 23). They meet their temporal destruction at the second advent of Christ (19:15, 17-21) and their eternal punishment at the Great White Throne (20:12-13). The kings of the earth have had the same character and destiny earlier in the book (6:15; 17:2, 18; 18:3, 9; 19:19). These portrayals appear incon-sistent with vv. 24 and 26 below and the participation of the two groups in the bride-city of the future.

The change of character of the nations and the kings prompts an investigation regarding their identity. (1) They may be the nations and kings that exist during the Millennium and come to Jerusalem in ac-cord with OT prophecy (Ps. 72:10-11; Isa. 60:3, 11; 66:12). They then join Satan in his rebellion at the end of the Millennium (Lee). The city now in view is the eternal city, though, not the millennial city spoken of in the cited OT prophecies. The rebels from the Millennium have already met their eternal destiny at the Great White Throne before this city descends from heaven. (2) Another line of thought makes these the ones who follow the Lamb and resist the beast (5:9; 7:9; 12:5; 15:3; 19:16), and consequently enter the blessings of the new creation (Johnson). The problem with this explanation is its inability to show why they are not inhabitants of the new Jerusalem rather than occa-sional visitors.

(3) Another possibility is that the nations are those who belong

109. Düsterdieck, *Revelation*, p. 483.
110. Beckwith, *Apocalypse*, p. 763; Robertson, *Word Pictures*, 6:477; Ford, *Rev-elation*, pp. 337-38.

spiritually, but not racially to the twelve tribes, and the kings are the martyr monarchs who reigned as successors to the heathen monarchs (20:4-6) (Kiddle). Yet this is inadequate because it is unjustified to exclude Israel as one of the nations in this group of occasional visitors to the city. (4) A further proposal has been that these will be the renewed-earth nations, organized under kings, and saved through the influences of the heavenly city (Alford). But to survive the Great White Throne judgment and enter the new creation, these nations would have to be saved *before* the abolishing of the old creation (20:11).

(5) The idea has come that these are the nations outside the city and on the new earth, whose names are in the Book of Life and who while on earth had striven against sin, but had not come to a knowledge of the Savior before the abolition of the old creation. In the new creation they do become willing subjects of God and the Lamb. This proposal leaves unanswered the question of how they were in the Book of Life at the final reckoning (20:11-15) without a personal relationship with Christ, however. It also leaves the mystery of how they could have striven against sin without an alliance with the Lamb. (6) That they are the nations that do not join with Gog and Magog in Rev. 20:8 during Satan's final rebellion is another theory (Bullinger). This theory may be good as far as it goes, but leaves open the question of whether these nations enter the eternal state in a state unchanged from their state in the old creation.

(7) A more extreme proposal is that the presence of the nations in the new order is an indication of universal salvation. The citizens of the city are those who were saved before the Great White Throne, and the nations and their kings are those who were not.[111] Yet this mention of access to the city for the Gentiles cannot teach universal salvation or even salvation of the majority of people (contra Morris). Such a scheme would nullify recent references to the lake of fire and brimstone as the eternal destiny of the lost (20:15; 21:8) and render meaningless the exclusion from the city spoken of in 21:27. Throughout Revelation salvation comes only to the loyal, not to the rebellious. The concept of universal salvation reads too much preconceived theology into incidental references which have better interpretations (Mounce).

(8) The explication that the mention of the nations and kings is solely for the purpose of emphasizing the universality of the knowledge of God and that details regarding their identity are meaningless has been another theory (Ladd). This approach dodges questions that deserve answers, however. It borders on the attributing of inconsisten-

---

111. William Barclay, *The Revelation of John*, 2d ed., 2 vols. (Philadelphia: Westminster, 1960), 2:276-78; Caird, *Revelation*, pp. 279-80.

cies to the text as some have done (e.g., Moffatt). (9) Another idea makes τὰ ἔθνη (ta ethnē, "the nations" or "Gentiles") refer to saved Gentiles who are not a part of the church (Walvoord). But if they are saved, they have as much right to be inhabitants of the city as do saved Israelites and saved members of the church.

None of the earlier proposals has any direct support. In fact, this is an issue on which the text of Revelation is silent, but there is one further theory which seems to satisfy the available criteria best. (10) This opinion holds that "the nations" are composed of saved people who survive the millennial kingdom without dying and without joining Satan's rebellion and who undergo some sort of transformation that suits them for life in the eternal state. They will be like Adam and Eve in the Garden of Eden prior to the Fall (cf. Govett, Seiss). They will be unresurrected human beings who will inhabit the new earth, Paradise restored (22:1-5), throughout eternity. These will be the ones over whom God's resurrected saints will reign (22:5). Nations, peoples, and men on earth must continue in the flesh as Adam and Eve did before the Fall (Seiss).

What conditions prevail outside the new Jerusalem in parts of the new earth from which the nations and the kings come to the city is not a matter of revelation. One can only assume that in the absence of the curse that plagued the former earth (22:3), conditions will be vastly superior to the world of the present order. Two features are certain: there will be no more sea (21:1) and no more night (21:25).

"The kings of the earth bring their glory" (οἱ βασιλεῖς τῆς γῆς φέρουσιν τὴν δόξαν αὐτῶν [hoi basileis tēs gēs pherousin tēn doxan autōn]) as their earlier counterparts did to Babylon before the abolition of the old creation (Johnson). The present tense of φέρουσιν (pherousin, "bring") marks this as habit and a matter of certainty in the new creation (Alford). Once again, a great metropolis will be the focus of the world and all lands will submit to her, but this time, under the exactly opposite moral conditions.

21:25 In a somewhat parenthetical way, the nonclosing of the city's gates (cf. Isa. 60:11) receives attention: καὶ οἱ πυλῶνες αὐτῆς οὐ μὴ κλεισθῶσιν ἡμέρας, νὺξ γὰρ οὐκ ἔσται ἐκεῖ (kai hoi pylōnes autēs ou mē kleisthōsin hēmeras, nyx gar ouk estai ekei, "and her gates will in no way be shut by day, for there will not be night there"). A future of emphatic negation, οὐ μὴ κλεισθῶσιν (ou mē kleisthōsin, "will in no way be shut") draws extra attention to the continued access for the nations and their leaders into the city. It also serves notice of the perfect security of the city (Lee). Would-be exploiters of the open city will be nonexistent.

The nonclosure will be by day only, but since "there will not be night there" (νὺξ . . . οὐκ ἔσται ἐκεῖ [nyx . . . ouk estai ekei]), this amounts to an around-the-clock access for the kings. The presence of νὺξ (*nyx*, "night") alongside ἡμέρα (*hēmera*, "day") has been customary throughout the book until now (cf. 4:8; 7:15; 12:10; 14:11; 20:10), but now the change in cycles has come. No nighttime will characterize the heavenly city because of the resident divine glory (21:11, 23; 22:5).[112]

21:26 Picking up its subject from the end of v. 24, οἴσουσιν (*oisousin*, "they will bring") returns attention to the action of the kings: καὶ οἴσουσιν τὴν δόξαν καὶ τὴν τιμὴν τῶν ἐθνῶν εἰς αὐτήν (*kai oisousin tēn doxan kai tēn timēn tōn ethnōn eis autēn*, "and they will bring the glory and honor of the nations into her"). The leaders of organized nations will have access to the Holy City and will pay regular tribute there. Τὴν δόξαν καὶ τὴν τιμὴν τῶν ἐθνῶν (*Tēn doxan kai tēn timēn tōn ethnōn*, "The glory and honor of the nations") refers to the choicest of their treasures, whatever they may be. In a time of uninhibited prosperity, their offerings will doubtless be very generous, though they will be different and special because of an increased productivity.

A viewpoint that they will be allowed to come up to the gate of the city, but not to enter the city itself[113] is difficult to sustain. The preposition εἰς (*eis*, "into") in the phrase εἰς αὐτήν (*eis autēn*, "into her") here and in v. 24 when following a verb of motion such as φέρω (*pherō*, "I bring") indicates penetration into the city. They will actually move about within the city (Govett, Walvoord).

21:27 Telling what will not enter the city is equally revealing to telling what will enter her: καὶ οὐ μὴ εἰσέλθῃ εἰς αὐτὴν πᾶν κοινὸν καὶ [ὅ] ποιῶν* βδέλυγμα καὶ ψεῦδος, εἰ μὴ οἱ γεγραμμένοι ἐν τῷ βιβλίῳ τῆς ζωῆς τοῦ ἀρνίου (*kai ou mē eiselthē eis autēn pan koinon kai [ho] poiōn bdelygma kai pseudos, ei mē hoi gegrammenoi en tō bibliō tēs zōēs tou arniou*, "and nothing unclean and no one doing an abomination and a lie will in any way enter into her, but those written in the book of life of the Lamb [will enter into her]"). Another future of emphatic negation, οὐ μὴ εἰσέλθῃ (*ou mē eiselthē*, "will [not] in any way enter"), dwells upon the characteristic purity of the city.[114] Even with wide open gates certain things will never gain access to the city. Though completely open, the city will exclude the works of darkness (Swete). To read into these words that lost people will roam about outside the city with an opportunity of eventual repentance and entrance into the city (Caird) is completely fallacious. The verse is rather intended as a warning to the reader that the only way to enter the city of the future is by becoming a loyal follower of the Lamb right now (cf. 21:7) (Johnson).

With the later οὐ μή (*ou mē*, "in no way"), πᾶν κοινὸν (*pan koinon*)

---

112. Lee, "Revelation," 4:830; Robertson, *Word Pictures*, 6:477.
113. William Kelly, *Lectures on the Revelation* (London: G. Morrish, n.d.), p. 481; Smith, *Revelation*, p. 292.
114. Robertson, *Word Pictures*, 6:477.

means "nothing unclean." The adjective κοινός (*koinos*) can refer to what is "common" to all (Titus 1:4), but in a number of places including here, it has passed over into an ethical meaning (Mark 7:2; Acts 10:14). No defiled entity will enter and contaminate the city (cf. 21:8; 22:15).[115]

Also barred from the city will be everyone "doing an abomination and a lie" (ποιῶν βδέλυγμα καὶ ψεῦδος [*poiōn bdelygma kai pseudos*]). Abominations will characterize future Babylon (17:4-5). God has already relegated those guilty of abominable behavior to the lake of fire and brimstone as He has liars who are in view in this same phrase (cf. 21:8). The latter will have a fuller description in 22:15 where πᾶς φιλῶν καὶ ποιῶν ψεῦδος (*pas philōn kai poiōn pseudos*, "everyone who loves and does a lie") identifies such a person.

Some interpret in John's continuing references to pagan life in contrast to life in the new Jerusalem a meaning that the abominable and liars are present on the new earth, but cannot gain access to the city (e.g., Charles). This is not valid, however, for John simply resorts to contemporary earthly idiom to describe a future eschatological situation (Ladd). Unwholesome lifestyles that oppose the truth will be totally denied entrance into the new order (cf. John 3:21; Rev. 14:5). Lying such as has marked the earlier existence of the false Christ will eliminate any possibility of a part in the bliss described in this context (1 John 2:22; cf. 2 Thess. 2:11) (Lee).

Earlier references to "the book of life of the Lamb" (τῷ βιβλίῳ τῆς ζωῆς τοῦ ἀρνίου [*tō bibliō tēs zōēs tou arniou*]) have come at 3:5; 13:8; 20:12, 15. The nations and the kings (vv. 24, 26) are unquestionably among those whose names will be in the book at the Great White Throne judgment (20:12, 15). This raises interesting questions regarding their relationship to redeemed Israel, the church, and other citizens of the bride-city itself (cf. Alford). The discussion of "the nations" at v. 24 above has explored some of these questions and has proposed that these are mortals surviving to the end of the Millennium and then having their mortality transformed to a new state resembling that of Adam and Eve before the entrance of sin in Genesis 3. The unmentioned transformation could occur in conjunction with God's work in creating the new heaven and the new earth (21:1, 5).

Inner life of the city (22:1-5). The final part of the intercalation about the Holy City focuses upon conditions within the city, particularly as pertains to the city's citizens.

---

115. Swete, *Apocalypse*, p. 297; Lee, "Revelation," 4:830; Beckwith, *Apocalypse*, p. 764; Robertson, *Word Pictures*, 6:477.

22:1 A pollution-free river is the first feature: Καὶ ἔδειξέν μοι πο-ταμὸν ὕδατος ζωῆς λαμπρὸν ὡς κρύσταλλον, ἐκπορευόμενον ἐκ τοῦ θρόν-ου τοῦ θεοῦ καὶ τοῦ ἀρνίου (*Kai edeixen moi potamon hydatos zōēs lampron hōs krystallon, ekporeuomenon ek tou thronou tou theou kai tou arniou*, "And he showed me a river of the water of life, bright as a crystal, proceeding from the throne of God and of the Lamb"). The words καὶ ἔδειξέν μοι (*kai edeixen moi*, "and he showed me") reflect a break in the description of the new Jerusalem. The angel now divulges to John a new aspect of the city (Hailey). This is the same angel who began this tour in 21:9-10 (cf. 21:15). The new details exhibit the Paradise-like qualities of the city (cf. 2:7). Aside from God and the Lamb, the Tree of Life and the water of life are her main distinguishing marks.[116]

The earliest description of Paradise is in Genesis 2. Man's banishment from it is in Genesis 3. Luke 23:43 tells of a restoration to it, and 2 Cor. 12:2, 4 speaks of a vision of it. A promise of a future enjoyment within it is in Rev. 2:7 (Bullinger). The five verses that begin Revelation 22 show that God's redemption will return the new creation to the Garden of Eden state and to the Creator's intention for humanity.[117] Earlier words about the city (21:9-27) have dealt with her visible splendors and relation to the nations of the earth. The account now turns to tell what nourishes and enriches the life of God's slaves who reside in her (Beckwith).

One of the twenty-four elders has earlier promised "the water of life" (τὸ ὕδωρ τῆς ζωῆς [*to hydōr zōēs*]) to the innumerable heavenly multitude (7:17). The same promise extends to anyone who is thirsty (21:6; 22:17; cf. John 4:11, 14; 7:38). The "river" (ποταμόν [*potamon*]) in which that water flows is a prominent part of the new city. This river recalls the one that flowed from the Garden of Eden and divided into four heads, one of which was the Euphrates (Gen. 2:10, 14). Such a river is a metaphor for refreshment during the millennial kingdom in Zech. 14:8. In Ezek. 47:9 the river's source is the temple-rock and its destination is the Dead Sea, which body of water it will convert into fresh water. A fountain of life that is akin to "the river of the water of life" appears in Jer. 2:13; 17:13; Ps. 36:9; Prov. 10:11; 13:14; 14:27; 16:22.[118] Metaphors involving water often in the OT describe future ideal conditions (e.g., Pss. 1:1-3; 46:4; Isa. 12:3; Jer. 17:7-8; Ezek. 47:1)

---

116. Bullinger, *Apocalypse*, p. 674; Robertson, *Word Pictures*, 6:479; Johnson, "Revelation," 12:599.
117. Caird, *Revelation*, p. 280; M. Eugene Boring, *Revelation* (Louisville: John Knox, 1989), p. 218; Wall, *Revelation*, pp. 255-56.
118. Swete, *Apocalypse*, p. 298; Robertson, *Word Pictures*, 6:479; Walvoord, *Revelation*, p. 329; Beasley-Murray, *Revelation*, p. 331.

(Johnson). Unlimited access to this life-giving water will assure residents of the new Jerusalem of an everlasting enjoyment of life. In the new creation the physical properties of water will impart the spiritual life which this creation can only portray through the metaphor of water. These are literal waters that are of such a nature and quality as to answer to the new Jerusalem to which they belong. Just as men on this earth have never known such a city, neither have they known such waters (Seiss).

The words λαμπρὸν ὡς κρύσταλλον (*lampron hōs krystallon,* "bright as a crystal") describe the river's appearance. The two words occur separately from each other, but never together elsewhere in the book. Λαμπρός (*Lampros,* "Bright") is in 15:6; 19:8; 22:16; and κρύσταλλος (*krystallos*) in 4:6. Together they envision the river as a sort of shimmering and sparkling stream of water as it passes over mountain rocks.[119]

The source of the river is τοῦ θρόνου τοῦ θεοῦ καὶ τοῦ ἀρνίου (*tou thronou tou theou kai tou arniou,* "the throne of God and of the Lamb"). Until now, the prophet has distinguished the Son from the Father who sits on the throne (cf. 5:6, 13; 6:16; 7:10, 17), but now they are together on the throne (Swete). Joint occupancy of the throne in heaven is the teaching of both 3:21 and 22:3 (cf. Heb. 1:3). Two persons sit on one throne, but they are not two separate entities. God is one (1 Tim. 2:5; Gal. 3:20), and the Father and the Son are one (John 10:30). Man in his finiteness cannot grasp the truth of the infinite being of the triune God.[120]

The water of life proceeding from the throne is similar to the picture in Ezek. 47:1 (cf. Zech. 14:8), where water comes from the temple (Johnson). This is fitting because God is the author of life.

No spiritual significance belongs to the water here (Charles). By using the water to typify the Holy Spirit, a theory is that the verse confirms the doctrine of the procession of the Spirit from the Father and the Son (Lee). No such typical significance is present, though. The point of the passage is to teach that in the eternal state God's people will live at the source of the life-giving stream, the very presence of God Himself (Mounce).

22:2 A good bit of uncertainty surrounds the city's layout as described in v. 2: ἐν μέσῳ τῆς πλατείας αὐτῆς καὶ τοῦ ποταμοῦ ἐντεῦθεν καὶ ἐκεῖθεν ξύλον ζωῆς ποιοῦν* καρποὺς δώδεκα, κατὰ μῆνα ἕκαστον ἀποδιδοῦν* τὸν καρπὸν αὐτοῦ, καὶ τὰ φύλλα τοῦ ξύλου εἰς θεραπείαν τῶν ἐθνῶν (*en mesō tēs plateias autēs kai tou potamou enteuthen kai ekeithen xylon*

---

119. Robertson, *Word Pictures,* 6:479.
120. Hughes, *Revelation,* p. 232.

zōēs poioun karpous dōdeka, kata mēna hekaston apodidoun ton karpon autou, kai ta phylla tou xylou eis therapeian tōn ethnōn, "in the middle of her street and of the river on this side and on that [was] a tree of life producing twelve fruit, yielding its fruit each month, and the leaves of the tree [were] for the healing of the nations"). At issue is the syntactical question of whether the words ἐν μέσῳ τῆς πλατείας αὐτῆς (*en mesō tēs plateias autēs*, "in the middle of her street") connect to v. 1 (Moffatt) and conclude that sentence or begin the new sentence that continues in v. 2 (Swete).

To take the phrase with v. 1 allows ξύλον (*xylon*, "tree") in v. 2 to be the direct object of the ἔδειξέν (*edeixen*) of v. 1 (Moffatt). It also follows the author's habit of introducing a new and distinct object with a καί (*kai*, "and"), the one before τοῦ ποταμοῦ (*tou potamou*, "the river") (Beckwith). A debilitating problem for this arrangement, however, is that it requires beginning a clause with a genitive *tou potamou*. This is very unusual. Also, it is very harsh to apply ἐν μέσῳ (*en mesō*, "in the middle") to τῆς πλατείας αὐτῆς (*tēs plateias autēs*, "her street") only, leaving καὶ τοῦ ποταμοῦ (*kai tou potamou*) to depend on ἐντεῦθεν καὶ ἐκεῖθεν (*enteuthen kai ekeithen*, "on this side and on that").[121]

To understand the expression as the beginning of the sentence in v. 2 presents several options. It could picture the river and the street as running side by side with the trees arranged in two rows, one on either bank, or placed on either side of the space between the street and the river. This arrangement would be rather unsymmetrical, however (Charles). Another possible understanding has a single tree standing between either side of the river which is envisioned as dividing into two branches, but if this is the picture, John has not expressed it very clearly (Beasley-Murray). The best analysis pictures a river flowing down the middle of the city's broad street with the trees on each side of the river in the middle of the space between the street and each of the river banks. This is the arrangement that has the support of the OT passage alluded to, Ezek. 47:7 (Alford, Swete). The absence of a *kai* to introduce v. 2 violates the pattern of this book and is somewhat of a problem to this view (Lee), but in light of the difficulties with other proposed layouts, this is not serious enough to rule the view out.

The idiom *enteuthen kai ekeithen* has the literal meaning of "from here and from there." It is the equivalent of ἔνθεν καὶ ἔνθεν (*enthen kai enthen*, "on one side and on the other") in Ezek. 47:12[LXX] (Beckwith). As an adverbial modifier, it completes the picture by locating rows of trees on each bank of the river.

The history of "the tree of life" (ξύλον ζωῆς [*xylon zōēs*]) goes back

---

121. Düsterdieck, *Revelation*, p. 488.

to Gen. 2:9, where God placed it in the original Garden of Eden. When man chose to disobey God, he lost his access to that tree (Gen. 3:22-24). During the period of no access to the tree, wisdom, the fruit of righteousness, and a soothing tongue are likened to it in a figurative way (Prov. 3:18; 11:30; 15:4), but in the eternal city restoration of access to the tree and even more privileges become reality. Ezekiel's account of the millennial river has all kinds of trees on both sides of the river, bearing food and leaves for healing month by month (Ezek. 47:12).[122] This account of the restored access to the Tree of Life retains the singular number of the noun ξύλον (*xylon*, "tree") from Gen. 2:9, but expands upon it through a description of a river lined with trees that resembles the picture in Ezekiel (Moffatt). It is an instance of the generic use of *xylon* to represent numerous trees (Swete, Lee, Beckwith). A suggested analogy between the cross of Christ and the Tree of Life[123] is baseless. The existence of the tree of life in the Garden of Eden long before the historical occasion of the tree of Calvary prohibit any reference to the latter here (Sweet).

The forest of trees will produce "twelve fruit" (καρποὺς δώδεκα [*karpous dōdeka*]), which may mean a twelvefold harvest of fruit—i.e., an abundant supply of fruit (Beckwith, Mounce)—or "twelve kinds of fruit" (Alford, Lee). The month-by-month output indicated by κατὰ μῆνα ἕκαστον (*kata mēna hekaston*, "every month") argues the probability of the latter meaning. The seasonal bearing of fruit familiar to this old creation will be a thing of the past (Ladd). Conditions of the new creation will be far different. The month-by-month harvest agrees with the picture of Ezek. 47:12 (Lee). The absence of the moon from the new creation (21:23) is not inconsistent with this reference to the twelve months of the year (contra Moffatt), because the new creation can have a basis for calendar reckoning entirely different from the lunar calculation familiar to the present creation.

Though eating the fruit of the Tree of Life is unmentioned here, the implication is that this is what brings immortality, the same as was true for Adam and Eve originally (Gen. 3:22). Conditions of future bliss will mean a return to the original glories and privileges of God's presence with man, before sin raised a barrier that prevented that direct contact.

The tree yields additional benefit through its leaves: τὰ φύλλα τοῦ ξύλου εἰς θεραπείαν τῶν ἐθνῶν (*ta phylla tou xylou eis therapeian tōn ethnōn*, "the leaves of the tree [were] for the healing of the nations"). The nations benefit from the health-giving qualities of the leaves

---

122. Robertson, *Word Pictures*, 6:479; Johnson, "Revelation," 12:599; Hughes, *Revelation*, p. 231.
123. Chilton, *Days of Vengeance*, pp. 567-68.

(Seiss). The statement of this benefit has created differences of opinion about chronology. The assignment of this benefit to the present era sees in it a reference to the healing virtues of the cross to the citizenship of fallen Babylon.[124] This perspective completely ignores the future focus of chapter 22 and other broader meanings of the context. Some of the particulars of this section have applications for the life of the church in the present, but these must be completely distinct from the primary meaning of the words.

Another viewpoint assigns this benefit of the tree's leaves to the period of the millennial kingdom (Charles). It reasons that healing is more suitable to the order of life in the Millennium than in the new creation where there will be no sickness (Beasley-Murray). Healing, however, does not necessarily indicate the presence of disease any more than the wiping away of tears (21:4) implies that sorrow still exists in the new Jerusalem. The tears were those caused by the troubles of this creation, tears that will no longer exist in the new creation. Likewise, the disease for which this healing provides is that of the former creation which no longer exists in the new Jerusalem.[125] The very next clause in v. 3 which tells of the absence of the curse demonstrates the impossibility of disease in the new order (Walvoord).

"Healing" (Θεραπείαν [*Therapeian*]), then, must connote a promoting of the health of the nations such as will be an ongoing service in the new creation (Govett, Seiss, Walvoord). This agrees with the identification of the nations proposed in the discussion of 21:24 above. Those who have entered the new heaven and the new earth in an unresurrected state will have a means for perpetuating their health.

22:3 The absence of the curse and the presence of God and of the Lamb further characterize the restoration of Paradise: καὶ πᾶν κατάθεμα οὐκ ἔσται ἔτι. καὶ ὁ θρόνος τοῦ θεοῦ καὶ τοῦ ἀρνίου ἐν αὐτῇ ἔσται, καὶ οἱ δοῦλοι αὐτοῦ λατρεύσουσιν αὐτῷ (*kai pan katathema ouk estai eti. kai ho thronos tou theou kai tou arniou en autē estai, kai hoi douloi autou latreusousin autō*, "and there will be no curse any longer. And the throne of God and of the Lamb will be in her, and His slaves will serve Him"). One way of relating πᾶν κατάθεμα οὐκ ἔσται ἔτι (*kai pan katathema ouk estai eti*, "and there will be no curse any longer") is to connect it with the next clause, resulting in the rationale, "because of the absence of the curse, divine rule will never terminate." The curse as a hindrance to man's fellowship with God will no longer exist (contra Gen. 3:8-9) (Swete, Lee).

This connection in thought would have required a δέ (*de*, "but") rather than a καί (*kai*, "and") to connect the two parts of v. 3, however.

---

124. Ibid., p. 569; Mulholland, *Revelation*, pp. 331-32.
125. Düsterdieck, *Revelation*, p. 489; Lee, "Revelation," 4:836.

It is better to relate the clause to the end of v. 2: the Tree of Life will heal the nations, and there will be no longer a curse from God on the nations, a curse imposed by Him in connection with the initial biblical appearance of the Tree of Life (Gen. 2:22-24) (Bullinger, Beckwith).

The "curse" (κατάθεμα [*katathema*]) imposed in Genesis 3 will no longer exist (Moffatt, Beasley-Murray, Johnson). This agrees with the anticipation of Zech. 14:11 (Hughes, *Revelation*, p. 233). *Katathema* occurs only here in the NT, but it is a cognate of ἀνάθεμα (*anathema*, "a curse") that occurs six times in the NT (Acts 23:14; Rom. 9:3; 1 Cor. 12:3; 16:22; Gal. 1:8, 9). The latter noun in all cases except Acts 23:14 refers to the object toward which a sentence is directed, but in Acts 23:14 it refers to the sentence itself (Swete). The latter meaning is more appropriate for *katathema*. The existence of a new creation lifts the bane that hung over the old creation throughout its existence after the Fall.

Nothing will remain to bar the residence of God among His people, so ὁ θρόνος τοῦ θεοῦ καὶ τοῦ ἀρνίου ἐν αὐτῇ ἔσται (*ho thronos tou theou kai tou arniou en autē estai*, "the throne of God and of the Lamb will be in her"). Repeated from v. 1, "the throne of God and of the Lamb" emphasizes the joint occupancy of the throne by the Father and the Lamb (cf. 21:22-23). The throne of Satan (2:13) will no longer have a place in the world (Johnson).

Because of the presence of His throne, "His slaves will serve Him" (οἱ δοῦλοι αὐτοῦ λατρεύσουσιν αὐτῷ [*hoi douloi autou latreusousin autō*]). John does not shun using the word for "slave" (δοῦλοι [*douloi*]) to describe the relationship of Christians to God any more than Paul did (Sweet). This is the broad usage of the term *douloi* to refer to all Christians as in its first occurrence of 1:1. The future tenses of λατρεύσουσιν (*latreusousin*, "will serve") and of the two occurrences of ἔσται (*estai*) in v. 3 changes from the descriptive style of vv. 1-2 to that of direct prediction (Lee). The tense usage is linear in nature: "they will keep on serving Him."[126] The usage of λατρεύω (*latreuō*, "I serve") in itself does not necessitate a reference to priestly service,[127] but broader contextual considerations require it to do so here (cf. 1:6; 5:10; 20:6) (Johnson). The destruction of the temple in A.D. 70 had dashed the hopes of any further priestly ministry for many Jews (cf. Acts 26:7), but the future state will see a realization of that hope for those who believe (Moffatt).

The singular pronoun αὐτῷ (*autō*, "Him") capitalizes on the unity of the Father and the Son (cf. John 10:30) (Lee). It is difficult to see this

---

126. Robertson, *Word Pictures*, 6:480.
127. Trench, *Synonyms*, pp. 126-27; Lee, "Revelation," 4:836.

priestly service rendered to one of the two persons to the exclusion of
the other (cf. 11:15) (Beckwith, Beasley-Murray).

22:4 Closeness to God and the Lamb will highlight the privileges of
the slaves: καὶ ὄψονται τὸ πρόσωπον αὐτοῦ, καὶ τὸ ὄνομα αὐτοῦ ἐπὶ τῶν
μετώπων αὐτῶν (*kai opsontai to prosōpon autou, kai to onoma autou epi
tōn metōpōn autōn*, "and they will see His face, and His name will be
on their foreheads"). After Adam and Eve sinned, they hid themselves
from God (Gen. 3:8). God did not allow Moses to view His face (Ex.
33:20, 23), but Jesus promised the privilege to the pure in heart (Matt.
5:8). It is possible only for those who are righteous and holy to view
God directly (Pss. 11:7; 17:15; Heb. 12:14; cf. 1 Cor. 13:12). Seeing
God's face is anthropomorphic language, but it is the best way available for expressing the essential goal of human existence.[128]

Viewing the glory of God is a limited privilege in the here and now
(Heb. 9:7; cf. 2 Cor. 3:18), but barriers will disappear when the redeemed enter the bride-city (cf. 1 John 3:2) (Johnson). Job entertained
this hope long ago (Job 19:25-27).[129] The question of whether this is
the face of God only or of God and the Lamb hinges on the antecedent
pronoun αὐτοῦ (*autou*, "His"). In light of the inclusion of both in the
autō that closes v. 3, the face probably belongs to both persons.

The same double reference applies to the "name" in the remainder
of v. 4. Having "His name" (τὸ ὄνομα αὐτοῦ [*to onoma autou*]) upon
one's forehead is a privilege seen three times earlier in Revelation. In
7:3 and 14:1 it was a privilege enjoyed in the old creation, but 3:12
looks forward to the fruition of Christian hope described here. The
144,000 who bore the name faced the constant threat of the beast and
those having his mark on their foreheads (13:16-17). However, no enemy will threaten God's slaves in the new Jerusalem (Kiddle). "Name"
and "glory" are two ways of referring to the presence of God in the
theophanic cloud, so both refer to the reflected likeness of God. To
note that citizens of the new Jerusalem bear the name of God and the
Lamb on their forehead is to say that they reflect the divine glory in
their persons.

22:5 The description of "Paradise restored" closes with a repeated
reference to the illuminating effect of God's presence and with a promise of an eternal reign for His slaves: καὶ νὺξ οὐκ ἔσται ἔτι, καὶ οὐκ
ἔχουσιν χρείαν φωτὸς* λύχνου καὶ φωτὸς* ἡλίου, ὅτι κύριος ὁ θεὸς
φωτίσει ἐπ᾽* αὐτούς, καὶ βασιλεύσουσιν εἰς τοὺς αἰῶνας τῶν αἰώνων (*kai
nyx ouk estai eti, kai ouk echousin chreian phōtos lychnou kai phōtos
hēliou, hoti kyrios ho theos phōtisei ep' autous, kai basileusousin eis*

---

128. Robertson, *Word Pictures*, 6:480; Beasley-Murray, *Revelation*, p. 332.
129. Hughes, *Revelation*, p. 233.

tous aiōnas tōn aiōnōn, "and there will not be night any longer, and they have no need of the light of a lamp and the light of the sun, because the Lord God will shine upon them, and they will reign forever and ever"). What was a somewhat parenthetical explanation in 21:25 now comes to the forefront of privileges in the new order in the words νὺξ οὐκ ἔσται ἔτι (*nyx ouk estai eti,* "there will not be night any longer") (Beckwith). This is a reminiscence of the condition described in Zech. 14:6-7 (Kiddle).

The words οὐκ ἔχουσιν χρείαν φωτὸς λύχνου καὶ φῶς ἡλίου (*ouk echousin chreian phōtos lychnou kai phōtos hēliou,* "they have no need of the light of a lamp and the light of the sun") repeat the gist of 21:23. In the earlier instance its setting focused on how unusual this new city will be. Here, however, attention is on the delight this condition will produce for the city's citizens (Beckwith).

The promise of the Lord God's personal illumination replaces the earlier one of illumination by His glory in 21:23. Another slight difference in the promise, "the Lord God will shine upon them" (κύριος ὁ θεὸς φωτίσει ἐπ᾽ αὐτούς [*kyrios ho theos phōtisei ep' autous*]), lies in the tenses of φωτίζω (*phōtizō,* "I illumine, shine"). The earlier occasion uses an aorist tense to describe what John saw (21:23), but here the future tense is a prediction of conditions that will prevail for people in the city.

The allusion of v. 5 to Ps. 118:27*a* commented on in the "Additional Notes" below is interesting. Since that Psalm reference is a shortened form of the priest's blessing in Num. 6:25, the fuller idea implied in Rev. 22:5 is, "The LORD will cause His face [cf. Rev. 22:4] to shine upon them" (Charles, Sweet). An added reason for seeing this as a partial allusion to Num 6:22-27 is that, in connection with that text, there was a fixed association of receiving the name of God (cf. Rev. 22:4) and living in the light of God (cf. Num. 6:25, 27) (Beasley-Murray).

The climaxing privilege of God's slaves is that of joining in the eternal reign of God: βασιλεύσουσιν εἰς τοὺς αἰῶνας τῶν αἰῶνων (*basileusousin eis tous aiōnas tōn aiōnōn,* "they will reign forever and ever"). This is an extension of the promise of a thousand-year reign given earlier (20:4, 6). Their eternal reign coincides with the eternal reign of Christ (1:6; 3:21; 11:15, 17; 12:10; cf. Luke 1:33).[130] This is the eventual fulfillment of God's command for man to rule over all creatures (Gen. 1:26).[131] The text is not explicit regarding those over whom God's slaves will rule, but presumably it will be "the nations" (v. 2) who will continue to populate the new earth just as Adam and Eve did the old earth before the Fall (Seiss).

---

130. Robertson, *Word Pictures,* 6:481; Mounce, *Revelation,* p. 388.
131. Beckwith, *Apocalypse,* p. 767; Wall, *Revelation,* pp. 257-58.

The promise of the eternal rule marks the end of John's visional experiences that began at 4:1. It is an appropriate note of triumph with which to terminate the account of the new Jerusalem. Many factors have required that the realization of these promises lies exclusively in the future, but some have made efforts to see a degree of their fulfillment in the present.[132] This practicc has introduced widespread confusion into the interpretation of this final vision. A better approach is to relegate the vision's fulfillment entirely to the future, with whatever parallels there are to the church's present experience treated as applications of the passage, not interpretations.

Additional Notes

21:9 Grammatically the participle τῶν γεμόντων agrees with the noun ἀγγέλων, rather than with φιάλας. This can mean that the angels, not the bowls, were full of the task committed to them, the seven last plagues (Lee, Swete). The sense of the passage, however, requires that the reference be to the bowls being full rather than the angels. The prominence of τῶν ἑπτὰ ἀγγέλων τῶν ἐχόντων earlier in the sentence explains the genitive case of τῶν γεμόντων (Beckwith). A similar grammatical surprise comes in 5:8 where the same verb is involved, though not directly: there the relative pronoun refers to the prayers, not to the bowls as the grammar might imply.

21:11 The nominative ὁ φωστὴρ that begins the description of the city's physical features changes constructions from the ἔδειξεν of v. 10 which if it had been continued, would have required an accusative. This is only one of several syntactical variations used to describe the city (Alford). The asyndeton with which the description begins provides additional emphasis to the already striking details of the city's architecture.

21:12 The participles ἔχουσα . . . ἔχουσα derive their feminine gender from the πόλιν of v. 10, the clause ὁ φωστὴρ . . . κρυσταλλίζοντι being somewhat parenthetical, but their nominative case rather than the accusative case of their noun antecedent and of the ἔχουσαν that begins v. 11 indicates that the two participles of v. 12 are functioning as finite verbs. They agree with an imaginary nominative subject ἡ πόλις in the mind of the author (Swete, Beckwith, Moffatt).

The words τὰ ονόματα following ἐστιν do not appear in Sinaiticus, the *Textus Receptus*, and a number of other sources, but their presence in Alexandrinus, 2053, and other authorities is sufficient to conclude that the words were original.

21:14 The masculine participle ἔχων modifies the neuter τὸ τεῖχος

---

132. E.g., Swete, *Apocalypse*, p. 302; Ladd, *Revelation*, pp. 291-92; Mounce, *Revelation*, pp. 390-91.

earlier in the verse. Its use is as a finite verb such as εἶχεν, a common practice in this book.[133] This author has a tendency to change case or gender in a participle in the direction of the nominative or masculine when he uses the participle of ἔχω.[134]

21:16 Sinaiticus and a few other MSS have omitted the καί following ὅσον, but its inclusion has the support of Alexandrinus and a number of other authorities. The latter reading is preferable.

The genitive σταδίων following ἐπί is probably the correct reading as attested in Sinaiticus along with other witnesses. Some witnesses including Alexandrinus read the more usual accusative σταδίους, but this reading creates confusion in light of the following genitive adjective χιλιάδων.

21:17 The genitive ἑκατὸν τεσσαράκοντα τεσσάρων πηχῶν is a genitive of quality, "as amounting to one hundred forty-four cubits." This is a rather rare use of the genitive case.[135]

21:18 The copula ἦν is present in Sinaiticus, 046, and a number of other MSS just after the initial καί in v. 18 (Ford), but MS evidence for inclusion is, on the whole, quite weak.

21:19 An asyndeton marks the change of discussion from the building materials of the wall and the city in v. 18 to the foundations in v. 19, though Sinaiticus, 051, and other MSS begin v. 19 with a καί (Ford). Textual evidence is insufficient to view the καί as original, however.

The participle κεκοσμημένοι functions as a finite verb in v. 19, in the absence of a copula ἦσαν to make it a periphrastic form.[136]

21:21 In the construction ἀνὰ εἷς ἕκαστος the ἀνά has its distributive force. It is an adverb used with the nominative εἷς ἕκαστος, as is κατά with the nominative in Mark 14:19; John 8:9; Rom. 12:5, instead of the more frequent use as a preposition with the accusative (e.g. Matt. 20:9, 10; Luke 9:3; Rev. 4:8), however.[137]

21:24 With only very slight MS support Erasmus in the early sixteenth century included the words τῶν σωζομένων immediately after τὰ ἔθνη. This reading eventually found its way into the *Textus Receptus* and the *King James Version*. The reason for the addition is obvious: a scribe or scribes felt the difficulty that no one else was left on earth except the inhabitants of the new Jerusalem, all previous national and

---

133. Robertson, *Word Pictures*, 6:472.
134. Beckwith, *Apocalypse*, p. 224.
135. Lee, "Revelation," 4:824; BDF, par. 165.
136. Robertson, *Word Pictures*, 6:474.
137. Archibald Thomas Robertson, *A Grammar of the Greek New Testament in the Light of Historical Research* (Nashville: Broadman, 1934), pp. 460, 555; idem, *Word Pictures*, 6:475; Charles, *Revelation*, 2:170.

religious distinctions having been erased. The addition was an attempt to help solve the problem.[138]

21:25 The term ἡμέρας is an adverbial genitive of time, telling the kind of time during which the gates will remain unshut.[139]

21:26 The verb οἴσουσιν could be impersonal as verbs in 10:11; 12:6 are,[140] but making "the kings" from v. 24 the subject gives a better sense (Walvoord).

21:27 It is unnecessary to adopt the reading of the neuter participle ποιοῦν found in 046, 2053, and other MSS. The masculine participle ποιῶν can join with the neuter πᾶν κοινὸν because the latter refers to a person who has become unclean, even though its gender is neuter (Beckwith). The masculine has the support of Sinaiticus, Alexandrinus, and a significant number of other MSS. In addition, it is necessary to include the bracketed article ὅ before ποιῶν as original, because the reading of Alexandrinus and others that excludes it results in a syntax whose difficulty renders it impossible.

This is a case where εἰ μή has its adversative meaning of "but" rather than its exceptive sense. The whole clause εἰ μὴ οἱ γεγραμμένοι ἐν τῷ βιβλίῳ τῆς ζωῆς τοῦ ἀρνίου is an example of *brachylogy*, whereby thought moves more rapidly than expression and the words crowd together in a compressed and terse way.[141] The compression implies the words "will enter into her" (or something comparable) that are supplied in brackets at the end of the translated verse.

22:2 In John 19:18 ἐντεῦθεν ("from here") is purely adverbial, but if καὶ τοῦ ποταμοῦ begins a new sentence as discussed above, ἐντεῦθεν here would have to function as a postpositive preposition. It is a preposition in Dan. 9:5 [Theodoret], but it is not postpostive there.[142] The probability of its being a preposition here is minimal.

Alexandrinus and a few other MSS have the nominative masculine participle ποιῶν rather than the neuter ποιοῦν. Sinaiticus and a number of other MSS have the nominative masculine participle ἀποδιδοῦς instead of the neuter ἀποδιδοῦν. The neuter is the correct reading in both cases, however, to give agreement with the neuter noun ξύλον.[143]

22:5 Various MSS read the nominative φῶς in both instances of the genitive φωτός. Alexandrinus is among those supporting the geni-

138. Lee, "Revelation," 4:829; Zane C. Hodges and Arthur L. Farstad, *The Greek New Testament according to the Majority Text* (Nashville: Nelson, 1982), p. 796.
139. Robertson, *Word Pictures*, 6:477.
140. Düsterdieck, *Revelation*, p. 484; Lee, "Revelation," 4:830.
141. Beckwith, *Apocalypse*, p. 764; Robertson, *Grammar*, p. 1203.
142. Robertson, *Word Pictures*, 6:479.
143. Ibid., 6:479, 480.

tive in the latter case. The weight of external authority as well as internal probability rests on the side of retaining the genitive in both cases, however.

Later MSS omit the preposition ἐπί because of the difficulty it creates following the verb φωτίσει, but almost all the earlier ones include it, showing it to be the correct reading. Its inclusion is probably a Hebraism patterned after the construction of Ps. 118:27a which utilizes the Hebrew ל after the verb. This is the verse to which John alludes here (Charles).

23
Final Words by an Angel, John, and Jesus

E. EPILOGUE (22:6-21)

A series of exchanges between one of the angels of the seven last plagues and John and between Jesus and John mark the Epilogue. Three repeated emphases characterize these exchanges: a confirmation of the genuineness of the prophecy (vv. 6-7, 8-9, 16, 18-19), a focus on the imminence of Jesus' return (vv. 6-7, 10, 12, 20), and a warning to the unfit and an invitation to enter the city (vv. 11-12, 15, 17-19).[1]

1. TESTIMONY OF THE ANGEL (22:6-7)

Verses 6-9 provide a conclusion to the intercalation devoted to the Holy City (21:9–22:5) as well as to the whole book.[2] Verses 8-9 relate more closely to the intercalation, with vv. 6-7 bearing more upon the

---

1. James Moffatt, "The Revelation of St. John the Divine," in *Expositor's Greek Testament*, ed. W. Robertson Nicoll (Grand Rapids: Eerdmans, n.d.), 5:488; Isbon T. Beckwith, *The Apocalypse of John* (New York: Macmillan, 1919), p. 771; George E. Ladd, *A Commentary on the Revelation of John* (Grand Rapids: Eerdmans, 1972), p. 289; G. R. Beasley-Murray, *The Book of Revelation*, NCB (Grand Rapids: Eerdmans, 1978), p. 334; Robert H. Mounce, *The Book of Revelation*, NICNT (Grand Rapids: Eerdmans, 1977), p. 380; Alan F. Johnson, "Revelation," in *EBC*, ed. Frank E. Gaebelein (Grand Rapids: Zondervan, 1981), 12:601.
2. For further discussion of this dual function of 22:6-9, see Excursus 5 at the end of this volume.

whole book (Moffatt), but these foci are not mutually exclusive of each other in either part.

Translation

6And he said to me, "These words are faithful and true, and the Lord, the God of the spirits of the prophets, sent His angel to show to His slaves the things that must happen soon." 7("And behold, I will come soon. Blessed is the one who keeps the words of the prophecy of this book.")

Exegesis and Exposition

This section has much in common with Revelation 1. The prophecy comes from God Himself (22:6; cf. 1:1) and from Jesus (22:6; cf. 1:1). It deals with things that must take place soon (22:6; cf. 1:1), using an angel (22:6, 16) as a means of communication with John (22:8; cf. 1:1), the book's author (22:8; cf. 1:1, 4, 9). Its message is genuine prophecy (22:6, 7, 9, 10, 18-19; cf. 1:3) delivered through a genuinely commissioned prophet (22:8, 9, 10; cf. 1:1, 9-11). The addressees are God's slaves (22:6; cf. 1:1) who will hear it read in their churches (22:16, 18; cf. 1:3, 11). It promises special blessing for those who obey its words (22:7, 12, 14; cf. 1:3) and warns of impending retribution to the unfaithful (22:11, 12, 18-19; cf. 1:7). Its message revolves around Christ (22:16, 18, 20; cf. 1:2, 5, 9), the Alpha and the Omega, the first and the last (22:13; cf. 1:17), who is the central figure (22:12, 13, 16; cf. 1:5, 7) and is coming soon (22:7, 10, 12, 20; cf. 1:3, 7). One aspect of the Epilogue that is missing from its earlier counterpart is the yearning cry of John and the church in response to the promise of the Lord's advent (22:17, 20). The above correspondences of the Epilogue to the book's Prologue demonstrate cohesion and rationality of thought that make this work a superior literary production.

Verses 6-7 state four distinct features of this book: an angelic sanction of the book's truthfulness (v. 6a), an angelic affirmation that God as the inspirer of prophecy has revealed to His slaves things that must happen shortly (v. 6b), Christ's assurance that the central promise of the Lord's coming is about to be fulfilled (v. 7a), and Christ's beatitude regarding those who heed this book's practical admonitions (v. 7b) (Beckwith).

22:6 Verse 6 uses the terminology of 1:1 to assure the truthfulness of what has been written:[3] Καὶ εἶπέν μοι, Οὗτοι οἱ λόγοι πιστοὶ καὶ ἀληθινοί, καὶ ὁ κύριος, ὁ θεὸς τῶν πνευμάτων τῶν προφητῶν, ἀπέστειλεν

---

3. Henry Alford, *The Greek Testament* (London: Longmans, Green, 1903), 4:746.

τὸν ἄγγελον αὐτοῦ δεῖξαι τοῖς δούλοις αὐτοῦ ἃ δεῖ γενέσθαι ἐν τάχει (*Kai eipen moi, Houtoi hoi logoi pistoi kai alēthinoi, kai ho kyrios, ho theos tōn pneumatōn tōn prophētōn, apesteilen ton angelon autou deixai tois doulois autou ha dei genesthai en tachei*, "And he said to me, 'These words are faithful and true, and the Lord, the God of the spirits of the prophets, sent His angel to show to His slaves the things that must happen soon'"). Variations in the identifications of speakers throughout this Epilogue have been frequent (cf. vv. 7, 12, 14, 17, 18), the present verse being no exception. One suggestion here has been the *Angelus Interpres* who has conveyed revelations throughout (cf. 1:1; 21:5*b*).[4] Another has said this is Christ Himself because of the words of v. 6*a*.[5] The best course, however, is to see this as a continuation of the part begun in 21:9-10 by one of the angels who had the seven bowls and continued by him in 21:15.[6] This follows the pattern of the conclusion to the earlier intercalation about Babylon, delivered by a comparable angel in 19:9-10.

Yet οὗτοι οἱ λόγοι πιστοὶ καὶ ἀληθινοί (*houtoi hoi logoi pistoi kai alēthinoi*, "these words are faithful and true") is not just an endorsement of 21:9–22:5 as the similar οὗτοι οἱ λόγοι ἀληθινοὶ τοῦ θεοῦ (*houtoi ho logoi alēthinoi tou theou*, "these words are the true [ones] of God") in 19:9 are for the earlier intercalation. The reference to ἃ δεῖ γενέσθαι ἐν τάχει (*ha dei genesthai en tachei*, "the things that must happen soon") a little later in v. 6 shows that this confirmation applies to the whole book (cf. Dan. 8:26).[7] The all-inclusive scope of "these words" provides a smooth transition from the glorious vision of the new Jerusalem to the conclusion of the book (Johnson). Πιστοί (*Pistoi*, "Faithful") and ἀληθινοί (*alēthinoi*, "true") have already received attention at 19:9 and 21:5. No book in the Bible has a more pointed attestation, a stronger safeguarding against tampering, or a more urgent recommendation for study and observance than does the Apocalypse, especially in its Epilogue.[8]

---

4. William Lee, "The Revelation of St. John," in *The Holy Bible*, ed. F. C. Cook (London: John Murray, 1881), 4:837; J. P. M. Sweet, *Revelation* (Philadelphia: Westminster, Pelican, 1979), p. 314; Homer Hailey, *Revelation, an Introduction and Commentary* (Grand Rapids: Baker, 1979), p. 425.

5. R. H. Charles, *The Revelation of St. John*, ICC (New York: Scribner's Sons, 1920), 2:217.

6. Henry Barclay Swete, *The Apocalypse of St. John* (London: Macmillan, 1906), p. 302; Beckwith, *Apocalypse*, p. 772; Archibald Thomas Robertson, *Word Pictures in the New Testament* (Nashville: Broadman, 1933), 6:481; Beasley-Murray, *Revelation*, p. 334.

7. Alford, *Greek Testament*, 4:746; Swete, *Apocalypse*, p. 302; Lee, "Revelation," 4:837; Beckwith, *Apocalypse*, p. 772; Robertson, *Word Pictures*, 6:481.

8. J. A. Seiss, *The Apocalypse* (New York: Charles C. Cook, 1909), 3:449-50.

The καί (*kai*, "and") that follows *alēthinoi* is quasi-epexegetic, because the clause that follows gives the reason why "these words" are faithful and true (Swete). Words approximating the remainder of v. 6—ὁ κύριος, ὁ θεὸς τῶν πνευμάτων τῶν προφητῶν . . . (*ho kyrios, ho theos tōn pneumatōn tōn prophētōn . . .*, "the Lord, the God of the spirits of the prophets . . ."*)*—were the words of John himself in 1:1 (Beckwith), but here they are a continuation of the words of the angel-guide who continued his part at the beginning of v. 6. Terminology related to the title "the God of the spirits of the prophets" (ὁ θεὸς τῶν πνευμάτων τῶν προφητῶν [*ho theos tōn pneumatōn tōn prophētōn*]) has occurred at 19:10. "The spirits of the prophets" are their own spirits—their cognitive faculties, particularly as reflected in their teaching—subjected to God, enlightened and inspired by the Holy Spirit as 19:10 indicates (10:7; 11:18; 22:9; cf. 1 Pet. 1:10-11; 2 Pet. 1:21; contra Num. 16:22).[9] This title for God designates one from whom all the prophets, including John, received their messages (Johnson), so this is an indirect certification of John's own word as genuine (Beckwith, Ladd). John associates himself with the whole body of Christian prophets, but not in such a way as to isolate the prophetic order from the rest of the church (Swete). In 1 Cor. 14:12, 32 πνεύματα (*pneumata*) has the sense of "spiritual gifts," a sense that fits comfortably in this context too.[10]

The words ἀπέστειλεν τὸν ἄγγελον αὐτοῦ δεῖξαι τοῖς δούλοις αὐτοῦ ἃ δεῖ γενέσθαι ἐν τάχει (*apesteilen ton angelon autou deixai tois doulois autou ha dei genesthai en tachei*, "sent His angel to show to His slaves the things that must happen soon") are a direct reference to 1:1 and the purpose of the book as a whole. The special function of a revealing angel does not receive explicit mention until 17:1, but in late Jewish thought, angels were viewed as intermediaries no matter what form the revelation took.[11] Words of this sort at the book's beginning and end wrap the content of the book in "a cloak of revealed certainty."[12]

More specifically, the verbal agreement of ἃ δεῖ γενέσθαι ἐν τάχει (*ha dei genesthai en tachei*, "the things that must happen soon") with the identical expression of 1:1 shows that this verse begins the conclu-

---

9. Friedrich Düsterdieck, *Critical and Exegetical Handbook to the Revelation of John*, in Meyer's Commentary, trans. and ed. Henry E. Jacobs (New York: Funk & Wagnalls, 1887), p. 490; Alford, *Greek Testament*, 4:746; Lee, "Revelation," 4:837; Beckwith, *Apocalypse*, p. 772; Robertson, *Word Pictures*, 6:481; Philip Edgcumbe Hughes, *The Book of the Revelation* (Grand Rapids: Eerdmans, 1990), p. 236.
10. E. W. Bullinger, *The Apocalypse or "The Day of the Lord"* (London: Eyre and Spottiswoode, n.d.), p. 678; Robert L. Thomas, *Understanding Spiritual Gifts* (Chicago: Moody, 1978), pp. 129, 155, 227-28.
11. Beckwith, *Apocalypse*, p. 773; Robertson, *Word Pictures*, 6:481.
12. Robert W. Wall, *Revelation*, New International Biblical Commentary (Peabody, Mass.: Hendrickson, 1991), p. 262.

sion of the whole book (Lee). The contents of the seven-sealed scroll in chapter 5 have now been exhausted. The seventh seal, seventh trumpet, and seventh bowl have concluded, and "the mystery of God" (10:7) has reached its climax. The miseries and conflicts described in the book will begin shortly (Hailey). The problem represented by the predicted nearness of the consummation (ἐν τάχει [*en tachei*, "soon"]) was a subject of consideration in 1:1. One should not divert attention away from the imminence of these events by suggesting that God is more interested in the fulfillment of His redemptive purposes in the present than in satisfying our viewpoint on timing (contra Mounce) or by thinking of Jesus' coming as occurring at a crisis in the life of an individual—particularly his death—or at a time when the state makes totalitarian demands that a Christian cannot follow (contra Ladd and Mounce). It is also wrong to state that imminence is a moral rather than a chronological Christian doctrine.[13] To be sure, it carries a moral mandate with it, but the fact that God has not furnished an infallible timetable for Christ's return should not eliminate the attitude of urgent expectation that has characterized the church throughout the centuries of her history (Mounce).

22:7 The sudden change in speakers reflected in the content of v. 7 marks the verse as parenthetical: καὶ ἰδοὺ ἔρχομαι ταχύ. μακάριος ὁ τηρῶν τοὺς λόγους τῆς προφητείας τοῦ βιβλίου τούτου (*kai idou erchomai tachy. makarios ho tērōn tous logous tēs prophēteias tou bibliou toutou*, "and behold, I will come soon. Blessed is the one who keeps the words of the prophecy of this book"). These words, perhaps reported by the angel, are nonetheless the words of Christ (cf. 11:3; 22:12) (Alford, Bullinger). With great similarity to 16:15, this is a case where the Lord speaks directly, the way the prophets sometimes injected utterances of God without the customary "says the LORD" (e.g., Isa. 16:10[end]; 61:8; cf. Rev. 1:8) (Swete, Beckwith).

Christ is undoubtedly the speaker of the words καὶ ἰδοὺ ἔρχομαι ταχύ (*idou erchomai tachy*, "behold, I will come soon"). He also speaks about His imminent coming without introduction in 22:12, 20. Very similar references to this coming are in 2:5, 16; 3:11; 16:15,[14] with still other mentions of an indirect sort in 1:1; 2:25; 3:3, 20. Reconstructionism (or, dominion theology) refers this imminence to the fall of Jerusalem in A.D. 70,[15] but to do this is totally without exegetical merit. The

---

13. F. F. Bruce, "The Revelation to John," in *A New Testament Commentary*, ed. G. C. D. Howley (Grand Rapids: Zondervan, 1969), p. 665.
14. Düsterdieck, *Revelation*, p. 490; Robertson, *Word Pictures*, 6:482.
15. David Chilton, *The Days of Vengeance* (Fort Worth, Tex.: Dominion, 1987), p. 575; Kenneth L. Gentry, Jr., *Before Jerusalem Fell* (Tyler, Tex.: Institute for Christian Economics, 1989), pp. 142-45.

imminence pertains to the personal advent of Jesus Christ that is still future. Ταχύ (*Tachy*, "Soon") has the same force as ἐν τάχει (*en tachei*, "soon") in v. 6. Immediacy was John's preoccupation. His message was and is one of life and death.[16]

Jesus continues by pronouncing a beatitude as He did in the parenthesis of 16:5: μακάριος ὁ τηρῶν τοὺς λόγους τῆς προφητείας τοῦ βιβλίου τούτου (*makarios ho tērōn tous logous tēs prophēteias tou bibliou toutou*, "blessed is the one who keeps the words of the prophecy of this book"). In substance this beatitude is very close to the one in 1:3, except here the singular replaces the plural of that earlier one.[17] Some think it more appropriate to attribute this beatitude to John, since he wrote the earlier one and it is somewhat inappropriate for the Lord from heaven to speak of "this book" when it lies before John on earth (Beckwith, Ladd). The parallel to 16:15 and the presence of the Lord beside the prophet as represented in chapter 1 make it preferable to have Christ as the speaker here, however.

John can now add the words τοῦ βιβλίου τούτου (*tou bibliou toutou*, "of this book [or scroll]") to what he wrote in the beatitude of 1:3, because he now has before him the all-but-completed scroll that he has written in obedience to the commands to write in 1:11, 19 (Alford, Lee). John has represented himself as writing his impressions as his visions have transpired (cf. 10:4) (Swete). This confirms that methodology of compiling the work. Verses 10, 18, 19 of this chapter (cf. 1:3) also define the nature of the work as "prophecy" (προφητείας [*prophēteias*]). The total expression τοὺς λόγους τῆς προφητείας τοῦ βιβλίου τούτου (*tous logous tēs prophēteias tou bibliou toutou*, "the words of the prophecy of this book") occurs again in vv. 10, 18, with the expression of v. 19 reversing the positions of τῆς προφητείας (*tēs prophēteias*, "of the prophecy") and τοῦ βιβλίου (*tou bibliou*, "of the book"). This beatitude reflects as well as anything the distinctly practical purpose of Revelation.

2. THE TESTIMONY OF JOHN (22:8-11)

Translation

8And I John am the one who heard and saw these things. And when I heard and saw them, I fell to worship before the feet of the angel who showed me these things. 9And he says to me, "See that

---

16. Martin Kiddle, *The Revelation of St. John*, HNTC (New York: Harper, 1940), p. 451.
17. Swete, *Apocalypse*, p. 303; Charles, *Revelation*, 2:218; Robertson, *Word Pictures*, 6:482; Walter Scott, *Exposition of the Revelation of Jesus Christ* (Swengel, Pa.: Bible Truth Depot, n.d.), p. 444.

you do not [do this]; I am the fellow-slave of you and of your brethren the prophets and of those who keep the words of this book; worship God." [10]And he says to me, "Do not seal up the words of the prophecy of this book, for the time is near. [11]Let the one who does wrong do wrong still, and let the filthy one be filthy still, and let the righteous one do righteousness still, and let the holy one be holy still."

Exegesis and Exposition

The next section records John's response to and dialogue with the angel at the conclusion of his overpowering visional experience.

22:8 John resumes the speaker's role for the first time since chapter 1 where he named himself three times (1:1, 4, 9): Κἀγὼ Ἰωάννης ὁ ἀκούων καὶ βλέπων ταῦτα. καὶ ὅτε ἤκουσα καὶ ἔβλεψα, ἔπεσα προσκυνῆσαι ἔμπροσθεν τῶν ποδῶν τοῦ ἀγγέλου τοῦ δεικνύοντός μοι ταῦτα (*Kagō Iōannēs ho akouōn kai blepōn tauta. kai hote ēkousa kai eblepsa, epesa proskynēsai emprosthen tōn podōn tou angelou tou deiknyontos moi tauta*, "And I John am the one who heard and saw these things. And when I heard and saw them, I fell to worship before the feet of the angel who showed me these things"). The writer adds his human guarantee to the superhuman words of authentication scattered through vv. 6-17 (Beckwith). This recalls a similar technique utilized by Daniel in his prophecy (Dan. 12:5; cf. Dan. 8:15) (Charles). Without using his name, John provides a similar authentication in his earlier description of the crucifixion (John 19:35). "I John" is the same two-word designation as occurs in 1:9.

The two participles ἀκούων καὶ βλέπων (*akouōn kai blepōn*, "heard and saw") reflect the two avenues through which he received his prophetic revelation—the ears and the eyes. This too is reminiscent of the emphasis on hearing and seeing by the same author in 1 John 1:1-3; 4:14 (cf. John 1:14; 19:35; 21:14). God has spoken and shown to the prophet in his state of prophetic trance all the things recorded between 4:1 and 22:5.[18] The use of such an autobiographical assertion (cf. Rom. 16:22; 1 Cor. 16:21; Gal. 6:11; Col. 4:18; 2 Thess. 3:17; Philem. 19) indicates the author's endorsement of what he has written and his opinion that it is true and useful.[19]

The antecedent of ταῦτα (*tauta*, "these things") is more specifically what he has just seen in the vision of the Holy City just concluded.[20] Now he *hears* the personal promise of Jesus' imminent return (v. 7a)

---

18. Düsterdieck, *Revelation*, p. 490; Lee, "Revelation," 4:838; Chilton, *Days of Vengeance*, p. 575.
19. Wall, *Revelation*, p. 263.
20. Hughes, *Revelation*, p. 236.

and *sees* the angel-guide whose apparel resembles that of Christ (cf. 1:13; 15:6). This may be what led to his confusion a second time in offering worship to the angel (21:8*b*; cf. 19:10). After all, he has already fallen at the feet of the glorified Christ once at the beginning of his visional experience without being reprimanded (1:17).

The description of John's response here—ἔπεσα προσκυνῆσαι ἔμπροσθεν τῶν ποδῶν τοῦ ἀγγέλου (*epesa proskynēsai emprosthen tōn podōn tou angelou*, "I fell to worship before the feet of the angel")—is in almost the same words as in 19:10. This time, it is not just the description of something monumental like a great city, but the vast scope and deep significance of his total prophetic experience on Patmos has overwhelmed him. Perhaps the brief word from Christ in 22:7 added to the impact of the occasion and created the lapse that led him to offer worship to the angel. Perhaps he thought he was worshiping Christ.[21] John's response apparently came immediately after the culmination of the vision of the glory of the new Jerusalem: the angel announces the vision's end in v. 6 with John bowing immediately thereafter (Beckwith). This was the sequence in 19:9-10. It only entails understanding the parenthetical nature of vv. 7-8*a* to have that sequence here.

The participial clause τοῦ δεικνύοντός μοι ταῦτα (*tou deiknyontos moi tauta*, "who showed me these things") identifies the angel to whom John offered the worship. It was the same one whose special task was to elaborate regarding the new Jerusalem (cf. 21:9, 10; 22:1, 6).

22:9 At v. 9 the same angel resumes the speaker's role in response to John's action: καὶ λέγει μοι, ῞Ορα μή· σύνδουλός σού εἰμι καὶ τῶν ἀδελφῶν σου τῶν προφητῶν καὶ τῶν τηρούντων τοὺς λόγους τοῦ βιβλίου τούτου· τῷ θεῷ προσκύνησον (*kai legei moi, Hora mē; syndoulos sou eimi kai tōn adelphōn sou tōn prophētōn kai tōn tērountōn tous logous tou bibliou toutou; tō theō proskynēson*, "and he says to me, 'See that you do not [do this]; I am the fellow-slave of you and of your brethren the prophets and of those who keep the words of this book; worship God'"). The words καὶ λέγει μοι (*kai legei moi*, "and he says to me") indicate the angel's resumption of the speaker's role. One of the angels who had the seven bowls, perhaps the same one as here, earlier issued the same corrective to John as here: ῞Ορα μή (*hora mē*, "see that you do not [do this]," 19:10).

He also follows the corrective with σύνδουλός σού εἰμι (*syndoulos sou eimi*, "I am the fellow-slave of you"), words that exalted especially John's prophetic office in 19:10. But here they exalt the prophetic office in general because of the addition of καὶ τῶν ἀδελφῶν σου τῶν

---

21. Düsterdieck, *Revelation*, p. 490; Seiss, *Apocalypse*, 3:455; Kiddle, *Revelation*, p. 448.

προφητῶν (*kai tōn adelphōn sou tōn prophētōn,* "and of your brethren the prophets"), an addition that differs slightly from the wording of 19:10 which has no explicit reference to other prophets.

A further extension adds a third group whom the angel joins as a fellow-slave, καὶ τῶν τηρούντων τοὺς λόγους τοῦ βιβλίου τούτοῦ (*kai tōn tērountōn tous logous tou bibliou toutou,* "and of those who keep the words of this book"). This makes a distinction between John's brethren who were prophets and his brethren who were not prophets but who keep the words of this book. The prophets are those with the special gift of prophecy, and the rest of the faithful compose the second group of brethren. This distinction between brethren has the effect of exalting the authority of John the prophet and consequently of this book which he is currently bringing to its conclusion (Lee, Beckwith, Beasley-Murray).

The angel's further command, τῷ θεῷ προσκύνησον (*tō theō pros-kynēson,* "worship God"), is a repetition from 19:10 also. The bewildered prophet for the moment has lost his bearings, and needs this reminder of something that he already knew quite well (cf. John 4:21-24).

22:10 The words καὶ λέγει μοι (*kai legei moi,* "and he says to me") indicate another continuation of the angel's speech: καὶ λέγει μοι, Μὴ σφραγίσῃς τοὺς λόγους τῆς προφητείας τοῦ βιβλίου τούτου, ὁ καιρὸς γὰρ ἐγγύς ἐστιν (*kai legei moi, Mē sphragisēs tous logous tēs prophēteias tou bibliou toutou, ho kairos gar engys estin,* "and he says to me, 'Do not seal up the words of the prophecy of this book, for the time is near'"). The combination does not indicate a resumption of Christ's speech (contra Charles). Rather the repetition of the introductory formula from v. 9 indicates the importance of what the angel has to say, as does a comparable repetition in 19:9.

It is vital for the scroll (or book) to remain open for all to read and not to be sealed up as John was commanded to do in 10:4.[22] The commands to Daniel were to seal up his book (Dan. 8:26; 12:4, 9-10), but John's Apocalypse is to meet an immediate crisis facing the churches as the seven messengers disseminated its contents to them. Other apocalypses, usually written in the name of some saint of old, did the same as Daniel by looking away to a distant fulfillment (e.g., *1 Enoch* 1.2). This is another feature that distinguishes Revelation from other apocalypses (Moffatt, Beasley-Murray, Johnson).

For John to publish what he had written follows through with the earlier command to send the written work to the seven churches (1:11). The availability of the volume to people in the churches would

---

22. Robertson, *Word Pictures,* 6:483.

enable them to read and hear its contents (1:3; 22:7) and to study its mysteries (13:18; 17:9). The angel heartily encourages these steps in communicating "the things that must happen soon" and the course of Christian behavior dictated by this urgency.

Lest anyone forget just how urgent the situation is, the angel repeats John's exact words from 1:3 with the addition of the copula ἐστιν (*estin*, "is"): ὁ καιρὸς γὰρ ἐγγύς ἐστιν (*ho kairos gar engys estin*, "for the time is near"). This is the exact opposite situation from that facing Daniel where the fulfillment was to come "many days [in the future]" (Dan. 8:26) (Alford).

22:11 The absence of a connective word to begin v. 11 heightens the urgent tone of the angel's words: ὁ ἀδικῶν ἀδικησάτω ἔτι, καὶ ὁ ῥυπαρὸς ῥυπανθήτω ἔτι, καὶ ὁ δίκαιος δικαιοσύνην ποιησάτω ἔτι, καὶ ὁ ἅγιος ἁγιασθήτω ἔτι (*ho adikōn adikēsato eti; kai ho hryparos hrypanthētō eti, kai ho dikaios dikaiosynēn poēsatō eti, kai ho hagios hagiasthētō eti*, "let the one who does wrong do wrong still, and let the filthy one be filthy still, and let the righteous one do righteousness still, and let the holy one be holy still"). The implied connection with v. 10 is that of cause and effect: "the time is short, so let people go their own way." This is another way of expressing the hopelessness of the final state of the wicked.[23]

Here is indirectly the formulation of a powerful warning against putting off one's decision to become a faithful follower of the Lamb. The time remaining is short, and once it is up, no more opportunity to change remains. Because of the imminence of Jesus' coming to initiate the events of this book, the response of a person to its message may very well be the decision that will carry him to his eternal state, whatever that may be (Johnson).

Throughout the career of the book after publication, however long that may be until its fulfillment, a persistence in evil or in good is all that is expected from the recipients. The angel anticipates no widespread change during the time lapse before the end (Moffatt). So the wise will respond with faithfulness and live their lives in readiness for Jesus' coming.[24] All four parts of v. 11 indicate with a tone of irony the fixity of state in which the good and the evil find themselves at a time when no further opportunity for repentance remains. The lesson is, "Change while there is time."[25]

Yet the imperatives of v. 11 are imperatives of permission, not

---

23. Bullinger, *Apocalypse*, p. 681; Robertson, *Word Pictures*, 6:483.
24. Hughes, *Revelation*, p. 237.
25. Düsterdieck, *Revelation*, p. 491; Alford, *Greek Testament*, 4:747; Swete, *Apocalypse*, p. 305; Lee, "Revelation," 4:839; Beckwith, *Apocalypse*, p. 775; Michael Wilcock, *The Message of Revelation*, ed. John R. W. Stott (Downers Grove, Ill.: InterVarsity, 1975), p. 216; Sweet, *Revelation*, p. 314.

imperatives of command.[26] The English language would term this usage the "let" of withdrawal instead of the "let" of positive exhortation.[27] It is a frightening prospect that at a given point, a considerable part of humanity will be left alone to reap the consequences of choosing the wrong lifestyle and consequently reaping divine contempt. The verse does not teach some kind of religious determinism that makes repentance and conversion impossible for some people (Beasley-Murray). The invitation of 22:17 makes clear that an opportunity for the right choice remains.[28] The teaching is simply that once a person makes that choice, he has sealed his eternal destiny for better or for worse.

The first individual singled out is "the one who does wrong" (ὁ ἀδικῶν [*ho adikōn*]). He has permission to keep on doing so "still" (ἔτι [*eti*]). He has sealed his own destiny by his personal choice, so he must continue in that state. The adverb *eti* in each of its four uses in v. 11 depicts the permanence of his character, condition, and destiny, but not necessarily an increase in the degree of his wrongdoing (Beckwith, Hailey).

The description of the second type builds on the word-group derived from ῥύπος (*hrypos*, "filth") (cf. 1 Pet. 3:21). Though commanded to put aside such moral pollution (James 1:21; cf. Zech. 3:4-5), some will cling to it. The verb ῥυπανθήτω (*hrypanthētō*, "let [him] be filthy") is passive in form, but has more of a middle force in this setting: "let the filthy one pollute himself still." The consequent state depends on the person's own choice (Alford, Lee).

The other side of the picture is that the righteous one will be marked by a continued practice of righteousness and the holy one by a continuation of being made holy. Like the state of evil, the state of good remains fixed after a person makes that all-important choice. The angel anticipates no second chance beyond the point marked by the events revealed to John in this series of visions.[29] The separate mentions of righteousness and holiness do not imply that the two can exist separately from one another. Their separate mention is just to provide a balance with the two opposite qualities depicted in *ho adikōn* and *ho hryparos* (Swete).

Additional Notes

22:11 The expression δικαιοσύνην ποιησάτω is the form of speech used by this same author in his first epistle (1 John 2:29; 3:7) (Lee).

---

26. H. E. Dana and Julius R. Mantey, *A Manual Grammar of the Greek New Testament* (New York: Macmillan, 1927), p. 176.
27. William Hendriksen, *More Than Conquerors* (Grand Rapids: Baker, 1944), pp. 251-52.
28. Wall, *Revelation*, pp. 264-65.
29. Robertson, *Word Pictures*, 6:483.

3. THE TESTIMONY OF JESUS AND JOHN'S RESPONSE (22:12-20)

Translation

¹²"Behold, I will come soon, and My reward is with Me, to give back to each one as his work is. ¹³I am the Alpha and the Omega, the first and the last, the beginning and the end. ¹⁴Blessed are those who wash their robes, that their authority may be over the tree of life and they may enter the gates into the city. ¹⁵Outside will be the dogs and the sorcerers and the fornicators and the murderers and the idolaters and everyone who loves and does a lie. ¹⁶I Jesus sent My angel to testify to you these things for the churches. I am the root and offspring of David, the bright morning star. ¹⁷And the Spirit and the bride say, 'Come.' And let the one who hears say, 'Come.' And let the one who thirsts come, let the one who desires take the water of life freely. ¹⁸I testify to everyone who hears the words of the prophecy of this book: if anyone adds to them, God will add to him the plagues which are written in this book; ¹⁹and if anyone takes away from the words of the book of this prophecy, God will take away his part from the tree of life and out of the holy city, which are written in this book."

²⁰The one who testifies these things says, "Yes, I will come soon." Amen, come, Lord Jesus.

Exegesis and Exposition

The substance of the statement in v. 12 reflects that Christ has suddenly begun speaking (Swete). This resembles the words introduced parenthetically at v. 7, but this time He apparently continues to speak through the end of v. 19.

22:12 An asyndeton beginning v. 12 emphasizes the fixity of spiritual states just outlined in v. 11. The verse dwells on the fact that the two possible outcomes in v. 11 depend on what a man has done in this present life:[30] Ἰδοὺ ἔρχομαι ταχύ, καὶ ὁ μισθός μου μετ' ἐμοῦ, ἀποδοῦναι ἑκάστῳ ὡς τὸ ἔργον ἐστὶν αὐτοῦ (*Idou erchomai tachy, kai ho misthos mou met' emou, apodounai hekastō hōs to ergon estin autou*, "Behold, I will come soon, and My reward is with Me, to give back to each one as his work is"). As He has just done in v. 7, Jesus promises His impending return in the words Ἰδοὺ ἔρχομαι ταχύ (*idou erchomai tachy*, "behold, I will come soon").

This time, however, instead of promising a blessing as He did in v. 7 (cf. 16:5 also), He promises a judgment that will differentiate between the evil and the righteous (Beasley-Murray). He is coming as a

---

30. Wilcock, *Revelation*, p. 216.

rewarder in both a positive and a negative sense. When He uses μου (*mou*, "My"), He does so with the idea of "the reward that it belongs to Me to give" (cf. 2 Tim. 4:8; Heb. 11:6) (Swete). The allusion of ὁ μισθός μου μετ᾽ ἐμοῦ (*ho misthos mou met᾽ emou*, "My reward is with Me") is to Isa. 40:10; 62:11.

The infinitival clause ἀποδοῦναι ἑκάστῳ ὡς τὸ ἔργον ἐστὶν αὐτοῦ (*apodounai hekastō hōs to ergon estin autou*, "to give back to each one as his work is") possibly expresses the purpose of His coming, but it is more likely that it is intended as a further definition of ὁ μισθός (*ho misthos*, "the reward") that comes after the promise of His coming. The thought is that the rightness or wrongness of the work will determine the nature of the reward (cf. 2:23; 2 Cor. 5:10; Rom. 2:26).[31] As noted already at 20:13, works are consistently the basis for future divine judgment. Here, however, the singular *ergon* views an entire lifetime as one continuous "work" (cf. the singular in 1 Cor. 3:12-15) (Lee). The adjective ἑκάστῳ (*hekastō*, "to each one") sounds the note of individual responsibility heard often in this book (2:23; 6:11; 20:13) (Swete).

22:13 The three titles Christ appropriates for Himself in v. 13 offer solemn assurance of His qualifications to reward each person: ἐγὼ τὸ Ἄλφα καὶ τὸ Ὦ, ὁ πρῶτος καὶ ὁ ἔσχατος, ἡ ἀρχὴ καὶ τὸ τέλος (*egō to Alpha kai to ⁻O, ho prōtos kai ho eschatos, hē archē kai to telos*, "I am the Alpha and the Omega, the first and the last, the beginning and the end"). They are the crowning attribution of divine prerogatives to the Son.

The first of the three, ἐγὼ τὸ Ἄλφα καὶ τὸ Ὦ (*egō to Alpha kai to ⁻O*, "I am the Alpha and the Omega"), is a title for God the Father in 1:8; 21:6.[32] Its symbolic force is, "I am He from whom all being has proceeded and to whom it will return" (Lee).

The second title, ὁ πρῶτος καὶ ὁ ἔσχατος (*ho prōtos kai ho eschatos*, "the first and the last"), applies only to Christ in this book (1:17; 2:8), but in Isa. 44:6; 48:12 it refers to the LORD (יהוה [*YHWH*]). Its symbolic meaning is, "I am the primal cause and the final aim of all history" (Lee).

The title ἡ ἀρχὴ καὶ τὸ τέλος (*hē archē kai to telos*, "the beginning and the end") applies to the Father in 21:6. A similar description of Christ is in Heb. 12:2: ὁ ἀρχηγὸς καὶ τελειωτὴς τῆς πίστεως (*ho archēgos kai teleiōtēs tēs pisteōs*, "the author and finisher of our faith"). What the Lord starts, He also finishes (Phil. 1:6).[33] This title has more of a

---

31. Alford, *Greek Testament*, 4:747; Robertson, *Word Pictures*, 6:484.
32. Swete, *Apocalypse*, p. 307; Robertson, *Word Pictures*, 6:484; Wall, *Revelation*, p. 265.
33. Hughes, *Revelation*, p. 238.

philosophical ring to it in conveying the essence, "I am the one who has created the world and who will perfect it" (Lee).

22:14 Following the appropriation of the three titles to Himself, Jesus pronounces the seventh and last beatitude of the book (cf. 1:3; 14:13; 16:15; 19:9; 20:6; 22:7): Μακάριοι οἱ πλύνοντες τὰς στολὰς αὐτῶν,* ἵνα ἔσται ἡ ἐξουσία αὐτῶν ἐπὶ τὸ ξύλον τῆς ζωῆς καὶ τοῖς πυλῶσιν εἰσέλθωσιν εἰς τὴν πόλιν (*Makarioi hoi plynontes tas stolas autōn, hina estai hē exousia autōn epi to xylon tēs zōēs kai tois pylōsin eiselthōsin eis tēn polin*, "Blessed are those who wash their robes, that their authority may be over the tree of life and they may enter the gates into the city"). Jesus is the one who pronounces the beatitudes at 16:15 and 22:6 too. John himself gives the beatitudes at 1:3 and 20:6. At 14:13 the beatitude comes from a heavenly voice, and the one at 19:9 is from one of the angels who have the seven bowls. The blessings of this book come from a variety of sources, all of them authoritative.

This final blessing deals with the ultimate issues of life—access to the Tree of Life (22:2) and entrance to the Holy City (21:25). The blessed ones are those "who wash their robes" (οἱ πλύνοντες τὰς στολὰς αὐτῶν [*hoi plynontes tas stolas autōn*]) in order to gain these supreme privileges. The allusion is to the heavenly multitude who in 7:14 have washed their robes and made them white in the blood of the Lamb. The need for this cleansing comes when people defile the spiritual apparel through sin, like most of the church of Sardis as cited in 3:4. These described in this beatitude have repented and clothed themselves in the pure white linen that stands for the righteous deeds of the saints (cf. 19:8) (Kiddle). They are all the believers in Christ, not just the martyrs as sometimes contended.[34]

The "authority . . . over" (ἐξουσία . . . ἐπὶ [*exousia . . . epi*]) the Tree of Life is presumably the authority to eat the fruit of the tree (Lee, Beckwith). The overcomer in the church of Ephesus receives a similar promise in 2:7. The sequence of placing authority over the Tree of Life before access through the gates of the city has seemed illogical to some, i.e., an apocalyptic way of thinking (e.g., Ladd), but this is not faulty logic. It is a case of referencing the greater privilege first because it includes all others, including entrance to the city. The suggestion that partaking of the Tree of Life pertains to the citizens within the city and entrance through the city's gates relates to the nations, is also faulty. Both are relevant to all believers: authority over the Tree of Life

---

34. Beasley-Murray, *Revelation*, p. 340; contra G. V. Caird, *A Commentary on the Revelation of St. John the Divine*, HNTC (New York: Harper & Row, 1966), p. 285

and access to the way that leads to it (Lee). The latter promise resembles that to the church of Philadelphia in 3:12.[35]

22:15 The opposite of the blessing promised in v. 14 is denial of access to the city: ἔξω οἱ κύνες καὶ οἱ φάρμακοι καὶ οἱ πόρνοι καὶ οἱ φονεῖς καὶ οἱ εἰδωλολάτραι καὶ πᾶς φιλῶν καὶ ποιῶν ψεῦδος (*exō hoi kynes kai hoi pharmakoi kai hoi pornoi kai hoi phoneis kai hoi eidōlolatrai kai pas philōn kai poiōn pseudos*, "outside will be the dogs and the sorcerers and the fornicators and the murderers and the idolaters and everyone who loves and does a lie"). Jesus continues His proclamation regarding eternal destiny by focusing on those who fail to qualify because they have never washed their robes. The adverb ἔξω (*exō*) refers to the position of those who are "outside" the wall of the city mentioned at the end of v. 14 (Mounce). To be outside the Holy City means a final destiny in the lake of fire (20:15; 21:8) (Beasley-Murray; Johnson). The abruptness caused by the lack of a conjunction to begin v. 15 adds emphasis to the horror of this future estate.

The verbal action implied in v. 15 is an implied future tense of εἰμί (*eimi*, "I am") because of the future frame of reference of v. 14. The city is not a reference to the present historical church (contra Caird), but to the new heaven and the new earth. The verse is not a command—"out, you dogs"—for the rebels to leave the city. This would have required an expressed verb. Such people could never have gained access to the city in the first place, because they are totally distinct from the new heaven and the new earth. They cannot be commanded to leave, since they are already outside (Swete, Beckwith).

"The dogs" (Οἱ κύνες [*Hoi kynes*]) is a metaphor for the morally impure as it is throughout Scripture. They represent male prostitutes (Deut. 23:18), Gentiles (Matt. 15:26), and Judaizers (Phil. 3:2-3), among other things (cf. 2 Kings 8:13; Ps. 22:16, 20; Isa. 56:10; Matt. 7:6; Mark 7:27). In the Orient dogs are scavengers and are objects of great contempt.[36] In this verse they are perhaps not just impure persons, but the impudently impure, those addicted to unnatural vices. This would account for their coming first in the list of other categories of sinners (Moffatt, Kiddle). "The dogs" replace the "abominable" in the list of 21:8. These are people contaminated through long contact with the base vices that permeated a pagan society (Swete). This promised fate certainly served as a warning to people in the churches not to fall into apostasy with its associated vices.[37]

---

35. Sweet, *Revelation*, p. 317.
36. Robertson, *Word Pictures*, 6:485; Johnson, "Revelation," 12:602.
37. Wall, *Revelation*, p. 266.

"The sorcerers" (Οἱ φάρμακοι [*Hoi pharmakoi*]) along with "the fornicators" (οἱ πόρνοι [*oi pornoi*]), "the murderers" (οἱ φονεῖς [*hoi phoneis*]), and "the idolaters" (οἱ εἰδωλολάτραι [*hoi eidōlolatrai*]) appear in the list of 21:8. Here they are "outside" the city; there they are "in the lake that burns with fire and brimstone, the second death." Both expressions reflect their presence in the place of eternal punishment and their eternal denial of fellowship with God. Jesus used the expression "outer darkness"—i.e., outside the lighted house—to speak of the abode of the condemned (Matt. 8:12; 22:13; 25:30). Another figure He used was that of a worm that does not die (Mark 9:48; cf. Isa. 66:24).[38] John's other references to these four vices come throughout the book—sorcery (9:21; 18:23; 21:8), fornication (2:14, 20, 21; 9:21; 14:8; 17:2, 4; 18:3, 9; 19:2; 21:8), murder (9:21; 21:8), and idolatry (2:14, 20; 9:21; 21:8).[39]

The phrase πᾶς φιλῶν καὶ ποιῶν ψεῦδος (*pas philōn kai poiōn pseudos*, "everyone who loves and does a lie") is an elaboration of πᾶσιν τοῖς ψευδέσιν (*pasin tois pseudesin*, "all liars") in 21:8 and of ποιῶν . . . ψεῦδος (*poiōn . . . pseudos*, "every liar") in 21:27. Satan is the father of lying (John 8:44), so his eternal home is a congenial place for those who love and practice lying (cf. 2 Thess. 2:12). The verb ποιέω (*poieō*, "I do") refers to not "doing" the truth in 1 John 1:6 and to "doing the truth" in John 3:21 (cf. Rom. 1:25; Eph. 4:25).[40] A proclivity toward falsehood appears earlier in this book several times (2:2; 3:9; contra 14:4). "Loving . . . a lie" (φιλῶν . . . ψεῦδος [*philōn . . . pseudos*]) is deeper than "doing" a lie, however. The person who loves falsehood has by that love demonstrated his kinship to it and his affinity to the false Christ and to Satan (Swete, Beasley-Murray).

22:16 Using a combination—"I Jesus"—found nowhere else in the NT, Jesus changes the subject to speak of His role in producing this book: Ἐγὼ Ἰησοῦς ἔπεμψα τὸν ἄγγελόν μου μαρτυρῆσαι ὑμῖν ταῦτα ἐπὶ ταῖς ἐκκλησίαις. ἐγώ εἰμι ἡ ῥίζα καὶ τὸ γένος Δαυίδ, ὁ ἀστὴρ ὁ λαμπρὸς ὁ πρωϊνός (*Egō Iēsous epempsa ton angelon mou martyrēsai hymin tauta epi tais ekklēsiais. egō eimi hē hriza kai to genos Dauid, ho astēr ho lampros ho prōinos*, "I Jesus sent My angel to testify to you these things for the churches. I am the root and offspring of David, the bright morning star"). The emphatic self-designation Ἐγὼ Ἰησοῦς (*Egō Iēsous*, "I Jesus") serves to put special attention on this, the last and most solemn attestation to His part in revealing the contents of the Apocalypse (cf. vv. 7, 12). The speaker is the historic Jesus—known

38. Robertson, *Word Pictures*, 6:485.
39. M. Robert Mulholland, *Revelation, Holy Living in an Unholy World* (Grand Rapids: Zondervan, 1990), p. 338 n. 4.
40. Robertson, *Word Pictures*, 6:485.

only to a few persons remaining alive since His earthly ministry—who is also the Christ of theology, the risen Christ, and the Lamb of God.[41] This, the only time in the book when the Lord calls Himself by his personal name, is to demonstrate that the book is not the product of an individual fancy (cf. 1 Pet. 1:21) (Moffatt). Such a personal word from the Lord bolsters John's case in the face of the strongly competitive atmosphere among prophets and professing prophets that prevailed in the churches of Asia at the time (e.g. 2:2, 20-21).

The verb ἔπεμψα (*epempsa*, "sent") is the same word as is used in John 20:21 for Jesus' sending of the apostles to represent Him. In that verse it appears alongside ἀποστέλλω (*apostellō*, "I send") which carries the added idea of being sent with a special commission, in that case the accomplished mission of Christ.[42] Here *epempsa* is a continuation of the ἀποστείλας (*aposteilas*, "sending") of Rev. 1:1 (cf. 22:6). It is enough to note who the sender is without the accessory connotation conveyed by *apostellō*.

"My angel" (Τὸν ἄγγελόν μου [*Ton angelon mou*]) is the same as "His angel" (τὸν ἄγγελον αὐτοῦ [*ton angelon autou*]) in 22:6. What God does, Jesus does also (Beasley-Murray). The plural number of ὑμῖν (*hymin*, "to you") recalls that John is not the sole beneficiary of the revelation (cf. 1:1). The ultimate objects were people in the seven churches who received these words through seven messengers who received them from John. This plural pronoun along with the τοῖς δούλοις αὐτοῦ (*tois doulois autou*, "His slaves") of 22:6 could imply that the book contains visions granted to some of the other prophets in the churches of Asia (Beckwith), but this is impossible in light of John's claim in 22:8 to be the sole instrument through whom the revelation came (Moffatt). The antecedent of ταῦτα (*tauta*, "these things") refers to the contents of the whole book, i.e., "things that must happen soon."[43]

A slight distinction between *hymin* and ταῖς ἐκκλησίαις (*tais ekklēsiais*, "the churches") is probable. The former term refers to people in the seven churches and the latter to the churches in general (Beasley-Murray). The latter is probably not limited to the seven churches in Asia, but since these seven are representatives of others, it may be John's way of referring to the church as a whole. Revelation never uses the singular *hē ekklēsia* to refer to the whole church as a unit the way Paul does. To do that, John uses the figure of the wife or the bride (19:7-8) (Swete). So this probably generalizes the destination of the Apocalypse both geographically and chronologically. What John

---

41. Ibid.; Hughes, *Revelation*, p. 239.
42. Edwin A. Abbott, *Johannine Vocabulary* (London: Adam and Charles Black, 1905), pp. 226-27.

wrote was for the seven churches in Asia then (1:4), but has come to be for the churches of the whole world, then and now.[44]

Jesus ties His claim to authority in revelation to His claim to Messiahship and His right to inaugurate the kingdom promised to David: ἐγώ εἰμι ἡ ῥίζα καὶ τὸ γένος Δαυίδ, ὁ ἀστὴρ ὁ λαμπρὸς ὁ πρωϊνός (*egō eimi hē hriza kai to genos Dauid, ho astēr ho lampros ho prōinos*, "I am the root and offspring of David, the bright morning star"). The pronoun *egō* is once again emphatic, being added to the first person singular subject of the verb εἰμί (*eimi*, "I am"). As David founded the first Jerusalem, Jesus will be founder of the new Jerusalem (cf. 2 Sam. 7:12-16; Ps. 132:11; Isa. 11:1, 10; Jer. 23:5; 33:15-16; Ezek. 34:23; 37:24-25; Hos. 3:5; Amos 9:11; Zech. 3:8; 6:12; Rom. 15:12) (Moffatt, Caird, Hailey). Revelation has mentioned "the root of David" earlier (5:5), but τὸ γένος (*to genos*) in the sense of "the offspring" (cf. Acts 17:28-29) is an addition here (cf. Matt. 22:42-25).[45] The allusion is to Isa. 11:1 where, contrary to the use of ἡ ῥίζα (*hē hriza*, "the root") here, the Messiah is a descendent of David rather than David's ancestor (Beasley-Murray, Johnson). Jesus is both the ancestor (*hē hriza*) and the descendant (*to genos*) of David, the beginning and the end of the economy associated with David.[46] Consequently, He fulfills all the Messianic promises associated with David's family (Charles). Numbers 24:17 and Luke 1:78 refer to the Davidic king as a star in this fashion (cf. 2 Pet. 1:19; *Test. Lev.* 18:3).

In this role He satisfies the promise to the Thyatiran overcomer (2:28). This is Christ's interpretation of His own earlier utterance where He calls himself "the morning star," but here He features the characteristic brightness of that star (ὁ λαμπρὸς [*ho lampros*, "bright"]). As the bright morning star, He is explicitly the brightest star in the whole galaxy.[47] He is the one whose return will remove the cold and dark hour before the sunrise and bring in the perfect day of God (Moffatt, Beckwith).

---

43. Hughes, *Revelation*, p. 239.
44. Beckwith, *Apocalypse*, p. 777; Robertson, *Word Pictures*, 6:485. David E. Aune ("The Prophetic Circle of John of Patmos and the Exegesis of Revelation 22.16," *JSNT* 37 [1989]: 103-16) identifies the ὑμῖν with a school of prophets associated with John and ταῖς ἐκκλησίας with the seven churches of Asia. The existence of such a prophetic school is quite uncertain, however, so the solution proposed Beckwith and Robertson remains the most viable.
45. Swete, *Apocalypse*, p. 309; Robertson, *Word Pictures*, 6:485-86.
46. Swete, *Apocalypse*, pp. 308-9; Wilcock, *Revelation*, p. 217.
47. Swete, *Apocalypse*, p. 310; Robertson, *Word Pictures*, 6:486; J. B. Smith, *A Revelation of Jesus Christ* (Scottdale, Pa.: Herald, 1961), p. 304; Caird, *Revelation*, p. 286; contra Michael S. Moore, "Jesus Christ, 'Superstar,'" *NovT* 24, no. 1 (1982): 85-91, who sees "the bright morning star" as coming from Chaldean, Ugarit, and Syrian sources rather than from the OT.

22:17 The words of Jesus continue with a change of focus from Himself to the Spirit and the bride: Καὶ τὸ πνεῦμα καὶ ἡ νύμφη λέγουσιν, Ἔρχου. καὶ ὁ ἀκούων εἰπάτω, Ἔρχου. καὶ ὁ διψῶν ἐρχέσθω, ὁ θέλων λαβέτω ὕδωρ ζωῆς δωρεάν (*Kai to pneuma kai hē nymphē legousin, Erchou. kai ho akouōn eipatō, Erchou. kai ho dipsōn erchesthō, ho thelōn labetō hydōr zōēs dōrean,* "And the Spirit and the bride say, 'Come.' And let the one who hears say, 'Come.' And let the one who thirsts come, let the one who desires take the water of life freely"). This verse could be the reply of John to the words of Christ in v. 16, especially in light of the series of declarations and responses in the Epilogue (vv. 10-11, 12-13, 14-15) (Alford, Beasley-Murray), but the flow of vv. 16-19 in their emphasis on the authority of the book and the identification of their speaker as Jesus in v. 20*a* make it more probable that these are Christ's words.

The Holy Spirit (τὸ πνεῦμα [*to pneuma*, "the Spirit"])—speaking either directly or through the prophets—who is also the Spirit of prophecy (2:7; 19:10), and "the bride" (ἡ νύμφη [*hē nymphē*]) (19:7-8; 21:2, 9), the people of God, join with the one speaking in inviting the Davidic King's return. After the picture of the heavenly city in 22:1-5, the prophets and the people of God to whom these two entities correspond (cf. 16:6; 18:24) long for the consummation of the marriage of the Lamb to His bride.[48] Until this point, *nymphē* has applied only to the triumphant people of God in the future, but with relevant oracles fresh in mind, John now applies the name to the church on earth as she awaits her redemption (cf. 2 Cor. 11:2; Eph. 5:31-32) (Moffatt).

Opinion is divided over the one whom ἔρχου (*erchou*, "come") addresses. The proposal that it invites the believing community to a greater devotion to Christ[49] rests on the faulty assumption that all in the seven churches are genuine believers and faithful followers of the Lamb. Earlier discussion of chapters 2-3 has shown this to be untrue. The view that the invitation addresses an unbelieving world to invite them to wash their robes in the blood of the Lamb rests principally on the last invitation of the verse which clearly has an evangelistic purpose.[50] However, this understanding fails to notice that the audience of the book is the church, not the unbelieving world.

To see *erchou* as a petition addressed to Christ, inviting His return, makes the best sense in a context that focuses on that event (22:7, 12, 20; cf. 22:6, 10). This approach also agrees with the dominant use of *erchomai* throughout the book (cf. 1:7 in particular). Taking the verb in

---

48. Swete, *Apocalypse*, p. 310; Robertson, *Word Pictures*, 6:486.
49. Wall, *Revelation*, p. 267.
50. Leon Morris, *The Revelation of St. John*, TNTC (Grand Rapids: Eerdmans, 1969), p. 261; Mounce, *Revelation*, p. 395.

a sense different from what it has in the last clause of the verse is justifiable because the subject of that verb, ἐρχέσθω (*erchesthō*, "let [him] come"), has the further qualification of ὁ θέλων λαβέτω . . . (*ho thelōn labetō* . . ., "let the one who desires take . . ."), compared to the earlier *erchou* which remains unqualified. The change from second person *erchou* to the third person *erchesthō* is also a significant difference.

Two questions might come regarding this viewpoint. Are these words of petition appropriate from the lips of Christ? The answer is yes, because to have Christ quoting the Holy Spirit and the bride in their petition to Himself is no more unusual than having John, who is part of the bride, or the angel doing so. Another question might be, why would the Spirit petition Christ to return? The answer here lies in the Spirit's ministry in revealing things to come (John 16:13) and in motivating the church toward a constant yearning for the fulfillment of events surrounding the second advent of Christ.[51]

Christ's command for a second petition for His own return addresses ὁ ἀκούων (*ho akouōn*, "the one who hears"). Everyone who hears the book read in the local assembly (cf. 1:3) is to repeat the call for Christ's second advent.[52] Not only the church in her corporateness —*hē nymphē*—but also every individual that makes up that church is to call for the fulfillment of Christ's promise to come soon (Swete). The hearing could have a narrower reference to the utterances of vv. 12-15 or to what the Spirit and the bride have just said, but the absolute use of the verb *ho akouōn* has a broader scope (Lee).

The verse's third invitation solicits the coming of "the one who thirsts" (ὁ διψῶν [*ho dipsōn*]). This sudden transition to exhort the hearers resembles those in 13:9-10 and 14:13 (Beckwith). Instead of welcoming the coming Christ, the thirsty one receives a summons to be welcomed by Christ (Swete). Διψάω (*Dipsaō*, "I thirst") refers to spiritual thirst in Matt. 5:6; Rev. 7:16; John 6:35; 7:37. It is a thirst for the water of life (21:6; 22:1; cf. Isa. 55:1).[53] Though this invitation could address the stranger who sometimes attended Christian worship (cf. 1 Cor. 14:23-24) (Moffatt), plenty of the regular attenders had not yet attained the category of an overcomer, as the seven messages of chapters 2-3 make very plain. They too needed to respond. The validity of this invitation remains to the very moment when history will transform into eternity, after which no further opportunity for a decision is available.

Ὁ θέλων (*Ho thelōn*, "The one who desires") is a clarification of

---

51. Düsterdieck, *Revelation*, p. 492; Seiss, *Apocalypse*, 3:478-79.
52. Beckwith, *Apocalypse*, p. 778; Robertson, *Word Pictures*, 6:486.
53. Robertson, *Word Pictures*, 6:486.

who "the thirsty one" is. The designation covers anyone who is conscious of a desire for a higher life, but who may not yet consider himself thirsty (Swete). Desire may lead to an earnest search which is tantamount to thirsting. Desire for the water of life is to have the desire to receive it (Jer. 29:13; Mark 7:6).[54] Even the one with this beginning inclination has an invitation to "take" (λαβέτω [*labetō*]) advantage of this provision which is free of charge (δωρεάν [*dōrean*, "freely"]) (cf. 21:6; Rom. 3:24). Here is a gracious and wide invitation to enjoy cheer immediately following a picture of gloom and despair for the doomed. Jesus invites all those in the seven churches to avail themselves of this free offer. The door of mercy is still open.[55]

22:18 Continuing with another emphatic *ego*, Jesus offers an extended word of testimony regarding the authority and finality of the prophecy He has commissioned John to write: Μαρτυρῶ ἐγὼ παντὶ τῷ ἀκούοντι τοὺς λόγους τῆς προφητείας τοῦ βιβλίου τούτου· ἐάν τις ἐπιθῇ ἐπ᾽ αὐτά, ἐπιθήσει ἐπ᾽ αὐτὸν ὁ θεὸς τὰς πληγὰς τὰς γεγραμμένας ἐν τῷ βιβλίῳ τούτῳ (*Martyrō egō panti tō̧ akouonti tous logous tēs prophēteias tou bibliou toutou; ean tis epithȩ̄ ep' auta, epithēsei ho theos ep' auton tas plēgas tas gegrammenas en tō̧ bibliō̧ toutō̧*, "I testify to everyone who hears the words of the prophecy of this book: if anyone adds to them, God will add to him the plagues which are written in this book").

Strong disagreement prevails regarding the source of vv. 18-19. One position has been that the words are an interpolation by a later editor that is out of harmony with the rest of the book and so are not genuine (Charles). The allegation is that copyists had a high view of Scripture and added these verses to try to protect the content of the Apocalypse during copying. If this had been the case, however, they violated their own standard by making the addition. The very fact that serious discrepancies existed in copies made as early as the time of Irenaeus is evidence against this view too (Moffatt). Another argument for tracing the words to a later copyist or editor is that such a severe warning against verbal fixedness is contradictory to the way John uses the OT in the book. Yet this severity derives from the source passage in Deut. 4:2 and seems to have been a conventional way of guarding the integrity of a book (Beckwith). Another facet said to be inconsistent with Revelation is that the penalty pronounced in this warning is temporal rather than eternal (Charles), but this observation fails to see that the warnings in both v. 18 and v. 19 are ultimately eternal in nature. A further objection to the words' authenticity compares them to the editorial postscript in John 21:24-25, which along with this warning indicate that when published or when added to the NT canon,

---

54. Hughes, *Revelation*, p. 240.
55. Robertson, *Word Pictures*, 6:487.

the books which they end needed special authentication. This can hardly be ground for assigning them to a later editor, however, because the words had become a stereotyped and vehement form of claiming a canonicity equal to the OT that John may have used himself (Moffatt). The view that the verses are spurious meets its waterloo by having no MSS to support their absence from the book. Revelation is never known to have circulated without them as an integral part.

The other two theories about the source of vv. 18-19 trace the verses to either John or Jesus. Choosing between the two is difficult because of the way 22:6-21 does not always identify speakers and changes speakers very abruptly without warning. If John had been the source of v. 17, it is quite possible that he continued his words in vv. 18-19. The reasoning is that after the statement of Jesus in v. 16 and John's response in v. 17, vv. 18-19 would be an impossible climax if they were the words of Jesus (Alford, Beckwith). But aside from the fact that John is not the ultimate source of v. 17, assigning vv. 18-19 to him cannot account for the emphatic *egō* in v. 18 and for the fact that John nowhere else in the Epilogue or even in the whole book assumes such an authoritative tone as these two verses have.

Making vv. 18-19 a continuation of Jesus' words begun probably as early as v. 12, but at least as early as v. 16, is more satisfactory. Only He has this kind of authority, a point accented by His use of the emphatic *egō*. The first part of v. 20 specifically identifies Him as the speaker, with ὁ μαρτυρῶν (*ho marturōn*, "the one who testifies") of v. 20 corresponding to μαρτυρῶ (*martyrō*, "I testify") of v. 18 and μαρτυρῆσαι (*martyrēsai*, "to testify") of v. 16. Throughout the book, Jesus has sent His angel to bear witness. Now He does so in person (Swete). Having Him as the speaker is only fitting in light of the solemnity of the injunctions in the two verses (Mounce).

This continuity of speaker in vv. 17-20 enhances the irreversibility of Christ's promised imminent return through the primacy it gives John's prophecy of that return.

The individualizing παντι τῷ ἀκούοντι τοὺς λόγους τῆς προφητείας τοῦ βιβλίου τούτου (*panti tō akouonti tous logous tēs prophēteias tou bibliou toutou*, "everyone who hears the words of the prophecy of this book") is an echo from 1:3 and refers to everyone in the seven churches who hears (Lee, Mounce). The words τῆς προφητείας (*tēs prophēteias*, "the prophecy"), which precede τοῦ βιβλίου τούτου (*tou bibliou toutou*, "this book") in v. 18 (the order being reversed in v. 19), put more emphasis on *tēs prophēteias*. "Prophecy" is the most significant part of the expression for what is heard and furnishes the justification for the severity of the threats in the two verses (Beckwith).

The substance of vv. 18-19 unquestionably comes from Deut. 4:2, which says, "You shall not add to the word which I am commanding you, nor take away from it" (cf. Deut. 7:15; 12:32; 28:27, 60; Prov. 30:5-6; Jer. 26:2). The adding and taking away have been objects of a number of different interpretations. One of them says the adding and taking away relate to the application to and reception by the readers of the practical lessons taught in the book. They are responsible to obey all the ethical standards advocated and not neglect or soft-pedal them through irrelevant and trifling explanations (Alford, Kiddle). The spirit of the Apocalypse is that of practical compliance just as was the case with Moses' injunction in Deut. 4:2 to which these warnings allude (Swete, Beckwith). The problem with this sense, however, is that this context does not deal directly with obeying Revelation's injunctions. The contextual flow requires that this warning concern itself with the substance of the book and not allowing that substance to be altered in any way.

The viewpoint that the warnings are intended as a formal threat to anyone who makes another copy of the book for the sake of new readers has merit, because it recognizes the contextual focus upon guarding the book's content. In the second century A.D. Irenaeus wrote,

> Whoever you are that are making a copy of this book, I adjure you by our Lord Jesus Christ and by his glorious advent when he comes to judge the living and the dead, that you compare your copy and correct it carefully by this original manuscript; and likewise transcribe this adjuration and set it in your copy.[56]

For Jews, one of the characteristics of Scripture was that its text should be regarded as inviolate. Deuteronomy twice makes such a declaration about the Torah (Deut. 4:2; 12:32; cf. *1 Enoch* civ. 10; *2 Enoch* xlviii. 7-8). Regarding the Greek translation of the Pentateuch, the Letter of Aristeas is relevant too:

> As soon as the scrolls had been read, the priests, the eldest of the translators, representatives of the commune, and the rulers of the people stood up and said: "Forasmuch as the translation has been well and piously carried out and with complete accuracy, it is right that it should be preserved in its present form, without any further revision." When all had assented to this proposal, they gave a ruling in accordance with their custom that an imprecation be imposed on any who should revise the text by addition, by any alteration whatsoever of what was written in it, or by subtraction.[57]

Both of these ancient quotations show the meticulous care used in copying, preserving, and transmitting Scripture.

---

56. Irenaeus, in Eusebius, *H.E.*, v. 20; cf. Swete, *Apocalypse*, p. 311; Caird, *Revelation*, pp. 287-88.
57. *Ep. Aris.*, 310-311; cf. Caird, *Revelation*, p. 287.

As persuasive as it might be to refer these warnings to later copyists of Revelation, the telling consideration against doing so is that it is explicitly addressed to "everyone who hears," i.e., people in the congregations of the seven churches. Copyists are not the ones warned.[58] Had the warnings been addressed to copyists, they would have signally failed, because no other NT book has a text that is rendered so uncertain because of its textual variants (Swete).

So the warnings about adding and taking away must pertain to teachers in the churches. They must be a prophetic protest against the spurious revelations that circulated through false teachers and false prophets in the name of the apostles. The commands here terminate any further prophecies that might arise through other prophets or prophetesses such as Jezebel (2:20). The error of Jezebel supports the need for this kind of warning[59] as does the "prophecy-conscious" condition of the churches in Asia at this time. John was one of a larger group of prophets who were vying for attention in that area.[60] First John 4:1 reflects a major problem created by the multiplication of prophets.[61] These were most likely secessionist deceivers who posed as authoritative divine mouthpieces.[62] Challenges to John's prophetic office surface in 2 John 10-11 and 3 John 9-10.[63] Other indications of the problem of false prophecy come out in Rev. 2:2, 6, 14-15, 24 in connection with the Nicolaitan heresy.[64] The contemporary tendency was to regard apostolic tradition as a body of authoritative doctrine not to be tampered with, so through vv. 18-19 John followed recognized precedent in guarding the prophetic content of this book (Moffatt).

It is commonly acknowledged that NT prophecy declined and eventually vanished shortly after the writing of this book. No other explanation in itself satisfactorily accounts for this disappearance.[65] Through His words in these two warnings, Jesus was concerned with attempted supplementation to[66] and subtraction from John's proph-

---

58. Düsterdieck, *Revelation*, p. 493; Beckwith, *Apocalypse*, pp. 778-79; Morris, *Revelation*, p. 262; Mounce, *Revelation*, p. 495; Ladd, *Revelation*, p. 295.
59. See Robert L. Thomas, "The Spiritual Gift of Prophecy in Rev. 22:18," *JETS* 32, no. 2 (June 1989): 208-9.
60. David Hill, "Prophecy and Prophets in the Revelation of St. John," *NTS* 18 (1971-72): 406; Thomas, "Spiritual Gift of Prophecy," p. 208.
61. Thomas, "Spiritual Gift of Prophecy," p. 209.
62. Raymond E. Brown, *The Epistles of John*, vol. 30 of AB (Garden City: Doubleday, 1982), p. 503.
63. Ibid., pp. 224-25, 744-45.
64. Thomas, "Spiritual Gift of Prophecy," pp. 209-10.
65. Ibid., pp. 213-15; F. David Farnell, "The Current Debate about New Testament Prophecy," *BSac* 149 (July-September 1992): 285-95; idem, "When Will the Gift of Prophecy Cease?" *BSac* 150 (April-June 1993): 185-202.
66. Smith, *Revelation*, p. 304.

ecy through an alleged exercise of the gift of the "discernings of spirits" (1 Cor. 12:10; 14:29). In the latter case those who falsely professed to have the gift of prophecy could claim the possession of discernment and thereby delete some of the elements John had written. John had already omitted one portion from his prophecy, though he carefully explained his reason for doing so (10:4). They might claim to find other parts to omit (Moffatt). John had already tried to terminate prophetic excesses (e.g., 1 John 4:1-6), but without success.[67] These words of Jesus head off any attempt to add or subtract from the book's content through deliberate falsification or distortions of its teaching (Swete, Ladd). They were bound to be unpopular with Jezebel and her followers (2:20 ff.), the propagators of Nicolaitanism (2:6, 15), those at Thyatira who had embraced "the deep things of Satan" (2:24), and the Jewish slanderers (3:9) (Kiddle, Sweet).

The relation of the warning of vv. 18-19 to the "canonization-formula" of Deut. 4:1 ff. is another good reason for concluding that John is forbidding any further use of the gift of prophecy. This is a canonizing of the book of Revelation parallel to the way the Deuteronomy passage came to apply to the whole OT canon.[68] Use of the canonical model is equivalent to saying that there was no more room for inspired messages.[69]

The comprehensive scope of Revelation's coverage of encouragement-parenesis (chaps. 2-3) and predictive elements (chaps. 4-22) and of the extensive time span from the first century to the eternal state also commends the view that vv. 18-19 anticipate no more prophecy.[70] The predictive portions project from John's lifetime all the way into the eternal state. Any type of prophetic utterance would intrude into the domain of this coverage and constitute either an addition to or subtraction from Revelation's content. So the final book of the Bible is also the concluding product of NT prophecy. It also marks the close of the NT canon since the prophetic gift was the divinely chosen means for communicating the inspired books of the canon.[71]

This is a warning not just to the would-be prophets themselves, who might try to continue prophetic ministries beyond the time of Revelation's writing, but also to "everyone who hears," i.e., those in the churches who needed to refuse any authority that challenged the divine authority, accuracy, and finality of this prophecy (Ladd). The

---

67. Thomas, "Spiritual Gift of Prophecy," pp. 210-11.
68. Moffatt, "Revelation," 5:492; Beasley-Murray, *Revelation*, p. 347; Hughes, *Revelation*, p. 241.
69. Thomas, "Spiritual Gift of Prophecy," p. 211.
70. Ibid.
71. Cf. Wayne Grudem, *The Gift of Prophecy in the New Testament and Today* (Weschester, Ill.: Crossway, 1988), p. 290.

observation is true that this warning applies specifically to the book of Revelation only,[72] but by extension it entails the termination of the gift of prophecy and the NT canon also.

The two uses of ἐπιτίθημι (*epitithēmi*, "I add" or "lay on") in this verse are a play on the two meanings of the word. The former—ἐπιθῇ (*epithē*, "adds")—has the sense of "add," similar to the verb προστίθημι (*prostithēmi*, "I add," cf. Prov. 30[24]:6[LXX]), in speaking of additions to the prophetic substance of this book. The latter—ἐπιθήσει (*epithēsei*, "will add")—does not have the sense of adding more plagues to the victim, but of "laying upon" the guilty individual the plagues described in the book (cf. Deut. 7:15[LXX]). To add to this book's contents is to incur the visitations which it threatens (Swete).

"The plagues which are written in this book" (Τὰς πληγὰς τὰς γεγραμμένας ἐν τῷ βιβλίῳ τούτῳ [*Tas plēgas tas gegrammenas en tō bibliō toutō*]) are, of course, the ones described in connection with the seals, trumpets, and bowls. Anyone guilty of not heeding this monumental warning will not experience the deliverance promised the Philadelphian church (3:10), but will remain behind to endure these plagues (Smith). The bowl-plagues are perhaps more directly in view, but this series presupposes the plagues that went before them.[73]

22:19 The other side of the warning is equal in severity to the first: καὶ ἐάν τις ἀφέλῃ ἀπὸ τῶν λόγων τοῦ βιβλίου τῆς προφητείας ταύτης, ἀφελεῖ ὁ θεὸς τὸ μέρος αὐτοῦ ἀπὸ τοῦ ξύλου* τῆς ζωῆς καὶ ἐκ τῆς πόλεως τῆς ἁγίας, τῶν γεγραμμένων ἐν τῷ βιβλίῳ τούτῳ (*kai ean tis aphelē apo tōn logōn tou bibliou tēs prophēteias tautēs, aphelei ho theos to meros autou apo tou xylou tēs zōēs kai ek tēs poleōs tēs hagias, tōn gegrammenōn en tō bibliō toutō*, "and if anyone takes away from the words of the book of this prophecy, God will take away his part from the tree of life and out of the holy city, which are written in this book"). Reversal of the positions of προφητείας (*prophēteias*, "prophecy") and βιβλίου (*bibliou*, "book") from what they have been (22:7, 10, 18) and putting *bibliou* first brings more attention to the almost completed scroll lying before John. Any sort of attempt to diminish the contents of this written piece will bring eternal damage to the offender.

"His part" (τὸ μέρος αὐτοῦ [*to meros autou*], cf. 20:6; 21:8) in the Tree of Life and the Holy City will be nonexistent. The taking away of his part (ἀφελεῖ . . . ἀπὸ . . . καὶ ἐκ [*aphelei . . . apo . . . kai ek*, "will take away . . . from . . . and out of"]) from the Tree of Life (22:2, 14) and out of the Holy City (21:2, 10; 22:14) is open to two possible meanings. It may mean that a saved person can lose his salvation by ignoring this warning (Mounce). The implication of the words is that

---

72. Robertson, *Word Pictures*, 6:487.
73. Düsterdieck, *Revelation*, p. 493; Wall, *Revelation*, p. 272.

people who at one point had a part in the Tree of Life and were on their way to the Holy City may falter along the way, and because of their extreme folly in subtracting from the words of Revelation, may find themselves in the lake of fire (Smith). Without looking beyond this verse, someone might reach this conclusion, but earlier discussion of the Book of Life—an entity related to the Tree of Life—at 3:5 has shown that everyone's name was originally in the Book of Life because of the unlimited atonement of Christ at Calvary. Removal from this book happens when a person fails to believe and follow through with a life that is faithful to that belief in Christ. Only a lack of working faith would permit a person to violate this warning, so the victims of this pronouncement are those who were never solidly a part of the faithful. A child of God would never tamper with these Scriptures.[74]

The act of adding to or taking away from this book, if deliberate, reflects a will that is out of harmony with the will of God. Such a rebellious one cannot receive the things of the Spirit of God now or later (Swete). Anyone with access to the Tree of Life and the Holy City will treat "the book of this prophecy" with utmost respect (Ladd).

The participle τῶν γεγραμμένων (*tōn gegrammenōn*, "which are written") is a genitive neuter plural modifying τοῦ ξύλου (*tou xylou*, "the tree") and τῆς πόλεως (*tēs poleōs*, "the city"). The section from 21:9 through 22:5 describes the Tree of Life and the Holy City. These two inheritances summarize all the bliss promised to the saints by this book.[75]

22:20 John's response to the far-reaching profundity of Jesus' words just concluded is a prayer for His soon return: Λέγει ὁ μαρτυρῶν ταῦτα, Ναί, ἔρχομαι ταχύ. Ἀμήν, ἔρχου, κύριε Ἰησοῦ (*Legei ho martyrōn tauta, Nai, erchomai tachy. Amēn, erchou, kyrie Iēsou*, "The one who testifies these things says, 'Yes, I will come soon.' Amen, come, Lord Jesus"). The λέγει (*legei*, "says") shows that the words of v. 20 are not the direct words of Jesus, but are a quotation by the writer (Beckwith).

The speaker identified by ὁ μαρτυρῶν ταῦτα (*ho martyrōn tauta*, "the one who testifies these things") is Jesus who has just spoken the words of vv. 18-19[76] as well as the earlier words in vv. 12-17. The ἔρχομαι ταχύ (*erchomai tachy*, "I will come soon") matches the same promise in 22:12 and proves vv. 12-19 to be an extended word directly from the Lord. This expression also confirms that Ἰησοῦ Χριστοῦ (*Iēsou Christou*, "Jesus Christ") is a subjective genitive in the expres-

---

74. John F. Walvoord, *The Revelation of Jesus Christ* (Chicago: Moody, 1966), p. 338.
75. Lee, "Revelation," 4:483; Swete, *Apocalypse*, p. 312; Beckwith, *Apocalypse*, p. 779; Robertson, *Word Pictures*, 6:487-88.
76. Robertson, *Word Pictures*, 6:488.

sion τὴν μαρτυρίαν Ἰησοῦ Χριστοῦ (*tēn martyrian Iēsou Christou*, "the testimony of Jesus Christ") in 1:2.[77] The pronoun ταῦτα (*tauta*, "these things") refers immediately to vv. 12-19, but indirectly and ultimately to the contents of the whole book (cf. John 21:24) (Lee, Hailey).

Another affirmation of the promise of 22:7, 12 comes in the words ναί, ἔρχομαι ταχύ (*nai, erchomai tachy*, "yes, I will come soon"). As in 1:7 ναί (*nai*, "yes") affirms the certainty of the book's theme, here it does so again in reference to Christ's coming.[78] This is Jesus' response to the Spirit, the bride, and the loyal hearers when they invite His coming in v. 17. His coming will be in swift retribution to His adversaries (2:5, 16), but in response to the needs of the faithful (3:11) (cf. Hailey).

John adds his ἀμήν (*amēn*, "amen") to Jesus' *nai* (cf. 1:7). This represents his absolute faith in Jesus' promise, just as *nai* expresses Jesus' assent to the call of *erchou* in v. 17 (Swete). John adds his personal invitation, ἔρχου (*erchou*, "come"), to those already extended.

His address of κύριε Ἰησοῦ (*kyrie Iēsou*, "Lord Jesus") rounds out a formula that must have been common among first century Christians. *Kyrie Iēsou* is a title used only here and in v. 21 in Revelation, but one that is quite frequent in the rest of the NT. It is an acknowledgement of Jesus' deity. Paul shared John's view of Jesus' deity and return (2 Tim. 4:8; Titus 2:13). The combination ἔρχου, κύριε (*erchou, kyrie*, "come, Lord") is the Greek equivalent of the Aramaic מָרְנָא תָא (*māranā᾽ tā᾽*, "the Lord comes") which was the watchword of the early church (1 Cor. 16:22) (Swete, Charles, Moffatt). The expression recognizes that as Lord, it is His right to come and judge (22:12), a theme held in common with Rom. 14:9-12. The judgment certainly includes the infliction of the curses pronounced in vv. 18-19, but it also includes a more positive connotation which is the hope of John in making this prayer for His coming (cf. v. 17) (Beasley-Murray).

Additional Notes

22:14 Instead of the reading πλύνοντες τὰς στολὰς αὐτῶν, 046, most minuscules, and some ancient versions read ποιοῦντες τὰς ἐντολὰς αὐτοῦ. The latter differs from the combination τηρεῖν τὰς ἐντολάς used by John elsewhere (12:17; 14:12; John 14:15, 21; 15:10; 1 John 2:3, 4; 3:22, 24; 5:3) when he expresses compliance with the commandments, but 1 John 5:2 does utilize this combination. Ποιοῦντες τὰς ἐντολὰς αὐτοῦ has the earmarks of a scribal emendation, with the copyist(s) being inclined toward a reading that required obedience instead of one

77. Wilcock, *Revelation*, p. 220-21.
78. Robertson, *Word Pictures*, 6:488.

that was a metaphor for faith in Christ and His cleansing blood. External testimony for πλύνοντες τὰς στολὰς αὐτῶν is strong, including Sinaiticus and Alexandrinus, so the preference favors this reading.[79]

The purpose clause with ἵνα has its verb in the future indicative in the case of ἔσται and the aorist subjunctive in the case of εἰσέλθωσιν. The future tense with ἵνα is frequent in Revelation (e.g., 6:4, 11; 9:5, 20; 13:12; 14:13). If there is a difference between the future indicative and the aorist subjunctive in this type of clause, it is a greater degree of *certainty* or the *actuality* of the result with the future compared to the *possibility* with the subjunctive.[80]

The instrumental case τοῖς πυλῶσιν is an associative instrumental meaning "by way of the gate towers."[81] This is an unusual independent use of this case (Beckwith).

22:18 In this setting the aorist subjunctive ἐπιθῇ is an instance of the *futurus exactus*. It is the equivalent of the future perfect: "if anyone *shall have added* to them" (Alford).

In both the protasis and the apodosis of v. 18, a separate preposition ἐπί adds to the force of the prepositional prefixes of the verb.[82]

22:19 The separate preposition ἀπό strengthens the ἀπό—prefix on the verbs in the protasis and in the apodosis—ἀφέλῃ and ἀφελεῖ. The form ἀφελεῖ is the future active indicative of ἀφαιρέω. It replaces the more usual form ἀφαιρήσει.[83]

The *Textus Receptus* reads βίβλου instead of ξύλου in v. 19, but MS support for that reading is all but nonexistent.[84]

4. THE BENEDICTION (22:21)

Translation

²¹The grace of the Lord Jesus be with all.

Exegesis and Exposition

22:21 John closes his Apocalypse on the note of transforming grace that enables the recipients to be faithful to Christ:[85] Ἡ χάρις τοῦ κυρίου ᾿Ιησοῦ* μετὰ πάντων* (*He charis tou kyriou Iēsou meta pantōn*, "The grace of the Lord Jesus be with all"). A benediction of this type is

---

79. Swete, *Apocalypse*, p. 307; Bruce M. Metzger, *A Textual Commentary on the Greek New Testament* (New York: United Bible Societies, 1971), pp. 767-68.
80. Swete, *Apocalypse*, pp. 307-8; Robertson, *Word Pictures*, 6:484.
81. Robertson, *Word Pictures*, 6:484.
82. Ibid., 6:487.
83. Ibid.
84. Zane C. Hodges and Arthur L. Farstad, *The Greek New Testament according to the Majority Text* (Nashville: Thomas Nelson, 1982), p. 779.
85. Wall, *Revelation*, pp. 269-70.

quite unusual at the conclusion of an apocalyptic writing, but it is quite fitting for this one which incorporates epistolary features for the churches and is to be read in them (1:3-4). This farewell word of grace corresponds to the initial one at the book's beginning (1:4). Χάρις (*Charis*, "Grace") is Paul's unvarying benediction in his letters as it is also in Heb. 13:25. It is an appropriate close for the description of God's gracious provision for His people in heaven and on earth.[86]

John's usual way of referring to believers in Christ is by οἱ ἅγιοι (*hoi hagioi*, "the saints") (8:3-4; 11:18; 13:7, 10; 14:12; 16:6; 17:6; 18:20, 24; 19:8; 20:9), but here he uses πάντων (*pantōn*, "all"). Perhaps he chooses a broader term here in hopes that many in the churches who have not yet attained to the standing of "saints" in God's eyes will respond to the repeated pleas of this book through repentance, faith, and washing their robes in the blood of the Lamb. It is possible for them to do this through the enabling "grace of the Lord Jesus."

"The Revelation of Jesus Christ" (1:1) has been the object of much derision, to the point that some critics "spit contempt" at those who study and teach its contents. Remarks to the effect that none but a madman would meddle with it and anyone who does will lose whatever wits he had when he started his study of the book[87] are typical of the insults leveled against students of the last book of the Bible. Yet the book is quite coherent, cohesive, logical, and well-organized. It is a more than worthy product of divine inspiration from the hand of the apostle-prophet John.

Additional Notes

22:21 The reading κυρίου Ἰησοῦ has the strong support of Sinaiticus, Alexandrinus, and about fifteen minuscules. Apparently a pious copyist expanded it by adding χριστοῦ after Ἰησοῦ and ἡμῶν after κυρίου. The omission of ἡ χάρις τοῦ κυρίου Ἰησοῦ in some MSS happened when a scribe's eye passed from the Ἰησοῦ at the end of v. 20 to the Ἰησοῦ in v. 21.[88]

The Greek MSS support seven different readings, including the

---

86. Düsterdieck, *Revelation*, p. 493; Swete, *Apocalypse*, p. 313; Beckwith, *Apocalypse*, p. 780; Robertson, *Word Pictures*, 6:488; Kiddle, *Revelation*, p. 457.
87. James Robertson in his 1730 book on Revelation, cited by Seiss, *Apocalypse*, 3:454. Recent sources continue to speak sarcastically about students of the Apocalypse with observations such as the following: the book "either finds you mad or leaves you mad. You have to be crazy to try to find out what it's all about, and if you're not you will be when you've finished" (H. J. Richards, *What the Spirit Says to the Churches: A Key to the Apocalypse of John* (London: G. Chapman, 1967), p. 94, cited with approval by Bernard P. Robinson, "The Two Persecuted Prophet-Witnesses of Rev. 11," *ScrB* 19, no. 1 (Winter 1988): 14.
88. Metzger, *Textual Commentary*, p. 768.

preferred μετὰ πάντων in v. 21. The others are μετὰ πάντων ὑμῶν, μετὰ πάντων ἡμῶν, μετὰ τῶν ἁγίων, μετὰ τῶν ἁγίων σου, μετὰ πάντων τῶν ἁγίων, and μετὰ πάντων τῶν ἁγίων αὐτοῦ. The reading μετὰ τῶν ἁγίων has the support of Sinaiticus and has the added support of being different from John's usual μετὰ πάντων τῶν ἁγίων in this book (e.g., 8:3). The reading of the *Textus Receptus* is μετὰ πάντων ἡμῶν, but it has only one Greek MS to support it and shows the influence of 2 Cor. 13:13; 2 Thess. 3:18. The reading μετὰ πάντων τῶν ἁγίων has the most extensive testimony, including 046, 051, and about 180 minuscules, but the reading appears to be a conflation of μετὰ πάντων and μετὰ τῶν ἁγίων. The other three readings—μετὰ πάντων ἡμῶν, μετὰ τῶν ἁγίων σου, and μετὰ πάντων τῶν ἁγίων αὐτοῦ—have insignificant external support. As the shortest reading and the one that best explains the origin of the others, μετὰ πάντων, supported by Alexandrinus, the Latin Vulgate, and Tyconius and Beatus, is the preferred reading.[89]

The choice of μετὰ πάντων as correct perhaps broadens the scope of the book to make it more universal. Whether it broadens beyond the seven churches to all congregations who might eventually read it[90] is questionable, however, because of the limitation placed in the introduction (1:4).[91] Swete prefers the reading μετὰ τῶν ἁγίων, reasoning that a scribe would hardly have changed this customary phraseology to πάντων (Swete), but with only Sinaiticus among the uncials to support this reading, it could hardly be correct.

Sinaiticus, 046, 051, almost all minuscules, and most ancient versions support the addition of ἀμήν at the end of v. 21. Yet it is difficult to explain how or why Alexandrinus and a number of other witnesses omitted it if it had been present originally. So the reading that omits the term is preferable.[92]

---

89. Ibid., pp. 768-69.
90. Wall, *Revelation*, p. 272.
91. Düsterdieck, *Revelation*, p. 494.
92. Metzger, *Textual Commentary*, p. 769.

Excursus 3: The Structure of the Apocalypse: Recapitulation or Progression?

Theories about the structure of the Apocalypse abound. Some propose that the organization of the book revolves around seven sections,[1] but another recommends a structure composed of six series of six.[2] Other proposals advance theories of eight basic visions in the book[3] or of five septenary patterns.[4] Still another method of division sees two divisions in the prophetic section, part one covering the first eleven chapters and part two the rest of the book.[5] A further plan is to divide

---

1. R. J. Loenertz, *The Apocalypse of St. John*, trans. H. J. Carpenter (London: Sheed & Ward, 1947), pp. xiii-xiv; John Wick Bowman, "The Revelation to John: Its Dramatic Structure and Message," *Int* 9, no. 4 (October 1955): 436-53; Leroy C. Spinks, "A Critical Examination of J. W. Bowman's Proposed Structure of the Revelation," *EvQ* 50, no. 3 (July-September 1978): 215-22; William Hendriksen, *More Than Conquerors* (Grand Rapids: Baker, 1967), pp. 22-25.
2. J. Massyngberde Ford, *The Book of Revelation*, vol. 38 of AB (Garden City, N.Y.: Doubleday, 1975), pp. 48-50.
3. Kenneth A. Strand, "The Eight Basic Visions in the Book of Revelation," *AUSS* 25, no. 1 (Spring 1987): 107-21; John G. Gager, "The Attainment of Millennial Bliss through Myth: *The Book of Revelation*," in *Visionaries and Their Apocalypses*, ed. Paul D. Hanson (Philadelphia: Fortress, 1983), pp. 149-50.
4. Jean-Pierre Charlier, "The Apocalypse of John: Last Times Scripture or Last Scripture?" *LV* 40 (1985): 184-90.
5. W. J. Harrington, *The Apocalypse of St. John* (n.p.: Chapman, 1969), pp. 31-40; Hendriksen, *More Than Conquerors*, pp. 29-31; Adela Yarbro Collins, *The Combat Myth in the Book of Revelation* (Missoula, Mont.: Scholars

the book into four septets, one consisting of the seven messages of chapters 2-3 and three consisting of one each of the seal, trumpet, and bowl series.[6] A further suggestion also sees another division into four parts but not four divisions of seven.[7] The division of the apocalyptic portion into three parts[8] varies from the four-septet scheme by omitting the seven messages of chapters 2-3.

Another issue of structural interest is the question of whether the author intended the sections of the book, however one may choose to divide it, to be parallel or consecutive. Some venture the opinion that they are parallel, each describing the same period from several different perspectives.[9] Most often, this scheme has been named "recapitulation."[10] The other option is to see chronological progression as entailed in the movement of chapters 4-22. Though not always the case,[11] this latter theory usually accompanies the telescopic or "dovetailing"[12] perspective regarding the expanded contents of the seventh

Press, 1976), p. 20; J. Dwight Pentecost, *Things to Come* (Findlay, Ohio: Dunham, 1959), pp. 187-88.

6. J. P. M. Sweet, *Revelation* (Philadelphia: Westminster, Pelican, 1979), pp. 44, 47; Eugenio Corsini, *The Apocalypse: The Perennial Revelation of Jesus Christ*, vol. 5 of Good News Studies (Wilmington, Del.: Michael Glazier, 1983), pp. 61-63.

7. Elisabeth Schüssler Fiorenza, "Composition and Structure of the Revelation of John," *CBQ* 39, no. 3 (July 1977): 363.

8. Jan Lambrecht, "A Structuration of Revelation 4,1–22,5," in *L'Apocalypse johannique et l'Apocalyptique dans le Nouveau Testament*, BETL 53 (Louvain, Belgium: Leuven Univ., 1980), pp. 84-86.

9. William Lee, "The Revelation of St. John," in *The Holy Bible*, ed. F. C. Cook (London: John Murray, 1881), p. 595; Hendriksen, *More Than Conquerors*, pp. 25, 28; G. R. Beasley-Murray, *The Book of Revelation*, NCB (Grand Rapids: Eerdmans, 1978), pp. 30-31.

10. J. Ramsey Michaels prefers the term "reiteration" to "recapitulation," because Irenaeus uses "recapitulation" to refer to going over the same grounds with different results—e.g., with reference to Christ's reparation of Adam's wrong (*Interpreting the Book of Revelation* [*Guides to New Testament Exegesis* 7, Scot McKnight, gen. ed.; Grand Rapids: Baker, 1992], pp. 53-54). "Recapitulation" has become so thoroughly established in speaking of the structure of Revelation, however, that a change in nomenclature at this point is inadvisable.

11. Lambrecht, "Structuration," pp. 88-90, in his theory of "encompassing technique" exemplifies a combining of recapitulation with linear sequence. He reconciles the contradictoriness of the two schemes by theorizing that John incorporated the contradiction as a signal to his readers not to expect a future historical realization of the events prophesied in the book (p. 104). This theory approximates the unusual hermeneutical assumptions characteristic of other theories that combine telescoping and recapitulation as discussed in a later section of this excursus. See also J. B. Smith, *A Revelation of Jesus Christ* (Scottdale, Pa.: Herald, 1961), p. 136, for an apparent example of combining telescoping with recapitulation.

12. "Dovetailing" is a term used by R. J. Loenertz, *Apocalypse*, pp. xiv-xvi.

seal and the seventh trumpet. A combining of these two options has proposed the possibility that both progression and recapitulation characterize the structure of the book.

The goal of the present study is to accumulate and evaluate whatever evidence the text will yield in deciding between those possibilities. Two phases of discussion are necessary: the former investigating the relationships between the seals and trumpets and the trumpets and bowls, and the latter isolating indications of chronological repetition or succession. The scope of this excursus will not permit an evaluation of the many proposals according to which the intercalations interspersed among the three numbered series are given consideration equal to the numbered series in the book's structure.[13] Yet relationships of some of these intercalations to the seals, trumpets, and bowls will be considered.[14] The assumption is that a *prima facie* understanding of the book dictates the structural dominance of the numbered series over visionary portions that are unnumbered.[15]

RELATIONSHIPS BETWEEN THE NUMBERED SERIES

THE THEORY OF RECAPITULATION

Strengths of recapitulation. A discussion of the relationships between the seals, trumpets, and bowls revolves mostly around the sig-

---

13. Revelation 1:19 divides the book into three major parts: 1:9-20, 2:1–3:22, and 4:1–22:5 (Robert L. Thomas, *Revelation 1-7, An Exegetical Commentary* [Chicago: Moody, 1992], pp. 113-16). Revelation 4:1–22:5 is the focus of this investigation, the assumption being that the structures of 1:1–3:22 and 22:6-21 are distinct from the central apocalyptic section. G. K. Beale ("The Interpretive Problem of Rev. 1:19," *NovT* 34, no. 4 [1992]: 367-75) reaches essentially the same conclusion regarding the book's broad structure by interpreting Rev. 1:19 as an allusion to Dan 2:28-29, 45.
14. See John A. McLean, "The Structure of the Book of Revelation and Its Implication for the Pre-wrath Rapture (Part One)," *Michigan Theological Journal* 2, no. 2 (Fall 1991): 138-67, for a helpful survey and evaluation of nine recent proposals analyzing the structure of Revelation.
15. G. V. Caird, *A Commentary on the Revelation of St. John the Divine*, HNTC (New York: Harper & Row, 1966), p. 106; Donald Guthrie, *The Relevance of John's Apocalypse* (Grand Rapids: Eerdmans, 1987), p. 25; Leland Ryken, *Words of Life: A Literary Introduction to the New Testament* (Grand Rapids: Baker, 1987), pp. 147-49. David L. Barr's comment is relevant here: "Many commentators cannot resist numbering one or two other sequences of seven which John apparently overlooked. Before one proceeds to help John in this way, the critic ought to ask why John chose not to number them. Then the critic ought to try to come to terms with John's own organization. We must read his work . . . ." ("The Apocalypse as a Symbolic Transformation of the World: A Literary Analysis," *Int* 38, no. 1 [January 1984]: 43).

nificance, content, or makeup of the seventh seal and of the seventh trumpet. (1) A recapitulatory interpretation rests on the assignment of the last seal and the last trumpet to the same time as the seventh bowl—i.e., the time of the end.[16] The most frequently cited proof of recapitulation notes the parallelism between the seventh trumpet and the seventh bowl, that both bring the reader to the time of Christ's second coming (cp. 11:16-18 with 16:17).[17] The key consideration in regard to the finality of the seventh seal is the impact of the sixth seal that allegedly "permits one interpretation alone: the last day has come."[18]

(2) Another line of reasoning to support recapitulation is the occurrence of the storm theophany in conjunction with each seventh member (8:5; 11:19; 16:18).[19] The conclusion drawn from this phenomenon is that it is necessary to assign each seventh member to the same climaxing of God's wrath. In 4:5 the writer previews that theophany as originating with the throne of God. The coincidence of the end of the first and second series shown by the theophany requires the first member of the next series to return to the beginning.

(3) A further proof of recapitulation compares the fourth trumpet (8:12) with the sixth seal (6:12-17) and states that the fourth trumpet cannot be subsequent to the sixth seal as the telescopic arrangement necessitates, because the darkening of the heavenly bodies under the former is impossible after the whole sun has become black as sackcloth under the latter.[20] The sequence demanded by this comparison requires placing the fourth trumpet *before* the sixth seal and permits only a recapitulatory relationship.

(4) A recent study has added a further argument to the recapitulation theory. It meticulously points out the tripartite unity of the sixth seal, sixth trumpet, and sixth bowl.[21] This observable unity requires that these parallel members of the three series cover the same ground rather than follow some sort of sequence.

---

16. Beasley-Murray, *Revelation*, pp. 30-31; R. C. H. Lenski, *The Interpretation of St. John's Revelation* (Columbus, Ohio: Lutheran Book Concern, 1935), pp. 267-68, 271; Alan F. Johnson, "Revelation," in *EBC*, ed. Frank E. Gaebelein (Grand Rapids: Zondervan, 1981), 12:490; Henry Alford, *The Greek Testament*, 4 vols. (London: Longmans, Green, 1903), 4:631-32; Philip Edgcumbe Hughes, *The Book of Revelation* (Grand Rapids: Eerdmans, 1990), p. 105.

17. Lenski, *Revelation*, p. 271; Beasley-Murray, *Revelation*, p. 30.

18. Beasley-Murray, Revelation, pp. 30-31; cf. Lenski, *Revelation*, pp. 267-68.

19. Alford, *Greek Testament*, 4:664-65.

20. Lee, "Revelation," 4:603.

21. Andrew E. Steinmann, "The Tripartite Structure of the Sixth Seal, the Sixth Trumpet, and the Sixth Bowl of John's Apocalypse" (Rev. 6:12–7:17; 9:13–11:14; 16:12-16)," *JETS* 35/1 (March 1992): 76.

Weaknesses of recapitulation. Although the theory that the seals, trumpets, and bowls are parallel does not lack support, it also faces difficulties. (1) If the three series are independent of each other as this hypothesis usually holds, the organic unity of the whole apocalyptic section of the book is impaired.[22] Ostensibly the vision of the seven-sealed scroll in chapter 5 introduces the remainder of the Apocalypse. A detachment of the trumpets and bowls from the seals leaves the last two cycles of judgment unrelated to the throne of God from which the seal judgments have proceeded. The detaching of the trumpet and bowl series leaves unanswered basic questions about their sources and their relationships with the rest of the book. This disconnection seems absurd and unworthy of a literary work. On the other hand, if the seventh seal includes the trumpets and bowls, the whole book is bound together into a literary unity.

(2) Another weakness of recapitulation is its inconsistent analysis of the nature and purpose of the seven seals. All seven are manifestations of wrath against "those who dwell on the earth," i.e., "the earth-dwellers" (3:10; cf. 6:10; 8:13; 11:10 [twice]; 13:8, 12, 14 [twice]; 17:2, 8). The theory is hard-pressed to explain the seventh seal as being a manifestaion of wrath on earth-dwellers and usually resorts to seeing it as a reference to the beginning of sabbatical rest[23] or a temporary suspension in the sequence of revelations given to John.[24] Both of these explanations relate the seventh seal to the faithful rather than the earth-dwellers. A further suggestion that the seventh seal is both introductory to the trumpets and simultaneous with the Parousia[25] is weak hermeneutically. It also fails to specify any particular temporal onslaught against the earth-dwellers. The seventh seal must be viewed as a temporal judgment against rebellious mankind.

(3) A third deficiency in recapitulation is its lack of an adequate explanation for the widely acknowledged increase in intensity from the seals to the trumpets to the bowls.[26] For example, the fourth seal

---

22. Friedrich Düsterdieck (*Critical and Exegetical Handbook to the Revelation of John*, Meyer's Commentary, trans. and ed. Henry E. Jacobs [New York: Funk & Wagnalls, 1887], pp. 261-62) sees recapitulation as causing "the organic connection of the visions as a whole [to be] rent."
23. Alford, *Greek Testament*, 4:630.
24. Henry Barclay Swete, *The Apocalypse of St. John* (London: Macmillan, 1906), p. 107.
25. Dale Ralph Davis, "The Relationship between the Seals, Trumpets, and Bowls in the Book of Revelation," *JETS* 16 (1973): 154-55.
26. E.g., Walter Scott, *Exposition of the Revelation of Jesus Christ* (Swengel, Pa.: Bible Truth Depot, n.d.), p. 176; J. A. Seiss, *The Apocalypse* (New York: Charles C. Cook, 1909), 2:17; Lenski, *Revelation*, p. 267; John F. Walvoord, *The Revelation of Jesus Christ* (Chicago: Moody, 1966), p. 231; Robert H. Mounce, *The Book of Revelation*, NICNT, gen. ed. F. F. Bruce (Grand Rapids: Eerdmans, 1977), p. 179; Davis, "Relationship," p. 149.

affects one-quarter of the earth's population, and the sixth trumpet afflicts one-third (6:8; 9:18). In contrast to these fractional and transitional punishments, the bowl judgments affect the totality of the earth and are ultimate in their consequences (e.g., cp. 8:8 with 16:3).[27] No theory of recapitulation has an adequate explanation for these increases.

(4) Each support for recapitulation cited above has an inherent weakness. (a) The observation that all three series *end* the same way does not necessitate that they begin at the same time. A similar or coinciding termination point is possible even if the three sequences *begin* at different times. They may still end together even though they are not parallel. (b) The same comment applies to the occurrence of the storm theophany (8:5; 11:19; 16:18; cf. 4:5) in conjunction with each seventh member. The seventh seal, seventh trumpet, and seventh bowl could end simultaneously without necessitating a parallelism of the three series *en toto*. (c) The fourth trumpet *could* follow the sixth seal if the darkening of the heavenly bodies under the sixth seal were only temporary. This interpretation that the sixth seal is *not* the immediate precursor of Christ's second coming is quite viable.[28] That would leave the heavenly bodies intact for a further manifestation of divine wrath *after* the cosmic upheavals of the sixth seal. (d) The alleged tripartite unity of the sixth seal, sixth trumpet, and sixth bowl rests on a merging of the intercalations following each sixth member with the divine visitation in each case.[29] These mergers are of doubtful validity because the material in the intercalations diverges widely from the judgments of the related seal, trumpet, and bowl. The announcement of the end of the second woe at 11:14, for instance, does not dictate the necessity of including 10:1–11:14 under the sixth trumpet (9:13-21). That announcement occurs at 11:14 so as to join it with the announcement of the third woe and seventh trumpet.[30]

The accumulation of evidence against the recapitulation theory is

---

27. See John A. McLean, "The Structure of the Book of Revelation and Its Implication for the Pre-Wrath Rapture (Part Two)," *Michigan Theological Journal* 3, no. 1 (Spring 1992): 7-8, for other indications of intensification from one series to the next.
28. Thomas, *Revelation 1-7*, pp. 451-52.
29. Steinmann, "Tripartite Structure," p. 70.
30. Isbon T. Beckwith, *The Apocalypse of John* (New York: Macmillan, 1919), pp. 607-8. Revelation 9:20-21 clearly marks the end of the sixth trumpet, making impossible the inclusion of 10:1–11:13 as part of that trumpet (Homer Hailey, *Revelation, an Introduction and Commentary* [Grand Rapids: Baker, 1979], p. 241). Inclusion of the intercalation within the trumpet fails to meet the criterion for each of the woes: the objects must be "those who dwell on the earth" (8:13). Nothing in 10:1–11:13 directly impacts all earth-dwellers the way 9:13-21 does.

considerable and outweighs its favorable points. That leads to a further search for the structural backbone of the Apocalypse.

THE TELESCOPIC THEORY

Strengths of telescoping. The telescopic or "dove-tailing" view sees the seventh seal as containing the seven trumpets and the seventh trumpet as containing the seven bowls. (1) This view turns for support principally to the absence of any immediate outpouring of wrath against the earth after the opening of the seventh seal (8:1) and after the sounding of the seventh trumpet (11:15). After the breaking of the seventh seal, no visitation against the earth-dwellers comes until the trumpet series begins.[31] This lull in judgment along with the preparation of the seven trumpet-angels that results from the seventh seal's opening provides a strong indication from the text that the content of the seventh seal is the seven trumpet-visitations (cf. 8:1-2).[32]

(2) The seventh trumpet provides the same scenario. Though some have identified the contents of the seventh trumpet with 11:16-18,[33] and others equate this trumpet with the woe pronounced in 12:12,[34] neither possibility can match the criteria required for a trumpet judgment. The visitation of the seventh trumpet is not in view until 16:1 ff., in the form of the seven bowl judgments.[35] The heavenly anthem of 11:16-18 cannot be the seventh trumpet because it is a proleptic celebration of what *will* have happened after the seventh trumpet.[36] The "woe" of 12:12 cannot be the last of the trumpet series because it alludes to the wrath of Satan, not of God. The third woe-judgment(s) (9:12; 11:14) remains unnoticed unless the content of the seventh trumpet is the seven bowls.[37]

(3) The three woes are pronounced against the earth-dwellers and are the same as the last three trumpets (8:12; cf. 9:12; 11:14). Since these people are the objects of God's wrath under the seven seals also

31. Merrill C. Tenney, *Interpreting Revelation*, pp. 71-72; George E. Ladd, *A Commentary on the Revelation of John* (Grand Rapids: Eerdmans, 1972), pp. 121-23; Davis, "Relationship" 151; McLean, "Structure (Part Two)," pp. 8-9.
32. Düsterdieck, *Revelation*, pp. 260-61; Ladd, *Revelation*, p. 123; M. Robert Mulholland, *Revelation, Holy Living in an Unholy World* (Grand Rapids: Zondervan, 1990), p. 185.
33. E.g., Beasley-Murray, *Revelation*, p. 30.
34. Mounce, *Revelation*, p. 190; Sweet, *Revelation*, p. 202.
35. E. W. Bullinger, *The Apocalypse* or *"The Day of the Lord"* (London: Eyre and Spottiswodde, n.d.), pp. 368-69; McLean, "Structure (Part Two)," p. 9.
36. Davis ("Relationship," p. 155) finds the content of the third woe in 11:18, but fails to recognize that this verse is part of a heavenly celebration and not an inflicting of misery on the earth-dwellers.
37. Ladd, *Revelation*, pp. 121-22; Johnson, "Revelation," 12:490-91.

(6:10; cf. 3:10), the identification of the seventh seal as the seven trumpets has further corroboration. Furthermore, the third woe must be the seven bowl judgments because those are referred to as "the seven *last* plagues" that complete the wrath of God (15:1).[38] The finality of the bowl judgments compared with the nonfinal characteristics of the seal and trumpet judgments brings further substantiation of the telescopic concept.

Other considerations coincide with a telescopic or progressive understanding of the seals, trumpets, and bowls. (4) If one accepts an identification of the first six seals with the "Little Apocalypse" of Christ (Matt. 24:1 ff.; Mark 13:1 ff.; Luke 21:5 ff.),[39] he must acknowledge that the first six seals are the beginning of birth pains that Christ spoke about (cf. Matt 24:8).[40] Compared with the seven *last* plagues (Rev. 15:1), the seals are earlier in "the hour of trial." Under this interpretation of progression, the first six seals come early and the bowls of wrath late in the future period of world tribulation.

(5) Telescopic progression also accounts well for the mounting intensity of wrathful manifestations from seals to trumpets to bowls. God's judgments against the earth become increasingly severe until they climax in temporal-become-eternal punishment at the personal return of the Warrior-King in chapters 19-21.

(6) The telescopic view also explains the occurrence of the storm theophany in conjunction with each seventh member (8:5; 11:19; 16:18; cf. 4:5). Since the seventh seal and the seventh trumpet each encompasses a following series of judgments, all three series end together and are marked by bolts of lightning, noises, peals of thunder, and sometimes an earthquake and large hailstones.[41] The initial scene in the throne room anticipates this climax to the visitations (4:5) when setting the tone for the seven-sealed scroll and the appearance of the Lamb (chap. 5). The other three references to the storm theophany (8:5; 11:19; 16:18)—each of which is also associated with the heavenly throne room—are reminders issued in conjunction with each of the seventh visitations. Each and every seventh visitation, when it has run

---

38. Johnson, "Revelation," 12:490-91; McLean, "Structure (Part Two)," p. 8.
39. Thomas, *Revelation 1-7*, p. 416.
40. John Andrew McLean, "The Seventieth Week of Daniel 9:27 as a Literary Key for Understanding the Structure of the Apocalypse of John" (unpublished Ph.D. diss., Univ. of Michigan, Ann Arbor, Mich., 1990), pp. 191-213.
41. A further indication of a simultaneous ending of the three series is the announcement of the end of delay and the culmination of the mystery of God in conjunction with the seventh trumpet (10:6-7) when compared with the finality of the seven bowls. Not only are the bowl judgments the seven *last* plagues (15:1), but when the final bowl is poured out, a loud voice from the temple and the throne proclaims, "It is done (γέγονεν)" (16:17).

its course, will mark the conclusion of God's punishments against the earth-dwellers. Only the telescopic arrangement can extend the purview of the initial throne room scene with its storm theophany to include the seal, trumpet, and bowl series.

(7) The telescopic theory also accounts for the differences between the seventh bowl on the one hand and the seventh seal and seventh trumpet on the other. The seventh bowl is the absolute end. It is the final stroke, but this is not true of the other two seventh members.[42] With the seventh seal, only silence in heaven is the immediate outcome. With the seventh trumpet, heavenly voices celebrating the victory of God's kingdom resound. But with the seventh bowl comes the dramatic announcement, γέγονεν (*gegonen*, "it has happened" or "it is done," 16:17). Recapitulation is at a loss to explain these differences among the seventh members of the three series. For recapitulation to be correct, the three final members should be at least approximately the same, but instead, they differ radically from one another.

Weaknesses of telescoping. Problems with the telescopic type of progression are at least three in number. (1) The end signaled by the seventh seal cannot be a period including the whole content of chapters 8-19, because events of chapters 12-14, part of the seventh trumpet, occur earlier than the first seal.[43] At least two happenings, the birth of the male child and His snatching away to God and His throne (12:5), have already passed and cannot belong to the future period of the seal judgments. Unless special allowance is made for the exceptional nature of Revelation's intercalations, progression in the strict sense is an unacceptable explanation of the book's structure.

(2) Matthew 24:29 clearly indicates that the events of the sixth seal (Rev. 6:12-17) occur "after the tribulation of those days" and just before Christ's second advent to earth.[44] That makes it impossible for the seventh seal with its trumpets and bowls to represent events later than the sixth seal. This formidable objection to telescopic progression rests on the identification of the sixth seal with the cosmic upheavals Christ spoke of in His Olivet Discourse. This identification has been questioned, however.[45]

---

42. Lambrecht, "Structuration," pp. 91-92.
43. Caird, *Revelation*, pp. 104-5.
44. Lenski, *Revelation*, pp. 266-68. Davis ("Relationship," pp. 153-54) notes the necessity of putting the sixth seal at the very end of the Tribulation as the immediate precursor of Christ's return, but strangely, he advocates progression in conjunction with the first five seals, the first six trumpets, and the first six bowls (ibid., pp. 157-58).
45. Thomas, *Revelation 1-7*, pp. 451-52; McLean, "Structure (Part Two)," pp. 19-23.

(3) Telescopic progression necessitates a rearrangement of the text to fit a strictly chronological scheme.[46] Citation of this weakness has in view scholars like R. H. Charles who felt that a later editor had carelessly rearranged the sequence of the text.[47] After weeding out and correcting those relocations, Charles proposed a strictly chronological sequence for Revelation's structure.[48] Charles's questioning of Revelation's accuracy in its present form and his liberties in arbitrarily shuffling verses and sections from one place to another are justifiably rejected. Yet one need not reject all structural proposals that may resemble Charles's view but which do not adopt his textual criticism.

THE THEORY COMBINING RECAPITULATION AND TELESCOPING

A third theory combines the other two theories. This one sees Revelation's series as neither systematically recapitulating each other nor consistently following each other in strict chronological sequence. Instead it allows for some of both. The most characteristic feature of this theory is its insistence on the book's *literary* quality—an emphasis on its artistry.[49] In its artistic arrangement, each new series both recapitulates previous visions and develops themes already introduced in those visions.[50] That allows for obvious progression and considerable restatement and detailed development of earlier material.[51]

The unique strength of this theory is its combining of valid elements in the two earlier theories and its nullifying of their weaknesses. When faced with a difficulty of chronological sequence in the text, it allows for a shift to a recapitulation mode. Conversely, when faced with a situation that recapitulation cannot account for, it explains the problem according to a progressive sequence.

Such vacillation, however, introduces a debilitating weakness for the view, because it presupposes the existence of conflicting criteria. It advocates an allowance for logical contradictions in the text of Revelation and necessitates dispensing with rational congruity in interpreting the book. It concurs with the opinion that the expression "a perfectly logical apocalypse" is an oxymoron.[52] It concludes that John's

---

46. Mounce, *Revelation*, p. 177.
47. R. H. Charles, *The Revelation of St. John*, ICC (New York: Scribner's Sons, 1920), 1:lv.
48. Ibid., 1:xxiii.
49. Martin Kiddle, *The Revelation of St. John*, HNTC (New York: Harper, 1940), pp. xxvii-xxx.
50. Caird, *Revelation*, p. 106.
51. Mounce, *Revelation*, p. 178.
52. Ibid.; E. F. Scott, *The Book of Revelation* (New York: Scribner, 1940), p. 26. Scott's exact statement is, "A logical apocalypse would be a contradiction in terms."

material cannot be forced into any system of chronological sequence or cycles[53] and that apocalyptic language and vision is generally surrealistic rather than rational and consistent.[54] An attempted justification for these unusual hermeneutical assumptions notes that to insist on a *systematic* presentation in Revelation would amount to implying that "John was more interested" in impressing his readers with "a work of literary subtlety than [in] sharing the awe-inspiring visions he experienced."[55]

As persuasive as that tactic may be, its underlying premise is fallacious. Wherein lies the necessity that literary art be logically contradictory?[56] Do the terms "artistic" and "rational" mutually exclude each other? Descriptions can be quite graphic and still conform to the strictures of human reason. Besides that, no adequate basis exists for relegating Revelation to an apocalyptic genre where normal hermeneutical principles do not apply.[57] The fact is that the book is more accurately characterized as prophetic rather than apocalyptic genre,

---

53. Caird, *Revelation*, p. 105.
54. Ladd, *Revelation*, p. 124.
55. Mounce, *Revelation*, p. 178.
56. The hermeneutical mood swing that tends at times to resort to artistic versus rational explanations in Revelation finds a parallel in the way many interpreters handle the gift of tongues in 1 Corinthians 12-14. An example of that occurs in Gordon Fee, *The First Epistle to the Corinthians*, NICNT, gen. ed., F. F. Bruce (Grand Rapids: Eerdmans, 1987), p. 645 n. 23: "It is perhaps an indictment of Western Christianity that we should consider 'mature' our rather totally cerebral and domesticated—but bland—brand of faith, with the concomitant absence of the Spirit in terms of his supernatural gifts! The Spirit, not Western rationalism, marks the turning of the ages, after all." Conversely, Richard B. Gaffin, Jr. (*Perspectives on Pentecost: New Testament Teaching on the Gifts of the Holy Spirit* [Phillipsburg, N.J.: Presb. & Ref., 1979], pp. 75-76), in commenting on 1 Cor. 14:4 and 14-19, observes the contemporary tendency to set in contrast the cognitive and preconceptual sides of man as a reaction against a secularized use of reason. Yet he concludes that as bad as the dehumanizing use of reason is, it does not warrant an overreaction against reason in biblical interpretation. He acknowledges that characteristics of an infinite God are beyond human logic, but an allegedly deeper aspect of personality than the mind (with its language capacities) is not where man copes with them. He observes, "Man is more than his mind; he is not an intellectualistic machine. But this 'more' is not inevitably in tension with the mind, nor does language necessarily distort or obscure the wholeness of experience" (p. 76). Gaffin's answer to the proposal that the gift of tongues consisted of some type of ecstatic utterances rather than foreign languages closely parallels an effective response to the proposal that logical consistency should not be required in the Apocalypse. Man's artistic appreciation is not innately opposed to his reasoning faculties any more than his allegedly "deeper aspect of personality" is in tension with his mind.
57. Thomas, *Revelation 1-7*, pp. 23-29.

so recourse to purported peculiarities of apocalyptic interpretation is baseless.

Interpretive presumption must lie on the side of rationality if the author's meaning is to emerge. Leaving the text's meaning in the hands of readers without controls imposed by logic can only bring multiplied interpretive conclusions, none of which might coincide with the text's originally intended meaning. John composed the Apocalypse for reasonable people, and the book must be interpreted accordingly.

CHRONOLOGICAL SUPPORT FOR PROGRESSION

A comparison of the three main theories regarding the seals, the trumpets, and the bowls leads to the conclusion that the form of progression known as telescoping or dove-tailing is superior to recapitulation and to a combination of recapitulation and progression. Chronological considerations add weight to this conclusion. As already noted, telescoping does not absolutely exclude recapitulation in the chronological fulfillment of the events predicted, though it does incline to do so. The suggestion that the sequence of the visions could differ from the sequence of the events fulfilling those visions contravenes normal expectation. The Apocalypse has a number of chronological indicators that confirm what is here called "normal," i.e., that the fulfillment of the visions should coincide with the sequence of the seal-trumpet-bowl visions.

(1) It is important to establish the successive nature of the seal and trumpet visitations. [a] Chronological sequence provides the most natural explanation of the numbering of the visitations from one to seven in each series.[58] [b] The most conspicuous confirmation of this explanation lies in the last three trumpets, otherwise known as the three woes (cf. 8:13). The text explicitly announces the completion of the first woe's fulfillment before the second begins (cf. 8:12), and of the second before the third begins (cf. 11:14).[59] [c] It is also obvious that warfare under the outworking of the second seal by its very nature must follow the peaceful conditions that prevail under the first seal. [d] Another indicator of the sequential nature of the trumpets is the five-month duration of the fifth trumpet's impact. This judgment has a definite period in which to run its course, thus implying that the same is true of the rest of the series. So the seals and trumpets occur one after the other in numerical sequence and are noncumulative, i.e.,

---

58. McLean, "Structure (Part Two)," p. 8.
59. Ibid.

each one finishes before the next one begins. This succession is the sequence of visions and requires the same sequence of fulfillment.[60]

The sequential nature of the bowl judgments is slightly different, however. The beginning of each visitation follows the same chronological sequence, but the bowl judgments are apparently cumulative rather than consecutive in the misery they create. Such a conclusion is necessary because by the time of the affliction of the fifth bowl, the earth-dwellers are still suffering from the effects of the first one (cf. 16:2, 10-11).[61] That feature makes two points: the bowls in their fulfillment follow one another in numerical sequence, and the effect of each remains even after the beginning of the next. Presumably, the second, third, and fourth bowls are causes of the ongoing pain of the fifth bowl also.[62] This cumulative relationship is the most natural explanation for the last three bowls too, and presents a contrast to the consecutive sequence of the last three trumpets.[63]

(2) Several internal time relationships add to this framework of sequence. The intercalation between the sixth and seventh seals (Rev. 7) is unnumbered and represents a pause in chronological advance. As with a similar insert between the sixth and seventh trumpets, it furnishes added perspectives that bear an indirect relationship to the manifestation of wrath in the seal just before and in the one to follow. The sixth seal has just closed with all classes of humanity expressing their futile plight and inability to cope with the great day of the wrath of God and the Lamb (6:16-17). The interlude that follows immediately answers the question of a panic-stricken world, "Who will be able to stand?" (6:17). Revelation 7:1-8 answers in essence, "The 144,000 servants of God will be able to stand." It pulls back for a moment and visualizes a group of saints on earth who are on God's side and consequently have God's seal of protection from the wrath yet to come.[64]

---

60. Davis derives the principle that "the order of the visions does not necessarily indicate the order of events" ("Relationship," p. 153), and cites the nonsequential nature of events in chaps. 12 ff. to prove his point. In doing so, however, he misses the point that chaps. 12 ff. are not a direct part of a numbered series and therefore present a different situation.
61. Alford, *Greek Testament*, 4:700; Moses Stuart, *A Commentary on the Apocalypse* (Edinburgh: Maclachlan, Stewart, 1847), p. 668.
62. Lenski, *Revelation*, p. 476.
63. William Henry Simcox, *The Revelation of St. John the Divine* (Cambridge: Cambridge Univ., 1893), p. 151.
64. Swete, *Apocalypse*, p. 95. Mounce calls the intercalation a parenthesis (Mounce, Revelation 164), terminology to which Lenski objects because the intercalation is an integral part of the book's movement (Lenski, *Revelation*, p. 244). Whatever the break in sequence of the seals is called, however, both agree that the function of chap. 7 is to reflect the status of the faithful as radically different from that of the world's rebels.

The connection of 7:1-8 with the sixth seal furnishes an important indication of chronological progression from the sixth seal to the first two trumpets. The four angels in 7:1 (cf. 7:3) are restraining the four winds lest they blow against the earth, the sea, and the trees. Those are the same parts of creation affected by the first and second trumpet visitations (8:6-9).[65] Evidently the restraint of the winds is a picturesque apocalyptic way of referring to the delay of the two plagues that are to come shortly.[66] The reason for no mention of the winds once the trumpet series begins is the fluidity of apocalyptic language that replaces the destructiveness of the four winds with the first two trumpet-angels and their judgments.[67]

The prescribed delay in releasing the four winds at the time of the sixth seal shows that time must elapse between the action of that seal and the implementation of the first trumpet. That furnishes proof of chronological sequence in the movement of seals to trumpets and conforms to the structural conclusion already reached—the seventh seal consists of the seven trumpets.

(3) Another temporal relationship hinges on factors in the intercalation of 7:1-8. That is the conferral of the seal in 7:3 before the release of the aforementioned winds (cf. 7:1). The sealing of the 144,000 must precede the trumpet plagues, especially the fifth one.[68] Otherwise, the plagues will hurt the faithful along with the earth-dwellers. Specifically, the fifth-trumpet description explains the protection of God's servants provided in the sealing connected with the sixth seal: "And it was said to them [i.e., the locusts] that they should not hurt the grass of the earth or any green thing or any tree, but [lit., 'except'] [they should hurt] the men who do not have the seal of God upon their foreheads" (9:4). That implicit reference to a sealed group can be none other than the 144,000 sealed earlier with a sealing that exempts them from the locust attack.[69]

That connection shows, once again, a temporal sequence from the seals to the trumpets. In particular, it reflects that the sixth seal precedes the fifth trumpet,[70] and by extension, the rest of the trumpets too. It coincides with the chronological progression of happenings portrayed in the seals and trumpets. It furnishes the added detail that the time span entailed is less than one generation—i.e., the persons

---

65. Alford, *Greek Testament*, 4:637; Swete, Apocalypse, p. 111.
66. Ladd, *Revelation*, p. 111.
67. Johnson, "Revelation," 12:478.
68. Davis, "Relationship," p. 150.
69. Swete, *Apocalypse*, p. 116; Smith, *Revelation*, p. 144; Sweet, *Revelation*, p. 168.
70. Johnson, "Revelation," 12:490.

protected at the sixth seal are still alive at the time of the fifth trumpet.[71] The predicted period cannot be expanded to hundreds of years.

(4) A comparison of the fifth seal with the days of the seventh trumpet's fulfillment also reflects chronological sequence in the progress of the book (cp. 6:11 with 10:6). The judgmental aspect of the fifth seal lies in the prayers of the martyrs under the altar for vengeance against the earth-dwellers. God's response to the martyrs' prayer (6:11) includes His instruction that they rest a little longer. This response, ἔτι χρόνος μικρόν (*eti chronon mikron,* "still a small delay" or "a little time yet"), points forward to a period whose conclusion is marked in 10:6 by χρόνος οὐκέτι ἔσται (*chronos ouketi estai,* "there will be delay no longer"). The latter expression marks the end of the delay spoken of under the fifth seal.[72] The use of χρόνος (*chronos*) in the sense of "delay" or "interval of time" in both places confirms the connection of those two announcements.

The very next statement after the announcement of the end of delay connects that end with the days ushered in by the seventh trumpet blast (10:7).[73] The whole series of trumpets is the answer to the martyrs' prayer for vengeance and that series is about to wind up.[74] That development adds a further point to the case for chronological

---

71. Lenski, *Revelation,* p. 284. Basing his conclusion on a view that the 144,000 in 14:1-5 have been preserved alive through severe persecution, Seiss notes another indication that the period from the opening of the sixth seal when the group was sealed (Revelation 7) to the sounding of the seventh trumpet when they appear on earth once again (Revelation 14) is no more than the normal length of one human life (*Apocalypse,* 3:20-21). That rests, however, on the questionable interpretation that the 144,000 do not die as martyrs.

72. Lee, "Revelation," 4:625. For other suggested identifications of the delay, see Thomas, *Revelation 1-7,* pp. 447-48.

73. Other proposed meanings of the angelic announcement of 10:6 include the suggestions that it proclaims the beginning of the reign of Antichrist (Charles, *Revelation,* 1:263-64) and that it indicates the absolute cessation of time (Lenski, *Revelation,* pp. 317-18). The former suggestion falters in its failure to take into account 10:7: completion of "the mystery of God" cannot be limited to the revelation of Antichrist. Furthermore, the seventh trumpet has not yet sounded (cf. 11:15), so there yet remains a progression of time beyond this announcement (Mounce, *Revelation,* p. 213). In regard to the latter suggestion, the ἀλλ' that begins 10:7, along with the contents of 10:7, requires that the meaning "delay" be assigned to χρόνος in 10:6 (Smith, *Revelation,* p. 159). Also, it is pointless for the angel to make such a solemn announcement about the timeless nature of eternity (Mounce, *Revelation,* p. 212).

74. Alford, *Greek Testament,* 4:652; Beckwith, *Apocalypse,* 582; Bullinger, *Apocalypse,* p. 339; Swete, *Apocalypse,* pp. 126-27; M. R. Vincent, *Word Studies in the New Testament* (McLean, Va.: McDonald, n.d.), 2:516; Hailey, *Revelation,* p. 244.

progression: a measurable period of time elapses between the fifth seal and the seventh trumpet.[75]

Leading chronological factors, including the sequential nature of the seals and trumpets, the priority of the sixth seal before the first two trumpets, the priority of the sixth seal before the fifth trumpet, and the priority of the fifth seal before the seventh trumpet, therefore, tend to bolster the case favoring structural and chronological progression rather than recapitulation in Revelation.

THE ROLE OF RECAPITULATION

The progressive sequence of the seals, the trumpets, and the bowls does not, however, rule out some measure of recapitulation in sections of intercalation.[76] In particular, the interlude in 11:1-13 regarding the two witnesses, the one in Revelation 12-14 between the sounding of the seventh trumpet (11:15) and the description of the seven bowls (chaps. 15-16), and the one in Revelation 17-18 between the announcement of the seventh bowl (16:17) and the personal intervention of the Warrior-King (19:11-16)—these three intercalations are partially recapitulatory.[77]

The passage about the two witnesses (11:1-13) presumably gives another perspective on the same period covered by the first six trumpets that precede it in the sequence of visions. That observation presupposes that the six trumpets carry to the time of the end described in the seven last plagues that compose the seventh trumpet.

In order to provide background leading up to the seven bowls, the interlude in Revelation 12-14 returns chronologically at least to the

---

75. Davis ("Relationship," p. 150) adds another indicator of chronological progress when he notes that men have already received the mark of the beast by the time of the first bowl (16:2). Since the marking occurs in 13:16-18 in an interlude between the conclusion of the trumpets and the beginning of the bowls, he takes that as another sign of progression. Yet he correctly notes that the interlude does not belong to a particular series of judgments and is, therefore, not a decisive factor. If the interlude composed of chaps. 12-14 furnishes a second perspective on the period of the trumpets, as will be suggested below, the imposition of the mark of the beast very possibly comes near the beginning of the trumpet series, not too long after the sealing of the 144,000 (Rev. 7:1-8) that is described in conjunction with the sixth seal. That would give every person one mark or the other to indicate his loyalty during the period of the trumpets.
76. McLean, "Structure (Part Two)," pp. 9-10.
77. Some would include the interlude of 7:1-17 among the intercalations that are recapitulatory (Bullinger, *Apocalypse*, p. 279; Caird, *Revelation*, p. 94; Johnson, "Revelation," 12:477). Their reason for doing so, however, rests largely on a misunderstanding of Zech. 6:5 (Thomas, *Revelation 1-7*, p. 463).

birth of the male child and perhaps even to a point before that. That clearly breaks the chronological sequence of the trumpet series, into which it is woven, by recourse to events long before the trumpet series begins. It also returns to give a third perspective on the period of the trumpets, assuming that the three and a half year period referred to three times in chapters 12-13 (12:6, 14; 13:5) is the same one spoken of in 11:2-3.

Revelation 17-18 turns aside to furnish background data regarding Babylon whose final wrathful visitation has just been forecast with the pouring out of the seventh bowl (16:19).[78] To do so, the section returns to review, among other things, more characteristics of the beast from the sea who has enjoyed greatest prominence during the period of the trumpets (cf. 17:7-12), though in sequence, the trumpet series comes earlier in the book.

That Revelation contains recapitulation in that sense is undeniable. But recapitulation is limited to the intercalatory portions of the book, with the main structure of the book revolving about the progressive sequence of the seals, the trumpets, and the bowls. Ladd's qualification of the book's progressive mode differs from that. He reasons that because the seals, the trumpets, and the bowls all carry through to the end and because the seventh seal contains the seven trumpets and the seventh trumpet the seven bowls, some measure of recapitulation is necessary.[79] That is a misleading use of the term "recapitulation." The encompassing nature of the seventh seal and seventh trumpet do not dictate a review of periods already covered. Rather they are another way of portraying progression. It may be granted that the three series are not strictly consecutive—i.e., the seventh member of one concluding before the first member of the next begins. But progress is portrayed when the trumpets begin later than the sixth seal, and the bowls later than the sixth trumpet.

THE RESULTANT STRUCTURAL SCHEME

The results of this study lead to the conclusion that the overriding structural plan of the Apocalypse is that of progression. It is the form

---

78. Charles H. Giblin is helpful in comparing 17:1 and 21:9 as beginnings and 19:9-10 and 22:6-9 as endings of two parallel subordinated interpretation-scenes that elaborate on what immediately precedes each section. The former interpretive-scene (Revelation 17-18) explicates God's wrath against Babylon under the seventh bowl (16:17-21), and the latter the bride of the Lamb who appears first in 21:2 (cf. 19:7, 9) ("Structural and Thematic Correlations in the Theology of Revelation 16-22," *Bib* 55, no. 4 [1974]: 488-504). See Excursus 5 later in this volume.
79. Ladd, *Revelation*, pp. 121-22.

of progression that entails "telescoping," i.e., the seventh seal consists of a number of parts as does a telescope when it is compressed, making the inner parts of the unit invisible. The same is true of the seventh trumpet. The chronological movement in the seals, the trumpets, and the bowls is always forward, never backward or static. The predictions forecast future events that will follow one right after the other in the same order as the book unfolds them.

Within this progressive structure, pauses occur when elements of recapitulation intervene. These pauses cannot be given equal weight in analyzing the book's structure, however. They function in supporting roles to add understanding to the happenings of the numbered series that compose the main skeleton of the Apocalypse.

Aside from the intercalations, however, there is forward movement in the book from chapter 6 toward a climax in the return of Christ and the establishment of His kingdom in 19:11–22:5.[80] When allowance is made for the intercalations of chapters 17-18 and 21:9–22:5, it is clear that the seventh bowl in its finality has three parts: (1) the fall of Babylon (16:17–19:10), (2) the final battles and judgments (19:11–20:15), and (3) the vision of the new creation and the new Jerusalem (21:1-8).[81] Within the scope of the last feature in the last plagues, progressive development is also clear.[82]

Figure 1 on the next page is a graphic representation of the relationships of the seals, the trumpets, and the bowls built on the conclusions reached above.

---

80. Cf. McLean, "The Structure of Revelation (Part One)," p. 158.
81. One feature that shows the inclusion of all three parts in the seventh bowl is the use in 21:6 of γέγοναν, a form almost identical with the γέγονεν of 16:17. Both words echo the theme of "lastness" that characterizes the bowl plagues as portrayed in 15:1 through the use of ἐσχάτας and ἐτελέσθη.
82. Lambrecht, "Structuration," p. 92. See Excursus 5 for a more detailed analysis of the seventh bowl.

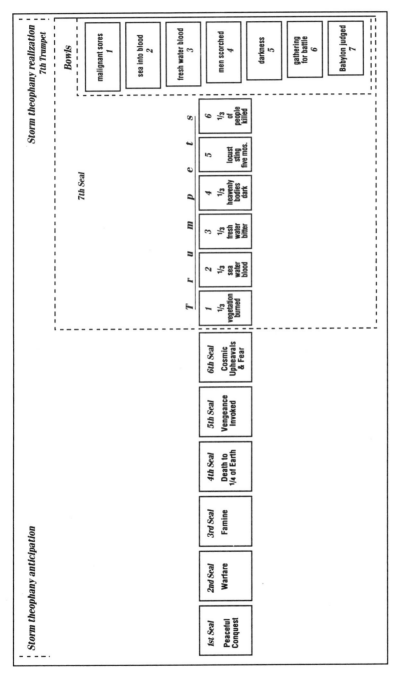

SEQUENCE OF THE SEALS, TRUMPETS, AND BOWLS

Figure 1

Excursus 4: The Kingdom of Christ in the Apocalypse

Any approach to the predictive portions of the Apocalypse must be with a full sense of limitations imposed on human comprehension of future events, even those spelled out in Scripture in nonapocalyptic terminology (cf. 1 Pet. 1:10-11). Yet the impossibility of comprehending enough details to satisfy all human curiosity must be balanced with the possibility of knowing as much as the Inspirer of Scripture intended. Sound doctrine regarding the future is strong motivation for intelligent Christian living and responsibility. Basic data about the future *are* discernible if care is exercised to avoid foregone conclusions.[1]

The text of John's Apocalypse yields satisfactory answers to at least four questions regarding one of its very prominent themes,[2] the kingdom of Christ: What are the time, location, nature, and duration of this kingdom? Too often studies related to the kingdom in Revelation have come only from a limited part of the book, Rev. 19:11–20:10 for exam-

---

1. Contrary to many current opinions on hermeneutics, preunderstanding is not an element to be factored into the hermeneutical process. It is rather the goal of the interpreter to repress personal bias and to let the text speak for itself.
2. McClain furnishes impressive statistical data that demonstrate the prominence of kingdom-related terminology in Revelation by itemizing the frequency of θρόνος, βασιλεία, διάδημα, στέφανος, βασιλεύω, ἐξουσία, ποιμαίνω, κρίνω, κρίσις, κρίμα, θυμός, and ὀργή (Alva J. McClain, *The Greatness of the Kingdom* [Grand Rapids: Zondervan, 1959], pp. 442-43).

ple.[3] Answers to the above questions should arise from a consideration of the whole book.

THE TIME OF THE KINGDOM

John speaks of being a "fellow partaker in the affliction and kingdom and endurance" with his readers (1:9). A common explanation of this expression has been that the present experience of tribulation is what brings in the kingdom (cf. Acts 14:22). However, endurance is mentioned here to remind the readers that the kingdom in its fullness has not arrived. A struggle yet remains.[4] Because of the governance of the three words by ἐν τῇ (*en tē*, "in the") in 1:9, perhaps a better view of the expression is to see the three as a *hendiatris*, i.e., the use of three words with only one thought intended. The major element is "affliction" and the other two words characterize that affliction as being not what the world experiences, but what is particularly connected with the kingdom (Acts 14:22; 2 Tim. 2:12; Rev. 20:6) and one which requires "endurance" or "patient waiting" (Rev. 3:2, 3, 10, 19; 13:10; 14:12).[5] No matter which explanation is adopted, with little or no dispute "kingdom" in 1:9 refers to the millennial kingdom described more fully in Rev. 20[6]—the future kingdom spoken of by Christ (e.g., Luke 12:32; 22:29), Paul (e.g., 1 Thess. 2:12; 2 Thess. 1:5), and James (e.g., James 2:5). Anticipation of this kingdom is an integral part of present Christian experience,[7] as is seen in the mention of "endurance" motivated by an expectation of coming deliverance (cf. "endurance of hope," 1 Thess. 1:3).

Yet the kingdom in Revelation is not only future. An isolated reference to the "kingdom" as a collective designation for believers in Christ during the present era occurs in the introductory doxology in 1:6. Such a corporate designation recalls a continuing NT theme traceable to the beginning of Jesus' parabolic teaching regarding the mysteries of the kingdom (cf. Matt. 13:1-52). This present kingdom is a theological entity noticed occasionally by other NT writers (e.g., Col. 1:13), but the present kingdom pales into minor significance in the rest of the Apoca-

---

3. E.g., R. Fowler White, "Reexamining the Evidence for Recapitulation in Rev. 20:1-10," *WTJ* 51(1989): 319-36.
4. Henry Alford, *The Greek Testament* (London: Longmans, Green, 1903), 4:553; Henry Barclay Swete, *The Apocalypse of St. John* (London: Macmillan, 1906), p. 12; Isbon T. Beckwith, *The Apocalypse of John* (New York: Macmillan, 1919), p. 443.
5. E. W. Bullinger, *The Apocalypse* or "*The Day of the Lord*" (London: Eyre and Spottiswoode, n.d.), p. 149.
6. R. H. Charles, *The Revelation of St. John*, ICC (New York: Harper, 1920), 1:21.
7. Swete, *Apocalypse*, p. 12.

lypse and may be construed as essentially negligible, since it serves only as a foreshadowing of the future kingdom.[8] Βασιλεία (*Basileia*, "Kingdom") in the LXX and the NT speaks most often of the Messianic rule and kingdom,[9] an emphasis which most vividly carries over into John's Revelation. It reaches its climax in chapter 20 where the future share of the saints in Christ's earthly rule is expressly described (Rev. 20:4; cf. 5:10; 11:15). The song of the elders in 11:16-18 is a proleptic anticipation of the millennial reign (20:6), the wrath of the nations (19:19; 20:8), the wrath of God (19:11-21; 20:10), the judgment of the dead (20:12), and the reward of the faithful (21:1–22:5).[10] It expands the comparable announcement of 11:15 that the kingdom of God and of His Christ will have arrived at the point anticipated. This end-time event is not to be confused with the progress of the kingdom of God on earth following Christ's incarnation.[11]

Other indicators of a dominant focus in the Apocalypse on the kingdom's futurity include the following:

(1) To the overcomers in Thyatira and elsewhere, Christ promises a future "authority over the nations" (2:26) based on their future destruction of them "with a rod of iron" (2:27).[12] This is a clear promise of a share in Christ's future rule over the nations (cf. 17:14; 19:14).[13]

---

8. Fiorenza describes the present and future kingdoms in the Apocalypse this way: "The Kingdom of God, which in the eschatological future will be realized in the entire cosmos, is now through the reality of the Christian community present on earth in the midst of the worldly demoɪ ɪc powers" (Elisabeth Fiorenza, "The Eschatology and Composition of the Apocalypse," *CBQ* 30, no. 4 [October 1968]: 559-60).

9. G. Abbott-Smith, *A Manual Greek Lexicon of the New Testament* (Edinburgh: T. & T. Clark, 1950), p. 77.

10. Lee, "Revelation," 4:645.

11. Cf. Lee, "Revelation," 4:645. It can hardly be accurate to conclude that the resumption of God's direct rule began at the birth of Jesus as Sweet assumes (J. P. M. Sweet, *Revelation* [Philadelphia: Westminster, Pelican, 1979], p. 192).

12. Some have preferred a milder meaning "shepherd" or "rule" for ποιμανεῖ in 2:27 (William Lee, "The Revelation of St. John," in *The Holy Bible*, ed. F. C. Cook [London: John Murray, 1881], 4:530; John F. Walvoord, *The Revelation of Jesus Christ* [Chicago: Moody, 1966], p. 77), but this is hardly strong enough to match the shattering of clay containers mentioned later in the verse (James Moffatt, "The Revelation of St. John the Divine," in *The Expositor's Greek Testament*, ed. W. Robertson Nicoll [Grand Rapids: Eerdmans, n.d.], 5:363; George Eldon Ladd, *A Commentary on the Revelation of John* [Grand Rapids: Eerdmans, 1972], p. 54). The same verb refers to actual destruction in 19:15 (Charles, *Revelation*, 1:76), and in the LXX rendering of Ps. 2:9 it translates the Hebrew רָעַע which means to "break" in the sense of "devastate" or "destroy" (BDB, p. 949; Alford, *Greek Testament*, 4:578; Charles, *Revelation*, 1:75-76). Charles points out how the translators of the LXX erred at Ps. 2:9, but how John avoided their error by rendering the Hebrew text independently.

13. Beckwith, *Apocalypse*, p. 470.

(2) To the overcomers in Laodicea and elsewhere, Christ promises the future privilege of sitting with Him on His throne (3:21). As with the rest of the promises to overcomers in Revelation 2-3, this one too points forward to conditions described in Revelation 19-22. Christ's throne is distinguished from the Father's throne in 3:21. The latter is in heaven, and the other is on earth, belonging to Christ as the son of David in the future millennial reign.[14] Because He is David's son, He will inherit David's throne (cf. Ps. 122:5; Ezek. 43:7; Luke 23:42).[15] Some reject this possibility. Bruce has written, "In all his [Jesus's] recorded teaching there is not one reference to the restoration of David's kingdom . . . ,"[16] but on the contrary, the Gospels and the rest of the NT are full of references to Christ's Davidic lineage. Christ emphasizes His own Davidic lineage and His role as David's Lord (Matt. 22:42-45; Mark 12:35-37; Luke 20:41-44), and Gabriel explicitly states that Jesus will occupy David's throne when He comes in His future glory (Luke 1:32; cf. Dan. 7:13-14; Matt. 25:31; Acts 2:30; Heb. 2:5-8; Rev. 20:4). The Gospels use "David" thirty-nine times, once calling him "David the king" (Matt. 1:6; cf. Acts 13:22; 15:16).

Likewise, from beginning to end, Revelation in particular emphasizes Christ's assumption of the Davidic throne (cf. 1:5, 7; 3:7; 5:5; 22:16). He promises the overcomer a share in this earthly throne.[17]

(3) Revelation 5:10 refers to the future kingdom again: "You have made[18] them a kingdom and priests to our God, and they shall reign on the earth." The redeemed people of God will not only be a people over whom He reigns, but also share in God's rule in the coming millennial kingdom (cf. 1 Cor. 4:8; 6:3).[19] The future tense of βα-

---

14. Bullinger, *Apocalypse*, pp. 209-10; Walvoord, *Revelation*, p. 99.
15. Bullinger, *Apocalypse*, p. 210.
16. F. F. Bruce, *New Testament History* (Garden City, N.Y.: Doubleday, 1971), p. 170.
17. The opinion based on Acts 2:32-35 that Jesus took His seat on David's throne at His resurrection (I. Howard Marshall, *Commentary on Luke*, NIGTC [Grand Rapids: Eerdmans, 1978], p. 68) rests on one of several interpretations of the Acts text. A preferable interpretation is that Peter's statement views Christ's resurrection as a necessary step to facilitate His ultimate assumption of the Davidic throne, but does not say He assumed that throne at the time of His resurrection. He is presently at the Father's right hand, not on David's throne, *until* His enemies become His footstool. Then He will ascend David's throne (McClain, *Greatness*, pp. 400-401).
18. Consensus is that ἐποίησας is a proleptic aorist: "you will have made them" (Swete, *Apocalypse*, p. 81; Beckwith, *Apocalypse*, pp. 512-13). As is commonly the case in heavenly songs of this book, this tense anticipates the culmination of the process that is in progress at the point the song is sung. Another possibility could be a constative aorist, in which case it would be a reference to the present kingdom as in 1:6. In this unlikely case, it would show the inseparability of the present kingdom and the future kingdom.
19. Charles, *Revelation*, 1:148; George Ladd, *A Commentary on the Revelation of John* (Grand Rapids: Eerdmans, 1972), pp. 91-92.

σιλεύσουσιν (*basileusousin*) in 5:10 shows this kingdom to be the goal toward which the program of God is advancing (cf. 20:4, 6). The present kingdom serves only as a faint preview of the ultimate kingdom that is future insofar as the Apocalypse is concerned, with only one reference in the entire book pointing to it (1:6). That believers will serve as reigning powers means that they will be the equivalent of kings in this forecast epoch.[20] Spelled out more particularly regarding the Millennium in 20:4 and the new heavens and new earth in 22:5, this means their joining with Christ in His millennial and eternal reign following His second advent.

The futurity of the kingdom is a foregone conclusion for John. It was future not only for him, but also for the entire period of the representative churches whom he addresses in the last decade of the first century.[21] Its futurity is expressed in all three types of literature in Revelation—the narrative (1:9), the epistolary (2:26-27), and the visional or apocalyptic (5:10). Raber's peremptory dismissal of futurism in the book's treatment of the kingdom[22] is oblivious to overwhelming evidence in the text. So thoroughly imbedded in John's words is this

---

20. Charles, *Revelation*, 1:16-17; Beckwith, *Apocalypse*, p. 429.
21. A recently revived theory of dating the Apocalypse in the A.D. 60s seeks to limit the period covered by the Apocalypse to only the very beginning of the church era. This date is suggested in lieu of the traditional date of the A.D. 90s. The early-date preference has characterized one element of the Theonomist movement (i.e., Reconstructionism) (David Chilton, *The Days of Vengeance, an Exposition of the Book of Revelation* [Fort Worth, Tex.: Dominion, 1987], p. 4; Kenneth L. Gentry, Jr., *Before Jerusalem Fell: Dating the Book of Revelation* [Fort Worth, Tex.: Institute for Christian Economics, 1989], pp. 1-353). This movement's postmillennial perspective and consequent optimism about Christianity's success in gaining control of secular society necessitates this dating because of Revelation's acknowledged pessimism about society's increasing hostility toward Christians. An early dating of the Apocalypse allows the Reconstructionist to seek fulfillment of its prophecies in the events culminating in the destruction of Jerusalem in A.D. 70, but leaves him to face an uphill battle forging a convincing argument that the book was written this early. Testimony of early Christianity opposes such an early date by putting the book's composition in the 90s (cf. G. B. Caird, *The Revelation of St. John the Divine*, HNTC [New York: Harper & Row, 1966], p. 6; G. R. Beasley-Murray, *Revelation*, NCB [Grand Rapids: Eerdmans, 1978], pp. 37-38; Sweet, *Revelation*, p. 27; Robert H. Mounce, *The Book of Revelation*, NICNT, gen. ed. F. F. Bruce [Grand Rapids: Eerdmans, 1977], p. 36; Helmut Koester, *Introduction to the New Testament*, 2 vols. [Philadelphia: Fortress, 1982], 2:250-51). Besides, an early date would create the unlikely probability of John's being side-by-side with Paul in simultaneous personal ministry to the churches of western Asia Minor. According to extant sources, John could not have arrived in this area in time to have written the Apocalypse from there during the 60s. (See Robert L. Thomas, "Theonomy and the Dating of Revelation," *The Master's Seminary Journal* 5, no. 2 [Fall 1994]: 185-202.)
22. Rudolph W. Raber, "Revelation 21:1-8," *Int* 40, no. 3 (July 1986): 297.

perspective that Ladd has written, "This is the central theme of the book of Revelation: the establishment of the Kingdom of God on the earth."[23] In light of the prevailing focus of the book, the kingdom can hardly be dated anytime but in the future. If Rev. 20:1-10 is that "ultimate institution" or a part of it, as subsequent discussion in this essay will verify, this fact in essence rules out any theory that Rev. 20:1-10 is in any sense a recapitulation of a previously described period before and including the personal return of Christ.[24]

THE LOCATION OF THE KINGDOM

The existence of God's kingdom in heaven cannot be questioned. When Jesus offered a model for the disciples' prayer—"Your kingdom come . . . as in heaven, [so] also on earth" (Matt. 6:10)—He verified the existence of such a kingdom in heaven, but in so doing, also gave notice of a future kingdom upon the earth to be modeled after it.[25]

Revelation is not a mythical or otherworldly book. Of eighty-two NT occurrences of γῆ (*gē*), the word for "earth," fifty come in Revelation, far more than in any other book. The key throne room scene in 4:1-11 portrays God as Creator of the earth, with the creation motif incorporated into other scenes as well (e.g., 10:5-6; 14:7). The Apocalypse is not otherworldly or dualistic. "The historical this-worldliness

---

23. Ladd, *Revelation*, p. 161. In essence, Fiorenza agrees with Ladd's assessment when she writes, "This main theme of the Apocalypse is shortly but precisely expressed in the hymn in 11,15-19" (Fiorenza, "Eschatology and Composition," p. 569), since the theme of this hymn is the future establishment of the kingdom of God on earth.
24. Contra White, "Evidence for Recapitulation," pp. 319-20, 343-44.
25. G. R. Beasley-Murray, *Jesus and the Kingdom of God* (Grand Rapids: Eerdmans, 1986), pp. 151-52; idem, "The Kingdom of God in the Teaching of Jesus" and "Comments on Craig Blomberg's Response to 'The Kingdom of God in the Teaching of Jesus,'" *JETS* 35, no. 1 (March 1992): 23-24, 37. To understand a kingdom to be established on earth is not contrary to Jesus' statement to Pilate, "My kingdom is not of this world" (John 18:36*a*), a statement not intended to designate the location of the kingdom, but rather the origin of it. To debate whether the kingdom referred to in John 18:36 is spatial or temporal (Robert Hodgson, Jr., "The Kingdom of God in the School of St. John," in *The Kingdom of God in Twentieth Century Interpretation*, ed. Wendell Willis [Peabody, Mass.: Hendrickson, 1987], p. 164) misses Jesus' point here. The preposition ἐκ conveys nothing about time or space. Immediately after those words about His kingdom, Jesus verified that His intended reference was to the source of the kingdom by adding "My kingdom is not *from this place* (ἐντεῦθεν)" (John 18:36*b*). The consummated kingdom of Christ on earth was the constant anticipation of early Christians (Mounce, *Revelation*, p. 358; Donald K. Campbell, "The Church in God's Prophetic Program," in *Essays in Honor of J. Dwight Pentecost*, ed. Stanley D. Toussaint and Charles H. Dyer [Chicago: Moody, 1986], p. 155).

of this [i.e., Revelation's] entire schema, including its extremities, should be clearly seen."[26]

The Apocalypse in a number of ways focuses on the earth in its expectation for the future:

(1) The explicit promise to the Thyatiran overcomer cited above (Rev. 2:26-27) is the exercise of authority over the nations after crushing them. The locale of the subjugated nations is the earth.

(2) The explicit promise to the Laodicean overcomer cited above is to join Christ in sitting on David's throne on earth (Rev. 3:21; cf. 3:7). Only by an unwarranted hermeneutical lapse can David's throne be said to be a heavenly one.[27] David ruled the first time on the earth, and His descendant will do so in the same place in the future (2 Sam. 7:12-16).

(3) The song of four living beings and twenty-four elders in 5:10 explicitly verifies that the redeemed "will reign *upon the earth.*" Words could hardly be plainer regarding the place of this future rule.

(4) According to the song of the heavenly voices and the twenty-four elders in 11:15-18, the future rule of God with His Christ will have as its subjects the nations, whose habitat is planet earth.

(5) The scene of the final battle resulting in the establishment of Christ's future kingdom is an earthly one. In 16:12 the drying up of the great river Euphrates, a specific geographical spot in this world, has a part in preparing the way for the kings from the East to be involved in this battle. Whether "east" means the territory currently known as Iraq and Iran or areas of the Far East with their heavy population, these are spatial designations in this world as currently known. Nor is it necessary to determine whether these kings from the East are distinct from or included among the kings of the whole earth in 16:14. The fact remains that οἰκουμένη (*oikoumenē*) (16:14) throughout Revelation denotes this world order as presently identified (cf. 3:10; 12:9).

Perhaps further evidence of the earthly location of the kingdom is unnecessary. An additional note regarding the kingdom of Christ extending into the new creation (22:5) must complete the picture, however. The passing of the old heaven and earth are a matter of record in 20:11 and the introduction of a new heaven and earth comes in 21:1.

---

26. M. Eugene Boring, "The Theology of Revelation: 'The Lord Our God the Almighty Reigns,'" *Int* 40, no. 3 (July 1986): 268.
27. Herbert W. Bateman IV ("Psalm 110:1 and the New Testament," *BSac* 149, no. 596 [October-December 1992]: 438-53) apparently locates the Davidic throne in heaven on the basis the words of the LORD in Ps. 110:1, "Sit at My right hand. . . ." Elliott E. Johnson ("Hermeneutical Principles and the Interpretation of Psalm 110," *BSac* 149, no. 596 [October-December 1992]: 428-37) details the weaknesses of this conclusion by pointing out distinctions between God's heavenly throne and David's earthly throne.

The presence of the throne of God and of the Lamb in this new order (22:3) dictates that the kingdom carry over into the new conditions also. Further confirmation of this extension is the participation of God's servants in His eternal reign in the new creation (22:5).

THE NATURE OF THE KINGDOM

The nature of the future kingdom on the earth according to the Apocalypse is discernible by several means: from the OT roots of the kingdom, from the means by which the kingdom is established, and from internal conditions with which it must cope.[28]

OLD TESTAMENT ROOTS OF THE KINGDOM

Revelation never quotes directly from the OT, but it has many allusions and much imagery that are thoroughly permeated with OT thought. Of the 404 verses in the book, 278 contain about 550 allusions to the Jewish Scriptures.[29] An investigation of several key OT passages provides insight regarding the nature of the kingdom in Revelation.

Of particular importance are the words ἃ δεῖ γενέσθαι (*ha dei genesthai*) in Rev. 1:1. This expression summarizes the broad content of the revelation to John[30] and depicts a theme of longstanding interest. These "things that must happen" appear first in Daniel's description and interpretation of Nebuchadnezzar's dream about the great statue (Dan 2:28[LXX]; cf. also 2:29, 45). The statue represents four kingdoms, and a stone cut without hands from the mountain that destroys the statue represents a kingdom that will supersede the other four. Using Nebuchadnezzar's dream as a vehicle, the prophecy predicts an eventual establishment of God's kingdom on earth.[31]

Jesus Himself on Tuesday of the week He was crucified picked up

---

28. In his discussion of the nature of the kingdom in the Apocalypse, McClain uses Rev. 20:4, 6 to conclude that the three governmental functions in the kingdom will be judicial, sacerdotal, and regal (McClain, *Greatness*, p. 497).
29. Swete, *Apocalypse*, p. cxl; McClain, *Greatness*, p. 443.
30. Beale goes so far as to call this expression the title of the book (G. K. Beale, "The Influence of Daniel upon the Structure and Theology of John's Apocalypse," *JETS* 27, no. 4 [December 1984]: 415).
31. Daniel 2 foresees the time when God's kingdom will intercept and replace the stream of human sovereignties. The predicted kingdom of God cannot be the church, because the church became a part of world history before the four kingdoms in Nebuchadnezzar's dream had run their course. The establishment of God's kingdom in Daniel's interpretation of the dream comes *after* the Roman Empire (Eugene H. Merrill, "Daniel as a Contribution to Kingdom Theology," in *Essays in Honor of J. Dwight Pentecost*, ed. Stanley D. Toussaint and Charles H. Dyer [Chicago: Moody, 1986], p. 222).

that theme from Daniel with the identical wording δεῖ γενέσθαι (*dei genesthai*) (Matt. 24:6; cf. Mark 13:7; Luke 21:9). Jesus pointed out that these things which "must happen," spoken of by Daniel, had not yet run their course. Happenings described generally in that Olivet Discourse, and more fully in the seven seal judgments, were still future. Jesus anticipated in summary fashion what He was to show John some six decades later on the island of Patmos.

John picked up the baton of communicating this long-awaited series of events and developed them in greater detail. The same expression from Daniel is used in Rev. 4:1 and 22:6 in marking off the central core of the book.

The revelation in this book, therefore, climaxes an expectation beginning at least as early as Daniel 2.[32] In fact, it is no overstatement to say that Daniel 2 pervades the fiber of the Apocalypse. This is the ultimate detailed account of events that must transpire in the outworking of God's program to institute the kingdom on earth that will replace other earthly kingdoms. This is the subject of the proleptic announcement of 11:15 that is sometimes taken as the main theme of the Apocalypse:[33] "The kingdom of the world has become [i.e., will have become] the kingdom of our Lord and of His Christ."

If the other kingdoms of Daniel 2 are political in nature, so will be the coming kingdom of Christ. The term "political" connotes "organized in governmental terms."[34] This is a governmentally organized kingdom with its accompanying social order as this world understands

---

32. Beale reaches essentially the same conclusion regarding the content of the Apocalypse: "Therefore if this allusion in Rev 1:1 is understood by John in the light of the eschatological context of Daniel 2—and there is good reason to believe this is the case—then he may be asserting that the following contents of the whole book are to be conceived of ultimately within the thematic framework of Daniel 2" (G. K. Beale, "Influence of Daniel," p. 416). He adds, "If it can be concluded that these Daniel 2 allusions in Revelation are intentional and draw with them the contextual idea of Daniel 2, then there is a basis for proposing that this idea provides the framework of thought for the whole of the Apocalypse—i.e., eschatological judgment of cosmic evil and consequent establishment of the eternal kingdom" (ibid., p. 420).

The Apocalypse has about ten additional allusions to Daniel 2 besides the one in Rev. 1:1: cp. 1:19 with Dan. 2:28-29; 1:20 with Dan. 2:29; 4:1 with Dan. 2:29, 45; 11:13 with Dan. 2:18; 11:15 with Dan. 2:44; 12:8 with Dan. 2:35; 17:14 and 19:19 with Dan. 2:47; 20:11 with Dan. 2:35; 22:6 with Dan. 2:28-29, 45.
33. Fiorenza, "Eschatology and Composition," p. 569. A comparable proleptic announcement celebrates the inauguration of the future kingdom when in 12:10 a significant step leading to that inauguration—the casting from heaven of the accuser of the brethren—is taken (Lee, "Revelation," 4:662; Lenski, *Revelation*, p. 378; Robertson, *Word Pictures*, 6:393).
34. *Webster's Ninth New Collegiate Dictionary*, p. 910.

such.[35] It is not a kingdom that is spiritual only. It is not a kingdom whose identity is hidden from most or even many. It is not a kingdom that is restricted to the recesses of human hearts. It will be one whose existence will be completely visible to earth's inhabitants just as Nebuchadnezzar's governmental authority and rule were quite evident to all the citizens of his kingdom. The goal toward which the Apocalypse moves is the institution of such a universally acknowledged government on earth.

Other OT Scriptures on which John builds his concept of the kingdom include the following:

(1) Immediately before his first reference to the kingdom in 1:6 he introduces Christ with three titles: "the faithful witness," "the firstborn from the dead," and "the ruler of the kings of the earth" (1:5). All three titles are from Psalm 89 whose fifty-two verses, particularly vv. 19-37, are a commentary on God's covenant with David recorded in 2 Sam. 7:8-16. The first—"the faithful witness"—is repeated in Rev. 3:14. It alludes to Ps. 89:37 where regarding the throne of David it is written, "It will be established forever like the moon, and the witness in the sky is faithful." Jesus Christ is the seed of David and will sit on the Davidic throne, which will endure forever as the sun (Ps. 89:36).

The second title—"the firstborn from the dead"—recalls God's promise to David's seed as God's firstborn. This is from Ps. 89:27 and is almost identical with the title of Christ in Col. 1:18. John follows Paul in adding to Christ's Davidic heritage an indication of His resurrection.

The third title—"the ruler of the kings of the earth"—also comes from Ps. 89:27. He, as David's seed, is "the highest of the kings of the earth." This is a clear foreshadowing of His future role as "King of kings and Lord of lords" (Rev. 19:16; cf. 17:14). The three titles taken together allude to Christ's future dominion over the earth,[36] but they contribute also to an understanding of the manner of His dominion. The nature of His kingdom will be the same as that of David's, i.e., a political rule. His dominion over other kings and lords speaks to the same effect, that is, His government will be of the same nature as governments have always been conceived in this world.

(2) Repeated references in the Apocalypse to His destruction of (or rule over) the nations recalls another OT passage where political rule is conspicuous: Psalm 2. Besides the promise of such authority to the

---

35. George Eldon Ladd, *The Last Things* (Grand Rapids: Eerdmans, 1978), p. 110, has written, "The idea seems to be that God has determined that there shall be a thousand year period *in history* before the Age to Come when Christ will extend his rule over the nations; that is, that there will be a period of political, social, and economic righteousness before the end."
36. Bullinger, *Apocalypse*, pp. 142-43.

Thyatiran overcomer (2:26-27; cf. Ps. 2:8-9), references to the psalm come in 11:15-18 where a transference of power from heathen nations to God is anticipated (cf. Ps. 2:2), in 12:5 where the male child's future destruction of the nations is anticipated (cf. Ps. 2:9), in 14:1 where the presence of the King on Mount Zion is described (cf. Ps. 2:6), in 16:14 where the kings of the earth set themselves against Him (cf. Ps. 2:2), in 17:18 where the world's kings align themselves for battle against the Lamb once again (cf. Ps. 2:2), and in 19:15 and 19 where the smiting of the nations and of the kings of the earth is once again described (cf. Ps. 2:2, 9).[37] The first Christians applied Psalm 2 to the treatment of Christ by political entities represented by Antipas and Pontius Pilate (Acts 4:25 ff.), but the outlook here is wider and more ultimate.[38] This is hostility of the whole world against God and God's response to it.

(3) The theme verse of the Apocalypse, 1:7, offers a further occasion to ascertain the nature of the future kingdom. The theme is a conflation of Dan. 7:13 and Zech. 12:10. Earlier Jesus used the same combination in His Olivet Discourse to describe His second advent (Matt. 24:30; cf. Mark 13:26; Luke 21:27), a statement heard by John about sixty-five years before penning these words (cf. Mark 13:3). The statement in Daniel 7 is part of a context describing the future coming of the Son of Man to assume rule over a worldwide kingdom that is to supersede all previous kingdoms under the whole heaven (Dan. 7:13-14, 27). Like Daniel 2, Daniel 7 looks forward to the crushing and displacement of the kingdom of Rome by the kingdom of God.[39] The text of Revelation alludes to various parts of Daniel's seventh chapter in over thirty instances besides the one in Rev. 1:7.[40] The allusion to Zech. 12:10 is from a context immediately after another prediction of

---

37. Sweet, *Revelation*, p. 191.
38. Swete, *Apocalypse*, p. 143. The uses of Psalm 2 in Acts 4:25 ff. and in the Apocalypse furnish a prime indication that a NT nonliteral application of an OT prophecy, in conjunction with Christ's first advent or the church, does not necessarily exhaust or nullify the divine intention of its ultimate and future fulfillment in a literal way. See note 41 below.
39. Merrill, "Daniel as a Contribution," pp. 222-23. Longman finds a continuation of an OT theme of the divine Warrior as a "Cloud Rider" in this verse because of its use of Dan. 7:13 (Tremper Longman III, "The Divine Warrior: the New Testament Use of an Old Testament Motif," *WTJ* 44/2 [Fall 1982]: 296). The Warrior image is a frequent one in Revelation, especially in 19:11 ff. (ibid., pp. 297-300). Beale also notes the prominence of Daniel 7 in the plan of the Apocalypse (Beale, "Influence of Daniel," p. 419 n. 31).
40. Cp. Rev. 1:13 with Dan. 7:13; 1:13 with Dan. 7:9; 5:11 with Dan. 7:10; 7:1 with Dan. 7:2; 11:7 with Dan. 7:3; 11:15 with Dan. 7:14, 27; 11:17 with Dan. 7:21; 12:3 with Dan. 7:7, 24; 12:13 with Dan. 7:25; 13:1 with Dan. 7:3, 7, 24; 13:2 with Dan. 7:4-6; 13:5 with Dan. 7:8, 11, 20; 13:6, 7 with Dan. 7:7, 21, 25; 14:13 with Dan. 7:13; 17:12 with Dan. 7:20, 24; 19:20 with Dan. 7:11; 20:3 with Dan. 7:9, 22, 27; 20:12 with Dan. 7:10; 22:5 with Dan. 7:18, 27.

the exaltation of the house of David and the defeat of nations that come against Jerusalem in the future day of the Lord (Zech. 12:8-9).

In none of these allusions to OT political entities does John drop even the slightest hint that he intends his words to be understood in a nonpolitical way. He in no way differentiates his kingdom from the kind of kingdom explicitly indicated in each of the respective contexts. Human governments of the future will be replaced by Christ's government in the existing order of creation as it is currently known.[41] Instead of cancelling the political overtones of these OT sources, the Apocalypse strengthens them as the following discussion will show.

MEANS BY WHICH THE KINGDOM IS ESTABLISHED

The forceful way by which Christ will gain control of His future kingdom is another indicator of its political nature. The proleptic song of the twenty-four elders in 11:17-18 celebrates the demonstration of God's great power at the sounding of the seventh trumpet. "Your great power" is not primarily the divine attribute of power, nor is it just the normal exercise of divine power. It is instead that final and overwhelming display to which all prophecy points.[42] This is the power of God on display as He overcomes His enemies in the final great conflict.[43] This is His resumption of direct rule over His creation. In 11:17 he is called "the Almighty" in recognition of the demonstration of naked power as His all-embracing sovereignty takes control.[44]

Human response to this display of unparalleled power is not positive. The nations are enraged by it (11:18) because it represents the institution of the hated kingdom of God on earth.[45] The hostility of

---

41. The suggestion that Israel has been superseded by the church and that fulfillment of OT prophecies will take an unexpected form (Joel B. Green, *How to Read Prophecy* [Downers Grove, Ill.: InterVarsity, 1984], pp. 103-5, 116-18; cf. Martin Kiddle, *The Revelation of St. John*, Moffatt New Testament Commentary [New York: Harper, 1940], pp. 325-28) can hardly be sustained. This assumption rests upon taking the NT application of various OT prophecies to Christ's first advent or the church as the exhaustive fulfillment, cancellation, or reversal of the grammatical-historical sense of these prophecies and is not well-founded. New Testament writers as authors of inspired books had the prerogative of seeing added meanings in these prophecies, but not of divesting them of their original sense. These citations did not "set aside, correct, or affect the literal interpretation of the OT prophets" as VanGemeren and others hold (Willem A. VanGemeren, "Israel as a Hermeneutical Crux in the Interpretation of Prophecy [II]," *WTJ* 46 [1984], pp. 271-97, esp. p. 272). See note 38 above.
42. Swete, *Apocalypse*, p. 143.
43. Mounce, *Revelation*, p. 231.
44. Leon Morris, *The Revelation of St. John*, TNTC (Grand Rapids: Eerdmans, 1969), p. 50.
45. Lee, "Revelation," 4:645.

earth's inhabitants against God is at its peak because, through this future visitation, He removes the world from their control and assumes control Himself. Their assault on His force is the fiercest ever, but it avails nothing against His omnipotent judgments.[46] Their kingdoms will become His kingdom despite their utmost efforts to resist the change in rulership (11:15).

Another perspective of the force to be utilized in the removal of the kings of the whole earth appears in Rev. 16:14, 16 and its sequel in 19:11-21. In the earlier passage the three unclean spirits gather the kings for "the battle of the great day of God Almighty." The battle is so named because in it the omnipotence of an almighty God will be fully displayed.[47] This day is explained in 19:17-21 as the day of God's reckoning with the nations led by the beast from the sea.[48] Almighty God assumes His power and begins to reign at this point.[49] The beast and the kings of the earth will gather to make war with Christ the returning divine Warrior, the same type of deadly warfare as waged against the saints just prior to Christ's return (cf. ποιῆσαι πόλεμον [*poiēsai polemon*], 13:7; and ποιῆσαι τὸν πόλεμον [*poiēsai ton polemon*], 19:19), and will fall victims to His righteous wrath (19:19-21). Included among the victims will be kings, chiliarchs, strong men, free men, slaves, the small, and the great (19:18). It will be an overwhelming show of power in battle such as the world has never seen.

Violence and warfare never provide a pretty picture, but they are almost inevitable whenever a sudden and radical change in governments occurs. The victor in battle becomes the new political ruler and institutes his laws and the means of enforcing them. This is the purpose of war in general, and the future victory of Christ is no exception. He returns as a victorious warrior and His kingdom on earth results from the battle.

INTERNAL CONDITIONS WITH WHICH THE KINGDOM MUST COPE

The removal of all enemies and the institution of Christ's government over the earth does not mean an end to all opposition, however. After a substantial period of His kingdom's existence on earth, Satan is able to muster an enormous army of those who have apparently resented Christ's authority over human affairs: "He [Satan] will go forth to deceive the nations who are in the four corners of the earth . . . and to gather them for battle" (20:8) against the existing government. This

---

46. Swete, *Apocalypse*, p. 143; Beckwith, *Apocalypse*, p. 609.
47. Walvoord, *Revelation*, p. 237.
48. Beckwith, *Apocalypse*, p. 684.
49. Mounce, *Revelation*, p. 300.

is a vivid indication that the future kingdom of Christ on earth will not be devoid of those who oppose the King.

This raises a question about the kinds of people who will inhabit the earth during the kingdom. Some might suppose the Apocalypse to be inconsistent with itself on this point, because Christ's enemies have all been killed in the final great battle before the kingdom (19:18, 21).[50] Those faithful to Christ, on the other hand, will have been martyred by the beast (13:15; cf. 13:9-10; 14:13; 16:6; 17:6; 19:2), so they will be unavailable to populate the kingdom.[51] Yet this is not the complete picture, because it ignores the woman who has been providentially preserved from the antagonism of the dragon (12:6, 13-17). She represents the protected remnant of mortals who will be left to populate the kingdom at its beginning. This remnant will survive in a mortal state when Christ comes to destroy His enemies (19:19-21) and will remain as a beginning for repopulating the earth.

This faithful remnant does not account directly for opposition to Christ's government in His kingdom, but it can do so indirectly. Presumably, among continuing generations to be born after the kingdom begins, some will not choose to be Christ's faithful followers. To be sure, outward rebellion against His throne will meet with immediate enforcement of kingdom laws, but secret rebellion may go undetected for extended periods. It is apparently from among such secret rebels that Satan will collect his "sands-of-the-seashore" army for a final desperate attempt to overthrow the King of kings and Lord of lords.

Whatever the source of the opposition, enemies will be present in the kingdom and will necessitate a political structure suitable for dealing with them.

THE DURATION OF THE KINGDOM

Does the kingdom have a fixed and limited duration? The answer to this question is in two parts: "yes" and "no." The "yes" answer pertains to the period immediately after Christ's second advent, and the "no" answer relates to eternal conditions in the new heavens and new earth.

THE PERIOD IMMEDIATELY AFTER CHRIST'S SECOND ADVENT

Is there an interval of time between Christ's second coming and the instigation of eternal conditions? Mounce concludes that John taught a

---

50. James Moffatt, "The Revelation of St. John the Divine," in *The Expositor's Greek Testament*, ed. W. Robertson Nicoll (Grand Rapids; Eerdmans, n.d.), 5:471; Arthur H. Lewis, *The Dark Side of the Millennium: The Problem of Evil in Rev. 20:1-10* (Grand Rapids: Baker, 1980), pp. 23-25.
51. Mounce, *Revelation*, pp. 355-56.

literal millennium, but that its essential meaning does not require a temporal fulfillment.[52] He denies that John's Millennium is the Messianic age foretold by the prophets of the OT.[53] This denial is hard to sustain, however, in light of the ultradeep roots of the Apocalypse in OT prophetic portions that foresee this future political entity.

One clear indicator that the future kingdom on earth does have duration, and that the return of Christ is not followed immediately by an eternal kingdom, is the above-mentioned revolt that occurs at the end of the thousand years. This Satan-led uprising has no place in an eternal kingdom, because by its very nature that kingdom is eternal and can tolerate no interruption. Besides, Satan will have been relegated to his eternal fate in the lake of fire before the eternal kingdom (20:10). A period separating Christ's removal of His enemies at His triumphant return and the end of the thousand years is necessary to account for a new group of rebels that arises and revolts against Him after the Millennium and preceding the eternal kingdom.[54] The revolt will end with "final and everlasting destruction of the forces of evil,"[55] paving the way for an eternal kingdom where no evil will exist.

Several other considerations require that the kingdom have a finite duration:

---

52. Ibid., p. 359.
53. Ibid.
54. White argues that 20:1-10 is a recapitulation of 19:11-21 by noticing that in 20:1-3 the binding of Satan is designed to prevent his deception of the nations that Christ has just removed in 19:19-21 ("Evidence for Recapitulation," p. 321). In his critique of premillennial explanations of the origin of the nations in 20:3, he disregards the possibility of an emergence of new nations to oppose the Lord in the generations subsequent to the first generation in the future kingdom, though he does mention the possibility of surviving believers after Armageddon (pp. 323-23 n. 10). He rightly insists on the destruction of all the wicked, but does not pursue the possibility of a role for the remaining righteous in repopulation after the Lord's second advent. The emergence of a new set of enemy nations is explained above under the heading "Internal Conditions with Which the Kingdom Must Cope."
55. Ladd, *Revelation*, pp. 270-71. In building his case to prove that the OT picture of the Messianic kingdom is void of evil and death, Lewis argues that Ps. 110:1, interpreted by Paul (1 Cor. 15:25-26, 54), eliminates death after Christ's return (Lewis, *Dark Side*, pp. 31-32). This is not true, however, because Isa. 65:20, a prophecy regarding the future Messianic kingdom, acknowledges the presence of death during the period. He tries to avoid the direct sense of this passage through vague inferences from the larger context of Isaiah 65 (ibid., p. 37), but the plain sense of the verse must be partly determinative of what the larger context expresses. Another example of an effort to delete evil from the coming kingdom is Lewis's denial that Zech. 14:17 indicates the presence of the wicked in the Millennium (ibid., 23). His rationalization simply evades the obvious meaning of the statement in this case too (cf. Jeffrey L. Townsend, "Is the Present Age the Millennium?" *BSac* 140 [1983]: 209-12).

(1) Two bodily resurrections separated by a thousand years in 20:4-5 are commonly acknowledged.[56] All efforts to dispute this explicit statement of the text[57] have proven fruitless. If two separate bodily resurrections will transpire, as validated in the text, the latter of the two must be separated from the former by a time lapse.

(2) The battle just before the Millennium is distinct from the defeat of the satanic army at its end.[58] The former victory comes through Christ's personal intervention, and the latter through fire from heaven that consumes the enemies. A significant amount of time must transpire for a second opposing force to arise, because at the beginning of the thousand years no opposing forces remain as the result of their utter destruction by Christ (19:20-21).[59] The location of the two battles differs also, the former being at Ἁρμαγεδών (*Harmagedōn*) (Rev. 16:16), a hard-to-identify location, and the latter in the vicinity of "the beloved city" Jerusalem.[60]

(3) In the climactic battle at Christ's second advent the beast and the false prophet will be cast into the lake of fire (19:20). At some time subsequent to this, a thousand years according to the text (20:7), the Devil will be cast into the lake of fire *where the beast and false prophet already are* (20:10). These are chronologically sequential events sepa-

---

56. Alford, *Greek Testament*, 4:732; Mounce, *Revelation*, p. 356. Walvoord correctly points out that the first of the two occurrences of ἔζησαν (20:4-5) cannot refer to the beginning of spiritual life as amillenarians so often assume, because included among the subjects of the verb are saints who have been beheaded by the beast. "People who receive the new birth are not those who have been beheaded" (John F. Walvoord, "The Theological Significance of Revelation 20:1-6," in *Essays in Honor of J. Dwight Pentecost*, p. 235).
57. E.g., Lewis, *Dark Side*, p. 58.
58. Charles, *Revelation*, 2:47. White's strongest argument that the battle of Rev. 19:17-20 and the one in Rev. 20:7-10 are identical is based on allusions to passages from Ezekiel 38-39 in connection with both battles (cf. also 16:17-21) ("Evidence for Recapitulation," pp. 326-28). He uses this as a basis for a *prima facie* assumption that the two are the same and that this proves the recapitulatory nature of 20:1-10. The weakness of his assumption is at least twofold: (1) its inadequate allowance for the characteristic of OT prophecy whereby it "compresses" or foreshortens future sequences without necessarily reflecting extended periods that may separate events named in the same prophecy; and (2) its inadequate consideration of John's independence in his allusions to OT Scripture. John's freedom in this latter regard negates the possibility of using any more than broad concepts of the OT to reach conclusions contrary to what Revelation more explicitly reflects. The distinctions between the two battles as outlined in the above discussion points clearly to two separate battles.
59. William Henry Simcox, *The Revelation of St. John the Divine* (Cambridge: Cambridge Univ., 1893), p. 184.
60. Swete, *Apocalypse*, p. 265.

rated by elapsed time.[61] The sequence makes inescapable the conclusion that the thousand years constitutes that interval of time.

The Length of the Period. A sixfold repetition of the thousand-year designation tells the duration of the period after Christ's second advent. Explicitly, it is the duration of Satan's binding (20:2), the duration of his imprisonment in the abyss (20:3), the duration of the resurrected saints' reign with Christ (20:4), the period separating the two resurrections (20:5), the period of the reign of those participating in the first resurrection (20:6), and the period before the loosing of Satan (20:7). Contextually, it is also the period between two battles pitting the forces of Satan against those of God. Also, a thousand years separate the casting of the beast and the false prophet into the lake of fire from the casting of Satan into that same lake.

Should the thousand years be understood as a literal one thousand calendar years or in a figurative way to designate a period of some other length? Augustine, at the beginning of the fifth century, was the earliest church father to view Revelation 20 in a nonfuturist fashion.[62] Yet at one point he still took a literal interpretation, making the period refer to a thousand years in the present era rather than to some future period.[63] Besides problems posed for Augustine's initial view by indi-

---

61. Wilbur B. Wallis, "The Coming of the Kingdom: A Survey of the Book of Revelation," *Presbyterion* 8, no. 1 (Spring 1982): 62-63; Townsend, "Is the Present Age the Millennium?" p. 213. Those who choose to see 20:1-10 as a return to a time prior to Christ's advent of 19:11-21 rather than as a sequel to it (e.g., Lewis, *Dark Side*, p. 49), whatever their reason, fail to account for this explicit indicator of chronological progression from chap. 19 to 20. White proposes that 20:10 requires that the Devil be cast into the lake of fire only a *short* time after the beast and the false prophet and thus does not preclude the possibility of 20:7-10 being a recapitulation of 19:17-20 ("Evidence for Recapitulation," p. 326). This reconstruction is quite improbable, however, because in the natural flow of the context one event precedes the thousand years and the other follows (cf. 20:7). It fails to explain why consecutive sections consign the beast and the false prophet to one fate (19:20) and the Devil to another (20:3) and then later assign the Devil to the same fate as the other two (20:10).

62. Some sources credit Origen with being the earliest to initiate allegorical interpretation and its consequent shift to amillennialism as the dominant method of interpretation in the church (Thomas Cornman, "The Development of Third-Century Hermeneutical Views in Relation to Eschatological Systems," *JETS* 20, no. 3 [September 1987]: 285), but Mounce indicates that Origen only rebuked those who looked forward to bodily pleasure and luxury in the Millennium (Mounce, *Revelation*, p. 358).

63. Aurelius Augustine, "City of God," in *Basic Writings of Saint Augustine*, ed. Whitney J. Oates (New York: Random House, 1948) 20.7, 22.30 (pp. 518, 663); idem, "Sermon 251" and "Sermon 259," in *The Fathers of the Church*, trans. M. S. Muldowney (New York: Fathers of the Church, 1959), 38:322,

cations of the period's futurity cited above, a present-era millennium supplies no suitable explanation of how Satan could be bound during the present.

Warfield rejected a literal interpretation, understanding it as a figurative way of referring to the intermediate state of the saints in heaven.[64] This ignores earlier indications in the Apocalypse that the future kingdom must be on earth.

Swete also took the period figuratively to refer to a long period of time of indefinite length, the duration of the triumph of Christianity.[65] The occurrence of bodily resurrection immediately before the period belies this understanding, however, as does the previously cited indication that the period is in the future, beyond the present era.

Kuyper took the language to refer to the exceeding fullness of divine action,[66] but his basis for that generalization was the prior assumption that no such period could transpire after Christ's future coming in judgment. Earlier discussion has shown this assumption to be fallacious.

No exegetical ground exists for any understanding of the thousand years in a nonfuturist, nonearthly, nonliteral way.[67] This is not an allegory.

Yet among those who recognize the literality of the thousand years, some do not conceive of the period in terms of a transient period of history.[68] They rather pursue a hermeneutical course of denying anything more specific in the millennial teaching than the truth that the martyr's steadfastness will win for him the highest life in union with God and Christ.[69] This perspective on a literal, nonallegorical understanding of the passage is said to reflect "the immediacy of the

---

368-69. Augustine later changed his view to a symbolic understanding of the thousand years, making the period to coincide with the whole interval between the first and second advents of Christ (cf. Swete, *Apocalypse,* pp. 265-66). Lewis calls his position the same as Augustine's later view and characterizes the position as "preterist" and "futurist" regarding the book of Revelation (Lewis, *Dark Side,* p. 55).

64. Benjamin Breckinridge Warfield, *Biblical Doctrines* (New York: Oxford Univ., 1929), p. 649.

65. Swete, *Apocalypse,* pp. 257, 263.

66. Abraham Kuyper, *The Revelation of St. John,* trans. John Hendrik de Vries (Grand Rapids: Eerdmans, 1935), p. 277.

67. Mounce, *Revelation,* p. 358.

68. Beckwith, *Apocalypse,* pp. 736-38; Mounce, *Revelation,* p. 359. Walvoord calls Mounce a premillenarian (Walvoord, "Theological Significance," p. 229), and White does the same ("Evidence for Recapitulation," p. 323), but this is questionable. Mounce specifically rejects the millennial reign as an actual period of political and social history to follow the return of Christ and denies that it is an eschatological era (Mounce, *Revelation,* p. 359).

69. Mounce, *Revelation,* p. 359.

culture" in which John lived. It suggests a distinction between the *form* of a literal Millennium and its *content*, a literal thousand years but no temporal fulfillment.[70]

Besides the difficulty in reconciling the seeming self-contradiction of such an explanation,[71] the explanation is vulnerable to the challenge of whether this was in fact the way people of John's time understood his words. Available evidence indicates they did not. Those closest to John's situation do not support that understanding.[72] Papias and Irenaeus who lived closest to the same period in the area where the Apocalypse was composed and received did not understand the Millennium that way.[73] Justin Martyr, Tertullian, and Nepos, who lived elsewhere in the Mediterranean world during the same general period, did not share this interpretation.[74] They all perceived of the Millennium as a future thousand-year period of history on earth—the climax of all other periods of world history.

The straightforward meaning of the text of Rev. 20:1-10 is the best and only logical answer. It speaks of a one-thousand-year period in the future political and social history of the world.

ETERNAL CONDITIONS IN THE NEW HEAVEN AND NEW EARTH

The promise that God and His Christ will reign forever and ever (Rev. 11:15; cf. Luke 1:33) finds its eventual fulfillment in the eternal kingdom portrayed in Rev. 21:1–22:5. The throne of God and of the Lamb will be in this new Holy City Jerusalem that descends from

---

70. Ibid.
71. This appears to be a case where some would recommend the hermeneutical principle of the primacy of imagination over reason, of treating the text as a picture book rather than as a theological treatise (Green, *How to Read*, p. 75). But is it not fallacious to put pictorial and rational faculties at odds with each other? Must the right brain be in opposition to the left brain?
72. See discussions of second-century opinions regarding the Millennium in Derwood C. Smith, "The Millennial Reign of Jesus Christ: Some Observations on Rev. 20:1-10," *ResQ* 16 (1973): 220-21; Barbara Wooten Snyder, "How Millennial Is the Millennium? A Study in the Background of the 1000 Years in Revelation 20," *Evangelical Journal* 9, no. 2 (Fall 1991): 51.
73. Papias, cited by Eusebius, *H.E.* 3.39.11-13; Irenaeus, *Adv. Haer.* 5.33.3-4, 5.28.3. Crutchfield lists seven second-century fathers as reputed premillenarians who were related in varying ways to Asia Minor and John the Apostle: Polycarp, Papias, Melito, Apollinaris, Ignatius, Justin Martyr, and Irenaeus. The premillennial views of Papias, Justin, and Irenaeus are explicit in their writings. The evidence for premillennialism in the other four is more indirect, but still convincing (Larry V. Crutchfield, "The Apostle John and Asia Minor as a Source of Premillennialism in the Early Church Fathers," *JETS* 31, no. 3 [December 1988]: 413-26).
74. Justin Martyr, *Dial.* 80-81; Tertullian, *Adv. Marc.* 3.24; Nepos, cited by Eusebius, *H.E.* 7.24.

heaven (22:3; cf. 21:2), and the servants of God will participate in this eternal reign (22:5). Several features differentiate the eternal kingdom from the millennial one:[75]

(1) No secret opposition such as that in the millennial kingdom will be tolerated in the eternal kingdom (21:8, 27; 22:15). Righteousness will prevail even in the inner recesses of the human heart, because conditions of mortality with its accompanying depravity will no longer exist.

(2) Unlike the millennial kingdom, the eternal kingdom will not pertain to the old creation, which will have been replaced by a new creation. There will be no further place for earth and heaven as currently known. God promises to make all things new, an apparent reference to the new heavens and the new earth (20:11; 21:1, 5).

(3) "The beloved city" (20:9) will be replaced by "the new Jerusalem" (21:2, 10). "The beloved city" is the scene of the final great conflict after the Millennium, and is most probably the Jerusalem that belongs to this creation.

(4) The reign of God's people in each of the two phases of the kingdom differs from that in the other. In one its extent is limited to a fixed period of a thousand years (20:4), and in the other it is described as lasting "forever and ever" and is therefore unlimited (22:5). Another difference is in the nature of the reigns. In the former phase the reign is one of kingship *and priesthood* (20:6), but in the latter it is a reign of kingship only (22:5).[76]

Details about conditions under the new order of creation defy definitive comprehension by finite minds, but enough is understandable to distinguish differences between the two phases of the future kingdom.

THE APOCALYPTIC KINGDOM SUMMARIZED

Without question, the kingdom described in the last book of the Bible is predominantly, but not exclusively, a future one. The sphere of its domain will be first the entire earth and then the new heavens and the new earth. Its nature will be political and social with a central government making and enforcing laws throughout the realm, yet a degree of secret opposition will exist without detection until the very end of the present world order. The duration of the kingdom will be one thousand years on the earth as currently known, but in the new order of creation beyond the thousand years its existence will be un-

---

75. For a similar description of differences, see Lewis, *Dark Side*, pp. 62-63.
76. Charles, *Revelation*, 2:186.

limited. Eventually it will be conspicuous to all that God and His Christ are sovereign over the present creation and the one to come. This assurance provides ample motivation for His servants to persevere through the trials of the present era, no matter how severe, as they await the coming kingdom.

Excursus 5: An Analysis of the Seventh Bowl of the Apocalypse

Throughout most of the visional portion of Revelation (4:1–22:5), the prevailing anticipation looks toward the establishment of a kingdom on earth over which God Himself will rule.[1] John reaches the climax of his expectation in a series of bowl judgments that issue from the seventh of seven trumpet judgments which, in turn, result from the seventh of seven seal judgments.[2] The spotlight of the present study is on the last of the seven bowl judgments with the goal of discovering the extent of the account describing that bowl, examining the structure of that special part, and deriving implications based on what is discovered.

THE EXTENT OF THE SEVENTH BOWL

The earliest word about the seventh bowl is in Rev. 16:17-21. The pouring of that bowl in the air leads to a loud voice out of the temple from the throne, proclaiming, "It is done," or better, "It has been and remains done" (Γέγονεν [*Gegonen*]). The action with its announce-

---

1. See Excursus 4 for details of how this anticipation expresses itself.
2. See Excursus 3 for an elaboration of the case to support progression as the overarching scheme of Revelation's structure. The present discussion of the seventh bowl does not depend solely on conclusions of this earlier study, but assumptions based on it will inevitably surface here and there.

ment indicates that the climax has come to be and remains so now and forever.[3] The storm-theophany, including the greatest earthquake yet, follows the utterance of that voice (cf. 6:12; 8:5; 11:13, 19).[4] The great city, probably Jerusalem,[5] undergoes a division into three parts, and the cities of the Gentiles fall. But an announcement that God has appointed Babylon to incur His intense wrath is the worst news of all for the earth. The flight of the islands and the disappearance of the mountains along with a pelting by unbelievably large hailstones conclude the initial announcement. The result is human blasphemy against God because of the plague of hailstones.

Most exegetes feel that the seventh-bowl description does not terminate at the end of chapter 16, but continues into chapters 17-18 with a detailing of Babylon's downfall.[6] Just how far it continues beyond that is, however, a point of obscurity. A definitive analysis of this issue from any perspective is hard to come by, so the present investigation, rather than evaluating several proposals to reach a decision, will advance what is hopefully an exegetically cogent theory with its supporting argumentation.

The thesis to be defended is that *the text all the way from 16:17 through 22:5 constitutes a description of the seventh bowl judgment*. The following rationale supports this thesis.

THE ANGELIC AGENT FOR SHOWING THE NEW JERUSALEM

The angel delegated to reveal special features of the descending Holy City in 21:9-10 is one of the angels of the seven last plagues, another name for the seven bowls.[7] The same identity holds for the angelic revealer in 17:1 where some would like to see him as the sev-

---

3. R. C. H. Lenski, *The Interpretation of St. John's Revelation* (Columbus, Ohio: Lutheran Book Concern, 1935), p. 482.
4. Henry Barclay Swete, *The Apocalypse of St. John* (London: Macmillan, 1906), p. 210.
5. James Moffatt, "The Revelation of St. John the Divine," in *The Expositor's Greek Testament*, ed. W. Robertson Nicoll (Grand Rapids: Eerdmans, n.d.), 5:449; J. Massyngberde Ford, "The Structure and Meaning of Revelation 16," *ExpTim* 98, no. 11 (August 1987): 329.
6. E.g., Swete, *Apocalypse*, p. 213; Walter Scott, *Exposition of the Revelation of Jesus Christ* (Swengel, Pa.: Bible Truth Depot, n.d.), p. 340; Martin Kiddle, *The Revelation of St. John*, HNTC (New York: Harper, 1940), p. 337; G. R. Beasley-Murray, *The Book of Revelation*, NCB (Grand Rapids: Erdmans, 1978), p. 248; Alan F. Johnson, "Revelation," in *EBC*, ed. Frank E. Gaebelein (Grand Rapids: Zondervan, 1981), 12:554; Robert W. Wall, *Revelation*, in New International Biblical Commentary, ed. W. Ward Gasque (Peabody, Mass.: Hendrickson, 1991), p. 204.
7. M. Robert Mulholland, *Revelation, Holy Living in an Unholy World* (Grand Rapids: Zondervan, 1990), p. 276.

enth of the seven bowl-angels because of the relevance of his revelation to Babylon, the main object of the seventh bowl.[8] The wording does not provide sufficient information to tell which of the seven it was in 17:1 or in 21:9, however. Nor does it identify the two with each other. The information can only tie these two revealers with the seven last plagues in a general way.

As noted above, the vast majority have endorsed that tie-in for the angel of 17:1 because of the immediate context.[9] Those willing to attach the account of the new Jerusalem in 21:9–22:5 as part of the seventh bowl have been more scarce, however, probably because of the contextual distance between 16:17 and 21:9.[10] Nevertheless, one of the angels commissioned to dispense the seven last plagues also had the charge of portraying divine love and fellowship in the heavenly city upon the new earth.[11]

This forges a strong link in the chain connecting the end with the beginning in the larger context of 16:17–22:5.

THE STRUCTURAL PATTERN OF THE TWO MAJOR INTERCALATIONS

Few if any have overlooked the major antithesis between the two women in the closing chapters of the Apocalypse.[12] The harlot Babylon receives detailed treatment in 17:1–18:24, and the bride of the Lamb in 21:9–22:5. Another element, a structural one, also marks the two major sections as parallel to one another, however. The wording of the introductory and concluding formulas for the two intercalations are to a remarkable degree either identical or nearly identical. These striking correspondences have been largely unnoticed or inoperative in analyses of the last chapters of the book.[13]

---

8. Friedrich Düsterdieck, *Critical and Exegetical Handbook to the Revelation of John*, in Meyer's Commentary, trans. and ed. Henry E. Jacobs (New York: Funk & Wagnalls, 1887), p. 428; Henry Alford, *The Greek Testament* (London: Longmans, Green, 1903), 4:704.
9. See note 6 above.
10. E.g., William Lee, "The Revelation of St. John," in *The Holy Bible*, ed. F. C. Cook (London: John Murray, 1881), 4:819; Mulholland, *Revelation*, p. 276.
11. Lee, "Revelation," 4:819.
12. Lee ("Revelation," 4:820), A. T. Robertson (*Word Pictures in the New Testament* [Nashville: Broadman, 1933], 6:470), and Mulholland (*Revelation*, p. 293) are among many who comment on the contrast between the two women. Richard Bauckham has also noted this contrast as well as the broad structural conclusions reached in this section ("The Economic Critique of Rome in Revelation 18," in *Images of Empire*, ed. Loveday Alexander [Sheffield: JSOT, 1991], pp. 47-48).
13. Cf. Charles H. Giblin, "Structural and Thematic Correlations in the Theology of Revelation 16–22," *Bib* 55, no. 4 (1974): 488-89. Most have noted some of the similarities, but only with isolated comments (e.g., Alford,

The introductory formulas to the sections contain twenty identical words in the same order and then five identical words in the same order followed by an analogous antithetical development: πόρνη (*pornē*, "harlot")—γυνή (*gynē*, "woman")/πόλις (*polis*, "city"); νύμφη (*nymphē*, "bride")—γυνή (*gynē*, "wife")/πόλις (*polis*, "city").[14] The extreme similarity of the introductions is evident in the following alignments of texts:

Rev. 17:1 Καὶ ἦλθεν εἷς ἐκ τῶν ἑπτὰ ἀγγέλων τῶν ἐχόντων τὰς
Rev. 21:9 Καὶ ἦλθεν εἷς ἐκ τῶν ἑπτὰ ἀγγέλων τῶν ἐχόντων τὰς
(Kai ēlthen heis ek tōn hepta angelōn tōn echontōn tas
(Kai ēlthen heis ek tōn hepta angelōn tōn echontōn tas

ἑπτὰ φιάλας,   καὶ ἐλάλησεν μετ᾽ ἐμοῦ λέγων, Δεῦρο, δείξω σοι
ἑπτὰ φιάλας, . . . καὶ ἐλάλησεν μετ᾽ ἐμοῦ λέγων, Δεῦρο, δείξω σοι
hepta phialas,   kai elalēsen met᾽ emou legōn, Deuro, deixō soi
hepta phialas, . . . kai elalēsen met᾽ emou legōn, Deuro, deixō soi

τὸ κρίμα τῆς πόρνης τῆς μεγάλης τῆς καθημένης ἐπὶ ὑδάτων πολλῶν,
τὴν νύμφην τὴν γυναῖκα τοῦ ἀρνίου.
to krima tēs pornēs tēs megalēs tēs kathēmenēs epi hydatōn pollōn,
tēn nymphēn tēn gynaika tou arniou

. . . Rev. 17:3 καὶ ἀπήνεγκέν με εἰς ἔρημον ἐν πνεύματι.
Rev. 21:10 καὶ ἀπήνεγκέν με ἐν πνεύματι ἐπὶ ὄρος μέγα καὶ ὑψηλόν,
kai apēnegken me eis erēmon en pneumati,)
kai apēnegken me en pneumati epi oros mega kai hypsēlon,)

As apparent, the first twenty words of 17:1 are the same as the first twenty of 21:9. Five words agree in form and order between 17:3 and 21:10, with the prepositional phrase εἰς ἔρημον (*eis erēmon*, "into the wilderness") preceding ἐν πνεύματι (*en pneumati*, "in the spirit") in 17:3 and ἐπὶ ὄρος (*epi oros*, "upon a mountain") following the same phrase in 21:10.

Certain parts of the concluding formulas exhibit a similarity almost as striking. Both have beatitudes, though the substance of the

---

Greek Testament, 4:739; Robert H. Mounce, *The Book of Revelation*, NICNT [Grand Rapids: Eerdmans, 1977], p. 307 n. 1; Mulholland, *Revelation*, pp. 26-30, 276). It has been extremely rare for any to trace the extent and implications of these correlations.

14. Giblin, "Structural and Thematic Correlations," p. 489; cf. Lee, "Revelation," 4:735; Wall, *Revelation*, p. 205.

two is different (19:9*a*; 22:7*b*). The following layout reflects verbal concurrences:

Rev. 19:9 . . . καὶ λέγει μοι, Οὗτοι οἱ λόγοι ἀληθινοὶ τοῦ θεοῦ εἰσιν.
Rev. 22:6*a* **Καὶ εἶπέν μοι, Οὗτοι οἱ λόγοι πιστοὶ καὶ ἀληθινοί,**
(kai legei moi, Houtoi hoi logoi alēthinoi tou theou eisin
(Kai eipen moi, Houtoi hoi logoi pistoi kai alēthinoi

Rev. 19:10 καὶ ἔπεσα ἔμπροσθεν τῶν ποδῶν αὐτοῦ προσκυνῆσαι
Rev. 22:8 . . . **ἔπεσα προσκυνῆσαι ἔμπροσθεν τῶν ποδῶν τοῦ ἀγγέλου τοῦ δεικνύοντός μοι ταῦτα.**
kai epesa emprosthen tōn podōn autou proskynēsai

. . . *epesa proskynēsai emprosthen tōn podōn tou angelou tou deiknyontos moi tauta*

καὶ λέγει μοι, Ὅρα μή· σύνδουλός σού εἰμι καὶ τῶν
Rev. 22:9 καὶ λέγει μοι, Ὅρα μή· σύνδουλός σού εἰμι καὶ τῶν
kai legei moi, Hora mē; syndoulos sou eimi kai tōn
kai legei moi, Hora mē; syndoulos sou eimi kai tōn

ἀδελφῶν σου τῶν ἐχόντων τὴν μαρτυρίαν Ἰησοῦ·
ἀδελφῶν σου τῶν προφητῶν καὶ τῶν τηρούντων τοὺς λόγους τοῦ βιβλίου τούτου·
adelphōn sou tōn echontōn tēn martyrian Iēsou
adelphōn sou tōn prophētōn kai tōn tērountōn tous logous tou bibliou toutou

τῷ θεῷ προσκύνησον.
τῷ θεῷ προσκύνησον.
tǭ theǭ proskynēson.
tǭ theǭ proskynēson.

ἡ γὰρ μαρτυρία Ἰησοῦ ἐστιν τὸ πνεῦμα τῆς προφητείας.
22:6*b* **καὶ ὁ κύριος, ὁ θεὸς τῶν πνευμάτων τῶν προφητῶν . . .**
hē gar martyria Iēsou estin to pneuma tēs prophēteias.)
kai ho kyrios, ho theos tōn pneumatōn tōn prophētōn.)

The first five words of 19:9*b* and 22:6*a* agree exactly with the subsequent concurrence of ἀληθινοί (*alēthinoi*, "true"). Five words of 19:10*a* are the same as five words of 22:8*b*, with a variation of word order. The first thirteen words of 19:10*b* and 22:9*a* are identical. Three words of 19:10*c* and 22:9*b* coincide exactly, and "the spirit of prophecy" in 19:10*d* is conceptually similar to "the spirits of the prophets" in

571

22:6*b*. The summation of 22:6 ff. appropriately concludes 21:1-8 and its elaboration in 21:9–22:5, just as 19:9*b*-10 summarizes and concludes 17:1–19:8.[15]

The resemblances are too close and too many to be accidental. Of course, the tactic of attributing the similarity to a later editor who copied one or the other from its companion passage[16] is a way to explain the correspondences, but endorsing the whole book to be the work of John as historically received has much greater plausibility than differing theories that partition the book into segments assigned to different scribes or editors. Those who respect the integrity of the Apocalypse must recognize the introductory and concluding formulas as intended to mark off the antithetical sections that elaborate on the background and destiny of the two women, both of whom relate to the seventh last plague.

In the closing formula of 22:6-9 two main obstacles seem to impede this otherwise clear-cut structural arrangement, however. The first consists of elements in the formula that make it a conclusion to the whole book rather than to just the vision of the heavenly city. To list a few, these include the expression δεῖξαι τοῖς δούλοις αὐτοῦ ἃ δεῖ γενέσθαι ἐν τάχει (*deiksai tois doulois autou ha dei genesthai en tachei*, "to show His slaves things that must happen soon") which refers back to the first verse of the book;[17] the statement ἰδοὺ ἔρχομαι ταχύ (*idou erchomai tachy*, "behold, I will come soon") that fits the tone of imminence in the book's earlier chapters (cf. 1:3; 2:5, 16; 3:11) and in the rest of the Epilogue (cf. 22:10, 12, 20);[18] and the expression "the words of the prophecy of this book," a clear reference to the whole Apocalypse (cf. 22:9, 10, 18, 19). If this formula parallels 19:9-10 as the conclusion to one of the two "woman-visions," why do these features project beyond the boundaries of the vision of the Lamb's bride in 21:9–22:5?

The apparent answer is that the author intends the words to accomplish both functions, i.e., to conclude the vision of the bride and to initiate the conclusion of the whole book too. He amplified this final formula so that it could perform a dual function.[19] The resemblances

---

15. Cf. James Moffatt, "*The Revelation of St. John* the Divine," in *The Expositor's Greek Testament*, ed. W. Robertson Nicoll (Grand Rapids: Eerdmans, n.d.), 5:478.
16. Moffatt, "Revelation," 5:489; R. H. Charles, *The Revelation of St. John*, ICC (New York: Scribner's Sons, 1920), 2:128-29.
17. Lee, "Revelation," 4:837, 839; Wall, *Revelation*, p. 262.
18. Düsterdieck, *Revelation*, p. 490; Swete, *Apocalypse*, p. 303; Robertson, *Word Pictures*, 6:482.
19. Cf. Giblin, "Structural and Thematic Correlations," p. 493.

to 19:9-10 on the one hand and to the rest of the book on the other, reflect this double intention.

The other obstacle to the absolute symmetry of the proposed structural arrangement is an apparent change in speakers in the closing formula of 22:6-9. The phenomenon of frequent unannounced changes in spokesmen in 22:6-21 is well known.[20] Agreement on who speaks at the beginning of 22:6 is not unanimous. Proposals have encompassed the *Angelus Interpres* who has been the general agent of revelation (cf. 1:1; 21:5)[21] and even Christ Himself because of the first person promise of His coming in 22:7*a*,[22] but the most probable identification is the angel who began speaking in 21:9-10.[23] In other words, it is still one of the angels who had the seven bowls.

The complication comes with the statement of 22:7*a*, "Behold, I will come soon"—clearly a statement of Jesus that is introduced simply by καί (*kai*, "and"). The first impression is that the speaker from v. 6 is continuing his conversation, but this poses the necessity that Jesus be the subject of εἶπεν (*eipen*, "he said") at the beginning of v. 6—an impossibility.

A possible solution to this dilemma is a phenomenon observable elsewhere in the Apocalypse, the "escalation" of an angelic spokesman to the role of a divine mouthpiece.[24] A good example of this comes when the angelic spokesman of 11:1-2 (cf. 10:9) continues in 11:3 after a simple introductory καί (*kai*, "and") by using δώσω (dōsō, "I will give") and a first person pronoun μου (*mou*, "My") as though God were the speaker.[25] Another possibility is to see this as an occasion when a prophet injected an utterance of God into his prophecy without the customary "thus saith the LORD" (e.g., Isa 16:10[end]; 61:8; cf. Rev. 1:8).[26]

Whichever is correct, the fact remains that one of the "seven last plague" angels is the primary spokesman, leaving the formula intact as a conclusion to the "bride" vision in 21:9–22:5. This resolution of matters leaves at least one other unanswered structural question: does the

---

20. E.g., see Isbon T. Beckwith, *The Apocalypse of John* (New York: Macmillan, 1919), p. 774.
21. Lee, "Revelation," 4:837; J. P. M. Sweet, *Revelation* (Philadelphia: Westminster, Pelican, 1979), p. 314; Homer Hailey, *Revelation, an Introduction and Commentary* (Grand Rapids: Baker, 1979), p. 425.
22. Charles, *Revelation*, 2:217.
23. Swete, *Apocalypse*, p. 302; Beckwith, *Apocalypse*, p. 772; Robertson, *Word Pictures*, 6:481; Beasley-Murray, *Revelation*, p. 334.
24. Giblin, "Structural and Thematic Correlations," p. 497; cf. Alford, *Greek Testament*, 4:745; E. W. Bullinger, *The Apocalypse* or *"The Day of the Lord"* (London: Eyre and Spottiswoode, n.d.), p. 678.
25. Düsterdieck, *Revelation*, p. 490.
26. Beckwith, *Apocalypse*, p. 774.

formula 22:6-9 combine with 21:9–22:5 as part of the intercalation (on the order of 19:9-10), or does it combine with 22:6-21 as part of the Epilogue to the book? The answer to this does not significantly affect the goal of the present study, but the ties to the Epilogue appear stronger. The formula is actually a bridge between the two, so that grouping it with either part is feasible.

MISCELLANEOUS INDICATIONS THAT 16:17–22:5 IS A UNIT

At least four other aspects solidify the conclusion that the seventh bowl encompasses all of the prophecy from 16:17 through 22:5: the two perfect tenses of γίνομαι (*ginomai*, "I become"), the battle of Armageddon with its final judgment of the beast, the final judgment of Satan, and the finality of the last of the last plagues.

The two perfect tenses of γίνομαι (*ginomai*, "I become"). Two utterances from God Himself,[27] γέγονεν (*gegonen*, "it is done") in 16:17 and γέγοναν (*gegonan*, "they are done") in 21:6, sound the note of finality in conjunction with this bowl. The former term refers to the whole series of plagues, of which the seventh bowl is a part.[28] With the pouring out of the seventh bowl, the series has come to an end. This has been taken to refer to the final act of God *before* the second coming of Christ,[29] but that does not satisfy the ultimacy of the pronouncement. No such limitation is appropriate, because these are the *last* plagues. When they are done, all is complete. Yet the declaration must be proleptic to account for the sequence that when the announcement comes, the seventh bowl has yet to run its course.[30]

Similarly, γέγοναν (*gegonan*, "they are done")[31] (21:6) signals finality, but at a later stage, at the conclusion of the summarizing introduction of the new creation. Whether the subject of the plural verb be taken as οὗτοι οἱ λόγοι (*houtoi hoi logoi*, "these words") (21:5)[32] or

---

27. Swete, *Apocalypse*, p. 210; Lee, "Revelation," 4:726; Robertson, *Word Pictures* 6:425, 468.
28. Swete, *Apocalypse*, p. 210; Robertson, *Word Pictures*, 6:425.
29. John F. Walvoord, *The Revelation of Jesus Christ* (Chicago: Moody, 1966), p. 240.
30. Alford, *Greek Testament*, 4:702; George E. Ladd, *A Commentary on the Revelation of John* (Grand Rapids: Eerdmans, 1972), p. 217.
31. Various MSS have differing endings for this verb—third person singular and first person singular as well as the third person plural. The third person plural is the choice for the correct reading because of being the hardest reading and because of respectable support from Alexandrinus and other authorities (Bruce M. Metzger, *A Textual Commentary on the Greek New Testament* [New York: United Bible Societies, 1971], p. 767).
32. Beckwith, *Apocalypse*, p. 752.

πάντα (*panta*, "all things") (21:5),[33] the coverage of its action reaches back to the proleptic γέγονεν (*gegonen*, "it is done") of 16:17. In either case the announcement is about the final days of the old creation and the bringing in of the new creation. The words just spoken have been fulfilled, and the state of completion now obtains. Since 21:9–22:5 is an expanded description of the new Jerusalem foreseen in 21:2,[34] the *gegonan* extends its coverage to that section too. So the *gegonen* of 16:17 anticipates the *gegonan* of 21:6, which in turn looks back to the *gegonen* of 16:17.[35] Between the two is the action of the seventh bowl judgment.

The battle of Armageddon. A consideration of the battle of Armageddon is of further help in fixing the extent of the *seventh* bowl (16:16). Recognition of the sixth bowl judgment as preparatory for this climactic confrontation is the regular interpretation.[36] The drying up of the Euphrates River and the mission of the three unclean spirits (16:12-15) pave the way for the battle of the great day of God Almighty. The former action facilitates passage to the battle scene for the kings from the east, and the latter involves the kings of the whole earth in conflict.

Yet preparation for battle is as far as the sixth bowl goes. It does not include the battle itself. It is a function of the seventh bowl to furnish a prophecy of the engagement itself. Stated in another way, the seventh bowl cannot terminate until after the description of the actual battle. A fixing of this point in the text is another means for determining how far the seventh bowl extends.

Dominant exegetical opinion correctly looks to the context of 19:17-21 as the culmination of the battle for which the sixth bowl prepares.[37] It is there that "the kings of the earth and their armies" (16:19) confront the warrior-King and His army and go down in ignominious defeat. If the seventh bowl fails to include this battle, the bowl-series as a whole is incomplete. As other considerations have already shown, however, it does encompass the account of that

---

33. Alford, *Greek Testament*, 4:737.
34. Bullinger, *Apocalypse*, 646; Robert Govett, *Govett on Revelation* (1981 reprint; Miami Springs, Fla.: Conley & Schoettle, 1861), p. 365; J. B. Smith, *A Revelation of Jesus Christ* (Scottdale, Pa.: Herald, 1961), p. 281; Walvoord, *Revelation*, 318; Johnson, "Revelation," 12:595.
35. Giblin, "Structural and Thematic Correlations," pp. 502-8.
36. E.g., Beckwith, *Apocalypse*, pp. 682, 685; Ladd, *Revelation*, p. 212; Kiddle, *Revelation*, p. 323; J. Massyngberde Ford, *Revelation*, vol. 38 of AB (Garden City, N.Y.: Doubleday, 1975), pp. 263-64.
37. E.g., Moffatt, "Revelation," 5:469; Beckwith, *Apocalypse*, p. 734; Mounce, *Revelation*, p. 349.

battle—an indication that the seventh bowl description extends at least through the end of chapter 19.[38]

But this is not all. A significant part of the battle of Armageddon is the assignment of the beast (i.e., the first beast of Rev. 13) to the lake of fire at the battle's conclusion (19:20). This must come under the scope of the bowl series in light of the fifth bowl's destination which is the throne of the beast (16:10). That bowl has its own torment, judgments against the demonic civilization of the last times,[39] but it is only temporary. The afflicted ones blaspheme God and do not repent of their evil works (16:11). Such a blasphemous response must have its supreme recompense before the series of "last" plagues ends. The leader of this God-defying element is especially deserving, and so has special recognition as he meets his final judgment (19:20). In this way, anticipatory implications of the fifth bowl corroborate that the seventh must extend at least through the end of chapter 19.

The final judgment of Satan. As part of the sixth bowl, the unholy trinity—the dragon, the beast, and the false prophet—plays a major part in the preparations for Armageddon (16:13). They are the ones who use the three unclean spirits to assemble a huge army for the battle of that great day. Revelation 12-13 shows decisively that Satan is the leader and energizer of this trio (cf. 13:2 especially).[40] Yet Satan's final judgment does not happen in connection with that of the beast and false prophet. For providential reasons, it occurs separately at a point after the thousand years of 20:1-6.

The seven "last" plagues are not over until this major instigator of rebellion is in his eternal place, the lake of fire and brimstone (20:10). Divine wrath has not finally quelled human and diabolic rebellion until it has dealt the deathblow to the final great revolt after the Millennium (20:7-9). So the seventh of the seven plagues must span at least through Rev. 20:10.[41] In this final encounter Satan escapes the doom of the armies he has mustered, only to face a more awful immediate end.[42] Here he receives his final and fatal blow as he joins his two

---

38. Beasley-Murray, *Revelation*, p. 277.
39. Ladd, *Revelation*, p. 212.
40. Swete, *Apocalypse*, p. 206; Robertson, *Word Pictures*, 6:423; Lenski, *Revelation*, p. 473; Michael Wilcock, *The Message of Revelation*, in The Bible Speaks Today, ed. John R. W. Stott (Downers Grove, Ill.: InterVarsity, 1975), p. 147.
41. Giblin also uses the disposal of these three major adversaries to demonstrate the unity of the larger section 19:11–21:8, but with a slightly different approach ("Structural and Thematic Correlations," pp. 500-501).
42. Swete, *Apocalypse*, p. 270.

cronies in reaching a destiny long appointed for him (cf. Matt. 25:41).[43]

Once again, the extended nature of the seventh bowl finds confirmation. Rather than excluding the dragon from this plague, this explanation involves him along with the beast and false prophet as part of the series whose climax includes a description of his doom.

The finality of the last of the last plagues. The text is reasonably explicit in its identification of the seven last plagues with the seven bowls (15:6-8; 21:9). If the angels with the seven last plagues are recipients of the seven golden bowls full of the wrath of God, the conclusion is inevitable that the bowl judgments and the last plagues are two ways of referring to the same series (cf. 15:1, 6-8; 16:1). Therefore, a study of the seventh bowl is also an examination of the last of the seven last plagues.

Expanding the seventh bowl to include the judgment of the Great White Throne at the end of Revelation 20 is the only way to do justice to the heavy emphasis on this plague series as being the very last one (15:1). Efforts to circumvent the plain statement about these being the ultimate, absolute, and universal termination of divine wrath (15:1) have rested on a predisposition to limit the text's meaning—to find the plagues' fulfillment in the A.D. 70 destruction of Jerusalem,[44] to interpret them in connection with the opening of the nineteenth-century French Revolution,[45] to limit their duration to the period just *before* the Second Coming,[46] or to employ some similar restriction. But no contextual features furnish hints to support any type of limitation. If the descriptive "last" (15:1) applies to the plagues, the meaning must be that no more are to follow. If they are the termination of God's wrath (15:1), the sequence of wrathful visitations ends only when they end. This comes with the relegation of all blasphemers (16:9, 11, 21) to the lake of fire in 20:12-15.

The ultimacy of the last of the last plagues is noticeable in another connection. The introductory announcement of the seventh bowl refers to the flight of every island and the disappearance of every mountain (16:20). The two verbs used, φύγειν (*phygein*, "to flee") and [οὐχ]

---

43. Lee, "Revelation," 4:801; Robertson, *Word Pictures*, 6:462; Johnson, "Revelation," 12:588.

44. David Chilton, *The Days of Vengeance* (Fort Worth, Tex.: Dominion, 1987), pp. 383-84.

45. E. B. Elliott, *Horae Apocalypticae*, 4 vols., 4th ed. (London: Seeleys, 1851), 3:448 ff.

46. Düsterdieck, *Revelation*, p. 408; Walvoord, *Revelation*, p. 226; Ladd, *Revelation*, p. 204; Mounce, *Revelation*, p. 285 n. 1.

εὑρεθῆναι ([*ouch*] *heurethēnai*, "not to be found"), occur nowhere else—not even in 6:12-17—to describe a cosmic event except in 20:11 (cf. 21:1) where they speak of the vanishing of the old earth and heaven.[47] So the introduction to the seventh bowl presages the complete disappearance of this creation.[48]

Since the removal of the old earth and heaven is in conjunction with the vision of the Great White Throne (20:11), another evidence for the broader range is in place. This is the fourth miscellaneous indication to verify the lengthened extent of the seventh bowl. It is the final element in an overwhelming case for concluding that 16:17–22:5 is the author's prophetic description of the seventh bowl judgment.[49]

POTENTIAL OBJECTIONS TO THE SEVENTH BOWL'S MAGNITUDE

Weaknesses of this theory must wear the label "potential" because its exposure to criticism has been so limited that objections have not had opportunity to materialize. One can only speculate on what direction those objections will take.

(1) One point probably to become an issue is how the millennial kingdom (20:4-6) and the new creation (21:1–22:5) can partake of the nature of a bowl judgment or a last plague. How can they be part of the outpouring of God's wrath? An answer could point to the consignment of the Devil to the lake of fire (20:8-10) as the reason for including the millennial account under the heading of divine wrath. It could also recognize the barring from the New Jerusalem of all who are in the lake of fire (21:8, 27; 22:15) as an explanation for the new creation's inclusion as part of a bowl of wrath.

(2) Another rejoinder to the theory of extending the seventh bowl into chapter 22 may be an objection to merging temporal punishment with eternal punishment. The seals, trumpets, and bowls deal predominantly with inflicting suffering on mankind in this life, but this theory extends the scope of the bowl to include punishment beyond this life. These two types of punishment differ in nature and do not belong in the same matrix of revelatory disclosure. An answer to this observation could call attention to the possibility that this account of the end of human history is of a special type. Eventually a time will come when God's temporal dealings with mankind will shift to an nontemporal basis as He prepares to instigate His new creation.

---

47. Giblin, "Structural and Thematic Correlations," p. 502; cf. Swete, *Apocalypse*, pp. 211, 271; Robertson, *Word Pictures*, 6:463.
48. Ladd, *Revelation*, p. 218.
49. Wilcock, *Revelation*, p. 150; Chilton, *Days of Vengeance*, p. 418.

(3) A further possible problem for extending the seventh bowl into the last chapter of Revelation is its erasing of an exact parallelism with Dan. 9:24-27 and the prophecy of Daniel's seventieth week. The climax of the seventieth week comes in chapter 19 with the coming of the Son of Man. If this climax was determinative in John's structural scheme, this too could mark the close of the seventh bowl judgment.[50] This does not allow the bowl to extend beyond chapter 19. An answer to this objection acknowledges John's heavy dependence on Daniel 9 for earlier parts of his structure, but asserts John's freedom to depart from that structure when the nature of his visions carries him beyond anything revealed in Daniel. The Millennium, the eternal state, and other aspects of Revelation 20-22 augment the prophecy of Daniel, so John's structural scheme had to allow for this additional revelation.

(4) A further potential objection comes in 19:4. Worship before the throne in heaven comes back into view in that verse, giving an indication that, in light of 15:8, the seven last plagues have come to an end. The indication of 15:8 is that no one could enter the heaven temple until the termination of these plagues.[51] An answer to this objection notes that 19:4 is part of an intercalation that does not follow the chronological sequence of the numbered-bowl series of which it is a parenthetical part. This act of worship could have been proleptic, preceding the temporal beginning of the bowl series, much the same as the announcement of Babylon's fall in 14:8. This then would not contradict the restriction on heavenly access placed in 15:8.

Each of these potential objections is worthy of attention, but none is as strong as the considerations supporting extending the seventh bowl through 22:5.

THE CORE OF THE SEVENTH BOWL

So far this examination of the seventh bowl has identified the introduction to the bowl description (16:17-21), two lengthy pictures of the harlot and the bride as supplemental background to the bowl (17:1–18:24; 21:9–22:5), and between the two intercalations a body of visional material with a number of ties to the seventh bowl that prove it to be an integral part of that bowl (19:11–21:8). It remains to examine that body of material which constitutes the "action" portion of the seventh bowl. This is the part that corresponds to the earthly outworking of the earlier bowls, trumpets, and seals.

---

50. John Andrew McLean, "The Seventieth Week of Daniel 9:27 as a Literary Key for Understanding the Structure of the Apocalypse of John" (unpublished Ph.D. diss., Univ. of Michigan, 1990), pp. 231, 255-58.
51. Hailey, *Revelation*, p. 375.

The section consists of eight visions,[52] each of which has καὶ εἶδον (*kai eidon*, "and I saw") to introduce it. In order, they are: [1] the return of Christ (19:11-16), [2] the invitation to the birds of prey (19:17-18), [3] the defeat of the beast (19:19-21), [4] the binding of Satan (20:1-3), [5] the Millennium and the final defeat of Satan (20:4-10), [6] the Great White Throne (20:11), [7] the judgment of those not in the Book of Life (20:12-15), and [8] the new heaven and the new earth (21:1-8). The far-reaching question is whether the sequence of these visions represents the sequence of their fulfillment.

Some have lodged objections to chronological sequence in these scenes. (1) One negative way of responding to such a sequence is to insist that the series deals with the complexity of Christ's second coming as a single event and does not chart a series of events over a period of time.[53] Each event portrays a separate aspect of that coming victory like an eschatological art gallery with seven [or eight] pictures of that victory at the end of history.[54] (2) Another reason for non-chronological fulfillment is the observation that the same Gog-Magog terminology occurs in the scene of 19:17-18 as does in the scene of 20:8.[55] (3) A further rationale for denying temporal sequence of fulfillment of the eight visions is to note the existence of nations in 20:1-3 after the same have died in the battle of 19:21.[56]

Proposed answers to the last two objections to consecutive fulfillment have already appeared.[57] The other reason is very presuppositional in nature and has little exegetical value.

Support for the successive fulfillment of these eight visions is of an exegetical nature. Putting aside earlier evidence for progression rather than recapitulation in this book,[58] one may use a thematic basis to present a good case for chronological sequence. A comparison of various pairs and combinations of scenes points inevitably to a consecutive trend in the visions:

(1) The return of Christ [1] must happen first, or else the invitation to the birds of prey [2] is pointless.

---

52. Swete and Moffatt divide a roughly comparable portion into three divisions (19:11-21; 20:1-6; 20:7-10), but do so on thematic rather than structural grounds (Swete, *Apocalypse*, p. 246; Moffatt, "Revelation," 5:466). Wall arrives at seven divisions by combining 19:17-18 and 19:19-21 into one section (*Revelation*, p. 227).
53. Wall, *Revelation*, p. 227.
54. M. Eugene Boring, *Revelation, A Bible Commentary for Teaching and Preaching* (Louisville: John Knox, 1989), p. 195.
55. Lee, "Revelation," 4:787.
56. R. Fowler White, "Reexamining the Evidence for Recapitulation in Rev. 20:1-10," *WTJ* 51, no. 2 (Fall 1989): 321.
57. See Excursus 4, pp. 815-16 nn. 54, 58.
58. See Excursus 3.

(2) The invitation to the birds [2] must occur before the defeat of the beast [3] in order for the birds to be present when the slaughter occurs (19:21*b*).

(3) The binding of Satan [4] must transpire before the Millennium and his release at the end [5] to account for his inactivity during the Millennium.

(4) All the first five scenes must take place before the appearance of the Great White Throne [6], because they relate to the old earth and heaven which depart when that throne appears.

(5) The Great White Throne [6] must be in place before it can be a scene for judging those absent from the Book of Life [7].

(6) The judgment of the lost [7] must come before the new heaven and the new earth [8] to explain the absence of all evil from the new creation.

(7) More broadly speaking, the second coming of Christ [1] is clearly the earliest of the series in its fulfillment, with the new creation [8] coming conspicuously last.

(8) The Millennium and its associated events [4 and 5] are obviously antecedent to the events of the Great White Throne [6 and 7] because they pertain to the present creation.

For about the last 1,700 years, the question has been, however, whether the second coming of Christ [1] and the battle of Armageddon [2 and 3] precede or are partially simultaneous with the Millennium [4 and 5]. Chronological fulfillment in every other comparison makes temporal precedence in 19:11-21 very probable. To add to this probability, one might argue that the beast's defeat and consignment to the lake of fire [3] must come before the binding of Satan [4] to explain the absence of the beast from the earth during the Millennium.

The debate is one-sided in favor of chronological sequence in these eight scenes.[59] This coincides with conclusions reached in another study dealing with the sequential fulfillment of the seventh seal and the seventh trumpet.[60] The difference here is, however, that these scenes are unnumbered.

RESULTANT STRUCTURE OF THE SEVENTH BOWL

If the above analysis of the seventh bowl is correct, the structural pattern of the seventh bowl is as follows:

---

59. Düsterdieck, *Revelation*, pp. 467-68; Charles, *Revelation*, 2:116; Beckwith, *Apocalypse*, pp. 98-100, 735; Walvoord, *Revelation*, pp. 289-90; Ladd, *Revelation*, p. 261; Mounce, *Revelation*, p. 353; Beasley-Murray, *Revelation*, pp. 287, 290; Johnson, "Revelation," 12:580-81.
60. See Excursus 3.

Announcement of the emptying of the bowl's contents (16:17-21)
[No direct inflicting of wrath occurs in this introductory announcement, only a number of terrifying phenomena that move men to blaspheme God. The central focus of the announcement is the proclaiming of the fall of Babylon (16:19c).]
a. *Intercalation #1: Detailed description of Babylon, her past, present, future* (17:1–19:10)
[The city whose destruction is foretold in the initial announcement is representative of a system of false religion and opposition to God and His people (chap. 17) and of godless materialism (chap. 18).]
  (1) The doom of religious Babylon (17:1-18)
  (2) The doom of commercial Babylon (18:1-24)
  (3) Heavenly rejoicing over the removal of Babylon and the institution of God's kingdom on earth (19:1-10)
b. *Events of the seventh bowl* (19:11–20:15)
[Now comes a series of eight scenes that furnish in sequence the steps in the chronological implementation of the seventh bowl-judgment.]
  (1) Second coming of Christ (19:11-16)
  (2) Summons of the birds to a human feast (19:17-18)
  (3) Slaughter of Christ's human opponents (19:19-21)
  (4) Satan's imprisonment (20:1-3)
  (5) Satan's release and final defeat (20:4-10)
  (6) Setting of the Great White Throne (20:11)
  (7) Sentencing to the lake of fire (20:12-15)
  (8) Sketch of the new Jerusalem (21:1-8)
c. *Intercalation #2: Detailed description of the new Jerusalem* (21:9–22:5)
[The new Jerusalem as part of the new creation is the divine counterpart to Babylon which was destroyed under this same seventh bowl.]
  (1) The city's physical features (21:9-21)
  (2) The city's illumination (21:22-27)
  (3) Paradise restored (22:1-5)

IMPLICATIONS OF THE SEVENTH BOWL

Several observations growing out of the conclusions of this study of the seventh bowl will provide further corroboration.

PARALLEL TO THE OTHER SEVENTH MEMBERS

First, the extended nature of the seventh bowl prophecy corresponds with the extended nature of the seventh seal and seventh trumpet. An earlier study has concluded on exegetical grounds other than those cited here, that the seventh seal consists of the seven trumpets, and the seventh trumpet includes the seven bowls.[61] It is altogether fitting that the seventh bowl should embody a series of its own.

The previous seventh members each had seven parts, but the seventh bowl has eight scenes. The first seven of these scenes pertain directly to the infliction of divine wrath on those in rebellion against God, corresponding to seven parts of the parallel segments. The eighth scene changes tone to sound the note of divine blessing in the new creation. This is the new beginning. The old creation has now been purged and replaced.

So the seventh-bowl account is compatible with earlier comparable portions of the Apocalypse.

RATIONAL INTEGRITY AND LITERARY CONCINNITY OF REVELATION

Students of Revelation have leveled a substantial number of aspersions against the logical merit of the book.[62] The understanding of the seventh bowl proposed here adds a significant factor to show, contrary to these criticisms, the complete reasonableness of this work of prophecy. It does so by providing closure to a literary plan laid out in Revelation 4-5.

Those two chapters supplied the design for the visional portion of this book when they described the throne room and introduced the seven-sealed scroll whose contents only the Lamb could divulge. This scroll purportedly contained all that John was to see regarding the destiny of the earth. Because the seventh bowl is part of the seventh trumpet which is part of the seventh seal, the interpretation of that bowl in the above discussion provides for the achievement of that objective by incorporating within the bowl events leading all the way into the eternal state of the future new creation.

Literary elegance and rational harmony in the Apocalypse thereby receive verification as the bowl that ends the visional portion matches the introductory portion, providing as a concluding wrap-up the revelatory data that the introduction promised it would.

CONFIRMATION OF THE PREMILLENNIAL RETURN OF CHRIST

Prominent elements in the events of the seventh bowl, as outlined above, are the second coming of Christ and the Millennium. Since

---

61. Ibid.
62. Ibid.; Robert L. Thomas, *Revelation 1-7, An Exegetical Commentary* (Chicago: Moody, 1992), pp. 23-29. Grant R. Osborne's hermeneutical scheme

these are also part of the last of the seven last plagues, another name for the bowl judgments, they too wear the attribute of "last." Few would dispute the futurity of Christ's return,[63] but if they do, they face the hopeless task of explaining how a returning warrior-King in the past is the last of the last plagues that prepare the way for the new creation.[64] If the Second Coming is future, as it surely is, then the Millennium must possess the same quality of "lastness" that belongs to the Second Coming.[65]

As a companion part of the last of the last plagues, the millennial description of 20:1-10 tells of the commitment of Satan to his eternal doom. Even apart from the validity of the above conclusion regarding the chronological sequence of the eight scenes of the seventh bowl, the Millennium must belong to the future, or else the term "last" would not accurately apply to it. It would be unfortunate to view any aspect of the present era as being the last of the seven last plagues in which the wrath of God is terminated. An apologetic for such a concept would be hard to construct. One would have to look for subtle or indirect clues and allow them to override what is plain exegetical data like that advanced in the discussion above.[66] A quest for such esoteric meanings is unnecessary and even harmful to the cause of accurate biblical exegesis.

---

of combining historicist, idealist, and futurist perspectives on Revelation and of seeing the book as both cyclical and linear seems irrational in the handling of details ("Theodicy in the Apocalypse," *Trinity Journal* 14, no. 1 (Spring 1993): 65.

63. Among those few are Chilton, who interprets 19:11-16 as an invitation to the church to have communion with Him and the progress of the gospel in the world (*Days of Vengeance*, pp. 240, 481-82), and Mulholland, who views the scene as picturing Christ in the midst of a rebellious order following His first advent (*Revelation*, p. 299).

64. Chilton brushes aside the finality of the terminology of 15:1 with the words, "There is no reason to assume that these must be the 'last' plagues in an ultimate, absolute, and universal sense" (*Days of Vengeance*, pp. 383-84). He does so by limiting the purpose and scope of Revelation as a whole to the Jewish people in the period of the first century A.D.

65. In his argument for recapitulation in Rev. 20:1-10, White uses 15:1 to prove that 20:7-10 is a recapitulation of 19:11-21, both being thereby relegated to the future (White, "Reexamining the Evidence," pp. 330-31). But what he fails to appreciate is that the Millennium with the associated binding of Satan is also a part of that last of the seven last plagues. To be consistent with himself, he must agree to a future Millennium rather than argue for a present one as he attempts to do through his theory of recapitulation.

66. Vern Sheridan Poythress likes White's recapitulatory alternative to the premillennial position but admits that it depends on contextual clues that are "subtle" or "indirect" ("Genre and Hermeneutics in Rev. 20:1-6," *JETS* 36, no. 1 [March 1993]: 53). In contrast to searching for obscure evidence, however, straightforward exegesis accepts the Millennium as part of the last of the last plagues as mandated by the text of the Apocalypse.

So the Millennium fits into the apocalyptic plan for the future, not the present, a judgment based on criteria different from that furnished in an earlier study.[67] It is then that the returning Christ will reign as King over the whole earth of the present creation. Freedom from satanic interference and immediate divine rule will make it the most ideal period of world history since the fall of man.

---

67. See Excursus 4.

Index of Selected Subjects

Unless italicized, page numbers are references to *Revelation 1-7*. Page numbers in italic are references to *Revelation 8-22*.

Index of Scripture

Unless italicized, page numbers are references to *Revelation 1-7*. Page numbers in italic are references to *Revelation 8-22*. Superscript numbers designate the number of occurences on a given page. The letter "n" following a page number refers to a footnote.

631

Index of Ancient Literature

Unless italicized, page numbers are references to *Revelation 1–7*. Page numbers in italic are references to *Revelation 8–22*. Superscript numbers designate the number of occurences on a given page. The letter "n" following a page number refers to a footnote.

Apocalypse of Baruch, 199^2, *206*
2 Apocalypse of Baruch, 448, *24*^{2}
Assumption of Moses, *276*
Athanasius, 21^2

3 Baruch, *172*
Book of Jubilees, *18, 29*

Cocceius, 507n

Ecclesiasticus, 172^2
1 Enoch, 73, 84, 98^2, 235, 324,
335, 361, 362, 364, 447,
448, 465^2, *7n, 20, 27*^{2}, *88,*
134, 252, 276, 433, 439,
501, 515
2 Enoch, 104, 172, 351, 352, 361^2,
447, *68*^{2}, *515*
Esdras, 73, 235
2 Esdras 92, 448
4 Esdras, *84, 88*

Eusebius, 2^5, 3^6, 4^2, 6^2, 7, 9^5, 9n,
18, 19n, 21, 171n, 183n

Hermas, 470n
Heroditus, *262n*
Hyppolytus, 10

Ignatius, 146
Irenaeus, 10, 20, 21^2, *184n, 185n,*
289

Jerome, 21
Josephus, 243n
Justin Martyr, 10^2

Letter of Aristeas, *515*

1 Maccabees, 172, 490^2
2 Maccabees, 199, 258, 490^2, *114*
3 Maccabees, 172, *181*
4 Maccabees, *134*

665

Index of Modern Authors

Unless italicized, page numbers are references to *Revelation 1–7*. Page numbers in italic are references to *Revelation 8–22*. Superscript numbers designate the number of occurences on a given page. The letter "n" following a page number refers to a footnote.

675

Robertson, A. T. (*continued*)
      135n, 137n^2, 138, 141n,
      142^2, 143n^3, 144n, 147n,
      148n, 150n^2, 151n, 153n^2,
      155n, 161n, 163, 164n,
      166n, 167n, 170n^2, 174n^2,
      178n, 186n, 187n^2, 190n,
      193n, 195n, 196n^2, 197n,
      198n, 199n^2, 201n^2, 202n,
      203n, 208n, 209n, 210n^2,
      211n, 212n^2, 214n, 215n^2,
      217n^3, 220n, 221n, 222n,
      223n, 226n^2, 227n^4, 229n,
      231n^2, 232n^2, 233n, 234n^2,
      235n, 237n^2, 247n, 248n,
      249n, 251n^2, 252n, 253n^2,
      254n, 255n^2, 257n, 258n,
      259n^3, 260n^2, 265n, 266,
      274n^2, 275n, 277n^2, 279n,
      281n, 284n, 288n, 289n,
      291n, 301n^2, 302n, 303n,
      307n^2, 310n, 312n^2, 313n,
      314n, 315n, 318n^2, 319n,
      321n, 323n, 325n^2, 326n,
      336n, 338n, 341n^2, 342n^2,
      349n, 359n^2, 360n^2, 364n,
      367n, 370n, 375n, 376n,
      382n, 383n^2, 386n, 388n,
      389n, 392^2, 393n, 394n,
      395, 400n, 401n, 403n,
      404n, 405n, 407n, 413n,
      414n, 415n, 416n, 417n^2,
      418n, 419n^2, 424n, 425n,
      429n, 430n, 432n, 434n,
      436n, 438n, 442n, 444n,
      445n, 447n^2, 451n, 455n,
      456n^2, 470n, 472n, 473n,
      475n, 487n, 488n^2, 490n,
      493n^2, 494n^2, 499n, 520n,
      2n, 3n, 6n^2, 7n, 11n^2,
      15n, 17n^2, 18n, 19n, 20n,
      21n, 22n, 24n^2, 25n^2, 28n^2,
      30n, 31n^2, 32n, 33n^4, 35n,
      36n, 37n, 39n, 40n^2, 43n^2,
      44n, 46n, 47n, 48n, 49n,
      50n^2, 51n, 52n, 58n, 65n,
      66n, 67n, 68n, 72n, 73n^2,
      74n^3, 75n^2, 76n^6, 77n^5,

79n^2, 83n, 87n, 90n^3, 91n,
94n, 95n, 96n, 97n, 98n,
99n, 100n^2, 101n^4, 102n,
105n, 106n^2, 107n, 109n^2,
112n, 114n, 115n^3, 119n,
121n^2, 122n^2, 123n, 124n,
125n^2, 127n, 130n^2, 131n,
132n, 133n, 136n, 138n,
140n, 141n, 142, 142n,
143n^2, 144n^2, 145n^4, 146n^6,
147n^2, 150n, 152n, 155n,
156n^2, 157n^2, 158n, 160n,
161n^2, 162n, 164n, 165n,
166n, 168n^2, 169n^3, 170n^4,
172n, 174n^2, 175n, 177n^2,
181n^2, 182n, 186n^3, 187n^2,
189n, 190n, 193n^3, 194n,
196n, 199n^2, 200n^2, 201n,
203n, 204, 205n, 206n,
209n, 210n^2, 212n, 213n^4,
214n, 215n, 216n, 219n^2,
221n, 222n, 223n, 225n^3,
226n^2, 231n, 234n^2, 236n,
237n, 239n, 240n, 243n,
250n^2, 252n, 255n, 256n,
257n, 258n^2, 259n, 260n,
261n, 264n, 265n, 266n,
268n^2, 274n, 276n, 285n,
287n, 288n, 291n, 292n,
294n, 298n, 299n, 301n,
302n, 307n, 308n^4, 309n^2,
310n, 314n, 316n, 317n,
319n, 321n^3, 322n, 325n^2,
326n^4, 329n^2, 330n, 332n^2,
334n^3, 336n, 337n^3, 338n,
339n^2, 344n^3, 345n, 346n,
347n, 348, 348n, 349n^2,
350n, 351n, 355n, 356n^2,
357n, 360n^2, 362n, 364n,
365n, 366n, 369n, 370n^2,
371n, 375n^3, 376n, 378n^2,
379n^3, 380n, 382n^2, 383n,
385n, 387n, 388n, 391n^2,
393n, 394n, 397n, 398n^2,
400n^3, 401n, 406n, 407n^2,
414n, 415n, 416n, 419n,
420n, 421n, 423n 424n,
425n^2, 426n, 427n, 428n^2,

Swete, Henry Barclay (*continued*)
110², 111³, 112², 114, 115n,
120², 121², 121n, 123³, 124,
126², 127, 129, 130², 133,
135, 135n, 136, 136n, 137,
138³, 138n, 140, 141, 143³,
144, 144n², 146², 150n,
153n, 155n, 156, 157,
157n², 160n, 161², 165,
166², 166n, 168, 170n, 172,
173², 174, 174n, 175n,
176², 177, 181, 182, 183,
186, 189, 189n, 190², 191,
193, 194, 196n, 197, 199²,
199n², 200, 202, 203²,
203n, 204³, 205, 206³, 207,
208, 209n, 210, 211², 212²,
213⁵, 215n, 216³, 218²,
219², 220, 221, 222², 224²,
225, 226n, 231, 231n, 232,
233, 234, 235², 239n, 241,
241n, 242, 243, 244, 245n,
246², 247, 247n², 250,
250n, 252, 252n, 253, 254,
255n, 256, 258, 260², 262n,
263, 264³, 264n, 265, 267,
271, 272², 273, 274, 274n²,
275², 276n, 277, 282n, 284,
284n, 286², 287³, 287n,
288, 288n, 290, 291, 294,
295, 297, 299, 302, 303,
304², 306, 308n, 314, 314n,
315, 316n, 317, 317n, 318,
319, 319n, 320, 320n, 324n,
325, 326n, 328, 329, 330n,
332, 334, 334n, 335, 336,
337n, 338, 339, 339n, 341,
342, 344n, 345², 345n, 346,
347², 349, 349n, 350n,
356n², 357n, 358, 358n,
359², 360, 360n², 361, 362²,
362n, 364, 365², 366n, 367,
367n, 369n, 370, 373, 374n,
375, 376n, 379n, 382²,
382n, 383n, 385, 385n,
386², 390², 391, 393, 394,
394n, 395, 397², 398n,

399n, 406², 406n, 407,
407n, 409n², 410, 411,
414n, 415, 418, 419², 421,
422, 425², 426, 428, 429²,
430n, 431, 432, 433², 434²,
435, 439n, 440, 441, 443n²,
444, 445, 446, 446n², 447,
447n, 448, 448n, 449²,
450n, 451³, 454n, 457,
459n, 460n, 462², 463,
464n, 466, 466n, 467, 468,
469², 470n, 471, 471n³,
472n⁵, 473², 474², 475, 479,
480n, 481n, 482, 483², 484,
485, 486, 489², 489n,
495n², 496², 497, 498,
498n, 502n, 503, 504, 505²,
505n, 507², 508, 509,
510n³, 511n, 512², 513,
514, 515, 515n, 516, 517,
518, 519, 519n, 520²,
521n², 522n, 523, 529n,
537n, 538n², 539n, 546n²,
548n, 552n, 555n, 556n,
557n, 560n, 562n², 568n³,
572n, 573n, 574n², 567n²,
578n, 580n

Tatford, Frederick A., 160n, 161n,
166n, 253n, 290n
Tenney, Merrill C., 22n, 31n, 32n,
39n, 70, 77, 129n², 130,
143n², 255n, 321n, *5n,*
118n, 406n, 531n
Thayer, Joseph Henry, 171n,
227n, 302n, 312n, 315n,
248n
Thiessen, Henry Clarence, 30n,
286n
Thomas, Robert L., 28n², 99n,
100n, 101n, 105n, 114n,
115n³, 120n, 121n, 128n²,
180n, 210n, 458n, 459n,
506n, *3n, 4n, 5², 8, 11n,*
15n, 16n², 21, 33, 49, 61,
61n, 62, 89, 95, 126, 142,
165n, 177, 191, 194, 199,